Nonverbal Communication

Forms and Functions

Second Edition

Peter A. Andersen
San Diego State University

WAVELAND
PRESS, INC.
Long Grove, Illinois

Nonverbal Communication

Second Edition

For information about this book, contact:
    Waveland Press, Inc.
    4180 IL Route 83, Suite 101
    Long Grove, IL 60047-9580
    (847) 634-0081
    info@waveland.com
    www.waveland.com

*This book is dedicated to the three women in my life who
taught me the fundamentals of nonverbal communication.
Their insights about people continue to amaze me.*

*To Mildred,
my mother, nonverbal communicator, and nurturer par excellence*

*To Janis,
my wife, co-author, life partner,
and the most insightful reader of nonverbal communication I know*

*To Kirsten,
my daughter, whose nonverbal behavior and
keen insights have always delighted*

Thank you!

Contents

PART II
Affective Exchanges:
Feelings and Nonverbal Communication   135

Preface

Across the millennia nonverbal communication has remained the primary means of human communication. Even in the age of the Internet, text messaging, Facebook, and instant messaging, face-to-face communication predominates. Likewise, as verbal media quickly morph into multichanneled media, it is nonverbal information that makes television, streaming video, face pages and YouTube so captivating and valuable.

It has been my privilege to be among a group of researchers and teachers on the cutting edge of research on nonverbal communication. For over a third of a century I have taught classes, conducted studies, and written books about nonverbal communication. Though my research has ranged from health communication campaigns to intimate relationships, nonverbal communication has been at the core of my research and teaching interests. My primary motivation for writing this book is to share with students my enthusiasm for and knowledge of this vital and interesting subject.

Research Orientation

This second edition of *Nonverbal Communication: Forms and Functions* is based on the best, latest, and most current theory and research in the field of nonverbal communication. Although this book is based on hundreds of studies of nonverbal communication, it is not a handbook of nonverbal behavior. The ever-expanding literature is far too extensive to cover every single study in an undergraduate text. The primary goal of this book is to make the huge body of research and theory on nonverbal communication accessible to undergraduates and graduate students.

Conceptual Organization

Most nonverbal communication texts are organized by the codes of nonverbal communication. This book employs a more intellectually interesting and practical approach: It is organized conceptually around the major functions, purposes, and uses of nonverbal communication. Although attention to the codes of nonverbal communication is necessary to orient the student to this field and its terminology, I adhere to the belief that a conceptual and functional orientation is most engaging, useful, and intellectually rich.

The book is organized into three parts with a total of twelve chapters. Part 1, "The Fundamental Forces of Nonverbal Communication," contains five chapters that introduce and orient students to the field of nonverbal communication. Chapter 1, "Nonverbal Communication and Language," provides the student with a unique, research-based definition of nonverbal communication that is based on the human brain and the structure of message codes. This chapter also outlines nineteen fundamental differences between nonverbal and verbal communication. Chapter 2, "The Body Codes of Nonverbal Communication," introduces the student to the primary ways we communicate: through our physical appearance, body motion (kinesics), eye behavior (oculesics), spatial behavior (proxemics), and touch (haptics). Chapter 3, "The Contextual Codes of Nonverbal Communication," outlines the contexts for all communication and serves as a bridge to the discussion of nonverbal functions; this chapter examines communication environments, chronemics, olfactics, and vocalics. Although culture as an aspect of nonverbal communication is emphasized throughout the book, chapter 4, "Cultural Cues," provides a foundational understanding of culture and emphasizes the ways in which nonverbal communication is used to convey and maintain culture. The chapter reviews briefly how different cultures employ the codes of nonverbal communication, and it focuses on six dimensions of culture that underlie all differences in nonverbal communication. Chapter 5, "Gender, Sex, and Nonverbal Communication," examines the similarities and differences between male and female nonverbal communication by exploring both biological and cultural differences.

Part 2, "Affective Exchanges: Feelings and Nonverbal Communication," contains four chapters that focus on this fundamental and often ignored macro-function of human communication, the exchange of emotion, for which nonverbal communication is primarily responsible. Chapter 6, "The Nonverbal Communication of Emotion," (1) introduces the student to the biological and cultural origins of emotion and its expression, (2) examines the face, voice, and body—nonverbal channels of emotional expression—(3) reviews the communication of fifteen emotions (happiness, sadness, fear, surprise, anger, disgust, contempt, pride, shame, embarrassment, guilt, love, jealousy, warmth, and sexual desire), and (4) discusses how emotions are a primary source and outcome of nonverbal communication. Chapter 7, "Communication and Stress," outlines the critical role arousal plays in nonverbal communication and provides an overview of the nonverbal aspects of three forms of communication avoidance: communication anxiety, social anxiety, and touch avoidance. Chapter 8, "Immediacy and Nonverbal Communication," focuses on the interpersonal communication of warmth, closeness, and involvement through the various body codes of nonverbal communication. Chapter 9, "Nonverbal Communication of Intimacy and Affection in Close Relationship" focuses on nonverbal communication in close relationships by examining the nature of affection, intimacy, introducing cognitive-valence theory—a model of intimacy development—and discussing the dialectics of intimate relationships in the context of nonverbal communication.

Part 3, "Implicit Influence: Nonverbal Cues of Persuasion, Deception, and Power," comprises three chapters that focus on the second major macrofunction of human communication—influence. Chapter 10, "Influencing Others through Nonverbal Communication," (1) reviews the often ignored nonverbal aspects of persuasion through an examination of the codes of nonverbal influence, (2) outlines the prominent theories of nonverbal persuasion, and (3) explores how we sell ourselves and the role of nonverbal communication in impression formation. Chapter 11, "Concealing and Revealing," gives an overview of the explosion of research on nonverbal communication. This chapter examines nonverbal deception cues and their inconsistency, individual differences in deception cues, contextual factors, an emerging theory of nonverbal deception cues, and the detection of deception. Chapter 12, "The Nonverbal Communication of Control, Power, and Status," reviews the codes of nonverbal communication in the context of one of the most central functions of nonverbal communication—the establishment of hierarchy, status, and power.

Other Features

Nonverbal Communication: Forms and Functions has important features that set it apart from other nonverbal communication textbooks. First, in addition to its emphasis on theory and research, this book provides strategies for students to improve their nonverbal communication. Many textbooks present a disembodied view of research and fail to offer advice on how the student can make changes that will improve her or his skill, sensitivity, or self-presentation. Accordingly, research-based advice is provided on such topics as coping with stress, caring for infants, increasing cultural sensitivity, and establishing intimacy.

Second, the book introduces and advocates such values as improving interpersonal relationships, creating and protecting the environment in which communication occurs, respecting culture and gender in the context of significant differences, and keeping an open mind to new perspectives without losing objectivity about the research findings.

Third, this book offers balanced theoretical positions to illuminate controversies in the social scientific literature. For instance, when considering the origins of nonverbal communication, gender differences, or emotional expression, the text encompasses both biological and cultural perspectives. Similarly, when reviewing culture or gender, the text notes both similarities and differences.

Fourth, each chapter begins with a real story or quote from literature or science to engage the reader. To facilitate comprehension, each chapter ends with a summary of the main points.

Acknowledgments

A number of people made this book possible. First I want to thank Gayle Zawilla, Carol Rowe, Neil Rowe, and the other people at Waveland Press who are extraordinarily talented, collaborative, and principled people. I want to thank my many nonverbal coauthors, especially Jan Andersen, David Buller, and Laura Guerrero, who helped me explore the frontiers on nonverbal communication. Finally, thanks to my many colleagues in communication and psychology who continue to demonstrate the power and importance of nonverbal communication.

Part I

The Fundamental Forces of Nonverbal Communication

1

Nonverbal Communication and Language
Distinctions and Connections

Human beings are talkative creatures. This is particularly true in America, where silence is seldom golden and people feel an obligation to chat continuously. Imagine a party or a date during which nobody talked! Years ago I invited my nonverbal communication class to spend a day at my home in complete silence. No talk, sign language, or written messages were permitted. At first, maintaining silence was impossible; it then became merely difficult and eventually possible, but barely so. Humans are nature's linguistic creatures, constantly talking and writing. Even the latest communication technologies favor written and spoken communication. The telephone, Internet, fax machine, voice mail, and answering machines are all primarily designed to transmit the "word."

Our verbal, language-using nature obscures an important fact: Much, perhaps most, of our communication doesn't rely on language at all! Although estimates vary, most communication researchers would agree that nonverbal communication is as important as verbal communication. In fact, most researchers believe that nonverbal communication is considerably more important. For example, research on interpersonal attraction suggests that 93 percent of the meaning or impact is communicated nonverbally (Mehrabian & Ferris, 1967; Mehrabian & Weiner, 1967). Scholars have justifiably criticized Mehrabian's methods (see Burgoon, Buller, & Woodall, 1996), but few challenge the basic concept: Nonverbal communication is an extremely powerful form of communication. Birdwhistell, one of the founders of the field of nonverbal communication, estimated that "no more than 30 to 35 percent of the social meaning of a conversation or interaction is carried by words" (1970, p. 158), leaving 65 to 70 percent of the meaning to be carried by the nonverbal channel. A better estimate of the relative importance of nonverbal communication comes from a statistical summary of studies by Philpot (1983), who reported that no more than 35 percent of conversational meaning comes from verbal communication. Philpot also reported that nonverbal commu-

3

nication is particularly potent in impression formation, emotional expression, and relational communication. Of course, all these estimates are a bit bogus; the relative importance depends on the task and the context.

The exact percentage of meaning carried by nonverbal communication isn't the issue. What is important is that numerous studies show that body movements, interpersonal distance, touch, facial expressions, and all the other components of nonverbal communication—separately or collectively, are *very* important. Nonverbal communication occurs beside language as a vital part of the communication process. Moreover, although it is an interesting academic exercise to deconstruct the relative impact of these two types of communication, verbal and nonverbal communication co-occur in almost every communication situation. Verbal communication and nonverbal communication, like respiration and circulation, exist side by side as two human processes that are part of the same system.

Nonverbal communication, as described in this book, includes all communication other than language. Language is a uniquely human form of communication that uses arbitrary symbols to convey meaning. These symbols consist of spoken or written words, arbitrary signs, computer symbols, mathematical symbols, or any other sign arbitrarily and definitionally related to its referent. Although some animals such as bees and monkeys do communicate using arbitrary codes, most animal communication is intrinsic and analogic. By contrast, humans in all cultures use language (Brown, 1991).

Nonverbal communication exists *beside language,* yet it is not language. It is present whenever we talk, but it is not talk. Although communication typically employs both nonverbal communication and language interactively, each method of communication derives from a different cognitive system, functions differently, and employs different codes. In this chapter we will examine definitions of nonverbal communication and explore the many differences between verbal and nonverbal communication.

DEFINING NONVERBAL COMMUNICATION

Differences That Make a Difference

Scholars have encountered several problems in defining nonverbal communication. One problem is that some definitions of communication exclude numerous forms of behavior, particularly nonverbal behavior, from consideration as forms of communication. Second, some scholars have failed to develop sound criteria for determining if a given act is nonverbal, resulting in long lists of potential nonverbal behaviors without any underlying reason for their inclusion on the list. Third, many behaviors are hybrids of nonverbal and verbal cues that make categorization difficult. Fourth, the degree to which a particular message is nonverbal is not always black and white. There is a gray area between verbal and nonverbal communication that sparks legitimate disagreement among researchers. Finally, because verbal communication developed from nonverbal communication, some communication that was once nonverbal and analogic is becoming verbal and digital.

The approach taken in this book is to provide a definition of nonverbal communication behaviors that is based on rigorous criteria for designating a particular action as nonverbal. In all, nineteen unique attributes of nonverbal communication are listed in this chapter, but for now, let's consider a definition based on three primary characteristics: Nonverbal messages include all communication that is *analogic, nonlinguistic,* and typically *governed by the right brain hemisphere* (Andersen, Garrison, & Andersen, 1975, 1979). "Analogic, nonlinguistic, and right hemispheric are all ways of describing an underlying nonverbal coding schema that unites a variety of communication behavior into one system" (P. A. Andersen et al., 1979, p. 83). This definition is consistent with Wilden's (1980) position:

> In human communication all non-conventionalized "gesture language," posture, facial expression, inflection, sequence, rhythm, cadence and indeed the CONTEXT within which human communication takes place is a type of analog or iconic communication in which the signal or sign has a necessary relation to what it "re-presents," whereas all denotative, linguistic communication is arbitrary and digital. (p. 163)

Gudykunst, Ting-Toomey, and Chua (1988) offered a conceptually based definition consistent with the definition employed in this book: "While verbal communication is a digital communication process, nonverbal communication is a multilayered, multimodal, multidimensional, analogic process" (p. 118).

Similarly, this book's definition is consistent with the traditional position taken by Watzlawick, Beavin, and Jackson (1967): Analogic communication "is virtually all nonverbal communication" (p. 62). This definition of nonverbal communication is almost identical to Buck's (1984, 1988; Buck & VanLear, 2002) "spontaneous" communication system, which is biologically shared, nonvoluntary, right-hemispheric, and nonpropositional. Although the definition employed in this book departs from many other conceptualizations of nonverbal communication, to paraphrase Bateson (1972), it is a difference that makes a difference. Purely nonverbal messages are analogic in nature.

Analogic Message Codes:
The Basis of Nonverbal Communication

Because analogic codes are the basis for nonverbal communication, it is important to understand the structure of these codes. First, analogic messages have a direct, nonarbitrary, intrinsic relationship to the thing they represent (Andersen, 1986; Watzlawick et al., 1967; Wilden, 1972). Such messages look or sound like what they refer to or represent. A pointed finger directs a person in an obvious direction. Usually, eye contact signals availability for communication. Analogic messages often are an abbreviated action: A clenched fist is an abbreviated punch, and a pat on the back is an abbreviated hug. Even these abbreviated actions directly signify meaning. These meanings are explained by the direct effects model (see chapter 8 for more about this model) or what Burgoon, Coker, and Coker (1986) described as the social meaning model of nonverbal communication.

Digital communication, by contrast, indirectly communicates information via arbitrary codes such as language. For example, any word can stand for "cat," the

English word *cat*, the Spanish word *gato,* or even a made-up word, say, *freem.* Most of you have never heard of the word *freem,* but since I have arbitrarily (for no good reason) chosen it to stand for *cat,* you will probably picture a cat when you read the word *freem* from this point on. Burgoon (1985b) explained that in digital coding systems,

> the connection between these semantic elements, or symbols, and their referent is arbitrary; there is no necessary or natural connection between the choice of sounds or letters and the thing for which they stand. Put another way, the meaning conveyed by symbols is socially defined rather than being derived from some instinctive meaning. (p. 272)

Analogic means of conveying love might include kissing, spending time together, prolonged eye contact, or smiling; whereas digital methods might entail writing or speaking a message such as "I love you."

A second quality of analogic messages is that each message can take on an infinite number of values or degrees. For example, a smile can range from a slight smirk to a broad grin. A vocal utterance can range from a whisper to a shout. Interpersonal distance can range from actually touching another person to being many feet or many miles apart. By contrast, digital codes possess just two values: present or absent, on or off, talking or silent. As such, digital messages are easy to repeat or reproduce, whereas analogic communication cannot be precisely replicated or easily relayed through several people with any degree of accuracy (Wilden, 1980).

Sign language is body language that actually is a language. (Photo courtesy of Robert Avery)

This book takes the position that by definition, nonverbal communication is analogically coded. Digital messages are linguistic or verbal, and messages with both analogic and digital properties are probably some combination of verbal and nonverbal messages. The distinguishing feature of nonverbal messages is the analogic code, not the channel. For example, gestures can be either nonverbal or verbal depending on the nature of the code (Andersen, 1991; Feyereisen, 1987; McNeill, 1985). Gestures that are used for emphasis—to show size, distance, or shape—and those that recreate bodily actions, such as pantomimes, are nonverbal. Note, however, that American Sign Language is linguistic and verbal (Poizner, Klima, & Bellugi, 1987) Sign language, like spoken and written language, is processed in the left brain hemisphere and is severely impaired by left-hemispheric but not right-hemispheric damage (Hickok, Love-Geffen & Klima,

2002). Likewise, the voice, which is usually associated with verbal communication, is nonverbal when it communicates analogically through grunts, screams, giggles, or vocal inflection during speech. The voice is involved in verbal communication only when it uses digital codes such as spoken words. The channel of communication is not a defining characteristic of nonverbal communication; rather, it is the type of message code that makes a meaningful difference (Table 1.1).

Table 1.1   Channels of Linguistic and Nonverbal Communication

Channel	Linguistic Messages	Nonverbal Messages
Kinesics:		
Gestures	Emblems, American Sign Language	Adaptors, illustrators
Facial movements	Lip reading, facial emblems	Spontaneous expressions
Voice	Talk, speech, language	Paralinguistics, vocalizations
Haptics	Braille, vibratese	Pats, hugs, strokes, squeezes
Music	Musical notation	Singing, melody, pitch
Space	"Keep Out" or "Welcome" Signs	Interpersonal distance
Physical appearance	T-shirt slogans, labels	Style of dress, physical attributes, facial recognition
Objects	Emblematic shapes, flags, road signs	Shapes, environments
Media	Verbal dialog, subtitles, letters, e-mail	Pictures, video, movies

The definition of nonverbal communication used in this book holds that purely nonverbal communication is analogic. Of course, it is rare that a message is purely verbal or purely nonverbal. Some messages fall in gray areas between these two message systems. Likewise, most communication is a combination of verbal and nonverbal communication. For some time, scholars have recognized that nonverbal communication has analogic properties (Birdwhistell, 1970; Koneya, 1977; Watzlawick et al., 1967; Wilden, 1972). Burgoon (1985b) argues that "many (though not all) nonverbal behaviors better qualify as analogic coding. They are nonarbitrary or natural behaviors that are continuous and infinite in form rather than discrete and finite" (p. 27). However, Burgoon, Buller, and Woodall (1996) argue that some nonverbal behaviors, such as the A-OK sign, are digital and arbitrary. Because such gestural emblems are primarily digital and arbitrary, they are usually considered a form of verbal communication, according to the perspective taken in this book (see Andersen, 1979; Koneya, 1977). It is important to recognize that gestural emblems represent gray areas, and some scholars are more likely to label them as a form of nonverbal communication while others may think they are really a form of verbal communication conveyed through a gestural modality like sign language.

As we will learn, all messages were probably analogic at one time. Thus, an emblem like the kill sign, made by running one's first finger across the throat, is quite analogic because it looks like what it stands for. Interestingly, this same sign might be used in a television studio or by a water-skier to signal "kill"; in these cases, the sign is becoming more arbitrary and digitalized. Such signs as the peace sign and nodding the head are now almost entirely arbitrary, and the origins of their meaning are fading with time.

Burgoon, Buller, and Woodall (1996) maintain that a number of nonverbal behaviors are discrete and symbolic, such as kisses, hairstyles, or postural shifts. The position held in this book is that these behaviors exist on an analogic continuum; there are an infinite number of hairstyles or hair colors and infinite degrees of kissing, from a peck on the cheek to a deep, lengthy kiss. These behaviors should be classified as nonverbal because they are many-valued, analogic acts that are largely relational in nature. The difference that makes a difference is that nonverbal behaviors use analogic codes that are processed by analogically oriented cognitive structures, whereas verbal communication employs digital codes and is processed by digitally oriented cognitive structures.

The Nonlinguistic Nature of Nonverbal Communication

A second defining characteristic of nonverbal communication is its nonlinguistic aspect. Almost forty years ago, Eisenberg and Smith (1971) put it well when they stated, "The real distinction between verbal and nonverbal communicative behavior lies in the system by which action is organized. Verbal behavior is organized by language systems, whereas nonverbal behavior is not" (p. 20). Language is an arbitrary, indirect system that is symbolic. Symbols stand for other things but may bear no natural relationship to the things they represent. Nonverbal communication is a natural, direct system that is not symbolic. Nonverbal signs naturally represent the things they stand for. This idea is consistent with the position that nonverbal communication is analogic and verbal communication is linguistic (P. A. Andersen et al., 1979). Indeed, Wilden (1980) contends that "natural language is the most highly organized form of digital communication" (p. 170).

Some scholars believe that many linguistic properties appear in nonverbal codes since some nonverbal codes are discrete and semantic (Burgoon 1985b). Here again, there are definitional disagreements as to what constitutes nonverbal communication. Head nods and peace symbols, by my definition, are linguistic, verbal forms of communication even though they employ a kinesic (body language) or pictorial modality. One should not assume that behaviors are nonverbal simply because they employ the face or hands—a problem with many noncriterial definitions of nonverbal communication. Recent research shows that skillful tool use, goal-oriented hand movements, semantics, and language are processed primarily in the mirror neurons of the left hemisphere regardless of channel/mode, visual or spoken (Baumgaertner, Buccino, Lange, McNamara, & Binkofski, 2007).

The position taken in this book is that behaviors must be analogic and nonlinguistic to qualify as nonverbal communication. Indeed, it is the unique character of nonverbal communication that necessitated a new set of research and theory separate from linguistic research and theory. As Siegman and Feldstein (1987) observe:

The concern with nonverbal communication is precisely a result of the increasing realization that there is more to communication than language. Infants communicate before they have even the rudimentary form of language and it is not unreasonable to assume that nonverbal communication predated verbal communication in the history of mankind as well. It will simply not do, therefore, to formulate a model of nonverbal communication based on verbal communication. (p. 4)

The Neurophysiological Basis of Nonverbal Communication

Perhaps the most compelling evidence of the difference between verbal and nonverbal communication comes from the field of neurophysiology, the study of the human brain and nervous system. Results of this research are summarized in an article by P. A. Andersen et al. (1979) that maintains, "Analogic, nonlinguistic, and right hemispheric are all ways of describing an underlying nonverbal coding schema that unites a variety of communication behaviors into one system" (p. 83). This nonverbal system is primarily governed by the right brain hemisphere. P. A. Andersen et al. (1975, 1979) reviewed research on brain-damaged split-brain patients (individuals whose corpus callosa are severed to prevent severe epileptic seizures), stutterers, and people with no neurological disabilities, concluding that nonverbal skills—including spatial relations, interpersonal touch, body motions, perceptions of clothing and objects, environmental sounds and music—are primarily governed by the right brain hemisphere. The right hemisphere excels at configurational, affective, nonverbal tasks, including melodic and vocalic qualities, facial expressions and recognition, and spatial perception and adjustment (Andersen, 1986; Blake, Duffy, Myers, and Tompkins, 2002; Bogen, 1977; Mandal & Ambady, 2004; Ogden, 1989; Pele, Kornreich, Foisy, & Dan, 2006; Sperli, Spinelli, Pollo, & Seeck, 2006; Vogel, Bowers, & Vogel, 2003). Aphasics, people with significant left hemispheric brain damage, cannot use symbolic or linguistic systems but are able to send and receive most nonverbal communication (P. A. Andersen et al., 1979; Saygin, Wilson, Dronkers, & Bates, 2004).

Research on communication deficits of brain-damaged persons and split-brain persons is particularly useful for identifying the neurophysiological distinction in the processing of verbal and nonverbal communication (for a complete review see P. A. Andersen et al., 1979). Severe damage, such as strokes or gunshot wounds to a particular part of the brain, results in lost communication functions. When the injury is to the left brain hemisphere, patients lose the ability to speak, read, and understand language or symbolic communication, leading researchers to conclude that the left hemisphere governs verbal and linguistic communication. In similar injuries to the right brain hemisphere, patients lose the

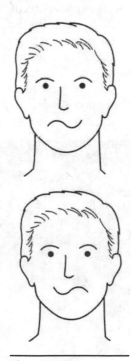

Figure 1.1
Which face looks happier? (See box on p. 11.)

ability to recognize familiar faces, to comprehend facial expression, to understand vocal inflections, to make sense of space and distance, and to create or understand music, leading to the conclusion that the right hemisphere governs nonverbal communication. Research shows that people who suffer from nonverbal learning disability syndrome and Asperger syndrome have some damage to the right brain hemisphere (Gunter, Ghaziuddin, & Ellis, 2002).

People with split brains have their corpus callosa (the nerve fibers that connect the right and left hemispheres) severed, leaving the right and left brain hemispheres out of contact with one another. Because the left visual field, left ear, and left side of the body are connected to the right brain hemisphere and the right visual field, right ear, and right side of the body are connected to the left brain hemisphere, researchers can selectively communicate with one brain hemisphere and not the other. The left visual field, the left ear, and the left hand can easily recognize objects and melodies but cannot name them since the right hemisphere has little linguistic ability. The right hand, right ear, and right visual field can identify verbal messages but have difficulty recognizing objects, faces, vocal intonation, and melody.

The research is consistent from these groups of brain-damaged persons as well as from studies of normal persons, leading to the conclusion that nonverbal communication is governed by the right brain hemisphere and verbal communication by the left brain hemisphere. In studies of normal people, for example, facial expressions of emotions mainly involved right hemispheric activity (Pizzagalli, Koenig, Regard, & Lehmann; 1998). Test this for yourself. Examine the photographs of the three faces below and the line drawings of the two faces on page 9. Answer the questions beneath each set of faces and then refer to the box "Nonverbal Communication and the Brain" on page 11.

In contrast to other definitions of nonverbal communication, P. A. Andersen and his colleagues (1979) propose that certain behaviors normally labeled nonver-

Chimeric faces: Which face looks most like the face on the left: the middle one or the one on the right? (See box on p. 11.)

> ### Nonverbal Communication and the Brain
>
> Chimeric faces are composites of two left halves or two right halves of a human face. Which face on page 10 do you think looks most like the face on the left (an unretouched photograph of a person's face)? Most people select the face in the middle, which consists of the two right halves of the person's face. The photograph on the right is a composite face made from the two left halves of the person's face. You see the right half of a person's face in your left visual field, and the information you receive in the left visual field is processed in your right brain hemisphere. Because your right brain hemisphere is much better at processing nonverbal information, including facial recognition, you derive a disproportionate share of information from the right half of someone's face. Thus, the right-halves composite (the photograph in the middle) looks more like the actual face (the photograph on the left) than the left-halves composite (the photograph on the right). Interestingly, both left- and right-handed parents cradle babies on the left side of their bodies, but not primarily due to the comforting sound of the parental heartbeat as once thought. Instead, left-side cradling of infants is due to the parent viewing the infant in their left visual field and right hemisphere, which processes nonverbal communication, the only kind of communication produced by infants (Sieratzki & Woll, 1996).
>
> For the same reason, most people think the bottom drawing on page 9 is happier than the top face. Just as we recognize faces in our left visual field and with our right brain hemisphere, so we recognize facial expressions more strongly from a person's right side of the face, because it appears in our left visual field and is processed in our right (nonverbal) brain hemisphere. Research suggests that the right side of the face exhibits strong, universal emotional displays as well (Mandal & Ambady, 2004).

bal are actually verbal if they employ a digital, linguistic, left-hemispheric code. Hand emblems, sign languages, lip reading, facial emblems, Braille type, musical notations, and slogans on T-shirts are forms of verbal communication because they use arbitrary symbols and are processed in the left brain hemisphere (Andersen, 1986; Hickok et al., 2002; Poizner et al., 1987; Wheeler, 1994). Although this perspective differs from some other definitions of nonverbal communication, it is supported by literally hundreds of neurophysiological studies (for summaries of this research see Andersen, 1986; P. A. Andersen et al., 1979; Bogen, 1977; Corballis, 2003; Lindell, 2006; Kimura, 1973; Knecht et al., 2001; Mandal & Ambady, 2004; Murphy & Venables, 1970; Poizner et al., 1987; Vogel et al., 2003). Moreover, evidence indicates "that there is relatively fixed [neural] architecture associated with the language module, although it is clearly spread across a number of different cortical and sub-cortical areas of the left hemisphere" (Marshall, 1984, p. 229). In other words, language is hardwired into the left hemisphere for most human beings.

This does not mean that the right hemisphere has no language ability. Lindell (2006) has recently shown that the right hemisphere has some linguistic ability and additionally contributes prosodic and paralinguistic information that compliments language. Stacks and Andersen (1989) summarize research that shows that although language is primarily left-hemispheric, the right hemisphere has a rudimentary conception of language. Analogously, a baseball pitcher can throw with either hand but usually can excel with only the dominant hand. So too with communication. The left hemisphere is specialized for language. Although the right hemisphere is specialized for nonverbal communication, it does have the linguistic ability of a preschooler.

Several criticisms have been targeted at the neurophysiological definition of nonverbal communication as being right-hemispheric. Some critics have argued that the two hemispheres are interdependent and that as such the hemispheric distinction is false. While Burgoon (1985a) maintained that "there is some hemispheric lateralization in the reception and production of verbal and nonverbal stimuli, with the left hemisphere typically more dominant for verbal signals and the right hemisphere for nonverbal ones" (p. 366), she also criticizes models that rigidly dichotomize brain function:

> However, there is growing evidence that the two hemispheres are highly interdependent in the processing of social information. The left-right distinction may therefore be more a matter of style differences, with the left showing a superiority in handling digital, symbolic, and rational stimuli and the right showing a superiority in encoding and interpreting analogic, visual gestalt, and emotional material. (p. 366)

This is an excellent point that is consistent with current neurophysiological research. Indeed, P. A. Andersen and his associates (1979) showed that "we do not have a split brain, but a whole brain with highly specialized parts" (p. 75). One textbook suggests a change in the way we conceive of the brain.

> Some texts use hemispheric differences (more commonly known as left brain/ right brain) to refer to processing differences; however, we prefer *hemispheric style*. . . . The left hemisphere of the brain is responsible for most people's verbal communication. This side of the brain is specialized in an abstract, logical, and analytical way which is best used in the analysis of language. The right hemisphere . . . is specialized for spatiotemporal, gestalt, emotive forms of communication for which nonverbal is best suited. (Hickson, Stacks, & Moore, 2004, p. 24)

The human brain is exceedingly complex and even capable of varying its own neural structure. Research suggests that the typical pattern of brain organization separates messages into linguistic and nonlinguistic categories and processes them in the hemisphere best suited for that code and cognition.

A second criticism of the neurophysiological approach to defining nonverbal communication is that some nonverbal behaviors originate in and are controlled by the left hemisphere, not the right (Burgoon, 1980; McNeill, 1985). Critics maintain that many nonverbal behaviors such as rhythmic gestures are actually processed in the left hemisphere. This criticism ignores two factors: (1) that one purpose of gestures is activation of cognitive processes (Wesp, Hesse, Keutmann, & Wheaton, 2001) and (2) the complex neurological basis of gestures among pairs of communicators during interpersonal interaction. Gestures accompanying speech are mainly right-handed and left-hemispheric (Vaid, Bellugi & Poizner, 1989; Kinsbourne, 2006). This phenomenon is explained by the fact that during face-to-face interaction, right-handed gestures are picked up in the *receiver's* left visual field and right hemisphere. The human brain evolved in such a way that important gestural information can be processed by the receiver's left visual field and nonverbal right hemisphere without interfering with the verbal, left hemisphere's decoding of talk (Jaffe, 1987; Kimura, 1973) and is even produced automatically by speakers who are blind from birth (Iverson & Goldin-Meadow, 1998). However, other gestures originate in the right brain hemisphere, particularly those that do not accompany speech (Kendon, 1983). According to Bavelas, Chovil, Coates, and Roe (1995), "interactive gestures assist the dialog itself rather than serving semantic or syntactic functions" (p. 404). In short, they are nonlinguistic and nonverbal.

As discussed previously, one type of gesture, the emblem (for example, the peace sign or hitchhiker's thumb), is usually a part of the verbal/left hemisphere system as are signs in American Sign Language. Koneya (1977) has shown that emblems are part of the verbal communication system because they are actually words that have precise dictionary meanings. "Emblems are held to be socially constructed, and differ extensively between cultures" (Kinsbourne, 2006). Emblems, along with Morse code, semaphores, smoke signals, and sign languages, are verbal, left-hemispheric communication codes. Indeed, extensive research (Hickok et al., 2002; Poizner et al., 1987) shows that left-hemispheric injuries disrupt all sign language and emblematic communication, whereas right-hemispheric injuries have little effect on these abilities. Poizner et al. (1987) concluded their book, *What the Hands Reveal about the Brain*, by stating:

> Right hemisphere damage disrupts spatial relations but spares syntactic ones; left hemisphere damage disrupts the use of space for syntactic relations but spares its use for spatial relations. Taken together these data suggest that the left cerebral hemisphere in humans may have an innate predisposition for the central components of language independent of language modality. (p. 212)

A third alleged problem with using neurophysiological criteria to define nonverbal communication is that many perceptual phenomena do not conform to a left-brain/right-brain split. Burgoon (1985b) asserted that rhythmic patterns and free movement are received by the left hemisphere. Research has shown that rhythm is received and processed by the left hemisphere only when speech sounds are involved but in the right hemisphere when the sounds are nonverbal (P. A. Andersen et al., 1979; Kimura, 1973; Murphy & Venables, 1970). Burgoon (1985b) also suggested that "the right hemisphere receives such 'speech tied' phenomena as note pitch and volume" (p. 271). This is true, but rate, pitch, and volume are nonverbal aspects of speech called vocalics (Burgoon & Saine, 1978) or paralinguistics, and they are a form of nonverbal communication (P. A. Andersen et al., 1979). Right hemispheric stroke impairs paralinguistic production and processing in both right-handers and lefties (Mackenzie & Brady, 2004). Buck (1984) summarized research that shows that affective tone of voice is a right-hemispheric function. However, Buck (1988) maintained that much of nonverbal communication is processed in subcortical brain regions of both hemispheres but particularly in the right brain hemisphere. Recent research on neural networks suggests that nonverbal communication is highly lateralized to the right brain hemisphere (Harle, Rockstroh, Keil, Wienbruch, & Elbert, 2004).

Scholars have defined nonverbal communication in many ways. The requirement in this text that nonverbal behavior should be analogic, nonlinguistic, and right-hemispheric is a narrower definition and suggests that a number of previously labeled nonverbal behaviors are actually verbal. These verbal behaviors include emblematic road signs, lip movements, some gestures such as emblems, musical notation, sign language, and Braille writing. However, some behaviors that at one time were labeled verbal would be considered nonverbal according to this definition. These nonverbal behaviors include some types of speech, such as greetings and curses, most phatic (emotionalized or ritualized) communication, singing, and of course vocalizations and paralinguistics (Table 1.1). Unlike the other definitions reviewed in the following section, this text's definition is based on properties of the message code itself, not on the channel or modality in which it occurs. It is irrelevant whether language is encoded with the voice, the hands, or the keyboard—it is still language. Variation in the message code is the *difference that makes a difference* and the definitive criterion of nonverbal communication used in this book.

Other Definitions of Nonverbal Communication

No disciplinary consensus has formed around a single definition of nonverbal communication. Thus, it is important to examine other definitions so that you, the reader, can understand and appreciate other approaches and develop your own definition.

Five groups of definitions have been offered by communication scholars. The most common definition considers all communication behavior other than words to be nonverbal communication (Burgoon & Saine, 1978; Eisenberg & Smith, 1971; Harrison, 1974; Knapp, 1972/1978; Mehrabian, 1972; Rosenfeld & Civikly, 1976). The fact that no recent texts primarily employ this definition (not even by the authors just cited) suggests that this definition may be losing favor. This definition classifies communication based on superficial criteria—the absence or presence of words—rather than on the distinction of message codes (for detailed criticisms see Andersen et al., 1975; Knapp & Hall, 1997; Noller, 1984; Richmond, McCroskey, & Payne, 1987). Words are but one class of rhetorical or symbolic messages; they are typically verbal but do not always fall in the verbal/linguistic domain. Words themselves have a number of nonverbal, paralinguistic aspects. Swearing, cursing, grunting, and singing, as you will learn, are produced orally but are really nonverbal forms of communication.

A second common approach that rarely appears in the literature today is to list various behaviors that allegedly constitute nonverbal communication (Barker & Collins, 1970; Benson & Frandsen, 1976; Leathers, 1976). The drawback to this approach is that it provides no underlying criteria for what behaviors actually belong on the list (Andersen et al., 1975).

A third approach defines nonverbal communication according to the sender orientation (Motley, 1990, 1991). This approach advocates that only intentional, symbolic behaviors should be considered communication. The problem is most nonverbal communication behaviors are in fact spontaneous, biologically based, and nonsymbolic (Andersen, 1991; Buck & VanLear, 2002, Cappella, 1991a). Indeed, the sender-orientation definition of communication would exclude most of behaviors described in this book. An even more serious problem with approach is that many, perhaps most, messages are sent without intentional, d erate encoding. Finally, it has been shown that senders, receivers, and even researchers cannot determine intent! We have no idea if a smile, for example, is symptomatic of a private feeling, a spontaneous communication behavior, or an intentional, symbolic act. As Bavelas (1990) has clearly stated regarding intentionality, "It is amazing to think how long we have let ourselves be dominated by a concept that its proponents admit they cannot adequately define or measure" (p. 595).

A fourth approach that continues to receive attention is that of Weiner, Devoe, Rubinow, and Geller (1972), who attempted to distinguish between nonverbal behavior and nonverbal communication. They define nonverbal communication as consisting of arbitrarily coded, intentional, and symbolic actions. Moreover, they require that these behaviors must exist in verbal contexts. This is certainly a restrictive definition that would exclude most nonverbal behavior described in this book. Indeed, this definition would limit the study of communication to arbitrary, digital, linguistic forms of communication, which are defined in this book as verbal! Some researchers have criticized Weiner et al. (1972) for their inappropriate use of a verbal model to define nonverbal communication (P. A. Andersen et al., 1979; Ellyson & Dovidio, 1985; Siegman & Feldstein, 1978). Others have criticized this type of definition because it is difficult to determine, even by interactants, which behaviors are intentional (Burgoon, 1985a; Harper et al., 1978). Certainly this definition is too restrictive for our purpose and, in fact, may actually exclude all nonverbal behavior from the realm of communication.

A less restrictive definition of nonverbal communication based on message orientation is provided by Burgoon and her associates (Burgoon, 1980, 1985a; Burgoon, Buller, & Woodall, 1996). Her definition is widely known and used by many scholars. According to this perspective, nonverbal communication is limited to behaviors that "are typically sent with intent, are used with regularity among members of a social community, are typically interpreted as intentional, and have consensually recognizable interpretations" (Burgoon, Buller, & Woodall, 1996, p. 13).

> The message orientation, with its focus on the code rather than encoders and decoders, rules out idiosyncratic mannerisms, behaviors that do not occur with any regularity, actions or attributes that are merely informative . . . and activities that do not regularly evoke the same interpretations across members of the social system engaging in them. (Burgoon, 1980, p. 180)

Burgoon's message orientation is based on the premise that the nonverbal system is an intentional system, derivative of language and containing some of the same basic elements as linguistic codes. Several problems devolve from this definition: (1) The requirement that nonverbal communication consist of typically intentionally sent actions eliminates most nonverbal actions from the realm of communication, including proxemic behaviors—an area in which Burgoon herself conducted research (see Burgoon & Jones, 1976; Burgoon & Aho, 1982)—which are typically unintentional unconscious acts (Bargh & Chartrand, 1999). (2) The requirement that no idiosyncratic behaviors be considered communication would rule out special codes or acts used by subcultures, as well as secret handshakes, expressions, or tokens used by intimate dyads (two-person groups) with special meaning only to that dyad. Clearly, our position is that nonverbal communication can be common to entire cultures or the entire human race or specific to a single dyad. (3) The message orientation is inherently ambiguous because individuals or researchers disagree about what is typically intentional, regularly used, and what behaviors have consistently recognizable interpretations. The requirement that nonverbal communication behaviors be typically sent with intent or typically received with intent is virtually impossible to determine. Indeed, in criticizing another perspective Burgoon (1985a) maintains, "One difficulty with this perspective is that it is very easy to deny intentionality for much of what goes on nonverbally. . . . The question then becomes who arbitrates what was intentional and what was not—the source, an 'objective' observer or who?" (p. 348).

A number of researchers take the position that the receiver determines if communication has occurred. Buck (1984) maintained that "behavior can be defined as communicative to the extent that it reduces uncertainty in the behavior of another" (p. 4). Buck argued that "many of the most interesting findings in the field of nonverbal communication involve influences via such spontaneous behaviors" (p. 5). Malandro, Barker, and Barker (1989) took a similar position that "nonverbal communication will be defined as the process by which nonverbal behaviors are used, either singly or in combination with verbal behaviors, in the exchange and interpretation of messages within a given situation or context" (p. 5). Similarly, Richmond and McCroskey (1995) summarized the receiver-based definition when they wrote, "nonverbal behavior becomes nonverbal communication if another person interprets the behavior as a message and assigns meaning to it" (p. 5).

This receiver-based definition has received criticism. For example, Burgoon, Buller, and Woodall (1989) maintain, "The main objection to this perspective is that it is too broad. . . . It permits treating as communication such involuntary and idiosyncratic behaviors as allergic sneezing and frequent blinking" (p. 16). However, under some circumstances, receivers might obtain meaning from these bizarre actions and treat them as messages. The position taken in this book is clear. *If a receiver obtains meaning from another's action, then communication has occurred. If this action is nonlinguistic and analogic, then nonverbal communication has occurred.*

The final and broadest position defines all behavior as communication (Wilden, 1972). Barker and Collins (1970) even argued that "nonverbal communication is much broader than nonverbal behavior. A room devoid of behaving, living things communicates atmosphere and function. Static clothing communicates the personality of the wearer" (p. 344). These broad definitions have been criticized widely. For example, Burgoon (1985a) argued that to treat all nonverbal behavior as communication "is the least productive, if for no other reason than a pragmatic one. It makes the task of discovering general principles of communication nearly impossible if every facet of human behavior must be accounted for" (p. 348). Certainly, many scholars agree with the position taken in this book that receivers must assign meaning to a particular behavior before it can be called communication.

DIFFERENCES BETWEEN VERBAL
AND NONVERBAL COMMUNICATION

What differences exist between verbal and nonverbal communication? Although both are parts of human communication and frequently occur simultaneously, they are based on different systems, each with a number of unique properties that are important for the student of communication to understand. Three distinctions between verbal and nonverbal communication have already been introduced:

Principle 1—Nonverbal communication is an analogic code; verbal communication is a digital code.

Principle 2—Nonverbal communication is nonlinguistic; verbal communication is a language system based on arbitrary meaning.

Principle 3—Nonverbal communication is processed primarily in the right brain hemisphere; verbal communication is processed primarily in the left brain hemisphere.

In the following section, we will examine sixteen additional distinctions between verbal and nonverbal communication (Table 1.2).

The Origin of Communication

Without much doubt, verbal and nonverbal communication did not evolve at the same time in the species, nor are they acquired simultaneously by individual communicators. This fact is underscored by evidence that verbal and nonverbal communication originated from different systems, which leads us to the next set of differences, based on biology.

THE BIOLOGICAL BASIS OF NONVERBAL COMMUNICATION

Principle 4—Nonverbal communication is primarily biologically based, whereas verbal communication is primarily culturally based. Most nonverbal code systems are biologically programmed. For example, Ekman and associates (Ekman & Friesen, 1975; Ekman, Friesen, & Ellsworth, 1972) identified a set of basic facial expressions that show little cultural variation around the world. Buck (1982, 1984, 1988, Buck & VanLear, 2002) demonstrated that the spontaneous, right-hemispheric system is founded on a biologically programmed set of signals. By contrast, although the capacity for language is innate, verbal and symbolic communication is based on a socially developed, socially learned, culturally shared communication system. This is why some nonverbal communication is universal and pancultural, whereas no universal verbal codes have been discovered. Right brain damage is disruptive of biologically based emotional and affective communication (Buck & VanLear, 2002; Mandal & Ambady, 2004). Cappella (1991a) showed that the process of stimulus regulation and emotional responsiveness are biological, automated forms of nonverbal interaction. This is not to say that cultural differences are nonexistent in nonverbal communication. Indeed, all cultures communicate at different distances, use different amounts of touch, and gesture somewhat differently, to mention but a few examples. (Chapter 4 includes a detailed discussion of how nonverbal communication displays culture.)

Table 1.2   Differences between Verbal and Nonverbal Communication Systems

	Verbal Communication Is:	Nonverbal Communication Is:
Fundamental Differences	1. Digital	1. Analogic
	2. Linguistic	2. Nonlinguistic
	3. Left-hemispheric	3. Right-hemispheric
Origins	4. Primarily culturally based	4. Primarily biologically based
	5. Phylogenetically recent	5. Phylogenetically ancient
	6. Developmentally secondary	6. Developmentally primary
	7. Culturally based system	7. Relatively universal system cross-culturally
Codes	8. Highly notational	8. Iconic
	9. Discontinuous/intermittent	9. Continuous
	10. Unitized	10. Nonunitized
Channel	11. Single-channeled	11. Multichanneled
	12. Awkwardly redundant	12. Simultaneously redundant
Cognition	13. Encoded/decoded discretely	13. Encoded/decoded as a gestalt
	14. Analytic	14. Syncretic
	15. Symbolic	15. Spontaneous
	16. Relatively manipulated	16. Relatively honest
Functional Distinctions	17. Used to convey precise information	17. Used to convey global meanings
	18. Logical and cognitive	18. Affective and emotional
	19. Content-oriented	19. Relational

The Phylogenetic Primacy of Nonverbal Communication

Principle 5—Nonverbal communication is an earlier genetic development than verbal communication. Scholars who study nonverbal processes generally agree that nonverbal communication evolved long before verbal communication in the human species (Andersen, 1986; Bateson, 1972; Burgoon, Buller, & Woodall, 1996; Watzlawick et al., 1967). Animals are adept nonverbal communicators, suggesting to some people that nonverbal is an intellectually inferior, lower-level type of communication. But this is not the case. Animals have evolved amazing nonverbal communication systems that entail heat sensors, sonar, great visual acuity, and powerful olfactory sensing. Although the evolution of verbal language has caused some nonverbal systems to decay in the human species—for example, our olfactory sense is only 1 percent as powerful as a dog's sense of smell—some forms of nonverbal communication have continued to develop right beside language. As Bateson (1972) maintained:

The kinesics of men [and women] have become richer and more complex, and paralanguage has blossomed side by side with the evolution of verbal language. Both kinesics and paralanguage have been elaborated into complex forms of art, music, ballet, poetry, and the like, and even in everyday life, the intricacies of human kinesic communication, facial expression, and vocal intonation far exceed anything any other animal is known to produce. The logician's dream that men should communicate only by unambiguous digital signals has not come true and is not likely to. (p. 412)

The evolutionary primacy of nonverbal communication suggests that we are biologically programmed to attend first to nonverbal signals and to give them greater weight in communication. This appears to be true particularly in times of danger or stress, when we revert to the older nonverbal system. As we will see, nonverbal communication has more personal validity than the more recent, more abstract verbal system (Watzlawick et al., 1967).

THE DEVELOPMENTAL PRIMACY OF NONVERBAL COMMUNICATION

Principle 6—Nonverbal communication precedes verbal communication in each individual.   Long before babies utter their first word or understand the words of others, they can send and receive nonverbal messages. Newborn infants can send and receive basic haptic (tactile), vocalic, kinesic, and olfactory messages (Andersen, Andersen, & Landgraf, 1985; Camras, 1982; Stern, 1980). Burgoon, Buller, and Woodall (1996) maintained that the early importance of nonverbal modes of expression at the crucial and dependent developmental stages from birth into early childhood may contribute to our continued reliance on nonverbal communication systems throughout life. Burgoon (1985a) summarized considerable evidence of the developmental and phylogenetic primacy of nonverbal communication and concluded, "Given that these behaviors largely precede the acquisition of language, their evolutionary and ontogenetic primacy should make them particularly potent communication vehicles" (p. 356).

THE CROSS-CULTURAL SIMILARITY OF NONVERBAL COMMUNICATION

Principle 7—Nonverbal communication displays considerable cross-cultural similarities; verbal communication does not.   A number of nonverbal actions show substantial cross-cultural similarity. This suggests a biological basis for nonverbal communication, although parallel cultural developmental patterns may account for some of the similarities. In an interesting set of experiments, Ekman and his associates showed pictures of facial expressions to people from different cultures around the world (Ekman & Friesen, 1975). In culture after culture, viewers labeled each facial expression similarly. The facial expression of basic emotions including fear, disgust, anger, sadness, happiness, and surprise showed striking cross-cultural consistency. Eibl-Eibesfeldt (1979) summarized his own research, which demonstrated that children who are blind from birth exhibit the same expressions of smiling, laughing, crying, fear, and anger as do sighted children, suggesting a biological origin of facial expression. Likewise, children who have been blind since birth and have never seen a gesture use the same number of gestures as sighted children (Iverson & Goldin-Meadow, 1998), suggesting the biological basis of gesturing.

Some hand gestures also appear to have universal cross-cultural meanings, such as the fist, a sign of anger and aggression; and the open palm, a sign of peace or greeting in most cultures. Frick (1985) reported that prosodic (rhythmic) aspects of the voice are virtually identical in every culture: "There is little evidence for either personal idiosyncrasies or cultural differences in the prosodic communication of emotion" (p. 414). Gestures are very similar across culture, "leaving only the details and refinements of execution to cultural choice" (Kinsbourne, 2006, p. 210).

The cross-cultural similarity of many nonverbal behaviors can significantly aid intercultural communication (although, as we will learn, cultural differences in nonverbal communication can be substantial; see chapter 4). Smiling, patting one's stomach, frowning, laughing, shrugging, and pointing are messages that can easily communicate when two interactants share no common language. Burgoon (1985a) concluded, "Because of their ability to bridge cultural differences, such nonverbal behaviors have a communicative power lacking from culture-bound verbal languages" (p. 352).

The Distinctive Coding of Verbal and Nonverbal Communication

One of the most basic and important differences between verbal and nonverbal communication is the way they are coded. As we discussed earlier, verbal codes are linguistic symbol systems, with each word bearing an arbitrary relationship to its referent. Nonverbal codes are direct, analogic, sometimes abbreviated signs that have an intrinsic relationship to their referent. Three other properties of nonverbal codes—iconicity, continuousness, and nonunitization—distinguish these codes from the verbal communication system.

ICONICITY

Principle 8—Nonverbal codes are iconic; verbal codes are notational. Virtually all nonverbal messages are iconic; that is, they directly resemble the object or event they represent (Andersen, Garrison, & Andersen, 1979; Bateson, 1972, Buck & Van-Lear, 2002). Statues, paintings, pantomimes, photographs, and facial expressions are examples of iconic codes because they directly resemble their referent. These codes are processed in the parts of the right brain hemisphere that are specialized for visual, nonverbal codes (P. A. Andersen et al., 1979; Marshall, 1984). According to Bateson (1972), most iconic messages are sent unconsciously and involuntarily. The graphic quality of iconic gestures and behaviors creates vivid, attention-getting messages that are missing from verbal communication (Burgoon, 1985a). Iconic signals tend to be easily interpreted by virtually all receivers cross-culturally because of their intrinsic meaning. Iconic communication is a principal mode of communication in animals and humans. As Wilden (1980) contended, "All non-linguistic communication through the senses, between person and person or person and world, with the single exception of conventionalized signals, involves analog and iconic communication" (p. 163). Writing, numbers, computer language, and Morse code are highly notational systems and part of the verbal domain. Computer icons, a form of nonverbal communication, are used rather than words because they directly resemble the function for which they stand.

CONTINUOUSNESS

Principle 9—Nonverbal communication is continuous; verbal communication is discontinuous. Purely nonverbal and analogic communication codes are continuous and cannot be turned off (Andersen, 1984; Eisenberg & Smith, 1971; Richmond et al., 1987). Words come and go and start and stop, but nonverbal and analogic messages are sent continuously. This is consistent with the receiver perspective explained earlier in this chapter. Nonverbal messages are continuously available to receivers; nonverbal communication begins when receivers assign meaning to these behaviors. Analogic systems cannot be shut off and have no form of negation, whereas digital systems introduce gaps into continuums (Wilden, 1980). It is for these reasons that one cannot choose not to communicate nonverbally (see Andersen, 1991).

There are no blank facial expressions. Attempts to create a blank expression are perceived by receivers as anger, sadness, or withdrawal. The face is continuously sending messages as long as another individual is present to receive them. Likewise, one cannot choose to stand a nondistance from another. The individual is always relatively near to or far from others and communicating through this proxemic system. Similarly, gestures cannot be shut off. Even folded or completely still hands send messages of composure or relaxation. Analogic systems, including nonverbal communication, represent the smallest differences that form a continuum along which all behaviors fall. Some scholars dispute the continuous nature of individual nonverbal behaviors. Richmond et al. (1987) contended, "Individual nonverbal messages indeed do stop. Gestures begin and end. Eye contact begins and ends" (p. 3). But this argument misses the point. Although a particular gesture may have a beginning and an end, the

A person can try to display a blank facial expression, but in reality there are no blank expressions. What are some messages that this young woman's face conveys to you?

gestural system is continuous. Non-gestures have the potential to signal relaxation or boredom. Similarly, eye contact can begin or end, but the oculesic (visual) channel is continuously sending messages. Little or no eye contact can signal boredom, rudeness, introversion, disinterest, and a variety of other messages. Even if you accept the fact that particular nonverbal messages can be discontinuous, most scholars concede that as a "package" of simultaneous messages, nonverbal communication is continuous (Richmond et al., 1987).

NONUNITIZATION

Principle 10—Nonverbal communication has no basic units; verbal communication is unitized. Whether verbal communication is spoken, signed, written, or computer-processed, the basic unit is the word or the morpheme (the smallest linguistic unit that carries meaning). If a verbal or linguistic message contains less than a morpheme, it has no meaning. Not so with nonverbal communication. Because nonverbal communication is continuous and non-unitized, the smallest segment of nonverbal behavior is potentially meaningful. A picture of a face taken at 1/400 of a second is still a face and contains a meaningful expression at that point in time. The face in a snapshot is not as meaningful as a videotaped face or a live face because its continuousness is frozen, and changes in expression cannot be captured by a single photograph. Nevertheless, any small slice of nonverbal communication may be meaningful because it does not require a complete morphemic unit, as does verbal communication. Indeed, recent research on "thin slicing" reveals that people are remarkably capable of making very accurate judgments about nonverbal behavior based on very short, "thin" slices of nonverbal behavior of a minute or even a few seconds in length (Ambady, Bernieri, & Richeson, 2000; Friedman, Oltmanns, Gleason, & Turkheimer, 2006; Murphy, 2005).

In her summary of nonverbal self-presentation research, DePaulo (1992) concluded, "It is impossible to regulate nonverbal behavior in such a way that no expression is conveyed. Thus, with regard to its attributional implications, nonverbal behavior is irrepressible" (p. 234). The nonunitized quality of nonverbal communication is why nonverbal analysis and research must abandon the linguistic model that was pioneered by Birdwhistell (1970). His linguistic model studied kinesics and established the kine as the basic unit of behavior. Language, however, is a poor model for nonverbal communication; and as such, Birdwhistell's linguistic model has led to no recent nonverbal research. "Unfortunately, kinesic communication is analogic and contains no basic unit of meaning" (P. A. Andersen et al., 1979, p. 85).

Channel Distinctions

A wink, a nod, a comment, and a gesture all communicate through different channels. In this section, we will explore how nonverbal communication is multichanneled, inherently redundant, and viewed as a gestalt. Verbal communication is single-channeled, awkwardly redundant, and processed as a discrete unit of meaning.

MULTICHANNELIZATION

Principle 11—Nonverbal communication is multichanneled; verbal communication is single-channeled. Virtually all nonverbal scholars agree about the multichanneled nature of nonverbal communication (Andersen, 1984; Burgoon, 1985a; LaFrance & Mayo, 1978). Most messages contain information in multiple nonverbal channels. For example, extreme excitement can be conveyed verbally with an expression such as, "Wow, I'm excited!" Such excitement may also be accompanied by a multiple set of nonverbal messages including giggles, wide eyes, smiles, clapping hands, running, open postures, jumping up and down, rapid movements, hands covering the mouth, an open mouth, expressive gestures, hugs, and loud or fast vocal utterances, to name only a few possibilities.

Consistent multichanneled messages communicate sincerity, honesty, and believability because each channel provides additional weight to the overall message. Also, it is hard to lie in ten channels, whereas verbal lies are relatively easy to achieve. These are some of the reasons that nonverbal communication is believed over verbal communication. However, this same multichanneled system has the capacity to send simultaneously contradictory messages such as approach and avoidance, ecstasy and guilt, joy and sorrow, or love and hate. Burgoon (1985a) maintained that these multimodal nonverbal messages give both encoders and decoders rich arrays of cues to send or to observe. Such multichanneled messages can increase both precision and ambiguity.

SIMULTANEOUS REDUNDANCY

Principle 12—Nonverbal communication is inherently redundant; verbal communication requires repetition for redundancy.   One of the basic principles of information theory (the major theory of information flow in communication) is that repetition and redundancy increase accuracy. Redundancy increases accuracy. Yes, redundancy increases accuracy. But verbal repetitiveness is fatiguing, nagging, and boring even though it increases accuracy. Verbal communication is poorly suited to redundancy because it is a single-channeled type of communication.

Cherry (1966) maintained that if a message "has zero redundancy, then any errors in transmission and reception owing to disturbance or noise will cause the receiver to make an uncorrectable and unidentifiable mistake" (p. 186). Redundancy increases accuracy (I know you're tired of reading that) because noise, poor reception, and inattention can prevent accurate communication. Redundant messages enhance the probability that one or more will be received, creating communication. As Bateson (1972) demonstrated, redundancy increases the signal/noise ratio and promotes communication.

Nonverbal communication is a highly redundant system. A person who is retreating, cowering, whimpering, and hunched over with a tearful facial expression is redundantly signaling fearfulness. Nonverbal messages often send simultaneous, multichanneled, consistent messages that are hard for even the most imperceptive receiver to miss. Thus, nonverbal communication is a highly efficient system. Nonverbal communication can also signal relational messages between interactants. If someone always walks the other way, avoids eye contact, turns away, or hides her or his face in your presence, negative relational messages are being clearly communicated. Bateson (1972) suggested that "human communication which increases redundancy in relationships between persons is still preponderantly iconic and is achieved by means of kinesics, paralinguistics, intention movements, actions, and the like" (p. 423). In short, nonverbal communication enables communication to overcome noise and define relationships with others.

Cognitive Differences

How do people mentally process and make sense of verbal and nonverbal messages? Research shows that the cognitive, or mental, processing of verbal and nonverbal communication is quite different. We have already reviewed research showing that verbal communication and nonverbal communication are processed in distinct neural structures, the left and right brain hemispheres, respectively. But several other important differences exist in the way these two types of messages are processed.

NONVERBAL GESTALTS

Principle 13—Nonverbal messages are processed as a gestalt; verbal messages are processed discretely. Gestalt processing means that we make sense of an interdependent whole rather than isolated parts. This is the way nonverbal communication is encoded and decoded, as a whole. It is likely that multichanneled gestalt impressions are the basis of human intuition (Andersen, 1985; Lieberman, 2000; Pell, 2005). Conversely, single-channeled, discrete verbal messages are the basis of logic.

Nonverbal behavior is decoded as a gestalt. Typically, we do not concentrate solely on, say, a person's feet or vocal pitch to detect nervousness or happiness. We take in the whole picture intuitively. Research shows that messages of nonverbal immediacy or warmth are processed as a gestalt. According to Andersen (1985), "It is quite clear that receivers do not count individual behaviors when judging the warmth or immediacy of interactants. Some sort of gestalt impression of immediacy is doubtlessly how receivers operate in real interactions" (p. 12). In a study by Gutsell and Andersen (1980), receivers were shown a videotaped lecture by a person who smiled either a lot, a little, or not at all. Receivers perceived that the person who smiled a lot touched the viewers more, gestured more, and stood closer to the viewers, even though he was actually in a completely still position with his hands out of view. Why did this occur? Receivers look for gestalt patterns in a communicator's behavior. If they receive information in only one or two channels, they *infer* that the other channels are congruent. This demonstrates the gestalt nature of nonverbal processing. Likewise, it is almost impossible not to encode nonverbal messages as a gestalt. Try to express affection with your body and face but not your hands or voice. It is very hard to accomplish.

SYNCRETIC PROCESSING

Principle 14—Nonverbal messages are processed syncretically; verbal messages are processed analytically. Syncretic cognition is a kind of thinking that takes in the whole picture. It is broad rather than deep and involves synthesis rather than analysis. This is consistent with the broad, synthetic nature of right-hemispheric, nonverbal processes and the gestalt nature of nonverbal communication. Tucker (1981) demonstrated that the right hemisphere is associated with imaginal, holistic, syncretic cognition. Buck (1982, 1988) maintained that nonverbal, right-hemispheric processes are associated with syncretic cognition that is sensitive to simultaneous, holistic information as opposed to sequential, verbal stimuli. By contrast, analytic processes, including verbal processes, are logical, sequential, and involve in-depth examination of a single idea or message. Logical analysis involves sequential reasoning through verbal premises to a rational conclusion.

The left hemisphere is specialized for dealing with things in sequence, such as causal relations or logical problems. The logical, sequential nature of verbal, linguistic, and mathematical processes predisposes the brain to process these types of information in the part of the brain best suited for such tasks—the left hemisphere (P. A. Andersen et al., 1979, p. 75).

So, two distinct types of cognitive processes coexist and cooperate during mental activity. Each is specialized for processing a particular aspect of a message.

SPONTANEOUS ENCODING

Principle 15—Nonverbal messages are spontaneous, whereas verbal systems are symbolic. Nonverbal actions are not symbolic. Most are signs or signals that are spontaneously produced. Burgoon (1985b) described this quality well:

> A final special property of nonverbal coding is its spontaneity, actual and perceived. Just as reception of nonverbal behavior is rapid and direct, so may its encoding be relatively uncontrolled and quick, especially for those behaviors that have intrinsically derived meaning. A byproduct is the popular belief that nonverbal behaviors are more spontaneous and thus more "truthful" than verbal expressions. (p. 279)

Buck (1984, 1988, Buck & VanLear, 2002) has described the spontaneous communication system in detail. Spontaneous communication is not symbolic because the referent is not arbitrary or socially determined. Spontaneous communication is made up mainly of signs that have a natural intrinsic relationship to their referent. Similarly, spontaneous communication is an automatic or reflexive response, is nonpropositional, and is related to the right hemisphere (Buck, 1984). According to research by Palmer and Simmons (1995), "nonverbal behaviors may be selected and enacted as a result of cognitive processing that occurs below the level of consciousness" (p. 131). Nonverbal communication and "biologically based gestures are not symbolic in that their relationship to their referents is not arbitrary" (Buck & VanLear, 2002, p. 524). Some nonverbal behaviors become "pseudospontaneous" when the sender intentionally manipulates their behavior, by deliberately smiling, acting, or imitating spontaneous displays (Buck & VanLear, 2002).

Symbolic communication, perhaps unique to humans and the province of the left hemisphere, is verbal and linguistic. Buck (1984, 1988, Buck & VanLear, 2002) has shown that symbolic communication is socially shared and learned, has arbitrary relationships to referents, and is processed in the left brain hemisphere. As Andersen (1991) concluded, "Symbolic messages have arbitrary relationships with their referents and are the creations of human beings in specific cultural contexts. Spontaneous messages have a natural, biological relationship with their referents" (p. 317).

AUTHENTICITY

Principle 16—Nonverbal communication is perceived to be more genuine and is more likely to be believed than is verbal communication. A final cognitive quality of nonverbal communication is its greater believability. Numerous studies show that people rely more on nonverbal communication than on verbal communication for social meaning, although the relative contribution varies from study to study (Amabile & Kabat, 1982; Archer & Akert, 1977; Hegstrom, 1979; Mehrabian & Weiner, 1967; Philpot, 1983). Indeed, Philpot's (1983) meta-analysis of 23 studies on the relative communicative contribution of verbal and nonverbal channels reported that slightly over 30 percent of the variance in meaning is attributable to verbal communication, with the remainder being attributable to nonverbal communication or an interaction among the verbal and nonverbal. Philpot (1983) stated that "the most fascinating finding of this meta-analysis is a consistent lack of a strong interaction between the verbal and nonverbal channels. Forty-five measures of these interactions are available in the literature. Only two of these interactions account for more than twenty percent of the variance" (p. 42). Evidently, most receivers process verbal and non-verbal communication separately and seldom use both together to make judgments.

Why do people believe the nonverbal channel more than the verbal channel, especially when the two conflict? First, because nonverbal communication is more spontaneous and less intentional than verbal communication, it is intuitively interpreted as more genuine. Sayings such as "The eyes are the window of the soul" show the extent to which nonverbal communication is believed to show one's "true feelings." Second, because the nonverbal system was an earlier, more basic genetic system, nonverbal perceptions may be neurophysiologically more powerful and basic. After all, virtually all communication among animals proceeds through nonverbal channels, and language is a fairly recent evolutionary development. Third, because nonverbal communication is present and active in interaction with newborns, humans learn to place stock in nonverbal communication long before verbal communication is interpretable. Finally, the multichanneled nature of nonverbal communication may give it more power as an individual seeks confirmation through redundant cues. As Bateson (1972) stated, "It is understandable that an early (in an evolutionary sense) method of creating redundancy would be the use of iconic part-for-whole coding" (p. 420).

Adults trust nonverbal communication more than spoken communication, especially when the channels conflict. Burgoon (1985a) summarized: "Adult reliance on nonverbal cues is greatest when the verbal and nonverbal messages conflict. . . . Congruency among channels just makes the verbal and nonverbal coding systems more equal in their contribution to meaning" (p. 347). Evidently, people put considerably more faith in the nonverbal message when the two channels conflict as a means of guarding against verbal deception (see chapter 11).

The pattern with children is somewhat different. Obviously, infants are entirely reliant on nonverbal communication because they cannot yet send or comprehend linguistic messages. However, interpersonal research clearly shows that once language develops, children rely primarily on *verbal* cues rather than on *nonverbal* ones (for summaries of this research see Burgoon, 1985a; Knapp, 1978). The onset of language provides such a powerful tool for children that for years they take comments literally, relying almost exclusively on verbal communication. This is why young children have difficulty with sarcastic messages, in which the nonverbal message (for example, tone of voice, facial expression) undercuts the verbal message. Blanck and Rosenthal's (1982) summary of research suggests that children are most reliant on verbal cues, less reliant on vocal cues, and much less reliant on visual cues and tend to take verbal communication literally in the case of sarcastic messages. Andersen, Andersen, Murphy, and Wendt-Wasco (1985) report that only 14 percent of kindergartners could understand a teacher's sarcasm as compared with 39 percent of third-graders, 52 percent of sixth-graders, 55 percent of ninth-graders, and 66 percent of twelfth-graders. Indeed, grade level explained almost 30 percent of the variance in understanding sarcasm. Similarly, television research shows that young children do pretty well with verbal information but have relatively more difficulty with nonverbal communication (Hoffner, Cantor, & Thornson, 1988). Together, these findings suggest that during preschool and the early elementary school years, children are primarily tuned in to verbal communication and steadily increase their ability to integrate nonverbal communication. By adulthood, nonverbal communication is the primary channel of communication.

Functional Distinctions

During interaction, we use our two major communication systems in different ways. The nonverbal system is more globally meaningful, basic, emotional, affective, and essential in all forms of communication regarding our relationships with others. Verbal communication is more precise, contains more information, and is logical and content-oriented.

THE INHERENT MEANINGFULNESS OF NONVERBAL COMMUNICATION

Principle 17—Nonverbal codes are more useful for global meanings and attributions; verbal communication is more useful for precise and factual information. The old saying "A picture is worth a thousand words" has been supported by communication research and theory. Global meanings regarding the situation, the relationship, the environment, or another person's state are gleaned more readily through nonverbal communication. Burgoon (1985a) concluded, "Verbal cues are more important for factual, abstract, and persuasive communications, whereas nonverbal cues are more important for relational, attributional, affective, and attitudinal messages" (p. 347). A highly technical lecture on research or theory must use verbal communication to convey abstract information. But understanding a new situation or the psychological state of a friend will be more meaningful if it is based on nonverbal observations. Wilden (1972) claimed that nonverbal and analogic communication "is pregnant with meaning whereas the digital domain of signification is relatively barren" (p. 58).

What happens when we must translate nonverbal cognitions to verbal codes or verbal cognitions to nonverbal codes? Watzlawick et al. (1967) claimed that there can "be no translation from the digital to analogic modes without great loss of information, but the opposite is also extraordinarily difficult: to *talk about* relationships requires translation from the analogic into the digital mode of communication" (p. 66). Wilden (1972, 1980) maintained that it is virtually impossible to translate the rich meanings of nonverbal and analogic messages into a digital or verbal form without great loss of meaning. Similarly, translation from the digital/verbal into an analogic/nonverbal message usually involves a great loss of information and precision.

THE AFFECTIVE PRIMACY OF NONVERBAL COMMUNICATION

Principle 18—Nonverbal messages are most useful for affective and emotional information; verbal messages are most useful for logical and cognitive information. To figure out a puzzle or to pass along detailed plans, verbal communication is clearly superior. Nonverbal communication lacks the precision and syntax to deal with these precise and logical issues. However, when the information involves affect, danger, emotion, or feelings, the nonverbal realm is superior. This may have been an evolutionary development. Before the emergence of language, nonverbal communication was used to communicate fear, anger, love, or other emotion. Even after language evolved, nonverbal expression provided fast feedback as to a person's emotional state and served as a survival advantage.

Recent research suggests that emotions are more than private experiences. Typically emotions are communicated through various forms of overt, direct nonverbal behaviors (see Andersen & Guerrero, 1998b). Burgoon suggests that the power and directness of nonverbal signals are due to their capacity for direct stimulation while circumventing the cognitive system entirely. Moreover, Zajonc (1984) has summarized considerable evidence which suggests that thinking and feeling are independent, that preferences need no inferences. He has also shown that emotional and nonverbal messages are processed faster than cognitive responses and operate on different neurophysiological and biochemical systems. This is why thinking too much about your romance or your tennis game may be counterproductive; these activities do not usually require considerable thinking, nor do they benefit from too much thinking. Evidence suggests that distinct brain modules may mediate the processes (Stacks & Andersen, 1989). In short, thoughts are much more likely to be part of the logical/verbal world, and feelings are more likely to be part of the emotional/nonverbal world.

THE RELATIONAL PRIMACY OF NONVERBAL COMMUNICATION

Principle 19—Nonverbal messages are the primary vehicle for relational communication; verbal messages are the primary vehicle for content communication. Using written or spoken words, try to describe a romantic relationship that has lasted months or years. It is nearly impossible to do without leaving out much of the detail. Watzlawick et al. (1967) believed that digital language lacks the meaning and semantics to communicate about relationships. Nonverbal, or analogic, communication is well equipped for conveying such relational content. Relationships are primarily a function of shared time and space, of meaningful movements and glances, of touch and smell. All relationships along romantic, status, power, relaxation, or friendship dimensions are best conveyed nonverbally. Bateson (1972) maintained:

> When boy says to girl, "I love you" he is using words to convey that which is more convincingly conveyed by his tone of voice and his movements; and the girl, if she has any sense, will pay more attention to those accompanying signs than to words. (p. 412)

Duck (1988) supported the notion that eye contact, smiling, and other nonverbal cues best communicate liking. The development of most relationships proceeds by these nonverbal, analogic means. As Eliza Doolittle said to Henry Higgins in *My Fair Lady*, "Don't talk at all, show me. When we sit together in the middle of the night, don't talk at all, just hold me tight. Anyone who's ever been in love can tell you that; this is no time for a chat."

The Complementary Relationship between Verbal and Nonverbal Communication

This chapter has focused on differences between verbal and nonverbal communication. However, these two systems work *beside* one another and share many characteristics. Both nonverbal communication and verbal communication complement one another in most cases. They are governed both by cultural rules and by laws of nature. Both verbal communication and nonverbal communication are influenced by culture and designed to perform many of the functions described in this book: to display culture, gender, and emotion, to signal arousal and anxiety, to send messages of warmth, intimacy and immediacy, to persuade, to deceive, and to dominate. Although this book focuses on the role played by nonverbal communication in the service of these functions, always remember that most things are accomplished through the complementary interplay of verbal and nonverbal communication.

SUMMARY

Although humans are talkative creatures, nonverbal communication may play a more important role than verbal communication in human interaction. The relative proportion of verbal versus nonverbal communication isn't very important; the important point is that nonverbal communication is a crucial, and often ignored, part of the communication process. Moreover, nonverbal communication coexists beside language and virtually always accompanies language.

This book defines nonverbal messages as all communication that is analogic, nonlinguistic, and governed by the right brain hemisphere. Other differences also distinguish verbal from nonverbal communication. Compared to verbal communication, nonverbal communication is a more basic, biologically based system, more widespread in living things, and is in an earlier development, in the history of the species and in each individual human.

Verbal communication and nonverbal communication represent different code systems. Nonverbal codes are analogic, iconic, continuously available, and nonunitized. Verbal codes are digital, notational, discontinuous, and unitized into words and morphemes. Verbal and nonverbal communication differ in channel capacity. Nonverbal communication is multichanneled, in both production and reception, and is simultaneously redundant. These properties may account for the relatively large impact of nonverbal messages in human communication.

Cognitively, nonverbal communication typically is encoded and decoded simultaneously and as a gestalt. It is processed holistically and syncretically. Verbal communication is encoded and decoded symbolically, intentionally, discretely, and analytically. As such, nonverbal communication is perceived as being more believable than verbal communication.

Finally, nonverbal communication and verbal communication perform different functions. Nonverbal communication is more meaningful and is the primary vehicle of interpersonal and relational communication. Verbal communication is more precise and information-laden and is the language of logic as well as the primary carrier of content-oriented communication. Paradoxically, although nonverbal and verbal systems are extraordinarily different in form and function, they necessarily coexist, co-occur, and collaborate in the process of human communication.

2

The Body Codes of
Nonverbal Communication

> Body language is nature's multimedia presentation. Unlike talk, which after all
> is just talk, body language is a rich form of communication involving every
> part of your body.
>
> —Peter Andersen, *The Complete Idiot's Guide to Body Language*

Though body language is not really a language, it is such a rich form of communication, that many people think of it as a language. The human body captivates us. It is hard to think of an activity in which the human body is not the center of attention. People are evaluated by how their bodies look. Sexual attraction is based in large part on bodily appearance. Sports consist of battling bodies. Television, movies, and magazines, in particular, are dominated by images of the human body. These images of the body analogically communicate without language to form powerful impressions (see chapter 1). As Morris (1985) observed in his book, *Bodywatching*:

> Nothing fascinates us quite as much as the human body. Whether we realize it
> or not, we are all obsessed with physical appearances. Even when we are
> engaged in a lively conversation and seem to be engrossed in purely verbal
> communication, we remain ardent body watchers. By the time we are adults
> we are all highly sensitive to the tiniest changes in expression, gesture, posture,
> and bodily adornment of our companions. We acquire this sensitivity in a
> rough and ready fashion, through intuition rather than analysis. If we took the
> trouble to make a more analytic study of body appearances we could become
> even more sensitized to them, and could avoid some of the pitfalls into which
> our intuition sometimes leads us. (p. 7)

This chapter provides an introduction to the body as a communication medium. Across the millennia, the body has provided humans and other animals with the primary vehicle for communication. Conscious or unconscious, intentional or unintentional, symptomatic, spontaneous, or symbolic, human communication is transmitted through a set of meaningful codes that observers make

31

sense of and interpret (Andersen, 1991; Motley, 1990, 1991). Codes form the basis of nonverbal communication. In later chapters you will learn how the body performs many important communication functions, but first, this chapter will explore five codes of the body: *physical appearance; kinesics*, or body movement; *oculesics*, or eye behavior; *proxemics*, or interpersonal spatial behavior; and *haptics*, or tactile communication.

Along with language, these nonverbal codes of the body provide the substance of human communication. Understanding these basic forms or codes of nonverbal communication behavior is essential to understanding communication. You may be surprised how much you already know about nonverbal communication; however, a thorough understanding of these nonverbal codes can make you far more effective in understanding and sending messages in everyday interaction.

PHYSICAL APPEARANCE

It is said that a person has only one opportunity to make a first impression. Our physical personae have a major impact on other people's initial impressions of us. Clothing style, race, sex, age, ethnicity, stature, body type, and mood all reveal one's physical persona. Right or wrong, receivers of this initial physical information make attributions about our attractiveness, competence, moral character, personality, social status, and warmth and friendliness (for more on this topic see chapter 10). Of course, these judgments are often based on stereotypes, and stereotypes can be wrong. But stereotyping others is an inevitable human process, a shortcut to evaluate other people before more information is available. Race and gender, for example, are biasing factors in initial impression. Research, for example, has repeatedly shown that African Americans and Hispanics are more likely to be stopped for traffic violations and twice as likely to be searched (Engel & Calnon, 2004), a phenomenon acerbically referred to as the "driving while colored" violation.

Uncertainty reduction theory suggests that during initial acquaintance, we are highly motivated to increase our certainty and familiarity with a person during interaction (Berger & Calabrese, 1975), and we use every possible cue that provides information about that person. Because physical appearance cues are so obvious, they serve as the primary source of information during initial interaction to reduce uncertainty. They may also be deeply ingrained in our biology. Several recent studies report that women dress sexier and more fashionably and are more attractive to men during the most fertile time in their monthly cycle (Grammer, Renninger, & Fischer; 2004; Haselton et al., 2007); they are also more sensitive to male sexual pheromones at that time of their cycle (see chapter 3).

Imagine a recent college graduate trying to get a job in a corporation or government agency. How would a potential employer evaluate a physically fit, attractive, appropriately dressed, well-groomed applicant compared to an overweight, unattractive, sloppily dressed, unkempt applicant? It would be no contest. Many of us would register only positive judgments about the first applicant's motivation, intelligence, character, and reliability. Of course, appearances can be deceiving, but that fact is almost beside the point. A communication perspective recognizes that subjective impressions by receivers are all that really matter. As Jackson Browne used to sing, "It's who you look like, not who you are."

In our postmodern world, our selves are embedded in a set of artifacts and body images that say "who we are." Critics justifiably worry about a world in which substance has been replaced by image, in which essence has yielded to illusion. The fact is that we have moved through the looking glass into a world where reality is loosely tied to outcome and perception rules supreme. The popularity of bodybuilding and fitness, fashionable clothes, makeup, designer labels, and such status symbols as homes and cars is more tied to their communication potential and image-creation value than to the intrinsic worth of fitness, fashion, or fanciness. The right athletic equipment, for example, along with the right sports body language, has been found to intimidate athletic opponents (Greenless et al., 2005).

As a student of communication, you might find these observations obvious. You may think that everyone dresses to communicate, that image is value. Surprisingly, many choices made by people have little to do with the symbolic value of appearance. Years ago, Aiken (1963) revealed that clothing choices are made for a variety of reasons other than image, including economy, conformity, and comfort. Morris (1977) suggested that, historically, clothing has also performed the functions of modesty and protection. Moreover, Andersen (1992b) contended that clothing is situationally appropriate, because clothing enhances one's positive qualities, conceals one's negative qualities, and makes a personal statement consistent with one's desired image. Likewise, bodily hairlessness is essential to women's images in Western culture, and this has become increasingly true for men as well; in short there is a war on hair (see chapter 5).

Similarly, the shape of one's body sends an important message to other interactants. Sheldon (1940) originally classified people into three general body types: *endomorphs* are rounded, soft, heavy people; *mesomorphs* are angular, muscular, athletic people; and *ectomorphs* are linear, thin, underweight people (Figure 2.1). In fact, various combinations and degrees of body types are possible, so that most people don't fit neatly into a single category, yet research has shown that discrimination exists against some body types—particularly endomorphs, who are often perceived as lazy, sloppy, slow, jolly, stupid, and unattractive (Andersen &

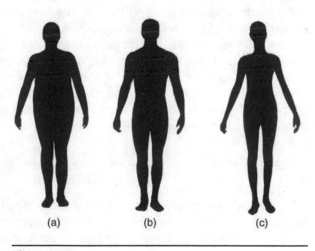

(a)   (b)   (c)

Figure 2.1

Body types: (a) endomorph, (b) mesomorph, and (c) ectomorph.

Singleton, 1978; Spiegel & Machotka, 1974; Wells & Siegel, 1961). These stereotypes have persisted for decades and are true not only for adults but also for children (Portnoy & Gardner, 1980) and even elderly adults (Portnoy, 1993). Ectomorphs, particularly male ectomorphs, are perceived as nervous, frail, weak, and sickly but also studious and intelligent (Andersen & Singleton, 1978). Female ectomorphs share some of these stereotypes but are perceived much more positively than males. Research has shown that female ectomorphs are more shy and fearful about communication. Additionally, the desire of many people, particularly women, to be thin despite more robust, genetic predispositions and bone structure has led in recent years to potentially life-threatening eating disorders such as anorexia and bulimia. Mesomorphs are the most positively perceived group because they are perceived as strong, forceful, and healthy, and they are frequently chosen as leaders. However, mesomorphs may be attributed negative qualities such as vanity and still must cope with the dumb jock stereotype. (For fun, complete the Body Type Survey that appears on the following page.)

Height, particularly for men, is perceived as a positive quality. Tall men are more likely to be hired, offered higher starting salaries, and given more prominent positions (Henley, 1977). Similarly, considerable data suggest that attractive people are perceived much more positively (Berscheid & Walster, 1978) and even afforded a "halo effect"—that is, people transfer their positive evaluations of a person's appearance to aspects of her or his personality. Good-looking people are perceived as more talented, kinder, smarter, more credible, and honest (Adams, 1977; Berscheid & Walster, 1978).

In sum, characteristics such as dress, attractiveness, height, body shape, race, and hairstyle are physical traits (Andersen, 1987) that form stereotypes. Dozens of studies indicate that even teachers think physically attractive kids are more intelligent, have more academic potential, have higher grades, and possess more social skills (Ritts, Patterson, & Tubbs, 1992). Some validity exists for such stereotypes, particularly since they can become self-fulfilling prophecies. For example, treating an attractive child as though he or she is more intelligent may eventually produce a more intelligent child, a result that is consistent with other people's expectations (see Rosenthal & Jacobson, 196). Of course, initial impressions based on physical cues are often erroneous. The wise communicator observes numerous verbal and nonverbal behaviors instead of relying solely on first impressions. Over time, the power of physical appearance attenuates, yielding to personal and relational cues that determine the eventual course of the interpersonal relationship.

KINESICS

Our body is capable of sending hundreds, if not thousands, of messages. The study of communication through body movement is called kinesics, which includes the study of facial expressions, gestures, the interactive synchrony of body movements, and sometimes eye behavior. Body movement cannot usually be translated directly as is the case with verbal behavior (Harrigan, 2005). Most kinesic behavior is analogic and nonlinguistic; when gestures stand for words, as in the

Body Type Survey*

Purpose: To demonstrate how body type affects behavior and communication.

Directions: Fill the three blanks following each statement with one of the twelve words listed below each statement. Although an exact word to fit you may not be in the list, select words that seem to fit most closely.

1. Most of the time I feel _____, _____, and _____.

calm	relaxed	complacent
anxious	confident	reticent
cheerful	tense	energetic
contented	impetuous	self-conscious

2. When I study or work, I seem to be _____, _____, and _____.

efficient	sluggish	precise
enthusiastic	competitive	determined
reflective	leisurely	thoughtful
placid	meticulous	cooperative

3. Socially, I am _____, _____, and _____.

outgoing	considerate	argumentative
affable	awkward	shy
tolerant	affected	talkative
gentle-tempered	soft-tempered	hot-tempered

4. I am rather _____, _____, and _____.

active	forgiving	sympathetic
warm	courageous	serious
domineering	suspicious	soft-hearted
introspective	cool	enterprising

5. Other people consider me rather _____, _____, and _____.

generous	optimistic	sensitive
adventurous	affectionate	kind
withdrawn	reckless	cautious
dominant	detached	dependent

6. Underline one word out of three in each of the following lines that most closely describes the way you are:

    (a) assertive, relaxed, tense

    (b) hot-tempered, cool, warm

    (c) withdrawn, sociable, active

    (d) confident, tactful, kind

    (e) dependent, dominant, detached

    (f) enterprising, affable, anxious

Source: Cortés & Gatti (1965)

*The scoring key for the survey appears at the end of the chapter.

case of emblems or sign languages, they are really verbal and linguistic. These are cases when so-called body language really is a language (Andersen, 2004). (Also see chapter 1 for a discussion of analogic and nonlinguistic communication).

Facial Expressions

The face is one of the richest sources of information available to humans. It is the best site for understanding feelings, communicating dozens of emotions between people. The face is far more than a window into our emotional world; it is a primary channel of interpersonal communication that has evolved as a clear and instantaneous form of human communication (Schmidt & Cohn, 2001).

Research by Ekman and his associates has convincingly established a basic set of at least six facial expressions that are innate, universal, and carry the same basic meaning throughout the world (Ekman & Friesen, 1975; Ekman, Friesen, & Ellsworth, 1972). As Crosby, Stills, and Nash once sang (probably without the benefit of Ekman's research), "If you smile at me I will understand, for that is something everybody, everywhere does in the same language." Research on children blind from birth by Eibl-Eibesfeldt (1972, 1979) revealed that these children employ very similar facial expressions to those of sighted children, suggesting that basic expressions are not learned but are part of an innate system of communication. Ekman and others have shown that at least six basic facial expressions are pancultural and universal: happiness, sadness, fear, anger, disgust, and surprise. Evidence shows that especially the first four of these facial expressions (happiness, sadness, fear, and anger) are easily identifiable across cultures (for a summary see Guerrero, Andersen, & Trost, 1998). Likewise, some other expressions, such as the eyebrow flash, a sign of recognition, have shown considerable cross-cultural consistency. There are, however, subtle cultural differences in the facial expression of some emotions, which we will explore in chapters 4 and 6.

Facial expressions are clearly social; they are most likely to be deployed during interaction, demonstrating that they are primarily communicative. Indeed, distinct and recognizable facial expressions are rare when a person is all alone. In an imaginative series of experiments, Kraut and Johnston (1979) studied the emotional reactions of bowlers and hockey fans. Hidden cameras demonstrated that when the bowlers got strikes, they exhibited little or no expression while facing the pins. When they turned to their friends, however, their faces lit up with smiles and excitement. Similarly, the hockey fans in this

Smiles communicate happiness but are usually displayed during interaction.

study were relatively poker-faced after their team scored a goal, but when they looked at their friends a second or two later, they showed intense facial happiness. Research has consistently shown that smiling occurs primarily in other people's presence and is not merely a reflection of internal emotional states (Parkinson, 2005). Indeed, the more involved people are with another person, the more they smile (Fridlund, 1991; Schmidt & Cohn, 2001); and the more positive the smile, the more positively the other person is evaluated (Frank, Ekman, & Friesen, 1993). Even babies under one year of age use anticipatory smiles to share positive emotions about an object (Venezia, Messinger, Thorp, & Mundy, 2004). This takes place when an infant looks at a funny or interesting object and then looks to a parent and smiles—clearly an invitation to share positive emotions with the other person.

Although basic facial expressions are primarily innate, their expression begins to be controlled and managed by cultural display rules as the individual matures. Infants and young children do little to monitor and manage their emotional displays, yet as they mature, they learn that manifesting certain emotions at specific times is situationally or socially inappropriate. They also learn that exaggerating or pretending to feel certain emotions can be functional in certain contexts. Likewise they learn to distinguish fake smiles from genuine, felt smiles (Schmidt & Cohn, 2001). During the preschool and early school years, children learn how and when to suppress and manage facial affect. (For more on the expression of emotion see chapter 6.) Management of facial affect is accomplished through the use of the following five display rules (Andersen, Andersen, & Landgraf, 1985; Ekman, 1978; Shennum & Bugental, 1982):

Simulation: showing feelings when you have no feelings.

Intensification: giving the appearance of more feelings than you actually have.

Neutralization or inhibition: giving the appearance of having no feeling when you really have a feeling.

Deintensification, or miniaturization: giving the appearance of having less feelings than you actually have.

Masking: covering one feeling with an expression of another feeling you are not experiencing.

Although these five display rules are initially employed during the preschool and early school years, they are not typically mastered until much later in life, if at all (for a summary see Guerrero et al., 1998). Most of the research has found that inhibition and deintensification increase as children develop. Interestingly, becoming an adult requires manifesting fewer outward emotions, particularly for men. Unfortunately, failing to express emotions is shown to cause an increase in detrimental physiological reactions, stress, and disease (Buck, 1979).

Gestures

Humans have uniquely dexterous and expressive hands. Not surprisingly, the hands are used extensively for communication. Recent research indicates that gestures may be superior to words for communication and problem solving because they are a more direct and embodied form of communication than words (Lozano

& Tversky, 2006). Ekman and Friesen (1969b) divided hand gestures into three broad categories: *adaptors*, touching behaviors that reveal internal states such as anxiety or nervousness; *emblems*, gestures with explicit meaning and dictionary definitions; and *illustrators*, nonverbal gestures that accompany speech.

There are three types of adaptors: self-adaptors, object adaptors, and other adaptors (sometimes called alter adaptors) (Ekman & Friesen, 1969b). Self-adaptors, or self-touching behaviors, such as scratching an itch, wringing one's hands, or pushing a strand of hair from one's eyes, are used to comfort oneself, cover or protect oneself, preen or groom one's body, send sexual signals, and alleviate nervousness (Morris, 1977). Self-adaptors are often a response to anxiety such as public speaking situations and are more common among men than in women (Heaven & McBrayer, 2000). Some research suggests that self-adaptors create negative impressions of nervousness and childishness, but other studies suggest that increased self-adaptors lead to impressions of honesty, sincerity, and warmth (Harrigan, 2005). Object adaptors are nervous behaviors that involve the manipulation of objects such as cigarettes, drinks, wedding rings, and watches. These adaptors can also signal boredom. Other adaptors involve adjusting or grooming others. These behaviors are common among all primates, including humans. Parents are particularly likely to use other adaptors such as hair grooming, lint removal, or buttoning a child's coat.

Emblems, like spoken words, have specific, recognized meaning within a culture. Called speech-independent gestures by some researchers (Knapp & Hall, 1997; Morris, 1977), emblems such as the hitchhiking sign, the A-OK sign, the upraised middle finger, and the peace sign have explicit verbal meanings within a given culture. Although classified as nonverbal communication by some researchers (Burgoon, Buller, & Woodall, 1996; Ekman, 1976; Knapp & Hall, 2006), as discussed in chapter 1, other researchers claim that emblems are linguistic, verbal forms of communication that take the form of gestures rather than spoken or written words (Andersen, Garrison, & Andersen, 1979; Koneya, 1977; McNeill, 1985).

The most common gestures are illustrators; arm and hand movements that accompany the flow of speech but usually cannot stand alone. These gestures assist

receivers in understanding a message, but they also facilitate speech and cognition in senders (Goldin-Meadow & Wagner, 2005, Stevanoni & Salmon, 2005). Illustrators increase when a receiver is present but are used to some degree even when a receiver is not present (Alibali, Heath, & Myers, 2001). In fact, gesturing is so biological and natural that congenitally blind people use them though they have never seen

Illustrators are gestures that accompany speech.

a gesture; they even use them with other blind people who cannot possibly see them (Iverson & Goldin-Meadow, 2001).

Eight kinds of illustrators are commonly used during speech (Ekman and Friesen, 1972).

- *Batons* are gestures that are used to emphasize a particular word or phrase. Watch the batons used by public speakers, particularly political candidates, such as chopping or punching gestures that coincide with the words they accent in their speech.

- *Ideographs* are gestures that sketch or trace the path of an idea or relationship. An economist may show the decline of unemployment by drawing an imaginary graph in the air. A communication professor may say "As anxiety increases, performance decreases" while raising one hand and lowering the other.

- *Pointers*, or deictic movements, point to an object, place, or event. For example, a parent may say "Clean up your room" while pointing in the direction of the room, or a teacher may point when calling on a student in class.

- *Spatials* are movements that depict size or distance relations. A fisherman widening his arms to show the size of his fish or a basketball coach using expansive gestures while saying "Spread the defense" are examples of spatials.

- *Rhythmic movements* are gestures that depict the rhythm, pacing, or timing of an event. For example, a person speaking about the chronology of events in a murder case may gesture to indicate when each event took place; similarly, a band leader may signal the tempo of a song with rhythmic gestures.

- *Kinetographics* are movements that depict bodily actions or a nonhuman physical action. Examples would include a surfer demonstrating how to keep one's balance when riding a particularly large wave or an eyewitness imitating the motions of the involved parties at a crime scene.

- *Pictographs* are movements that draw a picture of the referent in the air. The classic example is a man tracing the hourglass shape of a woman's body in the air. Likewise, if the previously mentioned surfer gesturally described the height and shape of a wave, she or he would be using a pictograph. A person indicating the physical topography of a region by sketching in the air would also be employing a pictograph.

- *Emblematic movements* employ a gestural emblem that is synonymous with a statement. Saying "You're dead" while symbolically slitting one's own throat, extending one's middle finger while saying "Up yours," or making a circular motion next to one's head while saying "He's crazy" are examples of emblematic movements.

Moreover, Ekman and Friesen (1972) correctly pointed out that these eight kinds of illustrators are not mutually exclusive but can occur simultaneously or fit into several categories.

Gestures can also stand alone. Often effective instruction in motor activities can employ gestures alone, as in the case of a basketball or tennis coach demonstrating a shot. Recent research suggests that gestures may facilitate tasks, such as putting together a TV table, for both the encoder and for the observer even better than speech alone or speech with gestures (Lozano & Tversky, 2006). Gestures that demonstrate actions are most effective in teaching such actions.

Gestures are both innate and learned. They are used in all cultures, tend to be tied to speech processes, and are usually automatic. Gestures are so habitual that communicators continue to gesture while talking on the telephone, even though they are invisible to their interaction partner (Alibali et al., 2001). While research shows that gestures may help receivers' comprehension of a message, research also suggests that speakers are more fluent and can retrieve more information if they are permitted to gesture (Alibali et al., 2001; Goldin-Meadow & Wagner, 2005; Harrigan, 2005). Speech and thought are facilitated by gestures, which explains the close association of speech and gesture in the left-hemispheric origin of the brain (Kinsbourne, 2006). Some experts even believe that speech and gesture evolved simultaneously as primary means of linguistic communication (Jaffe, 1987; Jaffe & Anderson, 1979).

Interactional Synchrony

One of the most intriguing aspects of kinesic behavior during interaction is how two individuals move almost as one. This phenomenon, called body synchrony, matching, postural echoes, reciprocity, or body congruence, has been observed by many scholars, although these are not equivalent terms (for summaries see Burgoon, Dillman, & Stern, 1993; Guerrero & Floyd, 2006). These behaviors are innate, though interaction between and infant and a caregiver is needed to sharpen these skills to produce competent interaction later in life (Kinsbourne, 2006). Interaction is like a dance in which partners engage in complex actions without stepping on one another's literal or metaphorical toes. Everyday rhetoric reveals that we are intuitively aware of such rhythms. When we're not in rhythm with someone we speak of being "on a different wavelength," being "out of sync," having "bad vibes," and "being rubbed the wrong way." Positive interactions are described as being "in tune," "clicking," "on the same wave length" and "hitting it off together."

Synchronous movements are a sign of identification or rapport. (Photo courtesy of Laura Guerrero)

Scheflen (1972) has shown that interactants often assume parallel postures and move synchronously, particularly when they're in rapport with one another. Condon and Ogston (1966) showed that people in

Synchronization of posture and gesture occurs spontaneously, even in intercultural communication. Note the similarity in posture and hands among this group.

rapport move together at up to forty-eight beats per second! Teachers often note that entire classes can be congruent and synchronous, indicating the students are in tune with one another or the teacher (Thompson, 1973). Even when very large groups of people congregate, synchronous action often takes place. Imagine, for example, church members sitting, standing, and kneeling together at certain times during a service or football fans doing the wave in a stadium or clapping in sync to a "DeeeeFense" chant. Although synchrony research has been criticized on methodological grounds in the past (McDowell, McDowell, & Hyendahl, 1980; Cappella, 1981), more recent research shows that synchronized interactions are evaluated more positively than less synchronized ones (Warner et al., 1987). Burgoon et al. (1993) recommend the term *matching* to refer to behavioral similarity among partners, regardless of the intentionality of partner influence.

Bavelas and her colleagues have also examined a similar communication phenomenon called motor mimicry. This occurs when, for example, a ball is thrown at your unsuspecting friend and *you* duck! If both your friend and the ball are visually accessible, you are likely to duck in the direction that your friend should duck to avoid getting hit by the ball. This behavior constitutes a clear, spontaneous communication message intended to influence the partner's movements. Motor mimicry is a unique communication behavior designed to unconsciously influence another's actions through nonverbal behavior (Bargh & Chartrand, 1999; Bavelas, Black, Lemery, & Mullett, 1986; Bavelas, Black, Chovil, Lemery, & Mullett, 1988).

New support for mimicry, synchronization, and connection comes from cutting-edge research on mirror neurons. In recent years researchers have discovered that if I wave my hand or smile at you, exactly the same sections of your brain are activated as if you yourself had waved or smiled (Rizzolatti & Arbib, 1998; Rizzolatti & Craighero, 2004). Mirror neurons may be one of the primary ways people learn to communicate and definitely are one of the ways that synchrony and matching provides connection between people.

Synchrony, reciprocity, and matching are behaviors that provide positive vibrations and interdependent rhythms among communicators. Our ability to synchronize our interactions with those of other people may be a fundamental way we develop close interpersonal relationships.

OCULESICS

During interaction, people focus their attention on the face and eyes of the other person. This is partly due to the fact that the face and eyes are highly expressive, sending myriad messages during interaction. It is also due to the fact that we perceive other people to be "located" just behind their eyes as opposed to other parts of the body. The eyes attend carefully to other communicators because vision, in addition to sound, is one of two primary channels through which humans receive nonverbal messages. But the eyes do more than receive messages; they send messages. While some scholars classify eye behavior as part of kinesics, oculesics is the term others use to label the study of how the eyes send messages. Because there is so much research on oculesics, it is treated as a separate area. Oculesics involves the study of the many nonlinguistic behaviors and messages sent by the eyes, including eye contact, pupil dilation, and eye movement.

Eye Contact

The most important aspect of oculesics is eye contact or mutual gaze. Eye contact is so basic that it is almost certainly innate. From birth infants can detect eye contact and gaze direction, as well as show a preference for faces that engage them in mutual gaze (Bakti et al., 2000; Farroni, Csibra, Simion, & Johnson, 2002). Recent research shows that newborn infants prefer to look at upright faces and upright eyes with direct gaze (Farroni, Menon, & Johnson, 2006; Senju & Hasegawa, 2006) and by three months of age infants use eye contact in elaborate interactive sequences with adult caregivers (Lavelli & Fogel, 2005). There is a subtle difference between eye contact and gazing. Eye contact occurs when *both* people look into one another's eyes; gazing occurs anytime one person looks at another. Interpersonal communication typically requires a considerable amount of eye contact. In fact, conversing without eye contact is perceived in many cultures as rude, disinterested, inattentive, shy, and/or deceptive. Eye contact is an invitation to communicate and an important immediacy cue, a sign of warmth and involvement (see chapters 8 and 9 for more on this). People attribute many personal qualities to another person based on eye contact, hence the terms *shifty eyes*, *evil eyes*, *bedroom eyes*, *all eyes*, and *sad eyes*. You can *give someone the eye*, *see eye to eye*, or *take an eye for an eye*—all metaphors that illustrate the centrality of the eyes in interpersonal relationships. Likewise, people as young as five can infer preferences of other people by watching whom and at what they gaze; the longer people gaze at someone or something, the more kids infer a preference for that person or object (Einav & Hood, 2006).

Eye contact performs numerous communication functions (Kendon, 1967): (1) it regulates interaction by providing turn-taking signals and eliciting or suppressing communication (Kendon, 1967); (2) it monitors interaction by receiving messages from one's interaction partner; (3) it signals cognitive activity when eye contact is broken during information processing; (4) it expresses involvement, because interest and connection are communicated by looking (see chapter 8); (5) it can create intimidation through the use of prolonged stares and negative facial expressions (Exline, Ellyson, & Long, 1975; see also chapter 5); (6) it initiates flirtation (Silver & Spitzberg, 1992); (7) it signals attentiveness (Einav & Hood, 2006; Fehr & Exline, 1987); (8) it increases interpersonal immediacy (Andersen, 1985, see also chapter 8); (9) it increases person perception by accessing interpersonal and stereotypical information from social memory (Macrae et al., 2002); (10) it facilitates the processing of positive emotional information from an interactant (Adams & Kleck, 2003); and (11) it increases the intimacy of an interaction (Andersen, et al., 2006; see chapter 9).

Pupil Dilation

A subtle but important eye behavior that affects interpersonal relationships is pupil dilation. The science of pupilometrics has discovered that individuals' pupils dilate when they experience arousal, positive affect, or attraction for another person (for a review see Andersen, Todd-Mancillas, & DiClemente, 1980; Hess, 1975; or Hess & Petrovich, 1987). For example, research shows that heterosexual males experience more pupil dilation when viewing photographs of women than of men, but homosexual males experience more pupil dilation when viewing photographs of men (Hess, Seltzer, & Schlien, 1965). Such research has been used extensively in the advertising and marketing industries to test consumer preferences.

Even more surprisingly, research has discovered that pupil dilation is unconsciously perceived during interaction and results in increased attraction (Andersen et al., 1980; Hess, 1975). If your romantic partner's pupils are dilated, your attraction to your partner may be heightened. Doubtlessly, this is part of the reason why moonlight, candlelight, and soft light from a fireplace increase romantic attraction.

Several studies have suggested that although the effect of pupil dilation on attraction is statistically significant, the effects are fairly small. Despite some methodological shortcomings of the study, Hensley (1991) reports that pupil dilation has a significant effect on attraction although the difference constitutes less than one point on a ten-point scale. Andersen and his colleagues (1980) conducted a more detailed analysis by using a multi-item, multidimensional measure of attraction. They report that pupil dilation has a significant effect on social attraction and physical attraction but not on task attraction (the degree to which a person enjoys working on a task with another person), although the size of these effects is small, accounting for only 2 to 3 percent of a person's judgments of physical attraction. Nevertheless, every study conducted to date has revealed a statistically significant effect for pupil dilation. And, of course, the cumulative effect of various subtle nonverbal cues can have a large effect on interpersonal attraction.

Perhaps the most remarkable study in this series was conducted by Hess and Goodwin (1974), who showed participants two photographs of a mother holding her baby. Both photographs were identical in all respects except that in one photograph the eyes were retouched; thus, in one photograph the mother's pupils were dilated and in the other constricted. Participants were asked, "Which mother loves her baby more?" Students unanimously chose the mother with dilated eyes! However, few could explain why. Most misattributed the source of their impressions by saying, "Her face is more pleasant," "She's holding her baby closer," or "She has a warmer smile." Pupil dilation is one of several subtle, unconscious nonverbal cues that can repel or attract us to other individuals. This is another example of how nonverbal communication is not only analogic and nonlinguistic but also at times unconsciously communicated.

Blinking

Previous research has associated blinking with mental activity, nervousness, and flirtatiousness (Andersen, 1999; Buller & Burgoon, 1998; DePaulo et al., 1985). Recent research has also found that receivers associate blinking with nervousness, carelessness, and unfriendliness (Omori & Myata, 2001).

Eye Movements

Eye movements can mean many things. A solid body of research suggests that lateral eye movements (LEMs) to the left are associated with nonverbal thinking and the right brain hemisphere (as described in chapter 1). Rightward LEMs are associated with verbal, linguistic, and left-hemispheric activity (Bakan, 1971; Bakan & Strayer, 1973; Gur & Gur, 1977). Other studies, however, have failed to consistently replicate these results (Ehrlichman, Weiner, & Baker, 1974; Ehrlichman & Weinberger, 1978). Researchers who subscribe to an approach called neurolinguistic programming (NLP) have a similar perspective (Bandler & Grinder, 1979), that is, that certain eye movements are associated with certain kinds of thought. As Knapp and Hall (1997) maintain, the scientific community has generally been skeptical of the NLP approach. At present, research suggests a tendency, particularly for males (Bakan, 1971), to look left when employing right-hemispheric visual or spatial thoughts and to look right when using left-hemispheric, linguistic cognitions.

PROXEMICS

The study of communication through interpersonal space and distance is called proxemics. Space is a powerful metaphor for interpersonal relationships. In relational rhetoric, we say "I feel closer to her than ever before," or "He seems so distant," or "They just need a little space in their relationship." Scholars have examined several areas of human spatial behavior, including territoriality, crowding and density, and personal space.

Territoriality

If someone sat at "your desk" or parked in "your parking space," you might be upset or at least wonder why this person failed to regard it as yours. The study of territoriality isn't limited to humans. Animals of all types occupy and maintain territory to defend themselves, protect their young, and conserve their food supply. Humans occupy and defend territory for much the same reasons. Indeed, the Fourth Amendment to the U.S. Constitution affirms "the right of the people to be secure in their persons, houses, papers, and effects" as a fundamental cornerstone of the Bill of Rights.

To defend our territory we employ an elaborate series of defensive signals. Some employ verbal warnings such as "no trespassing," "no soliciting," or "beware of dog" signs designed to discourage intruders. Others defend their territory with barriers such as gates, fences, walls, doors, and locks. These barriers are sometimes referred to as boundary markers. People even defend temporary space, such as library tables, classroom desks, stadium or theater seats, and lunch tables. Research suggests that people rarely use verbal communication to defend temporary space (Sommer, 1967a, 1969); instead, they use physical objects as "markers" (see Becker, 1973), such as leaving coats on theater seats, blankets on bleachers at football games, and books, purses, or backpacks on classroom seats or cafeteria tables. These types of markers are sometimes referred to as central markers because they are placed in a central location within the territory. Markers must appear to intentionally designate territory. Several of my own unreported experiments have found that a full cup or can of soda can reserve a space in a university cafeteria for over an hour but that a half-full cup rarely works longer than ten minutes, probably because it is perceived as someone's garbage rather than a territorial marker. Tenure, the length of time a person occupies a place, also helps lay claim to territory. Students who regularly occupy the same table in the cafeteria or library often get upset when someone sits at "their table." Although I don't assign seats in my classes, students are quick to establish their territory and return to it day after day. If an unperceptive student occupies "another's" seat, the affected student often appears angry, upset, or disoriented as he or she searches for a new seat. Territory becomes a status symbol and is defended against intrusion, as in the case of Archie Bunker's famous favorite chair. In a more serious vein, even the homeless claim territorial rights under bridge overpasses and on steam vents. Gang members defend their territories against intruders, and invasion of gang territory can result in violence (see chapter 12 for more on these issues).

Crowding and Density

When lots of people occupy our environment, we may feel crowded due to our subjective feelings of having our space invaded. Density is an objective measure of the number of people per square foot or square mile. Generally, perceptions of crowding are related to the density of a space, but not always. People from some environments such as parts of Asia or urban areas throughout the world may not feel as crowded as their American or rural counterparts under similar density levels. Moreover, attendees of such events as rock concerts, the Rose Parade, and the Super Bowl expect and even desire high density levels without experiencing the negative feelings associated with crowding. In general, however, high density is uncomfortable and stressful (Aiello, 1987; Sinha & Nayyar, 2000).

Aiello (1976) examined children in four-person groups at various grade levels in a small room (4 × 21 feet) and a large room (10 × 12 feet). At all grade levels, students characterized the small room more negatively, as more crowded, and as less

Although, in general, the Japanese touch very little and strive to maintain their personal space, extreme crowding during rush hour in Tokyo is quite common and accepted as normal by urban commuters.
(© DK Images)

comfortable than the large room. Aiello, Epstein, and Karlin (1975) studied identical dormitory rooms occupied by either two or three residents. Students in the three-person rooms felt more crowded and less satisfied than those in the two-person rooms. Moreover, physiological stress tests (measuring chemicals in the urine that indicate stress) showed increased stress levels for the students in the more- versus less-dense rooms. The results, however, did not show a disadvantage in work productivity in the socially dense environments.

Research has shown that crowding can result in social pathology and criminal behavior. Galle and Gove's (1979) studies of juvenile delinquency in Chicago revealed that density explains significant increases in delinquency independent of other factors such as poverty or education. In a study by Dean, Pugh, and Gunderson (1975), military personnel in high-density settings had more accidents than those living in less-dense settings.

Calhoun (1962) showed that crowding in rat populations produces miscarriage, violence, homosexuality, and eating disorders. Do such behavioral changes occur in human populations? Although behavioral changes are not as extreme in humans, the tentative answer is yes (see Baum, Davis, & Valins, 1979; Sadalla, 1978). To some degree humans can adapt to high density situations, particularly when they perceive a lot of social support from others around them (Sinha & Nayyar, 2000).

Personal Space

Wherever we go, whatever we do, we are surrounded by an invisible bubble called our personal space. The bubble in North America has a radius of about 3 feet and is slightly egg-shaped, being larger in front. The bubble is invisible but is recognized as an interpersonal and psychological reality. When individuals penetrate this invisible bubble, reactions are generally negative. The exceptions, of course, are friends, lovers, and family members, who have much freer access to us.

Hall (1968) maintains that in North America there are four zones of interaction that indicate the type of relationship that exists between interactants. The closest zone, *intimate distance*, extends from bodily contact out to about 18 inches. Typically, the only people allowed within this zone are intimate friends and family members. An exception to this rule are small children, who have yet to learn about personal space boundaries; whether relations or not, small children are free to penetrate adults' personal space zone and often climb or crawl right over adults.

The distance at which most of our interactions occur, *casual/personal distance*, extends from about 1½ feet to 4 feet from one's body. This distance, not coincidently at about an arm's length, makes touch difficult and defines interactions that occur in this zone as relatively nonintimate. Andersen and Sull (1985) have also shown that people with an aversion to touch maintain even greater distances that are "out of touch" with potential interactants.

The third zone of interaction is *social-consulting distance*, which extends from about 4 to 8 feet. Business people, salespersons, and professors typically use social space to convey an aura of professionalism and avoid creating feelings of spatial invasion or the impression of an intimate relationship. Social-consulting distance also occurs between most people during group interaction or business meetings.

The final zone, *public distance*, extends from about 8 feet and beyond and is reserved for the president and other high-ranking officials, public speakers, celebrities, and executives. The secret service gets noticeably agitated when the president wades into a crowd to shake hands, because the protective buffer of the public interaction zone is eliminated, creating a security problem. Public speakers maintain public distances not only to signify their role as the center of attention, but to create better visual access for their audience. Celebrities gain status and protection from distancing the public, yet like executives and elected officials they risk "losing contact" with their audiences, organizations, and constituencies with too much distance. Executive privacy, although advantageous in many respects, can result in loneliness, social isolation, and poor information flow (Andersen & Bowman, 1990; Kanter, 1979; Mehrabian, 1976).

When personal space is invaded, an interactant will seek to restore a comfortable, relationally appropriate distance through a variety of means, including retreats, changes in body orientation, reductions in immediacy, and the use of body buffers. A number of studies have shown that interactants will retreat and depart if invaded by a stranger (Russo, 1967; Sommer, 1969), particularly if the stranger is male. Similarly, people orient themselves away from an invading stranger, literally giving her or him the cold shoulder rather than a sensitive front loaded with multisensory inputs. Invasions of space also result in compensatory responses in other channels such as reductions in eye contact (Andersen, 1985; Burgoon & Jones, 1976). More recently, studies of reactions to spatial invasion in artificial, virtual environments have shown that people react very similarly by retreating and leaning away, particularly when virtual avatars invaded from the front and when avatars used eye contact (Bailenson, Blascovich, Beall, & Loomis,

2003). These compensatory reductions in immediacy (more on this in chapters 8 and 9) are an attempt to reduce the overall intimacy of an encounter. Finally, invaded interactants will use body buffers such as boxes, purses, briefcases, or even folded arms to protect vital body parts and ward off spatial invaders. Buffers and other compensatory responses are almost always nonverbal, analogic behaviors. Rarely do people resort to language to defend their territory.

Of course, the closest interpersonal distance is no distance, or actual touch. Tactile communication, or haptics, a highly intimate personal code, is examined next.

HAPTICS

The incredible power of touch is obvious to people the world over. The embrace of a close friend, the stroke of a lover's hand, the firm handshake of a business associate, or the warm hug of a family member in a time of bereavement communicate with an intensity that other forms of communication lack. Touch also has the potential to dominate, harass, and even injure. The news is full of stories of child abuse, sexual harassment, and domestic violence, situations in which touch was used destructively.

Perhaps no mode of human interaction has the same potential to communicate love, warmth, and intimacy as actual body contact. For adults touch typically conveys positive feelings of composure, immediacy, warmth, informality, and affection (Burgoon, 1991). Research has shown that touch is inherently rewarding or reinforcing in even the youngest infants (Field, 2002).

Humans are born into a world of touch. Infants are almost continually touched while being fed, played with, changed, held, cuddled, and comforted. Adults touch infants who are three- to nine-month-olds about 67 percent of the time (Muir, 2002). Touch evokes eye contact and facial expressions in an infant. During interaction infants who are touched exhibit more smiling and vocalizing as well as less crying. Touch is the primary form of infant-adult interaction. Studies have also shown that babies who are rarely or never touched are more susceptible to illness and even die from failure-to-thrive syndrome. Numerous studies indicate that touch is beneficial to infant and child development and even

Touch is the closest, most intimate nonverbal behavior, though space, eye contact, and touch work together to increase intimacy.

necessary for life itself. Infants confined to orphanages who were not touched regularly are often maladjusted, quiet, and unable to learn, gain weight, or mature normally (Frank, 1957; Montagu, 1971/1978; Morris, 1971; Shevrin & Toussieng, 1965). In an experimental study in which premature babies were assigned to either a touch or no-touch group, the touched babies gained 21 percent more weight and were discharged from the hospital five days earlier than nontouched babies (Scafidi, Field, Schanberg, & Bauer, 1990). Unfortunately, harsh touch in infancy is associated with behavioral problems, violence, and mental illness later in life (Field, 2002).

Experimental studies of premature babies who need incubator care show that intermittent skin-to-skin contact between the baby and the mother, called kangaroo care, has social and emotional benefits for both the mother and the infant (Feldman, Weller, Sirota, & Eidelman, 2003). Unfortunately, American children are touched far less than children in other cultures. Not surprisingly, America has correspondingly far more violence and homicide than most other countries as well (Field, 2002).

The extraordinary yet subtle power of touch was illustrated by a study conducted in a college library by Fisher, Rytting, and Heslin (1976). College librarians inconspicuously touched or did not touch students as they returned their library cards. After students exited the library, they were asked to complete a survey regarding the library and the librarians. Students, particularly females, evaluated the library and staff more positively when they were in the touch rather than the no-touch group. Similarly, in a bogus ESP experiment in which researchers were actually observing the effects of touch, participants (college women) in the touch (as opposed to the no-touch) group found their experimental partner more responsive, likable, and attractive and indicated they would like to have the same partner again (Boderman, Freed, & Kinnucan, 1972).

Touch can have influential and persuasive effects as well (see chapter 10 for a more detailed discussion). Willis and Hamm (1980) reported that people were more willing to sign a petition when they were touched by the circulator. Research has also shown that waitresses receive bigger tips when they touch patrons (Crusco & Wetzel, 1984), that psychologists who touch patients obtain greater compliance (Patterson, Powell, & Lenihan, 1986), and that shoppers purchase more when they are appropriately touched (Smith, Gier, & Willis, 1982). One experiment showed that complete strangers are more willing to comply when touch is employed; in this experiment, strangers who found dimes in phone booths were likely to return the coins to their owners (that is, the experimenters) when the request was accompanied by touch than when the request was unaccompanied by touch (Kleinke, 1977).

Types of Touch

Of course, not all kinds of touch are created equal or employed for the same purpose. Heslin (1974) separates touch into five major categories based on function, usage, and intensity. The least-intense touch is *functional-professional* (or instrumental) touch, which occurs between physicians and patients, physical therapists and clients, tailors and customers, coaches and athletes, and barbers and customers. Although this kind of touch is done in a professional and businesslike manner, it actually has therapeutic and interpersonal implications. Of course, the types of touch as well as the zones of the body touched are quite limited.

The *social-polite* function of touch occurs in initial-acquaintance situations, business relationships, and formal occasions. The classic example of social-polite touch is the handshake. Of course, too weak or too powerful a handshake can start a relationship off poorly, so the relational implications of these initial touches should not be underemphasized. Social-polite touch conveys recognition of the equality and humanity of the other person and signals inclusion and respect.

The *friendship-warmth* function of touch is simultaneously the most important and the most ambiguous. Because it is less formalized than social-polite touch, the type and amount of touch is negotiated relationally between partners. Too much touch or touch that is too intimate conveys love or sexual interest, whereas too little touch may suggest coldness and unfriendliness and arrest the chance for relational escalation. In private situations, friendly touches have an even greater potential for being perceived as sexual, particularly by males who perceive more sexual connotations with touch (Fromme et al., 1986; Hatfield, 1984; Stier & Hall, 1984).

The *love-intimacy* function of touch is increasingly personal, intimate, and unique. This touch is so special that it can be exchanged only by a few people, such as very good friends, close family members, lovers, and spouses, and it is unique to each particular person. When you lay your hand on another person's cheek, hold hands, or engage in a full frontal embrace, you are conveying intimacy. Typically, this type of touch is nonsexual, although in some relationships, such as romances or marriages, it may blend with sexual touch. High levels of immediacy (discussed in chapter 8) are conveyed by this type of touch, resulting in increased psychological closeness and warmth.

Sexually arousing touch is the most personal and intimate form of touch. Often reserved for one special person or limited to only a few persons for most people, sexual touch is the most stimulating and the most anxiety-arousing type of touch. Key to this type of touch is mutual consent, a high level of attraction, and a desire to stimulate and be stimulated by one's partner. It has become increasingly common over the past several decades for most sexually active individuals to practice serial monogamy—a relationship that is sexually exclusive until it ends, whereupon the individuals move on to new sexually exclusive relationships (Rathus, Nevid, & Fichner-Rathus, 1993; Sorensen, 1973).

Touch Avoidance

Individuals differ dramatically in the degree to which they like or dislike touch (see chapter 7 for more on this topic). Touch avoidance (Andersen & Leibowitz, 1978; Andersen, 2005) is the degree to which an individual likes and approaches touch or dislikes and avoids it. Touch avoiders of opposite-sex touch tend to be female and same-sex touch avoiders tend to be male (Andersen, Andersen, & Lustig, 1987). In a related study, Andersen and Sull (1985) interviewed undergraduates regarding their television-viewing preferences. Upon arriving at the interview, students were asked to pick up a folding chair and set it up near the interviewer. Students scoring high on a previously administered touch-avoidance measure set up their chairs twice as far away from the interviewer as students scoring low on the measure. Touch avoiders stay "out of touch" through larger interpersonal distances and tend to manifest less touch and less overall intimacy (Andersen et al., 1987; Andersen & Leibowitz, 1978; Guerrero & Andersen, 1991). Similarly, touch avoiders are less open, less expressive, somewhat lower in self-esteem, and more religious. Moreover, touch avoiders judge people who touch them less favorably than do touch approachers (Sorensen, 1979).

Touch and Relationships

Field research by Guerrero and Andersen (1991) reveals that opposite-sex touch is most likely to occur at the intermediate stages of a relationship, when people are "going out" or are engaged. By contrast, at both the initial stages of acquaintance and among married people, touch is dramatically lower. To collect this data, couples were unobtrusively observed while they waited in lines at theaters and amusement parks. After the amount and location of touch were recorded, the couples were approached and the partners were asked to separately complete a series of questions that included items about their relationship. Of course, these findings are limited to public touch, which was observed by the experimental assistants.

More recently, however, Emmers and Dindia (1995) conducted a questionnaire study designed to measure the amount of touch in private situations. Interestingly, the pattern of results was very similar to that of the Guerrero and Andersen study, with most private touch occurring during the serious dating and the engagement stages and slightly less touch occurring in the married stage. Research conducted in a field setting, namely an international airport, confirms the two previous studies (McDaniel & Andersen, 1998). Travelers from thirty-seven countries employed the most touch if they were close friends or lovers and less touch if they were initial acquaintances or married couples.

One other recent study has found that partners' public touch is highly correlated (Guerrero & Andersen, 1994).

Affectionate and sexual touches are immediacy behaviors that signal intimacy and bondedness.

This research indicates that in a public setting, if one person touches her or his partner, the other partner is pretty certain to match the touch level. This pattern holds true regardless of an individual's personality or touch-avoidance level; moreover, it strengthens across more intimate relationship stages. Marital touch, or lack thereof, is almost completely matched between partners. Taken together, these studies reveal that the highest level of tactile matching occurs in long-term, committed relationships such as marriages, whereas the highest frequency of touch occurs in intimate relationships at intermediate or escalating levels of acquaintance.

Touch Taboos

Because touch is such an intimate behavior, much of it is prohibited. Jones (1994) discusses seven forbidden forms of touch in the United States. First, strangers should avoid touch unless they are being introduced or giving aid. Nonfunctional touch by strangers is perceived as excessively intimate and creates negative attributions. Second, hurtful touches should be avoided at all times, even accidental touches. When they occur, an apology is surely required. Third, one should avoid startling another person with touch. Some people sneak up behind friends to startle them as a joke, but the friends rarely think it's funny. Fourth, interrupting touches should be avoided. Kissing your wife or husband during a phone call, hugging a child in the middle of her or his homework, or fondling your lover in the middle of a favorite television show are more annoying than affectionate forms of touch. Fifth, one should avoid moving people out of the way with touch alone. People who do this are perceived as rude or pushy. Placing a hand on someone's back while saying "excuse me" as you move through a crowded party is much more acceptable. Even hurrying a child through a door can be perceived as an aggressive violation. Sixth, playful aggression should seem more playful than aggressive. Family members who wrestle should keep this in mind. If someone is in pain or injured, the horseplay has gone too far. Mock strangleholds and armlocks can also be very scary. Nobody should get hurt physically or psychologically during playful aggression. Seventh, critical statements should not be accompanied by negative touch. Such a "double whammy" is unsupportive and unnecessarily aggressive. Finally, I must add that people should refrain from any touch that the receiver dislikes, rebuffs, or asks to be stopped. Remember, *No means no.* Respect people's right not to be touched.

SUMMARY

The human body is fascinating in its ability to communicate without language. During initial acquaintance, the most salient code of nonverbal communication is physical appearance. Right or wrong, other people judge your physical appearance and then make attributions about your social attractiveness, intelligence, motivation, social habits, health, and character based on your appearance. Although these attributions may be incorrect, they are what people believe to be true, and frequently that is all that really matters. Research that examines different body types has found that endomorphs, who are heavy and round, are perceived most negatively within the American culture. Mesomorphs, who are strong and muscular, are most positively perceived, followed by ectomorphs, who are thin, linear people. Tall people, especially tall men, are perceived more positively and tend to hold higher-status positions. Appearance can result in stereotypes, which sometimes become self-fulfilling prophecies.

Bodies in motion emit expressions, gestures, and synchronous movements that are examined by researchers studying kinesics. Research has shown that a set of basic facial expressions are universal and cross-cultural. Facial expressions are more than private muscular reactions. Facial expressions of distinct emotions occur mainly in social situations when other people are looking. As we develop and mature, we are less likely to show facial expressions than we did as young children. We learn display rules that simulate, intensify, inhibit, miniaturize, and mask our feelings.

Gestures are both innate and learned. They come in many forms, including emblems, or signs with dictionary definitions; adaptors, or self- or other-touching behaviors; and illustrators, gestures that accompany speech. Like partners at a dance, communicators match, or synchronize, their movement. People who are in rapport or who are attracted to each other are "in sync" or "on the same wave-length." One form of synchrony is motor mimicry, kinesic action designed to be imitated by one's partner.

Oculesics is the study of eye behavior, including eye contact, pupil dilation, and eye movements. Eye contact, the most important aspect of oculesics, is an invitation to communication that signals immediacy and warmth, expresses involvement, sends flirtatious messages, regulates interaction, and monitors communication. Under certain circumstances, eye contact can send intimidating messages. Pupil dilation occurs in dim light and when people experience arousal, positive affect, or attraction. More importantly, people with dilated pupils are perceived as warmer and more attractive, even though pupil dilation is perceived at low levels of awareness. Lateral eye movements are associated with cognition in the opposite brain hemisphere and can even stimulate thought.

Proxemics, the study of communication through interpersonal space and distance, is subdivided into territoriality, crowding and density, and personal space. Territoriality deals with fixed space that individuals own or occupy. Territory is reserved more often nonverbally than verbally through markers and tenure. Crowding is a subjective feeling that a space is overpopulated. Crowding has been shown to result in discomfort, stress, and even violence. Personal space, an invisible bubble that surrounds the body, is divided into four zones. Intimate distance extends from tactile contact to 18 inches and is generally reserved for children and people with whom we share very close relationships. Casual/personal distance, which extends from 2 to 4 feet, is where most of our daily interactions occur. Social-consulting distance, which extends from 4 to 8 feet, is used for many business relationships. Finally, public distance, reserved for high-ranking officials, public speakers, celebrities, and executives, extends from about 8 feet and beyond. When personal space is invaded, individuals attempt to restore a comfortable distance through retreat, reductions in immediacy, and the use of body buffers.

Haptics, or tactile communication, is the most intimate of the nonverbal codes. It has the power to comfort, arouse, or repel. Touch can produce compliance, create intimacy, and is necessary for healthy child development. The functions of touch include functional-professional, social-polite, friendship-warmth, love-intimacy, and sexually arousing. Touch avoidance is the degree to which an individual likes and approaches touch or dislikes and avoids touch. Touch avoiders maintain greater interpersonal distances, manifest less touch, and engage in fewer intimacy behaviors. Touch peaks in romantic relationships at the intermediate stages. Public touch is highly reciprocal; most people touch their romantic partners about the same amount as their partners touch them. Many forms of touch are taboo, so when a person says "Don't touch," you should respect her or his right not to be touched.

Scoring Your Body Type Survey

Directions: Locate the words you selected to fill in the blanks on the survey. Give yourself one point for each word you selected from the endomorphy column; one point for each word from the mesomorphy column; and so on. Total your points for each column. These relative totals should reflect your own body type. Do they? How much do they differ from your perception of yourself?

Endomorphy	Mesomorphy	Ectomorphy
affable	active	anxious
affected	adventurous	awkward
affectionate	argumentative	cautious
calm	assertive	considerate
complacent	cheerful	cool
contented	competitive	detached
cooperative	confident	gentle-tempered
dependent	courageous	introspective
forgiving	determined	meticulous
generous	dominant	precise
kind	domineering	reflective
leisurely	efficient	reticent
placid	energetic	self-conscious
relaxed	enterprising	sensitive
sluggish	enthusiastic	serious
sociable	hot-tempered	shy
soft-hearted	impetuous	suspicious
soft-tempered	optimistic	tactful
sympathetic	outgoing	tense
tolerant	reckless	thoughtful
warm	talkative	withdrawn

Source: Cortés & Gatti (1965).

3

The Contextual Codes of Nonverbal Communication

Without context there is no communication.

—Gregory Bateson, *Steps to an Ecology of Mind*

Context is vital for human understanding. "It has become axiomatic that any human action cannot be successfully interpreted outside of its context. The term 'out of context' has become synonymous with meaningless or misleading" (Andersen, 1989, p. 27). According to Bateson (1972), nonverbal communication provides the context, or frame, for all other behaviors.

So much of what is considered "inappropriate" is communication that is out of context: making a sexual proposition to an employee, proposing to an already married person, laughing at a funeral, interrupting another person mid-sentence, arriving late for a special ceremony, or giving a person a compliment in a sarcastic voice. The reason you wait for your turn to talk, put on deodorant, or clean your apartment for guests involves a sensitivity to the contexts of communication. Writing about competent communication, Spitzberg and Cupach (1989) stated, "Flexibility involves the adaptation of actions to the physical, social, or relational context . . . competence judgments are intrinsically contextual" (p. 22). Adaptability means adjusting to environmental factors such as heat, noise, group size, climate, and culture. Accordingly, our discussion begins here with the environments in which communication takes place.

In chapter 2 we explored the nonverbal, analogic codes of the body. In this chapter we will examine additional types of codes used to send multichanneled nonverbal messages. Contextual codes include macroenvironments, microenvironments, chronemics, olfactics, and vocalics. Like the body codes of nonverbal communication, contextual codes are analogic, nonlinguistic, and multichanneled. Body and contextual codes are also multifunctional and can communicate meaning in the absence of verbal communication. Although body codes provide some context for other nonverbal and verbal messages of communication, the primary function of contextual codes is to provide the context for all communication.

Communication is uninterpretable without context, environment, vocal inflection, and timing. As discussed in chapters 1 and 2, it is important to remember that nonverbal communication codes combined with verbal communication are packaged together to form an entire message, and communication messages are sent and received packages, or gestalts.

VOCALICS

Human speech is the main vehicle by which verbal and linguistic communication is transmitted; but speech is uninterpretable without the nonverbal inflection which can completely change the meaning of words. In my nonverbal communication class, we conduct an exercise in which we see how many ways we can say the single word "yes." Try it. Depending on one's tone of voice, the word "yes" can signal agreement, affirmation, reluctance, hostility, confusion, intimacy, boredom, seduction, affection, impatience, and a multitude of other messages. The class is generally able to find over twenty-five independent meanings associated with the various pronunciations of the word yes. As this exercise illustrates, the meaning of a word has less to do with its content than with the way it is spoken.

Vocal qualities such as pitch, rhythm, tempo, resonance, control, and accent lend meaning to the spoken word. The study of these nonverbal elements of the voice is called vocalics or paralinguistics. Vocal expression provides instant context and meaning for human communication. Throughout human history, before and during the evolution of language, the voice—and music as well—provided instant emotional communication between people (Juslin & Laukka, 2003). The study of vocalics examines other purely nonverbal characteristics such as laughing, screaming, inhaling or exhaling, sighing, yawning, and crying, as well as vocal segregates such as "uh-huh," "uh-uh," "ah," and "um" (Trager, 1958) and singing (Andersen, Garrison, & Andersen, 1979). Moreover, every person has a unique voice. A person's *vocal signature* is as distinctive to each individual as a fingerprint. No two voices are exactly alike (Burgoon, Buller, & Woodall, 1996). Each has its distinct combination of pitch, regional accent, volume, resonance, and other vocal qualities.

Among all of the contextual codes, vocalics may be the most important because it provides the context for everything we say. Bateson (1972) claimed that "paralanguage has blossomed side by side with verbal communication . . . [our] vocal intonation far exceeds anything that any other animal is known to produce" (p. 412). Jaffe (1987) suggested that the human brain evolved in such a way that the left hemisphere deals with content while the right hemisphere deals with the emotional quality available through nonverbal cues such as vocalics:

> If the left brains of both speaker and listener are saturated by the linguistic processing of the conversation, do their right brains remain available for the kinesic and paralinguistic phenomena that calibrate the emotional quality of a conversation? Intriguing support for such speculation has been provided. (p. 29)

Sadly, damage to the right hemisphere through injury or stroke reduces or eliminates vocalic or paralinguistic intonation from speech. Though patients can communicate verbally, their speech becomes a monotone because intonation is processed in the right brain hemisphere (Andersen et al., 1979; Blake et al., 2002).

Vocalics modifies everything that is said verbally. The tone of voice is essential for communicating emotion, humor, sarcasm, urgency, and comforting through what are called prosodic or paralinguistic features (Pell, 2005). Research shows that politeness is a major function of vocalic communication (LaPlante & Ambady, 2003). In fact, recent research shows that e-mail is significantly more polite than voice mail because e-mail can be edited and does not contain vocalic cues which sometimes carry messages of impoliteness (Duthler, 2006).

Vocalics, along with the kinesic cues described in chapter 2, contextualize every utterance. This was recognized early by one of the fathers of nonverbal communication, Ray Birdwhistell (1970), who examined parakinesic and paralinguistic cues:

> These cross-referencing signals amplify, emphasize, or modify the formal constructions, and/or make statements about the context of the message situation. In the latter instance, they help to define the context of the interaction by identifying the actor or his audience, and furthermore, they usually convey information about the larger context in which the interaction takes place. (p. 117)

Like other forms of nonverbal communication, vocalics exists beside language and interacts with language. Researchers have established six primary ways that nonverbal communication, and vocalics in particular, contextualizes and influences verbal communication (Ekman, 1965). First, nonverbal cues serve a *repetition* or redundancy function. Vocalic cues, such as an enthusiastic tone of voice, combined with the kinesic cue of nodding, repeat and reinforce the word yes to signal affirmation or positivity. Because repetition increases accuracy, one's nonverbal communication should repeat verbal communication to increase accuracy and clarify a message.

Complementarity, or modification, is the second function of vocalics. Nonverbal messages may elaborate or modify verbal messages. Telling a child not to do something in a loud or angry voice complements but also strengthens a verbal message. Complementarity is similar to the repetition function when considering vocalic cues. The difference between the two is clearer when kinesics are added to the picture. For example, if a child asks if she can have a piece of candy right before dinner, the mother might shake her head (repetition) while saying no, and she might say no in a stern manner (complementarity).

The third function, *accenting* or emphasizing, involves using vocalics to stress a certain part of a verbal message. The most important word in a sentence is often accented (such as italicized words in written communication) by saying the word more loudly, carefully, or slowly. Imagine a parent saying, "Please don't fall down that hillside." By accenting a particular word, such as *please* or *that*, the meaning of the sentence, as well as the emotion conveyed, changes.

Substitution, or replacement, is the fourth vocalic function. Sometimes nonverbal or vocalic information can replace verbal communication entirely. Vocalic expressions such as "uh-huh" replace the words "I understand what you're saying." Yawns can substitute for verbal expressions of boredom, and laughs can replace appreciative or derisive comments. In the example of the child asking for a piece of candy, if the mother shakes her head without verbalizing "no," substitution, rather than complementarity, has occurred.

Regulation, the fifth function of vocalics, entails the use of nonverbal cues that regulate or control verbal communication. Filler pauses such as "ah" or "um" and audible inhalations of air at the end of a sentence may prevent another speaker from interjecting or interrupting. Likewise, silent pauses or exhalations of air signal to other speakers that it's their turn.

The final function of vocalics is *contradiction*, which occurs when a person's vocalic messages contradict what the person says verbally. If a person says "I'll go to the dance" in a bored or lackadaisical tone of voice, the nonverbal message may be stronger than the verbal one. (See chapter 1 for a detailed discussion on contradictory cues.)

One frequently misunderstood vocalic cue is sarcasm, a message which is often conveyed by overaccenting a verbal statement. For example, overstating "Oh, great!" when the opposing team scores a touchdown is understood to mean just the opposite. Several studies (Andersen, Andersen, Murphy, & Wendt-Wasco, 1985; Blanck & Rosenthal, 1982) suggest that young children have great difficulty detecting sarcasm, resulting in confusion about what a sarcastic speaker really means. Likewise, people with very low intelligence or little education may take sarcastic messages literally. Occasionally, it is difficult for anyone to tell if a message is meant to be sarcastic or serious. This is particularly true if the receiver does not know the sender's personality.

Finally, nonverbal messages associated with the voice may create very distinct impressions of the individual communicator. Attractive, influential voices are more resonant and calm, less monotonous, lower-pitched (especially for males), less regionally accented, less nasal, less shrill, and more relaxed (Addington, 1968; Pearce, 1971; Zuckerman & Driver, 1989; Zuckerman, Hodgins, & Miyake, 1990). Midwestern voices tend to be the most accent-free, which is why many toll-free phone lines originate from Nebraska and employ Nebraska operators. Nasality in particular seems to be a quality that elicits numerous perceptions of negative characteristics.

MACROENVIRONMENTS

> After a while one notices something different about otherwise familiar objects: Colors are deeper, metals are shinier, the air is cleaner, and the brilliant California sun seems to jump from every surface. Before long everyday scenes begin to look like technicolor scenes. If London fog can make the English "moody and introspective," what must the California sun do to the Californians? (Hale & Eisen, 1968, p. xiii)

California isn't Illinois. In Southern California, where I live, the sun does affect people, their lifestyle, and their communication. Sitting here in California and reflecting on my youth in Illinois, the differences are extreme. Everything in the Midwest is more subdued and less extreme than in California. Poet Dave Etter (Davis, 1992) of Illinois writes:

> Here in . . . Illinois
> I'm living in the middle,
> standing on the courthouse lawn
> in the middle of town
> in the middle of my life
> a self-confessed middle brow
> a member of the middle class
> and of course Middle Western
> the middle, you see, the middle
> believing in the middle way.

The larger environmental context, called macroenvironments, affects every interaction in numerous ways. For years, scholars have reported that the climate of a region exerts considerable impact on communicative behavior. It was Hippocrates who noted:

> I hold that Asia (Minor) differs widely from Europe in the nature of all its inhabitants and all its vegetation . . . the one region is less wild than the other, the character of the inhabitants is milder and more gentle. The cause of this is the temperate climate, because it lies toward the east midway between the risings of the sun, further away than is Europe from the cold. (Biswas, 1984, p. 6)

In his seminal book on climate, Ward (1918) reported that in Aristotle's day, climate (*klima*) referred to the inclination of the earth toward the sun, commonly called latitude. Klima, according to Ward, is highly correlated with development. Ward maintains that in both the United States and Europe, northerners are more serious, industrious, enterprising, pessimistic, and mature, whereas southerners are more cheerful, genial, impulsive, generous, easygoing, and lazy.

Thomas Jefferson described southerners as being much more "fiery, voluptuary, indolent, unsteady, zealous for their own liberties but trampling on those of

Global warming is melting glacial ice throughout the world and altering humans' macroenvironnent. Glaciers are retreating rapidly and sea levels are rising.

others, generous and candid" than northerners (O'Brien, 1979, p. 3). The great philosopher and social observer of the early 1800s, Alexis de Tocqueville, reported, "The American of the South is fond of grandeur, luxury, and renown, of gaiety, pleasure and above all, of idleness; nothing obliges him to exert himself in order to subsist" (1835/1945, p. 411).

In his classic study of civilization, Huntington (1945) reported that mid-latitudes produce the highest efficiency and productivity, whereas high and low latitudes produce reduced efficiency due to their extremes in temperature. In a major study of world economics, John Kenneth Galbraith (1951) noted that a climatic belt several thousand miles wide, encircling the earth at the equator, contains countries with the lowest living standards, least development, and shortest life spans.

More recently in a study of college students at forty U.S. universities, Andersen, Lustig, and Andersen (1990) reported that across all of the United States, "southern culture is characterized by communication that is more dramatic and stimulating but more socially isolated and communication apprehensive than northern culture" (p. 305). Quite likely, the results are explained by both environmental determinism and conscious choice. Environment certainly exerts a huge influence on behavior, affecting mood and emotion (see Thorson & Kasworm, 1984; Whybrow, 1984) through the neuroendocrine system (for a summary see Andersen et al., 1990). In recent years, seasonal affective disorder (appropriately abbreviated SAD) has been recognized as a major source of depression in northern latitudes and is often treated with light therapy. SAD is common in such places as Seattle, which has one of the highest percentages of mostly cloudy days, but uncommon in such places as Tucson, which has one of the highest percentages of sunny days.

Of course, people frequently choose their environments. Someone who is prone to SAD may choose to live in Arizona rather than in Washington State. Someone who enjoys snow skiing and snowboarding might live in Colorado, whereas someone who enjoys sailing and snorkeling might live in South Florida. My wife and I, who grew up in Illinois but live in San Diego, California, often say, only half-jokingly, that we were always Californians inside, just waiting to come out. Others shun the West Coast and Southwest in favor of places that have distinct changes of season, complete with white Christmases and April showers. Some people like big, exciting cities; others prefer safe and cozy small towns. Thus, many individuals make voluntary migrations based on their own needs and preferences. Sometimes, large groups of people even migrate to the same place. The movement of Mormons and Christians to Utah, of intellectuals and artists to New York City, of gays and lesbians to San Francisco, of outdoor enthusiasts to Montana and Alaska, and of certain musical groups to the Pacific Northwest provides an additional explanation for the link between macroenvironments and communication.

MICROENVIRONMENTS

Microenvironments are smaller, local arenas constructed by people, such as buildings, rooms, parks, gardens, and patios. Microenvironments are communicative in two ways. First, they may actually communicate analogic messages. A well-decorated house is more inviting to guests than a trashed one; and it directly communicates a message to guests. Second, microenvironments provide the context for all other types of nonverbal and verbal communication that take place within that environment. Considerable research has shown that such microenvironmental factors as temperature, color, lighting, and sound (1) affect communication by providing context and (2) constitute nonverbal messages in and of themselves.

Communication scholars and environmental psychologists are understandably aware of the important role of microenvironment in communication, but others are not. For example, when I was a communication doctoral student, a well-known political science professor asked me why students in his seminar never talked. I replied that for starters, he had them in a traditional, front-facing, classroom environment. When he switched to a circular seminar table, sure enough, classroom interaction picked up considerably. Sometime later, a lawyer for whom I was consulting asked me why her clients didn't open up to her and frequently failed to return after their first visit. She posed this question in a dingy, poorly lit office, from behind huge piles of law books and files cluttering her desk; indeed, throughout most of our interaction I could hardly see her. Her practice improved dramatically after heeding my suggestion that she clear her desk, put the books on the shelf, and make eye contact with her clients! What was common sense for a communication major was a divine revelation for these otherwise bright professionals.

Microenvironments are designed to produce certain reactions in communicators. The bright lights, loud music, uncomfortable seats, and minimal service of a fast-food restaurant nonverbally communicate, "Eat quickly and make room for the next customer." The soft lights, soothing music, comfortable seats, and attentive service of a fine restaurant say, "Stay a while, relax, enjoy, spend money."

Malandro and Barker (1983) use Las Vegas as an example of a microenvironment that arouses customers and creates the emotional state of a king or queen entering a castle. Through the creation of an "unreal" environment, otherwise

Casinos are artificial microenvironments designed to produce uninhibited behavior and alter ordinary perceptions.

normal adults are encouraged to squander their money, stay up most of the night, and go to exotic shows. Hunter Thompson (1971) describes the bizarre environment of the Circus-Circus Casino:

> The ground floor is full of gambling tables like all the other casinos . . . but the place is about four stories high, in the style of a circus tent, and all manner of strange County-fair/Polish Carnival madness is going on up in this space. Right above the gambling tables Forty Flying Carazito Brothers are doing a high-wire trapeze act along with four muzzled Wolverines and the Six Nymphet Sisters from San Diego . . . so you're down on the main floor playing blackjack, and the stakes are getting high when suddenly you look up, and there right smack above your head is a half-naked fourteen-year-old girl being chased through the air by a snarling wolverine. (p. 46)

Of course, virtual reality experiences, otherworldly pirate journeys, lobby zoos, water parks, and replicas of New York, Paris, or Venice are a few other elements that add to the bizarre nature of the Las Vegas environment.

Sociopetal/Sociofugal Environments

Certain microenvironments have the effect of facilitating communication. *Sociopetal* environments (Sommer, 1967b) bring people together and stimulate interaction. By contrast, *sociofugal* environments inhibit communication and keep people apart. Sociopetal arrangements tend to be low in noise, have high levels of privacy, contain few barriers, and permit communicators to see one another and face each other directly. A semicircle of chairs by a fireplace, a hot tub, and a quiet table for two at a nice restaurant are examples of sociopetal environments. Although it can be stimulating, a crowded party with loud music is sociofugal because it makes communication difficult. In a series of interesting experiments, Mehrabian (1976) found that a straight-line bar is a sociofugal environment except at the corners, where patrons can face each other and converse more easily. Circular and zigzag bars provide more face-to-face positioning, facilitate eye contact, and enhance communication.

The typical American living room with furniture lining the walls is actually a sociofugal environment because interactants are beyond the normal 3- to 4-foot interaction range. Groups of chairs in a nook or surrounding a fireplace are far more sociopetal because they provide optimal interaction distances, feel warmer and cozier, and exclude distractions and uninvited people. Similarly, a couch is a fairly sociofugal environmental fixture when it is occupied by three or four people; eye contact among the group is virtually impossible. The maximum sociopetal seating capacity of a sofa is two; both occupants can converse as well as maximize many various forms of nonverbal communication.

Seating Arrangements

Whether in churches or homes, bars or schools, seating arrangements have a major impact on the quality and quantity of communication. In classrooms, interaction is facilitated by arrangements that promote interaction. Hence, the typical seminar is conducted around an oblong or circular table. In one study in which

The head of the table communicates leadership and power, as do steepling gestures.

students were given the opportunity to assemble chairs in a classroom to facilitate interaction, they chose a U-shaped configuration (Heston & Garner, 1972). Research has shown that such horseshoe-shaped classroom arrangements actually do facilitate interaction because every student has an equivalent position. In the traditional, front-facing classroom, students in the front and center are in much better communication positions, and they interact more (Hurt, Scott, & McCroskey, 1978; Rosenfeld & Civikly, 1976).

A whole group of studies shows that leaders select high-interaction positions, usually the head of a table (Heckel, 1973; LaFrance & Mayo, 1978; Sommer, 1967a). These positions have more visibility and are correlated with increased interaction (Ward, 1968). According to one study, persons who occupied focal positions were more likely to be selected as jury foremen (Strodtbeck & Hook, 1961; see chapter 12 for more about positions of power).

Temperature

Indoor temperature also influences communication. Harner's (1973) summary of research concludes that students show significant decreases in reading speed and comprehension when the room temperature rises above 77 degrees. Todd-Mancillas (1982) recommends that classroom temperatures be kept between 66 and 72 degrees to maintain optimal classroom performance. He also recommends that a "serious effort should be made to provide air conditioning in the classroom, especially during summer months" (p. 85). Similarly, Griffitt (1970) has noted that individuals' interpersonal attraction to other students decreases as temperatures and humidity become excessive.

Color

The color of an environment also exerts a substantial impact on our behavior. I knew a couple who attributed their frequent fights and sleeplessness to their orange bedroom. In Table 3.1, Burgoon and Saine (1978) provided a guide to moods and meanings associated with color. Sure enough, orange creates unpleasant, exciting, and disturbed moods. Bedrooms and studies, where relaxation and concentration are emphasized, should be white, light blue, or light green.

In his summary of research on color in the classroom, Todd-Mancillas (1982) concluded that bright, warm colors facilitate learning and improve affect in ele-

Table 3.1 The Moods and Meanings Associated with Color in the Environment

Color	Moods	Symbolic Meanings
Red	Hot, affectionate, angry, defiant, contrary, hostile, full of vitality, excitement, love	Happiness, lust, intimacy, love, restlessness, agitation, royalty, rage, sin, blood
Blue	Cool, pleasant, leisurely, distant, infinite, secure, transcendent, calm, tender	Dignity, sadness, tenderness, truth
Yellow	Unpleasant, exciting, hostile, cheerful, joyful, jovial	Superficial glamour, sun, light, wisdom, masculinity, royalty (in China), age (in Greece), prostitution (in Italy), famine (in Egypt)
Orange	Unpleasant, exciting, disturbed, distressed, upset, defiant, contrary, hostile, stimulating	Sun, fruitfulness, harvest, thoughtfulness
Purple	Depressed, sad, dignified, stately	Wisdom, victory, pomp, wealth, humility, tragedy
Green	Cool, pleasant, leisurely, in control	Security, peace, jealousy, hate, aggressiveness, calm
Black	Sad, intense, anxious, fearful, despondent, dejected, melancholy, unhappy	Darkness, power, mastery, protection, decay, mystery, wisdom, death, atonement
Brown	Sad, not tender, despondent, dejected, melancholy, unhappy, neutral	Melancholy, protection, autumn, decay, humility, atonement
White	Joyful, light, neutral, cold	Solemnity, purity, chastity, femininity, humility, joy, light, innocence, fidelity, cowardice

Source: Burgoon & Saine (1978).

mentary school classrooms. This summary concludes that even children's IQ scores can be enhanced by learning environments that are attractive and colorful. Color affects consumer behavior as well. Malandro and Barker (1983) asserted that sugar doesn't sell well in green packages, probably because consumers want mostly white packages that remind them of purity and sugar itself. Beauty aids in brown jars fail to sell well because brown is not perceived by consumers as a clean or beautiful color. Safety, too, is affected by color. White and orange cars are safest in summer months due to their high visibility, but green cars, which blend in with the foliage, are quite dangerous. Conversely, in snow, green cars are quite safe and highly visible but white cars are dangerous.

Lighting

Earlier in this chapter, we discussed the importance of sunlight to mood and mental health. Light has other important effects in communication environments as well. Dim, low lights create environments conducive to relaxation, intimacy, and romance. Bright lights have positive effects in work environments because they are stimulating. Indeed, experiments have shown that well-lit environments increase talk (Gergen, Gergen, & Barton, 1973).

In classroom environments, lighting should be bright and full-spectrum (non-fluorescent) for optimal performance. Fluorescent lighting has been shown to produce fatigue, inattention, hyperactivity, and decreased classroom performance (for a full summary see Todd-Mancillas, 1982).

Sound

Environmental sounds permeate our daily life. Sounds made by people, vehicles, appliances, televisions, radios, and so on are everywhere in our urban, mechanical, mediated world. Silence is such an uncommon condition for most people that when they camp or visit a rural area, they are shocked, even disturbed, by the silence.

A number of studies have shown that background music, particularly instrumental music, has numerous beneficial effects in a variety of business settings. Muzak, a company that specializes in producing background music for use in stores, restaurants, and offices, has been a multimillion-dollar industry for decades, serving millions of clients. Selections are carefully tailored to each business environment. The music is played intermittently to prevent workers or customers from becoming bored or fatigued. Research has shown that Muzak improves work performance and concentration, lessens tension, reduces absenteeism, and increases consumer spending (Rosenfeld & Civikly, 1976).

Schools also can utilize background music effectively. In his review of research on music in the school environment, Todd-Mancillas (1982) concluded that music can reduce boredom, improve social interaction, heighten pleasant feelings, and improve work performance in students from elementary school through college. It has also been successfully used in reinforcing positive classroom behavior.

By definition, noise is unwanted sound that either interferes with hearing desirable sounds or produces irritation. It can also cause hearing loss and disrupt concentration. White noise is sound—such as that produced by a clothes dryer or lawn mower—that drowns out other noise. Sometimes white noise has been shown to improve work performance, but many employees actually find it an additional source of irritation (Malandro & Barker, 1983).

Quiet elementary school environments are essential for good student performance, particularly for kids from disadvantaged environments (Heft, 1979; Todd-Mancillas, 1982). Quiet environments are less important for older students; however, sudden loud noises are very disruptive to all students' concentration and should be minimized. Schools should have sufficient soundproofing to minimize distractions from outside environments and other classrooms.

Environmental Efficacy

It is very important that we not underestimate the effect of our built environment on our personal welfare and interpersonal interaction. This is certainly true for internal environments, which residents, managers, school administrators, teachers, business people, and government officials can design as pleasant, attractive environments that improve interpersonal relations and facilitate social interaction.

Global climate change, Hurricane Katrina, and the recent Live Earth concerts are reminders of the importance and fragility of our environment. The global and local environment can benefit from our help. Students need to learn that every bag of garbage we contribute to a landfill, every time we travel by car rather than by bicycle or on foot, and every light we turn on has negative environmental consequences. Fortunately, this message is being spread in schools, where teachers are including environmental education in their curricula and through such wonderful books as *50 Simple Things Kids Can Do To Save the Earth* (Earthworks Group, 1990), which are widely available and replete with excellent ideas. Indeed, *50 Simple Things* suggests diffusion strategies in an entire section entitled "Spreading the Word" and prefigurative strategies in a chapter entitled "Teach Your Parents Well." Al Gore (1992) includes as a primary strategic goal of his global Marshall Plan "the establishment of a cooperative plan for educating the world's citizens about our global environment" (p. 306) and has organized a global initiative to deal with climate change. Communication specialists have an important role to play in designing optimal, objective, nonpropagandistic strategies that will create a generation of citizens capable of making critical choices in their daily lives about the planetary ecosystem.

It is also essential for urban dwellers, who increasingly live indoors and stay connected via cyberspace and mediated communication, to reexperience outdoor environments. A consciousness of the global environment is enhanced by understanding our natural context, through outdoor experiences and rituals. As Gore (1992) describes it, our detachment and alienation take many forms:

> Something was lost along the way, because the amount of attention necessary for this mental work detracted from the attention we paid to the context of communication. . . . The more information we consumed the more our mental lives were dominated by direct experience with information representing the world rather than direct experience of the world itself. . . . It is interesting to note that similarity between the crisis in our relationship to information and our crisis in our relationship to the natural world. (pp. 199–200)

Increasingly, we as human beings have become estranged from our natural environment, forgetting that we are part of it, not masters over it. Andersen (1993b) contends:

> This estrangement has caused a collective amnesia about the natural world. Gone is the smell of conifer or chaparral, the feel of sunshine or rain, the struggle and pleasure of walking in mud or snow. Our world is a world of indirect experience and our knowledge of the planet is sophisticated but incomplete, accurate but remote. (p. 17)

It is because of this estrangement from the natural world that a central feature of the Sierra Club, America's largest environmental group, is the outing—excursions into the natural world, backpacking, hiking, mountaineering, rafting, and camping. The organization's philosophy holds that one cannot really know the natural world without firsthand experience.

We must all be more conscious of environmental destruction and foster communication that protects habitats and species that have no voice or power over decisions to develop, destroy, or protect. We need to do this not only for all other living things but to ensure our own survival and the survival of our children as well.

Likewise, companies, schools, hospitals, architects, and city planners have an obligation to create microenvironments that facilitate interpersonal communication and enhance the human spirit. If, indeed, environments can communicate, what is communicated by a dirty, dilapidated ghetto and a messy, poorly maintained school versus a rehabilitated and renovated neighborhood and a clean, inviting school that facilitates interaction? The many microenvironments throughout the world that lack any sense of aesthetics and inhibit quality communication stand as visual testimonials of the ignorance people often have regarding the importance of the environment in our everyday communication.

CHRONEMICS

Chronemics is the study of the way we structure time and the meanings we attach to time during interpersonal interaction. In the United States, time is viewed as a commodity that can be manipulated. Think for a moment about the phrase "Let's spend some time together." This sort of rhetoric suggests that time is a tangible resource, a bank account that can be "budgeted." In the United States, parents and teachers frequently implore us to "budget" our time. Most Americans also try to "save" time. Actually, time irrevocably moves on, yet we persist in the illusion that time can be saved. What we really mean is that we hurry through unpleasant activities such as commuting and housekeeping so that we can get to the activities we really enjoy such as recreating, socializing, or relaxing. But we must be careful with our "commodified" time because recreating and relaxing may be perceived as "wasting" time. And of course, time marches on, so we must "capture the moment." Psychologically and rhetorically, most Americans treat time like their most prized possession or like money itself: something to be earned, saved, spent, and treasured. As we will learn in chapter 4, other cultures have no such conception of time. Indeed, each culture or subculture has its own sense of time, which is part of the reason each culture "marches to a different drummer" and vibes between cultures are sometimes characterized by friction.

Waiting Time

Not surprisingly, cultures that "commodify" time also value being prompt. Burgoon, Buller, and Woodall (1996) argued that "being on time for a business appointment most often means literally arriving at the appointed time. Arriving more than five minutes late is a violation of this rule and often requires an apology" (p. 129). However, such a rule is not the case in many parts of the world, including Latin America, where individuals may wait an hour or even a day for a business appointment. For some high-status individuals, such as doctors or executives, making people wait reinforces the individual's status. Insel and Lindgren (1978) maintained that "another psychological dimension to the distress of waiting is the effect of subordination. One who is in the position to cause another to wait has power over him. To be kept waiting implies that one's own time is less valuable than that of the one who imposes the wait" (p. 105). Chronically late subordinates are particularly reviled and can actually put their evaluations and positions at risk.

Spending Time

Spending time with another person is a powerful nonverbal cue that communicates warmth, friendliness, understanding, and love. In this day and age, although many parents tell their children they love them, they proceed to spend time on dozens of activities while spending little time with their children. Not surprisingly, many of these children feel unloved despite their parents' words. In a major study of nonverbal warmth and immediacy, Andersen, Andersen, and Jensen (1979) reported that spending time with someone was a major component of immediacy and psychological closeness. Burgoon and Aho (1982) suggested that because of the premium placed on time in our culture, the amount of time an individual spends in conversation indicates her or his interest in the other person. Stelzner and Egland (1995) found that among dozens of nonverbal behaviors, spending time with someone was the leading predictor of both relational satisfaction and relational understanding.

Talk Time

Conversational time, or talk time, has an important effect on how we are perceived. We can all think of a date or an acquaintance who wouldn't let us get a word in edgewise or a group member who totally dominated the conversation. Such people are perceived as rude, bossy, self-centered, and dominant. Similarly, a person who never speaks is perceived as shy, disinterested, and uninvolved. Persons who talk a little more (but not a lot more) than their share are perceived as more competent, confident, interested, influential, and credible (for summaries see Harper, Weins, & Matarazzo, 1978; Hayes & Metzger, 1972; see also chapters 10 and 12). A good rule of thumb is to talk your share or a bit more (for example, 50 percent plus in a dyad, or 20 percent plus in a five-person group).

Body Speed

Humans vary greatly in body speed, a characteristic that communicates much about people. Individuals who move slowly are labeled *hypokinetic*, and those who move rapidly are termed *hyperkinetic* (Barker, Cegala, Kibler, & Wahlers, 1979). A number of factors produce slow or fast body speeds. Metabolic differences are certainly important. Hyperkinetic people are most likely to be found in the North rather than in the South, in developed rather than in undeveloped countries, and in cities rather than in rural areas. Barker et al. (1979) outlined the problem when these different individuals work with one another:

> Hypokinetic group members and hyperkinetic group members potentially are annoying to each other. For example, you may have wondered how a particular person could talk so fast (or so slowly). However both a rapidly moving

> group member and a more slowly moving group member may be frustrated if they must work on a task together. . . . In extreme cases the two individuals cannot work together. Therefore, you should keep individual differences in movements in mind as group members are assigned to different tasks. (p. 192)

Similarly, some people have much longer response latency, the time it takes to respond to another person's statement or question. A longer response latency is not necessarily a sign of stupidity but rather a difference in style. Some people are more thoughtful, while others respond rapidly and spontaneously. Deceptive communicators also have longer response latencies (see chapter 11). Interestingly, even in deception, longer response latencies and hesitations are not always perceived negatively. Burgoon, Buller, and Guerrero (1995) found that hesitancy is actually positively associated with believability when other nonverbal cues (such as expressiveness) are positive. They argue that in some cases hesitancy may be interpreted as signaling thoughtfulness rather than a lack of knowledge.

Research has also shown that fast talkers slow down when interacting with slow talkers and slow talkers speed up when talking with fast talkers. These processes are called *convergence*, or *communication accommodation* (Street & Giles, 1982). Research has shown that speakers who converge to others' rates are more attractive and persuasive (Buller & Aune, 1988a).

Speaking rate has a major effect on first impressions. Generally, faster speakers are perceived as more credible, intelligent, and competent (Buller & Aune, 1988a; Street & Brady, 1982) but less honest and trustworthy than slower speakers (Burgoon, 1978).

Other Types of Time

Time has many meanings and dimensions. E. T. Hall (1984) classifies time into eight categories, each having its own social rules and interpersonal meanings. The first of these categories, *biological time*, deals with the rhythms of living things. Fiddler crabs are tuned in to tidal cycles; deciduous trees, to the rhythms of the seasons. Similarly, we humans have circadian (daily) rhythms of sleeping and wakefulness and monthly rhythms of menstruation and activity. Disruption of our biorhythms, as in the case of jet lag, throws off our cycles and may result in negative physical, psychological, and interpersonal consequences.

Personal time is the way individuals experience time in different contexts and cultures. Personal time is subjective. For example, during the last six miles of a marathon or the final days of a visit from a boring relative, time may seem to drag. By contrast, a vacation in Hawaii or a student's summer break usually seems to fly by. In addition, people have different orientations toward time. Those with future-time orientations are not likely to want to spend as much time looking at old photographs and letters as those with past-time orientations.

Physical time has to do with fixed geophysical cycles such as seasons or days. Ancient peoples erected observatories such as Stonehenge in England and medicine wheels in the American West to track the passage of the seasons, probably for religious, migratory, or agricultural reasons. As discussed earlier, seasonal patterns related to sunlight have been shown to affect human cycles of sociability, activity, alcohol use, and psychological well-being (for a summary see Andersen,

Lustig, & Andersen, 1990). Seasonal affective disorder has been shown to result in depression and even suicide during long winters in high latitudes (Thorson & Kasworm, 1984).

Metaphysical time includes many paranormal phenomena—such as pre-science, astral projection, and the recall of former lives—in which people claim to transcend time and space. Although such abilities are met with skepticism by scientists, they are very real to millions of people who report experiencing paranormal phenomena.

Sync time occurs when interaction partners are in rhythm. In our previous discussion of kinesics, we discussed the phenomenon of interactional synchrony, an important aspect of sync time. The African American expression "She's right on time," the whole notion of being "in sync," and the concept of "smooth" interaction all refer to the fundamental synchronization that is so vital to human interaction.

Microtime is the time frame used by a particular culture. According to E. T. Hall (1984), polychronic people maintain flexible schedules (or no set schedule at all), move in rhythm to nature, and do several things at once. Monochronic people (like northern Europeans and Americans) schedule one thing at a time, live by the clock, and believe they can conserve and spend time.

Sacred time, or mythic time, is imaginary, rooted in legend, and difficult for most Americans to comprehend. When Native Americans participate in tribal ceremonies, they cease to exist in ordinary, mundane time. Being really "into" an activity such as reading an engrossing book, watching a movie, or playing a sport may be as close as most Americans get to sacred time. Meditation and prayer are additional activities that can put people into a sacred time frame.

Profane time, or mundane time, consists of the seconds, minutes, hours, weeks, years, decades, centuries, and millennia to which we are so wedded. These time frames are only partly physical. The week, for example, has little or no geophysical counterpart, but each day seems quite different in industrial societies where people: say "thank goodness it's Friday," get through the Wednesday "hump day," and bemoan "Monday malaise."

Metatime is the intellectual study and discussion of time by philosophers, scholars, historians, and futurists. Metatime consists of abstractions and constructs of time. Einstein's theories, for example, suggest that contrary to our personal experience, time need not run forward. Concepts such as time warps are also part of the scientific study of metatime.

In communication, timing is everything. Chronemic cues manage the most subtle interactions, create lasting interpersonal perceptions, and facilitate or inhibit interaction. Time not only provides a context for other messages, it often *is the message*.

OLFACTICS

Recent research has begun to show the importance of nonverbal communication via olfactics, the study of nonverbal communication through scent and smell. Although smell has traditionally been overlooked by most researchers in psychology and communication, its importance is not lost on the American public, who spend billions of dollars annually on scents such as perfume, cologne, aftershave, breath spray, deodorant, and other fragrances. Advertisements urge us to suppress and replace the odors of our underarms, mouths, hair, genitals, feet, and bodies. Any orifice or surface seems to be fair game for Madison Avenue messages, which have made Americans the most heavily and artificially scented society in the world. According to Doty (1974), smells are meaningful on a single evaluative continuum, good to bad. Americans are rarely neutral about smell; body odors, in particular, carry strong negative connotations. This may be due to the ancient origins of our sense of smell, including its positive effect in mating and its functionality in helping us avoid spoiled, rotten, or contaminated substances, particularly food.

One of the most interesting aspects of olfaction research is the consistent finding that smells are memory triggers, producing instant associations with past events. Meerloo (1971) suggests that many smells are nostalgic connections to previously subconscious memories of places, relationships, and activities. In their comprehensive review of olfaction, Richardson and Zucco (1989) conclude that "odors have the extraordinary ability to remind us of a sometimes far distant past. These memories are often characterized by strong emotive connotation" (p. 352).

It is my experience that vivid memories can be evoked by a variety of smells: my childhood room, the smell of a perfume that was worn by an old girlfriend, lilacs in the spring, and even the smell of an old coffee factory near my boyhood home. I'm amazed by the number of people who have nostalgic memories of even toxic smells. After a camping trip, two friends of mine smelled the toxic smoke of steel mills at the edge of their hometown and were overcome by pleasant, nostalgic memories. Research supports these subjective experiences. Richardson and Zucco's (1989) review suggests that autobiographic memories are more likely to be evoked by smell than by either visual or verbal cues.

In the most extensive smell survey to date, Gilbert and Wysocki (1987) surveyed 1.5 million worldwide *National Geographic* readers and concluded:

> We found that the stronger the odor, the more likely it was to bring to mind a vivid memory. And just as women found all odors stronger, they also reported more memories than men for every odor but gas. Are foul odors as likely to evoke a memory as a pleasant one? They are. As it turned out, extremely pleasant and extremely unpleasant odors were both more likely to evoke memories than odors with a so-so rating. . . . A Coloradoan wrote, "One of my favorite smells is cow manure. Yes! It brings back memories of me on my aunt's farm in Southern Ohio. The vacations I spent there were the happiest of my childhood, and any farm smell evokes wonderful memories." (p. 524)

Smell can certainly stimulate recall, but can it also be a form of nonverbal communication? The answer seems to be yes. In a summary of research on odor, Engen (1987) concluded, "Odor perception is characterized by adaptability and a relatively concrete but open-ended nonverbal coding system" (p. 501). Similarly Elliot and Jensen (1979) conclude, "The evidence presented in this discussion suggests that humans possess a significant potential for the utilization of the olfactory communication channel, however current usage appears to be considerably below this potential" (p. 16). Certainly, the writers of nonverbal communication books who include a chapter on olfaction believe it is nonverbal communication (Guerrero & Hecht, 2008; Knapp & Hall, 2006; Malandro & Barker, 1983; Richmond, McCroskey, & Payne, 1987), and American communicators, who so carefully apply their daily combination of perfumes, aftershaves, and deodorants, are clearly believers in the power of olfactory communication.

In many animals, including all primates, olfaction is a primary means of communicating sexual attraction. Considerable evidence now suggest that olfaction, particularly via pheromones, plays an important role in human communication as well. The word *pheromone* was coined from the Greek *pherein* ("to carry") and *hormon* ("to stimulate or excite"; Malandro & Barker, 1983). Pheromones are external chemical messengers that are the external equivocate of hormones. Increasing evidence suggests that humans each carry a smell signature. Some individuals, such as the legendary Helen Keller, supposedly are able to identify friends and visitors by their unique smell (Weiner, 1966). Dogs have no difficulty distinguishing between the unique smell of individuals except in the case of identical twins, who smell the same to dogs (Davis, 1973; Kloek, 1961). Several research summaries report studies in which infants recognize the smell of their mother's breast but not that of a stranger (Knapp & Hall, 1997; Malandro & Barker, 1983) and adolescents can recognize their own smell, the smell of a relative, and the smell of friends at above-chance levels (Olson, Barnard, & Turri, 2006).

Many female animals prepare to mate when presented with a male sexual hormone or pheromone (external chemical messenger). Female hogs will assume a mating position when smelling male swine pheromone (Angier, 1995). Interestingly, swine pheromones are considered a pleasant smell by women but a foul smell by men (Doty, 1974). Women, but not men, smell and react to androstenone (andro), a male sex hormone (Vollmer & Gordon, 1975). Interestingly, a recent study showed that fertile women were much more sensitive to andro than to a floral environmental odor, though non-fertile women, including women on birth control pills, were more sensitive to the environmental odor than to andro (Lundstrom, McClintock, & Olsson, 2006). Women who are sensitive to smell show greater brain responses to male pheromones like andro than women without much sense of smell (Pause, Rogalski, Sojka, & Ferstl, 1999). Interestingly, the sexual region of the brains of both women and homosexual men, but not heterosexual men, are activated by the male pheromone andro. These same brain regions activate when heterosexual men, but not homosexual men or women, smell estrogen (Savic, Berglund, & Lindstrom, 2005; Savic, Berglund, Gulyas, & Roland, 2001). Likewise, the smell of estrogen activated the same sexual regions of the brain in lesbians as in heterosexual men (Bergland, Lindstrom, & Savic, 2006).

Experiments show that both women and homosexual men, but not heterosexual men, are more likely to select seats sprayed with andro (Pause, 2004). These findings demonstrate the power of sexual pheromones and also provide insight into the biological basis of homosexuality. A double-blind study showed that men who use andro in their aftershave lotion had more sexual activity with the opposite sex than men in a placebo condition, though there was no difference in masturbatory activity, suggesting that andro improved men's social and sexual attraction (Cutler, Friedman, & McCoy, 1998). Similarly, a double-blind study of females found that those who used a perfume containing their own pheromones had more sexual intercourse, slept more with their partner, and had more dates, although there was no increase in masturbation (McCoy & Pitino, 2002). Likewise, female exposure to andro and estrogen, as compared to control substances, has been shown to increase sexual arousal during sexual movie scenes (Bensafi, Brown, Khan, Levenson, & Sobel, 2004), and exposure to andro has been found to increase female attraction to vignettes and photos of males, compared to a control condition (Thorne, Neave, Scholey, Moss, & Fink, 2002). Several studies have shown that women's mood is positively affected by non-detectable amounts of andro (Lundstrom, Goncalves, Esteves, & Olsson, 2003), but one recent study showed that this effect only occurs in the presence of a male experimenter, not a female experimenter (Lundstrom & Olsson, 2006). These findings illustrate that pheromonal communication is more than a mere chemical reaction—it is an interpersonal process mediated by other nonverbal cues.

Research shows that human females are more sensitive to smell, particularly pheromones, during ovulation than during menstruation and less sensitive to smell during pregnancy, suggesting a role for smell in human reproduction (Doty, Snyder, Huggins, & Lowry, 1981; Gilbert & Wysocki, 1987; Regan & Berscheid, 1996; Richardson & Zucco, 1989, Stockhorst & Pietrowsky, 2004). Likewise, in blind smell experiments men are more attracted to the smell of a female during her most fertile period than during any other point in her menstrual cycle (Havlicek, Dvorakova, Bartos, & Flegr, 2006). Henkin's research, reported by Richmond, McCroskey, and Payne (1987), shows that 25 percent of people who have smell disorders lose interest in sex. One substance, exaltolide, which is used as a perfume base, may be a human sexual pheromone (Engen, 1973). Smell probably played a much greater role in sexual attraction in our ancestral past than it does today. Moreover, compared with touch or vision, smell is a distinctly inferior form of sexual communication.

We discussed previously that people are more physically and sexually attracted to symmetrical faces and bodies. During ovulation, their most fertile period, women have greater preferences for the male scents on T-shirts worn by symmetrical men than by nonsymmetrical men, suggesting that smell may be an interpersonal marker for attraction to the most genetically fit mates (Gangestad & Thornhill, 1998; Thornhill & Gangestad, 1999). Women on birth control pills, which regulate their hormone cycle and change their body chemistry, did not demonstrate this pattern. Both males and females were most attracted to opposite-sex scents of people with high facial attractiveness as independently judged from photos (Rikowski & Grammer, 1999; Thornhill & Gangestad, 1999). This finding was most pronounced for women during ovulation. This indicates positive association among bodily symmetry, sexual attraction, pheromones, and reproductive fitness (Thornhill & Gangestad, 2003). In short, in other species as well as humans, more symmetrical people have greater success with the opposite sex, tend to be more physically fit, are more attractive, and are able to detect some of these qualities through smell!

Several studies of women in group-living situations suggest that, over time, women coordinate their menstrual cycles, which are attributed to pheromonal cues (McClintock, 1971; Burton, 1976; Stockhorst & Pietrowsky, 2004). Menstrual synchronization provides strong evidence for the interpersonal effects of pheromones. In fact, every time I discuss this phenomenon in a nonverbal communication class, sorority women are quick to share that this has happened in their sorority houses.

Pheromones may have played a major role in human evolution and mate selection, and sexual attraction may still be a function of these chemical cues. A person's smell is associated with an individual's major histocompatibility complex (MHC), the chemical structure of an individual's immune response. Amazingly, research has shown that animals, including humans, are more attracted to potential mates if they have a different MHC than their own (Penn, 2002, Thornhill, et al., 2003, Grammer, Fink, & Neave, 2005). Indeed, recent research showed that as a couple's MHC compatibility increased, women's sexual responsiveness to their partner decreased (Garver-Apgar et al., 2006). The study also revealed that in couples with similar MHC, women are more likely to be attracted to men other than their primary partner and to have more extrarelational sexual liaisons. Research has shown that a greater variety of MHC is associated with more resistance to disease (Penn, 2002). Attraction to the smell of someone different than yourself may be a biological protection against incest and may produce stronger offspring with a more diverse and resilient immune system (Penn, 2002). When people say there was or was not "chemistry" in a romantic relationship, they may actually be tuning into their attraction or repulsion based on such subconscious pheromonal cues.

Unfortunately, many people suffer from an inability to smell, a syndrome known as smell blindness or *amnosia*. All of us may experience temporary or partial amnosia, such as during a severe cold. Smell sensitivity varies greatly. Some individuals are highly sensitive to certain smells, and others are virtually unaware of them. If another person detects a strong smell but you do not, it may be that you are completely impervious to that smell. In the previously mentioned *National Geographic* study of smell, nearly two-thirds of the worldwide respondents reported a period of virtually complete smell loss, and smokers displayed reduced sensitivity to most smells (Gilbert & Wysocki, 1987). Over 25 percent of participants in this study failed to detect the smell of sweat or of musk. Additional research shows that when people are exposed to a certain smell (particularly if it is negative) for an extended period of time, they adapt by losing their ability to detect that particular smell (Knapp & Hall, 1997).

Interestingly, a number of studies indicate that women are more sensitive to smell than men (Stockhorst & Pietrowsky, 2004). It is unclear if these are biological differences, if women are socialized to be more smell sensitive, or some combination. In a study by Cain (1990), women significantly outperformed men in identifying a variety of smells in test tubes; however, men in this study avoided a total shutout by more accurately identifying bourbon, Brut aftershave, Crayola crayons, horseradish, rubbing alcohol, soap, and Vicks Vaporub. This supports dozens of research studies (see summaries by Elliot & Jensen, 1979; Gilbert & Wysocki, 1987; Richardson & Zucco, 1989; Stockhorst & Pietrowsky, 2004).

SUMMARY

Like the body codes of nonverbal communication, the contextual codes provide the rich, analogic, multichanneled messages of human communication. Although contextual codes perform many functions, such as creating intimacy and persuasive influence, their primary function is to provide context for all of the other nonverbal and verbal messages we communicate.

Macroenvironments, the large environmental contexts that set the stage and provide the background for our many communicative actions, include landforms, climate, sunlight, and geographic regions. Macroenvironments greatly influence how people in that environment will communicate. Through voluntary migration, some people actively seek macroenvironments that facilitate the types of communication and relationships they value.

Microenvironments are smaller, local human contexts that both have impact on other messages and are messages in and of themselves. Certain environments are sociopetal, that is, they facilitate interaction; others are sociofugal, that is, they inhibit communication. Seating arrangements in homes, schools, bars, or churches directly affect the types of communication that will occur. Room temperature and color, lighting, and sound provide the context for certain types of communication; at the same time, such characteristics can virtually preclude other kinds of communication. It is important not to underestimate the significance of environments. We should all be active agents in creating communicative, pleasant, and sustainable macroenvironments and microenvironments.

Chronemics, the study of how we structure and use time, has become even more important in the time-pressed twenty-first century. In America, time is a commodity that we believe can be wasted, saved, spent, and even treasured. An aspect of chronemics is waiting time, which sends messages of interest, politeness, status, and responsibility. Spending time with another person is a powerful relational message and is associated with love and closeness. Talk time is extremely important in nonverbal communication; too much talk or too little talk can be perceived negatively. One's speech rate also affects receivers' comprehension and interpersonal perceptions. Some dimensions of time include biological time, personal time, physical time, metaphysical time, sync time, microtime, sacred time, profane time, and metatime. In communication, timing is everything because it contextualizes most, if not every, communication behavior.

Olfactics is a largely neglected area of nonverbal communication that examines smell. Americans annually spend billions of dollars on products to suppress and replace body odors. Natural body odors are taboo in most situations. Smells also create nostalgia and trigger old, sometimes hidden memories. Moreover, smell plays some role in human sexual attraction, although less so than it does in other mammals. Humans have individual smell signatures that play a role in interpersonal communication, particularly for infants. Pheromones, external chemical messengers, also have interpersonal effects in communication.

Finally, vocalics, or paralinguistics, is the study of nonverbal elements of the voice—such as pitch, rhythm, tempo, resonance, control, and accent—that modify and contextualize every verbal utterance. Vocalics also comprises such nonverbal vocal behaviors as laughing, screaming, and crying. Vocalics can repeat, complement, modify, accent, replace, regulate, and contradict verbal communication. Vocal qualities, such as pitch and volume, are powerful elicitors of personality judgments.

This chapter completes our discussion of the codes of nonverbal communication and introduces the first function of nonverbal communication: providing context for other communication. Throughout the rest of the book, we will examine the other functions performed by nonverbal communication: communicating our culture and gender in a diverse world; communicating affect and emotion; sending and suppressing signals of stress, anxiety, and arousal; expressing messages of immediacy, involvement, and intimacy; influencing others by persuading and gaining compliance; concealing and revealing deception; and establishing power, control, and status relationships.

4

Cultural Cues
Nonverbal Communication
in a Diverse World

In most countries we are neither liked nor respected. It is time that Americans learned how to communicate effectively with foreign nationals. It is time we stopped alienating people with whom we are trying to work.

—Edward Hall, *The Silent Language*

The emigrants that came at different periods to occupy the territory now covered by the American Union differed from each other in many respects.

—Alexis de Tocqueville, *Democracy in America*

It is no surprise that the second most commonly asked question after "What's your name?" is "Where are you from?"

—Joel Garreau, *The Nine Nations of North America*

America has always been one of the most culturally diverse nations on earth, yet Americans still have difficulty with people from other cultures. Although some Americans grow up in ethnically homogeneous communities, most of us live and work in communities that are ethnically and culturally diverse. Look around your classroom or your workplace. Chances are there are people who grew up in many regions of the United States, as well as people from different ethnic and racial backgrounds than your own. If you don't like living in a culturally diverse place, you are living in the wrong country. America has always been diverse and is becoming more diverse, not less. Intolerance and prejudice against various ethnic groups has been a problem throughout much of U.S. history, yet diversity has served as one of our nation's greatest strengths. Americans have benefited from the rich mix of traditions, modes of thinking, religions, foods, music, and technology of people from many backgrounds. We are both emulated and hated by many people in the world. We are a magnet for people seeking opportunity, yet most of world's people think of America today as a bully and a threat. It is because of this perception that improving intercultural communication is so vital.

Americans are the most mobile people on earth. According to Dinnerstein and Reimers (1975), "Never before—and in no other country—have as many varied ethnic groups congregated and amalgamated as they have in the United States" (p. 1). Moreover, once immigrants settle in America, they and their families frequently move to new states and regions. More than 20 percent of Americans move annually (Fielding, 1974), and this has been true for centuries (Lewis, 1972; Zelinsky, 1973). One of the biggest communication challenges you will face is effectively interacting with people from different cultural backgrounds than your own. Indeed, without ever leaving the United States, you are likely to communicate with people from dozens of different ethnic and cultural traditions. Lustig and Koester (2003) concluded:

> The twenty-first century is upon us, and competence in intercultural communication has become an absolute necessity. In both your private and public lives, in all of your personal and professional endeavors, it is imperative that you learn to communicate with people whose cultural heritages make them vastly different from you. (p. ix)

Not only are people immigrating, they also are traveling today in record numbers, and international trade is at an all-time high (Brown, Kane, & Roodman, 1994). Never before have so many people from so many cultures had so much contact with one another. Language differences constitute a major barrier to effective intercultural communication, yet they are just the tip of the iceberg. Nonverbal behaviors are both biological (for discussions on the biological basis of nonverbal communication see chapters 1, 5, and 7) and cultural in origin. Because cultural differences exist in each channel of nonverbal behavior and because nonverbal behaviors are multichanneled, the chance for intercultural misunderstandings in nonverbal communication is substantial.

Culture is mainly an implicit, spontaneous, nonverbal phenomenon. Most aspects of one's culture are learned through observation and imitation rather than through explicit verbal instruction or expression. The primary level of culture is communicated implicitly, without awareness, by primarily nonverbal means (Andersen, Hecht, Hoobler, & Smallwood, 2002; Andersen & Wang, 2006; E. T. Hall, 1984; Sapir, 1928). For example, cultural customs such as how to wait in line, what foods to eat, how to treat one's elders, and how to greet other people are communicated nonverbally from adults to children, often with no verbal instruction. In fact, *one of the most basic and obvious functions of nonverbal communication is to communicate one's culture.* People cling tenaciously to cultural, religious, and ethnic customs and are unwilling to give up important aspects of their culture, including language, dress, gestures, tactile behaviors, and the many other aspects of nonverbal behavior that you will read about in this chapter. Indeed, culture is such a powerful force that throughout history people have gone to war to preserve cultural customs and behaviors.

Until people communicate interculturally, they are unaware of most of their own nonverbal behaviors, because these behaviors are enacted mindlessly, spontaneously, and unconsciously (Andersen, 1986; Burgoon, 1985a; Samovar & Porter, 2001; see also chapter 1). Indeed, Edward Sapir stated many years ago, "We respond to gestures with an extreme alertness and, one might almost say, in accordance with an elaborate and secret code that is written nowhere, known to none and understood by all" (1928, p. 556). In fact, "culture is so basic, learned at such a tender age, and so taken-for-granted, that it is often confused with human nature itself" (Andersen, 1997, p. 224). Because we are not usually aware of our own nonverbal behavior, which we take for granted, we have great difficulty understanding or learning the nonverbal behavior of another culture. Frequently, people feel uncomfortable in other cultures because they intuitively think "something isn't right." "Because nonverbal behaviors are rarely conscious phenomena, it may be difficult for us to know exactly why they [people from other cultures] are feeling uncomfortable" (Gudykunst & Kim, 1992, p. 172).

In this chapter, we will focus on six conceptual differences among cultures that provide a theoretical explanation for *why* cultures differ in their nonverbal communication. Indeed, a multitude of nonverbal differences exist between cultures, and detailing these myriad differences would be impossible and somewhat trivial. To begin, we will briefly explore intercultural interactions in terms of the nonverbal codes that were discussed in chapters 2 and 3. Following that, we will examine in detail the six cultural dimensions that help explain differences in nonverbal communication across cultures.

CULTURAL DIFFERENCES IN NONVERBAL COMMUNICATION CODES

Chronemics

According to Edward Hall, the founder of the intercultural communication field, "time talks. It speaks more plainly than words" (1959, p. 15). In the following extract, Hall (1959) described an American diplomat in a Latin country arriving for an appointment to see a cabinet minister of the government:

> Arriving a little before the hour (an American respect pattern), he waited. The hour came and passed—five minutes—ten minutes—fifteen minutes. At this point he suggested to the secretary that perhaps the minister did not know he was waiting in the outer office . . . thirty minutes—forty-five minutes (the insult period)! He jumped up and told the secretary that he had been "cooling his heels" in an outer office for forty-five minutes and he was "damned sick and tired" of this type of treatment. The message was relayed to the minister who said, in effect, "Let him cool his heels." The attaché's stay in the country was not a happy one. The principal source of misunderstanding lay in the fact that in the country in question the five-minute delay interval was not significant. Forty-five minutes, on the other hand, instead of being at the tail end of the waiting scale, was just at the beginning. (p. 18)

Cultures march to different drummers. Chronemics is probably the most-discussed and best-researched nonverbal code in the intercultural literature (Albert & Ah-Ha, 2004; Bruneau, 1979; Burgoon, Buller, & Woodall, 1996; Gudykunst & Kim, 1992; Hall, 1959, 1976, 1984). Although each culture is unique in its use of time, Hall (1984) maintains that the big cultural gulf is between monochronic (or M-time) cultures and polychronic (or P-time) cultures. M-time cultures, including countries in northern Europe or with northern European roots (for example, England, Germany, Finland, Norway, Sweden, Canada, and the United States), believe in doing one thing at a time. In contrast, P-time cultures have little regard for artificial schedules and stress informality, people-centeredness, multiple simultaneous activities, and the importance of context.

Many years ago on a trip to some remote island in the Bahamas (a P-time culture), I (being from an M-time culture) was surprised to discover that life in the islands totally stops when it rains. Until the rain stopped, the ground crew at the airport would not unload our airplane, nor would gas station attendants pump gas. We American college students who were visiting the island on our short one-week spring break were upset by this behavior. But our anger was useless, for we were up against a cultural (P-time) custom of the Caribbean people. As this story illustrates, the time frames of cultures vary so substantially that even if only chronemic differences existed, intercultural misunderstandings would still be considerable. As described in chapter 3, people in the United States view time as a commodity that can be wasted, spent, saved, and used wisely. Of course, many cultures have no concept of time as being segmented into arbitrary units (seconds, minutes, hours, weeks, months, and so on). In many third-world cultures, life moves to the rhythms of nature: the day, the weather, the tides, and such. Things are experienced polychronically and simultaneously. By contrast, in Western cultures time is modularized, and events are scheduled sequentially, not simultaneously. It is thus very important to remember when interacting with people from different cultures that the march of their lives may be to the beat of a totally different drummer. As an American visiting a third-world culture, it would be safe to assume that all your assumptions about time are false.

Proxemics

Research on proxemics has shown that cultures differ substantially in their use of interpersonal space, in their regard for territory, and in the meanings they assign to proxemic behavior (Burgoon, Buller, & Woodall, 1996; Gudykunst & Kim, 1992; Hall, 1959, 1976; Malandro & Barker, 1983; Scheflen, 1974; see chapter 2 for more on proxemic behavior). For example, according to Lustig and Koester (2003), people from colder climates typically maintain larger interpersonal distances when they communicate, whereas those from warmer climates prefer closer interpersonal distances. Recent research on sitting distances during interviews has shown that Anglo-Saxon people from the United Kingdom, the United States, and English Canada maintain the largest distances of any cultural group. Asians maintain somewhat closer distances, but people with southern European origins, including French Canadians and Brazilians, maintain the closest distances (Beaulieu, 2004).

One Saturday night in Mexico City many years ago, I rode in a subway train with several other Americans. As thousands of people boarded the train and the crush became intense, the Americans showed signs of pain and claustrophobia, yet the Mexicans remained blasé, though somewhat amused by our discomfort. It is common for Americans to perceive Mexicans as rude and Arabs as pushy because they maintain close personal-space boundaries and expect and employ closer interpersonal distances than do Americans. Conversely, Arabs and Mexicans may perceive Americans as aloof and unfriendly because of cultural differences in proxemic behavior.

Kinesics

Substantial cultural differences have been observed in all aspects of people's kinesic behavior, including facial expressions, body movements, gestures, and conversational regulators (Burgoon, Buller, & Woodall, 1989; Gudykunst & Kim, 1992; Hall, 1976; Jensen, 1985; Samovar, Porter, & Jain, 1981; Scheflen, 1974). The greatest intercultural differences in gestures are found in emblems, word-like gestures with dictionary meanings. For example, the A-OK sign, which is formed by making a circle with the thumb and index finger, is familiar to all Americans. When Richard Nixon visited Venezuela as the U.S. vice president in 1956 and gave two A-OK signs to a crowd of demonstrators in Caracas, a huge riot erupted. Nixon was later informed that the A-OK sign actually had a different meaning in Venezuela, similar to that of an upraised middle finger in America. In Italy, China, and Colombia goodbye is signaled by moving the palm and fingers back and forth toward one's body, a gesture that means "come here" in the United States (Jandt, 1995). Such culturally-based emblematic gestures are best recognized by people from the same culture, although outsiders who have spent more time in a culture and people with greater intercultural communication competence are more likely to understand emblematic gestures as well (Molinsky, Krabbenhoft, Ambady, & Choi, 2005).

Northern Europeans and northeast Asians engage in much more restrained nonverbal displays than, for example, Africans, southern Europeans, or Mexicans. Gestures and movements differ dramatically in meaning, extensiveness, and intensity. Americans and northern Europeans seem "square" and unexpressive to most Italians, Greeks, or Egyptians. Conversely, the gestural behavior of people from the Mediterranean seems almost undignified and overly emotional to most Americans.

The most significant kinesic behavior, facial expressions of emotion, shows considerable cross-cultural similarity in meaning (Ekman, 1972; Elfenbein & Ambady, 2003a, 2003b; Marsh, Elfenbein, & Ambady, 2003; Matsu-

Emblems are gestures with a dictionary definition within a given culture.

moto, 2006; also see chapter 8). Some evidence suggests that facial expressions of emotion are most accurately recognized by members of one's own cultural group (Dovidio, Hebl, Richeson, & Shelton, 2006; Elfenbein & Ambady, 2002, 2003a, 2003b; Mandal & Ambady, 2004) but other research suggests that there is no support for this in-group hypothesis (Beaupre & Hess, 2005; Matsumoto, 2002, 2006). Research does suggest that there are nonverbal "accents," much like linguistic accents, that give a subtle cultural flavor to facial expressions; but even with these "accents" facial expressions are highly recognizable across culture (Elfenbein & Ambady, 2002; Marsh et al., 2003). Training people to recognize facial expressions provides the most effective results in understanding cultures other than one's own (Elfenbein et al., 2006) suggesting there are cultural "accents." Finally, it has recently been suggested that the neurology of the face might help disentangle this controversy (Mandal & Ambady, 2004). The right side of the face displays more universal expressions for the benefit of the receivers' left visual field and right hemisphere where reading of facial expressions is most likely to occur, and these expressions are under more conscious control of the left hemisphere. The left side of the face, which is run led by the more spontaneous right hemisphere, is more uninhibited and intense emotionally but may "learn" more spontaneous expression from its culture through imitation.

Cultures do differ in degree of facial expressivity. Asians, for example, are much less facially expressive than Americans or people from Southern Europe. Childhood socialization is the most important force in promoting or discouraging facial expressivity. A study by Camras et al. (1998) of 11-month-old babies found that Chinese babies were significantly less emotionally expressive than either Japanese or European-American babies. While genetic differences cannot be ruled out, the fact that Japanese babies were more like European-American babies than like Chinese babies suggests that early socialization and enculturation explain these differences. Recent research on three-year-olds found that native Chinese children are less likely to express emotions facially than Chinese children adopted in American families, who in turn were less expressive than native American children (Camras, Chen, Bakeman, Norris, & Cain, 2006).

Haptics

Research has discovered that interpersonal patterns of tactile communication, or haptics, show considerable intercultural variation (Andersen & Leibowitz, 1978; Field, 1999; Malandro & Barker, 1983; Miller, Commons, & Gutheil, 2006; Prosser, 1978; Samovar, Porter, & Jain, 1981). Studies reveal differences in international and intercultural touch in amount, location, type of touch, and whether it is manifested in public or in private (Albert & Ah-Ha, 2004; Jones, 1994; McDaniel & Andersen, 1998). The consensus of these studies suggests that Asia is the most touch avoidant region of the world, and countries in the Mediterranean region are the most touch oriented.

Touch behavior represents a major source of diversity among couples from different cultures. During a recent data-collection session at an international airport, a colleague and I observed incredibly diverse tactile behaviors between people of many cultural backgrounds (see McDaniel & Andersen, 1998). A family leaving for Tonga formed a circle, wove their arms around each others' backs, and prayed and chanted together. A tearful man returning to Bosnia repeatedly tried to leave his sobbing wife; each time he turned back to her, they would grip each other by the fingertips and exchange a passionate, tearful kiss and a powerful embrace. Two Korean couples departed without any touch, despite the prolonged separation that lay ahead of them.

Physical Appearance

Physical appearance, the most salient nonverbal code during initial encounters, is crucial because many intercultural encounters are based on stereotypes and superficial physical cues. People use features of physical appearance such as skin color, hairstyle, clothing, and facial hair to recognize people from their in-group and others from an out-group. These impressions occur quickly and form the basis of cultural stereotypes and even prejudices.

Within a culture, clothes have subtle but important meanings. For many Jews a yarmulke is an important expression of their religiosity. Some young Mormon women grow their hair long as a sign of faith. In northern India the level of a woman's veil signifies sexual interest or disinterest (Lambert & Wood, 2005).

Certainly, what is "beautiful" varies greatly from culture to culture, particularly in terms of clothing, artifacts, body ornamentation, body type, and body shape (see Burgoon, Buller, & Woodall, 1996; Hatfield & Sprecher, 1986; Samovar, Porter, & Jain, 1981). There is considerable cross-cultural similarity in what constitutes an attractive face (Cunningham, Roberts, Barbee, & Druen, 1995) and the hourglass figure for a woman is preferred by men worldwide (see chapter 5). But cultural difference can be substantial. Ubangi women insert pieces of wood into their mouths to create lips up to ten inches in diameter. In China during much of the twentieth century, women often had their feet bound and deformed, which

Clothing communicates culture. What does the attire of these men communicate?

prevented walking outside the home. This culturally imposed deformity was considered a very desirable trait in China, although most Americans would consider such a tradition grotesque and even evil.

The amount of body and facial hair that is desirable also varies greatly from culture to culture. American advertisers have been quite successful in convincing women that hair on their legs or underarms is unsightly, and they have been somewhat successful in convincing men, particularly in the business world, that facial hair is unprofessional. Indeed, body hair is out of vogue for both men and women in American culture and much of the developed world (see chapter 5). By contrast, African or middle Eastern women are much less likely than American women to remove the hair from their legs and underarms, and businessmen in central Asian and Arab cultures are much more likely to have mustaches or beards than are American businessmen. And although T-shirts, blue jeans, business suits, and basketball shoes are now internationally popular attire, many cultures still observe local dress customs. Recently, during the previously mentioned field study at an international airport, I witnessed Tongans in multicultural ceremonial gowns, Sikhs in white turbans, Hasidic Jews in blue yarmulkes, and Africans in white dashikis—alongside Californians in bikini tops.

One vital part of interpersonal communication is facial recognition. Most of us are better at recognizing a face than at remembering a name. When it comes to intercultural communication, a number of studies have shown that people are better at recognizing faces of people in their own ethnic or racial group than the faces of people of other races (Meissner & Brigham, 2001; Sporer, 2001a, 2001b). Regardless of your own ethnicity you have probably heard people say when referring to members of another ethnic group, "all those people look alike to me." These studies also reveal a tendency for people to think they recognize someone of another ethnic or racial group when they have never seen them before (Sporer, 2001a). This can result in a major problem in courts of law where people often claim they recognize a defendant, when in fact they have never seen the person before. The cross-race effect, or own-race bias, is caused by several forces. First is the contact hypothesis: Studies tend to show that increased intercultural and interracial contact diminishes the cross-race effect (Sporer, 2001a). In one interesting study white basketball fans were much better able than white nonfans at distinguishing among black NBA basketball players, suggesting that the quantity and quality of contact is a primary reason for the cross-race effect (Dunning, Li, & Milpass, 1998, as cited in Sporer, 2001a), and suggesting that contact can break down stereotypes. This body of research also suggests that prejudice may be at work here. Openness to intercultural contact and the lack of prejudice against other groups seem to diminish the cross-race effect (Sporer, 2001a). Prejudiced people not only have less contact with other groups, they also tend to disregard people of other races and fail to focus carefully on their faces.

Oculesics

Oculesics, the study of messages sent by the eyes through eye contact, blinks, eye movements, and pupil dilation, has received only marginal attention by intercultural communication scholars (Gudykunst & Kim, 1992; Jensen, 1985; Samovar,

Porter, & Jain, 1981). Because eye contact has been called an "invitation to communicate," its cross-cultural variation is an important communication topic, yet most books on intercultural communication fail to cite any eye-contact research.

Many years ago I served as an instructor for a university-wide orientation for teaching assistants. Among the participants were two young women from France who were in America for the first time. These very attractive young women expressed their disappointment to the class that during their brief stay they had received no attention at all from American men. "They don't even look at us," one complained. "Are American men gay?" queried the other. These women were used to the eye behavior of men in France, where staring at a woman's body is quite acceptable and, in certain contexts, even flattering. Such staring would be considered rude in America, where men take fleeting glances at a woman's body and try not to get caught looking.

Vocalics

Vocalics, or paralinguistics—the tones, pitches, and other nonverbal elements of the voice—has received relatively little attention in intercultural communication research (Gudykunst & Kim, 1992; LaBarre, 1985; Rich, 1974; Scheflen, 1972; Samovar, Porter, & Jain, 1981). The sounds of the human voice vary greatly from culture to culture. For example, to speakers of other languages, German speakers sound domineering and angry. Americans often erroneously perceive Saudi Arabians to be excited or angry due to their intonation patterns (Lustig & Koester, 2003). Despite the linguistic similarity between the Scandinavian languages Swedish and Danish, the differences in pronunciation cause Swedes to joke that "Danes don't speak, they just make animal sounds!" Italians and Mexicans complain that the tones of English are unromantic and difficult to use to communicate intimacy.

Silence, the absence of any vocalization, is interpreted very differently across culture. In Asia silence is an indication of respect, and less talk is associated with wisdom (Lebra, 1987). Likewise, Latin children use silence as a sign of respect (Albert & Ah-Ha, 2004). By contrast, Americans view silence as uncomfortable and fill the void with small talk if there is nothing more important to say.

Music and singing, universal forms of nonverbal communication, have been almost completely overlooked in intercultural research, except for one excellent study (Lomax, 1968) that identified several groups of worldwide cultures through differences and similarities in their folk sounds. Lomax's research is so thorough that migration and diffusion patterns among cultures can be studied by examining his data.

Accents are one aspect of vocalics that has been widely researched (for a summary see Giles & Street, 1994). Research shows that although regional, ethnic, and blue-collar accents are preferred by members of one's own group, such accents are thought of as signs of low intelligence, low education, low status, and low success by the dominant or "mainstream" culture. This research on vocalic stereotyping has been conducted in a number of countries, with similar patterns emerging regardless of the country.

Olfactics

Olfactic differences among cultures have not been widely studied. Reports of chemical and olfactic communication are given only cursory treatment in contemporary intercultural textbooks because of the limited research on this topic (see Gudykunst & Kim, 1992; Jandt, 1995; Lustig & Koester, 2003). One thing we do know is that North Americans are arguably the most aromaphobic people on earth. To them, no body odor is a good body odor. In America and much of Europe and Asia, "To err is human, to smell is a crime" (Andersen, 2004, p. 103). Not so in other places. In the Middle East communication is so much more intense than in Europe and in the United States and Canada. According to Hall (1966b), in Arab cultures, "Not only is the sheer noise level much higher, but the piercing look of the eyes, the touch of the hands, and the mutual bathing in the warm, moist breath represent stepped-up sensory inputs to a level Europeans find unbearably intense" (p. 158). The feel and smell of another's breath, considered obnoxious and offensive by Americans and Canadians, is an intimacy cue in the Middle East, much like eye contact and nodding in the United States.

LOCATING AND DEFINING CULTURE

The word *culture* is frequently used in a variety of ways. To avoid confusion, culture is defined in this book as "the enduring influence of the social world on one's behavior, including interpersonal communication behavior" (Andersen, 1997, p. 246). Culture, along with the social situation and the individual's personal traits and internal state, is one of the four primary antecedents of interpersonal behavior (Andersen, 1987, 1997; Figure 4.1). Culture has been defined as "a shared system of socially transmitted behavior that describes, defines, and guides people's ways of life, communicated from one generation to the next" (Matsumoto, 2006, p. 220). Culture exerts a considerable force on individual behavior through what Geertz (1973) calls "control mechanisms—plans, recipes, rules, instructions (what computer engineers call 'programs')—for the governing of behavior" (p. 44). Culture has persuasive effects on members who live in its sphere, although not all people are affected uniformly. Culture is usually an intergenerational phenomenon, because the family and the community inculcate in children the views, rules, norms, and folkways of their culture. "Culture can be behav-

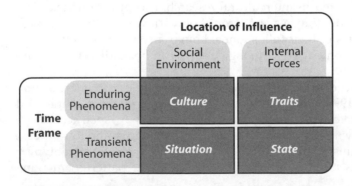

Figure 4.1   Sources of Influence on Interpersonal Behavior

iorally observed by contrasting intragroup homogeneity with intergroup heterogeneity" (Andersen, Lustig, & Andersen, 1986, p. 11).

Culture is often confused with personal traits because both are enduring influences on a person's nonverbal behavior (Andersen, 1987, 1997). Personal traits, however, derive from multiple sources (Andersen, 1987), including genetics, environmental influences, and individual consciousness, as well as culture. Culture is also sometimes confused with the situation because both are part of one's social environment. Culture, however, is an enduring phenomenon, whereas each situation is a transient experience with an observable beginning and end. Culture, along with genetics, is the most enduring, powerful, and invisible shaper of our communication behavior.

DIMENSIONS OF CULTURE

Each culture manifests thousands of nonverbal behavioral differences—some small and subtle, some large and obvious—that distinguish it from every other culture. Because there are hundreds of different cultures on earth, the list of these differences is almost endless. Fortunately, there is a way to organize these differences into meaningful dimensions or groups. Researchers have identified a set of six dimensions that may explain why cultures differ in their nonverbal behavior (Andersen et al., 2002; Andersen & Wang, 2006; Hofstede, 1982). Arguably, most cultural variations in nonverbal behavior, including those discussed in the first part of this chapter, are the result of these fundamental dimensions.

Immediacy Orientation

Immediacy behaviors are defined as actions that simultaneously communicate warmth, closeness, and availability for communication and signal approach rather than avoidance and closeness rather than distance (see chapter 8 for more on nonverbal immediacy). Cultures that display considerable interpersonal closeness or immediacy have been labeled contact cultures; people in these cultures stand closer to each other, touch more (Hall, 1966b), and are generally more expressive than are people in noncontact cultures, who tend to stand farther apart, touch less, and manifest less nonverbal expressiveness. Patterson (1983) maintained:

> These habitual patterns of relating to the world permeate all aspects of everyday life, but their effects on social behavior define the manner in which people relate to one another. In the case of contact cultures, this general tendency is manifested in closer approaches so that tactile and olfactory information may be gained easily. (p. 145)

Cultures also differ in the degree of sensory stimulation they prefer. Contact cultures create immediacy by increasing sensory input, whereas noncontact cultures prefer less sensory involvement.

Although much has been written about contact and noncontact cultures, only a handful of studies have examined the immediacy dimension of culture. As shown in Figure 4.2, research indicates that contact cultures include Indonesia,

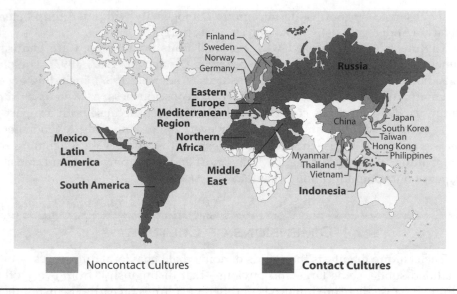

Figure 4.2   **Immediacy Orientations of Selected Countries and Regions**

most Arab countries (including those in northern Africa), as well as countries in the Mediterranean region (including France, Greece, Italy, Portugal, and Spain), the Middle East, eastern Europe (including Russia), and virtually all of Latin America (including Mexico; Andersen et al., 2002; Andersen & Wang, 2006; Condon and Yousef, 1983; Jones, 1994; Jones & Remland, 1982; Mehrabian, 1971a; Patterson, 1983; Samovar, Porter, & Jain, 1981; Scheflen, 1972). Australians are moderate in their cultural-contact level. Noncontact cultures include most of northern Europe (including Norway, Sweden, Finland, Germany, and Great Britain), Anglo-Americans (the predominant culture of the United States), as well as virtually every Asian country (including Myanmar—formerly Burma—China, Hong Kong, Japan, South Korea, the Philippines, Taiwan, Thailand, and Vietnam (Andersen, Andersen, & Lustig, 1987; Heslin & Alper, 1983; Jones, 1994; Jones & Remland, 1982; McDaniel & Andersen, 1995; Mehrabian, 1971a; Patterson, 1983; Samovar, Porter, & Jain, 1981; Scheflen, 1972).

Two studies (McDaniel & Andersen, 1998; Remland, Jones, & Brickman, 1991) suggest that residents of the United States, Canada, and Great Britain may actually fall under the contact category. According to this research, these cultures engage in considerable touch and maintain relatively close interpersonal distances. These studies question Hall's (1966b) research and suggest that his original designation of some cultures—such as Europe and North America (excluding Mexico)—as noncontact cultures was an oversimplification. One explanation for these conflicting findings is that younger people—that is, those born after World War II—in England and the United States exhibit much higher contact and more nonverbally expressive behaviors than their parents and grandparents do. Members of the baby-boomer generation and generations that followed have grown up in a culture permeated by international and intercultural media, intercultural contact, mediated sports celebrations replete with physical contact, rock and roll, and a counterculture ideologically predisposed to contact. Try giving a hug or a high five to a person over 65 (with the exception of family members) and see if I'm right. A person in her or his 20s—that is, a member of a contact culture—is much more likely to respond to your high five. It may not be that Hall's findings about Europe and North America were wrong; instead, they may have simply failed to detect the dramatic culture change that was simultaneously occurring in our globally mediated world.

Contact cultures tend to be located in the Middle East, the Mediterranean region, and in lower latitudes near the equator. Research has identified several factors—including energy level, climate, sunlight, and metabolism—that may explain such latitudinal variations (Andersen, Lustig, & Andersen, 1990). Cultures in cooler climates tend to be more task-oriented and interpersonally "cool," whereas cultures in warmer climates tend to be more interpersonally oriented and interpersonally "warm." Even within the United States, more-immediate cultures tend to be located in the warmer latitudes. Andersen, Lustig, and Andersen (1990) report a .31 correlation between latitude and touch avoidance among American university students. These data suggest that students attending universities located in the Sun Belt are more touch-oriented and thus constitute contact cultures or subcultures. Furthermore, research suggests that African Americans tend to be warmer, more expressive, and more immediate than European Americans (Lustig & Koester, 2003).

Pennebaker, Rime, and Sproul (1994) found a correlation between latitude and expressiveness *within* dozens of countries. Their studies show that northerners are less expressive in Belgium, Croatia, France, Germany, Italy, Japan, Serbia, Spain, Switzerland, and the United States than are southerners in these countries; in fact, a difference in expressiveness has been found to exist across the entire northern hemisphere. Pennebaker et al. (1994) conclude:

> Logically, climate must profoundly affect social processes. People living in cold climates devote more time to dressing, to providing warmth, to planning ahead for food provisions during the winter months. . . . In warm climates, people are more likely to see, hear, and interact with neighbors year round. Emotional expressiveness, then, would be more of a requirement. (pp. 15–16)

Similarly, Andersen, Lustig, and Andersen (1990) conclude:

> In Northern latitudes societies must be more structured, more ordered, more constrained, and more organized if the individuals are to survive harsh weather forces. . . . In contrast, southern latitudes may attract or produce a culture characterized by social extravagance and flamboyance that has no strong inclination to constrain or order their world. (p. 307)

McDaniel and Andersen's (1998) data on public touch suggest the biggest cultural difference in immediacy is between Asians, who rarely touch in public, and people from virtually every other culture, all of whom manifest higher degrees of public touching. These findings are consistent with other research that suggests that China and Japan are distinctly nontouch cultures (Barnland, 1978; Jones, 1994). Research by Klopf and Thompson (1991) reveals that Japanese students reported themselves to be significantly less immediate than either Finnish or American students. This provides additional evidence that Asia is a low-immediacy, noncontact region and that northern Europe and North America—excluding Mexico—may be higher-immediacy regions than previously believed, though not as highly immediate as cultures located in Latin America, the Mediterranean, or the Middle East.

Why is Asia such a low-immediacy culture? McDaniel and Andersen (1995) speculate that Confucianism, with its emphasis on self-control, respect, decorum, and proper behavior, may restrain the expressiveness of cultures under its influence. Perhaps the Asian emphasis on collectivism (discussed in the following section) is a primary force that emphasizes respect of others at the expense of individual expressiveness.

To summarize the cultural differences in immediacy: in general, northern countries, northern parts of individual countries, traditional cultures, and Asian countries are the least immediate and expressive; southern regions, modern countries, and non-Asian cultures are the most expressive and immediate. Obviously, these findings are painted with a fairly broad brush and must await a more detailed cultural portrait.

Individualism versus Collectivism

Perhaps the most fundamental dimensions along which cultures differ is their degree to which the core values of a culture center on individualism versus collectivism. This dimension explains the ways in which people live (for example, alone, in families, in villages or tribes) their values, how they think, and how they communicate, including how they communicate nonverbally (Hofstede, 1982; Nisbett, Peng, Choi, & Nerenzayan, 2001). Individualistic cultures value space, privacy, emotional expression, and personal choice of nonverbal behavior. Collectivist cultures value contact, togetherness, and restrained individual expression of emotion, particularly the expression of negative emotion. Collectivists engage in nonverbal behaviors that benefit the group.

In his landmark study of forty noncommunist countries, Hofstede (1982) reported that the nine most individualistic nations are (in order) the United States, Australia, Great Britain, Canada, the Netherlands, New Zealand, Italy, Belgium, and Denmark—all of which are Western, developed cultures with predominantly European roots (Figure 4.3). The nine most collectivist nations are (in order) Venezuela, Colombia, Pakistan, Peru, Taiwan, Thailand, Singapore, Chile, and Hong Kong—all Asian or South American cultures. Similarly, Sitaram and Codgell (1976) reported individuality to be of primary importance in Western cultures, of secondary importance in African cultures, and of lesser importance in Eastern and Muslim cultures. Nisbett et al. (2001) stated: "China and other East Asian societies remain collectivist and oriented toward the group, whereas American and other European-influenced societies are more individualistic in orientation" (p. 395).

Individualism is one of the fundamental dimensions that distinguish cultures, particularly Eastern cultures from Western cultures. "There is little doubt that

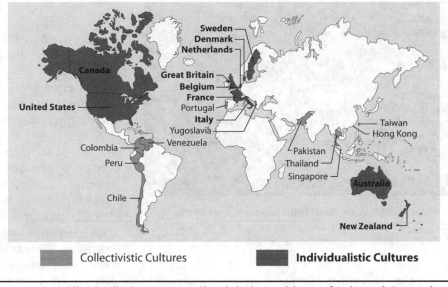

Figure 4.3   Individualistic versus Collectivistic Rankings of Selected Countries
(Hofstede, 1982)

Western culture is individualistic, so people rely on personal judgments. Eastern cultures emphasize harmony among people, between people and nature, and value collective judgments" (Hecht, Andersen, & Ribeau, 1989, p. 170). Tomkins (1984) argued that an individual's psychological makeup is the result of this cultural dimension. He states, "Human beings, in Western Civilization, have tended toward self-celebration, positive or negative. In Oriental thought another alternative is represented, that of harmony between man and nature" (p. 182). According to Lustig and Koester (2003), individualism is characterized by the key words *"independence, privacy, self* and the all-important *I"* (p. 123). By contrast, collectivist cultures emphasize *we* and a sense of connection and belonging. According to Jandt (1995), the Japanese concept of *amea* best typifies collectivist cultures. *Amea* is characterized by nurturing concern, dependence on others, and a wish to be loved and cared for unconditionally.

For better or worse, Americans are individualists. According to the U.S. census of 1990, the most common American household consisted of one person and the second most common household comprised two people. Americans see individualism as a blessing and have elevated it to the status of a national religion (Andersen, 1988). From the early days of the American republic, individualism has been celebrated. In his writings about America in the 1830s, the French philosopher Alexis de Tocqueville (1835/1945) noted:

> Individualism is a mature and calm feeling, which disposes each member of the community to sever himself from the mass of his fellows and to draw apart with his family and friends, so that he has thus formed a little circle of his own, . . . he willingly leaves society at large to itself (p. 104).

The United States is the most individualistic culture on earth. Despite traffic jams and air pollution, individualistic Americans typically commute one person to a car.

The best and the worst of American culture are attributable to individualism. Proponents of individualism have argued that it is the basis of liberty, democracy, freedom, and economic incentive and that it serves as a protection against tyranny. Conversely, individualism has been blamed for our alienation from one another, loneliness, selfishness, crime, and narcissism.

Indeed, Hall (1976) has claimed that as an extreme individualist, "Western man has created chaos by denying that part of his self that integrates while enshrining the parts that fragment experience" (p. 9).

Although the United States is the most individualistic country on earth (Andersen, 1988; Hofstede, 1982; Prosser, 1978), regions of the United States vary in their degree of individualism. Elazar (1972) has shown that the central Midwest and mid-Atlantic regions are the most individualistic political culture, whereas the Southeast is the most traditionalistic and least individualistic. Remember, however, that these findings are all relative; by world standards, even Mississippi is an individualistic culture. Bellah, Madsen, Sullivan, Swidler, and Tipton (1985) stated:

> Individualism lies at the very core of American culture. . . . Anything that would violate our right to think for ourselves, judge for ourselves, make our own decisions, live our lives as we see fit, is not only morally wrong, it is sacrilegious. (p. 142)

Just as geographical regions of the United States differ in their degree of individualism, so too do various ethnic groups. African Americans, for example, emphasize individualism, whereas Mexican Americans emphasize group and relational solidarity (Hecht, Andersen, & Ribeau, 1989). Indeed, extreme individualism makes it difficult for most Americans to interact with and understand people from other cultures. As Condon and Yousef (1983) stated, "The fusion of individualism and equality is so valued and so basic that many Americans find it most difficult to relate to contrasting values in other cultures where interdependence greatly determines a person's sense of self" (p. 65).

Whether a culture is individualistic or collectivist affects the nonverbal behavior of that culture in every way. First, people from individualistic cultures are more remote proxemically. Collectivist cultures are interdependent, and as a result, people work, play, live, and sleep in close proximity to each other. Hofstede (1982) cited research that suggests that as hunters and gatherers, people lived apart in individualistic, nuclear families. As agricultural societies developed, the interdependent extended family began living in close proximity in large family or tribal units. Urban-industrial societies later returned to the norm of individualism, nuclear families, and lack of proximity to one's neighbors, friends, and coworkers.

Kinesic behavior tends to be more synchronized in collectivist cultures. Where families work collectively, movements, schedules, and actions need to be highly coordinated (Argyle, 1975). In developed, urban cultures, family members often "do their own thing," coming and going, working and playing, eating and sleeping, all on different schedules. People in individualistic cultures also smile more than in normatively or collectively oriented cultures, according to Tomkins (1984). This is probably due to the fact that individualists are responsible for their relationships and their own happiness, whereas collectively oriented people regard compliance with norms as a primary value and personal or interpersonal happiness as a secondary value (Andersen, 1988). Matsumoto (1991) contends that "collective cultures will foster emotional displays of their members that maintain and facilitate group cohesion, harmony, or cooperation, to a greater degree than individualistic cultures" (p. 132). A series of studies reported by Matsumoto (2006) indicates that collectivists restrain and moderate their facial expression, as is the case in most Asian cultures. By contrast, in individualistic cultures like the United States, individuals freely display facial expressions of emotion. People in collectivist cultures may suppress both positive and negative emotional displays that are contrary to the mood of the group, because maintaining the group's cohesion is a primary value (Andersen, 1988). Bond (1993) reports that the Chinese culture is lower in frequency, intensity, and duration of emotional expression. Bond contends that "the expression of emotion is carefully regulated out of a concern for its capacity to disrupt group harmony and status hierarchies" (p. 245). Likewise, people from collectivist cultures like Asia are also less likely to recognize facial expressions, especially negative ones, a result of display rules that proscribe the production and display of individual and especially negative emotions (Beaupre & Hess, 2005; also see chapter 6).

People in individualistic cultures are encouraged to express emotions nonverbally, especially in their faces and voices, because individual freedom is a paramount value. Research suggests that people in individualistic cultures are nonverbally affiliative. Intuitively, the reason for this is not obvious, because individualism doesn't require affiliation. However, as Hofstede (1982) explains:

> In less individualistic countries where traditional social ties, like those with extended family members, continue to exist, people have less of a need to make specific friendships. One's friends are predetermined by the social relationships into which one is born. In the more individualistic countries, however, affective relationships are not socially predetermined but must be acquired by each individual personally. (p. 163)

In individualistic countries, affiliation, dating, flirting, small talk, smiling, and initial acquaintance are more important than in collectivist countries, where the social network is more fixed and less reliant on individual initiative. Bellah et al. (1985) maintain that over the centuries, the individualistic and mobile nature of

U.S. society has enabled people to meet more easily and maintain more open communication; at the same time, however, it has caused their relationships to be more casual and transient.

Similarly, Lustig and Koester (2003) maintain that "people from individualistic cultures are more likely than those from collectivist cultures to use confrontational strategies when dealing with interpersonal problems; those with a collectivist orientation are likely to use avoidance, third-party intermediaries, or other face-saving techniques" (p. 127).

People in individualistic cultures where personal success is the most important outcome place more emphasis on physical appearance, including hairstyles, body shape, makeup, and clothing. Interestingly, recent research shows that young adults in Japan are dissatisfied with their bodies, partly because they come from a collectivistic culture that deemphasizes self-enhancement, but also because they perceive their bodies to be far from the ideal as portrayed in the media, especially Western media (Kowner, 2004). Interestingly, people in other Asian cultures with less media exposure do not experience the same degree of body dissatisfaction as do the Japanese.

Finally, in an impressive study of dozens of cultures, Lomax (1968) found that song and dance styles of a country were related to its level of social cohesion and collectivism. Collectivist cultures exhibit higher cohesiveness in their singing styles and more synchrony in their dance styles (Lomax, 1968). It isn't surprising that rock and hip-hop dancing, which emphasizes separateness and "doing your own thing," evolved in such individualistic cultures as England and the United States. Americans' style of dancing may serve as a metaphor for the whole U.S. culture, which emphasizes individuality more than any other country in the world (Andersen & Wang, 2006).

Gender Orientation

The gender orientation of culture has a huge impact on many aspects of communication, including nonverbal behavior. Although gender is largely a biologically determined trait—each of us is born as a male or female—it is also regulated by the gender rules of each culture. In most cultures, males are socialized into so-called masculine roles that emphasize qualities such as power and dominance, and females are socialized into traditionally feminine roles that emphasize qualities such as nurturance and compassion. Gender roles regulate (1) the types of expressions permitted by each sex, (2) occupational status, (3) nonverbal aspects of power, (4) the ability to interact with strangers or acquaintances of the opposite sex, and (5) all aspects of interpersonal relationships between men and women. "While numerous studies have focused on gender as an individual characteristic, gender has been neglected as a cultural dimension" (Hecht, Andersen, & Ribeau, 1989, p. 171).

As conceptualized here, gender orientation refers to the degree of masculinity or femininity exhibited by a culture. In rigidly masculine cultures, positive traits typically include strength, assertiveness, competitiveness, and ambitiousness; less valued are typically feminine traits such as affection, compassion, nurturance, and emotionality (Bern, 1974; Hofstede, 1982). Masculine cultures also regard power and materialism as important values (Gudykunst & Kim, 1992; Hofstede, 1982). People in masculine cultures believe in ostentatious manliness (Lustig & Koester, 2003). Masculine Latino countries such as Mexico and Venezuela emphasize *machismo*, or macho male characteristics. Similarly, masculine Germanic countries such as Austria, Germany, and Switzerland value "manly" men—as satirically depicted in the classic "Hans and Frans" routine on *Saturday Night Live*, in which bodybuilders Hans and Frans are "all pumped up," not "girlie men."

By contrast, feminine (also called androgynous) cultures emphasize nurturance, compassion, and quality of life (Hofstede, 1982). These cultures have more flexible sex roles and allow both men and women to express more diverse, less stereotyped sex-role behaviors. Not surprisingly, women have more rights and privileges in feminine cultures.

Hofstede (1982) has measured the degree to which a culture endorses masculine or feminine goals. The masculinity of a culture is negatively correlated with a high percentage of women in technical and professional jobs and positively correlated with segregation of sexes in higher education (Hofstede, 1982).

The countries in the study with the nine highest masculinity index scores, according to Hofstede (1982), are (in order) Japan, Austria, Venezuela, Italy, Switzerland, Mexico, Ireland, Great Britain, and Germany (Figure 4.4), though many Middle Eastern countries would be considered highly masculine as well. The majority of the countries in this list are located in western and central Europe and the Caribbean region. The nine countries with the highest feminine scores are (in order) Sweden, Norway, the Netherlands, Denmark, Yugoslavia, Finland, Chile, Portugal, and Thailand—a good percentage of these countries being located in northern Europe. Compared to low-masculinity countries, high-masculinity countries have fewer women in the labor force, have only recently afforded voting

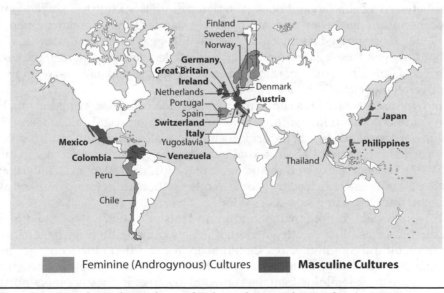

Feminine (Androgynous) Cultures   **Masculine Cultures**

Figure 4.4   Gender Orientations of Selected Countries (Hofstede, 1982)

privileges to women, and are least likely to consider wife rape a crime (Seager & Olson, 1986).

Why don't most South American cultures manifest stronger masculine orientations and the Latin pattern of machismo? Hofstede (1982) suggests that machismo is more prevalent in the Caribbean-bordering countries than in the remainder of South America. In fact, South America, as compared to Central America, has a much higher percentage of working women, much higher school attendance by girls, and more women in higher education (Seager & Olson, 1986). Furthermore, Brazil—the largest country in South America—manifests considerable Portuguese influence in its language and culture. Because Portugal tends to be feminine in its gender orientations, its values may still be evident in contemporary Brazilian behavior.

Research suggests that androgynous patterns of behavior (that are both feminine and masculine) result in higher levels of self-esteem, social competence, success, and intellectual development for both males and females (Andersen & Wang, 2006) and may even lead to greater physical health, because both masculine strength and fitness and feminine expressiveness and nurturance are associated with good health. Is it a coincidence that the more androgynous (feminine) countries are associated with longer life expectancies? Perhaps not. Nonverbal styles that allow both men and women alike to express both masculine traits (such as dominance and strength) and feminine attributes (such as warmth and emotionality) are likely to contribute to physical and emotional well-being. Buck (1984) has demonstrated that many males may harm their health by internalizing emotions rather than externalizing them as women usually do. Internalized emotions that aren't expressed result in more stress and higher blood pressure. Interestingly, more-masculine countries show higher levels of stress (Hofstede, 1982).

Considerable research has demonstrated significant nonverbal vocalic differences between egalitarian and nonegalitarian countries. Countries where women are economically important and where sexual standards for women are permissive show more relaxed vocal patterns than less-egalitarian countries (Lomax, 1968). Moreover, these egalitarian countries show less tension between the sexes, more vocal solidarity and coordination in their songs, and more synchrony in their overall movement (Lomax, 1968).

In feminine countries, as compared to masculine countries, same-sex touch is more common. Masculine cultures tend to have a more rigid and unaccepting view toward same-sex touch, particularly among males. Feminine countries have more permissive attitudes about sexual behavior, particularly for women (Hofstede, 1982). Indeed, many of the most feminine countries, such as Denmark and the Netherlands, are criticized by people of other nationalities for their liberal attitudes and laws regarding sexual behavior.

It is important to note that, according to Hofstede (1982), the United States tends to be a masculine country, although it is not among the very most masculine. Intercultural communicators should keep in mind that other countries may be either more or less sexually egalitarian than the United States. Because most countries are more feminine than the United States (that is, they are more nurturing and compassionate), Americans of both sexes frequently seem dominant, loud, aggressive, and competitive by world standards, conveying the image of the "ugly American." Likewise, Americans' attitude toward women may seem sexist in extremely feminine cultures such as Scandinavia.

Power-Distance Orientation

A fourth basic dimension of intercultural communication is power distance. Power distance—the degree to which power, prestige, and wealth are unequally distributed in a culture—has been measured in a number of cultures using Hofstede's (1982) Power Distance Index (PDI). In cultures with high PDI scores, power, wealth, and influence are concentrated in the hands of a few rather than being more equally distributed throughout the population. Condon and Yousef (1983) distinguished among three cultural patterns: democratic, authority-centered, and authoritarian. The PDI is highly correlated (.80) with authoritarianism (Hofstede, 1982).

According to Hofstede (1982), the highest-PDI countries are (in order) the Philippines, Mexico, Venezuela, India, Yugoslavia, Singapore, Brazil, France, Hong Kong, and Colombia (Figure 4.5). This list is dominated by countries located in the low latitudes of Asia and the Americas. Gudykunst and Kim (1992) reported that both African and Asian cultures usually establish hierarchical relationships. Asian students are expected to be modest and deferent nonverbally in the presence of their instructors. Likewise, the Vietnamese consider teachers and employers to be their mentors and will not question orders. The nine lowest PDI countries are (in order) Austria, Israel, Denmark, New Zealand, Ireland, Sweden, Norway, Finland, and Switzerland (Hofstede, 1982). Most of the countries in this list are middle-class, developed democracies located at high latitudes.

A primary determiner of power distance is weather and climate (for a discussion of these macroenvironmental nonverbal factors see chapter 3). Hofstede

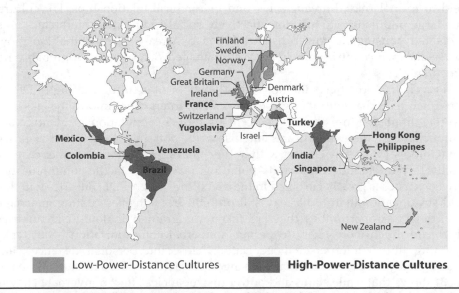

Figure 4.5   Power-Distance Orientations of Selected Countries (Hofstede, 1982)

(1982) claims that latitude and climate are major forces that shape a culture. He maintains that the key intervening variable is climate. For example, in colder climates, technology is needed for survival. This produces a chain of events in which people come to rely on each other rather than on authority figures. Education, teamwork, and individual initiative are necessary to survive in harsh, variable climates, as are creative solutions to problems and changing conditions, rather than simple obedience to authority. The result is that most low-PDI cultures are found in high latitudes and harsh climates; in fact, Hofstede (1982) reports a –.65 correlation between PDI and latitude! In a study conducted at forty U.S. universities, Andersen, Lustig, and Andersen (1990) reported a –.47 correlation between latitude and intolerance for ambiguity and a –.45 correlation between latitude and authoritarianism. This suggests that residents of the northern United States are less authoritarian and more tolerant of ambiguity than those in the southern United States. Northern U.S. cultures, like their international counterparts, may have to be less autocratic and more cooperative to ensure collaboration and survival in harsher climates.

The United States scores slightly lower than the median on the PDI, indicating lesser status differentials than many countries but more inequality than some others. Cultures differ in terms of how status is acquired. In many countries, such as India, one's status is historically ascribed according to class. In the United States, however, power and status are typically achieved through monetary success and manifested by conspicuous displays of materialism (Andersen, 2008).

The population of a country or a culture may be another predictor of power distance. Generally, larger cultures score higher on the PDI (Lustig & Koester, 2003). As the size of any group increases, it becomes unwieldy and difficult to manage informally. This is even true of larger classrooms, larger governments, and larger organizations. In larger aggregations, informal relationships must yield to formal rules, bureaucracies, and hierarchical relationships. For cultures with large populations to function effectively, social and political hierarchies must be created, causing the power-distance factor to increase. The fact that most low-power-distance countries are small, well-managed democracies is probably not coincidental.

Power distance affects the nonverbal behavior of a culture. In high-PDI cultures such as India, with its rigid caste system, interaction among the classes is severely limited. More than 20 percent of India's population is identified as "untouchables"; these individuals languish at the bottom of India's five-caste system (Chinoy, 1967). Any contact with untouchables by members of other castes is strictly forbidden and considered "polluting." Certainly, tactile communication between castes is greatly curtailed in Indian culture. High-PDI countries with less rigid stratification than India may still prohibit free interclass dating, marriage, and contact—opportunities that are taken for granted in low-PDI countries, which are much more likely to permit nonverbal communication of all types, including liberal interpersonal association, close interpersonal distances, and greater tactile contact and visual exchanges. Research by Kowner and Wiseman (2003) shows that while status and power discrepancies affect nonverbal behavior in both low-PDI countries like the United States and high-PDI countries like

Japan, status differences have more effect on nonverbal behavior in high-PDI countries. For example, Japanese workers may be startled by the fact that American workers would sit while addressing a seated superior.

Civilizations with large power discrepancies produce different kinesic behavior. High-PDI cultures foster and encourage emotions that underscore status differences. In high-PDI cultures, people are expected to show only positive emotions to others with high status and to display negative emotions to others with low status (Matsumoto, 1991; Porter & Samovar, 1998). According to Andersen (2008), the bodily tension of subordinates is more obvious in power-discrepant relationships. Similarly, Andersen (2008) reported that in power-discrepant circumstances, subordinates smile more in an effort to appease superiors and appear polite. The ever present smiles on many Asians' faces constitute a culturally inculcated behavior of appeasing superiors and smoothing social relations; this nonverbal behavior is in keeping with a high-PDI cultural profile.

Vocalic, or paralinguistic, cues also vary according to the power-distance dimension of a given culture. Citizens of low-PDI cultures are generally less aware that vocal loudness may be offensive to others. American vocal tones are often perceived as noisy, exaggerated, and childlike (Condon & Yousef, 1983). Lomax (1968) has shown that in countries where political authority is highly centralized, singing voices are tighter and the voice box is more closed; by contrast, more permissive societies produce more relaxed, open, and clear sounds.

Uncertainty Orientation

People in all cultures face change, unpredictability, and uncertainty. Uncertainty orientation is a cultural predisposition toward risk and ambiguity (Hecht, Andersen, & Ribeau, 1989). Cultures with high uncertainty avoidance dislike ambiguity and uncertainty and believe that certain rules and beliefs will reduce uncertainty; at the individual level, this predisposition is often called tolerance or intolerance for ambiguity (Martin & Westie, 1959). People with intolerance for ambiguity or with high levels of uncertainty avoidance want clear, black-and-white answers, fear change, and dread the future. People with a high tolerance for ambiguity and with low levels of uncertainty avoidance are more tolerant, accept ambiguous answers, see many shades of gray, and embrace future change. Hofstede (1982) demonstrated that a country's uncertainty avoidance is highly correlated with a high incidence of neuroticism and anxiety in its population. High uncertainty avoidance is negatively correlated with risk taking and positively correlated with fear of failure.

Countries vary greatly in their tolerance for uncertainty. In some cultures, freedom leads to uncertainty, which leads to stress and anxiety. Hofstede (1982) maintained that intolerance of ambiguity and dogmatism are primarily a function of the uncertainty-avoidance dimension rather than the power-distance dimension. According to Hofstede (1982), the nine countries with the highest levels of uncertainty avoidance are (in order) Greece, Portugal, Belgium, Japan, Yugoslavia, Peru, Argentina, Chile, and France (Figure 4.6); this list is dominated by southern European and South American countries. The nine countries with the highest levels of uncertainty tolerance are (in order) Singapore, Denmark, Sweden, Hong

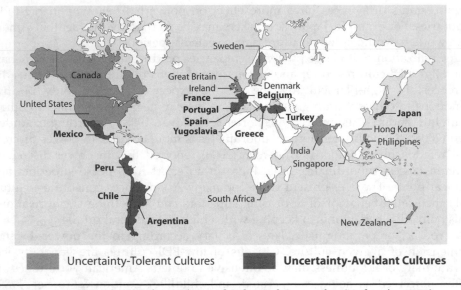

Uncertainty-Tolerant Cultures   **Uncertainty-Avoidant Cultures**

Figure 4.6   Uncertainty Orientations of Selected Countries (Hofstede, 1982)

Kong, Ireland, Great Britain, India, the Philippines, and the United States; this list is dominated by northern European and Southeast Asian cultures. Hofstede (1982) also reported that Catholic countries are high in uncertainty avoidance, whereas Protestant, Hindu, and Buddhist countries tend to be more accepting of uncertainty; Eastern religions and Protestantism tend to be less "absolute" than Catholicism. Andersen, Lustig, and Andersen (1990) reported that intolerance for ambiguity is much higher in the southern United States than in the north; this tendency reflects the international pattern of tolerance at higher latitudes.

Fewer studies have examined the uncertainty dimension of nonverbal behavior than the other dimensions of culture. However, some research has shown that emotional displays are associated with uncertainty avoidance. Hofstede (1982) maintains that uncertainty-avoidant countries tend to display emotions more than do uncertainty-tolerant countries. Furthermore, he reports that uncertainty-avoidant countries are less tolerant in their attitudes toward young people and their emotional displays. According to Gudykunst and Kim (1992), when consensus or uniformity breaks down in high-uncertainty-avoidant countries, people become upset and show their emotions more than do residents of uncertainty-tolerant countries, who are more likely to tolerate change or nonconformity. Residents of high-uncertainty-avoidant cultures, such as Greece or France, are most likely to experience and exhibit stress and anxiety cues (Hofstede, 1982; see chapter 7 for a complete discussion of these behaviors).

Certainly, disagreement and nonconformity are not appreciated in high-uncertainty-avoidant countries. Moreover, such cultures seem to prefer verbal behavior over nonverbal behavior. Indeed, Hofstede (1982) reported that in high-uncertainty-avoidant countries, rituals are created to provide "pseudo-certainty," or the illusion of certainty. Such cultures place great importance on memos and reports and structured information collection and dissemination procedures—all with the intent of creating the illusion, if not the reality, of certainty.

Similarly, nonverbal behavior is more likely to be codified and rule-governed in high-uncertainty-avoidant countries. This means that kinesic and proxemic behaviors, for example, follow a strict set of rules and rituals. Such a profile seems to fit a high-uncertainty-avoidant country like Japan but remains to be tested and is somewhat speculative. Hofstede (1982) found that high-uncertainty-avoidant nations report more stylized and ritualized behavior, so we should expect nonverbal behavior to be more proscribed in these cultures. When communicating with people from a high-uncertainty-avoidant country such as Japan or France, Americans may come across as excessively unconventional and lacking in manners; at the same time, Americans may view their Japanese or French counterparts as too controlled and rigid (Lustig & Koester, 2003).

High Context versus Low Context

Context is the final important dimension of intercultural communication. Context provides situational or environmental cues that frame any communication and influence its meaning (see chapter 3 for more about the contextual codes of nonverbal communication). E. T. Hall (1976, 1984) has described high- and low-context cultures in considerable detail. "A high context (HC) communication or message is one in which most of the information is either in the physical context or internalized in the person, while very little is in the coded, explicit, transmitted parts of the message" (Hall, 1976, p. 91). Lifelong friends often use high-context, or implicit, messages that are nearly impossible for an outsider to understand. The situation itself, a smile, or a glance provides implicit meaning that does not need to be articulated. "In a high-context culture, much more is taken for granted and assumed to be shared, and consequently the overwhelming preponderance of messages are coded in such a way that they don't have to be explicitly and verbally transmitted" (Lustig & Koester, 2003, p. 113). In high-context situations or cultures, information is gleaned from the environment, the context, the situation, and from nonverbal cues that give the message meaning in the absence of explicit verbal utterance.

Low-context messages are just the opposite of high-context messages; most of the information is provided in the explicit code (Hall, 1976). Low-context messages must be elaborated, clearly communicated, and highly specific. Unlike personal relationships, which tend to utilize high-context message systems, institutions such as courts of law and formal systems such as mathematics and computer language require explicit, low-context message systems (E. T. Hall, 1984).

In a high-context country, the power structure is well known, and people behave with great deference toward their superiors. By contrast, in a low-context culture, people are oblivious to the power structure until they are told who is powerful and who is not. In a high-context culture, a negative facial expression or lack of enthusiasm may signal the cancellation of a business deal, whereas written notification would be required in the same case in a low-context culture.

Cultures vary considerably in the degree of context used in communication. As shown in Figure 4.7, the lowest-context cultures are Germany, Switzerland, the United States, Sweden, Norway, Finland, Denmark, and Canada (Hall, 1976, 1984;

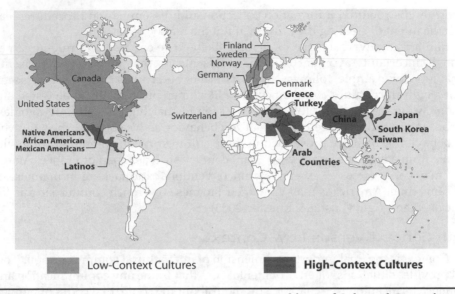

Figure 4.7   High-Context versus Low-Context Rankings of Selected Countries

Gudykunst & Kim, 1992; Nisbett et al., 2001). These cultures are preoccupied with specifics, details, literalness, and precise time schedules at the expense of context. They utilize behavior systems built around Aristotelian logic and linear thinking (E. T. Hall, 1984). These cultures also tend to be pathologically verbal, that is, they may miss subtle cues from other people, or from the environment, which are more meaningful than words (see chapter 1 for more on the differences between verbal and nonverbal communication). Countries that exhibit characteristics of both high-context and low-context message systems include France, Great Britain, and Italy (Gudykunst & Kim, 1992); these countries are somewhat less explicit than far-northern European and Scandinavian cultures.

The highest-context cultures are found in Asia. China, Japan, South Korea, and Taiwan are extremely high-context cultures (Elliot, Scott, Jensen, & McDonough, 1982; Gudykunst & Kim, 1992; E. T. Hall, 1976, 1984; Nisbett et al., 2001). Native Americans, African Americans, Mexican Americans, and Latinos are also fairly high-context groups (Lustig & Koester, 2003). Usually, *language* implies an explicit message system, but the Chinese language is unique in that it is an implicit, high-context system. To use a Chinese dictionary, one must understand thousands of characters, which change meaning when used in varying combinations with other characters. Perhaps the best example of high-context communication is the Japanese tea ceremony, in which every behavior of both the host and the guests is carefully prescribed. The tea ceremony is a highly ritualized experience that is almost incomprehensible to those who do not understand the meanings of the most subtle behaviors (Lustig & Koester, 2003). According to Jandt (1995), in the tea ceremony "nothing is spoken; all meanings are in context. A typical response from a low-context observer is 'hurry up and drink your tea'" (p. 203).

In the highly ritual-
ized Japanese tea cere-
mony, every body
movement and ges-
ture—no matter how
subtle—has a meaning.

Asian cultures are so reliant on context partly because they have been highly influenced by Buddhism, which places a high value on silence, lack of emotional expression, and the unspoken, nonverbal parts of communication (Burgoon, Buller, & Woodall, 1996; Camras et al., 2006; McDaniel & Andersen, 1998). Americans frequently complain that the Japanese never "get to the point," yet they fail to recognize that high-context cultures rely on the context and setting and let the point evolve (E. T. Hall, 1984). In a study of tactile behavior during international airport farewells, McDaniel and Andersen (1998) found Asians to be the least tactile of any cultural group on earth. The influences of Confucianism and Buddhism and the value placed on context rather than on emotional expression probably explain this finding. Native American cultures with ancestral migratory roots in East Asia are remarkably similar to contemporary Asian cultures in several ways, especially in their use of high-context communication (E. T. Hall, 1984).

Before meeting with a small group of Native Americans on their reservation near my home in Southern California, I instructed my Anglo-American friends to sit silently and not make a lot of idle small talk. Complying with my instructions, my friends and I sat in a circle under a pepper tree and listened to the wind and the birds before the meeting commenced. From our perspective, considerable time passed (probably only about five minutes). The Native Americans subsequently welcomed us back to the reservation for other ceremonies, projects, and meetings. By observing their high-context rules for communication, we had gained their trust.

Not surprisingly, most Latin American cultures, a fusion of Iberian (Portuguese-Spanish) and Native American traditions, are also high-context cultures. Eastern Mediterranean (including Greece and Turkey) and Arab cultures tend to fall under the high-context category as well.

Obviously, communication is quite different in high- and low-context cultures. First, explicit forms of communication such as verbal codes are more prevalent in low-context cultures such as the United States and northern Europe.

Research by Ting-Toomey (1991) showed that U.S. respondents are more likely to express love overtly and explicitly through verbal communication than are French or Japanese respondents. These findings are consistent with low-context communication patterns. People from low-context cultures are often perceived as excessively talkative, belaboring of the obvious, and redundant. People from high-context cultures may be perceived as nondisclosive, wasteful of time, sneaky, and mysterious. Second, high-context cultures do not value verbal communication as highly as low-context cultures. Elliot et al. (1982) found that more-verbal people were perceived as more attractive by people in the United States (a low-context culture), but that less-verbal people were perceived as more attractive in Korea (a high-context culture). Third, high-context cultures are more likely to tune into and utilize nonverbal communication. Members of low-context cultures, particularly men, fail to perceive as much nonverbal communication as members of high-context cultures do. Nonverbal communication provides the context for all communication (Watzlawick, Beavin, & Jackson, 1967; see also chapter 3), but people from high-context cultures are particularly affected by these contextual cues. Thus, facial expressions, tension, movements, speed of interaction, location of interaction, and other subtle "vibes" are likely to be perceived by and have more meaning for people from high-context cultures. Finally, people in high-context cultures expect more from their interaction partners than do people in low-context cultures (Hall, 1976): people in high-context cultures expect their interaction partners to pick up on unarticulated feelings, subtle gestures, and environmental cues, which people from low-context cultures simply do not process. Unfortunately, both cultural extremes fail to recognize these basic differences in behavior, communication, and context and are quick to misattribute the causes for their behavior.

THE PRACTICAL BENEFITS OF UNDERSTANDING INTERCULTURAL COMMUNICATION DIFFERENCES

Simply reading about these six cultural dimensions of nonverbal communication will not ensure intercultural communication competence. Combining research-based knowledge from intercultural articles and courses with actual encounters with people from other cultures is the best way to gain intercultural communication competence. International travel, even travel within the United States, provides an opportunity to gain perspective on one's own behavior and the behavior of others that will help lead to intercultural communication competence. Research suggests that intercultural competence is highly valued by people of various cultures and especially to Americans who value approachability, attentiveness, and immediacy even more than people from other cultures (Leclerc & Martin, 2004).

Practical understanding of the dimensions along which cultures differ, as well as knowledge of how specific communication acts differ cross-culturally, has several practical benefits. First, such knowledge will highlight and challenge assumptions about our own behavior. The structure of our own behavior is invisible and taken for granted until it is exposed and challenged through actual intercultural encounters. Indeed, Hall (1976) argued that diversity in inter-ethnic communication can be a source of strength and self-discovery.

Second, this chapter should convince you that conclusions about the nonverbal communication of people from other cultures are generalized observations, not ironclad rules. No dictionary or code of intercultural behavior exists. You cannot read people like books, not even people from your own culture. However, understanding that another person is from a masculine, collectivist, or high-context culture may help shape your perception of her or his behavior as less confusing, more interpretable, and less bizarre.

Finally, understanding intercultural communication and actually engaging in intercultural encounters are bound to reduce ethnocentrism and make strangers from other cultures seem less threatening. Fear is often based on ignorance and misunderstanding. In your future life, I guarantee that you will continue to meet and communicate with many people from other cultures than your own. Learn from these differences. Intercultural diversity is a source of joy and optimism about the number of possible ways to be human.

SUMMARY

The diversity of U.S. culture requires that Americans understand intercultural communication in order to communicate effectively. Differences in language are only the tip of the intercultural iceberg; many of the most important cultural differences are in nonverbal communication.

The codes of nonverbal communication, discussed in chapters 2 and 3, are used differently by people in various cultures. Chronemically, the more developed cultures such as countries in Europe and North America employ monochronic time, a time orientation in which one thing gets done at a time and time is treated like a commodity. People in lesser-developed countries do not structure time so rigidly; such cultures employ polychronic time, a time orientation that emphasizes informality and multiple simultaneous activities. Proxemically, people from cooler, northerly climates tend to be more distant and remote interpersonally, whereas people from tropical regions tend to prefer closer interpersonal distances. Kinesically, cultures differ as greatly in their use of emblems (gestures with verbal meanings) as in their languages. People in warmer climates use more expressive gestures and movements than do people in cooler climates. Haptic behavior varies dramatically from one culture to the next; for example, Asian cultures engage in very little touch, whereas Mediterranean and South American cultures employ a great deal of touch in their interpersonal interactions (Miller et al., 2006). The physical appearance of people around the world in terms of hairstyle, clothing, facial hair, artifacts, and body decorations is extremely varied. Cultures also differ greatly in their use of oculesics. For example, many Mediterranean cultures use much more direct eye contact than do Americans or Asians. Vocalics also shows considerable cultural variation in intonation, loudness, pitch, and tone. In terms of olfactics, Americans are much more tuned in to smell than are most of the world's people.

Nonverbal differences across cultures center on six dimensions of human behavior. Cultures differ in immediacy, the degree to which nonverbal behavior communicates warmth, closeness, and availability for communications. Cultures high in immediacy—contact cultures—stand close to each other, touch more, and are generally more expressive. Cultures low in immediacy—noncontact cultures—tend to stand farther apart, touch less, and manifest less nonverbal expressiveness. Individualistic cultures value independence and privacy and manifest these values in their nonverbal behavior. Conversely, collectivist cultures value interpersonal connection and group behavior and reflect these values in their nonverbal behavior. Gender orientation is the degree to which a culture emphasizes typically masculine traits or typically feminine traits. The nonverbal behavior of a masculine culture emphasizes assertiveness, competitiveness, and ambitiousness. Cultures that are more feminine exhibit nonverbal behavior that stresses equality, nurturance, emotionality, and compassion.

Cultures also differ in power distance, the degree to which wealth and prestige are equally or unequally distributed in a culture. High-power-distance cultures have more formal, hierarchical relationships and show only positive emotions to authority figures. Low-power-distance cultures exhibit nonverbal behavior that is more informal and not structured along class lines. Uncertainty orientation is a cultural predisposition toward risk and ambiguity. Uncertainty-avoidant cultures are more controlled and ritualized in their behavior but exhibit more nonverbal emotional displays when under stress. Uncertainty-tolerant cultures tend to exhibit fewer prescribed nonverbal behaviors and greater tolerance toward young people and their emotional displays. Context is the final dimension of intercultural communication. In low-context cultures, verbal communication is emphasized and nonverbal communication is more informal. In high-context cultures, nonverbal communication is highly stylized and replete with meaning.

5

Gender, Sex, and Nonverbal Communication

Popular books today would have us believe that men and women are completely different—members of different cultures or perhaps even creatures from different planets like Mars and Venus. Likewise, traditional stereotypes often lead people to believe that men and women are cut out for completely different roles. Research has shown that these are oversimplified and erroneous views of reality. A more accurate though less sensationalistic view is offered by Dindia (2006), who claims that men are from South Dakota and women from North Dakota. To North Dakotans, those South Dakotans seem pretty strange, and vice versa. But to Texans, Californians, Floridians, New Yorkers, or residents from any other place in the world, all those Dakotans seem pretty much alike.

Certainly men and women are different. These differences, including differences in the way men and women communicate, are governed by a complex set of forces, including biology, culture, stereotypes, and prejudice. But men and women are certainly not from different planets. Four overriding principles can be used to organize the complex body of theory and research on sex differences in nonverbal communication:

1. Men and women are far more similar than they are different.
2. Biological sex differences exist.
3. Learned gender differences occur in every culture.
4. Men and women can consciously alter their nonverbal behavior.

SIMILARITIES BETWEEN THE SEXES

Men and women behave similarly in most respects. Indeed, statistical summaries of research indicate that the similarities far outweigh the differences between the sexes (Canary & Hause, 1993; Dindia, 2006; Hyde, 2005; Wilkins & Andersen, 1991). Men and women easily recognize each other's facial expressions, learn similar norms for the use of touch and space in interpersonal interaction, and maintain fairly continuous eye contact when listening and alternate between gaze and gaze aversion when speaking. Men and women both use gestures, reveal emotions on their faces, hug their children, enjoy sexual intimacy in the right relational contexts, and are conscious of interpersonal meanings of time, space, smell, and appearance. The nonverbal behaviors of both men and women are synchronized to a remarkable degree during interaction. Recent research shows that men and women have very similar expectations and standards for their partners' behavior in romantic relationships (Vangelisti & Daly, 1997). These behaviors are hardly the alien expressions of creatures from different planets. They are familiar, universal ways that all humans communicate. The gestures, touches, and facial expressions of men and women are recognizable behaviors of Earthlings, not Martians or Venusians.

A number of recent analyses have statistically summarized hundreds of previous studies on sex and gender differences in communication (see Canary & Hause, 1993; Halberstadt & Saitta, 1987; Hall, 1985; Stier & Hall, 1984; Hyde, 2005; Wilkins & Andersen, 1991). These studies have found significant differences between the communication behavior of men and women, but the differences are usually tiny. Overall, sex differences in communication are so small that men and women are about 99 percent similar and only 1 percent different,

A few larger sex differences do exist, which we will discuss in this chapter. Sex differences in communication are the result of the biology of men and women, and gender differences are the result of cultural role socialization. In summary, the communication of men and women is exceedingly similar. Communicatively speaking, men and women inhabit the same planet and have the ability to communicate effectively with one another. This chapter examines sex differences due to the "nurture of nature" and gender differences due to the "nature of nurture" (Andersen, 2004, pp. 307–309).

BIOLOGICAL SEX DIFFERENCES: THE NURTURE OF NATURE

In animal species, two sexes exist for the purpose of reproduction. The search for sex differences in communication should always begin with the most basic biological differences: the differences in each sex's reproductive role or related differences that are indirect consequences of reproduction. Years ago, Birdwhistell (1970), one of the founders of the field of nonverbal communication, discussed three types of differences in the nonverbal communication behavior of men and women: (1) primary differences that relate to the production of ova or spermatozoa; (2) secondary differences that are anatomical but not directly related to reproduction, such as muscle mass, body fat, throwing ability, body hair, and physical size; and (3) tertiary differences that are learned patterns of social behavior.

Politics, Prejudice, and Biology

An examination of textbooks on sex, gender, and communication reveals an almost complete evasion of biological sex differences. Usually these books ignore the topic entirely or devote a paragraph or two before dismissing biology as a meaningless source of gender behavior. I have said on several occasions that books in our field are in a state of "biological denial" (Andersen, 1998a; 2006). Many people fear the forthright discussion of biological differences between men and women for political reasons. It is important for many reasons to ascertain if men and women are all that different and, if so, why.

Because of our commitment to equality, many of us in American universities have been part of a worthwhile project to eradicate prejudice and ensure that men and women have an equal opportunity to succeed in college and in life. This goal has been so important that some people fear that discussing biological differences between men and women will be used as a pretext for denying people (usually women) equal opportunity. Unfortunately, it is increasingly difficult to write or speak the truth about gender, and many academics have lost their reputations and even jobs because their views are not politically correct.

These concerns are understandable: Biological differences have been used by many hate groups such as the Nazis and the Ku Klux Klan to justify racism and sexism, even though these differences have not shown one group of people to be any more intelligent than another. Just decades ago, women in communication were denied access to graduate school because of a perception that the woman's role in society was as homemaker and mother.

Hopefully, we are at a point in the history of the field of communication when a real discussion of biological differences can take place. Understanding real differences makes it easier to refute bogus differences. Identifying differences does not imply the superiority or inferiority of either males or females. Additionally, most of the differences that have been discovered are relatively small. Remember, the similarities between the sexes are much more substantial than are the differences. Finally, the recognition of differences provides the opportunity for men and women to remediate behavioral differences and enhance their skills as effective communicators.

Biological Differences between the Sexes

As stated earlier, the primary biological difference between men and women is reproductive. Men can ejaculate and impregnate, and women can menstruate, gestate, and lactate. These differences lead to other basic differences between men and women. Women have proportionally wider hips, more subcutaneous fat, and larger breasts than men. Men have greater size, more muscle mass, and greater throwing ability. Some people believe that women are more innately nurturant than men due to their role in breast-feeding and caring for young children.

What about other differences? Why are men taller, more muscular, hairier, shorter-lived, better throwers, more spatially aware, and seemingly more violent than women? Why are women more socially perceptive, more tuned into nonverbal communication, and more nurturant than men? It is likely that some of these differences are attributable to evolutionary, sex-linked variations in men and women.

Over several million years of human evolution, men and women have played different roles in maintaining the survivability of the species (Andersen, 2006). Today, we share our genetic and biological heritage with ancestors who spent several million years adapting to hunting, gathering, and scavenging. Comparatively, we have spent just several thousand years as agricultural people and only a few hundred years as urban people. Our modern culture is a relatively new development, but our biology dates back to before the Stone Age.

Throughout most of our history, growing old was a luxury few humans enjoyed. For hundreds of thousands of years, human life expectancy was less than 30 years (for a summary of this literature see Andersen, 2006). Even during the more recent agrarian period (when most people were subsistence farmers), life was short, brutish, and nasty (Whicker & Kronenfeld, 1986). Up until the last several generations, short life expectancy, high infant mortality, and—ultimately—the survival of the species meant that most women were pregnant throughout most of their dozen or so childbearing years. Likewise, women were almost continuously nursing and caring for infants and toddlers. Women who failed to bear and nurse children had no genetic legacy to be passed along.

Males were not occupied with the pregnancy and nursing that limited women's mobility, so men became largely responsible for hunting, gathering, scavenging, and combat. The larger, more muscular physiques of men evolved so they could be relatively more efficient hunters, gatherers, and combatants than women. One of the largest biological differences between men and women is in throwing velocity and distance, accounting for several standard deviations (Hyde, 2005). Likewise, navigational and spatial skills were more essential for hunters and combatants. Men of low muscle mass, small stature, poor throwing ability, or a poor sense of space and direction were unlikely to survive to father many offspring.

Of course, in contemporary society few men choose to be hunters, scavengers, or combatants, though some do. Most men work in offices, classrooms, boardrooms, and factories where their survival skills must be adapted to modern life. Likewise, few women spend their entire adult life pregnant and mothering. Their social skills are increasingly employed in the same roles and occupations held by men, although all too frequently at lower salaries than men receive. Humans are incredibly adaptable. Women can be hunters and soldiers, and men can nurture their children and be preschool teachers. Nonetheless, some of our behavior is biological, a relic of our pre–Stone Age evolutionary heritage. Women's somewhat superior nonverbal sending and receiving ability and men's superior visuospatial abilities are vestiges of our evolutionary past.

GENDER DIFFERENCES: CULTURAL EXPLANATIONS

As underscored earlier in this chapter, men and women are Earthlings and members of the same human species, yet continuing debate questions whether men and women are from the same culture (see Vangelisti & Daly, 1997: Wood, 1997a). Whether or not men and women come from different cultures, American culture (and most other cultures) treats men and women differently. Differential rearing, socialization, and treatment result in variations between male and female behaviors and perceptions.

Men and women are aware that gender differences exist. In a fascinating study, Briton and Hall (1995) found that men and women are quite accurate in identifying sex differences in nonverbal behavior. When asked to name behaviors they believed were generally different between men and women, men's beliefs correlated .68 with actual, observed sex differences and women's beliefs correlated .74 with actual, observed sex differences. As expected, women were more accurate in identifying differences, but the real news here is how closely our stereotypes and beliefs conform to reality. (To see how closely your stereotypes and beliefs conform to reality, complete the checklist in Box 5.1 entitled "Behaviors Performed by Men and Women," and Box 5.2, "Communicating Dominance and

Box 5.1
Gendered Gestures?
Behaviors Performed by Men and Women

Directions: You have spent much of your life observing men and women. You have probably noticed differences between males and females in terms of their gestures, body postures, and facial expressions. Identify the following nonverbal behaviors predominantly performed by males, predominantly performed by females, or are performed equally by each sex. Be honest. Check the behaviors that are *actually* performed by one sex or the other, rather than *behaviors stereotypically associated with one of the sexes.*

Predominantly Performed by Males	Predominantly Performed by Females	Performed by Both Males and Females	Nonverbal Communication Behavior
_____	_____	_____	1. Smiling
_____	_____	_____	2. Gazing
_____	_____	_____	3. Eye contact
_____	_____	_____	4. Frowning
_____	_____	_____	5. Smiling
_____	_____	_____	6. Tilting one's head
_____	_____	_____	7. Gesturing
_____	_____	_____	8. Yielding (moving out of another person's way)
_____	_____	_____	9. Opposite-sex touch
_____	_____	_____	10. Averting another's gaze
_____	_____	_____	11. Occupying space
_____	_____	_____	12. Initiating touch
_____	_____	_____	13. Raising brows
_____	_____	_____	14. Loud voice
_____	_____	_____	15. Blinking
_____	_____	_____	16. Holding one's head erect
_____	_____	_____	17. Close interaction distance
_____	_____	_____	18. Open body posture
_____	_____	_____	19. Self-touch
_____	_____	_____	20. Nodding

Warmth." Comparing the results of the two boxes will give you added insight about gendered nonverbal communication behavior.) These interesting findings do not reveal, however, which came first, the beliefs or the behaviors. On one hand, these beliefs may simply reflect that people accurately perceived differences between men and women. On the other hand, beliefs about sex differences influence behavior and attitudes and serve as powerful socializing agents that maintain "gender-appropriate" behavior. For instance, Plant, Hyde, Keltner and Devine (2000) reported that women are typically stereotyped as emotional even when they are not.

Without a doubt, most societies treat men and women differently. Some scholars believe that the bulk of sex-differentiated nonverbal behavior is learned (Henley, 2002). The difference in the treatment of men and women in our society is the result of many forces: exaggerations of biological differences, patriarchal sexism designed to maintain gender inequality, and unconscious socialization processes that perpetuate gender differences in general and in nonverbal behavior in particular.

Box 5.2
Communicating Dominance and Warmth

Directions: Decide if each of these nonverbal communication behaviors expresses dominance, warmth, or is capable of communicating both.

A Strong, Dominant Communication Behavior	A Warm, Affiliative Communication Behavior	Communicates both Warmth and Dominance	
_____	_____	_____	1. Smiling
_____	_____	_____	2. Gazing
_____	_____	_____	3. Eye contact
_____	_____	_____	4. Frowning
_____	_____	_____	5. Smiling
_____	_____	_____	6. Tilting one's head
_____	_____	_____	7. Gesturing
_____	_____	_____	8. Yielding (moving out of another person's way
_____	_____	_____	9. Opposite-sex touch
_____	_____	_____	10. Averting another's gaze
_____	_____	_____	11. Occupying space
_____	_____	_____	12. Initiating touch
_____	_____	_____	13. Raising brows
_____	_____	_____	14. Loud voice
_____	_____	_____	15. Blinking
_____	_____	_____	16. Holding one's head erect
_____	_____	_____	17. Close interaction distance
_____	_____	_____	18. Open body posture
_____	_____	_____	19. Self touch
_____	_____	_____	20. Nodding

Exaggerations of Biological Differences

Sometimes cultural forces exaggerate preexisting biological differences between men and women. There are numerous ways in which women and men accentuate their biological sex. For example, women wear push-up bras and shave their legs, and men wear elevator shoes and shoulder pads. Women and men employ other nonverbal gender-role behaviors to underscore their biological differences. Men often speak in deep, loud voices, whereas women speak in soft, breathy tones to exaggerate already present sex differences in the size of the vocal cords and the pitch of the voice. Likewise, to accentuate their size men use space more expansively than women when sitting, standing, and gesturing. "Ladylike" positions—for example, women sitting with the arms and legs together—emphasize a woman's relatively smaller size.

Our society rewards us for behaving consistently with our sex roles. Feminine men are considered strange in a homophobic culture where gay and transsexual men face harassment and even violence. Gay men are called names like *queer* and *fag* because they threaten highly gendered definitions of what it means to be a

Masculine nonverbal behavior is communicated by lack of facial expressions and expansive body positions.

Our society rewards us for behaving consistently with our sex roles. However, tolerance of gays and transsexuals is increasing and is celebrated by such events as Gay Pride parades. (© AP Images/Noah Berger)

man. Similarly, lesbians are called *dykes* and other derogatory terms because they threaten our definition of what it means to be female and also because they are unavailable to men sexually, a cardinal sin among patriarchal men.

A Patriarchal and Oppressive Sexism

People in positions of power rarely relinquish it. Just as slavery and racism benefited certain powerful ethnic groups, so sexism sometimes benefits those in positions of power. Some men seek to exploit the lower status of women by requiring them to serve their needs and satisfy them sexually. The old double standard that says women should be faithful and monogamous but men can sow their wild oats is just one example of exploitative sexism.

The home is another locus of exploitation by men. In their review of research, Canary, Emmers-Sommer, and Faulkner (1997) reported that the division of labor in the home still exploits women. Women work an hour or two more each day than men. Although this gap has narrowed, women are still more likely than men to be domestic servants; in other words, they tend to be limited in their movements and social networks by the requirements of home and family. Chronemically, women are more likely to accommodate to men's schedules than vice-versa. This is not to say that women never exploit men. Indeed, women exploit men for money and status, whereas men are more likely to exploit women sexually. In balance, however, women as a social class historically have been exploited by men, who have often viewed women as a resource in terms of both labor and sexuality.

Unconscious Socialization

Societal expectations about gender are very prevalent but not always particularly obvious. These unconscious expectations about what it means to be a man or a woman create gender roles that are generally consistent with biological sex differences. As Wood (1997b) contended, "To be feminine is to be attractive, deferential, unassertive, emotional, nurturing, and concerned with people and relationships" (p. 27). Women are supposed to look pretty or sexy; old, homely, or fat women are devalued in our society. By contrast, men are expected to be strong, unemotional, aggressive, brave, successful, and wealthy. Pity the poor fellow who is perceived as weak, unsuccessful, or poor, for he fails to meet society's expectations of what it means to be masculine and is thus devalued.

From the time we are infants, our gender roles are shaped. Girls are given dolls and dishes, told to be ladylike, and discouraged from roughhousing. Boys are given trucks and guns, told to take pain "like a man," and warned not to let others push them around. A boy's aspiring masculinity or a girl's evolving femininity becomes a fixed aspect of one's identity (for summaries of this research see Pearson, West, & Turner, 1995; Wood, 1997b). Parents, families, church, school, and peers all send consistent messages about "appropriate" feminine and masculine behavior. Sometimes these messages are very subtle: a smile or a nod provides a silent message of approval for a particular behavior; a frown, a furrowed brow, or the lack of approval discourages another behavior. Society does not have to work actively to produce manly men and womanly women; the process is subtle yet pervasive.

Gender is continuously modeled for us. At home, mother and father model what it means to be masculine and feminine (see Wood, 1997b). At one time, this meant that boys were socialized to be breadwinners and women to be housewives, because that was the predominant gender role of the day. Increasingly, the norm has moved toward dual-career couples. These changes are slowly but surely altering the model of what constitutes male and female roles in the family.

The omnipresent mass media of television, radio, film, and popular music send powerful and quite consistent gender messages that are emulated by viewers, especially young viewers (see Pearson et al., 1995; Wood, 1997b). Gerbner's cultivation theory has shown that repeated exposure to media messages creates attitudes and behavior consistent with those messages (see Gerbner, Gross, Morgan, & Signiorelli, 1986). The images cultivated by the media usually portray men and women in traditional roles.

Boys are socialized to play with "masculine" toys like footballs, guns, or trucks.

Girls are socialized in traditionally feminine activities like tap dancing or ballet.

As Wood (1997b) stated:

> Media continue to present both women and men in stereotyped ways that limit our perceptions of human possibilities. Typically men are portrayed as active, adventurous, powerful, sexually aggressive, and largely uninvolved in human relationships. . . . Female characters devote their primary energies to improving their appearances and taking care of homes and people. (p. 279)

These stereotypes are changing slowly in America. At no time in U.S. history have men and women had greater opportunity to free themselves from the constraints of either biology or culture. Indeed, in a creative study a masked videoclip was used to compare the nonverbal behavior of men and women and their impact on leadership. Interestingly, this study showed that when the identical nonverbal leadership behaviors are attributed to either men or women, women are perceived as more competent as leaders (Koch, 2004), suggesting that we may now be overcompensating by valuing competent women more than competent men.

SEX DIFFERENCES (AND SIMILARITIES) IN NONVERBAL BEHAVIOR

Despite the numerous similarities between men and women, some differences do exist in nonverbal communication, resulting from the twin forces of biology and culture. In this section, these sex differences will be reviewed for each nonverbal code. Additionally, we will examine how men and women differ in their ability to send and receive nonverbal messages, in their interpersonal perceptions and attributions and in their relational communication.

Physical Appearance

When we meet a person, perhaps the most salient cue is gender. From the time children can talk and throughout life, whether we are male or female affects every interaction we have. How does appearance communicate our gender?

PHYSICAL ATTRACTIVNESS

In her book, *Moving Beyond Words*, feminist Gloria Steinem (1994) recalled, "I and other women of my generation grew up believing—as many girls still do—that the most important thing about the female body is not what it does but how it looks. The power lies not within us but within the gaze of the observer" (p. 93). Without a doubt, physical attractiveness is important to both sexes. In chapter 2, we discussed how attractive people generally have considerable advantage over unattractive people. "What's beautiful is good" is an important principle, particularly in beauty-conscious America, where image is often, unfortunately, more important to the success of a person or product than is substance (see chapter 10 to for a detailed discussion of how we sell ourselves).

Gender plays an important role in the power of physical attraction in important ways. First, research has shown that a woman's physical attractiveness is even more important to men than a man's physical attractiveness is to women (for a complete review of this literature see Feingold, 1990). Research on human mating patterns throughout the world shows that men prefer young, nubile women. Having a physically attractive mate is a sign of status for men. Although a man's attractiveness is also important to women, wealth and social status are much more important (Kenrick & Keefe, 1992).

Why is physical attractiveness of women so important to men? The sociobiological explanation is that youth and beauty are innately attractive to men because they are signs of health and fertility that women display. Interestingly, recent research shows that women actively engage in more grooming, ornamentation and attractive dress during ovulation than at over times of the month (Haselton et al., 2006). Moreover, the closer a woman is to ovulation the more attractive men find her (Haselton et al., 2006). According to the social evolutionary view, men are programmed unconsciously and biologically to seek attractive mates with attractive qualities, which explains why men in all cultures value youth and beauty— which are signs of fertility and health in a mate. Women, on the other hand, are inclined to select men with sufficient resources to care for them, which may explain why women of all cultures are attracted to wealth, power, and status (see Trost & Alberts, 2006, for a longer discussion of these issues).

The socialization that takes place within a patriarchal male society offers another explanation for the difference between men's and women's perceptions of physical appearance. Today, although many men are not sexists, much of society still subscribes to sexist patriarchal attitudes. In keeping with the traditional patriarchal view, men like attractive, compliant women who are sex objects. Because men control the resources and the power structure, women are socialized to maintain and display their physical appearance to please men and gain access to the resources that men control. The tragic increase in life-threatening eating disorders occurring overwhelmingly in young women is, in part, a product of our culture's preoccupation with thinness and physical beauty. Of course, family communication patterns, genetic predispositions, and control issues also play a part in the heightened incidence of anorexia and bulimia; nevertheless, these diseases were unheard of in the days before beautiful, thin models dominated our mass media. Our cultural expectations cause women to be preoccupied with their own beauty and men's reactions to their appearance. Teen magazines are mostly manuals for fashion, grooming, makeup, and dieting (Wood, 1997b). In a survey of 33,000 young women, 42 percent said that losing weight would make them happier than would success at work (Wooley & Wooley, 1984). Of course, the biological and cultural explanations for sex differences in physical attraction are not mutually exclusive. It is likely that sexual and romantic attraction is affected by a combination of biological and sociocultural forces.

A second, equally disturbing finding is that the higher a woman's occupational status, the more her physical attractiveness becomes a disadvantage! Although receptionists, secretaries and even celebrities and newscasters are likely to profit from good looks, a woman's attractiveness actually may be a disadvantage in positions of leadership, particularly managerial positions. To paraphrase Heilman and Saruwatari (1979), beauty can be beastly; these researchers found that attractiveness was an advantage for all men but an advantage for only those women seeking low-level, nonmanagerial positions. So society creates a double bind for women by requiring them to be beautiful but precluding beautiful women from high-status positions!

Few highly attractive women have succeeded on the political scene—both in the United States and worldwide—though Hillary Clinton is both physically attractive and a serious contender to become president at the time of this writing (see chapter 10 for more on physical attractiveness and selling oneself). Some research, however, paints a somewhat more optimistic picture for female political candidates. A study by Lewis and Bierly (1990) had people rate black-and-white photographs of forty-four male and female candidates serving in the House of Representatives in the late 1980s. Men were equally likely to rate male and female candidates positively, although women showed a preference for female candidates, rating them more competent than males. Although prior research had shown that attractiveness was a disadvantage for women seeking high-status positions, results of this study showed that the more attractive male and female candidates were rated as more competent. Perhaps women are escaping from the double bind that turns beauty into a positive or negative trait depending on a woman's career status. Although it is disturbing that attractiveness is still so highly associated with competence, it is heartening that Lewis and Bierly's (1990) data revealed little sexism: Attractive men and women were rated as more competent by both men and women. Perhaps our society is ready for women who are both attractive *and* competent.

Biology and Appearance

There are obvious biological differences between the physiques of men and women. In general, women are shorter, less muscular, more rounded, wider in the hips, and narrower in the waist and shoulders; they also have larger breasts, female reproductive organs, less body hair, and a lower incidence of receding hairlines. Sex researchers from both the social structural camp and from the social evolutionary camp agree that these are biological differences, and both camps agree that biology interacts with social structure to produce larger sex differences (Eagly & Wood, 1999). In many cultures, including our own, these biological qualities have been exaggerated to communicate gender even more clearly (Morris, 1977). In past years, women wore corsets to exaggerate their narrow waists and to enhance their breasts and bustles to increase their hip size. Men have worn shoulder pads and epaulets to give the appearance of wider shoulders, codpieces to exaggerate the size of their penises, and elevator shoes to unobtrusively add to their height. Women have shaved their legs and armpits for centuries—and today almost their entire bodies—in a virtual war on hair, to amplify the fact that they have less body hair than men.

The War on Hair

Hair is a powerful secondary, biological sex characteristic; men have significantly more facial and body hair than women. Hairiness has always been associated with masculinity and hairlessness with femininity. In many parts of the world, especially in Western cultures and the United States in particular, women have emphasized their femininity by the removal of body hair, particularly on the face, legs, and under the arms. This practice dates back to a number of ancient societies in Greece, Rome, Turkey, and the Pacific Islands (Toerien, Wilkenson, & Choi, 2005). John Ruskin, the Victorian writer and critic, reportedly fainted on his wedding night when his wife displayed pubic hair and was not smooth and hairless like the classic statues of Greece and Rome (Kingston, 1999). Hairlessness is a textbook example of tertiary gender cue; hair removal for women accentuates a secondary, biological difference between men and women.

In the United States and other countries such as Australia, England and much of the Western world, more than 90% of women routinely and regularly remove the hair from their legs, underarms, pubic region, and face (Toerien et al., 2005). In fact, depilation is now normatively and routinely associated with femininity such that women would feel embarrassed and unattractive without the removal of most body hair. American women spend half a billion dollars a year at spas and medical centers removing their hair (Stainburn,

Increasingly throughout the world, women remove body hair to accentuate stereotypical femininity.

2006). The normal, unaltered female body is now believed by men and women to be unfit for public presentation and associated with poor hygiene and disgust (Tiggemann & Lewis, 2004; Toerien et al., 2005). It is also widely believed that starting in adolescence body hair creates the perception of women as less sociable, less happy, unfeminine, animalistic, more aggressive, and less attractive, particularly to men (Basow & Braman, 1998; Tiggemann & Kenyon, 1998; Tiggemann & Lewis, 2004; Toerien & Wilkenson, 2003). Interestingly, even feminist women subscribe to these beliefs about the benefits of hairlessness (Basow & Braman, 1998). In short, the supposedly "ideal" woman of today is virtually hairless, like her prepubescent state, and as far from the mammalian heritage as possible.

Today the war on hair has been extended to the male body. Although ancient Greek and Roman cultures placed a premium on a hairless male body (Boroughs, Cafri, & Thompson, 2005), throughout most of human history a hairy body was a sign of masculinity (Toerien et al., 2005). Recently this has begun to change; male hairlessness is "in." Of course, shaving the face has been a common practice by many men during many periods of history, producing a more "civilized," less animalistic, and more feminine appearance in men. However, in the United States and other Western countries, the war on hair has been extended to men's entire bodies, particularly to their chests and backs, though not to their legs. During most of the twentieth century hairy chests were a sign of masculine pride, virility, and strength. Today, hairy chests and backs are considered nasty, unclean, and out of fashion. Recent research indicates that almost two-thirds of American men engaged in body depilation below the neck, particularly the abdomen, chest, and even the groin (Boroughs et al., 2005). In Japan men's-only *estute* salons are widely used to remove body hair. Men that try greater hairlessness report increased feelings of cleanliness, sex appeal, and muscular definition (Miller, 2003). Japanese women believe that body hair, especially back and chest hair, is gross and they describe the ideal man as smooth. In America more than half the men who had body hair removed reported that friends and acquaintances had noticed their depilation and normally reacted favorably (Boroughs et al., 2005).

Proxemic Behavior

INTERPERSONAL DISTANCE

A number of studies have shown that in same-sex dyads, women interact at closer distances than do men (for a summary see J. A. Hall, 1984), although men are more likely than women to lean forward during interaction (Guerrero, 1997). Because women are generally smaller than men, one would expect them to interact at closer distances. But size is not the entire explanation. Even when controlling for body size, research has found that women still interact at closer distances than men. Even though women's arms are shorter than men's, women tend to interact at distances closer than an arm's length, whereas men interact with other men at more than arm's length (Aiello, 1987). The belief that women are more interactively intimate than men may be due in part to their tendency toward closer, more intimate interaction distances. One recent study, however, found that psychological gender is a better predictor of interpersonal distance than biological sex, with feminine people interacting at closer distances regardless of sex (Uzell & Horne, 2006). Since closer distances are associated with more, not less power (Hall et al., 2005), this may be one arena where women are more dominant than men.

Interestingly, when men and women interact with one another, they adopt the closer, more intimate interaction distance that women, not men, typically employ. Opposite-sex interaction is an area where women often have more power than men: the power to make men interact more intimately than they typically would man to man. Indeed, women may have a unique effect on men—the ability to make men more sensitive and intimate.

Men require and are given more space than women. They tend to have larger offices and use more space when they are working, relaxing, sitting, and standing (see Aiello, 1987; see also chapter 12). Some researchers have attributed men's greater spatial needs to their larger body sizes, but these differences seem to be based in part on power and status differences between men and women. Even today women, despite so much progress in the workplace, hold few of the very top jobs in business and politics. Because men hold the majority of very high-status jobs and because with status comes greater, more remote, and more commanding space, men at the top have larger territories than most women. Likewise, sex-role socialization encourages boys to venture out and explore their environment, whereas girls are encouraged to stay closer to home.

BODY ORIENTATION

Research has also shown that women are more likely to face their interaction partners than are men (Guerrero, 1997; Hall, 1984). A more direct orientation is perceived as warmer and more immediate and may make it easier for women to receive nonverbal cues from their interaction partners.

CROWDING

Studies of crowding and density have shown a fairly consistent sex difference. Interpersonal density is an objective measure of the number of people in a given area. As the number of people in an area increase, humans often experience crowding, a negative, subjective feeling of not having enough space. Women seem to experience less negative feelings of crowding in high-density situations (Aiello, 1987). Men are more likely to react negatively to crowding and even become physically violent when crowding is excessive.

SPATIAL ABILITY

One of the larger differences between the sexes is spatial ability. Just as it is likely that women's general superiority in nonverbal receiving ability (more on this later in the chapter) is primarily a biological difference, so it is likely that men's greater ability in spatial and navigational skills is also biologically based (see Andersen, 1998a, 2006; Gaulin, 1992). Gaulin (1992) concluded that among well-documented sex differences, men are more adept than women at visuospatial tasks. Gaulin contends, "Such explanations can only be evolutionary. When psychological features under study are widely distributed across human societies and are also present in nonhuman mammals the argument that they are cultural epiphenomena is substantially weakened" (1992, p. 127). This male advantage appears across an impressive array of spatial tasks, including object rotation, water-pouring and water-tipping tasks, field independence, tracking tasks, and spatial memory tasks (Andersen, 1998a, 2006; Voyer, Nolan, & Voyer, 2000). Although men's greater competence in some of these tasks may be due to practice, other tasks, such as the water-tipping task, are not stereotypically "male tasks." Halpern (1986) reasoned, "It does not seem likely that males have more or better experience with a tipped glass of water. In fact, one could argue that females, the primary cooks and dishwashers in many homes, might have more related experience with tipped glasses of water and other liquids than males" (p. 151).

Men and women generally employ different strategies when attempting to perform spatial tasks. Men try to visualize the entire pattern. When finding their way while driving or walking, most men tend to view themselves on a map of the entire terrain, whereas women tend to rely on landmarks and verbal labels (Gaulin, 1992).

As we will see later in the chapter, women's right brain hemispheres may have evolved to be particularly sensitive to interpersonal nonverbal cues, whereas men's right brain hemispheres may have evolved to specialize in nonverbal cues involving spatial perception (see chapter 1 for more on this issue). Of course, none of this means that men are insensitive or that women can't navigate, only that each sex has some general predispositions that are likely biologically based.

Kinesic Behavior

FACIAL EXPRESSIONS

Men and women clearly differ is in their use of facial expressions. Studies have shown that women are much more expressive in the face than men and reveal their emotions more accurately and more frequently than men (Brody & Hall, 1993; Broverman, Vogel, Broverman, Clarkson, & Rosenkrantz, 1972; Hall, 1978; Hess, Adams & Kleck, 2005; Thunberg & Dimberg, 2000). Men believe it is important to hide or conceal their emotions, even in close relationships (Aune & Aune, 1997). However, some of the difference is perceived rather than real; research shows that women's facial expressions are sometimes misinterpreted, consistent with the stereotype of the emotional female (Plant et al. 2000, Plant, Kling & Smith, 2004).

Perhaps the biggest gender difference in facial expressions is in smiling. Women smile considerably more than men (Ellis, 2006; Hall, 1984, 1998, 2006; Hall, LeBeau, Reinoso, & Thayer, 2001; LaFrance, 2002; LaFrance, Hecht & Paluck, 2003; Luxen, 2005; Weisfeld & Stack, 2002). It is more appropriate, even expected, that women smile (Hess, Adams & Kleck, 2005; LaFrance, 2002), and women are much more likely to smile when they are happy than are men (Coates & Feldman, 1996). The difference is most pronounced is in adolescence, when girls smile significantly more frequently than boys (LaFrance et al., 2003), but the effects persist in long-term married couples (Weisfeld & Stack, 2002). The fact that women smile more may be an advantage because people like people who show positive emotions. Women may be more able to communicate warmth and be more persuasive because they smile more than men (see chapter 10). However, women should not overdo it! When women overreact to happy events they are perceived as less appropriate and sincere than when men overreact to happiness (Hutson-Comeaux & Kelly, 2002), supporting a theory that gender-inconsistent emotional expressions are more sincere.

During interaction women typically display more emotion than men.

Women's ability to communicate positive emotions through their facial expressions may be due to a number of factors. If, indeed, women are more innately nurturant than men, positive facial expressions (including smiling) may have evolved as nurturing, comforting, and caregiving behaviors. Smiling, however, has many functions, so this may be only part of the story. Research has shown that smiling evolved in primates as a display of submission or appeasement, a sign of friendliness and harmlessness. Given the history of the oppression of women, smiling may have evolved as an important, naturally selected display to appease the larger, more aggressive males. Finally, research has shown that girls are rewarded for emotional expression, especially positive expressions like smiling, whereas young boys are rewarded for suppressing emotional displays. Women are more likely than men to smile in many contexts, including flirtation (McCormick & Jones, 1989). The coy smile in flirtation sequences is very characteristic of female but not male flirtation (Grammer, Kruck, Juette, & Fink, 2000). While to some degree these sex differences are certainly based on cultural gender roles, some research and theory suggests that testosterone inhibits smiling and evolved because smiling interfered with males' ability to intimidate rivals (Ellis, 2006).

Anger is one facial expression that men use more than women. A study by Coates and Feldman (1996) indicated that men are more likely to show their anger while they are feeling angry than are women. Whether men's higher level of anger expression is biological, cultural, or both is not certain. Women are perfectly capable of showing anger. When shown slides of angry facial expressions of men and women, people recognize anger regardless of gender, though angry men are perceived as angrier than angry women and angry women are often perceived as sad (Algoe, Buswell, & DeLamater, 2000; Plant et al., 2000; 2004). Anger is perceived as a more expected expression for men than for women, even for submissive men (Hess et al., 2005). Likewise, anger in men's facial expression is more quickly and easily recognized than anger displayed in the face of a woman (Goos & Silverman, 2002). Anger is a more socially acceptable emotion for men to exhibit but also may have roots in men's traditional biological sex role, the intimidation of rivals or threats, which may have genetically evolved (Ellis, 2006; Guerrero, Jones, & Boburka, 2006). But men must be careful. When men overreacted to angry events they were perceived as less appropriate and sincere than when women displayed excessive anger (Hutson-Comeaux & Kelly, 2002), again showing that gender-inconsistent emotional expressions are judged as more sincere.

The expression of other emotions is also gender related. Fear is displayed more frequently by women than by men, though there is no difference in the experience of fear (Thunberg & Dimberg, 2000). Research has shown that it is more appropriate for women than men to react with sadness in negative emotional situations, to cry and withdraw, and to express shame and guilt (Hess et al., 2000). By contrast, the study found that men should express happiness or serenity during negative emotional situations.

GESTURES

Gender differences in gestural behavior also exist (Hall, 1984). As with other areas of expressive behavior, women are more likely to gesture than are men, although men tend to use larger, more expansive gestures. Not all studies, however, have shown a gender difference in gestural behavior (see Kennedy & Camden, 1983), so it is likely that this gender difference may vary from context to context. Overall, Hall's (1985) comprehensive review of gender differences shows that women gesture more than men.

BODY MOVEMENTS

Another kinesic gender difference is that men more often exhibit restless, fidgety hands and feet than do women (Hall, 1984). Probably, women are socialized to suppress such cues because they are not "ladylike." Men may be more restless in confined social situations because they have a greater predisposition to action and disinclination to quiet interaction. Some research suggests that women display more erect posture and use more forward leans than men (Hall et al., 2001). Research suggests that walking style distinguishes male and female walkers, and both a feminine body and more body motion while walking are associated with femininity and attraction (Johnson & Tassinary, 2005, 2007).

Considerable research suggests that women are better listeners than men; and a recent study of American college students suggests that women nod more during conversation than men, supporting the idea that women are more sensitive and responsive receivers (Hellweg-Larsen, Cunningham, Carrico, & Pergram, 2004). A study of South African students found no sex differences between backchannel behaviors, such as nods, for men and women. However, both sexes tended to backchannel more to women speakers than to men (Dixon & Foster, 1998). In both the previous studies lower-status people nodded more to higher-status people, suggesting that power may be more predictive of nodding than is sex or gender.

KINESIC DIFFERENCES IN DOMINANCE AND AFFILIATION

Research has extensively examined gender differences in the communication of dominance and affiliation. In general, women show more affiliative kinesic behavior including more laughing, smiling, and open body postures (Algoe et al., 2000; Halberstadt and Saitta, 1987; Hess et al., 2005; Luxen, 2005; Weisfeld & Stack, 2002). However, these are not necessarily submissive; smiling and laughing are often dominant behaviors (Hall et al., 2005; Mast & Hall, 2004a). Men show more dominant behaviors including side-to-side head shaking, anger and disgust expressions, and sitting in a closed posture (Hess et al., 2005; Luxen, 2005). Women display some dominant kinesic behaviors as well, such as more facial expressiveness (Hall et al., 2005). Like other behaviors, some researchers find more similarities than differences in kinesic behavior between men and women and little association with dominance (Halberstadt & Saitta, 1987, Hall et al., 2005). The situation is probably more important than gender in predicting behavior, for as Halberstadt and Saitta (1987) concluded, "Males' and females' nonverbal behaviors are very similar when observed in natural settings" (p. 268).

Oculesic Behavior

As we saw in chapter 2, women are much more visually oriented than are men. Women look more at other people, attempt to make more eye contact, and are also looked at more than men. This is the case when they are speaking, listening, during silences, and even while flirting (Bente, Donaghy, & Suwelack, 1998; Grammer et al., 2000; Guerrero, 1997; Hall, 1984; McCormick & Jones, 1989; Mulac, Studley, Wiemann, & Bradac, 1987). Women use more short glances than men in flirtation situations to signal interest in a man (Grammer et al., 2000), but women's greater eye contact persists in long-term married couples (Weisfeld & Stack, 2002). The highest levels of eye contact occur between two conversing women, the lowest levels between two men; the level is somewhere in between for male-female interactions. The considerably higher level of oculesic activity that occurs between two women partly explains why women are more sensitive to nonverbal communication cues, particularly since so many nonverbal cues are visual. Mulac et al. (1987) have found, however, that although female-female dyads exhibit high levels of gaze, female-male dyads (like male-male dyads) exhibit less gaze. Unlike proxemic behavior in mixed-sex dyads—in which males adopt the female interpersonal distance—gaze behavior shows that females in mixed-sex dyads accommodate to the male oculesic norm.

Several explanations have been offered for women's greater oculesic activity. Primate studies have shown that more submissive, less powerful members of a species are more visually attentive because they are wary of the stronger, more dominant animals. Given women's history of oppression by men, visual attentiveness may have evolved as both a naturally selected, genetic behavior and a learned response within oppressive cultures. However, gazing is sometimes associated with more power, not less (Hall et al., 2005). Other perspectives suggest that as women learn to be more socially oriented and responsive, they accordingly use more eye contact. Finally, listeners look more than speakers during interaction, and women both listen more and listen more attentively than men.

Vocalic Behavior

One fairly basic biological difference between men and women is the pitch of the voice. After puberty, men's vocal cords thicken, producing a biological difference in pitch between men's and women's voices. Like the physical-appearance cues discussed earlier, men and women may exaggerate these sex differences according to their specific gender roles. Many men speak in low-pitched or harsh voices to exaggerate their masculinity, and many women use high-pitched, breathy voices to emphasize their femininity. However, some gay males may speak in a higher pitch to distinguish themselves from straight men as a gender group.

LaFrance and Mayo (1978) have shown that women are socialized to use their voices differently than men. Women use more vocal variation (Hall et al., 2005) and often end sentences in a rising pitch, implying a qualified answer or a lack of certainty (Lakoff, 1975). Men are more likely to use louder voices, consistently associated with power (Hall et al., 2005). In chapter 3 we discussed positive and negative aspects of the voice. Research has shown that men are more likely than women to lapse into negatively perceived vocal dysfluencies, such as false starts, stutters, and speech interruptions (Hall, 1984). Likewise, men speak in louder voices than women.

Some studies have shown that men interrupt more than women during conversations (Burgoon, Buller, & Woodall, 1996; Crawford, 1994; Hall et al., 2005). Men's alleged tendency to interrupt may be due to (1) their need to assert dominance, (2) the belief that women's talk is unimportant, or (3) insensitivity to others' turns at talking. Researchers, however, do not consistently find sex differences in interrupting. For example, Dindia (1987) reported no sex differences in terms of interrupting or being interrupted. Instead, in her very thorough study, she reports that both sexes are more likely to engage in cross-sex interruptions rather than same-sex interruptions.

Haptic Behavior

Contrary to common stereotypes, there is little evidence that men touch women more than women touch men. Where touch-related sex differences are found, they are very small (Guerrero & Andersen, 1994; J. Hall, 1984, 1996; Hall & Veccia, 1992; Major, Schmidlin, & Williams, 1990; Stier & Hall, 1984). There is, however, evidence that men initiate touch more than women in casual dating relationships and that women initiate touch more than men in marital relationships (Willis & Briggs, 1992). Some evidence shows that women are the recipients of more touch from both men and women (Major et al., 1990), although more recent data suggest that this is true only in the early stages of a relationship. Overall, research has found cross-sex touch to be almost entirely reciprocal (Guerrero & Andersen, 1994): That is, in couples in which one person doesn't touch very much, neither does the partner; in couples in which one person touches a lot, so does the partner. This evidence suggests mutual causality; men and women select individuals with similar touch preferences, and couples become more like each other as the relationship develops.

Despite beliefs to the contrary, there is also little evidence that touch primarily communicates power (see chapter 12) or that males touch females more when they are in positions of power (Hall & Veccia, 1992). Touch, especially opposite-sex touch, is much more likely to be perceived and employed as an immediacy or intimacy cue (see chapter 8) than as a power cue. Touch by waitresses, for example, has been consistently shown to be a warm behavior that increases tips (Ebesu-Hubbard, Tsuji, Williams, & Seatriz, 2003). Although touch is a behavior that mostly conveys immediacy and intimacy, it can also convey sexuality, comfort, and commitment for both males and females. One difference between the genders is that increasingly intimate touch—particularly intimate sexual touch— is more likely to be viewed as a sign of commitment by females than by males (Johnson & Edwards, 1991). As such, the potential for miscommunication increases in heterosexual relationships as tactile behavior escalates. During flirtation, women are more likely than men to use brief touches, whereas men are more likely than women to employ intimate touching.

A number of studies have shown that female-female touch is much more prevalent than male-male touch (Andersen & Leibowitz, 1978; Kneidinger, Maple, & Tross, 2001; Major et al., 1990; see chapter 7). Sports seems to be one area where men are more free to touch other men. Research shows, however, that women on sports teams actually touch each other more than do men, so even in this context same-sex touch is higher for women (Kneidinger et al., 2001). These findings are also consistent with research on touch attitudes. Studies show that men have more positive attitudes towards opposite-sex touch than do women. Conversely, women have more positive attitudes towards same-sex touch than do men, although these differences appear to be more pronounced in the United States than in other countries (Andersen, Andersen, & Lustig, 1987; Andersen & Leibowitz, 1978; Larsen & LeRoux, 1984; Willis & Rawdon, 1994; see chapter 7). Another take on these findings implies that both men and women are reluctant to touch men, a tendency that may lead to feelings of tactile deprivation among males.

Regarding self-touching behaviors, research shows that women are more likely to touch themselves than are men (Hall, 1984). Because self-touching behaviors are perceived as sensual or sexual by many observers, it could be that these cues are courtship or flirtation behaviors that call attention to a woman's body (Grammer et al., 2000; McCormick & Jones, 1989; Morris, 1977). However, self-touching behavior is also associated with anxiety and subordination, which given women's traditionally lower social status may provide an alternative explanation for women's self-touching patterns.

Nonverbal Receiving Ability

One of the most robust differences between the sexes is women's superior nonverbal receiving ability. Numerous studies have shown that women throughout the world are more accurate, sensitive receivers of nonverbal communication than are men, and they recall more nonverbal cues than men do (Hall, 1979, 1984, 1998, 2006; Hall, Murphy, & Mast, 2006; Keeley-Dyerson, Burgoon, & Bailey, 1991; Rosenthal, Hall, DiMatteo, Rogers, & Archer, 1979; Rosip & Hall, 2004). Research by Rosenthal and DePaulo (1979) showed a consistent female advantage in nonverbal receiving ability across eleven diverse nations. Hall (1979) also found that this female advantage was stable across the decades in which the study was conducted. Likewise, research suggests that these differences emerge early in life. Studies have found that 1- to 3-day-old girls tend to cry more than boys in response to another infant's cries but not to other sounds (Rosenthal et al., 1979).

Recently Hall et al. (2006) also found that women have better recall ability for nonverbal cues than do men. Interestingly, nonverbal recall ability was also correlated with better moods and increased smiling, suggesting that the ability to recall nonverbal behavior is associated with positive affective states. Alternatively, both increased smiling and nonverbal recall ability may be accidentally correlated and simply are both traits possessed by women.

Although it is probable that these differences are the result of both learned skills and biological differences, it is likely that receiving ability primarily represents a biological difference between men and women. Recent research in the field of genetics (Skuse, James, Bishop, & Coppin, 1997) suggests that the women's skill may be inherited through the X chromosome that women receive from their father! Women missing their father's X chromosome are socially inept and communicatively insensitive. Boys, of course, have only one X chromosome, and it comes from their mother. Unfortunately, the mother's X chromosome is not the one on which social skill is carried. This is not to say that sex differences of this type cannot be remediated. In the context of a laboratory experiment on nonverbal decoding, Keeley-Dyerson et al. (1991) reported that men's decoding ability improved after several trials, suggesting to the experimenters that there exists "the possibility that with practice, men can improve their decoding ability" (p. 601). This finding comports with research by Rosenthal et al. (1979), who found that some of the best decoders were students—men *and* women—who had completed a single course in nonverbal communication!

Several other explanations for women's superior nonverbal receiving ability have been offered: the gender explanation, the oppression hypothesis, and the social-rules perspective. The gender explanation says that differences in nonverbal receiving ability are due to a person's psychological gender rather than a person's biological sex. This does not seem to be the case, however. In her meta-analysis of eleven studies that correlated masculinity and femininity scores with nonverbal receiving ability, Hall (1979) concluded, "Overall the correlations between masculinity and femininity measured on unipolar scales with nonverbal decoding ability were small and nonsignificant" (p. 52). In short, nonverbal receiving ability is associated with being female but not with being feminine.

The oppression hypothesis posits that because of their low status and oppressed state, women must be more sensitive to nonverbal cues to ensure their survival. However, the data do not seem to support this hypothesis either. Hall (1978) revealed one flaw of the oppression hypothesis by showing that there is no age effect for the female advantage in nonverbal sensitivity: "That young girls should be better judges of nonverbal communication than young boys is inconsistent with this hypothesis, unless one seriously believes that young girls as well as women are oppressed in our society" (p. 354).

Other evidence casts further doubt on the oppression hypothesis. Hall (1979) has shown that women with more egalitarian attitudes are more, not less, sensitive to nonverbal communication. Similarly, she reports that women who subscribe to traditional sex roles have lower nonverbal receiving scores than less traditional women. Likewise, Hall and Halberstadt (1994) found that less subordinate women are better decoders of nonverbal communication than are more subordinate women. They conclude, "Although the subordination hypothesis has frequently been cited as an explanation for women's greater decoding skill compared to men, our results reveal serious difficulties for any simple version of this hypothesis" (p. 163).

Some scholars support the oppression, or subordination, hypothesis and offer methodological and conceptual criticisms of Hall's work (see LaFrance & Henley, 1997). Although the oppression hypothesis has not fared well in empirical tests, it should not be completely dismissed (see Hall & Halberstadt, 1997). Sex differences are complex processes and may be the result of complementary factors that enhance sex differences or competing factors that minimize sex differences.

The most plausible, nonbiological explanation for women's superior nonverbal receiving ability is the social-rules perspective (Noller, 1986). Noller provides evidence that women's decoding advantage disappears under certain circumstances: Men are just as accurate as women when they know the sender. Similarly, no sex difference is generally observed in detecting deception (see chapter 11). Noller maintains that women know the social rules for a situation better than men do, so that in situations that are rule-governed, they are more accurate decoders. In deceptive situations, however, the rules are ambiguous and often strategically manipulated, and in acquaintance situations general rules are unnecessary because unique relational rules govern the interaction. Of course, this perspective fails to specify how women acquire these rules. It may be that women are better observers, are socialized to be more empathic, or are genetically programmed to better process such information.

While little mention is made of biological explanations in the literature, there may be sex differences that produce greater nonverbal sensitivity in women. Hall (1978) concluded:

> Another kind of explanation, in its simplest form, would hold that females are wired from birth to be especially sensitive to nonverbal cues or especially quick learners of such cues. This would make evolutionary sense, because nonverbal sensitivity on a mother's part might enable her to detect distress in her youngsters or threatening signals from other adults, thus enhancing the survival chances of her offspring. (p. 854)

Andersen (2006) suggested that three mechanisms could produce sex-linked differences in nonverbal receiving ability: brain lateralization, chromosomal differences, and hormonal differences. Which, if any, of these mechanisms can explain sex differences in nonverbal receiving ability is a subject for future research.

Among the many advantages women have in nonverbal receiving ability is their greater skill at recognizing faces (Hall, 1984). It is unclear whether this is mainly an innate difference or whether women are socialized to, look more at others' faces and focus more on their appearance. Women's accuracy—but not men's accuracy—in receiving nonverbal messages is enhanced by the presence of an expressive, immediate sender (Bush & Connolly, 1984). This "nonverbal recall facilitation effect" may help explain why interactions among women are often highly involved, animated, and satisfying.

Nonverbal Sending Ability

As is the case with nonverbal receiving ability, women are better, more accurate senders of nonverbal messages than men (Buck, Miller, & Caul, 1974; Hall, 1984). Research has shown that women are generally more expressive than men (Buck, 1984). This is particularly true for positive emotional messages (Noller, 1986) conveyed through both facial expressions and other nonverbal channels as well, such as through vocal inflection, gestures, and attire. As discussed earlier, women are much more likely than men to smile across a wide variety of situations (Hall, 1984). Women are also more likely than men to encode virtually every facial expression except anger (Guerrero & Reiter, 1998). In general, women's nonverbal sending ability is an advantage because it allows others, particularly friends and family, to read the sender's mood. Sometimes, however, being poker-faced is beneficial, putting men at an advantage in some circumstances, such as during a business negotiation or during a confrontation with an adversary. Of course, how men and women send nonverbal messages is a function of maturation; as children and adolescents mature, they learn display rules and gradually reduce their sending of unmonitored nonverbal messages (Andersen, Andersen, & Mayton, 1985; see chapter 11).

Nonverbal Perceptions and Attributions

In the opening chapter of her book, *Gendered Relationships*, Julia Wood (1996) recalled a conversation with her four-year-old niece:

> When I asked her who she was she immediately replied, "I'm a girl." Only after declaring her sex did she proceed to describe her likes and dislikes, fam-

ily and so forth. In Western society, gender is fundamental to social life and to individuals' identities, roles and options. The influence of gender is evident in everything from social policies and laws to intimate interaction. (p. 3)

Our sex and gender roles affect our perceptions in many ways. As males and females, we perceive the world in different ways. Moreover, we are taught to view our own behavior and behavioral options through the lens of gender.

For years, literature on communication and gender has shown that boys and girls are taught to view their potential in different ways. Boys are taught to develop a view of themselves that features independence, assertiveness, and a virtually unlimited choice of potential occupations. Girls have traditionally been taught to view themselves as being dependent on family and on men, being submissive, and having a narrower range of potential occupational choices. Although women today have greater choices and more independence than at any time in history, they still are socialized into narrower and more conventional roles than men.

Another difference between men and women has to do with their perceptions regarding sexuality. Research has shown that men are much more likely to see sexual intent in the behavior of women than women intend to convey (Haselton, 2003; Levesque, Nave, & Lowe, 2006; Koukounas & Letch, 2001) though there is little difference based on psychological gender (Levesque et al., 2006). Men are more likely than women to view closer interpersonal distances, eye contact, increased touch, revealing clothing, and a variety of other warmth and friendship cues as more sexual in intent (Abbey & Melby, 1986; Koukounas & Letch, 2001; Major & Heslin, 1982; Metts & Spitzberg, 1996). For instance, men are much more likely than women to attribute sexual intent to a smile. In fact, men overattribute sexuality to situations that have no sexual intent, whereas women are likely to underattribute sexuality to situations that have sexual intent. Recent research suggests that physical attractiveness is overinterpreted as a sign of sexual interest to a greater degree than is friendliness (Levesque et al., 2006).

Differences in the perception of sexual intent in nonverbal behavior may help explain some common misunderstandings and behaviors. Because men overattribute sexuality to the behavior of female friends, they often suffer disappointment when a woman's warm nonverbal behavior is just a manifestation of friendliness, not sexual intent. Indeed, research has shown that socially incompetent men may engage in sexual coercion or assault when their expectations about receiving sex are not met (Spitzberg, 1998).

It is difficult to know if discrepant attributions about sexuality in everyday interaction represent biological or cultural differences between males and females. Sociobiologists contend that because frequent mating has greater biological value for males than for females, men are biologically programmed to see many nonverbal communication behaviors as sexual. Advocates of the different-cultures perspective argue that our society raises men and women to fulfill different roles; that is, society treats men and women as if they were members of different cultures (see Wood, 1997a). These different socialization and enculturation processes result in genders with different orientations, expectations, and worldviews.

Perceptual differences between men and women also occur in organizational settings. In a study by Eagly, Makhijani, and Klonsky (1992), men and women were asked to evaluate female and male managers. The managers were instructed to display either typically feminine or typically masculine leadership styles. The evaluators—particularly male evaluators—rated female managers more negatively than male managers when the leadership was carried out in a typically masculine style (that is, an autocratic or directive style). This sort of finding reveals that female managers may be in a bind due to these sexist views: They must either limit their repertoire of behaviors to traditionally feminine leadership styles or risk negative evaluation. Of course, females should not be evaluated on different or more stringent criteria than are males.

Relational Communication

A central function (perhaps the primary function) of nonverbal communication is the establishment of close interpersonal relationships with others (see chapter 9). Research shows that males and females are likely to establish somewhat different relationships with people of the same sex. Most of this research has suggested that women establish closer relationships with other women than men do with other men (see Wood & Inman, 1993). These findings may be due in part to two differences discussed earlier: Women are emotionally more expressive than men, particularly in communicating positive emotions; and women are more likely to accurately perceive emotions in other people. Thus, the highest exchange of warm emotional communication typically occurs in interactions between women. This suggests that women may develop closer, more intimate relationships than men.

Another perspective suggests that part of this difference is actually a bias in favor of the way women express intimacy (Bate, 1988; Wood & Inman, 1993). Whereas women express intimacy through physical expression, nonverbal warmth, and emotional expression, men convey intimacy through shared activities and experiences (Duck, 1988). For men, intimacy may be more likely to occur between teammates during a sports event or between friends going for a run or taking a fishing trip. Helping one another out or partying and drinking together may be more masculine ways of communicating closeness. This suggests that from a man's perspective, there is no distinction between emotionally expressive communication and task communication; sharing a task or activity is expressive communication. In fact, when men and boys express intimacy, it may look more like aggression than affection. Males may punch each other in the arm, give each other high fives, or play fight as expressions of affection.

Always remember that men and women are more similar in their intimacy needs than they are different. Although men tend to express intimacy in terms of shared activity more than women do, both men and women find disclosure and emotional expression more important than activity sharing. As Wood and Inman (1993) noted, men and women both value friendship, seek intimacy, and desire warm, close, validating, and satisfying connections. As is so often the case in "sex differences" research, the similarities between men and women outnumber the differences.

REMEDIATION OF SEXISM

Though considerable progress has been made in raising people's consciousness about sexism, much remains to be done. A number of successful measures are being taken to defeat the negative effects of sexual stereotyping. Many couples are actively practicing role sharing. At one time, few women worked outside the home as either primary or secondary breadwinners. Today, the vast majority of women are in the workforce, many with excellent careers as businesswomen and professionals. At the same time, men are realizing that child rearing and even homemaking are fulfilling functions missed by many men who rarely spend much time with the family or in the home. Moreover, recent advances in telecommuting have made it possible for both men and women to integrate family, home, and work.

Although sexual harassment has probably diminished in the last several decades, it still occurs and is unacceptable. Even when men are not engaging in sexual harassment, a woman in the presence of highly dominant male nonverbal behavior, such as nearly continuous gaze while speaking, may perceive harassment with the possible result of reducing her job performance (Kelly, Murphy, Craig, & Driscoll, 2005). Male supervisors would be wise to tone down their most dominant nonverbal behaviors so as not to be perceived as harassing and possibly impairing their employees' performance.

Another imperative change facing our society is freeing women from the nightmare of sexual assault. Statistics reveal the horrifying fact that every woman has a one-in-three chance of being the victim of sexual assault in her lifetime (Ullman & Knight, 1992). Moreover, virtually all women live with the fear of sexual assault and often limit their activity as a result. Limitations on women's proxemic and chronemic freedoms may be the ultimate form of sexism. In the past few decades, women have taken a number of proactive measures to stop this sexual terrorism. Women have insisted on the prosecution of sexual predators, armed themselves, taken self-defense classes, and organized rallies to "take back the night."

Several studies have shown that conscious alterations in a woman's nonverbal behavior can reduce the chance of becoming the victim of an attack or sexual assault. Studies report that rape victims often signal their vulnerability to rapists through the use of submissive nonverbal behaviors and revealing clothing (Edmonds & Cahoon, 1986; Grayson & Stein, 1981; Richards, Rollerson, & Phillips, 1992). Murzynski and Degelman (1996) found that students and police officers perceived that women with either longer or shorter strides, more lateral weight shifts, more one-sided limb movements, and more lifted-foot movements were more vulnerable to rape. Research that surveyed convicted felons found that they use a number of nonverbal cues to identify potential assault victims. The felon's most likely victim is a female who is wearing fancy clothing or visible jewelry, appears intoxicated, looks physically weak, takes short steps, and does not swing her arms. Similarly, looking worried, looking away, and avoiding stares were associated with victimization (Mezzakappa & Andersen, 1996). Knowledge of these subtle nonverbal behaviors may offer protection for both women and men against the horror of assault.

SUMMARY

Men and women are not from different planets. Although some sex differences in nonverbal communication do exist, men and women are far more similar than they are different. Furthermore, these relatively small differences are due to both biology and learned, cultural differences. Men and women can be active agents in changing their nonverbal behavior to become more effective communicators.

Men and women are somewhat different in physical appearance. Men are larger and more muscular, have more body hair, and have male sex organs. Women have wider hips, larger breasts, more subcutaneous body fat, and female sex organs. Beyond these anatomical differences, women have been socialized to be more concerned than men about their physical appearance. Disturbingly, women have traditionally been valued for how their bodies look, not what they can do: Women's physical attractiveness is more important to men than men's physical attractiveness is to women. A second disturbing finding is that despite all this emphasis on physical beauty, the more successful a woman is occupationally, the more her physical attractiveness is a disadvantage rather than an advantage, which poses a genuine double bind for women.

Men stand farther apart from one another than do women during interaction. However, when a man and a woman interact with each other, the man adopts the interaction distance of the woman. Women are more likely to face their interaction partner directly. In general, men have better spatial and navigational skills than women; this may be a biologically based sex difference.

Women are more facially expressive than men and more attuned to the facial expressions of others. This is particularly true for smiling, which women do more frequently than men. Men are more likely to show anger in their faces. Women tend to gesture more than men, although men's gestures are more expansive than women's. Despite these differences, the kinesic behavior of men and women is highly similar.

Women look at other people more than men do and are looked at more than men are; this is true while they are speaking or listening and even during silences. Women are probably better senders and receivers of nonverbal communication because they look more and are looked at more.

Men have deeper voices than women. Both men and women tend to exaggerate these biological differences to emphasize their masculinity and femininity, respectively. Women speak more softly than men and often use vocal variations that qualify an answer and signal uncertainty. Some studies suggest that men interrupt more than women.

Men and women exhibit fewer differences in tactile behavior than once assumed, and those differences that do exist are often due to other factors such as relational stage. Men initiate more touch in the beginning stages of a romantic relationship, whereas women initiate more touch in marital relationships. Touch is more likely to signal immediacy and warmth than power when used by men or women. In opposite-sex relationships, touch is highly reciprocal; men and women touch each other about the same amount. In same-sex relationships, women touch considerably more than men, at least in American culture.

Women are better receivers of virtually every type of nonverbal behavior than are men. This heightened sensitivity to nonverbal communication by women is probably biologically based but increased by socialization.

Regardless of the origins of sex differences in nonverbal communication, biology is not destiny. Men and women can alter their abilities, attitudes, and behaviors to become more effective nonverbal communicators.

Part II

Affective Exchanges

FEELINGS AND NONVERBAL COMMUNICATION

6

Nonverbal Communication of Emotion

"So, what—your advice is . . . hire someone I'm not happy with and be happy?"
—Dr. Gregory House from *House MD*

"You mope around like a dog that likes to get kicked. You make me sick."
—Alex from *Grey's Anatomy*

". . . those feelings are starting to bleed into my business."
—Tony Soprano from *The Sopranos*

In the media as in everyday interaction, emotional expression is a central aspect of life. Emotional communication is mostly nonverbal, which evolved so that people can quickly read our emotions and we can read theirs. In daily communication, talking about our feelings is common, but spontaneously revealing feelings through nonverbal communication is much more common. Revealing our feelings verbally is too personal and "uncool." The natural system of communicating emotion is nonlinguistic, analogic, nonverbal communication (see chapter 1). Research suggests that emotions are more than private experiences; they are interpersonal information to be shared (Andersen & Guerrero, 1998b; Parkinson, 2005).

The brain is hardwired to communicate our emotions through nonverbal communication. Yet increasingly research suggests that nonverbal communication is much more than expression (Russell, Bachorowski, & Fernandez-Dols, 2003); emotions communicate intent that is designed biologically and individually to influence others. There are close connections between emotions and nonverbal communication. You learned in chapter 1 that nonverbal communication is primarily processed in the right brain hemisphere. Not surprisingly, as Silberman and Weingartner (1986) stated, "the right hemisphere is specialized for processing the emotional aspects of communication" (p. 323). Likewise, Mandal and Ambady (2004) stated, "the evidence for right hemisphere involvement in emotional perception and expression is overwhelming (p. 26). Pizzagalli et al. (1998), who studied the electrical activity in the brains of normal people, concluded that affect [emotion] is associated with the right brain hemisphere. Furthermore, the right hemisphere seems to have greater control over negative emotions (Mandal & Ambady, 2004; Pizzagalli et al., 1998). In this chapter we will explore the complex interrelationship between emotion and nonverbal communication. Although we will examine each emotion separately, in reality our feelings are complex combinations of many emotions. Rarely do we experience one emotion in isolation; rather, our feelings are complex arrays of mixed emotions.

Our discussion will begin with an examination of the genetic and cultural origins of emotions, including emotional intelligence and control. Next, we'll look at the three primary channels of emotional expression—the face, the voice, and the body—and then review fifteen separate emotions and their expression. Finally, we'll examine three principles that govern the inextricable relationship between emotional and nonverbal communication.

THE BASIC CHARACTERISTICS OF EMOTION

Although scholars differ to some extent on what makes up an emotion, six fundamental characteristics appear to comprise every human emotion.

1. *Emotions involve subjective experiences or feelings.* We know when we are experiencing an emotion because we feel angry, happy, ashamed, guilty, or one of many other feelings.

2. *Emotions are inherently valenced affectively*; that is, they always produce positive or negative feelings (see chapter 9 for more on this topic). There are no neutral emotions; all emotions involve pleasure or displeasure in response to stimuli (Guerrero, Andersen, & Trost, 1998).

3. *Emotions involve physiological arousal* and other physical reactions. Emotions can be monitored via changes in one's heart rate, respiration, electrical conductivity of the skin, brain temperature, and a host of other physiological functions.

4. *Most emotions interrupt our thoughts*, intrude on our cognitions, and require appraisals of the emotion and our reactions to it. People weigh the significance of an emotion cognitively; they judge whether it is desirable or undesirable, acceptable or unacceptable, controllable or uncontrollable, and so forth (Frijda, Kuipers, & ter Schure, 1989).

5. *Emotions are expressed behaviorally* (Andersen & Guerrero, 1998b). In virtually all cases, emotions produce intentional or unintentional changes in our behavior that result in the transmission of our emotional state to other people.

6. *Emotions are adaptive* in that they are innate reactions to stimuli that motivate the organism to adapt to the situation or the environment (Burgoon, Buller, & Woodall, 1996). In the evolution of humans and other primates, facial expressions associated with good and bad tastes warned others to avoid spoiled foods and to benefit from good foods (Erickson & Schulkin,

2003). Emotions motivate us to flee, fight, mate, express remorse, grieve, and to enact dozens of other beneficial human responses. If we as human beings were not biologically programmed to experience emotions, to act upon these feelings, and to share them with others, our ability to survive would be impaired—which brings us to the genetic and biological origins of emotional communication.

THE GENETIC ORIGINS OF EMOTIONAL COMMUNICATION

Emotions are internal control mechanisms, but they are much more than that. Emotions evolved as universal communication systems that promote the individual and group survival of human beings. Past research has revealed a high degree of similarity in the expression of emotions across virtually all cultures (Ekman, 1993; Izard, 1992; Scherer & Wallbott, 1994) and suggested that any behavior that is highly similar across many diverse cultures is likely to be biologically based.

More recent research suggests that accuracy is higher within cultures or groups, suggesting that emotional expressions are not all that universal (Dovidio, Hebl, Richeson, & Shelton, 2006; Elfenbein & Ambady, 2002), but other research points to methodological and conceptual problems with those studies and suggests that expressions are universal across culture (Beaupre & Hess, 2005; Matsumoto, 2002, 2006). Instantly recognizable displays of emotion had survival value for our species or they would not have evolved. Humans are hardwired to express their emotions through nonverbal communication (Andersen & Guerrero, 1998b; Dillard, 1998). As DePaulo (1992) stated, "There may be automatic links between the elicitation of an emotion for nonverbal but not for verbal behavior" (p. 205). Instant nonverbal emotional communication allows us to understand the moods and emotional states of other people and to adjust our behavior accordingly. When people communicate their anger, we can avoid them and thus avert potentially dangerous—and even deadly—conflicts. People who express warm, happy emotions show they are available as friends, partners, or mates (see chapter 9 for more on nonverbal communication in intimate relationships). Indeed it is believed that emotional expressivity not only creates attraction and positive first impressions, it also stimulates specific regional brain activity that engenders trust and positive feelings (Boone & Buck, 2003), creating a more cohesive and resilient dyad or group. Similarly, people who express shame or guilt for their transgressions have a greater chance of being accepted back into the group rather than being isolated, ostracized, or even killed.

Emotional recognition is a spontaneous, genetic, nonsymbolic, nonlinguistic process that is one of the most basic functions of nonverbal communication (Andersen, Garrison, & Andersen, 1979; Buck, 1984; Schmidt & Cohn, 2001). In an imaginative study Scherer and Ceschi (2000) secretly videotaped the behavior of people who lost their luggage at an international airport. Later he also interviewed both the agent filing the lost luggage reports and the passengers who had lost their luggage. Interestingly, the nonverbal behavior of the passengers correlated more substantially with the agents' rating of their emotions than with their own rating of their emotions. Emotions are more than private experiences; emotions are expressions that are produced communicatively for the benefit others. Emotional communication permits most people to adjust to the behavior of others to facilitate cooperative rather than conflictual relationships. Most humans are remarkably successful in harmoniously adjusting to their social group and culture.

Finally, as we will learn later in the chapter, emotions are contagious. Seven different mechanisms posit explanations for the contagiousness of emotions, but this much we know: When people communicate they are likely to imitate each other and like each other better as a result (Chartrand & Bargh 1999; Lakin, Jefferis, Cheng, & Chartrand, 2003) and experience similar emotions. These universal mechanisms of alignment are central to all the processes of human communication and gave humans an advantage over less social and aligned creatures. This brings us to the next foundation of emotional expression—socialization and culture.

SOCIALIZATION, CULTURE, AND EMOTIONAL EXPRESSION

In every culture, children learn the appropriate expressions of emotions and how to read emotions through a process called socialization. All over the world, infants and very young children differ little in how, when, and where they express their emotions. A compilation of studies reveals that family emotional expressiveness and children's emotional expressiveness are highly correlated particularly for positive expressiveness (Halberstadt & Eaton, 2002), suggesting that socialization of emotional expression is strong. As children mature, each culture and family shapes and teaches children rules for emotional expression. Children that are secure in their early attachment are more open, happy, and expressive than children with insecure attachments (Becker-Stoll, Delius, & Scheitenberger, 2001; also see chapter 9). Children are great imitators, and as they grow up they imitate the behaviors modeled by their parents, siblings, and friends (Andersen & Guerrero, 1998b; Saarni, 1993). They learn how to express and read emotions in the context of their families. Interestingly, a meta-analysis by Halberstadt and Eaton (2002) showed that family and children's negative expressiveness is curvilinearly related to age; young children are very much like their parents, pre-teens and teens are less like their parents, and young adults again are similar in expressiveness to their parents. This is consistent with abundant research which shows that teens actively try to act different than their parents only to become like them again as adults.

Sadly, some parents are poor at recognizing emotions in their offspring, and this can put their children at risk in several ways. One study has shown that severely obese children are more likely than normal-weight children to come from homes where mothers have poor ability to read emotions and provide food to treat every kind of distress (Baldero, Rossi, Caterina, Codispoti, Balsomo, & Trombini, 2003). Recently, a dyadic effect has been observed for the ability to read emotions in interpersonal interaction (Elfenbein, Foo, Boldry, & Tan, 2006). This means that some interacting dyads are more or less accurate than others, something which could not be accounted for with their individual scores. In short, some people click emotionally and others are not in sync with each other.

A major agent for the socialization of emotional expression is the media, particularly television, film, and the Internet (Wilson & Smith, 1998). Of course, this is why many parents are concerned about the content of television, film, and even the Internet, because children are apt to imitate even mediated behaviors, particularly those they view frequently.

Emotional Intelligence

Over the past decade emotional intelligence has become recognized as a vital component of social skill and a real aspect of human intelligence (Mayer, Solovey, Caruso, & Sitarenios, 2001). Researchers have recognized that emotional intelligence is actually a set of abilities that are vital to effective functioning in interpersonal relationships as well as one's career.

Step 1: Recognizing Emotions.   Some people are emotionally clueless. Emotionally intelligent people can recognize their own emotions and those of others. Failure to recognize emotions in oneself, and especially in others, leads to social incompetence and risks incorrectly perceiving anger, sadness, love, and a host of other emotions. People are better at judging the emotions of friends than of strangers. In judging concealed negative emotions we can read casual friends better than we read close friends, probably because of the distress that reading negative emotion in a close friend could produce (Sternglanz & DePaulo, 2004). As will be illustrated throughout this chapter, emotions are mostly communicated nonverbally; so the most emotionally intelligent people must tune into facial expression, tone of voice, gestures, and other sources of nonverbal emotional information.

We usually think of doctors as intelligent people, but many doctors do a poor job of reading the emotions of their patients—a skill that has proved to be critical to patient healing and satisfaction (Roter, Frankel, Hall, & Sluyter, 2006). This may be because doctors have little training in communication or because they are looking at the medical chart and not at the patient.

People with right hemispheric problems such as strokes and brain injuries (P. A. Andersen et al., 1979) and attention-deficit hyperactivity disorder (Pele et al., 2006) have considerable difficulty recognizing common facial expressions of emotion. This suggests that emotional intelligence resides in a different part of the brain than linguistic skill or logic.

Step 2: Emotions as Data.   Recognizing emotions is one thing; interpreting their meaning and significance is another. The data in our emotions is as important as a textbook or a spreadsheet; they contain a wealth of information. Our emotions and those of other people should be thought of as a window into what makes people tick and should determine how we react interpersonally. Asking why you feel angry, frightened, or joyful will provide some important insights.

Step 3: Thinking about Emotions.   Generally emotions are all about feelings, not about thought. As indicated above, emotions evolved to produce quick reactions. Human survival depended on quick emotional responses. Today, however, you cannot flee a stressful meeting, attack a romantic rival, or cry every time someone at work says something hurtful. Emotional intelligence means that once we receive emotional data, we must next try to understand what it means. The attribution, appraisal, and processing of emotional information is at the heart of emotional intelligence.

Step 4: Managing Emotions. Of critical importance is how we behave in an emotional situation. On one hand, denying emotions can lead to emotional stress, emotional labor, and ill health. But showing every emotion we feel makes us act and look like a two-year-old, and nobody likes a romantic partner or a coworker that is an emotional basket case. As we mature we learn to control our emotions, though some people are far more successful in managing emotions than others. In the next section we move to a discussion of display rules: conventions for the effective and appropriate presentations of emotions.

Display Rules

A crucial part of emotional intelligence is learning when and when not to show emotions. Early in life most parents covertly and overtly shape the emotional behavior of their children. For example, mothers frequently gesture or whisper to their children to be quiet, to cheer up, or to stop making faces. Sometimes these are overt verbal instructions such as "Wipe that smile off your face," "Be a man, don't cry," or "That's not a very ladylike way to act!" In America, children—particularly girls—are punished for negative emotions such as anger (Guerrero & Reiter, 1998; Lemerise & Dodge, 1993). Fear and sadness are also discouraged, but most often for boys. These numerous processes of socialization modify the nonverbal expression of emotions through the use of display rules.

The socialization of emotional communication produces culturally based display rules (see chapter 11 for more on display rules relating to interpersonal deception). Facial expressions of emotion are pretty universal across human cultures except in cases where cultural display rules interfere (Mandal & Ambady, 2004). These learned display rules govern the appropriate expression or suppression of emotional communication displays (Andersen, Andersen, & Landgraf, 1985; Ekman & Friesen, 1975; Saarni, 1993). For example, exaggerated anger displays may be appropriate on a football field but not in the classroom. Public displays of affection may be considered inappropriate and "tacky," but the same affectionate displays might be appropriate and desirable in private. Humans control the expression of emotion by employing the following five display rules.

SIMULATION

Simulation occurs when we show emotions we are not feeling (Andersen, Andersen, & Landgraf, 1985; Shennum & Bugental, 1982). We may smile when receiving a gift even before opening it so as not to hurt the giver's feelings. We may feign astonishment at a surprise party that we knew about in advance. And we may laugh at a boss's joke, even if it wasn't funny, just to be polite. Children learn these behaviors early. For example, toddlers cry to get attention even when they are not hurt.

INTENSIFICATION

Sometimes we need to show stronger feelings than we are experiencing internally, a process called intensification or maximization (Andersen, Andersen, &

Landgraf, 1985; Saarni, 1985). Unlike simulation, intensification involves experiencing a milder form of the emotion than one communicates. Examples of intensification would be crying at the funeral of an uncle you neither knew very well nor liked, or acting warmly and affectionately toward your boyfriend or girlfriend even though you're physically and emotionally exhausted at the end of a hard day.

MINIATURIZATION

The opposite of intensification is miniaturization, also known as minimization or deintensification (Andersen, Andersen, & Landgraf, 1985; Saarni, 1993). Miniaturization is a product of socialization. As children develop and mature, they gradually decrease their show of emotion (Andersen, Andersen, & Mayton, 1985). Children as young as two years old use miniaturization (Saarni, 1993). Examples of miniaturization in children include frowning rather than throwing a temper tantrum and showing less fear than they are actually experiencing. Teens may smile faintly at a really funny joke or express less overt affection for a partner that they really like in order to "play it cool." Adults show only mild pride to appear humble when receiving an award of which they are very proud. Similarly, people may show only mild surprise even though they are intensely surprised over the news of a friend's divorce. Recent research indicates that the full surprise expression is rarely seen in social interaction by adults or infants; instead surprise is often miniaturized, completely inhibited, or manifested through attentiveness or stillness (Camras et al., 2002; Reisenzein, Bordgen, Holtbernd, & Matz; 2006).

INHIBITION

Sometimes, to be socially appropriate, people attempt to show no emotion even though they are truly experiencing an emotion—a process called inhibition or neutralization (Andersen, Andersen, & Landgraf, 1985; Ekman, 1978). Examples include hiding your attraction to someone else when your boyfriend or girlfriend is present, holding back tears when you are really upset and ready to cry, and keeping a straight face when you think something is really funny. Inhibition is also evident during deception, when guilt, shame, duping delight, anxiety, and other emotions are concealed to avoid detection (Buller & Burgoon, 1998; O'Hair & Cody, 1994; see also chapter 11 for more on deception). Similarly, suspicious receivers of deceptive messages use inhibition to avoid tipping off the sender (Buller & Burgoon, 1998).

Inhibition of emotions is not always healthy. Boys' failure to show negative expressions to slides of violent or disgusting scenes is associated with a variety of violent and negative behaviors (Eisenberg et al., 2001). Kids from violent homes are less able to express emotions and are poorer decoders of others' emotions (Hodgins & Belch, 2000). Inhibited emotions may lead to violent outbursts. It is very rare to find reports of a mass murderer who is described as outgoing and expressive; inhibited, expressionless, and quiet are much more likely descriptors. Research on children who were victims of childhood sexual abuse shows that children who did not voluntarily disclose the abuse are much more likely to show shame and polite smiles than survivors who disclosed it (Bonanno et al., 2002). Internalizing emotions is often a dangerous thing (Buck, 1984) because failure to express emotions is associated with potentially dangerous physiological symptoms such as high blood pressure. Moreover, research showed that women who experience ambivalence about showing emotional expressions actually showed more negative expressions during conflict, producing negative reactions by their boyfriends (Heisel & Mongrain, 2004). Evidently, internalizing emotions leads to more negativity under stress.

MASKING

Sometimes people show a completely different emotion than they are feeling, a process called masking or substitution (Ekman, 1978; Saarni, 1993). Masking appears later in the developmental cycle than other display rules because it requires considerable communication skill to show a totally different emotion than one is experiencing (Saarni, 1993). Showing disappointment instead of glee over the straight flush you've been dealt when playing poker or feigning sadness over an enemy's misfortune are examples of masking. During deception, masking is a vital skill when substituting joy for guilt or calmness for anxiety (Buller & Burgoon, 1998; O'Hair & Cody, 1994, also see chapter 11).

Biological evolution and cultural socialization both play important roles in the communication of emotion. In the following sections, we will take a close look at the channels of emotional expression as well as the individual emotions and how they are communicated.

NONVERBAL CHANNELS OF EMOTION

The Face

For many people the communication of emotion is virtually synonymous with facial expressions (Planalp, 1998). Such a view is not naive, because the face is the main site of emotional communication. We are most likely to look at another person's face during social interaction to quickly assess her or his emotional state. Certainly, on some occasions the face directly expresses feelings; however more and more research suggests that the presence of receivers increases the likelihood of emotional expression, though on other occasions the presence of people deters emotional expression (Andersen & Guerrero, 1998b; Kraut & Johnston, 1979; Parkinson, 2005; Schmidt & Cohn, 2001). Studies show that bowlers rarely smile when they get a strike; only when they turn to face their friends does smiling occur (Kraut & Johnston, 1979; Ruiz-Belda, Fernandez-Dols, Carrera, & Barchard, 2003). Studies of Olympic gold medal winners show that both before and during the ceremony they smile only a very small percentage of the time, despite the fact they are certainly experiencing happiness (Fernandez-Dolz & Ruiz-Belda, 1995). After soccer goals and hockey goals fans rarely smile; it is only after they turn to their friends that smiling occurs (Kraut & Johnston, 1979; Ruiz-Belda, Fernandez-Dols, Carrera, & Barchard, 2003). These studies suggest that facial expressions are more than manifestations of internal states; they are socially stimulated nonverbal communication designed for viewing by communication receivers. This does not mean that most facial expressions are conscious or intentional. Remember, non-verbal communication is usually spontaneous and operates at low levels of awareness. As children mature, however, they develop posed smiles that look increasingly like spontaneous smiles, but interestingly, these are only deployed when others are watching (Schmidt & Cohn, 2001).

How do we know that a person's face conveys messages of affection, anger, fear, sadness, or joy? Ekman and Friesen (1975) discovered six basic facial expressions that are cross-culturally and universally identifiable: anger, surprise, disgust, fear, happiness, and sadness. In his taxonomy, Izard (1977) included Ekman's six basic expressions but argues for four additional basic emotions—contempt, shame, shyness, and guilt—each with its own unique facial display. The cross-cultural recognizability of these basic emotions suggests their innate, nonverbal, right-hemispheric origins (see chapter 1). Humans worldwide compare facial expressions to the ideal form of that expression to derive its meaning (Horstman, 2002). Facial expressions interact with eye contact such that approach-oriented emotions are more accurately perceived when accompanied by direct contact; avoidance-oriented emotions like fear and sadness are more easily read when eye contact is averted (Adams & Kleck, 2003, 2005).

Of course, practice or training in reading emotional facial expressions can improve recognition scores (Elfenbein, 2006; Grinspan, Hemphill, & Nowicki, 2003). Training in reading expressions has positive benefits for girls, improving their self-concept and lowering anxiety. For boys, however, training lowered social anxiety but also lowered self-concept (Grinspan et al., 2003). Evidently, in a boy's world it is not always beneficial to know what others are feeling! Research suggests that training in the recognition of facial expressions from cultures other than one's own provided the biggest benefits (Elfenbein, 2006). Practice in facial expression is also beneficial. Schnall and Laird (2003) had undergraduates practice one of three facial expressions—happiness, anger, and sadness—for four minutes, and then after two minutes rest had them pose the expression for four more minutes. Subsequent testing revealed that participants felt the emotion they portrayed, and they recalled more life events associated with that emotion as compared with other groups that did not have a chance to practice. In short, we feel what we express and we train ourselves to experience certain emotions.

Facial expressions are usually spontaneously communicated to others without conscious thought or linguistic representation. However, as we discussed previously, we clever humans can simulate facial expressions for feelings we don't have. Indeed, a primary form of strategic deception behavior involves managing facial displays. Deception researchers found that smiling and other pleasant facial expressions are often used to conceal deceit; positive facial expressions are more commonly used by deceivers than by truth tellers (Buller & Burgoon, 1998; see chapter 11). Most people, however, are unable to continuously control their facial expression and frequently leak their emotions for others to read. People also differ greatly in their ability to send messages of emotion facially. Likewise, a dyadic effect occurs in sending and receiving emotional facial expressions; some dyads are (better or worse) than one would expect from knowing their sending or receiving ability (Elfenbein, Foo, Boldry, & Tan, 2006).

The Voice

Everyone who has used a telephone knows that the voice conveys emotion; even when vocalic cues are the only available nonverbal behavior, we can still accurately identify other people's emotions. In fact, research shows that our accuracy in detecting emotions through vocal cues is nearly as good as our accuracy in identifying emotions through facial expressions, though vocal expressions of emotion are somewhat more easily recognized within one's own culture than cross-culturally (Planalp, 1998, Scherer, 2003). The ability to correctly interpret vocal cues increases over the years, and from preschool to adulthood it is associated with social competence and interpersonal adjustment (Rothman & Nowicki, 2004).

There is mounting evidence, however, that human vocalic behavior, like animal calls, is hardwired into our brains to produce beneficial communication. Recent research suggests that many forms of nonlinguistic vocal behavior have evolved to positively influence the emotions of other people (Owren & Bachorowski, 2003). A major recent summary of research shows that the voice is a primary channel of emotional communication and evolved as an instantaneous channel of nonverbal emotional information (Juslin & Laukka, 2003). Their summary also reveals that music has powerful cross-cultural emotional meaning and has been part of the same communication code system as vocal expression before the evolution of language.

Studies have shown that harsh tones of voice usually elicit crying in young infants throughout the world (Magai & McFadden, 1995), suggesting that emotional communication by voice is a hardwired, innate behavior. Research by Scherer and Wallbott (1994) has shown a cross-cultural similarity in the vocal expression of several emotions. Anger is expressed by yelling, screaming, shouting, and considerable vocal variation. Joy, for instance, is accompanied by higher pitch, more vocal variation, and, of course, laughing. Laughter is a fairly common interpersonal behavior occurring more than once every two minutes, which typically occurs following a person's own verbal expressions as well as those of others (Vettin & Todt, 2004). Laughter positively influences other people's emotions and creates positive impressions of the laugher. Laughing and smiling, but not verbal expressions of humor, also increase pain tolerance (Zweyer, Velker, & Ruch, 2004). Laughter is even produced in deaf and blind children, suggesting its evolutionary roots (Owren & Bachorowski, 2003). An entire profile of vocalic behaviors characterizes depression, including slower, quieter, halting speech; lower pitch; more vocal interruptions or hesitations (such as ah or um); and a more monotonous tone of voice (Segrin, 1998). Sadness is often expressed by crying or weeping, although it sometimes is expressed through silence. Interestingly, four emotions—fear, disgust, shame, and silence—are all communicated primarily through silence (Scherer & Wallbott, 1994). This illustrates the power of emotion not only to promote communication but also to inhibit or interrupt it (Guerrero, Andersen, & Trost, 1998).

Planalp and her associates (1998; Planalp, DeFrancisco, & Rutherford, 1996) showed that vocal cues are the most recognizable sign of emotions. Loudness and speed of talking were the most commonly reported vocal cues that indicated emotion was being expressed. Interestingly, unlike vocal cues, direct verbal cues were reported to be very uncommon in interpersonal interaction (for example, "Boy, I'm angry."). Vocal cues that last longer than half a second interact with facial expressions to determine the mood of an interactant (Pell, 2005).

One's voice is crucial in helping to comfort a person who is upset. Research by Burleson and Goldsmith (1998) showed that people are most successful in comforting an upset person when they provide emotional support, affection, and concern. Patients are more likely to heal more slowly, be dissatisfied, and file malpractice claims if health-care providers fail to be emotionally expressive and available (Roter, Frankel, Hall, & Sluyter, 2006). An important aspect of comforting is helping upset individuals to express themselves by asking leading questions and providing encouragement vocally with nonverbal backchannel cues (such as uh-huh and mm-hmm) that both legitimize a person's feelings and encourage verbal expression.

The Body

Like the face and the voice, the body is quite capable of expressing emotions. Planalp (1998) reports that people can easily interpret a person's emotional state from cues such as "being physically energetic, bouncy, jumping up and down, clenching hands or fists, making threatening movements, holding the body rigidly, shuffling, or having a slumped, droopy posture, dancing around, and using hand emblems" (p. 34). Research has revealed that certain postures convey attitudes. Studies by Bull (1987) have revealed that folded arms typically convey disagreement, whereas crossing one's legs is associated with positive affective interpretations such as friendliness and relaxation.

Although sign language is a verbal, linguistic form of communication (see chapter 1), research shows that signs also carry nonverbal emotional information much like the voice employs intonation (Hietanen, Leppanen, & Lehtonen, 2004). Recent research used computer-generated mannequins from which observers can infer a variety of emotions (Coulson, 2004). Researchers have also developed a test to measure the ability to judge emotions from people in both standing and sitting postures (Pitterman & Nowicki, 2004). Emotions can be reliably identified from postures, though the ability seems to develop over time, since younger individuals scored lowest in postural identification. Like other tests of nonverbal receiving ability, women tended to score better on this test (see chapter 5).

Some bodily shapes and movements seem to convey innate meanings. Round shapes, patterns, and movements of all types—including the eyes, breasts, oval faces, and smooth gestures—communicate warmth. Even newborn babies find rounded objects pleasant, suggesting that this is an instinctive preference. Angular or diagonal movements and bodily shapes, such as angry frowns and tense muscles, tend to convey threat (Aronoff, Woike, & Hyman, 1992).

Immediacy cues (see chapter 8) such as happy facial expressions, enthusiastic gestures, closer interpersonal distances, and friendly touches are potent indicators of warmth (Andersen & Guerrero, 1998a). Such cues have been shown to increase affection, intimacy, and attention in both interpersonal and classroom interactions, and they contagiously affect the emotional states of others. Recent research has shown that touch can convey at least six emotions—anger, fear, disgust, love, gratitude, and sympathy—in the absence of any other cues, at rates similar to those conveyed by facial expressions (Hertenstein et al., 2006). Moreover, outside observers watching such touches also can accurately identify their emotional meaning.

A number of physiological behaviors convey emotional states: blushing may convey shame or embarrassment; trembling often communicates fear or anxiety; penile erections and vaginal secretions may indicate sexual desire; heavy breathing can reveal sexual arousal or physical exertion; sweating often signals nervousness; and fidgeting may communicate anticipation or anxiety. No exact correspondence has been established between these behaviors and singular emotions, so caution should be exercised in interpreting such cues; many of these behaviors can convey more than one emotional state. For instance, although crying usually communicates sadness, in some social settings it can communicate sentimentality or even joy, such as crying at weddings or upon reuniting with old friends.

COMMUNICATING HUMAN EMOTIONS

Happiness

Happiness is one of the most positive human emotions. Happiness is so important to Americans that the Declaration of Independence guarantees "the pursuit of happiness" as "inalienable." Happiness is the only emotion given the status of a human right. Researchers all include happiness on their list of basic human emotions, and when people are asked to list words that fit the category "emotion," *happiness* and *joy* are among the most frequently mentioned words (Fehr & Russell, 1984; Shaver, Schwartz, Kirson, & O'Connor, 1987). Researchers who have examined the emotion joy (Izard, 1977; Scherer & Wallbott, 1994) found that both the conceptualization and expression of joy are virtually identical with those of happiness.

Among facial expressions, happiness is one of the most basic and most universally recognized emotions. Ekman and Friesen (1975) have found that people worldwide are able to recognize and name the facial expression of happiness. The corresponding facial expression, smiling, involves a widening and upturning of the lips and mouth. Genuine smiles, also called Duchenne smiles, not only include the upturned mouth but also involve raising the cheek muscles and squinting the eyes, producing smile lines at the corners of the eyes. Smile lines may be temporary or more permanently etched on the face of a person who smiles frequently.

Everyone smiles—babies, teenagers, and adults—because smiling is an innate part of our biological heritage (Konner, 1987). Babies show both the full Duchenne smile and the mouth-only smile, which is often a prelude to the full Duchenne smile (Messinger, Fogel, & Dickson, 1999). Babies attract caregivers, potential victims appease attackers, and young adults attract mates with the most pleasant of facial expressions, the smile.

Aside from smiling, happiness produces other changes in a person's nonverbal behavior, including increased vocal pitch, intensity, and rate, a more melodious tone of voice, a lighter walking style, closer interpersonal distances, and increased laughter (Planalp, 1998; Scherer & Wallbott, 1994). In a study using computer-generated figures, happiness has been displayed by backward head tilts without forward leans and by raised arms (Coulson, 2004). Happy people touch more, hug their friends and family, and refrain from violent behavior (Andersen & Guerrero, 1998b; Shaver et al., 1987).

Happy expressions rarely occur when a person is alone; instead, they are reserved for social occasions when they can be shared with other people (Kraut & Johnston, 1979; Rime, Mesquita, Philippot, & Boca, 1991; Kraut & Johnston, 1979; Ruiz-Belda, Fernandez-Dols, Carrera, & Barchard, 2003). Likewise, positive relationships with friends, colleagues, and family are the major source

The smile is a universal expression of happiness, joy, and the exchange of positive emotion. But is this a genuine smile?

of one's own happiness and its expression (Andersen & Guerrero, 1998b; Taraban, Hendrick, & Hendrick, 1998). It is difficult to think of a really joyous or happy moment that was not shared with significant others. Sharing happiness may have provided the human species with a survival advantage: people tend not to be dangerous when they are displaying positive emotions. In fact, among all primates, including humans, smiling is a primary display of appeasement and submission, designed to calm and build positive relationships with other members of the species (Schmidt & Cohn, 2001, Van Hoofe, 1972) suggesting an evolutionary basis for smiling.

Sadness

Like its opposite, happiness, sadness is a basic emotion (Fehr & Russell, 1984; Shaver et al., 1987). Depression, a similar emotion, is typified by chronic, sad affect, melancholy feelings, and a host of other symptoms (Russell, 1989; Segrin, 1998). Grief, a similar melancholic emotion, is a special form of sadness involving the loss of a loved one through death or separation, and it activates the same regions of the brain as sadness or depression (Najib et al., 2004). Sadness is experienced as a loss of an object or person closely associated with one's identity where there is typically no blame for the loss (Burleson & Goldsmith, 1998) and no way to reverse the loss aside from accepting it. If blame is involved, typically the emotion becomes anger (blame of another) or guilt and shame (blame of oneself). Sadness and depression

Sadness and melancholy are communicated by downcast eyes, avoidance, and the classic sad face.

are associated with impaired accuracy in relational and nonverbal communication (Ambady & Gray, 2002). Long-term sadness reduces focus on other people and impairs judgments about others' personality and moods.

Sadness is displayed nonverbally in several ways. The sad face, easily drawn by any schoolchild, includes a downturned mouth and downturned eyes. The facial expression of sadness is easily recognized by people of virtually every culture, suggesting its universality (Ekman & Friesen, 1975; Scherer & Wallbott, 1994). Behavioral indications of sadness include a slumping posture, frowning, moping, a lowered head, forward chest bends, prolonged silences, withdrawal, social isolation, talking in a monotone, lower vocal volume, decreased smiling, reduced eye contact, and, in more extreme cases, crying, sobbing, and throwing oneself on the ground (Coulson, 2004; Guerrero et al., 1998; Magai & McFadden, 1995; Segrin, 1998).

Sad people look pitiful, and the main function of expressed sadness may be to elicit support and comforting (Planalp, 1998). Comforting involves verbal and nonverbal communication that alleviates distress, such as sadness, in another person (Burleson & Goldsmith, 1998). Offering nonverbal or verbal solace and spending time listening to a sad person is probably the most effective comforting behavior.

Sadness is an interpersonal emotion in another way: The main cause of sadness is relationship loss (Andersen & Guerrero, 1998b; Shaver et al., 1987). Similarly, depression is almost always associated with social isolation, lack of interpersonal intimacy, and a shortage of social support, although these factors are probably both the cause and the effect of depression (McCann & Lalonde, 1993: Segrin, 1998).

Fear

A considerable amount of research has been conducted on the experience, effects, and expression of fear. Fear is a transitory, negative emotion characterized by avoidance of painful or dangerous stimuli (Gaines et al., 1998). Everyone experiences fear. Studies show that when asked to list basic emotions, virtually all respondents include fear on their list (Fehr & Russell, 1984; Shaver et al., 1987). Fear is probably essential for survival because it activates the human body to respond to impending danger. The expression of fear also serves as an instant warning to other members of one's social group, enabling them to take the necessary actions. Thus, the experience and expression of fear evolved due to its survival benefits for individuals, for group members, and for their future offspring.

Fear typically occurs in the presence of an external threat, but phobic or paranoid states can also produce feelings of fear. At one time in the history of the human species, fear was primarily induced by nature in the form of large predators and severe storms, for example. Fear today, however, is often socially induced, resulting from interpersonal stimuli, such as a threatening teacher, a scary movie, and anxiety-producing social situations (Andersen & Guerrero, 1998b; Wilson & Smith, 1998), as well as close calls on the freeway (see chapter 7 for more on arousal, anxiety, and nonverbal communication). Moreover, parents, doctors, politicians, police officers, and advertisers use fear appeals to persuade us to eat less fat,

Fear is a universally recognized facial expression.

practice safe sex, wear seat belts, and support the war on terrorism (see Witte, 1998).

Fear is usually accompanied by an increased heart rate, muscular tension, changes in breathing patterns, perspiration, trembling, increased skin conductivity, and cold extremities (Scherer & Wallbott, 1994). In human beings, fear produces an especially recognizable facial expression. The expression of fear is characterized by raised eyebrows. The upper eyelids are raised, the lower eyelids are tightened, and the lips and mouth are stretched horizontally to reveal the lower teeth (Dillard, 1994; Ekman & Friesen, 1975). Fear is also manifested through various forms of defensive avoidance, including outright flight, cowering, protecting the body, covering the face, and hiding. In studies of computer-generated figures fear is characterized kinesically by a backward head tilt and a backward transfer of weight (Coulson, 2004). Research suggests that fear and anxiety can be reliably recognized in "thin slices" of brief nonverbal interactions lasting only a few seconds (Ambady & Krabbenhoft, 2006).

Numerous studies have shown that both the experience and expression of fear is cross-culturally universal (Ekman & Friesen, 1975; Scherer & Wallbott, 1994), suggesting that fear is an innate, unlearned expression. Of course, as with all emotional expression, the circumstances under which we reveal or conceal fear are governed by culture.

Surprise

For more than a century nonverbal communication researchers have included surprise on their lists of basic emotions (Darwin, 1872/1904). Surprise is one of Ekman's (1972) six basic emotions, and it also appeared on Tomkins' (1962) and Izard's (1977) lists of basic emotions (for a summary see Guerrero et al., 1998). Shaver, Wu, and Schwartz (1992) have suggested that because surprise doesn't always produce the same feelings, it may not be a basic emotion. Unlike other emotions, surprise can be negative (for example, getting an unexpected, bad grade on a test) or positive (for example, getting an unexpected pay raise). According to this view, surprise is not a pure emotion but a fuzzy one that may be part of many emotions. Most researchers, however, consider surprise a basic emotion.

Surprise is the most transient of human emotions (Ervin & Martin, 1986). By definition, one cannot be continuously surprised. The facial expression of surprise is universally recognized, though not viewed initially as either positive or negative (Ekman, 1972; Ekman & Friesen, 1975). Surprise is displayed by a rapid opening of the eyes and a raising of the eyebrows, such that the sclera, the area above the iris, is exposed. The mouth opens rapidly, the jaw drops, and the teeth are slightly parted. Research suggests that the full-blown surprise expression is relatively rare; instead, a slight raising of the eyebrows is most common (Reisenzein et al., 2006). Even in infants the full surprise expression is rarely seen, even in response to an unexpected event. When a toy was secretly switched underneath a cloth, young infants failed to show the classic surprise face—instead they usually showed partial surprise, behavioral stilling, or sudden attentiveness (Camras et al., 2002). This suggests that there is not always a one-to-one correspondence between and emotion and a facial expression. Because the surprise facial expression is fleeting, it changes quickly to another expression such as fear, joy, excite-

Surprise is a fleeting facial expression that quickly morphs into another emotional expression. The surprise expression on the right is blending into happiness.

ment, embarrassment, or anger. In a computer-generated posture study, surprise was manifested with backward head and torso leans and straight forearms with raised arms (Coulson, 2004).

Anger

Anger is an intense feeling of displeasure that typically results from being injured, offended, or mistreated by another person. In a study examining anger, respondents were asked to describe their experience of anger. In 95 percent of their accounts, respondents reported having been harmed illegitimately as the source of their anger (Canary, Spitzberg, & Semic, 1998). Anger's manifestations are often aggression or revengeful displeasure. Although anger can occur outside of interpersonal interaction, it is usually the result of a troubling interpersonal circumstance (Andersen & Guerrero, 1998b) and most often the result of interpersonal communication (Canary et al., 1998; Guerrero, 1994). The most common causes of anger are physical or verbal attacks; thoughtless, inconsiderate, and rude behavior; the frustration of one's goals by another; threats to one's identity; and relationship threats such as unfaithfulness and disloyalty.

Excitement is communicated by animated facial expressions, active body movements, and active gestures.

Anger has a unique facial expression: knit and lowered brows, a direct stare, narrowed eyes, and a tense jaw, often with the mouth open and the teeth exposed. Like the other basic facial expressions, this behavior is universally and cross-culturally recognized, indicating its biological origins. Anger also incurs changes in the voice. Vocalic behavior is louder, harsher, and often deeper in pitch. Anger behaviors may also include breaking things, slamming doors, stomping one's feet, making threatening gestures, clenching one's fists, staring at someone in a hostile fashion, "getting in someone's face," giving someone the "silent treatment," and walking out on someone (Andersen & Guerrero, 1998b; Canary et al., 1998; Guerrero, 1994; Shaver et al., 1987). In research using computer-generated figures, anger was characterized by backward head tilt, erect posture and arms raised (Coulson, 2004).

Research has consistently shown that anger displays usually occur during social interaction rather than when one is alone (Canary et al., 1998; Shaver et al., 1987). Researchers believe that the anger expression evolved as a way to warn other individuals of—and thus avert—an impending attack (Andersen & Guerrero, 1998b; Darwin, 1872/1904; Planalp, 1998). Today, as in years past, attacks without warning can result in death or injury to one of the combatants. But warn-

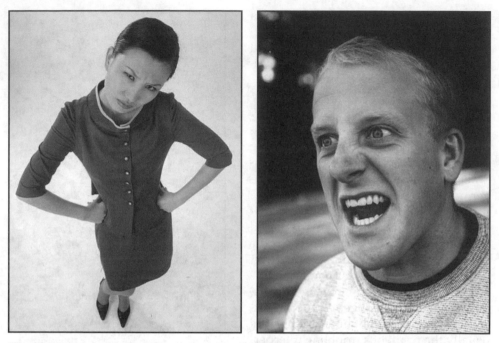

The face, head, and arms of the woman on the left all show anger. The angry facial expression on the right is inherited from our animal ancestors and recognizable interculturally.

ings through the expression of anger result in symbolic combat, aggression displays, or flight by one or both parties. According to this evolutionary perspective, individuals who express emotions like anger have a better chance of avoiding potentially life-threatening combat and have a greater likelihood of passing their genes on to the next generation.

Disgust

In the distant past, humans originally experienced disgust when they encountered a foul taste or smell; human infants show disgusted expressions in response to bitter tastes and smiles in response to sweet ones (Erickson & Schulkin 2003). Today, although we are still disgusted by some tastes and smells, we experience disgust in new contexts; disgust now also applies to people, groups, situations, and interactions. Disgust is deeply ingrained and prewired in human nature. According to numerous theorists and researchers, disgust is a basic emotion (Darwin, 1872/1904; Ekman, 1972; Izard, 1977; Tomkins, 1963).

In interpersonal communication, feelings of disgust are reserved for individuals with extremely obnoxious personal qualities. Disgust is closely associated with rejection and leads to interpersonal avoidance (Gaines et al., 1998). Like disgusting smells or tastes, disgusting people are rejected and avoided.

The facial expression of disgust is well known to everyone, even preschoolers: The eyes are nearly shut, the nose is wrinkled, and the mouth is turned down; in extreme disgust, the tongue protrudes outward and downward. In the 1980s, a cartoon version of this facial expression was portrayed in the form of "Mr. Yuck," an icon featured on containers of toxic household substances. Research has demonstrated that disgust is a universal facial expression (Ekman, 1972; Porter & Samovar, 1998), produced and recognized in all cultures.

Contempt

Scholars have debated whether contempt is an independent emotion or a blend of other emotions. Izard (1977) includes contempt among his primary emotions, yet some scholars have suggested it is a secondary emotion, a blending

Modified disgust expressions are common in social interaction.

of anger and disgust (Plutchik, 1980). In their early work, Ekman, Friesen, and Ellsworth (1972) classified contempt as a variation of disgust; in their later work, however, Ekman and Friesen (1986) argued, like Izard, that contempt is a freestanding emotion. In his circumplex model, Plutchik (1980) classified contempt as the opposite of submission.

According to some researchers, contempt produces a recognizable facial expression: a blank expression accompanied by a tightened, curled lip (Ekman & Friesen, 1986). Other researchers (Russell, 1991) have failed to support the existence of a contempt expression. Gaines et al. (1998) concluded that there is no consensus regarding the existence of a distinct contempt expression. Pittam and Scherer (1993) have identified a vocal profile of shame but admit that the contempt profile is mostly undifferentiated arousal.

Pride

Pride is often overlooked by researchers as a human emotion, despite its inclusion as one of the "seven deadly sins" (Andersen & Guerrero, 1998b). Pride isn't entirely negative but is really a mixture of good and evil. On the dark side, too much pride can make someone seem arrogant and boastful; excessively proud people are warned that "pride comes before a fall." Pride is often a barrier to seeking social support or help with one's problems (Barbee, Rowatt, & Cunningham, 1998). However, too little pride can be injurious to one's self-esteem. On the bright side, pride can be a very constructive reaction to the compliments and approval of others and to socially valued accomplishments (for more on this topic see Andersen & Guerrero, 1998b). According to Gaines et al. (1998), pride is a subset of a cluster of "delight" emotions. Pride, a highly interpersonal emotion, has been characterized as one of the most "social" emotions (Barrett, 1995) because it is typically dependent on a social audience (Greenwood, 1994). Under the rare instances of private pride, an audience is usually imagined.

Although little research has been done on pride, some studies have identified nonverbal behaviors that are associated with the experience of pride: proud individuals stand taller, make themselves larger, elevate the chin, tilt back the head, and exhibit signs of strength (Andersen & Guerrero, 1998b; Tracy, Robbins, & Lagattuta, 2005). Proud individuals display their body to others, smile broadly, and produce celebratory gestures such as the high-five sign (Mascolo & Fischer, 1995; Tracy et al., 2005). Like adults, children display their pride nonverbally with broad smiles, increased eye contact, and conspicuous kinesic displays designed to attract attention from others. Recent research has shown that pride is recognizable to both adults and to children as young as four years old (Tracy & Robbins, 2004, Tracy, Robbins & Lagattuta, 2005).

Shame

Shame is an intensely negative feeling that one is inferior to others and has lost their respect due to one's own immoral behavior or incompetence (Andersen & Guerrero, 1998b). Shame typically involves global negative feelings about oneself rather than about one's actions. Shamed individuals experience a substantial loss of face and feel unworthy of the respect or love of others. Shame involves an overall loss of self-esteem and is accompanied by persistent feelings of worthlessness (Lewis, 1995). According to many theorists and researchers, shame is a basic emotion (Darwin, 1872/1904; Izard, 1977; Tomkins, 1962), although others would classify it as a secondary emotion or an emotional blend (Ekman, 1982). Shame is usually accompanied by other emotions, including dejection, sadness, depression, helplessness, and sometimes anger (Ferguson & Stegge, 1995).

Shame does not occur in solitude. It is always the product of one's perceived transgressions against others and their negative interpersonal reactions. Shame, like its cousins embarrassment and guilt, is a so-called self-conscious emotion because it frequently fosters moral behavior and inhibits transgressions against others (Tangney, 1995). Self-conscious emotions evolved to protect the group against the immoral or injurious behavior of an individual. Were there no guilt, embarrassment, or shame, people would be emotionally unrestrained in behaviors that are damaging to other people and to their primary group. Throughout the ages, people who experienced distress over the impressions they made on others were more likely to survive as reproductive members of the group than those who felt disdain or disregard for other people's feelings (Miller & Leary, 1992).

Shamed individuals engage in a number of nonverbal behaviors best characterized by the desire to disappear, hide, and avoid observation by others. People who feel shame are motivated to avoid interpersonal contact and experience overwhelming feelings of pain and loss of face. Avoidance reactions include shrinking one's body (by exhaling air from the chest, for example), covering the face with one's hands, avoiding eye contact, slouching, lowering one's head, and fleeing from social contact (Andersen & Guerrero, 1998b). Some other avoidance reactions include blushing (although this is a more common reaction to embarrassment), self-control behaviors such as biting or licking one's lips, wrinkling one's forehead, increased facial touching, and forced, weak smiling (Keltner, 1995; Leary & Meadows, 1991; Scheff, 1995).

Embarrassment

Like shame, embarrassment is expressed through numerous nonverbal behaviors. As mentioned in chapter 1, most nonverbal behaviors are analogic. Many of the nonverbal reactions to embarrassment, such as smiling, are analogic apologies designed to maintain face in an embarrassing situation. Other behaviors are designed to appease onlookers, avoid observation, and release tension: avoiding gaze and eye contact; covering one's mouth, eyes, or entire face; pressing the lips together making fake, feeble, or silly smiles; laughing halfheartedly; blushing; interrupting others; lowering one's head; glancing down, turning one's face or body away from others; withdrawing and making moves to depart (Andersen & Guerrero, 1998b; Costa, Dinsbach, Manstead, & Bitti, 2001; Cupach & Metts, 1990, 1994; Keltner, 1995; Miller & Leary, 1992; Schmidt & Cohn, 2001). Interestingly, these human behaviors are very similar to primate appeasement displays, suggesting their genetic origins (Schmidt & Cohn, 2001). In an experiment where participants consented to view pictures of nude men and women and sexual activity, participants *displayed* more embarrassment when they were alone than when they were with others, but actually *experienced* more embarrassment when they were with other people than when they were alone (Costa et al., 2001). With embarrassment, as with other emotions, what is felt is not always what is expressed.

Guilt

Guilt is an interpersonal emotion. In fact, it is hard to imagine how one could experience guilt except in reference to other people. Although intrapersonal guilt does exist (for example, eating a second piece of cake when one is home alone), it usually involves an interpersonal failure (for example, feeling gluttonous or ashamed of excessive weight gain because you eat too much). One typically experiences guilt as the result of a perceived transgression against another person, especially when the transgression (such as sexual infidelity) occurs in the context of a close relationship (Metts, 1994; Vangelisti & Sprague, 1998). Guilty emotions occur when a person has unjustly deceived, injured, cheated, hurt, or failed to help someone (Friedman, 1985; Vangelisti & Sprague, 1998). Guilt is most likely to occur when in the presence of other people and often works to strengthen a relationship after an offense has occurred (Baumeister, Reis, & Delaspaul, 1995). People may feel guilty that they have received too many benefits (Andersen & Guerrero, 1998b; Metts, 1994). Guilt may also occur when people mistakenly take responsibility for a transgression; even victims can experience guilt. For example, Holocaust survivors, who were themselves victims, often feel deep, crippling guilt even though they could have done nothing to prevent the deaths of other victims (for a summary of these findings see Vangelisti & Sprague, 1998).

Guilt shares some similarities with regret, shame, and embarrassment (White & Mullen, 1989) and may sometimes accompany these other emotions. Research conducted in thirty-seven countries by Scherer and Wallbott (1994) found that guilt occurs in virtually all cultures. Guilt is considered a basic, primary emotion by some researchers (Izard, 1977) because it can occur by itself. It frequently appears as one of the basic, or prototypic, emotions.

Responses to guilt are likewise highly interpersonal in nature. Guilty individuals may engage in interpersonal avoidance or seek to make up for their behavior through apologies, repairs, or promises to change their behavior. Indeed, recent conceptualizations of guilt suggest it is a phenomenon that "happens between people rather than just inside them" (Baumeister, Stillwell, & Heatherton, 1994, p. 243).

Guilt is an emotion that functions to exert social control over one person's actions in a group. Indeed, Miller and Leary (1992) suggested that social emotions such as guilt are functional because they show remorse to the injured party rather than a disregard for others. Those who act with consistent disregard for others may be ostracized, banished, or even killed. Guilty behavior, however, demonstrates a remorseful attitude that may be reassuring to other group members. Guilt also serves to prevent others from engaging in behavior that deviates too greatly from social standards (Andersen & Guerrero, 1998b). Moreover, guilt is used as a strategic behavior to manipulate or persuade or to change the behavior of another person (Vangelisti & Sprague, 1998).

Most of the literature on guilt deals either with guilt's internal experience or with many verbal responses to guilt (see Vangelisti & Sprague, 1998). Relatively little has been written about nonverbal responses to guilt. There is no single facial expression associated with guilt (Izard, 1977); however, sad or worried facial expressions, a lump in one's throat, and remorseful and sorry expressions accompanying apologies are common reactions to guilt. Avoidance and silence are other behavioral responses to guilt across a variety of cultures (Scherer & Wallbott, 1994). Guilt often produces actions that are designed to repair the situation, redeem the guilty person, or reduce the guilty feelings, although guilty nonverbal behaviors, including reduced smiling and less pleasant tones of voice and facial expressions, may evoke suspicion in others and lead to perceptions of deception (Buller & Burgoon, 1998).

Love

Love is one of the most basic and culturally universal human emotions (Scherer & Wallbott, 1994; Taraban et al., 1998). Love is part of our emotional heritage; it is built into the fabric of our genetic structure. Love is perhaps the strongest positive emotion that a person can experience (Shaver et al., 1987; Taraban et al., 1998). Although most scholars consider love a basic or primary emotion, Plutchik (1980) maintains that it is actually a combination of two positive emotions: joy and acceptance. Shaver et al. (1987) classified love as a basic emotion closely related to adoration, affection, fondness, liking, attraction, arousal, desire, lust, and longing.

Love is typically experienced in the context of interpersonal relationships (although one could experience a love for nature or a love for God that is independent of interpersonal influence). Love creates in each of us a desire to reinforce social bonds and to establish and maintain close relationships. Love serves the social purpose of creating feelings of connectedness, and messages of love begin the process of creating close interpersonal ties. Love is an inherently interpersonal emotion because it occurs in relation to a particular other and is always associated with the desire to maintain a close relationship with another person (Andersen & Guerrero, 1998b). Love can take many forms, from familial to dyadic, from intimate to passionate (see the section on sexual desire later in this chapter; for more on the many aspects of love see Sternberg, 1986; Taraban et al., 1998).

Love is such a basic emotion that we are motivated to extremes by the desire to protect and nurture loved ones. Emotional appeals to love are frequently employed in persuasive communication: tire commercials (whose message is "So much is riding on your tires") feature babies sitting in sturdy radials, and phone commercials (which implore us to "Reach out and touch someone") picture elderly relatives weeping over calls from their grandchildren (see chapter 10 for more on nonverbal communication and persuasion).

Love is communicated in a variety of ways: through verbal expression and through various obvious and subtle nonverbal behavioral displays. Although no single facial expression of love has been identified (Fischer & Tangney, 1995), nonverbal manifestations of love include prolonged eye contact, closer interpersonal distances, increased time spent with the loved one, blushing, pupil dilation, increased smiling, and increased and prolonged touch across many areas of the loved one's body (for more about these behaviors see Andersen & Guerrero, 1998a; see also chapters 8 and 9). Couples who are falling in love, "going out," and newly married actually touch more than couples who have been married for many years (Emmers & Dindia, 1995; Guerrero & Andersen, 1991; McDaniel & Andersen, 1998). As compared to secure, stable, long-term relationships, the intensity of new love relationships makes visible displays of love more essential. In relationships of all durations, touching, hugging, kissing, and caressing are vital to the communication of love. According to research on "love ways" by Marsden, Hecht, and Robers (1987), touch is especially important to the communication of love, as is smiling, making eye contact, and spending time together. One study (Egland, Stelzner, Andersen, & Spitzberg, 1997) showed that one of the most important behaviors in establishing understanding and in creating long-term relational satisfaction is spending more time together.

Nonverbal behavior, evidently, is more important in the communication of love than is verbal communication: "nonverbal behaviors are viewed as less strategic, more spontaneous, and therefore more honest than verbal behaviors" (Montgomery, 1988, p. 348). Love is expressed best through nonverbal behavior.

Jealousy

Just as it has its bright sides, so too does love have its dark sides. One of love's darkest sides is jealousy, an emotion that occurs when a real or perceived rival threatens a close relationship, usually a romantic one. Jealousy likely has a genetic basis because it is a ubiquitous, cross-cultural phenomenon (Hupka, 1981; White & Mullen, 1989). Sociobiologists argue that paternity certainty and mate retention are genetically based and essential to the survival of one's genes (Buss, 1988; Daly & Wilson, 1987). Jealousy certainly has a long history; it is central to classic writing—from Homer to Shakespeare to Hawthorne, to name only a few (see Guerrero & Andersen, 1998a).

Jealousy occurs in close interpersonal relationships and involves communication among members of a jealous triangle. People communicate feelings of jealousy in many ways, including through nonverbal communication. Immediately upon experiencing jealousy, people report feeling a jealousy flash—an intense, hot feeling due to sudden increases in physiological arousal. They also report feeling a blend of anger, fear, sadness (Izard, 1977), and hurt simultaneously.

But jealous communication is more than immediate feelings and reactions. In a series of studies, my colleagues and I examined jealous communication and its consequences (see Andersen, Eloy, Guerrero, & Spitzberg, 1995; Guerrero & Andersen, 1998a, 1998b; Guerrero, Andersen, Jorgensen, Spitzberg, & Eloy, 1995). People communicate their jealousy in many ways, including through nonverbal communication. Among the fourteen sets of communicative responses to jealousy we discovered, eight responses were entirely or partly nonverbal in nature, including:

1. *Negative-affect expression*, including crying, pouting, appearing hurt, and exhibiting displeasure facially;
2. *Active distancing*, such as leaving the scene, storming out of a room, giving the partner cold looks, using the silent treatment, and withholding sex;
3. *Avoidance/denial*, such as acting nonchalant about a rival, avoiding jealousy-inducing situations, and decreasing contact with the partner;
4. *Violent communication/threats*, including threatening to hit the partner, pulling the partner away from a rival, and pushing, punching or slapping a rival;
5. *Signs of possession*, such as always appearing in public with the partner, wearing rings or other "tie" signs, and holding or kissing the partner in the presence of potential rivals;
6. *Surveillance/restriction*, such as spying on the partner, searching through the partner's belongings, and restricting the partner's access to rivals at parties;
7. *Manipulation moves*, such as flirting with others to make the partner jealous or going out with rivals in retaliation; and
8. *Violence toward objects*, such as slamming doors, breaking dishes, or throwing the partner's possessions against a wall.

How do these nonverbal behaviors, or even verbal behaviors, affect relationship satisfaction? Our results suggest that all forms of jealousy are associated with relational dissatisfaction. Moreover, all of the previously listed responses to jealousy seem to make matters worse by reducing relational satisfaction, with one important exception: A combination of integrative verbal communication combined with negative-affect expression seems to counteract the deleterious effects of jealousy. Our results suggest that the best approach to dealing with jealous emotions is to express one's concerns and show negative emotions in a constructive way (Andersen, Eloy, Guerrero, & Spitzberg, 1995).

Warmth

In the presence of others about whom we care deeply, we experience pleasant, cozy feelings that some researchers call warmth (Andersen & Guerrero, 1998a). The emotion warmth has received sparse attention by researchers, yet it is perhaps the most social of all the emotions. Interpersonal warmth is universally experienced but goes by a variety of labels, including intimacy, closeness, bonding, attachment, involvement, confirmation, and validation, although these terms are not exact equivalents (see chapter 9). *Warmth*, admittedly, is a vague and arbitrary term used to describe a specific emotion (see chapter 9). Sternberg (1986, 1988) employed thermal metaphors to describe passion (*hot*), commitment (*cool*), and intimacy (*warm*). According to Sternberg (1988), intimacy refers to feelings of warmth that "promote closeness, bondedness, and connectedness" (p. 38).

Obviously, interpersonal warmth can occur only in the context of close relationships, although warm, contented feelings may be generated by a cozy house, feeling connected to nature and natural beauty, or reading a good book on a rainy day. Warmth, as conceptualized here, refers to the flood of good, soothing, pleasant feelings that occur when you are with a group of people or an individual about whom you care deeply.

Warmth is expressed primarily through nonverbal immediacy behaviors, which are covered extensively in chapter 8, so only a brief mention will be made of them here. Warmth is conveyed by spending time together, maintaining closer interpersonal distances, smiling, nodding, using warm, reinforcing vocal tones, touching, interacting synchronously, and a number of other verbal and nonverbal behaviors (Andersen & Guerrero, 1998a).

Sexual Desire

In contrast to warmth, sexual arousal is passionate and hot. Whether sexual desire is an emotion is still debated among researchers. Sexual desire clearly includes arousal, the interpretation of the arousal as sexually stimulating, the activation of cognitive schemata associated with desire, and subjective feelings that seem to be distinguishable from other emotions. Certainly, sexual desire is a multifaceted experience accompanied by subjective feelings, emotions, situational responses, physiological reactions, thoughts, interpersonal interactions, and nonverbal behaviors (Metts, Sprecher, & Regan, 1998). In one study, very few sexually active college students defined sexual desire in terms of psychological arousal or sexual activity; most defined sexual desire as a motivational state, and many defined it as an emotional state or part of an emotional syndrome (Ragan & Berscheid, 1996).

Sexual desire is associated with many other emotions, including love, happiness, loneliness, jealousy, and guilt. Romantic love typically involves sexual desire as a major component. Similarly, having a partner who is sexually attractive and sexually satisfying is essential to the experience of passionate or romantic love (Sternberg, 1987). Sexual jealousy is one of the most common types of jealousy, particularly for men, and is a leading precursor of violent behavior (Guerrero & Andersen, 1998a, 1998b). Conflicts over sexual feelings and behaviors have long been recognized as a primary source of guilt (see Freud, 1930/1961; Vangelisti & Sprague, 1998). Similarly, sexual rejection is associated with feelings of hurt and even depression (Baumeister & Wotman, 1992; Vangelisti & Sprague, 1998).

Sexual desire has a number of behavioral manifestations, including obvious physiological reactions such as erection of the penis, clitoris, and nipples, genital

Flirtation behaviors are courtship cues, signaled through close proximity, self-touching, touching one's partner, and eye contact.

secretions, flushed skin, increased heart rate and respiration, and various vocal behaviors (Masters & Johnson, 1966; Rathus, Nevid, & Fichner-Rathus, 1993). Of course, sexual desire does more than prompt physiological reactions. It is also a vital component of flirting, sexual behavior (including intercourse), dating, and marriage.

Some of the most interesting nonverbal behaviors occur during flirtation and courtship. Sexual desire is expressed through eye contact and a whole set of interesting courtship-readiness behaviors: preening behaviors, such as touching, combing, or flipping one's hair or smoothing one's clothing; open-palm presentations; head cocking; pelvis rolling; and postural adjustments such as standing straighter, expanding or protruding one's chest, crossing one's legs, pulling in one's stomach, and revealing more of one's body (Scheflen, 1965, 1974).

EMOTION AS COMMUNICATION

Traditionally, emotions have been thought of as purely internal, subjective experiences. Certainly, emotions can be experienced in private, yet recent research has shown that in many ways nonverbal communication is an inherent part of the emotional experience (Andersen & Guerrero, 1998b; Dillard, 1998; Planalp, 1998; Fischer & Tangney, 1995). In this final section, we will explore three important principles that govern the relationship between emotion and nonverbal communication: (1) most emotions are the result of interpersonal nonverbal communication; (2) emotions are typically expressed through nonverbal communication; and (3) emotions are contagious.

Emotions Result from Interpersonal Nonverbal Communication

In recent years, studies have shown that the primary source of our emotional state is our interactions with others (Andersen & Guerrero, 1998b; Metha & Clark, 1994). Bowlby (1979) has shown that our most intense emotional experiences occur during the formation, maintenance, disruption, termination, or renewal of close relationships. The formation of close, new relationships involves increases in time spent together, eye contact, touch, proxemic closeness, and other forms of nonverbal communication; such experiences create joy, happiness, excitement, and warmth. The disruption of interpersonal relationships results in emotions such as jealousy, hurt, sadness, anxiety, and anger. And the loss of a relationship, which involves decreased nonverbal communication, results in grief, hurt, sadness, and depression. Even the recall of intimate touch, of spending an evening with someone close, or of the visual image of someone you love can create waves of emotion.

Emotions Are Expressed through Nonverbal Communication

As we learned earlier in this chapter, every emotion can be communicated nonverbally. But the relationship between nonverbal communication and emotion is stronger than that. The *primary* means through which emotions are expressed is nonverbal communication, and studies show that emotional expression is much more likely to occur when others are present than when we are alone (Kraut & Johnston, 1979; Planalp, 1998). Like it or not, when we are in the presence of other people, it is difficult not to reveal our emotions nonverbally. As Andersen and Guerrero (1998b) stated:

> Even when the nonverbal expression of emotion is unintended, it can send a clear message to a receiver. Indeed, emotions so automatically generate communicative displays that they can be problematic for the maintenance of competent self-presentations during interaction, particularly when negative emotions are unwittingly revealed. (p. 73)

Although concealing all our emotions is impossible to do, revealing our every emotion would be a sign of immaturity and incompetence. It takes great skill and years of practice to learn and deploy the display rules examined earlier. We all feel emotions we'd rather not show. We may prefer not to reveal our physical attraction for our spouse's best friend, our glee at a "perfect" coworker's misfortune, or our eagerness to sign a business deal still under negotiation. Likewise, as a receiver, detecting unintended nonverbal communication can be disadvantageous. Some emotions are better left undetected; picking up on guilty deception from a close friend, subtle sexual interest from one's boss, or hostility from a coworker can cause hard feelings and awkwardness.

Sometimes, however, the automatic expression of emotion through nonverbal communication can be advantageous to both senders and receivers. Sometimes nonverbal leakage can send messages that one might not have the courage or competence to intentionally reveal: you may communicate subtle dissatisfaction at work and prompt your boss to give you a pay raise, or you may inadvertently show romantic interest in a friend that sparks off a romantic relationship. As receivers, tuning in to subtle displays of emotion can be equally advantageous. Remember, in the main, "emotions exist so that one's affective states can be shared to ready others for parallel action, to forewarn others of individual feelings, and to create a particular affective atmosphere for communicating" (Andersen & Guerrero, 1998b, p. 73).

Emotions Are Contagious

Patterns of reciprocity or matching generally govern the communication of emotion (Andersen & Guerrero, 1998b; Burgoon, Stern, & Dillman, 1995). For example, it is easier to be happy when your relational partner is happy and easy to feel negative when your partner is negative (Oatley & Johnson-Laird, 1987; Tickle-Dengen & Puccinelli, 1999). Likewise, fear spreads quickly in a group, and depressed individuals increase the depression of those around them (Segrin, 1998). Some researchers have called this the "chameleon effect," whereby one individual mirrors or adopts the postures expressions and feelings of another (Chartrand & Bargh, 1999; Lakin, Jefferis, Cheng, & Chartrand, 2003). How does this take place? At least seven processes may account for the contagiousness of emotions (Andersen & Guerrero, 1998b, Rizzolatti & Craighero, 2004). One thing is certain, however: emotional matching is no mere coincidence.

SOCIAL REFERENCING

One explanation for the contagious nature of emotions is called social referencing (Klinnert, Campos, Sorce, Emde, & Svedja, 1983). When we try to make sense of any event (a funeral, a meeting, a party), we look to others for cues as to how we should behave and what we should feel. Cialdini (1984) discussed a similar concept called social proof, a process whereby people determine what to do and feel based on the actions of others. This process can explain phenomena as diverse as mass hysteria and why it is that bystanders fail to come to the aid of an assault or rape victim. In the latter case, more than fear is at work. If someone were being assaulted while bystanders continued going their merry way, the conclusion that most people would draw is that the situation is not too serious. In the case of mass hysteria, the observation that everyone else is experiencing fear and panic would make it seem foolish to stay calm.

CONTAGION

Research on emotional contagion has attempted to provide an explanation for a whole group of processes, including mob panic, mass euphoria, contagious laughter, group grief, and collective panic (Hatfield, Cacioppo, & Rapson, 1994). Contagion occurs in dyads as well (Magai & McFadden, 1995). Although the exact process underlying contagion is not entirely understood, the emotions sadness, fear, joy, and anxiety seem particularly susceptible to the phenomenon (Klinnert et al., 1983).

IMITATION

People of all ages, particularly children, imitate the behavior of others. Magai and McFadden (1995) maintained, "The literature on the proclivity of infants to match the facial and vocal expressions of their caregivers is now quite substantial" (p. 282). Imitation is the primary process in modeling and plays a significant role in all human learning. Although it is frequently unconscious, imitation can also be intentional. Imitation is most pronounced when the person being imitated is of high status or prestige. This process occurs in various settings. Many professors, for example, have protégés who move and act exactly like the professor. Observe children watching a football or basketball game; they will imitate the moves and behavior of their heroes, from how they unsnap their helmet to how they spike a football or dunk a basketball.

MOTOR MIMICRY

One mechanism that may explain the contagiousness of emotions is motor mimicry. Bavelas and her colleagues have shown that affect or emotional sharing is a common communication behavior (Bavelas et al., 1986, 1988). In a series of imaginative laboratory experiments, Bavelas and her colleagues were able, for example, to get observers to wince when a television was placed on another person's hand and to duck when a ball was thrown at another person's head. These researchers suggest that motor mimicry is more than mere empathy; it is a powerful form of communication by an observer that conveys appropriate affect to the observed person or warns the person of a dangerous situation. In the vast majority of cases, the observer simultaneously and symmetrically mirrors the other's emotional response. Because this reaction often occurs earlier in the observer than in the person being observed, it is not mere imitation. Motor mimicry is a parallel process between two communicators that puts the interactants in highly similar emotional states. This is particularly true in light of the next process, Cappella's (1993) interpersonal facial feedback hypothesis (IFFH).

THE INTERPERSONAL FACIAL FEEDBACK HYPOTHESIS

The IFFH is based on considerable research that demonstrates that people match or mimic each other's facial expressions (see, for example, Bavelas et al., 1988; Cappella & Palmer, 1990). The IFFH is also based on the original facial feedback hypothesis, which has demonstrated that as a person's facial expression changes, so her or his mood changes in the direction of the facial expression (Buck, 1995; Izard, 1991; Schnall & Laird, 2003). Cappella (1993) has shown that when people smile, they feel more affection toward their interaction partner. The IFFH contends that because people match the expressions of their partners and because facial expressions provide facial feedback that alters one's mood, the result is, ultimately, matched emotions.

CONGRUENT INTERPRETATIONS

Finally, emotions may be interpersonally contagious because both interactants interpret the other's emotions as the same as their own (Metha & Clark, 1994). Happy people think other people are happy. Sexually aroused interactants often erroneously believe that their partners are similarly aroused. Grieving people believe that others share their grief. In one study of this process, researchers had two groups—one group had exercised, the other had not—view a target person (Clark, Milberg, & Erber, 1984). The exercising group perceived the target person as having stronger emotions than the nonexercising group (for example, joy versus contentment). In short, if we are angry, we see others as angry. If we are happy, we see others as happy. These self-fulfilling expectancies may help explain why we believe we are experiencing the same emotions as others.

MIRROR NEURONS

As described previously in chapter 2, research on mirror neurons using PET scans, CAT scans, and other brain imaging techniques provide a neurophysiological explanation for emotional contagion (Rizzolatti & Arbib, 1998; Rizzolatti & Craighero, 2004). If you view fear in my face, your brain activates exactly the same areas as if you felt fear yourself. The same is true for gesturing, walking, and for other facial emotions. Amazingly, what occurs in the brain of a person expressing an emotion or enacting a gesture occurs in the brains of receivers as well! Interestingly the receiver's spinal cord usually blocks enactment of the same behavior, but sometimes not. The common phenomenon of friends imitating each other, communicators getting in sync with each other, and people experiencing similar emotions is due, in part, to mirror neurons.

SUMMARY

Nonverbal communication and emotion are inseparable. It is almost impossible not to express emotions nonverbally. The natural system of communicating emotion is analogic, nonlinguistic, nonverbal communication. The nonverbal communication of emotion is a biologically based genetic system that provides both an internal control system for each of us and a means of communicating these emotions to others. Emotions and their expression have provided humans with a survival advantage; by allowing us to adjust our behavior to the emotions of others, we can prevent dangerous and deadly conflicts, promote the well-being of the individual and group, and initiate mating relationships to ensure the survival of the species.

Emotions are socialized differently in each culture. Display rules that govern emotional expression include simulating nonexistent emotions, intensifying mild emotions, miniaturizing strong emotions, inhibiting emotions that are inappropriate to express, and masking one's felt emotion with the display of another emotion.

The primary channel of emotional expression is the face. Facial expressions show great consistency among cultures, indicating their genetic, biological origins. At least six basic expressions—anger, surprise, disgust, fear, happiness, and sadness—are recognizable across cultures. The face is not the only nonverbal channel for emotional expression. The voice and the body also carry considerable emotional information. Nonverbal communication is used to convey fifteen emotions described in this chapter: happiness, sadness, fear, surprise, anger, disgust, contempt, pride, shame, embarrassment, guilt, love, jealousy, warmth, and sexual desire.

Three important principles govern the relationship between emotion and nonverbal communication: Emotions are the result of interpersonal, nonverbal communication; emotions are expressed through nonverbal communication; and emotions are contagious. Theories regarding the contagiousness of emotions include social referencing, contagion, imitation, motor mimicry, the interpersonal facial feedback hypothesis (IFFH), congruent interpretations, and mirror neurons.

7

Communication and Stress
Nonverbal Reactions
to Arousal and Anxiety

Fifty years ago the concept of stress was first researched by Hans Selye (1956), who wrote:

> I believe that the mere fact of understanding the general rules about the way stress acts on the mind and body, with a few remarks about the way this has been used as a basis for one man's personal philosophy, can help others, better than fixed rules, to formulate their own solutions. . . . The study of stress has shown that complete rest is not good, either for the body as a whole, or even for any organ within the body. Stress, applied in moderation, is necessary for life. Besides, enforced inactivity may be very harmful and cause more stress than normal activity. (pp. 294, 300)

Every human being walks a tightrope between boredom and stress, between stimulation and relaxation, between maintaining privacy and avoiding loneliness. Imagine spending a few days resting alone, without friends or family. At first it would be fine, but the need for stimulation and companionship would quickly return. From infancy through adulthood, we all desire human contact; too little human contact can lead to loneliness, boredom, and depression. Stern (1980) maintained that humans "from birth, will seek out stimulation and even work for it. In fact, the seeking of stimulation has now achieved the status of a drive or motivational tendency not unlike that of hunger" (p. 52). Now imagine having out-of-town guests who planned to stay for a month during a particularly hectic time of the year. Privacy would become nonexistent, and soon you would feel like hiding, fleeing, or attacking. Interpersonal overstimulation, so common in our present-day world, is one source of stress, anxiety, and apprehension.

Finding and maintaining a balance between understimulation and overstimulation is the key to personal sanity and interpersonal harmony. Each person must find her or his own mix of privacy and interpersonal interaction (for more on these relational dialectics and paradoxes see chapter 9). Because introverts, high communication apprehensives (discussed later in this chapter), and stimulation avoiders are individuals who have much lower stimulation thresholds, they are more likely to suffer from overstimulation and stress. By contrast, sensation seekers, low communication apprehensives, and extroverts have much higher stimulation thresholds and are more likely to suffer from loneliness and boredom.

The stress of modern life is taking its toll on today's college students. According to a survey conducted by the UCLA Higher Education Research Institute (Weiss, 1997), the class of 2000 was more stressed than any previous college class. This survey, completed by over one quarter of a million freshmen, revealed that 29.4 percent of respondents feel "overwhelmed by all they have to do"—up from 16 percent in 1985. Much of the stress seems to be self-inflicted: a record 66.3 percent of freshmen planned to go on to graduate school, 49 percent intended to maintain at least a B average in college, and 72 percent reported being involved in volunteer work.

AROUSAL AND MOOD

Arousal is the degree to which a person is stimulated or activated. Internal signs of arousal, such as increased heart rate, brain temperature, and blood pressure, prepare the body for action. Feelings of excitement, anxiety, stress, or stimulation are also part of arousal. As we will learn in this chapter, arousal is also accompanied by behavior changes, including many nonverbal communication behaviors.

Moderate arousal feels best. Research and theory have established a curvilinear relationship between arousal and mood (Cappella & Greene, 1982; Eysenck, 1976). As illustrated in Figure 7.1, moderate arousal is generally experienced neutrally or positively. Low arousal and the accompanying feelings of boredom, understimulation, and loneliness tend to be unpleasant and may motivate an individual to seek higher levels of stimulation and human contact. Very high arousal or sharply increasing arousal creates fear, anxiety, and stress and is generally aversive and unpleasant.

This theory regarding the relationship between arousal and mood may help explain a diverse set of nonverbal behaviors and reactions. For example, a sexual encounter with your relational partner should result in optimal sexual arousal. But sexual dysfunction can result from understimulation that is insufficient to support sexual arousal and that may cause feelings of boredom. Similarly, sexual dysfunction can be the result of overstimulation, which may produce feelings of anxiety, unease, or

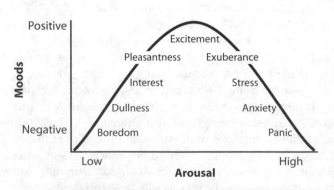

Figure 7.1   The Relationship between Arousal and Mood

fear. This theory also explains the use and abuse of many drugs and alcohol. Small doses of the substances generally produce increases in positive subjective feelings, but large doses may produce anxiety, stress, and psychosis (Eysenck, 1963). Optimal arousal can be achieved by driving fast in a car or boat, but at some point the excitement turns to fear if the speed becomes excessive. Achieving optimal arousal levels is critical to achieving more positive states of mind and more pleasant interpersonal relationships. The relationship between arousal and mood may also be important in explaining much of what we still do not understand about human communication.

Nonverbal Communication and Arousal

Nonverbal communication among humans leads to increases in arousal. Andersen's (1985) review of two dozen studies concludes that "the research generally supports a positive relationship between nonverbal immediacy increases and increases in arousal" (p. 15). Physiological arousal results from increased gaze and eye contact, closer interpersonal distances, face-to-face seating, more-direct body orientations, greater crowding and density, more smiling, and increased touch (Andersen, 1998; Osato & Ogawa, 2003).

A number of models and theories attempt to explain how these nonverbal processes work in interpersonal communication, including cognitive valence theory, explained in chapter 9. Both cognitive valence theory and discrepancy arousal theory posit that moderate arousal is pleasurable but that very high arousal leads to stress and anxiety. This position has stimulated a number of efforts at theory building that have been at least moderately successful (see Andersen & Andersen, 1984; Burgoon, Stern, & Dillman, 1995). These models all recognize that nonverbal involvement produces arousal and that under some conditions, arousal fuels and promotes positive interpersonal relationships. Communication that promotes positive arousal leads to harmonious interpersonal relationships. This principle is useful in such diverse arenas as dating behavior and infant communication.

In dating behavior, negative arousal has detrimental relational effects. Most people are happy or flattered to be asked out on a date or to have another person accept their invitation to go out on a date. Dating can be fun, exciting, and can even lead to long-term friendship or romance. However, when things move too fast, particularly in terms of tactile involvement, one person may get "cold feet" (an indication of negative arousal) and become an involvement reducer. The "involver" may want to spend all of her or his time with the other, become more sexually involved than the partner desires, engage in conversational entrapment, or manifest desperate cues such as jealousy and surveillance. The "reducer" then becomes overstimulated and stressed and tries to reduce involvement. Fearing that her or his autonomy and individuality are in danger, the reducer withdraws. The involver views this withdrawal as a sign of rejection and potential breakup, which in turn leads the involver to become more desperate and seek even more closeness. The reducer then engages in defensiveness, compensation, and withdrawal and feels reduced attraction for the involver. To the reducer, the involver may seem pathetic and desperate, and these negative attributions about the involver's mental health and seemingly insatiable need for a relationship may cause additional relational decay. These moves and countermoves illustrate how easily negative arousal can spiral within interpersonal relationships (for more on cognitive valence theory, see chapter 9).

Assessing another person's readiness for involvement in a close relationship is an important nonverbal skill. Too much or too little touch, too close or too remote an interpersonal distance, too much or too little eye contact fails to produce optimal, symbiotic relationships. The appropriate amount of nonverbal involvement produces the best relationships (see chapter 9). Perceiving a partner's optimal arousal level and producing the right amount of involvement are difficult interpersonal skills to develop, yet their mastery contributes to the success of interpersonal relationships.

Optimal stimulation and involvement are important in all types of relationships. Take, for example, a parent's nonverbal interaction with a fussy infant who won't stop crying. After checking to see if the baby is wet, hungry, or pinned to the diaper, the parent may give up hope of calming her or his infant. Because stimulation is as basic a need as hunger, the fussy baby may simply be seeking contact. After all, being a baby can be pretty boring. Lying in a crib hour after hour looking at the sheets or ceiling can't be very exciting. "Just as food is needed for the body to grow, stimulation is needed to provide the brain with the 'raw materials' required for the maturation of perceptual, cognitive, and sensorimotor processes" (Stern, 1980, p. 52). So, when a baby fusses, one cause might be understimulation and a need for interpersonal contact. Many babies respond positively to playful tactile contact, exaggerated facial expressions, and games such as peek-a-boo. However, babies can also be overstimulated and overaroused, so bouncing a baby on one's knee or shaking a rattle in her or his face may just make matters worse. For an overstimulated infant, nonverbal behaviors such as gentle rocking or soft, firm hugs may be the necessary responses to comfort and to reduce arousal and stress.

Reading Nonverbal Arousal Cues

Unfortunately, most communicators, including most parents, are unaware of the concepts of overarousal and underarousal. Nonetheless, most parents do a pretty good job of intuitively reading an infant's nonverbal cues and responding to her or his needs. Less-skilled parents are unable to read an infant's nonverbal cues, and they often respond habitually with gentle rocking or aggressive bouncing or by simply ignoring the baby. Assessing a baby's stimulation level by reading her or his nonverbal behavior and then responding appropriately with arousal-increasing or arousal-decreasing actions may be the key to positive parent-infant relations.

Oftentimes, parents are so thankful when their baby stops crying that they fail to touch or interact with their happy baby. Unfortunately, such a response is misguided. First, if parents interact with their babies only when they are crying, then crying is behaviorally reinforced and more crying occurs. The infants learn that crying results in attention and stimulation. Second, parents may develop more positive relationships with their babies if they interact with them when they're happy and playful as well as when they are distressed. Third, playing with babies when they're happy reinforces happy, positive, and prosocial communication.

Letting happy babies lie has intuitive merit but may be a poor strategy
in the long run.

Some scholars actually believe
that raising a child is a process in
which the baby trains the parents
how to be caregivers; indeed, the
child already knows how to be a
baby. This paradigm suggests that
the infant may actually be more powerful and influential than her or his
parents. This position was elaborated
in an excellent series of articles edited
by Lewis and Rosenblum (1974) on
The Effect of the Infant on Its Caregiver.
Of course, parents can be proactive in
shaping their infant's behavior, as the
previous discussion suggests.

Understimulated babies respond positively
to playful eye contact, facial expressions, and
touch.

Recent work has examined nonverbal indications of arousal. Some
indices of arousal are emerging,
although research on arousal is difficult and controversial (see the debate between
Burgoon & LePoire, 1992; Greene & Sparks, 1992; Sparks & Greene, 1992). Unfortunately, arousal behaviors, whether they are behavioral or physiological, rarely
correlate very highly among one another (Buller, Jorgensen, Andersen, & Guerrero, 1995; Sparks & Greene, 1992). Increases in negatively valenced arousal have
been found to produce a number of changes in nonverbal behavior, including
increased random movement, more self-touching behaviors (called self-adaptors),
less immediacy, less attentiveness, reduced body coordination, more vocal tension, and less vocal warmth (Burgoon, 1994; Burgoon, Kelley, Newton, & Keeley-
Dyerson, 1989; Burgoon, LePoire, Beutler, Bergan, & Engle, 1992; Heaven &
McBrayer, 2000); these studies, however, have been criticized for failing to correlate any of these indices with physiological arousal (Sparks & Greene, 1992).
Alternatively, Burgoon and her associates have correlated nonverbal behavior
with observers' ratings of arousal. Buller et al. (1995) observed the reactions of
female/male dyads in a laboratory setting. One of the people in each dyad had
been told to increase intimacy with her or his partner. Observers' ratings of the
partners' positive arousal were associated with greater nonverbal immediacy and
fewer self-adaptors. Reduced pulse volume—a measure of increased arousal—
was associated with nonverbal immediacy and fewer self-adaptors. The search for
a valid profile of arousal is difficult, but strides are being made.

For some individuals, communication is too arousing and communication
anxiety develops. These people inherit and/or develop an extreme aversion to
various forms of communication. The next two sections of this chapter explore the
nonverbal behavior of people with two types of aversion to communication: communication anxiety and touch avoidance.

COMMUNICATION ANXIETY, APPREHENSION, AND AVOIDANCE

In the early evolution of the human species, anxiety was often a functional, beneficial reaction. When attacked by an animal or another human, an individual might have responded by fleeing, retreating, or counterattacking. Rapid increases in arousal accompanied by a faster heart rate, surges in adrenaline, and increased blood pressure motivated the individual to defend herself or himself. For hundreds of thousands of years, these reactions increased one's chance for survival. More recently, the accelerating rate of change in modern society has made anxiety a more common phenomenon. Gone are the days of solitude and boredom. Today the senses are overloaded by people, media, technology, deadlines, change, and the competing demands for one's job, family, and self. We may feel an adrenaline surge telling us to flee when we're on a crowded freeway, in the middle of a difficult exam, in an argument with our spouse, or in a tense discussion with a business client. Usually we suppress such responses, leading to greater internal pressures within the body, such as an increased heart rate and higher blood pressure (see Buck, 1984), or we avoid situations that lead to stress by cutting class, skipping meetings, or avoiding our spouse. Avoidance, however, is not usually a viable alternative.

Today, one of the most common forms of anxiety actually results from communication. This type of anxiety has been variously labeled CA (communication anxiety), SA (social anxiety), or unwillingness to communicate. Recent surveys indicate that various forms of communication are the leading sources of anxiety for Americans today. The most severe form of such anxiety is CA, which extends across situations. CA results in stress not only during actual communication but also whenever an individual thinks about communicating (see McCroskey, 1982). Even temporary, "state" apprehension can be problematic, creating patterns of avoidance and incompetence. CA is exceedingly common; virtually everyone experiences temporary, state CA. This trait, with its many debilitating effects, afflicts fifty million Americans and is arguably one of the most prevalent social or psychological problems in our society. Moreover, CA is at least as common in other cultures as it is in America.

SA occurs in even more situations than does CA. Anytime a person appears in public, the potential exists for SA to occur. Researchers have developed a self-presentational theory to explain the widespread existence of SA (see Leary & Kowalski, 1995; Schlenker & Leary, 1982). People are likely to feel some increase in SA when they are observed nonverbally, particularly when they want to make a good impression (see chapter 10 for more on self-presentation and impression maintenance). SA tends to occur more in people who are highly self-conscious, in settings where a person is conspicuous, in circumstances during which a person is being evaluated, in novel situations such as the first day of a new job or a first date, and in larger audiences of observers. High levels of SA occur during adolescence; adolescents must adjust to more adult roles and expectations, cope with bodily changes and their developing sexuality, and deal with the novelty of dating and possibly holding a job. Moreover, changes in physical appearance make adolescence an awkward time (see chapters 2, 5, and 10 for more on the importance of physical appearance as a nonverbal cue). Finally, researchers have discovered that people who are lower in social skills and who nonverbally present themselves poorly are more prone to SA. Of course, this may start a negative spiral, with poor nonverbal skills leading to anxiety and anxiety undermining a person's nonverbal skills.

Research reveals that three predominant communication patterns are experienced by communicatively apprehensive (CA) or socially anxious (SA) individuals: withdrawal, reduced awareness, and tension (see Andersen & Guerrero, 1989). The following sections discuss these three patterns in detail.

The Withdrawal Response

Fear and stress are unpleasant, even painful emotions. It is natural to withdraw from, or avoid entirely, situations or activities that produce fear. The most basic responses to CA and SA are escape, avoidance, and withdrawal. SAs and CAs avoid social encounters, make themselves nonverbally inaccessible, avoid touch, and use architecture and objects to isolate themselves (for reviews of some of this research see Leary & Kowalski, 1995; McCroskey, 1976; Ohman, 1993; Wilhelm, Kochar, Roth, & Gross, 2001). Usually, avoidance is considered a dysfunctional behavior because communication is vital to functioning in today's world. Dates, interviews, service encounters (for example, a waiter taking an order or a customer checking into a hotel), meetings, classes, parties, and presentations all require communication. Many of us find that interaction is anxiety producing, which is why people report communication as the most potent stressor in today's world.

Withdrawal during interaction is a typical response to anxiety. In a study by Daly (1978), high school students high in SA talked less during interviews than their less-anxious counterparts. Schlenker and Leary (1985) show that high SAs fail to participate fully in interaction, exhibit introversion or reticence, and physically or psychologically withdraw from situations. Burgoon and Koper (1984) report that among reticents and CAs, "cues of detachment, nonaffiliation, and nonintimacy were more pronounced" (p. 615). Even in romantic relationships, SA may lead to withdrawal and detachment. Guerrero (1996) found that individuals who characterize themselves as avoidant (that is, they feel uncomfortable when others get too close to them) tend to exhibit low levels of immediacy/affection, fewer forward leans, less gaze, and decreased facial pleasantness and attentiveness when interacting with their romantic partners.

A number of studies have reported that high CAs and SAs avoid eye contact and face-to-face communication (for a summary see Patterson & Ritts, 1997). Daly (1978) reported that high SAs make less eye contact and exhibit shorter periods of eye contact than less-anxious subjects. Andersen and Coussoule (1980) maintained that high CAs fail to perceive immediacy and intimacy cues because of their low levels of eye contact. In several experiments, Burgoon and Koper (1984) showed that CA and reticence are negatively correlated with eye contact. Studies have also shown that experimentally induced interpersonal stress is associated with low levels of eye contact (Exline & Winters, 1965; Slane, Dragan, Crandall, &

Payne, 1980). Indeed, all types of anxiety, including general trait anxiety, which is experienced by people who are chronically anxious, are associated with decreased eye contact (Eckman, 1978; Leary & Kowalski, 1995).

Other nonverbal avoidance behaviors are correlated with increased CA and SA. Burgoon and Koper (1984) demonstrated that during interaction, CA and reticence are associated with more backward leaning, more body blocking or barrier behaviors, and more face covering. Across a series of forty geographically diverse samples, Andersen, Andersen, and Lustig (1987) reported evidence that CA is associated with touch avoidance (a concept discussed later in this chapter). Wilhelm et al. (2001) also reported avoidance of, discomfort with, and anxiety regarding touch associated with SA. A study of the conversational behavior of high CAs shows that they exhibit more silences and longer silences than more-self-confident speakers. Not surprisingly, CAs are perceived as nonaffiliative by others (Burgoon & Koper, 1984).

CA also affects interpersonal distancing behavior in an unusual, sometimes counterintuitive, pattern. Because high CAs seek to avoid interaction, one would predict intuitively that they would maintain greater distances, thereby reducing the chances of interaction. Some evidence supports the position that CAs are spatially remote, but other evidence indicates they are less remote.

On one hand, several studies report that high CAs tend to select low-interaction seats on the periphery of classes, meetings, and group discussions (McCroskey & Sheahan, 1976; McCroskey & McVetta, 1978; Patterson & Ritts, 1997; Weiner, 1973). Carducci and Webber (1979) reported that shy persons tend to maintain large interpersonal distances. A study by Slane et al. (1980), exploring the behavior of stress repressors and stress sensitizers, found that stress-sensitive individuals maintain greater interpersonal distances. Patterson and Edinger (1987) reported several studies that found a relationship between SA and distance such that subjects with higher anxiety maintained greater distances. In their recent summary of correlates of SA, Patterson and Ritts (1997) stated that "reducing gaze and interacting at greater distances allow socially anxious individuals to disengage partially from social interactions yet remain in the encounters. Socially anxious individuals may totally disengage by withdrawing from social encounters or attempting to avoid them altogether" (p. 273).

On the other hand, three studies have found that high CAs actually maintain closer distances than other individuals (Cardot & Dodd, 1979; McCroskey, Richmond, & Young, 1977; Schwarzwald, Kavish, Shoham, & Waysman, 1977). Cardot and Dodd (1979) paired students in three same-sex dyadic combinations consisting of two high CAs, two low CAs, or a high CA paired with a low CA. Results showed that the high-CA dyads maintained closer distances (12 to 18 inches) than mixed-CA dyads (30 to 51 inches). Participants' apprehension level accounted for over 70 percent of the variance in interpersonal distance. Why did high CAs sit so close to one another? Cardot and Dodd (1979) reported that 47 percent of the high-CA dyads—but none of the low-CA or mixed-CA dyads—spoke so softly that they were virtually inaudible through laboratory microphones. They concluded that the high-CA dyads were forced to sit close together in order to hear each other speak. A similar finding with a different explanation is offered by

Schwarzwald et al. (1977), who reported that in a fear-induction condition, subjects sit closer to same-sex individuals but not to opposite-sex individuals. The experimenters suggest that in a fear-provoking situation, people tend to associate and identify with "like" individuals. Perhaps the most compelling explanation was provided by McCroskey et al. (1977), who demonstrated that high-CA males preferred smaller interaction distances than low-CA males by about 6 to 9 inches. The authors explain that because eye contact invites interaction and intimacy, high CAs are more comfortable at distances that are so close as to discourage eye contact and communication.

The research on proxemic correlates of anxiety and apprehension are seemingly contradictory and certainly complex. A number of variables such as sex, task, partner type, and method interact to produce this complex pattern. In any case, the simplistic prediction that high CAs always maintain large interpersonal distances is probably incorrect. High CAs are not stupid; they cleverly use proxemics to avoid communication. Instead of maintaining normative interaction distances, they strategically employ excessively near or far distances to inhibit communication.

The avoidance behavior of high SAs is perhaps most evident in their back-channel behaviors—receiver actions that encourage senders while they are speaking. Burgoon and Koper (1984) reported a series of correlations, all of which indicate that CAs and SAs display significantly less nodding, less interest, and less involvement during interaction. These behaviors, which normally increase interactants' desire for communication, are exactly the behaviors that high CAs and SAs fail to manifest.

Clearly, the evidence suggests that the nonverbal behavior of high CAs constitutes an attempt to avoid communication. But because communication is often important or required in many settings, strong approach-avoidance forces compete within these individuals. The avoidance behavior of high CAs and SAs represents the classic flight response of humans and other animals. The simplest way to avoid fear and anxiety is to withdraw. Unfortunately, social situations are rarely simple. Various avoidance responses, short of full-blown flight, may be the most effective and appropriate defense.

Reduced Awareness

A series of studies demonstrate that high CAs and SAs are oblivious to various social and environmental cues. An anxious, frightened individual in a threatening situation would profit from increased social awareness because more social information would facilitate functional adaptations and adjustments. Unfortunately, the excess anxiety experienced by CAs and SAs produces responses that actually screen out relevant social information, creating a cycle of increased confusion and anxiety.

Several studies have suggested that during interaction, CAs become self-focused and self-conscious rather than other-focused (Andersen & Coussoule, 1980; Andersen & Singleton, 1978; Daly & Stafford, 1984; Greene & Sparks, 1983; Patterson, 1995). A study by Guerrero (1996) reported that avoidant individuals who characterized themselves as uncomfortable with social interaction tended to be fairly inattentive when communicating with their romantic partners. Avoidant individuals also tended not to engage in forward leaning, which may impair both actual and perceived listening. Andersen and Singleton (1978) summarized several studies that suggest that CAs are cerebrotonic, a trait characterized by excessive self-focus, introversion, and tension. Andersen and Coussoule (1980) reported the results of an experiment on the interpersonal perceptions of high CAs; the study concluded that "high CA individuals did not generally perceive significant differences between gaze conditions, even though gaze was operationalized as two extreme conditions." High CAs are preoccupied with their own internal states. Thus, as Patterson (1995) summarized: "as cognitive resources are invested in concerns other than the immediate interaction, fewer resources are available to attend and process information about the partner" (p. 18). SA children seem to suffer as well; research indicates that the have a reduced ability to process nonverbal and social information, particularly vocal and emotional cues (McClure & Nowicki, 2001).

Research suggests that a focus on the self rather than on others is generally viewed as an incompetent communication strategy. Andersen (1986) suggested that extreme self-awareness and self-consciousness are detrimental to effective communication and concludes that "economy in consciousness is essential to competence in communication" (p. 97). This is particularly true for self-consciousness. Similarly, Spitzberg and Cupach (1984) contended that self-consciousness is particularly detrimental to communication competence and typically increases one's anxiety. Cappella (1985) reported that SAs are cognitively overloaded. When faced with a complex cognitive task, their performance deteriorates. He reports that anxious, cognitively overloaded people display more nervous self-touching behaviors and more hesitations and pauses than nonanxious, cognitively overloaded people. Evidence also suggests that high SAs not only are self-focused but also are preoccupied with negative aspects of their performance (Patterson & Ritts, 1997; Ritts & Patterson, 1996). Schlenker and Leary (1985) concluded that when SAs are threatened, "their minds race with thoughts about the unreachable goal and their problems in attaining it; they become self-preoccupied and self-focused, continually re-examining their limitations" (p. 18). Research shows that SAs become preoccupied with how other people evaluate them (Smith, Ingram, & Brehm, 1983). In short, SA produces a debilitating cycle of excessive self-awareness, reduced skill, and increased anxiety.

Other research suggests that a syndrome of problematic defensive reactions produces a cycle of anxiety and incompetence in cases of high CA (Andersen & Guerrero, 1989). Anxious individuals' lack of eye contact compounds their inability to receive relevant social information (Andersen & Coussoule, 1980). Their backward leans and facial covering further limit the sending and receiving of important social information. Their excessive self-focus prevents psychological attention to the other and the situation. Keeley-Dyerson, Bailey, and Burgoon (1988) confirmed that experimentally induced stress reduces nonverbal decoding accuracy over time. In their study, the biggest effects occurred late in the conversations, suggesting that anxiety during interaction may be cumulatively detrimental to nonverbal decoding accuracy. Moreover, they found that the greatest decrease in decoding ability was in the vocal channel, suggesting that decreased sensitivity is a function not only of decreased eye contact but also of decreased cognitive processing.

The apprehension syndrome of increased self-focus, decreased other-focus, reduced visual monitoring, partial withdrawal from the situation, and inefficient cognitive processing of social information produces a spiral of fear, negativity, panic, incompetence, and confusion. This results in avoidance of valuable interaction and decreased performance as a communicator.

Tension

The third behavioral pattern exhibited by high CAs and SAs is increased tension. Tension has the simultaneous effects of (1) increasing anxiety through somatic feedback, (2) limiting blood flow to various parts of the body, including the brain, and (3) sending negative, confusing messages to conversational partners.

The tension felt by people experiencing communication anxiety ranges from mild excitement to sheer panic. Some evidence suggests that mild anxiety during social interaction or even public speaking may get a person "up" for the interaction, but if arousal and fear increase, any positive feelings quickly become negative. The experience of SA is universally unpleasant. Indeed, Leary and Kowalski (1995) explained:

> With increasing levels of anxiety, people are able to detect physiological signs of arousal (such as heart palpitations or bodily tension) that are often unpleasant. When anxious, people sometimes experience a sinking or nauseated feeling in their stomachs, or feelings of weakness or dizziness. (p. 137)

To understand the feelings that extremely high CAs and SAs experience, imagine yourself falling off a cliff, going 90 miles per hour on skis, or being buried alive. Some people actually experience trembling, heart palpitations, or fainting when they encounter SA (Leary & Kowalski, 1995).

Studies demonstrate a relational pattern between increased tension and nervous behaviors in high CAs. Burgoon, Pfau, Birk, and Manusov (1987) demonstrated that the bodies of high CAs are significantly more tense than less-apprehensive individuals. Because bodily relaxation is an immediacy cue that leads to more positive, intimate interactions (Andersen, 1985; see chapter 8) and contributes to perceptions of increased credibility and attraction (Jensen & Andersen, 1979), tension has certain negative interpersonal consequences. Excessive tension may be perceived as a signal of emotional buildup that later may be manifested in aggressive or hostile actions (Eibl-Eibesfeldt, 1974).

Schlenker and Leary (1985) reported that "high social anxiety is associated with an array of nervous responses including fidgeting, self-manipulation, perspiring, and the appearance of overall tension" (p. 178). We have all witnessed a nervous speaker who plays with a pen or strokes her or his hair. Nervous communicators repeatedly touch their hands or face. It is unclear whether CAs exhibit more self-manipulations and self-adaptors than others without CA; one article reports several significant correlations between communication anxiety and self-touching (Burgoon & Koper, 1984), but two other studies fail to find such a relationship in the laboratory (Burgoon, Pfau, Birk, & Manusov, 1987; Comadena & Andersen, 1978). Nonetheless, the preponderance of evidence suggests that high CAs manifest nervousness nonverbally. Burgoon and Koper (1984) concluded that

Anxiety and apprehension are visible in the face, posture, and hands of a nervous speaker.

high CAs, compared to others, "tend to show more negative forms of arousal through increased bodily tension, more self-touching and more protective behaviors" (p. 618).

Several other changes in nonverbal behavior occur because of the tension experienced by SAs. One common, visible response to SA is blushing, particularly the "creeping blush," which appears as splotches of red on a person's cheek, neck, or jaw (Leary & Kowalski, 1995; Patterson & Ritts, 1997). Blushing sends involuntary messages of anxiety and overarousal and, ironically, usually makes the poor, anxious blusher even more embarrassed and anxious. Tension also restricts blood flow to the extremities, often resulting in cold, clammy hands. Because handshakes are obligatory in many social situations, clammy hands send a tactile message of tension and anxiety to interaction partners. Other signs of tension may include jiggling feet, rapid breathing, pale skin, dysfluent speech, higher vocal pitch, and negative facial expressions (Leary & Kowalski, 1995; Mulac & Wiemann, 1984). For example, Guerrero's (1996) research suggested that SAs display more vocal tension than their more socially secure counterparts. She also shows that SAs who fear intimacy are especially likely to engage in nonfluent speech characterized by long response latencies.

There may also be a relationship between apprehension and the use of power and/or force. Aida (1993) reported that high CA couples use more unilateral, noninteractive negative power strategies in their marriages than do non-apprehensive couples. Few high CAs are dangerous to others; however, many mass murderers are described as nice, shy, quiet people who never disturbed anyone previously. It may be that for some severely disturbed individuals, their inability to communicate verbally, along with excessive tension, leads to the most destructive nonverbal response possible: murder.

Coping with Communication Apprehension and Social Anxiety

Most people who experience CA or SA do a pretty good job of dealing with it. They lead relatively quiet but satisfying lives. They are less likely to get into conflicts and confrontations, and they like it that way. They seek lifestyles and occupations that offer them less social contact.

Sometimes, however, CA or SA limits a person's social life, occupational growth, financial success, and relational satisfaction. What can these people do to feel more comfortable about social interaction when they desire it? Several books offer sound, research-based advice (Leary & Kowalski, 1995; Richmond & McCroskey, 1985). First, nearly everyone gets the jitters or feels nervous before a public speech, yet most of us do very well once we get underway; after awhile, the butterflies begin to go away. A similar, calming progression occurs during a first date; after a few hours (and especially after a few dates), the initial nervousness is ancient history.

To overcome CA and SA, there are several guidelines to follow without needing to seek professional help:

- *Reduce self-awareness.* Avoid focusing on your performance; instead, think of the task or person at hand and "get out of yourself." Most good communicators nearly forget about themselves during an interaction because they are so focused on their audience or topic.

- *Breathe.* Anxious individuals tend to hold their breath or engage in shallow breathing. Watch a basketball player at the free-throw line or an Olympic diver; they often take a deep breath to alleviate the jitters and make sure enough oxygen gets to the brain.

- *Relax.* Stretching techniques reduce the physical tension that accompanies CA and SA. Hatha yoga, athletic stretching, or even just reaching your arms high above your head or opening or closing your fists may help you relax.

- *Be prepared.* Anxiety is often the result of poor preparation. Whether you are facing a job interview, presentation, or speech, being prepared can greatly reduce your anxiety.

For some people with persistent traitlike CA or SA, self-help is not enough. Fortunately, several therapies have proven to be quite successful: (1) relaxation therapies, especially systematic desensitization; (2) skills training, which helps individuals develop more competence, a key to overcoming anxiety; (3) cognitive therapies, particularly cognitive restructuring, which can change negative internal dialog into positive internal dialog; and (4) role playing and practice interactions, which help individuals "rehearse" appropriate behaviors under less threatening conditions. (For more about these methods see Leary & Kowalski, 1995; Richmond and McCroskey, 1985.) Fortunately, some of these methods do not require expensive psychiatric treatment and may be offered through your college communication department or counseling center.

Touch Avoidance

The preceding discussion focused on verbal CA and general SA, along with the nonverbal behaviors that accompany anxiety and avoidance. A similar sort of fear and negativity relates to intimate nonverbal communication, particularly touch. Researchers have examined a concept called touch avoidance, a negative attitude toward touch that also affects an individual's proxemic behavior and other types of nonverbal communication.

Few would argue that touch is a crucial part of personal and intimate relationships. For example, imagine a mother who never touched her baby or an engaged couple who never touched one another. Such relationships would be considered abnormal, even pathological. Investigators of tactile communication have equated touch with intimacy itself (Morris, 1971) and have suggested that love cannot be successfully conveyed in the absence of touch (Montagu, 1971/1978). Touch deprivation has been associated with a host of undesirable consequences, including increased mental illness in adults, and both a failure to thrive and even death in infants. Instrumental and comforting touch, in the nursing profession for example, is associated with greater patient satisfaction, safety, comfort, and self-confidence (Lower, 1980; Routasalo & Isola, 1996).

Anxiety about touch or avoidance of touch undoubtedly has a negative impact on an individual's personal relationships. Numerous communication researchers have investigated how people develop attitudes toward touch, what behaviors are associated with these attitudes, and what consequences occur for those who are anxious or avoidant of touch. Jourard and Rubin (1968) were the first to examine the notion of "touchability" and touch avoidance and suggested that separate sender-receiver and opposite-sex/same-sex dimensions may exist for touchability and touch readiness. A series of investigations followed, which examined the related constructs of touch avoidance (Andersen, 2005; Andersen, Andersen, & Lustig, 1987; Andersen & Leibowitz, 1978; Andersen & Sull, 1985; Guerrero & Andersen, 1991; Jones & Brown, 1996; Leibowitz & Andersen, 1976), tactile attitudes (Deethardt & Hines, 1983; Larsen & LeRoux, 1984), and touch comfort (Fromme et al., 1986, 1989). We are just beginning to understand the causes and consequences of negative attitudes toward touch. "The touch avoidance construct is not a direct index of how much a person touches or avoids being touched. Instead, it is an index of a person's affect toward touch" (Andersen, Andersen, & Lustig, 1987, p. 90). So, touch avoidance is an attitudinal measure of how much a person likes or dislikes touch.

Research consistently shows that two independent dimensions of touch attitudes exist, an opposite-sex dimension and a same-sex dimension. Research has shown the avoidance and repugnance regarding same-sex touch is, in part a function of homophobia (Floyd, 2000). Separate sending and receiving dimensions have not been discovered (Andersen & Leibowitz, 1978; Fromme et al., 1986; Jones & Brown, 1996). Evidently, most people have generally similar attitudes toward both being touched and touching others.

How do negative attitudes toward touching develop? Andersen and Leibowitz (1978) reported that the cultural roles people perform as a function of their sex, age, marital status, and religion are associated with their touch-avoidance levels. Older persons, married persons, and Protestants generally are more touch avoidant than others. Several studies suggest that parental attitudes toward touch are the critical determiners of their offspring's attitudes toward touch. Fromme et al. (1986) reported that an individual's touch comfort is associated with perceived parental touch comfort, particularly with the comfort level of the father. Another study (Spradlin & Fromme, 1989) showed a very strong relationship between parents' and children's attitudes toward touch, accounting for 50 to 90 percent of the variance between the two sets of measures. Evidently, parental attitudes are critical determiners of children's tactile attitudes; however, other variables play a role as well. Research has shown that children who experienced hitting while growing up or had been physically abused had much more negative attitudes toward touch and had much greater need for larger personal-space bubbles (Fromme et al., 1989; Vranic, 2003). This is consistent with the observation that child abuse is an intergenerational phenomenon.

Peoples' self-reports of touch avoidance or touch comfort correlate with actual behavior. In one experiment, Sorensen (1979) conducted school-related interviews with volunteers who had previously filled out a touch-avoidance instrument. (A sample touch-avoidance instrument appears in Box 7.1, and a scoring key is at the end of the chapter for you to complete and score your answers.) At the conclusion of the experiment, as the interviewees were being thanked for

---

Box 7.1
Touch-Avoidance Questionnaire

Directions: This instrument is composed of eighteen statements concerning feelings about touching other people and being touched. Please indicate the degree to which each statement applies to you by circling whether you (1) strongly agree, (2) agree, (3) are undecided, (4) disagree, or (5) strongly disagree with each statement. Although some of these statements may seem repetitious, take your time and try to be as honest as possible.

1 2 3 4 5   1. A hug from a same-sex friend is a true sign of friendship.

1 2 3 4 5   2. Opposite-sex friends enjoy it when I touch them.

1 2 3 4 5   3. I often put my arm around friends of the same sex.

1 2 3 4 5   4. When I see two people of the same sex hugging it revolts me.

1 2 3 4 5   5. I like it when members of the opposite sex touch me.

1 2 3 4 5   6. People shouldn't be so uptight about touching persons of the same sex.

1 2 3 4 5   7. I think it is vulgar when members of the opposite sex touch me.

1 2 3 4 5   8. When a member of the opposite sex touches me I find it unpleasant.

1 2 3 4 5   9. I wish I were free to show emotions by touching members of the same sex.

1 2 3 4 5   10. I'd enjoy giving a massage to an opposite-sex friend.

1 2 3 4 5   11. I enjoy kissing a person of the same sex.

1 2 3 4 5   12. I like to touch friends who are the same sex as I am.

1 2 3 4 5   13. Touching a friend of the same sex does not make me uncomfortable.

1 2 3 4 5   14. I find it enjoyable when my date and I embrace.

1 2 3 4 5   15. I enjoy getting a back rub from a member of the opposite sex.

1 2 3 4 5   16. I dislike kissing relatives of the same sex.

1 2 3 4 5   17. Intimate touching with members of the opposite sex is pleasurable.

1 2 3 4 5   18. I find it difficult to be touched by a member of my own sex.

their participation, half were touched by the experimenter and the other half were not. Sorensen found that touch avoiders had significantly more negative attitudes toward the experimenter when touched than when not touched, but touch approachers had more positive attitudes toward an experimenter when touched than when not touched. In another lab study, Wilhelm et al. (2001) found that scores on a social touch aversion measure were correlated with dislike for touch in an experimental situation. In yet another laboratory study, Andersen and Sull (1985) reported that touch-avoidance scores were fairly good predictors of inter-personal distance: Touch avoiders chose to interact at greater distances than touch approachers. Guerrero and Andersen (1991) found that people's touch-avoidance scores correlated with their actual touch behavior. In this study, experimenters unobtrusively observed and recorded the tactile behaviors of people waiting in theater and zoo lines. The observed people were then asked to complete a ques-tionnaire about their perceptions of their own touch behavior. Similar experi-ments found that the touch-comfort test significantly predicted personal space (Fromme et al., 1986, 1989): these studies demonstrated that college students with higher touch-comfort scores were more likely to volunteer to participate in a "hugging experiment." Moreover, even among the volunteers, people with greater touch-comfort scores rated hugs more positively than those with lower touch-comfort scores.

Touch avoidance and touch comfort may actually be an index of a person's general intimacy or immediacy level. Interpersonal touch is a critical component of both intimacy and immediacy (Andersen, 1985; Thayer, 1986; Jones, 1994; see also chapters 8 and 9). As Andersen and Leibowitz (1978) originally argued, "The failure to utilize touch is indicative of interpersonal avoidance and lack of inter-personal closeness" (p. 90). Thayer (1986) contended,

> If intimacy is proximity, then nothing comes closer than touch, the most inti-mate knowledge of another. The expression to know someone in the biblical sense is equivalent to having been sexually intimate with them, to have known their body. (p. 12)

Hall (1966a) suggested that touch and close interpersonal space are indices of intimacy because at the closest distances, one can actually grasp or hold the other person. As noted previously, several studies show that touch avoiders maintain greater interpersonal distances, literally staying out of touch and out of reach from others. Fromme et al. (1989) suggested that "touch comfort reflects a more active interpersonal style and more satisfactory social relationships in general" (p. 18). Wilhelm and colleagues (2001) report a set of relationships between negative attitudes toward touch, SA, and negative attitudes toward affection.

What other factors seem to be associated with touch comfort or avoidance? Andersen and Leibowitz (1978) found that married, older, and Christian people reported relatively more negative, avoidant attitudes toward touch. Similarly, Fromme et al. (1986) reported that touch comfort was lower for older people, peo-ple of high socioeconomic status, and younger, later-born children in families. However, family size was positively related to touch comfort. Touch comfort is positively correlated with social success and happiness, life satisfaction, self-satis-

faction, self-confidence, assertiveness, active problem solving, and social acceptance (Fromme et al., 1989). In short, positive tactile attitudes seem to be related to
a healthy personality, successful social relations, and intimate personal relationships. Research demonstrates that touch avoidance is negatively associated with
social self-confidence (Jones & Brown, 1996). In other words, people who enjoy
and use touch are better adjusted and more socially confident across a wide variety of situations.

Some evidence (Fromme et al., 1986; Jones, 1994; Noller, 1978) showed that
females are generally more comfortable with touch than males. However, this is
probably because females have more positive attitudes toward same-sex touch
than do males. Research has shown that attitudes toward same-sex and opposite-
sex touch are not meaningfully associated; therefore, we will examine these two
bodies of research separately.

Same-Sex Touch Avoidance

Considerable evidence suggests that males have far more negative attitudes
then females toward same-sex touch. Derlega, Lewis, Harrison, Winstead, and
Costanza (1989) reported that in friendships, males display less tactile intimacy
with males than with females and less tactile intimacy than females display with
other females. Several studies conclude that males are more touch avoidant of
same-sex individuals than are females, regardless of age, religion, or marital status (Andersen & Leibowitz, 1978; Silverman, Pressman, & Bartell, 1973). In an
intercultural study of touch avoidance, Jones and Remland (1982) reported that
both Asian and American females were less averse to same-sex touch than were
males from either cultural group. In a study of touch avoidance among nurses,
Lower (1980) found that male nurses had significantly more same-sex touch
avoidance than female nurses. Similarly, Larsen and LeRoux (1984) show that
females have more positive scores on the same-sex touching scale than do males.
Fromme et al. (1986) report a series of significant correlations, all demonstrating
that women are comfortable with same-sex touch, particularly in such areas as the
face, buttocks, outer thighs, and knees.

Evidently same-sex touching is more threatening, anxiety provoking, and
repugnant for males than it is for females. One explanation is homophobia—the
fear of homosexuals or of even appearing to be homosexual (Andersen & Leibowitz, 1978).The extreme avoidance of other males by males, according to one study,
is probably the result of homophobia (Derlega et al., 1989). Males may overcompensate for this fear by developing negative attitudes toward same-sex touch and
by avoiding intimacy with other men. A second related explanation is that
because men are more likely to associate touch with sexuality than are women
(Fromme at al., 1986), men find opposite-sex touch to be socially appropriate but
not same-sex touch. With the exception of roughhousing, males are quite reluctant
to touch other males. This may be because observers perceive male-male touch to
be sexual but make no such assumptions about female-female touch (Derlega et
al., 1989). A third explanation is that many men avoid gentle, loving, or nurturant
communication acts because these activities are not masculine as traditionally
defined. When male-male touch does occur, it is often in the form of roughhousing

or contact sports such as football, basketball, and hockey. In this way, males are permitted to touch in a manner they perceive to be sex-role appropriate.

A final explanation for men's high levels of same-sex touch avoidance may stem from the fact that in many primate species, including humans, males are more aggressive and hostile than females. Whether male aggressiveness is biologically or culturally induced is a matter of considerable debate (see Andersen, 1998). Such differences may be due to low parental involvement and reproductive advantages for aggressive males. In other words, women carry a child during pregnancy and often breast-feed the infant after birth. As such, women have a greater parental investment from a biological standpoint than men. Moreover, males may attempt to have several mates without investing much time or material resources in any mate. In his book on universals of human behavior, Brown (1991) explains:

> In mammals it is almost always the male that invests less, is larger, is more actively competitive and is prone to seek multiple mates. . . . The greater aggressiveness of males is at least partly a result of sexual selection, aggression being an effective male strategy in competition for females. (pp. 108–110)

If this evolutionary argument is valid, then males have a propensity to be combative or competitive with one another. Male-male touch then can be seen as a hostile, aggressive act, a challenge for dominant status. Even well-socialized males may be predisposed to avoid male touch.

Both men and women with certain types of personalities are more likely to be same-sex touch avoiders. Same-sex touch avoiders of both sexes are more authoritarian and rigid (Larsen & LeRoux, 1984), suggesting more intolerant, autocratic orientations among these individuals. Similarly, same-sex touch avoiders of both sexes have more socially undesirable conceptions of femininity, suggesting less nurturance and less responsiveness among touch avoiders. Male same-sex touch avoiders have been found to possess an external locus of control—that is, they conform to others' wishes and attitudes—as opposed to an internal locus of control, which is characterized by self-confidence and self-direction. This suggests that conformity to sex-role norms may be an issue with these individuals. Female same-sex touch avoiders appear lower in self-esteem and more conservative than touch approachers (Larsen & LeRoux, 1984). Same-sex touch avoiders also tend to be less androgynous than touch approachers (Crawford, 1994). People who are rigidly masculine or feminine view same-sex touch as a violation of their definition of appropriate sex roles (for more on sex and gender roles see chapter 5).

A number of studies have reported that negative attitudes toward same-sex touch are associated with religiosity. Montagu (1971/1978) suggested that Christian religions, particularly fundamentalist Christian religions, discourage interpersonal touch. In a study by Andersen and Leibowitz (1978), Protestants were found to be more avoidant of same-sex touch than were non-Protestants. Their data show that people with no religious affiliation were the least touch avoidant. In a study by Lower (1980), Jewish nursing students were significantly less same-sex touch avoidant than their Protestant or Catholic counterparts. Larsen and LeRoux (1984) reported that same-sex touch avoidance correlates with religious orthodoxy of males but not of females. This body of research suggests that religiousness, particularly for Christian religions, is associated with same-sex touch avoidance.

Some limited intercultural research suggests that Americans may be less touch avoidant than residents of Mediterranean countries, India, Pakistan, and Asia (Jones & Remland, 1982; see chapter 4). The restrictive religious prohibitions against touch in these parts of the world may explain this cultural variation. Far Easterners are even more touch avoidant, supporting findings that Asian countries are noncontact cultures. McDaniel and Andersen (1998) reported that Asians touch less than any other group.

Some light has been shed on the development of same-sex touch avoidance by Fromme et al. (1986), who found that if mothers and fathers are comfortable with same-sex touch, their children reported more comfort with same-sex touch. This effect is particularly true for the father but also is strong for the mother. In general, if your family is comfortable with same-sex touching, you will be too.

Opposite-Sex Touch Avoidance

Although a number of studies (J. A. Hall, 1984, 1985; Stier & Hall, 1984) have shown small or nonexistent sex differences in actual touch (observed touch behavior), other studies demonstrate that women are more reluctant about and have more negative attitudes toward opposite-sex touch than men do (Guerrero & Andersen, 1991; Hall, 1985; Henley, 1977; Silverman et al., 1973). Research shows that females have significantly higher levels of opposite-sex touch avoidance than males across numerous diverse samples (Andersen & Leibowitz, 1978; Andersen, Andersen, & Lustig, 1987). Fromme et al. (1986) report that "regardless of body area or degree of acquaintance, men are more comfortable than women with opposite-sex touch" (p. 56). Andersen et al. (1987) collected samples from 40 American universities and found that for 39 of the 40 samples, females reported more opposite-sex touch avoidance than males, with 32 of the 40 samples showing statistically significant differences.

Why do females have more touch-avoidant attitudes toward opposite-sex touch than men do? One possibility is that females' natural expressiveness and immediacy are tempered by restrictive attitudes toward touch. A corollary explanation is that opposite-sex touch is most likely to have sexual connotations. Traditionally, women have been enculturated to believe that employing "forward" touch is out-of-role and excessively aggressive. A woman in one of my classes explained this finding by saying, "I don't touch men; men don't need any encouragement." In their exhaustive study of American couples, Blumstein and Schwartz (1983) found that, regardless of marital status, males reported initiating considerably more sexual contact than females; this finding held true in reports from both males and females. Indeed, their research supports the traditional position that females exert a restraint on sexual behavior, whereas males play an initiator role. One final explanation for greater female touch avoidance of males concerns psychological sex roles. In a study by Eman, Dierks-Stewart, and Tucker (1978), androgynous and masculine individuals reported less touch avoidance than feminine or undifferentiated (neither feminine nor masculine) individuals. Evidently, individuals with more masculine psychological profiles are less touch avoidant in opposite-sex relationships, suggesting that biological sex is less important than sex-role orientation.

Lower touch-avoidance scores for opposite-sex relationships are related to a number of other attitudes and predispositions. Results suggest that touch approachers are better adjusted, have better communication relationships, and are more relaxed (Larsen & LeRoux, 1984). Evidence by Andersen et al. (1987) shows that among 40 geographically diverse samples, opposite-sex touch avoidance was negatively correlated with self-esteem in 38 of these samples, 32 of which were statistically significant. Evidently, individuals with more self-worth and self-esteem are more likely to have positive attitudes toward opposite-sex touch. A series of findings also has shown that opposite-sex touch avoiders are more communicatively apprehensive, less predisposed to verbal behavior (Andersen et al., 1987) and more reticent (Fromme et al., 1989) than other individuals. This portrait suggests that opposite-sex touch avoiders find it difficult and anxiety producing to communicate with others of the opposite sex. Touch avoiders have also been found to have less open communication styles, confirming their noncommunicative nature (Andersen et al., 1987).

One study suggests that actual touch behaviors and touch-avoidance scores are correlated in dating relationships (Guerrero & Andersen, 1994). This study found significant correlations in touch-avoidance scores between partners in both dating and married relationships, suggesting that people tend to find romantic partners with the same tactile attitudes as their own. More importantly, this study found that touch was highly correlated across all relational levels ($r = .88$), suggesting that individuals' own attitudes toward touch become much less important than the relationship itself. People tend to reciprocate their partner's touch level, whether it is high or low. As the relationship grows, so does the reciprocity of touch. Dating couples showed highly reciprocal tactile behavior ($r = .81$); seriously dating couples showed even more tactile similarity ($r = .88$); and married couples showed almost entirely reciprocal tactile behavior ($r = .96$). Evidently, becoming a committed relational partner involves a virtual merging of intimacy levels between partners. This may be the real meaning of relational intimacy (for more on relational intimacy see chapter 9).

TECHNOLOGY, OVERAROUSAL, AND STRESS

In our not-so-distant past, interpersonal relationships were few, limited to the social confines of the family, tribe, or village. Today, because of technological advances in communication and transportation, our circle of interpersonal interaction has expanded to include not only close friends and intimate loved ones but also innumerable acquaintances and strangers with whom we come into contact via telephones, fax machines, the Internet, airplanes, and so on. We are living in what McLuhan (1969) called a global village, a place where contact with virtually every other human being is possible. Human relationships have been devalued by their abundance, and stress is one of the most commonly used words in our vocabularies. Overarousal and anxiety are common characteristics of everyday life. Kenneth Gergen (1991) observed:

As a result of the technological development just described, life is a swirling sea of social relations. Words thunder in by radio, television, newspaper, mail, radio, telephone, fax, wire service, electronic mail, billboards, Federal Express, and more. Waves of new faces everywhere—in town for a day, visiting for the weekend, at the Rotary lunch, at the church social—and incessantly and incandescently on television. Long weeks in a single community are unusual; a full day in a single neighborhood is becoming rare. . . . As this increase becomes extreme we reach a state of social saturation. (p. 61)

Overstimulation and overarousal are everywhere. The greatest challenge most of us face is how to live in a world of information and interpersonal overload.

A personal experience helps illustrate how overstimulation and overarousal function in people's everyday lives. I called my secretary one morning. Upon inquiring how she was, I was informed that she was drowning in a sea of papers. I empathized and replied that it is a sign of the times and told her how my desk was a paper disaster as well, scattered with grant proposals, student papers, memos from our director, newsletters, warnings from campus security. But the blizzard of paper was only the tip of the iceberg, I explained. I had dozens of unanswered messages to deal with as well.

It was the first week of fall classes at San Diego State University, and as I returned to my office, I realized I hadn't checked my voice mail or e-mail. Voice mail, the high-tech version of the answering machine, permits message storage, retrieval, transfer, and, best of all, noninteractive responses—all with the touch of a button. I picked up my phone to listen to my messages with trepidation; I hadn't picked them up for eight hours, and I didn't know what to expect. The virtual voice of the cyberoperator answered my prompt, "You have 22 messages." Forty minutes later I had finished hearing all my messages. I had not responded to them, but at least I had heard them. Next, I turned to my e-mail, which contained 140 new messages. I began to process the messages, discarding the obsolete and irrelevant, making lists—one for urgent, one for nonurgent, and one for longer conversations with friends and colleagues with whom I actually wanted to chat. The goal of all this, however, was not communication; it was emptying in-boxes. In the last few years, I have observed an interesting phenomenon. I get more satisfaction from discarding my mail than reading it and responding to it. And I'm an extrovert. Pity the poor sufferer of CA!

But the problem is more than information overload. The unfortunate reality of modern communication is a retreat from the sources of information themselves—colleagues, teachers, politicians, and so on, who all complain they can't "get their message across." As I observed recently at a campus task force meeting, we are living in an information purgatory. At work, I read my mail and messages from my secretary, browse my e-mail messages, listen to voice mail, check my fax machine, and go home. Heading home, I realize I will face more of the same: more mail, e-mail, voice mail, and faxes, not to mention the 88 (soon to be 500) channels of cable television to which I've been upgraded.

Demands are made on our time by other forms of communication as well. At one time, humans desired close contact with others and longed for the sight and feel of close friends. Today, the cancelled dinner party, date, or concert is as likely

Increasingly stressed-out urbanites seek solitude and emotional renewal in remote places.

to bring feelings of relief as disappointment. In fact, it is only during my solitary, daily long-distance runs that I feel refuge from this communication crisis.

If we once walked a tightrope between boredom and stress, we are far less likely to stumble into boredom today. Nonverbal intimacy is becoming increasingly hard to achieve, and we are awash in a sea of relationships, most of them nonintimate and indirect. Finding special relationships may be harder now than at any time in history.

The popularity of ecovacations in the wilderness, of weekends at country inns, of cross-country skiing, of solitary runs, of trips to the mountains shouldn't be surprising. One of the hot topics in communication research is privacy maintenance (see Petronio, 1993). I have written that we would do well to leave our desks, computers, and conference tables to swim in the ocean, climb a mountain, touch a glacier (Andersen, 1993b). The challenge of the next century will be to maintain close relationships while avoiding the perils of excess arousal and anxiety. This may make quiet, nonverbal forms of communication even more important in our close relationships. Quiet sharing of eye contact, space, and touch and an exchange of warm, genuine, caring smiles may be the ultimate antidote to the stress of our fast-paced technological world.

SUMMARY

Humans thrive on interpersonal arousal and stimulation. Too little contact with others produces loneliness and boredom. Too much contact produces stress and anxiety. For each person, an optimal level of arousal exists. Introverts become easily overstimulated and often choose to avoid contact with others. Extroverts require more stimulation and seek verbal and nonverbal interaction. For all of us, overarousal is stressful. Being able to assess and respond appropriately to another person's arousal cues is an important interpersonal skill. Overaroused people need calming; underaroused people need stimulation.

Two of the most widespread forms of anxiety are known as communication anxiety (CA) and social anxiety (SA). For high CAs and SAs, communication is anxiety provoking and elicits the following responses: withdrawal, reduced awareness, and tension. Each of these responses is accompanied by its own distinctive array of nonverbal behaviors. High CAs and SAs withdraw from communication by talking less, avoiding other people, invading or avoiding the interaction space of others, reducing eye contact, leaning backward, and creating body barriers that impede interaction. These individuals are also so preoccupied with feelings of anxiety that they become self-focused, self-conscious, and oblivious to the nonverbal behavior of interaction partners. They experience cognitive overload and fail to process external information. This produces a spiral of additional anxiety, confusion, and incompetence. The tension felt by high CAs and SAs produces negative nonverbal behaviors that are perceived negatively by interactional partners. Their nervous movements, blushing, halting speech, and clammy hands send negative nonverbal messages to other interactants.

The most widely researched form of nonverbal anxiety and withdrawal is touch avoidance, a negative predisposition to touch that is nonverbally manifested in less touch, greater interpersonal distances, and reduced intimacy. Touch approachers tend to experience less communication anxiety, better social relationships, and better psychological adjustment. In close relationships, touch avoiders touch their partners frequently, even though they touch somewhat less than touch approachers. Touch avoiders also touch at the same level as their partners, suggesting that reciprocal touch is vital to relational intimacy and that people can often overcome anxious feelings in the context of close relationships.

Scoring Your Touch-Avoidance Questionnaire

1. Label each question as an A, B, X, or Y in this manner.

Question 1 = Y	10 = B
2 = B	11 = Y
3 = Y	12 = Y
4 = X	13 = Y
5 = B	14 = B
6 = Y	15 = B
7 = A	16 = X
8 = A	17 = B
9 = Y	18 = X

2. Total separately your responses for all A questions, all B questions, all X questions, and all Y questions. In other words, see what number you circled to answer questions 7 and 8. Add those two numbers together and that's your A total.

3. To arrive at your touch-avoidance measure for same-sex touch (TAM1), use the following formula:

$$TAM1 = 15 + Y - X$$

To figure out your touch-avoidance measure for opposite-sex touch (TAM2), use the following formula:

$$TAM2 = 10 + B - A$$

Following are some experimental findings based on the use of this touch-avoidance instrument:

- The male average for same-sex touch avoidance is 26.4; the female average is 21.7.
- The male average for opposite-sex touch avoidance is 12.9; the female average is 14.9.
- The Protestant group average for touch avoidance is 15.0.
- The non-Protestant group average for touch avoidance is 12.9.
- The highest touch avoiders are married, Protestant females with an average score of 15.8.
- The lowest touch avoiders are married, non-Protestant males with an average score of 9.8.

8

Immediacy and Nonverbal Communication

There is language in her eye, her cheek, her lip.

—William Shakespeare, *Troilus and Cressida*

The human communication which creates redundancy in relationships between persons is still preponderantly iconic and is achieved through the means of kinesics, paralinguistics, intention movements, action and the like.

—Gregory Bateson, *Steps to an Ecology of Mind*

Nonverbal behaviors provide the most basic connections between humans. Warm, involving, engaging nonverbal signals, called immediacy behaviors, provide connection and positive affect in all human relationships. Immediacy behaviors create connection, signal interest in communicating, and create closeness between interactants. The exchange of nonverbal immediacy is perhaps *the* most central function of nonverbal behavior. The term *immediacy* describes messages that signal feelings of warmth, closeness, and involvement with other people. Mehrabian (1971a) first developed the immediacy principle, which states, "People are drawn toward persons and things they like, evaluate highly and prefer" (p. 1). What communication behaviors convey these warm, positive feelings to others? Andersen and colleagues (Andersen, 1985, Andersen & Andersen, 2005; Andersen, Andersen, & Jensen, 1979) have conceptualized and measured immediacy behaviors that simultaneously perform four functions: signal availability and inclusion, communicate approach and involvement, increase sensory stimulation, and communicate warmth and positive affect.

Immediacy behaviors signal availability and inclusion. Immediacy behaviors signal availability for communication and include others in the interaction (Andersen, 1985; Burgoon & Hale, 1984). Behaviors such as eye contact, close interpersonal distances, and touch, as well as open, direct body positions, communicate availability and inclusion and invite communication from others. Conversely, avoiding eye contact, distancing oneself, facing away from another person, and avoiding touch all signal exclusion and unavailability and are nonimmediacy behaviors.

191

Immediacy behaviors communicate approach and involvement. Actions that communicate physical or psychological closeness to another person are considered immediacy behaviors (Andersen, 1985). Burgoon and Hale (1984) suggested that involvement is an essential aspect of immediacy. Cappella (1983) and Burgoon (1994) have taken the position that immediacy is a part of involvement, not the reverse. Involvement has been defined as the degree to which an individual is engaged and interested in the conversation at hand. Cappella and Burgoon both maintain that involvement behaviors are not always perceived positively; how they are perceived depends on situational, relational, and individual factors. Nevertheless, although it is certainly true that involvement behaviors can take on new meanings in light of other behaviors, personal factors, or relational factors, in general are perceived positively as predicted by the direct effects model or social meaning model (Andersen, 1985, 1999; Andersen, Guerrero, & Jones, 2006; Burgoon, Coker, & Coker, 1986). The basic immediacy behaviors that signal approach and liking are hardwired into the human species. In dyadic interaction, eye contact, joint symmetrical actions such as high fives, and face-to-face imitation are approach behaviors. They all serve to orient two people to a shared perspective or state of mind (Kinsbourne, 2006).

Immediacy behaviors increase sensory stimulation. When someone looks at us, smiles at us, or touches us, physiological changes occur in our body. Interpersonal gazes, close distances, direct body positions, touches, and smiles cause increases in our heart rate, brain activity, blood pressure, and bodily movements (Andersen, 1985). Because immediacy behaviors are typically multichanneled and occur in clusters, we show considerable activation and arousal when others communicate immediacy to us.

Joint symmetrical actions such as high fives are approach behaviors that serve to orient two people to a shared perspective or state of mind.

Immediacy behaviors communicate interpersonal warmth and positive affect. Interpersonal warmth, intimacy, friendship, trust, and love are communicated by immediacy behaviors (Andersen, 1985; Andersen & Guerrero, 1998b; Boone & Buck, 2003). Gifford (1994) showed that receivers attribute warmth to smiles, attentiveness, reclining postures, extended hands, the absence of nervous movements, and head nods, among other behaviors. In positive relationships, immediacy is the vehicle for propelling a relationship to higher levels of intimacy and closeness. Imagine yourself in a new dating relationship. You really like your partner a lot. During the evening, your date looks into your eyes, touches you on several occasions, sits very near to you, and speaks in a warm, affectionate voice. Chances are these immediacy behaviors will increase your level of closeness. Moreover, you are likely to reciprocate with your own set of immediacy behaviors, which will take the relationship to a higher level of intimacy. (More on this process will be discussed in chapter 9). Warm, affectively positive immediacy behaviors are unconsciously communicated to people we like. In an experiment by Palmer and Simmons (1995), people were induced to show liking for another person. Though they successfully communicated liking through immediacy and involvement cues, less than one-quarter of the participants were consciously aware of how they communicated liking.

In less positive or overstimulated interactions, immediacy cues carry messages of too much closeness and are perceived as threatening, stressful, anxiety provoking, suffocating, overwhelming, and even harassing. (See chapters 7 and 9 for more on what happens when immediacy is unwanted). Nevertheless, regardless of the reaction produced, immediacy messages in general are intended by the sender to convey warm, positive, and intimate feelings. The power of immediacy was illustrated in Manusov's (1991) study of interpersonal conversations. Results show that immediacy behaviors lead to more favorable evaluations of a communicator's social skills, competence, and pleasantness. Manusov reports that interactants believe immediacy behaviors to be natural, unintentional, spontaneous behaviors that signal positive feelings.

COMPONENTS OF NONVERBAL IMMEDIACY

Nonverbal immediacy is typically encoded and decoded as a set of redundant, interrelated behaviors. In this section, the components of nonverbal immediacy will be examined carefully for conceptual purposes. But keep in mind that this is an artificial fragmentation; immediacy behaviors are sent and received as a gestalt, a multichanneled set of nonverbal behaviors that signal availability and warmth, decrease interpersonal distance, and provide increased stimulation (Andersen, 1985; also see chapter 1). For example, when you feel attraction for a person on a date, you send more than positive verbal messages; you communicate your attraction in more than one channel. You might touch your date, move closer, make eye contact, talk in warm tones, and face in your date's direction. Immediacy is typically a mindless, spontaneous expression of positive affection for another person that is encoded as a combination of cues. The following excerpt illustrates this principle:

> A few years ago, when this author was training experimental confederates to use continuous (90 percent) or averted (15 percent) gaze, an interesting and troubling experience occurred. The validations of our manipulations revealed that the confederates in the continuous gaze condition used more forward leans, more vocal enthusiasm, and more smiles. Only after considerable training were some confederates able to suppress these collateral immediacy cues. Some were unable to suppress immediacy in other channels and weren't used

> in the experiments. Other researchers have reported similar problems. . . . The
> point is that immediacy cues are encoded and decoded as a conceptual, behav-
> ioral gestalt. (Andersen, 1985, p. 13)

Human perception is rarely a direct function of the objects or events we receive through our senses. In fact, when something is missing from a sentence, a scene, or an interaction, our minds often fill in the missing information. These principles were illustrated nicely in the following immediacy experiment. In a study of televised immediacy, Janis Andersen and one of her graduate students were attempting to determine if smiling faces were perceived as happier, more credible, and more immediate than "straight" faces. The experimenters video-taped a person giving a speech twice—once with a smiling face and the other time with a straight face. Viewers were given a set of measures to complete, including the Behavioral Indicants of Immediacy scale (BII; J. F. Andersen et al., 1979). The BII contains items on smiling, as well as items on fourteen other immediacy behaviors. To the researchers' surprise, people seeing the smiling face, as opposed to the straight face, reported that the smiling person also stood closer, gestured more, touched more, and stood facing them more directly. None of these cues had been visible to the viewers! These results suggest that receivers fill in the blanks with plausible responses. When immediacy is increased in one channel, we infer that it increased in other channels as well. The principle here is that immediacy is decoded as a gestalt, not behavior by behavior. Keep this principle in mind as we now turn to the individual behaviors that contribute to this gestalt.

Oculesics

Oculesics or eye behavior is a vital channel of nonverbal immediacy. During interaction, we usually focus our attention on the eyes of the other interactant. In fact most people believe that a person's conscious essence is located in or behind the eyes. Eye contact is a vital connection between people; it is your window to other people's nonverbal behavior, and your eye behavior constitutes a vital social cue to others. Research suggests that the human mind contains a special structure called the eye direction detector that senses other people's eye contact instantly (Langston, Watt, & Bruce, 2000). Have you ever noticed how quickly other drivers notice you are looking at them on the freeway? That is the eye direction detector at work!

EYE CONTACT

One of the behaviors most central to the immediacy construct is eye contact, or mutual gaze, which occurs when two communicators both look at each other's eyes or faces. Eye contact does more than signal availability; it is an invitation to communicate. The literature on interpersonal gaze is so extensive that it is only possible to provide a brief overview of this research (for a classic review see Fehr & Exline, 1987). Gaze, which occurs when one person looks at another, performs a number of functions, including monitoring interaction and turn-taking, dominat-ing and threatening others, and receiving feedback. Nonetheless, its primary function is to convey immediacy (Andersen, 1985). Very young infants are more likely to gaze at eyes or images of eyes than at other objects and by four months can discriminate between direct and averted gaze (Langston et al., 2000)

Immediacy is
communicated
via positive
facial expres-
sions, eye con-
tact, forward
leans, and signs
of connection.

Eye contact typically produces positive perceptions in receivers and observers, although some studies reveal that very high levels of eye contact are not necessarily perceived more positively than moderate levels. In a study by Goldberg,
Kiesler, and Collins (1969) people who spent more time gazing at an interviewer
received higher socioemotional evaluations from the interviewer. Mehrabian
(1968a, 1970, 1971b) demonstrated that increased eye contact communicates a
more positive interpersonal attitude and increases affiliative behavior. Kleinke,
Meeker, and Fong (1974) reported that gazing couples were rated more positively
by observers on all evaluative dimensions than nongazing couples. Thayer and
Schiff (1974) found that dyads who engaged in more extended or reciprocated eye
contact were perceived to have more enduring relationships. Noller (1980)
showed that happily married couples looked at each other frequently during the
exchange of positive messages and less frequently during negative exchanges
than did less-happily married couples. Beebe (1980) found increased eye contact
to be associated with greater perceived dynamism, and believability. Mason, Tatkow and Macrae (2005) established that gaze is associated with likability and
attraction. One study showed that general gaze aversion communicates negative
relational messages, including dissimilarity, superficiality, nonaffection, nonre-
ceptivity, lack of trust, and nonimmediacy (Burgoon et al., 1986). A study of the
nonverbal behavior of therapists found that increased eye contact improved
respondents' ratings of the therapists' trustworthiness, expertness, and attractiveness, as well as increasing the likelihood that participants would revisit the therapist (Ziegler-Kratz & Marshall, 1990). In general, eye contact is perceived as
positive, immediate behavior in interpersonal interaction.

A similar body of literature suggests that eye contact is used strategically to
send messages of positive affect. When Mehrabian and Friar (1969) asked experimental subjects to role-play "liking" for an interactant, they substantially

increased their eye contact. Similarly, when people are requested in experiments to increase their conversational involvement or liking for another person, they gaze more at their partner (Burgoon & Coker, 1988; Coker & Burgoon, 1987; Ray & Floyd, 2006). Likewise, people spontaneously engage in more mutual gaze with friends and people they like than with strangers or people they dislike (Coutts & Schneider, 1976; Exline & Winters, 1965). Guerrero (1997) also demonstrated that people tend to gaze more at their dating partners than at their same-sex or oppo-site-sex friends. At the same time, however, people sometimes look less at their partners with whom they share highly committed and very intimate relation-ships. Dindia, Fitzpatrick, and Attridge (1989) found that people engage in less eye contact and gaze with their spouses than with opposite-sex strangers. This is similar to several findings that show that spouses touch less after they are mar-ried than when they were engaged or dating. This behavior is true for both public touch (Guerrero & Andersen, 1991) and private touch (Emmers & Dindia, 1995). Three reasons explain this decrease in eye contact and touch in long-term relation-ships. First, marriage is a commitment, so spouses may not need such constant reassurances as eye contact and touch, which are vital in dating relationships. Sec-ond, once people are married, other symbols of the relationships (such as wed-ding rings and children) serve as reminders of the partners' commitment to each other. In serious dating relationships, other "tie" signs, such as hand holding and long stares, may signal unavailability to potential rivals. Third, many married people simply take their spouses for granted. This shouldn't be the case, but with familiarity and comfort may come less excitement and immediacy.

Although eye contact is perceived as a positive nonverbal behavior and occurs most in positive relationships, this is not always the case. Eye contact interacts with other variables to intensify other meanings. Under some circumstances—such as prolonged gaze or gaze accompanied by an angry facial expression—it is perceived as a threat display (Exline, Ellyson, & Long, 1975). Studies have shown that in hostile interactions or in negative relationships, increased eye contact leads to negative affect (Scherwitz & Helmreich, 1973; Noller, 1980).

PUPIL DILATION

Pupil-dilation research, or pupilometrics, has shown that pupil dilation is both the result of positive interpersonal feelings and a subconscious immediacy cue (Hess, 1965, 1975). In one classic study, Hess and Goodwin (1974) showed peo-ple two identical pictures of a mother with her infant; in one photograph the mother's pupils were retouched to appear dilated, and in the other photograph they were retouched to appear constricted. Subjects overwhelmingly perceived that the mother with the dilated pupils loved her baby more. Interestingly, few subjects reported having detected any cues from the eyes. Many said the mother's face was warmer or that she was holding her baby more closely, although these characteristics were identical in the two photographs. This and other experiments illustrate that some immediacy cues are encoded and decoded at very low levels of awareness. In a study by Andersen, Todd-Mancillas, and DiClemente (1980), subjects were shown pairs of identical photographs of a woman—identical, that is, except for the pupils, which were retouched to be constricted in one photograph and dilated in the other—and asked to rate the woman's attractiveness. Although pupil dilation did not increase subjects' perceptions of the woman's task attractiveness (the desire to work with the woman), it did significantly increase their perceptions of her social and physical attractiveness. This suggests that immediacy cues may be more important in interpersonal relationships as opposed to role relationships. The observation that pupil dilation does not enhance task attraction suggests that this display occurs only for the benefit of relationally intimate people rather than nonintimates such as store clerks, secretaries, or salespeople.

Proxemics

Like oculesic behavior, proxemic behaviors are primary messages of immediacy. Indeed, by definition, an immediacy behavior decreases psychological or physical distance. Several different proxemic behaviors communicate immediacy.

PHYSICAL DISTANCE

First among Argyle's (1972) five primary intimacy (or immediacy) cues is physical proximity. In many subsequent studies of immediacy, close interpersonal distances are at the core of what people perceive as immediacy (Andersen, 1979; J. F. Andersen et al., 1979).

Closer interpersonal distances typically result in more attraction, more warmth, and more immediacy. Mehrabian and Ksionsky (1970) reported several studies that show closer distances of various kinds result in more-positive interpersonal attitudes. One study found that closer residential distances elicited greater friendship and liking among dormitory residents (Priest & Sawyer, 1967). Another study found that when a speaker stood at a closer interpersonal distance, a receiver's nonverbal agreement responses increased (Kleck, 1970). This effect of proximity on attraction and immediacy is most powerful among friends and other "rewarding" people (people who we find attractive, credible, wealthy, or high in status), is less powerful among strangers, and is negative among enemies or threatening people. Morton (1977) reported that although acquaintances prefer close interpersonal distances, unacquainted people are more intimate and comfortable at intermediate distances. In a series of studies, Burgoon and her associates report more compliance and positive affect in response to rewarding people at distances closer than typical norms. By contrast, nonrewarding people are perceived more positively at normative distances (Burgoon, 1978, 1983; Burgoon & Aho, 1982; Burgoon, Manusov, Mineo, & Hale, 1985). Evidently, close interpersonal distances produce an intensification effect that makes negative interactions more negative and positive interactions more positive (Schiffenbauer & Shiavo, 1976). In a study by Stelzner and Egland (1995), closer interpersonal distance was the leading predictor of relational satisfaction. Because most of our interactions occur in the context of positive relationships (such as between friends and family), closer interpersonal distances are generally perceived as positive, immediate behaviors.

Just as proxemically close interactions generally produce positive impressions, positive relationships produce proxemically closer interactions. Studies have consistently shown that communicators are most likely to interact at close distances with people they like (Coker & Burgoon, 1987; Mehrabian and Friar,

1967; Ray & Floyd, 2006). Furthermore, Guerrero (1997) demonstrated that individuals sit closer to romantic partners than to friends. Conversely, insecure people attempt to maintain excessive proximity (Schachner, Shaver, & Mikulincer, 2005).

THE PHYSICAL PLANE

Immediacy is also communicated by interacting on the same level or physical plane as another person (Andersen, 1985). When people tower over us, it increases their power and our submissiveness (more about this in chapter 12), and it makes them seem less warm and approachable and more psychologically distant. Interacting on the same physical plane is particularly problematic in interactions between young children and adults who tower over them (Andersen & Andersen, 1982) and between disabled people—particularly people in wheelchairs—and nondisabled people. One way people can increase their immediacy is to sit or lean in a manner that minimizes height differences. Brown (1965) has suggested that interacting on the same plane is a manifestation of interpersonal solidarity and closeness.

BODY ORIENTATION

Whether you face someone directly, at an angle, or literally give them the "cold shoulder" (as opposed to a nice, warm front), your body angle communicates more or less immediacy. People are interpersonally cold, unavailable, and uninvolved in side-to-side and back-to-back positions. When an interactant wants to reduce the immediacy of an encounter that is too close, he or she frequently compensates with a less direct body orientation (Patterson, 1973a, 1977). Conversely, one of the main ways people increase involvement and immediacy is to assume a more direct body orientation (Coker & Burgoon, 1987). Stelzner and Egland (1995) reported that a direct body position is one of the three behaviors that best predicts relational satisfaction.

FORWARD LEANS

A number of scholars have included forward leans on their lists of nonverbal behaviors that convey immediacy (Andersen, 1985; Mehrabian, 1971a). Several studies have reported that forward leans communicate greater rapport and immediacy than upright positions or backward leans (Burgoon, Buller, Hale, & deTurck, 1984; Trout & Rosenfeld, 1980). In a study in which subjects were asked to increase involvement or immediacy, the one behavior they increased significantly was the forward lean (Coker & Burgoon, 1987). Forward leans produce closer interpersonal distances and more involvement. Interactants typically feel more warmth and friendship for people who lean forward slightly during conversations.

Haptics

Tactile communication is probably the most important intimate and involving immediacy behavior, but it can be one of the most threatening behaviors as well. Touch is threatening because it is the only immediacy behavior that can physically harm a person and because it often has sexual connotations. Reactions to touch are dependent on cultural and personal norms as well as the specific interpersonal relationship (Andersen & Leibowitz, 1978; Jourard, 1966; Thayer, 1986; Trenholm & Petrie, 1980). Normative, appropriate touch, however, is usually perceived as a warm, immediate behavior. Certainly, a large number of scholars include touch on their lists of primary immediacy behaviors (Andersen, 1979; J. F. Andersen et al., 1979; Andersen & Leibowitz, 1978; Heslin, 1974; Heslin & Boss, 1980; Mehrabian, 1971a; Patterson, 1977).

A number of studies using a variety of methods have been conducted on tactile communication. Interestingly, regardless of the method used, the results are fairly similar. The entire body of research, based on laboratory studies, questionnaires, field studies, and diary studies, reveals that touch communicates intimacy and immediacy.

In a laboratory study by Burgoon et al. (1984), subjects viewed videotaped interactions, one in which the interactants touched and another in which they

Hugs are a prototypical immediacy cue.

didn't touch. Subjects rated the people in the touch condition as more intimate and immediate than the interactants in the no-touch condition. Research by Burgoon, Walther, and Baesler (1992) showed that even slight touches generally result in increased credibility and attraction toward the toucher for all individuals and particularly for well-groomed, high-status, and expert communicators. Jones (1994) demonstrated that touch is the central behavior in human bonding and the development of close relationships.

A number of studies that examined attitudes toward touch show that individuals who approach and like touch are generally more self-confident, warmer people who enjoy intimacy and physical closeness (Andersen & Leibowitz, 1978; Andersen & Sull, 1985; Andersen, Andersen, & Lustig, 1987; Jones & Brown, 1996; see also chapter 7). A study by Fromme et al. (1989) revealed that a touch-comfort test could predict whether or not students would volunteer to participate in a study on hugging. Moreover, among the volunteers, subjects with higher touch-comfort scores rated hugging most positively. Finally, touch comfort is related to an active interpersonal style and the degree to which one's relationships are satisfactory.

A study by Pisano, Wall, and Foster (1986) employed a questionnaire to rate thirty-one descriptions of nonreciprocated touch in romantic relationships. Subjects rated most touch as indications of warmth or love, followed by playfulness, sexual desire, and comfort. Interestingly, all of these functions suggest that touch is typically interpreted as an immediacy behavior. Similarly, in their study of the functions of touch, Heslin and Alper (1983) classified friendship/warmth as one of the five basic meanings associated with touch.

In an extensive field study, Jones and Yarbrough (1985) had undergraduates record all their touch behaviors. The researchers then separated the meanings of touch into six categories: positive affect, playful, controlling, ritualistic, hybrid, and task-related. The study revealed that positive-affect touch is the most common of these types. Positive-affect touch includes five basic touch subtypes, which follow:

- *Support touches:* behaviors that serve to nurture, reassure, or promise protection. This form of touch is most common in close relationships and generally involves touching, patting, or holding the other person by the hand or arm. Verbalization often accompanies support touch; for example, a person may say, "It's okay," or ask, "Are you all right?"

- *Appreciation touches:* tactile messages of thanks that are often followed by verbalization. This form of touch is most common in close, opposite-sex relationships and mainly involves hugging or holding.

- *Inclusion touches:* behaviors that seek to bring people together and enhance psychological closeness. This form of touch is used by close friends and sexual intimates and mainly consists of holding or pressing up against another person.

- *Sexual touches:* behaviors that seek to express sexual interest or physical attraction mostly among people with a sexually intimate relationship. These tactile behaviors include touching the genitals, buttocks, or a woman's chest and usually involve holding or stroking. A study (Henchy & Falk, 1995) indicated that although sexual touch is a fairly common behavior observed in both heterosexual and lesbian bars, it is significantly more common in lesbian bars.

- *Affectionate touches:* the most common form of positive-affect touch, which sends messages of positive regard beyond mere greeting. This form of touch primarily occurs in opposite-sex relationships (and, secondarily, in same-sex relationships between females) and is often expressed in the form of kisses, hugs, caresses, tactile reinforcers, and pats. Touching the face or cheek is seen as most affectionate, but also most threatening and harassing in the wrong kind of relationship (Lee & Guerrero, 2001).

In addition to Jones and Yarbrough's (1985) functions of touch, Afifi and Johnson (1993) suggested that some types of touch function as relationship-presentation tools. Their study, which was conducted in college bars, suggests that touch, particularly male touch, sometimes functions to publicly communicate that one's partner is taken. Of course, not all touch functions to convey positive affect or to display relational intimacy to others. Some types of touch function to display aggression, hostility, or negative responses. For example, in an observational study on children's touch, Guerrero and Ebesu (1993) found that children used two forms of negative-affect touch: aggression (such as hitting and kicking) and affection withdrawal (such as pushing someone's comforting hand away). They also found that more younger children than older children used negative-affect touch, suggesting that as people mature, they use aggressive touch less frequently, presumably because they learn that such touch is socially inappropriate.

In sum, although prior research indicated that touch is a dominant behavior used (particularly by males) to manipulate and control (Henley, 1977), subsequent research suggests that the principal function of touch is to convey immediacy and positive affect. Recent research also disputes the belief that males engage in more opposite-sex touch than females. In fact, there is no sex difference in opposite-sex touch between males and females (Hall & Veccia, 1992a). Jones and Yarbrough (1985) did identify a category called control touch, but this was only one of five major categories of touch. Similarly, Guerrero and Ebesu (1993) found children to display more intimate touch than controlling or aggressive touch. Moreover, they found that most of the control touch was not used in an attempt to dominate but rather to get attention (Guerrero & Ebesu, 1993), in other words to signal availability for communication.

Other studies have found little effect of touch on perceptions of dominance. Forden (1981) showed college students three videotapes of a conversation. In the first videotape, a male touched a female on the shoulder; in the second, a female touched a male on the shoulder; and in the third, no touch occurred. Subjects perceived the females who touched to be more dominant and the males who were touched to be more passive. Contrary to Henley's (1977) gender hypothesis, men were not perceived as more dominant when they touched. In a similar experiment by Burgoon et al. (1984), interpersonal touch increased subjects' perceptions of composure, relaxation, and informality but not dominance. Finally, Pisano et al. (1986) found that subjects often perceived touch as communicating warmth and love but rarely as expressing dominance and control. In sum, although tactile behaviors convey multiple messages, they are typically perceived as immediate or intimate behaviors rather than dominant or powerful ones.

Kinesics

Communicative movements of our face, head, body, and hands (called kinesics) have considerable impact on the perceived immediacy of interaction. At one time, *kinesics* referred to almost all nonverbal behavior; kinesics was the nonverbal counterpart to linguistics. But over the last several decades, the study of nonverbal communication has expanded to include other forms of nonverbal communication. Nonetheless, the study of kinesics, the body in motion, is central to the study of nonverbal communication and, specifically, immediacy.

SMILES

Another central immediacy cue is the smile. No expression communicates as much warmth, or provides such a strong invitation to interact as does the smile. Bayes (1970) reported that the best single predictor of interpersonal warmth is frequency of smiling, which is a fairly stable behavior quality of individuals (Komsi et al., 2006). In a number of investigations, smiles are classified as a crucial part of nonverbal immediacy and liking (J. F. Andersen et al. 1979; Andersen, 1985; Mehrabian, 1971a; Patterson, 1978, Ray & Floyd, 2006), intimacy (Argyle, 1972), and warmth (Reece & Whitman, 1962). Studies examining the interactions between therapists and their patients found that the more frequently the therapists smiled, the greater their patients' perceptions were of their expertise, trustworthiness, and interpersonal acceptance. The therapists' increased smiling also increased the likelihood that the patients would return to the therapist in the future (Reece & Whitman, 1962; Ziegler-Kratz & Marshall, 1990).

Several studies have also reported that smiling is a primary means of communicating interpersonal affiliation (Mehrabian, 1971b; Mehrabian & Ferris, 1967; Rosenfeld, 1966a, 1966b). In one study, a speaker lectured to classes while either smiling or not smiling. Results showed that increased smiling produced higher perceptions of immediacy and affiliation (Gutsell & Andersen, 1980). Similarly, Burgoon et al. (1984) showed that the absence of smiling communicates less immediacy than does smiling during dyadic interactions. When Coker and Burgoon (1987) asked participants to increase their conversational involvement, a number of immediacy behaviors increased, including smiling. Finally, smiling is a contagious immediacy cue. Several studies report that smiles are reciprocated during interaction (Kendon, 1967; Rosenfeld, 1966a, 1967).

HEAD NODS

In North America, nodding is a sign of agreement and rapport. Research shows that monkeys and apes, as well as humans, use ritualistic bowing gestures to signal submission and friendliness (Eibl-Eibesfeldt, 1974, 1979). Listeners signal warmth and agreement by nodding. Nodding is a type of backchannel behavior, or reinforcing listener response (Dittman, 1972). In studies in which subjects were asked to simulate approval seeking (Rosenfeld, 1966a, 1966b) and conversational involvement (Coker & Burgoon, 1987), subjects exhibited frequent head nods. Like smiling, nodding is contagious and tends to be reciprocated during interaction (Rosenfeld, 1966a, 1966b).

BODILY RELAXATION

When you seem relaxed during interaction, people are likely to perceive you as more available, warmer, and friendlier. Tension and stress signal nonimmediacy and are often perceived as emotional buildup that can potentially lead to an aggressive release of tension (Eibl-Eibesfeldt, 1974). In interactions between patients and therapists, patients perceived therapists' relaxed, nonaggressive behavior as a sign of warmth (Reece & Whitman, 1961). One study shows that still, relaxed hands are one type of behavior that communicates warmth (Reece & Whitman, 1962). Several major studies have found relaxation and tension reduction to be important components of nonverbal immediacy (J. F. Andersen et al., 1979; Mehrabian, 1968b). Relaxation is perceived positively during interaction. Mehrabian (1968a, 1969) found that relaxed body positions communicate more liking than do tense positions. Similarly, Jensen and Andersen (1979) reported that relaxation behaviors are associated with higher credibility and attractiveness. One caveat, however, is in order: *Extremely* relaxed body positions may sometimes convey boredom and detachment (such as slumping back in a chair), especially when coupled with nonimmediacy cues such as decreased eye contact. Therefore, Burgoon (1994) argued, moderately high relaxation conveys the most warmth, interest, and involvement.

GESTURES

When you gesture with your hands, others perceive you as more involved and interested in the interaction. Several studies have shown that increases in gestural activity communicate increased affiliativeness (Mehrabian, 1971b) and

In Asia, bowing and exchanging business cards are important rituals of communication, warmth, and respect.

immediacy (J. F. Andersen et al., 1979). In studies in which subjects were asked to seek approval from or increase involvement with others, they responded with increased gesturing (Coker & Burgoon, 1987; Rosenfeld, 1966a, 1966b).

BODY SYNCHRONY

Like good dancers, good communicators act almost as one, rarely stepping on one another's toes, flowing smoothly, and emitting positive "vibes." Good communicators attune and adjust their movements to other interactants. In a study by LaFrance and Mayo (1978) synchronous posture sharing between students and instructors increased interpersonal rapport. Research indicates that body congruence and mimicry produce more positive affect and rapport in interactions ranging from mothers and infants, to therapists and patients, to interpersonal friendships (Andersen & Guerrero, 1998a; Lakin & Chartrand, 2005; Scheflen, 1972; Kinsbourne, 2006; Trout & Rosenfeld, 1980). In a laboratory experiment, confederates producing congruous movements were perceived as more competent, composed, trustworthy, extroverted, and sociable than confederates who enacted incongruous movements (Woodall & Burgoon, 1981). Interestingly, socially ostracized or excluded individuals unconsciously mimic other people in an effort to regain acceptance (Lakin & Chartrand, 2005). Another study showed that unconscious interpersonal mimicry was more likely to occur when a person has an affiliation goal and when someone has failed to affiliate with another, compared with someone who has already succeeded (Lakin & Chartrand, 2003). Likewise, research shows that unconscious mimicry occurs with other people who we like implicitly (Yabar, Johnston, Miles, & Peace, 2006)

GAIT

A number of our interpersonal interactions occur while walking. Moreover, even in the absence of verbal interaction, how we walk communicates a considerable amount of information about us. Our gait or walking style affects an interactant's perception of immediacy. In one study, happy moods were associated with arm swinging, moderate-length strides, light-footedness, and erect posture (Montepare, Goldstein, & Clausen, 1987). It is likely that people are perceived as more approachable when they display an animated but unhurried walking style.

OPEN BODY POSITIONS

When people have their heads down, their arms folded, and their legs crossed, they convey little warmth or availability. Open body positions symbolize openness for interaction. Morris (1977) used the term *barrier signals* to describe a set of gestures and positions that communicate defensiveness and avoidance in social situations. In children, these positions are quite obvious, such as hiding behind a mother's skirt. As adults, these barrier signals, or body buffers, become abbreviated, such as folding one's arms, crossing one's legs, adjusting one's cuffs, and covering one's face. In a study by Mehrabian (1969), females who used more open arm and leg positions were perceived by receivers to have a more positive attitude. In a study of marital communication, Beier and Sternberg (1977) report that close, well-adjusted couples used more open leg positions than couples experiencing conflict. In most cases, holding one's legs tightly together and folding one's arms communicates defensiveness and unapproachability rather than immediacy.

Closed body position signals unavailability, avoidance, and lack of immediacy.

Vocalics

Research shows that nonverbal elements of the voice play a major role in communicating interpersonal liking and nonverbal immediacy (Mehrabian, 1971a; Mehrabian & Ferris, 1967; Ray & Floyd, 2006). In fact, one study found that vocal expressiveness is the behavior most central to immediacy (J. F. Andersen et al., 1979).

Using an electronic synthesizer to vary the pitch, amplitude, duration, and tempo of nonverbal sounds, Scherer (1979) showed that affect and emotion are primarily the result of vocal changes in pitch and tempo. Beebe's (1980) study shows that pitch variation has a major effect on liking. Similarly, Burgoon and Aho (1982) report that increased vocal fluency, pleasantness, clarity, and variety increase a speaker's credibility as well as perceptions of the speaker's sociability. Even with infants, warm, pleasant voices produce more attentiveness than unpleasant voices (Milmoe, Novey, Kagan, & Rosenthal, 1974).

BABY TALK

Certain vocalic behaviors produce very high levels of intimacy and immediacy. Perhaps the most interesting vocalic behavior is baby talk—a varied, high-pitched, imitation of children's speech used by adults when they communicate with infants and small children. Sometimes baby talk involves the use of nonsense phrases (such as "kutch-ee-kutch-ee-koo") accompanied by touch or smiles. At other times, ordinary phrases, such as "You're my little sweetie," are simply accented with baby-talk vocalics.

Interestingly, baby talk is not used only when talking to infants or children. One study has shown that baby talk is commonly used when communicating with the elderly (Caporael, 1981). Baby talk, which employs immature pronunciation and high vocal pitch, typically is perceived by the elderly as conveying affection and nurturance. But communicators must be careful: Research shows that slow, loud speech may be perceived as patronizing by the elderly (Ryan, Bourhis, & Knops, 1991). Baby talk is also common among lovers during sexual foreplay, during phone conversations, and during face-to-face interactions. Shaver and Hazan (1988) suggested that in both parent-child and adult romantic relationships, baby talk is used to communicate attachment and bondedness. Ferguson (1964) showed that baby talk is used worldwide in languages as diverse as Arabic and Comanche.

BACKCHANNELING

As discussed earlier, backchannel behaviors, or reinforcing listener responses, are behaviors performed by listeners while another person is talking. These behaviors are not attempts to talk or to gain the floor, but rather they provide feedback and encouragement to the speaker, often signaling her or him to continue speaking. Frequently, such backchannel behaviors are vocalic. Utterances such as "hum" and "uh-huh" are clearly backchannel behaviors. Utterances such as "yeah" and "okay" are probably more nonverbal than verbal, although some scholars would disagree. One study found that the backchannel utterance "mm-hmm" belongs to a set of reinforcing nonverbal behaviors that actually cause an increase in the length of another's speaking turns (Matarazzo, Weins, & Saslow, 1965). A number of cultural differences exist in backchannelling (see chapter 4). In sum, vocal backchanneling increases immediacy, signals that the listener comprehends the speaker's message, and reinforces the speaker's role in a conversation. One exception, however, should be noted. When backchannel behaviors such as "mm hmm" and "uh huh" are used in rapid succession, they sometimes signal that the listener understands the point and wants the speaker to stop talking.

VOCAL SYNCHRONY

Communicators who are in rapport with one another are able to converse, backchannel, take turns talking, and laugh without interrupting each other or getting out of sync. Although it was indicated earlier that synchrony involves kinesic behavior, vocal synchrony is an essential part of establishing immediacy as well. People who like one another manifest vocal convergence (LaFrance & Mayo, 1978; Street & Giles, 1982), a similarity in pitch, rate, and accent during a conversation. Vocal convergence is a common phenomenon in which, over time, people start to communicate like one another. For example, as a boy from Illinois, I sometimes spent summer vacations in Massachusetts. My Illinois friends often told me I had picked up a New England accent over my vacation. Fast talkers slow down when talking to slow talkers, and slow talkers speed up when talking to fast talkers. Vocal convergence is a form of immediacy that brings people even closer together. A sure way to reduce warmth, rapport, and immediacy is to get out of vocal sync with another person by interrupting, talking simultaneously, or yelling when the other person is whispering.

Chronemics

The way we use time communicates a lot about our relationship with another person. In the United States, Canada, and northern Europe, time is treated like a commodity. People believe that time can be wasted, spent, saved, and invested as if it were money. A number of studies suggest that immediacy can be communicated through such chronemic cues (J. F. Andersen, 1984; Andersen & Andersen, 1982; Burgoon & Aho, 1982).

Spending time with someone is perhaps the best way to signal immediacy because it involves availability and closeness (J. F. Andersen et al., 1979). A study by Egland, Stelzner, Andersen, and Spitzberg (1995) reported that the immediacy behavior most associated with relational satisfaction is spending time together. As I discussed in the opening chapter, spending time with another person is a major indicator of that person's importance. Another interpersonal chronemic cue that signals immediacy is pause time, the length of time between utterances in a conversation. Pause time is an immediacy cue because it allows for interaction from one's partner and signals an other-orientation.

Punctuality is another important chronemic immediacy cue, particularly in classroom contexts (Todd-Mancillas, 1982). Students who arrive to class late are perceived as low in immediacy, inconsiderate, and incompetent. One study of secretaries by Baxter and Ward (1975) demonstrated that late arrivers were perceived as low in competence, composure, friendliness, and sociability. Friends and romantic partners who constantly arrive late or do not call at a specified time may also be evaluated negatively.

Finally, monochronic (as opposed to polychronic) use of time, which involves focusing on only one thing during a particular time span, may be considered an immediacy behavior in American culture. We like others to concentrate on the conversation at hand rather than busy themselves with other tasks while they listen. For example, hearing your conversation partner typing on a computer in the background while you are talking on the phone might anger you—after all, the person you are talking to should be paying full attention to you, not working on something else!

ANTECEDENTS OF IMMEDIACY

What causes a person to communicate nonverbal immediacy to another person? Two of these antecedents, or causes of immediacy behaviors—culture (see chapter 4) and interpersonal valence (see chapter 7)—were discussed earlier in the book. Next, we focus on four other antecedents of immediacy: the relationship, individual differences, the situation, and temporary states.

The Relationship

We are most likely to touch, gaze at, approach, and smile at individuals with whom we share positive relationships. But relationships are tricky things. For one thing, both people must have similar perceptions of the relationship if the display of immediacy behavior is to be reciprocal. For example, immediacy behaviors that are normally reserved for close friends or lovers would be inappropriate if used between business associates or relatively new acquaintances (see chapter 9 for more on this topic).

Most theories of relationship development maintain that as a relationship grows, communication becomes more immediate (Altman & Taylor, 1973; Berger & Calabrese, 1975; Duck, 1988; Knapp, 1984). Likewise, research shows that when two individuals increase their immediacy, observers infer that they have an extended, stable relationship (Thayer & Schiff, 1974). A body of empirical evidence suggests that across the early stages of a relationship, nonverbal communication becomes more intimate. Hays (1985) reported that hugging increases during the first three months of a relationship. Levinger (1980) showed that intimate couples touch more than strangers do when working together on projects. Gendrin and Honeycutt (1988) discovered in their experimental interactions that acquaintances smiled more at each other than did strangers. Similarly, a study by Hill, Blackman, and Crane (1982) demonstrated that married couples stood closer than did strangers during experimental interactions. None of these findings are too remarkable. Among individuals in well-acquainted or intimate relationships, nonverbal immediacy is higher than among new acquaintances.

A number of scholars question whether immediacy continues to increase linearly as people become more acquainted or have more-bonded relationships. Several scholars, however, characterize relational communication as capricious and nonlinear (Guerrero & Andersen, 1991; Duck & Miell, 1986; Honeycutt, Cantrill, & Greene, 1989).

Various studies on touch have shown that greater immediacy is not necessarily characteristic of well-developed, stable relationships. Recall the study by Dindia et al. (1989), which showed that we gaze less at our spouses than at opposite-sex strangers. Burgoon, Buller, and Woodall (1989) reported that tie-signs such as holding hands, linking arms, or putting arms around one another "are more prevalent among dating and courting couples than among marrieds" (p. 318). Guerrero and Andersen's (1991) field study showed a curvilinear relationship between relational stage and touch among dating and married couples: Couples who were engaged or seriously dating touched each other significantly more than did couples who had either just started dating or were married, a finding confirmed by Willis and Briggs (1992). More recently, Emmers and Dindia (1995) reported a similar finding based on a questionnaire study of private, intimate touch. Couples' touch behaviors rise from the casual dating stage to the serious dating stage and then diminish slightly during marriage. Burgoon, Buller, and Woodall (1989) provided an explanation for this type of finding: "Once a relationship is well established, the need for public displays of affection is no longer necessary" (p. 318). Likewise, Patterson (1988) maintained, "It is as though relationship intimacy gives individuals some license to ignore their partner" (p. 52).

Immediacy behaviors are also vital in interpersonal comforting and support. Comforting strategies are messages that are intended to alleviate or moderate another's distressed emotional state (Burleson & Goldsmith, 1998). Studies indicate that most nonverbal comforting strategies make use of immediacy behaviors, including hugs, pats, other forms of touch, eye contact, attentiveness, sympathetic facial expressions, and close interpersonal distances (Bullis & Horn, 1995; Dolin & Booth-Butterfield, 1993; Hertenstein, 2002). Studies report experimental evidence that nonverbal immediacy is associated with emotional improvement during comforting and social support (Jones, 2004; Jones & Guerrero, 2001; Jones & Wirtz, 2006). The closer we are to someone, the more likely we are to use immediacy behaviors as a form of comfort.

Nonverbal immediacy increases as relationships develop, but only up to a point. In close, stable, long-term relationships, high immediacy levels are not needed to constantly define the relationship. Close friends, family members, and married couples, however, must be careful not to show so little immediacy as to signal distancing or deterioration of these close relationships.

Individual Differences

Individuals vary greatly in the degree to which they send immediacy messages, even in close relationships. Some individuals rarely smile, touch, stand at close interpersonal distances, or make eye contact. Others, however, regularly produce such immediacy behaviors during interaction. Why is this? Some evidence suggests that inherited *biological differences* are part of the explanation. Eysenck (1967, 1971) showed that extroverts seek more social interaction and adventure because they have chronically low cortical arousal levels. Introverts manifest a pattern of interaction avoidance and stimulation inhibition due to their chronically high arousal levels. The same pattern may be true for high communication apprehensives, who decrease arousal by reducing immediacy during interaction (Andersen, 1987; Andersen & Coussoule, 1980). Recent research suggests that several immediacy cues like laughing and smiling are relatively consistent throughout infancy and childhood (Komsi et al., 2006).

Another explanation for individual differences in immediacy levels is *cultural background*. Based on research conducted over the past four decades, certain groups—ethnic, national, and regional—have been identified as contact cultures; that is, touch and high levels of immediacy are the norm among group members (Hall, 1959, 1966a; see chapter 4 for a detailed discussion on this dimension of culture). Contact cultures interact at close interpersonal distances, touch frequently, and are generally more demonstrative and immediate. Interestingly, most contact cultures are located in relatively warm climates at low latitudes (Andersen, 1988; Hecht, Andersen, & Ribeau, 1989). By contrast, most noncontact cultures are located in cool climates at high latitudes. Evidently, cooler climates produce interpersonally "cooler" and more task-oriented cultures. Differences between contact and noncontact groups have been found even within the United States. Those living in warmer zones of the United States report being more dramatic, more expressive, and more positive toward touch than do those living in cooler zones (Andersen, Lustig, & Andersen, 1990).

In addition to physiology and culture, individual differences in immediacy are also the result of *interpersonal environments* that model, reward, and punish various immediacy behaviors. Immediacy behaviors are shaped during infancy and childhood and often result in lifelong patterns of behavior. In particular, tactile immediacy is very important to infant communication and development (Hertenstein, 2002). At one extreme are abused children, who may have difficulty interacting in a warm, immediate style after experiencing the trauma of abuse. In one study abused children, and abused girls in particular, exhibited less touch and greater interpersonal distances and generally had less social engagement than nonabused children (Hecht et al., 1986). Research suggests that parental attachment style predicts immediacy cues, including adult kinesic and vocalic behavior, with securely attached individuals displaying the most warmth and immediacy (LePoire, Shepard, & Duggan, 1999). Similarly, Guerrero (1996) found that individuals with anxious attachment styles showed less immediacy and affection than more securely attached individuals.

Regardless of the cause, a number of studies show that individual differences in immediacy usage prevail across interactions with different relational partners. Patterson (1973b) reported that individuals are highly stable in their use of interpersonal distance, body orientation, eye contact, and body leans regardless of their interaction partner. Crouch (1980) also reported that individuals maintain similar levels of eye contact regardless of their partner. In a study by Guerrero (1997), subjects were videotaped interacting with three different relational partners: a close same-sex friend, a close opposite-sex friend, and a romantic partner. Despite several differences due to relationship type, Guerrero found that behaviors such as smiling, vocal warmth, proxemic distancing, bodily relaxation, composure, head nods, relaxed laughter, body orientation, and conversational fluency were correlated across all three interactions. Patterson (1973b, 1978) reviewed a number of studies that also show that people maintain about the same amount of personal space across various relationships. Even children show a number of consistent nonverbal immediacy behaviors in interviews with different people, including gazes, smiles, bodily movements, facial expressions, and head nods (Feldstein, 1972; Takala, 1977). Gallaher (1992) reported that individuals are very consistent in their level of expressiveness. Over time and across interactions, people exhibit consistent individual differences in immediacy behaviors regardless of the partner with whom they are interacting.

A number of personality measures are related to immediacy behaviors. For example, extroverts stand closer to others than do introverts (Patterson, 1978), and approval seekers position themselves closer to others than do people who do not seek approval (Rosenfeld, 1965). Additionally, the tendency to be affiliative is related to using closer interpersonal distances (Mehrabian & Diamond, 1971), and both communication apprehension and touch avoidance are negatively related to close interpersonal distance (Andersen & Sull, 1985; Cardot & Dodd, 1979).

People's tactile orientations may also be a general index of immediacy. Touch avoiders, defined as people with negative attitudes toward interpersonal touch, not only engage in less touch (Guerrero & Andersen, 1991) and maintain greater conversational distances (Andersen & Sull, 1985), but they are also less predisposed toward interaction and have lower self-esteem (Andersen, Andersen, & Lustig, 1987). Conversely, Deethardt and Hines (1983) reported that touch approachers are more talkative, cheerful, and optimistic and less fearful of affection. Andersen and Sull (1985) concluded that the "touch avoidance measure probably taps into an underlying trait of approach and avoidance of nonverbal communication generally" (p. 69).

Research has shown that some individuals are more predisposed to experience aversive states than others, a trait called negative affectivity (Watson & Clark, 1984). Negative affectivity encompasses trait anxiety, neuroticism, weak ego strength, repression, and general maladjustment. High-negative-affectivity individuals tend to be distressed and upset, have a negative self-concept, and manifest withdrawal and nonimmediacy in interpersonal interaction. Simply put, some people just aren't very immediate.

One final personal trait that is highly linked to immediacy is biological sex. Women in our society are generally expressive and immediate, whereas men tend to be more poker-faced and withdrawn. Buck (1984) has summarized numerous studies that suggest that women are much more likely than men to send positive-affect messages as well as more accurate in sending such messages. In a study of nonverbal communication between men and women in college bars, Afifi and Johnson (1993) showed that women manifested more nonverbal affection displays than men. In particular, women smiled more and initiated more tie-signs than men. These findings suggest that women tend to externalize and display their emotions, whereas men tend to internalize and hide their emotions (also see chapter 5).

The Situation

The situation is an important variable that determines whether immediacy is expressed. Formal, public, negative, or conspicuous situations inhibit the expression of immediacy. The situation has a lot to do with why people engage in certain communication behaviors (Funder & Ozer, 1983). Interacting individuals use situ-

Proxemic, haptic, and kinesic immediacy are all displayed in this historic Middle East peace-agreement meeting between Yitzhak Rabin, Bill Clinton, and Yasir Arafat. (© Paul Conklin/PhotoEdit Inc.)

ational information to restrain or display immediacy behavior. Acitelli and Duck (1987) maintained that a critical variable in the expression of intimacy "is the perspective on it that is taken by the participants, particularly their judgments about the level of intimacy appropriate for a given situation or occasion" (p. 301). Andersen (1989) suggested that situationally inappropriate intimacy or immediacy behaviors are viewed negatively and decrease closeness and attraction: "When intimacy behaviors are perceived to be situationally inappropriate, the episode will be negatively valenced, whereas when intimacy behaviors are perceived to be situationally appropriate, the episode will be positively valenced" (p. 28). Obviously, certain immediacy behaviors with high intimacy value, such as affectionate or sexual touching and prolonged eye contact, are constrained in certain situations.

Temporary States

We all go through moods or temporary states that alter our communication behavior. Studies have shown that drugs, foods, amount of sleep, the quality of one's interpersonal relations, and one's self-image are among the factors that have an impact on temporary states (Andersen, 1987). Temporary states have a definite impact on immediacy or intimacy, as Acitelli and Duck (1987) described:

> Intimacy as a process is seen to develop, fluctuate and change over time. . . . The very notion of process implies that there will be changes in subjects' reports about their feelings and behaviors over time. A relationship may be intimate overall, but interactions can be intimate at one moment and not intimate the next. (p. 300)

Andersen (1985) showed that others' moods are related to how much immediacy they desire: "A fight with one's boss, a headache, a raise, a heavy workload, or any number of temporary factors can cause immediacy behaviors to be valenced either more positively or more negatively" (p. 28). Badzinski (1986) concluded that moods affect the messages we send, the judgments we make about others, and the judgments others make about us such that our actions and evaluations shift in the direction of our mood. Thus, when we are in a bad mood, we are likely to be less enthusiastic and less vocally expressive and to exhibit negative facial displays. Other people also react to our bad moods. In other words, if we are in a "bad mood," we may cause our partner to reduce her or his immediacy.

THE DIRECT EFFECTS MODEL OF IMMEDIACY

In general, immediacy behaviors produce direct, positive effects on other people. This *direct effects model* suggests that in most circumstances, immediate interactants are perceived as warmer, friendlier, more intimate, and more attractive. Many of our interactions occur with one of two types of partner: friend or stranger. In either of these relational situations, immediacy cues usually are perceived positively (Andersen, 1985, 1999; Coutts, Schneider, & Montgomery, 1980). Research supports a similar model of nonverbal immediacy, the *social meaning model* (Burgoon, Coker, & Coker, 1986; Burgoon & LePoire, 1999; Burgoon & Newton, 1991). According to the social meaning model, many nonverbal behaviors have such a clear social meaning that most interactants react in the same way across most relationships.

Support for the direct effects and social meaning models have been accumulating, suggesting that immediacy behaviors have strong positive meanings in social interaction that are similar for the source, the receiver, and observers. Of course, immediacy behaviors interact with personal or situational variables in some circumstances. As Andersen (1985) pointed out, "When approach behaviors are employed in negative or hostile relationships they will not be perceived as immediacy cues at all, but will most likely generate negative affect and compensating responses" (p. 3). So, although immediacy behaviors can produce negative effects in negative relationships, the norm is for immediacy behaviors to produce direct, positive effects across most sorts of relationships. More recently Floyd & Erbert (2003) reported support for the direct effects or social meaning model by showing that senders, receivers, and observers all tend to agree about the meaning of immediacy behaviors which seem to be intrinsically meaningful. But what positive effects are likely to occur as a result of increased immediacy?

Interpersonal Effects

Our most common interactions occur with acquaintances, friends, loved ones, and romantic partners. In these relationships, immediacy behaviors are the primary means by which we exchange positive feelings. Following are several types of interpersonal effects generated by immediacy behaviors.

INTERPERSONAL ATTRACTION

Studies consistently show that warm, immediate, expressive individuals, even strangers, are perceived as more attractive than their reserved, inexpressive counterparts. Sabatelli and Rubin (1986) reported that nonverbal expressiveness, or the degree to which people show their feelings, correlates positively with interpersonal attraction, warmth, and likability, independent of physical attractiveness. Both unattractive and attractive communicators seem to benefit from increased expressiveness. Sabatelli and Rubin concluded, "These findings also suggest, however, that nonverbal expressiveness may in some way compensate for an absence of physical attractiveness as a factor impacting on initial interpersonal impression" (p. 132). In one study, subjects reported that their interaction partner's nonverbal immediacy behaviors, including gestures and eye contact, signaled their interactional involvement (Cegala & Sillars, 1989). In a similar study, Remland and Jones (1989) found that nonverbal involvement behaviors, particularly backchanneling, forward leans, direct body angles, and other-directed gaze, produced large increases in interactants' attraction; and this was true for all people, whether shy or outgoing. Remland and Jones conclude, "The difference between high and low levels of NVI [nonverbal involvement] was substantial enough, even in a short interview, to result in differential attributions of interpersonal regard" (p. 181). Hale, Lundy, and Mongeau (1989) reported that immediacy is a leading predictor of relational intimacy, particularly for best friends.

Perhaps the most dramatic illustration of the power of immediacy on initial attraction was Fisher, Rytting, and Heslin's (1976) library study. Subjects in this experiment, particularly females, felt much more positive toward librarians who briefly touched their hand during the exchange of a library card than they did toward librarians who did not touch them. So, even a single immediacy cue in one channel can have positive effects on interpersonal attraction. Burgoon and Saine (1978) put it well when they described how attraction occurs among humans: "The messages used to communicate attraction and liking are a mixture of inclusion, confirmation, and affection messages" (p. 140). Interestingly, these are the primary components of nonverbal immediacy messages.

Relational Messages

Once a relationship is established, immediacy behaviors continue to signal positive messages between relational partners and help them maintain their relationship and move it toward even greater levels of intimacy. Patterson (1983) reviewed a large number of studies that collectively show that interactions between friends are more immediate than between either acquaintances or strangers. He summarized by stating, "The expected pattern of higher involvement in developed relationships than in initial relationships is well supported by empirical research" (p. 91). Bell and Daly (1984) reported that one of the strategies that people typically employ to get others to like them is to display nonverbal immediacy behaviors. Similarly, nonverbal immediacy behaviors, including attentiveness, eye contact, concerned vocal tones, empathic facial expressions, closer interpersonal distances, hugs, pats, and other forms of touch, are associated with interpersonal comforting (Bullis & Horn, 1995; Dolin & Booth-Butterfield, 1993). Guerrero and Andersen (1991) showed that touch occurs most frequently among steadily dating or engaged couples—as compared to early-dating or married couples—suggesting that immediacy is vital in close, developing relationships. Moreover, one's comfort with another person's immediacy is important to relational growth. Fromme et al. (1989) reported that touch comfort is related to the establishment of intimate relationships and is even correlated with the ability to establish satisfactory relationships of any type. Stelzner and Egland (1995) showed that immediacy is highly related to relational satisfaction for friends, casual daters, serious daters, and marriage-bound relational partners. Sending and receiving immediacy messages appear to be essential to bonding and growth in all types of relationships.

Sexual Involvement

Sexual interaction, including flirtation, courtship, and actual sexual encounters, is predicated on high levels of immediacy. Indeed, the initiation of sexual interaction involves every immediacy behavior discussed so far; however, these behaviors are often exaggerated and convey higher levels of intimacy and or sexuality. For example, in sexual interaction, touch and gaze may be prolonged and directed to more private areas. Flirtation cues occur in combinations such as prolonged gazes and smiles, or close interpersonal distance, touch, and relaxed posture.

A number of studies suggest that immediacy cues are the most potent attractors in cross-sex relationships. Kahn and McGaughey (1977) reported that closer interpersonal distances result in greater attraction in opposite-sex pairs but not in same-sex pairs. Johnson and Edwards (1991) showed that escalating levels of sexually intimate touch are highly associated with relational commitment for both sexes, particularly for females. Patterson (1983) summarized the research in this area: "As the intimacy of the relationship increases in romantic relationships, greater involvement is typically expressed in a variety of behaviors. However, mutual gaze and touch are particularly important in facilitating a high level of involvement" (p. 96).

Studies of flirting have shed even more light on the role of immediacy behaviors. Condra (1988) showed that flirtation behaviors are important signals from a sociobiological standpoint; they enable mating rituals, which ultimately lead to reproduction of the species. Condra maintains, "It is clear that nonverbal communication may play a critical, maybe even defining, role in what is considered flirtatious" (p. 4). In her study, she reports that flirting is positively correlated with the number of dates spent together and negatively correlated with sociability, shyness, and loneliness (Condra, 1988). Males were more likely to be successful flirts and make contact with women in bars if they engaged in more eye gaze, glancing, moved closer, touched their other male friends, and had open body positions (Renninger, Wade, & Grammer, 2004). Moreover, men were more likely to engage in these behaviors when women were present than when they were not present, suggesting that men intuitively know what flirtation cues are effective. Nonverbal flirtation cues, however, are interpreted differently by men and women. Women are more likely to flirt for fun or to initiate a relationship, whereas men view flirtation in more sexual terms than do women (Henningsen, 2004).

Several studies have carefully examined the cues that convey interest and attraction in dating among college students (Afifi & Johnson, 1993; Moore & Butler, 1989; Muehlenhard, Koralewski, Andrews, & Burdick, 1986). These studies report that most courtship or dating cues are immediacy behaviors, including eye contact, room-encompassing glances, smiling, forward leans, sideways leans, direct shoulder orientation, closer interpersonal distances, touching, smoothing another's hair, catching another's eye, humor, attentiveness, frequent nodding, and animated speech. Research shows that acceptance of sexual initiation is usually done nonverbally, whereas rejection of sexual overtures is typically done verbally (Byers & Heinlein, 1989; Cupach & Metts, 1991; Metts, Cupach, & Imahori, 1992). Sexual involvement often proceeds without much verbal communication, yet when verbal communication is used to tell a partner to stop escalating sexual involvement, it is important to ignore nonverbal cues of sexual arousal and to stop the behavior. Sexual harassment or date rape can result from ignoring these explicit verbal cues in favor of nonverbal cues that seem positive and encouraging. We should all be aware: "Stop" means stop and "no" means no.

MARITAL SATISFACTION

Obviously, immediacy is important in marital relationships, as it is in friendships and dating relationships. However, contrary to common sense, immediacy may not be *as* important in marriage as it is in somewhat less established relationships. Burgoon, Buller, and Woodall (1989) reported that "tie-signs are more prevalent among dating and courting couples than among marrieds. Once a relationship is well established, the need for public displays of affection and oneness are no longer necessary" (p. 318). As noted earlier, research on touch has confirmed this tendency by showing that public touch is over twice as common among couples "going out" or engaged couples than among marrieds (Guerrero & Andersen, 1991). Married couples are bound together formally and legally; their home, investments, children, history, and relationship provide tangible reminders of their closeness to each other. Less established couples need more reassurance about their relationships, so immediacy behaviors become a primary vehicle for conveying involvement, attraction, and closeness.

Although married couples may not exhibit as much immediacy as engaged couples, several studies show that happily married couples manifest more immediacy than their less-happy counterparts. In a study by Beier and Sternberg (1977), close, well-adjusted couples sat closer together, looked at each other more, touched more frequently, and maintained more open body positions than couples experiencing disagreement. Similarly, research by Noller (1987) on marital adjustment (happiness or compatibility) showed that "the greater degree of pleasantness of the high marital adjustment subjects stands in contrast to the intense negativity in the behavior of the low marital adjustment subjects" (p.170). Evidently, she continues, "high marital adjustment subjects leak their comfortable happy feelings in their interactions with a spouse, while low marital adjustment couples leak their unhappiness and resentment" (p. 170). Although immediacy is less important in marital relationships than in earlier-stage relationships, it is still important. Reducing immediacy too much can signal marital distress and actually threaten the marriage.

Finally, research also shows that receiving immediacy cues is as important as sending them in marital relationships. Noller (1987) found that happily married couples are more successful at decoding nonverbal communication than are unhappy couples. Particularly important to marital satisfaction is the husband's ability to both send and receive nonverbal messages. Dissatisfied wives want more nonverbal affection, appreciation, and attention, all of which are communicated as nonverbal immediacy behaviors.

Instructional Effects

Some of the most fruitful research on nonverbal immediacy has been conducted in the classroom. The primary conclusion of this research is that immediate teachers are the most effective teachers—contradicting conventional mythology that asserts that stern teachers are the most effective. Andersen and Andersen (1987) addressed this myth:

> Perhaps the most frequently quoted admonition to new teachers is "Don't smile until after Christmas!" Although well-intentioned, this advice is a misdirected attempt to enhance instructional effectiveness. Somehow an instructional myth has been created which suggests a trade-off between being nice and being effective in the classroom. . . . Regardless of how the myth began or is sustained, recent research in instructional effectiveness requires the destruction of this myth. Our research and that of our colleagues clearly demonstrate

> that nice teachers are highly effective. This research demonstrates that contrary to much popular opinion, students respond best to "nice" teachers—to teachers who are warm, friendly, immediate, approachable, affiliative and fostering of close, professionally appropriate personal relationships. (p. 57)

In fact, the recent educational trends requiring more discipline, less personal closeness, and more homework may be counterproductive in producing educational gains. The following sections review the research on nonverbal immediacy and its positive relationship to instructional outcomes.

AFFECTIVE LEARNING

Perhaps the most basic finding of seventy years of behavioral psychology is that people are drawn to things they like and avoid things they dislike. So it is with learning. We learn to like certain kinds of material and to dislike others. This process, called affective learning, may have more to do with learning over the long term than so-called cognitive learning. Likable schools, teachers, books, and subjects attract students and keep their interest. Moreover, high, positive affect and positive attitudes create commitment and, as we will see, produce lifelong learning.

Research suggests that it is the teacher who is most responsible for affective learning. Indeed, immediacy behaviors are the primary way to promote positive student attitudes. Early studies showed that college students preferred teachers who interacted warmly with them as opposed to cool and formal teachers (Beck & Lambert, 1977; Hyman, 1968). Leeds (1950) reported that creating a friendly atmosphere is one of the two most important elements of teaching, across all grade levels. Similarly, Ryans (1960, 1964) showed that teacher warmth and friendliness are important predictors of positive student response. A teacher's immediacy level is one of the main reasons why students like a class, a teacher, or a subject,.

In her classic study, Andersen (1979) reported that teacher immediacy was a powerful predictor of students' attitudes toward the teacher, the course, and the subject matter in general. Students with immediate teachers reported about 20 percent higher satisfaction in their attitude toward the teacher. A number of other studies have supported this finding. In a study by Plax, Kearney, McCroskey, and Richmond (1986), students of highly immediate teachers reported a 50 percent increase in liking for the course at both the high school and college levels. Immediacy is strongly related to positive affect for the course content and for the instructor in both secondary school and college classrooms. Giglio and Lustig (1987) reported that in introductory college communication courses, teacher immediacy increased students' positive attitudes toward class by over 30 percent. Frymier (1994) showed that nonverbal immediacy promotes positive affect and increases student motivation, which may lead to long-term student learning. Research also suggests that teacher immediacy interacts with teacher credibility to produce increases in affective learning (Pogue & AhYun, 2006).

A recent study of primarily Hispanic students found that more teacher immediacy increases teacher credibility, including competence and trustworthiness, in the eyes of students (Glascock & Ruggiero, 2006). Sanders and Wiseman (1990) have found that higher levels of teacher immediacy increased affect and positive attitudes for white, Asian, Hispanic, and African American students. Although all types of students responded positively to immediate teachers, Hispanic students had the most positive responses to instructional immediacy. Similarly, immediacy is an important instructional behavior in Chinese culture, though recent research suggests that the Chinese distinguish between instructional, relational, and personal immediacy (Zhang & Oetzel, 2006).

Comstock, Rowell, and Bowers (1995), found that a high-immediacy condition produced more affective learning than did a low-immediacy condition; students in a moderately high immediacy condition reported more motivation, more positive attitudes toward the course content, and more positive attitudes toward the teacher than did students in a low-immediacy condition (Comstock et al., 1995). Interestingly, a *very* high immediacy condition resulted in slightly less affective learning than the *moderately* high immediacy condition, suggesting that teachers can be too immediate. A recent meta-analysis that compiled the results of 81 studies of immediacy showed a strong correlation between teacher nonverbal immediacy and affective learning (Witt, Wheeless, & Allen, 2004). Parallel research from the field of education also shows that teacher enthusiasm, operationalized very similarly to immediacy, has yield similar result on positive student affect and better teaching evaluations (Babad, 2005). Interestingly, student immediacy works much the same way as teacher immediacy. Student nonverbal immediacy and responsiveness were a major predictor of teacher self-confidence and job satisfaction (Mottet, Beebe, Raffeld, & Medlock, 2004).

Even in mediated, distance-learning environments, immediacy and nonverbal involvement is important. A more immediate televised lecturer compared with a non-immediate one was shown to increase liking for a course by 22 percent (Andersen & Withrow, 1981). Likewise a study of videotaped distance learning lectures found that more immediate teacher presentation enhanced the likability and trustworthiness of the teacher, as well as the interest level and perceived value of the course (Guerrero & Miller, 1996). In a study on interactive distance learning Mottet (2000) reported that interactive video does not allow capture of the nonverbal cues necessary for communicating immediacy and interactivity. There is more nonverbal interactivity and responsiveness in face-to-face learning situations. These data suggest that the vocal nonverbal cues may be better communicated by such technologies than are visual cues. Likewise, Mottet found that if teachers perceived students as more nonverbally responsive in distance learning, the teaching was more interactive, satisfying, and effective.

Studies have even shown that increasing immediacy in only a single nonverbal channel produces a significant improvement in student affect. In an experimental study on teacher-student conferences, teachers either touched students on the arm at the beginning and at the end of the conference or did not touch students at all. Students rated the conferences much more positively in the touch condition than in the no-touch condition; in fact, touch accounted for almost a 25 percent increase in students' conference evaluation scores (Steward & Lupfer, 1987). However, other research suggests that touch in the classroom is more complicated. Lanutti, Laliker, and Hale (2001) reported some generally supportive effects for touch, but not for male teachers with female students—particularly if the touch was increasingly immediate.

In a similar study, subjects were divided into two groups. In one group's meetings with a teacher, a desk was placed between the interactants; in the other group's meetings, there was no desk blocking the teacher from the students. The result was that the students in the no-desk situation rated the teacher much higher than did the students in the other group (Zweigenhaft, 1976).

Most importantly, teachers can be trained to be more immediate and, as a result, produce more positive student affect. Richmond, McCroskey, Plax, and Kearney (1986) compared teachers with immediacy training to teachers with no such training and discovered that students had more positive affect toward the teachers who had been trained to be nonverbally immediate. Babad (2004) likewise showed that teacher training can improve the quality of their nonverbal communication.

BEHAVIORAL COMMITMENT

Students with more positive affect become more committed students. Studies have shown that students are more likely to become motivated, committed, long-time learners as their positive affect for a class or instruction increases. As Andersen and Andersen (1987) stated:

> Warm, affiliative teachers are likely to produce lifelong learners. Students under the tutelage of "nice" teachers are more likely to engage in continued reading and studying after the homework is done and the school year is ended. Teachers who engage in affiliative behavior motivate self-initiated work by students and create a desire for further coursework in the subject area. (p. 58)

Studies have actually shown that in classes with immediate teachers, students substantially increase their likelihood of continued reading in that area, enrolling in future classes as opposed to dropping out, increasing their motivation to study, and engaging in behaviors recommended by the teacher (Andersen, 1979; Andersen, Norton, & Nussbaum, 1981; Babad, 2005; Beck & Lambert, 1977; Comstock et al., 1995; Gorham, 1988; Pogue & AhYun, 2006; Richmond et al., 1986). Comstock et al. (1995) have demonstrated that—as with affective learning—very high immediacy is slightly less effective than moderately high immediacy in producing behavioral commitment.

PERCEIVED COGNITIVE LEARNING

Research shows that students are more likely to enjoy school and become committed students if they have immediate, affiliative teachers. Moreover, a series of studies has shown that students certainly believe they learn more from immediate and affiliative teachers. Over four decades ago, Harrington (1955) reported that parents believed kindergarten teachers were more effective if the teachers smiled more. A study by Powell and Harville (1990) showed that increased teacher immediacy generally improved teacher clarity or the degree to which teachers avoided ambiguous and unclear messages. This finding varied across different ethnic groups, but the effect was highly positive for white students and even more powerful for Latino and Asian American students. Similarly, Sanders and Wiseman (1990) found that perceived cognitive learning was increased by immediate teachers for white, Asian, Hispanic, and African American students. Studies show that students report they learn up to 50 percent more from immediate teachers than from nonimmediate ones (Giglio & Lustig, 1987; Gorham, 1988; Gorham & Christofel, 1988; Gorham & Azkahi, 1990; Richmond, Gorham, & McCroskey, 1987). The most important immediacy behaviors that correlate with increased perceived learning are vocal expressiveness, smiling at the class, relaxed body positions, looking at the class, and moving around the classroom (Richmond, Gorham, & McCroskey, 1987). In their recent meta-analysis Witt et al. (2004) reported a strong relationship between teacher nonverbal immediacy and perceived learning.

ACTUAL COGNITIVE LEARNING

Studies certainly show that students think they learn more from immediate teachers, but do they really learn more? Some studies show that students do learn more from immediate teachers, but other studies have failed to find a statistically significant relationship. Early studies showed that some immediacy behaviors did increase student learning. For example, lecturer eye contact with students increased student comprehension (Breed, Christiansen, & Larson, 1972); speaker dynamism increased information recall by students (Coats & Smidchens, 1966); lectures accompanied by gestures improved listening comprehension (Gauger, 1952); proximity, smiling, and touch in one-on-one counseling increased learning (Kleinfeld, 1974); and positive rather than negative kinesics increased learning but only if the teacher was female (Esp, 1978). Steward and Lupfer (1987) reported a small but significant increase in examination scores for students who had received touch rather than those who had not been touched by their instructors.

Unfortunately, a number of studies using measures of immediacy have failed to find increases in short term cognitive learning (Andersen, 1979; Andersen & Withrow, 1981; Giglio & Lustig, 1987). All of these studies used multiple-choice tests to measure short-term learning of course content. Perhaps other factors, such as study time and reading ability, wipe out the effects of teacher immediacy on objective test measures. Medley and Mitzel (1958) reported no long-term differences in intellectual growth between students who had warm teachers and those who had cold teachers.

Nevertheless, studies have shown that actual student learning may be associated with teacher immediacy. Christiansen (1960) found a positive relationship between teacher warmth and both vocabulary and arithmetic achievement in grade school children. McDowell, McDowell, Hyendahl, and Steil (1980) reported a small but significant increase in cognitive learning in high school students taught by more immediate teachers. The strongest evidence for an immediacy–cognitive-learning relationship is provided by Kelley and Gorham (1988), who report that eye contact and physical immediacy produced a nearly 20 percent increase in college students' short-term recall. The overall verdict is provided in the recent meta-analysis of 81 studies by Witt et al. (2004): Across studies there is a statistically significant relationship between teacher nonverbal immediacy and actual cognitive learning; however, it represents only about a 3 percent increase in cognitive learning.

Other evidence for a positive relationship between teacher immediacy and learning is provided by Comstock et al. (1995), who report that a lecturer moderately high in immediacy produced more retention of material than a low-immediacy lecturer. However, a very high immediacy condition resulted in less learning than the moderately high immediacy condition, suggesting that a lecturer can be too immediate. Still, the very high immediacy condition produced significantly more cognitive learning than the low-immediacy condition. This suggests that lecturers and teachers should strive to be highly immediate; erring in the direction of very high immediacy is still far better than erring in the direction of low immediacy.

The pattern of findings is somewhat less consistent for the immediacy–cognitive-learning relationship than for the relationship between immediacy and affective learning, behavioral commitment, and perceived learning. Nonetheless, none of the studies suggest that immediacy reduces cognitive learning, and the cumulative findings suggest that actual teacher nonverbal immediacy produces slight increases in cognitive learning.

Institutional Effects

Institutional communication in organizations, on the job, or in customer-service-provider encounters differs somewhat from communication in interpersonal relationships or instructional environments. Institutional communication—which involves interactions between such people as doctor and patient, subordinate and superior, or police officer and citizen—is less spontaneous and more rule-governed. Nonetheless, research has shown that nonverbal immediacy has positive benefits even in impersonal institutional encounters. Recall the Fisher et al. (1976) study, which found that subtle touch from librarians improved students' attitudes toward librarians and the library in general. Research on immediacy in organizational communication by Koermer, Goldstein, and Fortson (1993) found that "supervisors who were communicatively immediate left subordinates with the impression that supervisors respected them, encouraged more input, valued their work, and wanted to get to know them professionally" (p. 277). Supervisors who were nonimmediate caused subordinates to feel betrayed, to feel like outcasts, and to regard work as a waste of time. As we will learn in chapter 12, immediacy cues from supervisors and other powerful people serve as particularly effective motivators.

Druckman, Rozelle, and Baxter (1982) reported a series of studies that showed that more-immediate behavior was beneficial even in police–citizen encounters. In the positive nonverbal condition, police were trained to employ relaxed postures, friendly facial expressions, head nods, and eye contact—all immediacy behaviors. The authors concluded:

> Results supported predictions that positive verbal and nonverbal encoding conditions would lead to more favorable ratings on interpersonal and job-related qualities of the police officer than would be the case for the standard presentation. In addition, nonverbal behaviors accounted for a greater proportion of the variance in the obtained ratings than did verbal behaviors. (p. 102)

In health-care settings, immediacy has several benefits. Studies consistently report a strong positive correlation between physician affiliativeness or immediacy and patient satisfaction and report (Conlee, Olvera, & Vagim, 1993; Griffin,

Wilson, Langer, & Haist, 2003; Harrigan, Oxman, and Rosenthal 1985; Street & Buller, 1988). Based on these studies doctors would be advised to utilize uncrossed legs and open, symmetrical body positions, directly face the patient, maintain closer interpersonal distances, smile, nod, be facially expressive, and use direct eye contact. A recent study reports that increase total touch and increased task touch from parents reduced children's pain and distress during painful cancer treatment procedures (Peterson et al., 2007). Even a doctor's tone of voice has been related to successful treatment of alcoholism, showing that a physician's nonverbal behavior is not trivial. Patients were likely to seek treatment if the doctor's voice was low in anger and high in anxiety or concern (Milmoe, Rosenthal, Blane, Chafetz, & Wolf, 1979). Burgoon and Saine (1978) summarized several studies that have shown psychiatrists and nurses to have the most rapport with patients when their upper bodies were in positions that mirrored their patients' upper-body positions. Similarly, Ziegler-Kratz and Marshall (1990) reported that potential clients were more likely to seek counseling from a therapist who smiled more or used more eye contact than from a less-immediate therapist. Only recently has the medical community realized the power of communication in patient satisfaction, patient compliance, and healing. Hopefully, immediacy training will become a standard part of the education of all health professionals.

SUMMARY

One of the most central functions of nonverbal communication is the communication of immediacy. Immediacy behaviors signal availability and inclusion, communicate approach and involvement, increase sensory stimulation, and send messages of warmth and positive affect. In some less positive relationships, immediacy behaviors are perceived as threatening and suffocating, but in most relationships they are perceived (and intended) as warm, positive behaviors that promote interpersonal closeness. Immediacy is usually a mindless, positive expression of warmth and involvement with another person, although it is sometimes displayed strategically.

We communicate immediacy primarily through a multichanneled set of nonverbal codes, including (1) oculesics, through gaze, eye contact, and even pupil dilation; (2) proxemics, by way of closer interpersonal distances, communicating on the same physical plane, orienting one's body toward one's partner, and forward leaning; (3) haptics, via various types of increased touch appropriate to one's relationship; (4) kinesics, by employing positive facial expressions, especially smiles, as well as head nods, bodily relaxation, gestures, body synchrony, a light and happy gait, and more-open body positions; (5) vocalics, by varying the pitch, amplitude, duration, and tempo of the voice, by maintaining vocal synchrony with others, and, in some relationships, by using baby talk; and (6) chronemics, by spending time with another person and being punctual.

Several factors affect the amount of immediacy expressed between interactants. (1) *The relationship*—close, positive relationships generally produce the most immediacy, although stable, long-term relationships often require less immediacy than developing ones. (2) *Individual differences*—a number of communication pre-dispositions or personality traits cause some people to show immediacy more overtly than others. Likewise, gender and cultural background have an impact on the amount of immediacy individuals display. (3) *The situation*—some settings are more conducive to immediacy expression than others. (4) *Temporary states*—moods and physical states determine the level of immediacy a person feels like expressing.

The direct effects model holds that immediacy generally is perceived as a warm, friendly, intimate, and attractive behavior. According to the social-meaning model (a similar model of immediacy), many nonverbal behaviors, including immediacy behaviors, have such a clear social meaning that most interactants react to them the same way across most relationships. Considerable support exists for these models.

Immediacy has positive interpersonal effects, including increased attraction for the person expressing immediacy, the maintenance of close relationships, sexual attraction and involvement, and improved marital satisfaction. Similarly, in the classroom students show substantially increased affective and behavioral learning and some increase in cognitive learning from more-immediate teachers. Finally, in organizational communication, immediacy has numerous positive effects, even in impersonal encounters.

9

Nonverbal Communication of Intimacy and Affection in Close Relationships

Writing about intimacy, Montgomery (1988) stated, "As sure as intimacy is the goal of this search, communication is its method. For it is through verbally and nonverbally sharing, disclosing, revealing, and expressing themselves that two people become intimate" (p. 347).

Exchanging intimate messages may be the essence of close relationships. In a chapter entitled "The Bright Side of Relational Communication," Andersen and Guerrero (1998a) maintained:

> Almost without exception, our relationships with friends and loved ones are the cornerstone of our lives and our emotional well-being. The warm feelings of an intimate conversation, a reassuring hug, seeing a close friend after a long absence, or sharing joy with one's family are experiences each of us has had. Indeed, the brightest side of life's experiences often occurs in close intimate relationships during the exchange of warm involving immediate messages. (p. 303)

It is through interactions with our closest relationships with friends, family, romantic partners, and spouses that we truly experience intimacy and affection. Close, intimate relationships enhance our lives, provide satisfaction, promote health, create security, and engender some of the most positive emotions humans can experience. It is through nonverbal behavior first and foremost that intimacy is communicated.

THE DIMENSIONS OF INTIMACY

Intimacy is a broad term that references warm, involving behaviors, interactions, experiences, and relations. Other terms that suggest intimacy include *love, warmth, closeness, affection, support, bonding, sexuality, attachment, immediacy, involve-*

ment, confirmation, validation, and *friendship* (Andersen & Guerrero, 1998a; Andersen, Guerrero & Jones, 2006; Prager, 1995). Intimacy can be any or all of these. In fact, intimacy—the expression of a truly close relationship—lies at the intersection of these concepts. So, if one of these other terms helps you understand close relationships better than the term intimacy, go with it. *Intimacy,* however, is the central term used by relationships researchers and in this chapter to refer to close relationships because it encapsulates what it means to have a unique, high-quality relationship with another person.

Intimacy has been characterized as the "proverbial elephant" by Acitelli and Duck (1987), who described intimacy researchers as a group of blind people who touch different parts of the same elephant and reach dramatically different conclusions about the shape of the beast. Intimacy is multifaceted; it entails dimensions of behavior, interaction, ideology, emotion, and relationships. Because intimacy *must* be communicated, our discussion begins with communication behaviors that convey intimacy in interpersonal interaction.

Intimacy as Communication Behavior

In chapter 8 we discussed nonverbal immediacy, the many ways that humans express interpersonal warmth, closeness, and involvement with one another. Our discussion of intimate behavior must start with nonverbal immediacy, the foundation of intimacy.

INTIMACY'S FOUNDATION: NONVERBAL IMMEDIACY

"The only way you can become closer and more intimate with others is via immediacy behaviors. Immediate body language is the means of sending messages of closeness, warmth and friendship" (Andersen, 2004, p. 193). Intimate behaviors are typically called immediacy behaviors (Andersen, 1989, 1998, 2008); intimate behaviors signal warmth, availability for interaction, and relational closeness. In chapter 8 we discussed how actions such as eye contact, smiling, touch, and interpersonal space communicate immediacy, so we won't repeat that discussion here. It is clear that *immediacy behaviors are the foundations by which intimate interactions and intimate relationships are created and sustained.* It is nonverbal communication in particular that creates intimacy. Andersen (1989) stated:

> Nonverbal communication is the primary means of relational communication. The multichannelled nature of nonverbal communication, its spontaneity, its phylogenetic and ontogenetic primacy, and the difficulty in concealing or controlling nonverbal cues, may be reasons why it has such heavy relational impact. (p. 5)

Research shows that nonverbal communication is the primary means of establishing and maintaining an intimate relationship. In their classic book, Watzlawick, Beavin, and Jackson (1967) showed that verbal and other forms of digital communication are far less important than nonverbal communication: "Wherever relationship is the central issue of communication, we find that digital language is almost meaningless" (p. 63). In chapter 1 we learned that nonverbal communication is as important as verbal communication. For relational interaction nonverbal communication is certainly *more* important. This does not suggest that some forms of verbal communication, such as self-disclosure (revealing private information about oneself), are irrelevant to relational closeness and intimacy. Indeed, scholars have long recognized that self-disclosure is a key component of relational closeness and intimacy (see Hatfield, 1984). However, Montgomery's (1988) review of the relationship literature shows that "the nonverbal mode of expression appears to be more closely linked to relationship quality than the verbal mode" (p. 348).

Research indicates that certain kinds of nonverbal behavior are vital to the communication of intimacy and the establishment of relational closeness. Certainly, the immediacy behaviors discussed in chapter 8 (including eye contact, touch, smiles, and close interpersonal distances) are essential to intimate communication and relational closeness, but immediate communication is also important in nonintimate relationships with strangers, acquaintances, classmates, coworkers, and customers. So, although immediacy is essential to intimacy, it is not enough. Intimacy and relational closeness are communicated when immediacy behaviors are *sustained* and *prolonged*. Research by Register and Henley (1992) showed that nonverbal behavior, in general, defines intimacy but that three particular kinds of nonverbal behavior are especially important to intimacy: prolonged time spent together, lingering gazes, and sustained touch. Other research has shown that total time spent with a relational partner is a vital part of relational satisfaction in marital and dating relationships (Egland, Stelzner, Andersen, & Spitzberg, 1997). Although gaze is an important nonverbal behavior, it is prolonged gaze that signals intimacy (Patterson, 1983). It is the sustained communication of immediacy that distinguishes the intimate relationship from one that is just mildly positive or socially polite.

Similarly, sustaining immediacy across many interactions and situations seems to be essential for relational intimacy to occur. Being immediate one moment and cold and aloof the next is not a recipe for intimacy. As Miller, Cody, and McLaughlin (1994) stated:

> It is very likely that high intimacy not only reflects a particular set of qualities
> of the relationship (emotional attachment and so on) but also reflects a greater
> number of shared situations; nonintimates communicate in a limited range of
> events while intimates experience more situations together as well as a wider
> range of them. (p. 183)

This, of course, does not mean that intimacy requires people to share every one of life's moments. In fact, some breathing space is necessary to help intimacy thrive and keep the relationship exciting. It does mean, however, that intimate behavior occurs across many diverse situations in which nonverbal immediacy is high.

INTIMACY AS AFFECTION

A vital part of intimacy is the communication of affection. During the last decade considerable research has focused on the importance of affection and how it is communicated nonverbally (For excellent summaries see Guerrero & Floyd, 2006; Pendell, 2002). Although affection can be communicated in any type of relationship, it is most commonly expressed in our closest relationships: in families, close friendships, romances, and marriages (Pendell, 2002).

Affection communicates warmth, positive regard, safety, support, comfort, relationship satisfaction, and closeness (Dolin & Booth-Butterfield, 1993; Floyd, Sargent, & DiCorcia, 2004; Gulledge, Gulledge, & Stahmann, 2003; Pendell, 2002) of infants as well as adults (Hertenstein, 2002). Genuine expression of affection results in intimacy, closeness, and relational connection. People frequently remember their first hug or first kiss, and affectionate communication is often appreciated and remembered in times of distress as a form of social support. Affection increases liking (Floyd & Voloudakis, 1999), creates feelings of warmth (Andersen & Guerrero, 1998a), and is central to the experience of intimacy in close relationships (Marston et al., 1998). Likewise, decreases in affection are even more noticeable than increases in affection and create negative attributions about the relational partner and the relationship (Floyd & Voloudakis, 1999), though decreases in affection were often attributed to the situation, not the person.

Research shows that while verbal affection and supportiveness are important parts of affection, its primary factor is comprised of *nonverbal* expressions of affection (Floyd & Morman, 1998; Guerrero & Floyd, 2006). Primary manifestations of affection are smiling, close interpersonal distances, support, touch, kissing, prolonged eye contact, and other interpersonally warm behaviors (Andersen & Guerrero 1998a, Floyd & Morman, 1998; Gonzaga et al., 2006; Gulledge, Gulledge, & Stahmann, 2003; Pendell, 2002). Tactile behavior is central to the expression of affection, from cuddling a baby to back rubs, stroking, holding hands and kissing with a partner, and even to sexual intercourse. Facial behavior sends messages of affection that include smiling, eye contact, expansiveness or animation in the face, head nodding, and winking (Floyd & Morman, 1998; Gulledge, Gulledge, & Stahmann, 2003; Guerrero & Floyd, 2006). Vocal affection is conveyed via low tones of voice, vocal variation as opposed to a monotone, and even baby talk that is expressed not only to babies but between romantic partners as well (Floyd & Ray, 2003; Guerrero & Floyd, 2006).

The need for affection is biological, an extension of nurturant behavior, and manifested in all cultures throughout the world (Guerrero & Floyd, 2006; Pendell, 2002). Offspring not only need affection; they bring out affection behavior in parents. Interestingly, fathers show more affection to their sons if the sons are more likely to have offspring (Floyd, Sargent, & DiCorcia, 2004) suggesting the biological basis of affection and explaining why homosexuals receive less affection from their fathers. Young animals, including young humans, thrive when caregivers manifest warm affectionate behaviors and fail to thrive in the absence of affection. Affection is vital in pair bonding, mating, and marriage that form the basis of human family and reproductive relationships. Humans need affection, and a number of studies have related it to everything from positive development in infancy to increased life expectancy (Pendell, 2002). Love and affection are more than just feelings; a complex biology underlies affection. Recent research shows that love and affiliation releases oxytocin (Gonzaga et al., 2006), a chemical associated with bonding among mammals (including humans) with their infants and romantic partners. Similarly, more frequent hugs from their partners were associated with a higher level of oxytocin and lower blood pressure in premenopausal women (Light, Grewen, & Amico, 2005), suggesting that tactile affection is highly beneficial to the relationship and to personal health.

Affection also has a social and cultural basis. People that grow up in affectionate families and cultures learn to be affectionate and manifest more affection (Pendell, 2002). High-immediacy or high-contact cultures such as those that derive from the Mediterranean region are much more nonverbally affectionate and expressive (Andersen & Wang, in press; also see chapter 4). Likewise, secure attachment forms the basis for affectionate behavior (Pendell, 2002; Schachner, Shaver, & Mikulincer, 2005).

One advantage of nonverbally communicating affection is ambiguity. Unlike saying "I love you," communicating affection via facial expression, vocal tones, or touch is more implicit and equivocal, certainly more mysterious, and some would say more romantic. Affectionate nonverbal communication, like all forms of nonverbal communication is more intuitive, multichanneled, spontaneous, and believable (see chapter 1).

INTIMACY AS CONTACT

Relational closeness and intimacy rely particularly on one nonverbal behavior, touch. As Morris (1971) noted in his classic book *Intimate Behavior*, "To be intimate means to be close, and I must make clear at the outset that I am treating this literally. In my terms, then, the act of intimacy occurs whenever two individuals come into bodily contact" (p. 9). Monsour (1992) maintained that physical contact is essential to intimacy for both friends and relational partners. Johnson and Edwards (1991) supported this position when they found that increasingly intimate touch was the major indicator of relational commitment. In all relationships—between parents and offspring, grandparents and grandchildren, close friends, teammates, sorority sisters, siblings, lovers, and married couples—touch is a vital part of communicating intimacy. Guerrero and Andersen (1991) established that touch is extremely important to the establishment of intimacy in developing and newly bonded relationships. A consensus has emerged that touch is an

Intimacy is communication via multiple nonverbal cues. At the core of intimacy are touch and eye contact.

essential component of all intimate relationships (Andersen et al., 2006; Montagu, 1978, Prager, 1995; Prager & Roberts, 2004).

In summary, intimacy requires three elements of nonverbal behavior. First, intimate relationships necessitate high levels of nonverbal involvement and immediacy beyond that which occurs in most relationships. Second, warm, immediate nonverbal behavior must be sustained over many interactions and situations. Finally, the most important behaviors needed to establish an intimate relationship involve affection and physical closeness, particularly touch.

Intimacy as Interaction

Of course, one person behaving intimately does not necessarily make for an intimate interaction. In fact, when people unilaterally move closer, smile, maintain eye contact, and/or touch their interaction partners, they may be perceived negatively—they may seem intrusive, overbearing, harassing, or even threatening—by their partners. In general, intimate interactions move slowly, with both partners gradually manifesting more immediacy and affection, sharing more space and time, and lowering their defenses. Intimate interaction is the essential foundation of intimate relationships, and intimacy is created interactionally (Andersen et al., 2006).

As we will see later in this chapter, building a relationship involves a complex series of moves and countermoves that gradually escalate the intimacy level and slowly build a truly intimate relationship. Most scholars have recognized that all social interaction is synchronously, rhythmically, and interactionally organized (Burgoon, Stern, & Dillman, 1995; Cappella, 1981, 1991b). Burgoon and her associates (1995) maintain that social interaction "entails regular *patterns* of behavior in which each interactant's behavior influences the other's behavior. The dyad rather than single individuals, and dynamic rather than static behaviors, are at the heart of synchrony" (p. 19). All interactants, especially intimate interactants, must synchronize and coordinate their communication behaviors to achieve good "vibes" and to be on the same "wavelength." Insecurely attached individuals are often excessively intimate and they intensely, often obnoxiously, try to attain attachment to potential friends or partners (Schachner et al., 2005), hardly the recipe for a strong reciprocal relationship that is truly on the same wavelength.

Although most of these synchronous patterns are reciprocal, some are not. Some are complementary: One person gives a back rub, and the other receives it; one person discloses, and the other listens and nods attentively. More often, though, synchronous nonverbal behaviors are reciprocal—for example, two lovers caressing one another while gazing into each other's eyes (Prager, 1995).

One problem with conceptualizing intimacy as an interactive concept is that both parties in an interaction have unique and separate points of view (see Acitelli & Duck, 1987; Prager, 1995). One person may find an interaction highly intimate, whereas the partner may find it only mildly intimate or not intimate at all. Partners have different cognitive schemata (social knowledge structures) for the relationship (Andersen, 1993a), and in their minds they may even have two distinct psychological relationships (Acitelli & Duck, 1987).

Although different psychological relationships and perspectives exist in all intimate interactions, it has been widely noted that males and females have different notions of intimacy (for more on gender differences and similarities see chapter 5). Traditionally, males find intimacy in recreational and task-related activities, whereas females find intimacy in sharing time with others and communicating with others verbally and nonverbally (Helgeson, Shaver, & Dyer, 1987; Monsour, 1992). Research, however, has shown more similarity than difference in males' and females' perceptions of intimacy in both same-sex and opposite-sex relationships (Koerner & Fitzpatrick, 2002; Monsour, 1992; Parks & Floyd, 1996). Burleson, Kunkel, Samter, and Werking (1996) found that males rated instrumental or task skills as more important than did females in close relationships; whereas females rated affective, or emotional, skills as more important than did males. However, both males and females overwhelmingly viewed affectively oriented skills as more relationally important than instrumental skills. Moreover, Burleson et al. found that "affectively oriented communication skills appear to be important for both genders in the conduct of intimacy—regardless of whether intimacy is realized in same-sex friendship or opposite-sex romances" (p. 218). Because nonverbal communication is the most important part of affective messages, nonverbal skills are a vital part of intimate interaction. This is similar to research reported by Koerner and Fitzpatrick (2002), who found that accuracy in decoding the positive and negative emotions of one's partner was related to marital satisfaction for the partner, particularly when husbands accurately decoded wives' emotions.

This, of course, does not mean that in any given interaction both parties will evaluate the interaction as equally intimate. Although intimacy is created in interaction, it exists in the minds of individuals. For this reason, I subscribe to the position taken by Acitelli and Duck (1987): "The question is whether intimacy is a quality of persons or interactions. Rather than decide between them, we opt for an amalgamation of the two—Intimacy can be a property of persons and interaction" (p. 298).

Intimacy as an Ideology

Throughout history, a set of beliefs have developed that made intimacy an important value. This "ideology of intimacy" suggests that life is incomplete without friends, mates, parents, and even children. Historically, we have been persuaded that intimate bonds and attendant feelings of intimacy are a basic need. McAdams (1988) has suggested that as individuals, we have an intimacy motive, "a recurrent preference or readiness for experiences of warm, close, communicative interchanges with others" (p. 19). Intimacy has come to be perceived as an end in itself, not as a means to an end. In recent decades, intimacy has even increased in importance! Bookstores are glutted with how-to manuals on intimate relationships; Internet chat lines are used primarily for personal, intimate conversations; and card companies have institutionalized the mandatory celebration of Mother's Day, Father's Day, Grandparents' Day, and so on.

Of course, when basic, individual needs are not being met, such as our need for food or shelter, intimacy doesn't seem very salient (Maslow, 1968). In today's developed world, even though most of our "basic" needs have been met, many people feel a longing for something less tangible. Loneliness, separation, alienation, stress, and uneasiness characterize our times. More than four times as many Americans today describe themselves as lonely than in 1957 (Twenge,

2006). People are searching for meaning. Although we come in contact with more people now than ever before in the history of humankind, our relationships have not necessarily become more intimate. Some would even say that relationships today are less intimate than ever before in spite of the high value society places on intimacy. This may be particularly true in America. A comparative study of American and French teenagers found that American teens engage in less affectionate touch and less positive facial behavior as well as more aggressive behavior than do French teens (Field, 1999). Lack of intimacy and affection is associated with an epidemic of depression being experienced by young Americans today (Twenge, 2006). Paradoxically, in a culture where intimacy is more important than ever, it is harder to find.

Since the 1960s, society's preoccupation with this "ideology of intimacy" has increased. This was described in some detail by Sennett (1977) and extended to communication by Parks (1982). Montgomery (1988) stated that "by the late 1970s people were placing more importance on interpersonal sources of happiness like being close to their children, 'really' getting to know their friends and having meaningful relationships" (p. 347). Having met our material needs, we have begun a quest for intimacy. Sennett (1977) suggested:

> The reigning belief is that closeness between persons is a moral good. The reigning aspiration today is to develop individual personality through the experience of closeness and warmth with others. The reigning myth today is that the evils of society can all be understood as evils of impersonality, alienation, and coldness. The sum of these three is an ideology of intimacy. (p. 259)

Today, most of us subscribe to this ideology. We recognize that acquaintances, friends, and lovers are essential—and the more the merrier. Most authors and professors (including myself) subscribe to this ideology to a greater or lesser degree. Parks (1982) suggested that the appeal of the ideology of intimacy "flows from larger critiques which decry the loss of feeling and the decline of community in modern life. Popular images of people hungry for close, meaningful relationships and of communities fragmented by rapid change and excessive mobility are not new" (p. 85). Parks warns that other values such as privacy, nonintimate relationships, and information control may be lost and individuals may be propelled into an unending and ultimately unsatisfying quest for intimacy. Paradoxically, effortful striving for intimacy may prevent us from ever finding it—or at least finding it satisfying (more on this later).

Of course, nonintimate relationships, including those between business associates and casual friends, can be very satisfying. However, Spitzberg and Cupach (1994) pointed out that an ideological assumption is that only closer relationships are valuable.

> Relationships are considered "on track" if they are progressing toward intimacy and togetherness and are disintegrating, decaying, dissipating, declining, dissolving, or dying if they are moving away from intimacy. Yet as the chapters on the dark side have argued, closeness often breeds undue influence, loss of identity, loss of privacy, frustration of individual goals and personal projects, and the possibilities of great psychological and physical harm. (p. 317)

There is, indeed, a dark side to intimate relationships. After all, most violence, including most murders, occurs within the confines of intimate relationships (see Marshall, 1994).

We strive today for more intimacy, yet our busy lives often preclude it. We are suffering from information overload, and our lives are "saturated." In Gergen's (1991) landmark book *The Saturated Self*, he discussed the geographically, interpersonally, and socially fragmented situation of the postmodern age. The multiple selves, fragmented lives, and busy schedules of postmodern humans prevent any "true" intimacy:

> In the context of social situation, one can see why both intimacy and commitment are vanishing from relationships. This began when commitment concepts of the person were ended by modernism. In the romantic period one could build a life around "true love" or "a powerful passion." With the advent of modernism, expressions of mysterious depths began to appear to be dubious. . . . Nowadays, to tell a romantic partner, "It is your soul I thirst" or "My passion is all consuming," might send him or her into a quick retreat. (pp. 175–179)

Human contact may be increasing dramatically, but our intimacy needs are unmet. We may not even know how to achieve intimacy. So, though intimacy is our quest, true intimacy may frighten us.

Intimacy as an Emotion

At the individual level intimacy is an experience; we think intimate thoughts and feel intimate emotions (Prager, 1995; Prager & Roberts, 2004). This is more than an ideology; scholars have begun conceptualizing intimacy as an emotion.

Reflect for a moment on an intimate interaction: a hug from an old friend or sharing time with family during the holidays. Tune in to your feelings. The emotion of intimacy you may be experiencing is often described as warmth. Andersen and Guerrero (1998a) have suggested that intimacy, or warmth, is a basic emotion. Although it is not listed in most studies as a basic emotion, English has no word with which to describe the nonverbal, ineffable feeling of intimacy that Andersen and Guerrero call interpersonal *warmth*. The Danish word *hugge* and the German *gemütlichkeit* come the closest in capturing the warm, pleasant, amiable, cozy feelings that are experienced in close relationships.

Most definitions of intimacy include feelings of warmth as a central component. Sternberg's (1986, 1988) theory of love employs three thermal metaphors: hot for passion, cool for commitment, and warm for intimacy. Warmth is the metaphor employed to describe feelings of intimacy, attachment, commitment, validation, closeness, and involvement. Scholars have recognized that intimacy has distinct emotional components. Acitelli and Duck (1987) recognized that love and intimacy can be located in both thoughts and emotions. In her book on intimacy, Prager (1995) recognized the centrality of intimacy as an emotion. It is primarily nonverbal behavior during intimate interaction that generates these warm feelings, although verbal behaviors also play a role. Patterson's (1983) review of research demonstrated that the quality of emotions or affect in close relationships is the result of nonverbal involvement, particularly touch communication such as kissing, hugging, and holding hands. Intimate, warm feelings can emotionally be experienced only through immediate interpersonal communication in positive situations with relationally significant others.

Intimacy in Relationships

Intimate relationships result from many episodes of warm, immediate interactions. As Prager (1995) maintained, "At the simplest level, an intimate relationship is one in which intimate interactions occur on a regular and predictable basis" (p. 23). Perhaps the most essential quality of intimate relationships is that each one is unique. Although many of our role relationships—such as our interactions with supermarket clerks, bank tellers, or classmates—are nonunique and replaceable, intimate relationships are difficult, if not impossible, to replace. Hendrick and Hendrick (1992) contended that intimacy "is characterized by genuineness and an absence of formal 'role' relationships" (p. 166). In intimate relationships, a unique pattern of nonverbal behavior develops. Special experiences are shared, and relational intimacy both enhances those experiences and is enhanced by them. More time and higher-quality time is spent together, creating a chronemic bond. Space—work space, home space, and conversational space—is also shared in distinct ways, creating proxemic intimacy. Even the sharing of food and the act of feeding another person are associated with intimacy (Miller, Rozin, & Fiske, 1998) though we may find such practices disgusting if they were performed with any random individual. Touch that would be offensive in role relationships is encouraged in intimate relationships, creating a special haptic bond. Intimate interactants display unique, implicit facial expressions whose meanings are clear only to each other. Interaction rhythms begin to merge.

Touch that would be inappropriate and offensive in role relationships is encouraged in intimate relationships, creating unique bonds.

Intimacy is the essence of friendship (Perlman & Fehr, 1987) typified by deep, intimate interconnections (Walster, Walster, & Berscheid, 1978) that are emotional, cognitive, and behavioral. Intimate relationships, including friendships, also involve a powerful, unspoken nonverbal comfortableness and unpretentiousness. Activities, schedules, and movements are highly synchronized and have pleasing, comfortable rhythms to them (see chapter 8).

Intimate relationships have a history; they often develop slowly over time as trust, warmth, and synchrony build. They also have a future. We expect our intimate relationships to

Intimate relationships are a function of repeated intimate interactions characterized by sharing of time, space, and touch.

play an important role in our lives for years to come; we want our intimate partners to be lifelong friends who will support us and comfort us, as well as engage us in talk and activity. When intimate relationships end through conflict, geographic separation, or death, we feel a deep loss, in part because the termination of a relationship robs our future of happy, intimate interactions with a treasured partner.

Studies show that nonverbal behaviors are crucial for sustaining intimate relationships. One study by Noller (1980) revealed the importance of gaze behavior in marital relations: Well-adjusted, intimate married couples spent less time looking at each other during negative messages than did poorly adjusted couples. This was true for speakers and listeners and suggests that although eye contact is generally positive, it is more intimate, deferent, and nonconfrontational to avert eye contact during conflict. Additionally, Noller (1980) reported that poorly adjusted couples look more when speaking and less when listening than did well-adjusted couples, indicating that poorly adjusted couples are more dominant and less intimate (see chapter 12 for more on the visual dominance ratio). Other research by Noller (1982) showed that well-adjusted couples sent more positive messages, fewer negative messages, and fewer discrepant messages (for example, positive visual behaviors accompanied by negative vocal behaviors) than did poorly adjusted couples. Similarly, other studies have found that unhappily married couples sent and reciprocated more negative messages than did happily married couples (Fitzpatrick & Badzinski, 1985; Gottman, 1979).

Intimate relationships may be one of our greatest stress reducers, a source of much of our creative energy, and the basis of our important plans and goals. Think of losing the three most intimate relationships you have. Would any of your plans or projects seem very important without them? Probably not! Our very physical and psychological health depends on intimate relationships. Severely depressed people tend to have highly disrupted and negative intimate relationships (Segrin, 1998). It is likely that a lack of intimacy produces depression and that a negative, depressed mood destroys feelings of intimacy. Such a negative spiral of depression and lack of intimacy can be difficult to break. Intimacy, however, has the ability to promote optimism and mental health and, consequently, lead to more intimacy.

In this section, we have examined five dimensions of intimacy: as a behavior, as a function of our closest interpersonal interactions, as an ideology, as an emotion, and as a key component of close relationships. Nonverbal immediacy cues are vital to intimacy. Immediacy behaviors that are prolonged and occur repeatedly over the course of a relationship both generate intimacy and result from intimacy. Touch is particularly indicative of intimacy. Intimacy cannot be achieved unilaterally; it must be interactionally reciprocal, held as a part of one's life philosophy, experienced emotionally, and sustained in an intimate interaction.

VERBAL AND NONVERBAL INTIMACY

Certainly, verbal behaviors can communicate intimacy. Verbal intimacy behaviors have been summarized by Andersen (2008; Andersen & Guerrero, 1998a). There are several types of verbal intimacy behaviors. *Positive interaction patterns,* in which both partners exert symmetrical or complementary patterns of control, are likely to result from and create close, intimate relationships (see Rogers & Millar, 1988). *Verbal immediacy behaviors,* including first-person plural pronouns (we versus you and me) and other linguistic devices, create relational bonds that help to establish and maintain interpersonal intimacy (Weiner & Mehrabian, 1968). *Self-disclosure* (such as telling your partner about your very personal fears and joys) is a primary means of communicating intimacy and escalating relational closeness (see Derlega, Metts, Petronio, & Margulis, 1993). *Personal forms of address* (for example, Tom as opposed to Mr. Knight or President Knight) have considerable relational significance (see King & Sereno, 1984). Finally, specific verbal *communication about the relationship* often enhances closeness and confirms relational commitment (for example, "I'm glad we're friends," or "I love you"). Despite these important verbal behaviors, it is nonverbal behaviors, with their greater authenticity, multichanneled redundancy, developmental primacy, and general spontaneity, that produce the greatest relational impact.

COGNITIVE VALENCE THEORY

How are intimate relationships formed and maintained? A number of theories of relationship development and interpersonal adaptation exist (for summaries see Andersen & Andersen, 1984; Burgoon et al., 1995; Guerrero & Floyd, 2006). Many of these theories have similar components, so I will focus on one explanation of intimacy development, *cognitive valence theory.* This theory describes and explains the process of intimacy exchange across a variety of relationships, including those between close colleagues, friends, intimate friends, romantic partners, married couples, and family members.

Relationships don't "just happen." They result from numerous positive interaction episodes. Intimate communication behavior is the primary vehicle for developing and increasing relational intimacy (Andersen & Andersen, 2005; Jones & Guerrero, 2001). All intimate relations begin with increases in immediacy, particularly nonverbal immediacy, by one of two partners. Of course, a person's immediacy behaviors must be perceived or noticed by her or his interaction partner to have any communicative significance. As the cognitive valence model (Figure 9.1) indicates, Person B must detect a change in Person A's behavioral immediacy level. In short, Person B must perceive that Person A's behavior is more intimate than usual. Reis and Shaver (1988) maintain that considerable research on perceptual filters has shown that expectations and schemata profoundly influence a partner's behavior. They also contend, "What matters for B's response is B's construal of A's expression" (p. 378). Perceived increases in intimacy behavior activate receivers physiologically, emotionally, and cognitively and also increase their arousal.

Arousal

Intimacy is in part biologically based; moderate increases in immediacy produce physiological arousal, which in turn activates cognitive processes (Guerrero & Floyd, 2006). In his summary of twenty-four studies on the relationship between immediacy increases and arousal, Andersen (1985) concluded, "The research generally supports a positive relationship between immediacy increases and increases in arousal" (p. 15). For example, if your boyfriend or girlfriend makes eye contact with you and smiles, you would show moderate increases in signs of physiological arousal. Arousal increases as a function of increased gaze, close proxemic distances, more direct body orientation, greater spatial density and crowding, increased smiling, and more touch. Research by Andersen, Guerrero, Buller, and Jorgensen (1998) revealed that an increase in multichanneled immediacy by one person significantly raises a partner's physiological arousal.

According to cognitive valence theory, when one interactant perceives increased intimacy from another interactant, physiological arousal increases. Very large arousal increases, however, are inherently aversive and stressful and lead to withdrawal and even flight. For example, a stranger invading your space on a dark street would cause you to experience high arousal and, possibly, to flee. Many studies have shown that rapid arousal increases are unpleasant and aversive (see Berlyne, 1960; Cappella & Greene, 1982; Eysenck, 1967, 1976) and that the resulting reactions can occur without any conscious thought (Zajonc, 1980, 1984). By contrast, small arousal changes produce little behavioral change.

Most intimate messages produce moderate increases in arousal that activate cognitive schemata, or social knowledge structures (Brehm, 1985; Mandler, 1975). People store knowledge about a given message's cultural appropriateness, their interpersonal relationship with the interaction partner, their interpersonal valence (positive or negative attitude toward the partner) the situational appropriateness of the message, their present physical or emotional state, and their predisposition toward a particular type of communication. Cognitive valence theory emphasizes that these cognitive schemata, or social knowledge structures, hold information about expected behavior. If the observed behavior fails to roughly match the expected behavior, the receiver will perceive the behavior as inappropriate, and

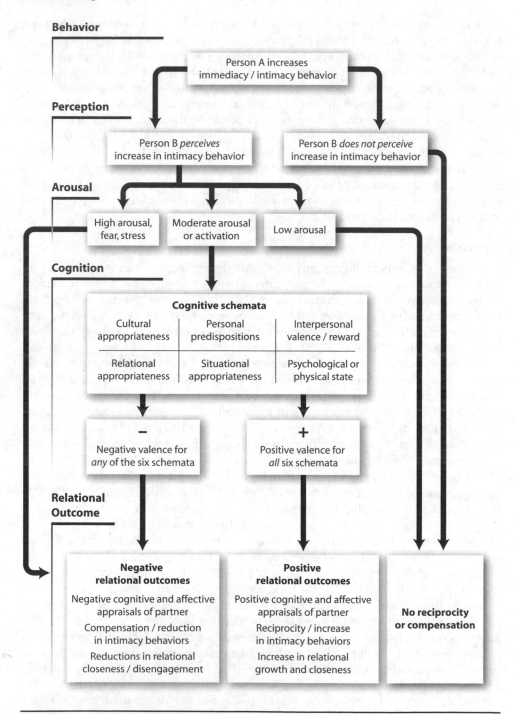

Behavior

Person A increases
immediacy / intimacy behavior

Perception

Person B *perceives*
increase in intimacy behavior

Person B *does not perceive*
increase in intimacy behavior

Arousal

High arousal,
fear, stress

Moderate arousal
or activation

Low arousal

Cognition

Cognitive schemata

| Cultural appropriateness | Personal predispositions | Interpersonal valence / reward |
| Relational appropriateness | Situational appropriateness | Psychological or physical state |

–
Negative valence for
any of the six schemata

+
Positive valence for
all six schemata

**Relational
Outcome**

**Negative
relational outcomes**

Negative cognitive and affective
appraisals of partner

Compensation / reduction
in intimacy behaviors

Reductions in relational
closeness / disengagement

**Positive
relational outcomes**

Positive cognitive and affective
appraisals of partner

Reciprocity / increase
in intimacy behaviors

Increase in relational
growth and closeness

**No reciprocity
or compensation**

Figure 9.1   Cognitive Valence Theory

negative relational outcomes will occur (see Figure 9.1). Six cognitive schemata are described here in detail.

Cognitive Schemata

Research has shown that six cognitive schemata work to determine the valence of an intimacy increase (see Andersen, 1993a; 2008). Valence is a term borrowed from chemistry, which means a positive or negative charge. Planalp (1985) suggested that relational schemata permit individuals to approach interactions with some sense of what behaviors are appropriate given the specific situation and relationship. Six types of cognitive schemata are employed by people to valence or evaluate intimacy increases: cultural schemata, self-schemata, interpersonal schemata, relational schemata, situational schemata, and state schemata.

CULTURAL SCHEMATA

Other than our membership in the human race itself, culture is the most basic force that shapes human development. Culture is such a basic and invisible force that it is often confused with human nature itself (see chapter 4, which examines the impact of culture on nonverbal communication). Hall (1976) argued that "there is not one aspect of human life that is not touched and altered by culture" (p. 16). Our cultural knowledge, or schemata, is so deeply ingrained in us that it is virtually impossible to think or behave transculturally.

Cultures differ dramatically in the degree to which they value and display intimacy (see chapter 4). For example, contact cultures use small interaction distances and considerable interpersonal touch. Noncontact cultures use little or no touch and maintain greater interpersonal distances. As a result of these cultural differences, Americans may view Arabs as pushy and intrusive, and Asians may perceive almost every other culture as too touch-oriented. These cultural communication norms are so automatic and overlearned that when an individual violates these norms, the reaction is negative. Thus, culturally inappropriate immediacy behaviors are negatively valenced by interaction partners.

SELF-SCHEMATA

Self-schemata, or individual schemata, often called personality, also influence our response to intimacy behaviors. Individuals differ greatly in personality and personal preferences for intimacy. Three groups of stable individual difference variables play a role in the intimacy exchange process: (1) *Personality traits or psychological predispositions* such as dogmatism, dominance, extroversion, and locus of control (whether a person is motivated by self or others) influence your reactions to immediacy behaviors from other people. For example, introversion causes an individual to avoid excessive stimulation and to seek tranquility (see chapter 7). Similarly, homophobia causes people to respond negatively to affectionate or immediate tactile behavior from people of the same sex (Floyd, 2000). Research suggests that independent as opposed to interdependent self-concept is associated with preference for less immediacy and greater interpersonal distance (Holland et al., 2004). (2) *Communication predispositions* such as communication apprehension, predispositions toward verbal behavior, shyness, and touch avoidance determine whether a person appreciates immediacy behaviors. For example, high touch avoiders prefer larger personal-space zones than touch approachers (Andersen & Sull, 1985). Similarly, people with an avoidant attachment style dislike close proximity to others and maintain larger interpersonal-space zones (Kaitz, Bar-Haim, Lehrer & Grossman, 2004). Likewise, insecurely attached individuals have difficulty encoding and decoding nonverbal communication resulting in inappropriate decisions about intimacy and closeness with others (Noller, 2006). (3) *Trait communication behavior*, or act frequencies (such as amount of eye contact or interpersonal distance) are consistent, intra-individual patterns of interpersonal actions (Andersen, 1987). Like cultural schemata, self-schemata are used to judge the appropriateness of intimacy behaviors. When an interaction partner's intimacy behaviors are judged to be personally inappropriate, they will be negatively valenced by the receiver. A shy person, for example, might respond negatively to immediacy increases from friends or acquaintances, whereas an extrovert might respond positively to immediacy increases. As indicated in chapter 7, traits such as communication apprehension and touch avoidance are likely to result in negative valencing of intimacy behaviors.

INTERPERSONAL SCHEMATA

During interpersonal interactions, we are quick to form impressions of other people. Considerable research shows that our perceptions about another person's qualities have dramatic effects on our valencing of intimacy behaviors. Compare these two extremes: being hugged by an unbathed, homeless person and being hugged by your boyfriend or girlfriend. These personal perceptions, or schemata, represent what we call interpersonal valence (Garrison, Sullivan, & Pate, 1976), an umbrella term that encompasses aspects of credibility (Andersen & Clevenger, 1963; McCroskey, 1966), attraction (McCroskey & McCain, 1974), and homophily or similarity (Andersen & Todd-Mancillas, 1978; Rogers & Shoemaker, 1971). Burgoon, Buller, and Woodall (1996) call these constructs "reward value." Credible, attractive, homophilous communicators are intrinsically "rewarding." It is important to distinguish reward value, or interpersonal valence, from the construct "relationship." Interpersonal valence is the evaluation of another person's qualities, not one's relationship with that person.

Interpersonal valence is a central construct in communication. Messages are not processed in a vacuum; they are always colored by evaluations of the source. Intimate actions are no exception. Our valencing of the *person* is critical to our evaluation of any attempt he or she makes to increase intimacy. If an immediacy behavior is displayed by a person with very low interpersonal valence or low reward value, we will valence the immediacy behavior negatively.

RELATIONAL SCHEMATA AND RELATIONAL TRAJECTORIES

In relational communication, the focus is on the dyad, or relationship, rather than the self or the other. Relational schemata are different from interpersonal schemata (Andersen, 1993a; Baldwin, 1992). Chelune, Robinson, and Kommor (1984) maintain that in a relationship, the focus shifts from "you and me" to "us" and thus creates a new system with its own unique properties. Intimate partners develop a sense of "we-ness" and thus create a metaperspective (Reis & Shaver, 1988). Relational schemata are the stores of knowledge we have about our relationships with others as they exist now. For example, a person might say, "We were just acquaintances but now we're getting a lot closer" or "We are engaged."

Evidence suggests that at least two kinds of relational schemata exist: relational type (for example, friend, lover, coworker, spouse, and so on) and relational trajectory (the direction in which the relationship is going; Baxter, 1987). Relational trajectory is a very important kind of relational schemata because it is one's expectation of where the relationship should be heading. Should the relationship be escalating or de-escalating? Should the relationship be on a steady and stable course? Immediacy behaviors that fall along the anticipated trajectory of future intimacy are most likely to be positively valenced. Take, for example, touch. Imagine you are in a new relationship and you *really* like your dating partner, but so far you have only held hands. Because you want the relationship to become more intimate, you will have a positive response when your date holds you close, puts her or his arm around you, and is attentive to you, even at a large party. In other words, you will judge most positively those immediacy behaviors that fall along your preferred relational trajectory, not just those that are appropriate to your current relational state. The key to relational success is to anticipate your partner's desired relational trajectory and to behave accordingly. If your partner desires more space and less intimacy, the relationship will benefit from giving your partner that space. If your partner anticipates and desires more intimacy, your relationship will benefit from being more intimate. The ability to accurately display and read one another's needs is a central feature of what characterizes secure, intimate relationships (Schachner et al., 2005).

Relational history has a powerful effect on the development of relational schemata and on the interpretation of specific actions by one's partner (Altman & Taylor, 1973; Andersen, 1993a; Baldwin, 1992; Knapp, 1978). Relationships are comprised of nonverbal metamessages that have precedence over literal messages (Chelune et al., 1984). Relational attributions that transcend interpersonal or situational attributions color the interpretation of each message. Planalp (1985) contended that cognitive background helps frame and interpret each message. She stated, "Relational schemata, then, are coherent frameworks of relational knowledge that are used to derive relational implications of messages" (p. 9). Relational schemata create expectations about a relationship (Park & Waters, 1988). Researchers believe that deviations from these expectations are essential to our interpretation of particular behaviors. Chelune et al. (1984) suggest, "Discrepancies and/or consistencies between current perceived behavior and expectations derived from past behaviors become meaningful and make a statement (metacommunication) about the relationship between the interactants" (p. 25). King and Sereno (1984) maintain that in more stable, long-term relationships, people recognize deviations from prior patterns, suggesting that relational schemata are more vital to developed relationships.

Research shows the critical importance of relational schemata: They are the *most important* determinants of intimacy acceptance or rejection. Heslin and Alper (1983) have shown that reactions to touch are totally dependent on the nature of the relationship. In very close relationships, intimate touch is expected, comfortable, and pleasurable. In moderately close relationships, intimate touch is unexpected and uncomfortable. Among strangers, most touch is extremely uncomfortable, particularly intimate touch. Studies of touch in the nursing profession have revealed that nurses need to establish a good nurse–patient relationship before using expressive touch. By contrast, instrumental, task-oriented touch requires no such prior relationship (McCann & McKenna, 1993).

In a study of excessive intimacy, Andersen (1992a) asked subjects to describe a situation in which they perceived intimacy to be excessive and to explain why they

perceived it to be excessive. Among the many reasons cited, 54 percent attributed their perception of excessive intimacy to the relationship, more than all the other schemata combined. Subjects reported that several nonverbal behaviors were inappropriate except in very intimate relationships, including several types of touch, prolonged eye gaze, and invasion of one's personal space. As Andersen (2008) concludes, "People overwhelmingly attribute the appropriateness of another individual's intimate behavior to the relationship, not to other qualities."

Inappropriate intimacy will result in avoidance and compensation.

Relational partners described behavior inappropriate to the relationship in the following ways: "I just didn't think it was right for my boss to touch me that way." "I saw our relationship as a friendship, nothing more." "The relationship happened too quickly, destroying any chance of 'chemistry.'" "Someone I barely knew shouldn't be standing so close." Indeed, in a study of sexual harassment, Wertin and Andersen (1996) found that behavior inappropriate to the relationship was the leading reason recipients perceived unwanted sexual attention as harassment. In the appropriate relational context, almost any immediacy behavior will be perceived positively. The wrong behavior for the relationship's current state or anticipated trajectory will be perceived as negative, excessive, and even harassing.

SITUATIONAL SCHEMATA

The situation, or the context, affects the meaning of every immediacy behavior. The expression "out of context" describes behaviors that are meaningless, difficult to interpret, or misleading. Close interpersonal distances and intimate touch might be appropriate behaviors for the bedroom or even the living room but not for the classroom or the boardroom. Behavior that is appropriate in private may be perceived as excessively intimate in public. Parents are often upset by their teenagers' public displays of affection because these behaviors seem inappropriate in the given context, or situation. Scholars have shown that contextual sensitivity is an essential component of communication competence (Goffman, 1959; Spitzberg & Cupach, 1989).

Some settings go with particular actions. Chelune et al. (1984) showed that some physical settings are more conducive to intimacy than others. Situational schemata are stored in our memories, along with behaviors judged to be appropriate or inappropriate in a given setting. Acitelli and Duck (1987) believe that intimacy is both personal and situational. Perceptions of the appropriateness of intimacy by participants are critical, "particularly their judgments about the level of intimacy appropriate for a given situation or occasion" (p. 301). "A situational schema is structured, intuitive knowledge about one's current context as an instance of a general class of similar contexts" (Andersen, 1993a, p. 20). Familiar contexts are meaningful, and behaviors appropriate to those contexts are easy to determine. Unfamiliar contexts produce anxiety, require mental effort, and lead to inappropriate nonverbal behaviors. Intimacy inappropriate to a particular situation, like kissing a girlfriend in front of her parents, may be tolerated in close relationships, particularly if the violations are in the direction of the overall relational trajectory. In general, however, intimacy inappropriate to the situation will be negatively valenced.

STATE SCHEMATA

We all experience changing moods, psychological states, and physical conditions. In a single day, we may feel tired, excited, bored, depressed, sexually stimulated, fearful, angry, or loving. Our thoughts and feelings related to being tired, happy, aroused, fearful, drunk, or sick are state schemata. Physical conditions, moods, and psychological states come and go. Like situations, states are temporary. States, however, represent intrapersonal, internal dispositions, whereas situations relate to external environments (for a more complete discussion see Andersen, 1988).

States affect perceptions of intimacy. A classic example is the wife who says to her passionate husband, "Not tonight, dear, I have a headache." A fight with one's boss, an illness, a loss by one's favorite basketball team, stress in one's life, noisy children, a hangover, excitement over a new job, an endorphin rush after a run, hunger, and a host of other factors affect how we respond to a partner's nonverbal expressions of intimacy. In general, negative physical or psychological states result in negative reactions to intimacy. Canary and Cody (1993) describe an instance of a state reaction: "If Tracy has the flu, for example, she may not feel up to reciprocating Brad's interactional intimacy" (p. 207). On occasion, negative states may be consistent with positive intimacy behaviors. Massaging a partner's sports injury or holding a sick friend's hand may be perceived quite positively. In general, though, positive, energetic states are most conducive to positive reactions to intimacy.

Valence

As mentioned previously, valence is a chemistry term that refers to positive or negative charges. Relationships, like subatomic particles, can be either negative or positive. Cognitive valence theory suggests that movement toward intimacy is possible only during positively valenced interaction. This movement toward intimacy is a precarious process: A negative valence in any one schema could arrest the process of intimacy development (see Figure 9.1). This is why Andersen (1989; 2008) described the process of intimacy development as "fragile." Burgoon et al. (1995) summarized how the valencing process works in cognitive valence theory:

> Positively valenced arousal leads to reciprocity—or increased immediacy. If a *single negative* valence occurs during the valencing process (such as five positive valences and one negative), then the overall valence of the arousal is negative. Thus, negative valencing carries more weight than positive valencing. The negatively valenced arousal leads to compensation and withdrawal. (p. 108)

Showing intimacy too soon in a relationship, violating a person's preference levels for intimacy, or displaying intimacy in an inappropriate situation will result in negative valence and send the relationship into a negative spiral. Research has shown that negative relational information is weighted more heavily than positive information (Andersen, 1998; Kellerman, 1989). "Precariousness of close relationships is a result of several factors. Negative spirals can result from inappropriate behavior for any of the six cognitive schemata" (Andersen, 1998; 2008).

Relational Outcomes

Positively valenced intimacy will result in three positive relational outcomes. First, an interactant will experience more positive interpersonal valence toward her or his partner. Positive, appropriate, relational intimacy will create higher attraction levels, more interpersonal closeness, perceived intimacy, and overall reward value for one's partner. Second, positively valenced immediacy behaviors will be reciprocated. Thus, if a person receives an appropriate, positively valenced hug from a relational partner, he or she is likely to return the hug or increase the intimacy in other ways, say, with a kiss or a smile. Numerous studies have shown this reciprocity effect (for summaries see Andersen, 1985; Burgoon et al., 1995; Patterson, 1973a, 1976). Third, appropriate intimacy creates greater relational closeness, not just attraction for one's partner but a feeling of closeness, warmth, and intimacy. This starts a cycle in which positive interpersonal perceptions and a positive relationship lead to a positive valencing of increased behavioral immediacy, which, in turn, leads to increased positive feelings toward one's partner and to the relationship (Andersen, 1998). Relations are built on positive cycles of appropriate, receiver-oriented immediacy behaviors. Close, satisfying relationships are characterized by positive intimacy spirals.

Negatively valenced intimacy results in three corresponding negative outcomes. First, negative cognitive and affective appraisals of one's partner result from negatively valenced behaviors. An interactant will respond negatively to a partner who is overbearing, shows too much intimacy in inappropriate situations, or shows intimacy prematurely in the relationship. Attraction to this person turns to repulsion. Reward value drops. Second, negatively valenced intimacy causes compensatory reactions, as shown in a whole host of theories (for summaries of research and theory see Andersen & Andersen, 1984; Burgoon et al., 1995). Too much intimacy—especially with the wrong person, at the wrong moment, or at the wrong stage of the relationship—causes the receiver to withdraw or even flee. Such withdrawals or compensatory reactions frequently provoke more immediacy behaviors by the sender. Often, these compensatory immediacy behaviors are perceived as desperate attempts to increase intimacy and are met with another round of compensation and flight. When a partner withdraws or compensates, the only possible course of action that may help the relationship is a gradual withdrawal to restore a comfortable level of intimacy to the relationship. Otherwise, the downward spiral of hide and seek/withdraw and approach will continue. Third, inappropriate intimacy also decreases relational closeness. Savvy relational partners look for signs of relational claustrophobia in their partners and give them space. Sensitivity to excessive intimacy is a major predictor of relational success. As Gibran (1923) has said of marriage, "Let there be space in your togetherness . . . for the pillars of the temple stand apart and the oak tree and the cypress grow not in each other's shadow" (pp. 16–17).

Cognitive valence theory is one way of conceptualizing or modeling relationships and their outcomes. The theory attempts to explain one of the most basic questions regarding human relationships: Why is intimacy appreciated and reciprocated in some instances and rebuffed and compensated in other occasions? The cognitive-valence process attempts to unite the research on immediacy behaviors, perception, physiological arousal, interpersonal cognition, and relational outcomes into a single, unified model of relational intimacy.

PARADOXES OF INTIMACY

Dialectic Theory

Successful relationships represent a balance between oppositional forces. Too much nonverbal immediacy, such as close interpersonal distances or touch, can cause claustrophobic reactions or interpersonal overload. Too little nonverbal immediacy can cause resentment, loss of closeness, and other relational ills. Dialectic theory has emerged as a way of understanding these oppositional and paradoxical forces.

Dialectics are contradictions, or paradoxes, that reinforce one another. Writing on dialectics, Rawlins (1992) said:

> These antagonistic yet interdependent aspects of communication among friends form the pulse of routine as well as volatile and transitional moments of such dyads . . . configurations of contradictions compose and organize friendships through an ongoing process of change across the life course. (pp. 7–8)

Dialectics are forces for change. They provide the energy by which relationships become more intimate. Likewise, dialectics provide the dynamic balance for relationship maintenance (Baxter, 1994). However, relational breakups also derive their energy from dialectic tension. As Andersen (1993a) has stated: "A primary reason that relationships are dynamic, nonlinear, and even turbulent is the nature of human dialectical cognition" (p. 9).

Human relationships themselves are paradoxes. With each new relationship, we become more than we were. The opportunities for companionship, dialog, cooperation, sexuality, reproduction, friendship, support, and intimacy are possible only in interpersonal relationships. At the same time, relationships make us less than we were. In relationships we lose freedom, other relationships, and that precious commodity, time. Relationships can cost money, create risks, and result in emotional distress. Relationships are paradoxical.

Intimacy exists in a set of these dialectical tensions. The fragile nature of intimacy was described earlier in this chapter. Most of our relationships are transitory, impersonal, and nonintimate. Few of our relationships ever attain high intimacy levels. To understand how we attain, maintain, and successfully terminate our intimate relationships, we need to consider relational dialectics.

Although dozens of paradoxes pervade and perplex our relationships, scholars have focused on a set of dialectics with particular significance for intimate relations. We will examine four dialectics here: (1) autonomy-connection, (2) novelty-predictability, (3) openness-closedness, and (4) risk-reward. Although both verbal communication and nonverbal communication are important in managing relational dialectics, this section will focus on the sometimes subtle, but always important, nonverbal aspects of dialectics.

AUTONOMY-CONNECTION

The first and most fundamental relational dialectic has been variously called autonomy/connection (Baxter, 1988), integration/separation (Baxter, 1994), individualism/collectivism (Lustig & Andersen, 1990b), and freedom to be independent/freedom to be dependent (Rawlins, 1992). This dialectic suggests the contradiction between seeking intimacy and avoiding it. As Rawlins (1992) states:

> In forming a relationship, each friend grants the other a pair of contradictory prerogatives. The freedom to be independent is the liberty to pursue one's life interests without the friend's interference or help. In contrast, the freedom to be dependent is the privilege of calling on or relying on one's friend in times of need. Both liberties engender choices for self and other. Yet, exercising individual options of independent or dependent behavior also poses de facto contingencies restricting the other's choices. (p. 16)

Intimate relationships involve sacrifice of one's individuality. As Baxter (1993) states, "No relationship can exist unless the parties forsake individual autonomy. However, too much connection paradoxically destroys the relationship because the individual entities become lost" (p. 89).

The autonomy-connection dialectic manifests itself continuously through nonverbal behaviors. Sharing proxemic space is a sign of togetherness, bonding, and intimacy, but it is also constraining and inhibiting. Relationships can also suffer chronemically: Too much time together may make a partner seem intrusive, boring, or inhibiting; however, too little time together may make a partner seem uncaring and may prevent relational closeness and intimacy. The tension between autonomy and connection is also evident in the eye behavior of newly intimate couples, which is characterized by periods of contact and avoidance. When the connection through eye contact becomes uncomfortable, partners avert their eyes and autonomy is restored. Soon, however, the need to connect returns, and eye contact bonds the couple in nonverbal intimacy.

Research demonstrates the push and pull of autonomy versus connection by showing that nonverbal immediacy behavior varies across relational stages as couples become more and less connected. Studies show that touch increases significantly during the stages of serious dating and engagement (Figure 9.2). By contrast, married couples touch less the longer they are married (Emmers & Dindia, 1995; Guerrero & Andersen, 1991). Married couples can show less tactile immediacy over the years because their relationship is so intimate.

Touch, however, does not equate with more intimacy. Emmers and Dindia (1995) reported that touch increases along with intimacy up to a point; then, as relationships become highly intimate, touch decreases! Guerrero and Andersen (1994) have found that although the frequency of touch peaks at intermediate stages (during serious dating and engagement), partners match one another's touch more in stable, married relationships. They conclude that the reciprocity of touch behavior, rather than the frequency of touch, may be the key component predicting intimacy in marital relationships.

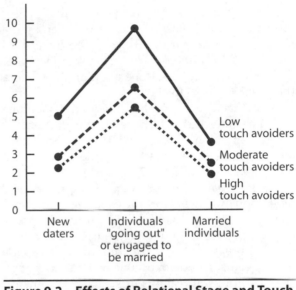

Figure 9.2   Effects of Relational Stage and Touch Avoidance on Interpersonal Touch

As Guerrero and Andersen (1991) stated, "touching may decrease in 'stable' relational stages, not from a loss of psychological intimacy or feelings of closeness but from a reduced need to continually communicate intimacy behaviorally" (p. 160). Sternberg (1986), in his triangular theory of love, discussed a similar process. According to Sternberg, relationships are characterized by both manifest intimacy, which is the physical intimacy that we show one another through behavioral displays (such as touching, smiling, and gazing), and latent intimacy, which is the psychological intimacy that we feel toward one another but cannot "see." Sternberg theorizes that in satisfying relationships, once the relationship is well established the manifest intimacy will drop off but the latent intimacy level will remain high or increase slightly. Paradoxically, couples may actually need less touch and more autonomy in their established relationships in order to avoid feeling "smothered."

Autonomy-connection is a relational tightrope act we all walk. Baxter (1993) reported that this dialectic is present in 88 percent of all relationships and particularly present in long-term relationships. As we will examine later in this chapter, several methods exist for coping with the fundamental relational dialectic of autonomy and connection.

NOVELTY-PREDICTABILITY

The second relational dialectic that affects intimate relationships is novelty-predictability. Our intimate friends must be predictable in a variety of ways. Loyalty, punctuality, concern for our welfare, reliability, and consistency are prerequisites to the experience of intimacy in a relationship. However, spontaneity, novelty, change, excitement, and adventure create more-attractive, more-interesting intimate relationships.

Theory and research have shown that in all relationships, but particularly in intimate relationships, partners are driven by the need for stability and certainty in their relational partner (Berger, 1988; Berger & Bradac, 1982). According to Baxter (1994), "conditions of intimacy are facilitated when partners have certainty and predictability about one another, their interactions together, and the state of their relationship" (p. 24).

However, research also shows that spontaneity and adventure are also valued. Learning theorists have shown that emotional deadening can result from excess repetition (Baxter, 1993). Sternberg (1988) maintained that "in order for love to survive there has to be some mystery—some degree of doubt about what will happen when" (p. 132).

Nonverbal behaviors are part and parcel of the novelty-predictability dialectic. Chronemic behavior, for example, can establish certainty and predictability, such as being available, being punctual, spending time together, and sharing important events. Conversely, surprises (such as parties, weekend trips, and so on) that break up and energize mundane, repetitive schedules are chronemically novel events. Although established patterns of proxemic and haptic behavior create trust, prevent feelings of sexual harassment, and provide certainty, on some occasions it is the surprises, sexual spontaneity, and intimate affection that provide much-needed novelty in a relationship.

Research has shown that the novelty-predictability dialectic exists for over three-fourths of all relationships and over 80 percent of longer-term relationships (Baxter, 1993). Another study suggests that failure to introduce sufficient novelty can be a major problem in long-term relationships. Hill, Rubin, and Peplau (1976) reported that the number-one reason for terminating a dating relationship is boredom with the relationship.

OPENNESS-CLOSEDNESS

Another dialectic that is extraordinarily important in intimate relationships is openness-closedness. Openness is the foundation of many theories and models of relational development (Altman & Taylor, 1973; Berger & Bradac, 1982; Knapp, 1978). Presumably, unless one is nonverbally and verbally open, intimacy is impossible to develop. However, critiques of the "ideology of intimacy" (discussed earlier in the chapter) suggest that nonstrategic or insensitive openness is not a recipe for intimacy. Instead, sensitive, strategic, tactical behaviors that maximize the benefits of openness and minimize injury are advised.

Eye contact is an invitation to communicate. Avoiding eye contact, called civil inattention, communicates avoidance.

Although openness has been equated frequently with verbal behaviors such as self-disclosure, nonverbal behaviors are crucial aspects of openness as well. Open body postures (Andersen, 1985; Morris, 1977) communicate openness, warmth, and intimacy, whereas folded arms, a covered face, and other barrier signals reduce intimacy and immediacy. Similarly, averting touch (see chapter 7) and eye contact (see chapter 2) are closed, inaccessible behaviors. Proxemic behaviors such as facing a person directly and maintaining appropriate interaction distances signal openness and lay the foundation for intimacy. Baxter and Montgomery (1996) maintained that behavioral openness includes "a variety of verbal and nonverbal signals that grant permission to explore specified aspects of the personal domain including behaviors such as appropriately timed eye contact, smiling, and other backchannel actions that say to the other person that he or she is being attended to" (p. 135). On the other hand, too much nonverbal openness, from inappropriate nudity to excessive eye contact, does not lay a sound foundation for intimacy.

Baxter (1993) has shown that 72 percent of relational partners report that the openness-closedness dialectic is present in their relationship. This is particularly true for new relationships. Because couples may simultaneously strive for privacy and self-control on the one hand and affiliation and connection on the other, it is not surprising that openness-closedness is an issue that must be dealt with in most intimate relationships.

RISK-REWARD

An old aphorism states, "It is better to have loved and lost than never to have loved at all." This optimistic view of relationships suggests that intimacy is unattainable without risk. The poet Gibran (1923) similarly advised, "When love beckons to you, follow him . . . even as he is for your growth so he is for your pruning" (p. 12). Although a partner's trust must be earned, all intimate relationships are a leap of faith. Holmes and Remple (1989) argued that "issues of trust have their origins in the dialectic between people's hopes and fears as close relationships develop" (p. 187). Wheeless (1978) showed that trust is essential to relational involvement and interpersonal solidarity. However, trust and intimacy can be unwarranted and risky.

People often fail to trust others. Engaging in immediate nonverbal communication requires trust. In terms of proxemics, going to a new boyfriend's (or girlfriend's) house or apartment requires trust. Touch in new relationships requires a suspension of fear, particularly in the case of sexual touch. Chronemic intimacy requires giving up precious time and excluding other relational opportunities. Most violence, including assault, rape, and even murder, occurs in intimate relationships (Marshall, 1994). AIDS, depression, unwanted pregnancies, infidelity, and abuse are just some the risks people encounter in intimate relationships. People want the reward to outweigh the risk in such relationships. They secretly and strategically test relationships to establish a baseline of trust, fidelity, and loyalty before increasing relational intimacy (Baxter & Wilmot, 1984). Many of these tests include searches for nonverbal cues of deception (see chapter 11). Relational tests include fidelity checks (such as spying and pushing the redial button on a partner's phone to see who he or she has been talking to) and testing to see if a partner will respond to one's emotional distress (Baxter & Wilmot, 1984; Guerrero, Andersen, Jorgensen, Spitzberg, & Eloy, 1995). Nonetheless, the risks involved with a new relationship may be part of the pleasure, the thrill of the hunt, the arousal of taking risks.

OTHER DIALECTICS

Certainly these aforementioned dialectics aren't the only tensions that exist in intimate relationships. Others include the ideal-real, instrumental-affectional, reciprocal-compensatory, and public-private dialectics (for the best summaries of relational dialectics see Baxter & Montgomery, 1996; Rawlins, 1992). Indeed, scholars have come to recognize that the potential number of relational contradictions is practically infinite (Billig, 1987; Baxter & Montgomery, 1996).

Managing Intimate Paradoxes

How do intimate partners cope with the paradoxes and contradictions present in all relationships? Scholars have found a number of ways—some functional, some dysfunctional—that people cope with intimate paradoxes.

CYCLICAL ALTERNATION

One way we cope with contradiction is to cycle between both dialectical poles to maintain balance. Couples will balance a period of autonomy with a period of connectedness. Openness will be followed by closedness for a time. Baxter (1993) discovered that cyclical alternation was the most common way of coping with the autonomy-connection dialectic and the second most common way to manage the novelty-predictability dialectic. One female respondent in Baxter's (1993) study reported cyclical alternation this way: "We kind of kept floundering around together . . . drifting towards each other and drifting apart again . . . kind of a cycle" (p. 97). These cycles appear to swing in a pendulum-like manner, alternating between autonomy-enhancing efforts and connection-enhancing efforts.

Nonverbal behaviors are critically important in cyclical alternation. Chronemic, proxemic, and haptic behaviors can create patterns of connection and autonomy. Whole clusters of immediacy behaviors signal periods of openness and closedness. Novelty and predictability can be established through touch or facial expressions. Indeed, it is quite normal, perhaps necessary, for relationships to experience cycles across all of the dialectics.

SEGMENTATION

Segmentation involves separating content or activity into distinct domains, appropriate to only one pole of a dialectic. Often, nonverbal behaviors are segmented to manage dialectical tension. For example, the junior-high student struggling with the autonomy-connection dialectic may let her parents kiss her goodbye at home but not at school. Similarly, some parents are very open with their children about politics or religion but completely closed about the "taboo" topics of drugs and sex. Some couples may decide that certain novel behaviors are okay in private but that predictable appropriateness is the only public face to show.

SELECTION

Selection is another method of coping with relational contradiction. In selection, partners perceive the coexistence of contradictions but transcend them by making one pole more dominant (Baxter, 1993). For example, recognizing that autonomy may threaten connection, partners may restrict each other's access to other people. Similarly, a couple may feel that it is more important to have a predictable, secure relationship than an exciting, novel relationship. Selection is a common strategy for coping with autonomy-connection, openness-closedness, and novelty-predictability (Baxter, 1993). Selection is most likely to be successful when both partners value the same side of the dialectic. If one partner values autonomy over connection and the other values connection over autonomy, selection is not a viable option.

UNITY OF OPPOSITES

Perhaps the best way to manage, even appreciate, relational dialectics is through understanding the unity of opposites (see Altman, Vinsel, & Brown, 1981; Hendrick & Hendrick, 1992). This is similar to the Chinese concept of yin (passive, yielding) and yang (dominant, active). Opposites are sustained by one another. Happiness is impossible without sadness; life exists only with death; and freedom couldn't even be a concept without oppression.

Without autonomy, connection would be logically impossible. Without closedness, openness would have no meaning. Relationships need to accept and even embrace paradox and change. It is, after all, separation that makes for a happy reunion or predictability that allows for novelty. Baxter (1988; Baxter & Montgomery, 1996) called the unity of opposites a process of reframing and reaffirmation; it involves accepting that paradoxical polarities cannot be reconciled and therefore must be appreciated. From this perspective, the tension is tolerated and the richness afforded by each polarity is celebrated. Moreover, the tensions are reframed so that they are viewed as complementary rather than contradictory. Allen et al. (1995) reported that autonomy and connection, novelty and predictability, indeed, all the dialectical poles are correlated in interpersonal relationships. Moreover, the pole of each dialectic is correlated with relational satisfaction. This empirical existence suggests that dialectics are, indeed, unities of opposites.

How can these contradictions create intimacy through communication? One way is to recognize that they are compatible though contradictory. A couple in love, for example, may be separated proxemically and chronemically by distance and time, yet during this separation the couple may exploit the advantages of autonomy. On one hand, he might work overtime, watch football (which she hates), and go out with his buddies—unconstrained by the connections and commitments he experiences when she is with him. On the other hand, she may study harder than ever, go to extra dance classes, and read that novel she never has time for. Upon reuniting, they will likely celebrate their connection through all of the multichanneled interconnections of communication. They may hug and kiss, look into each other's eyes longingly, stay with each other for days, manifest their joy through facial expressions of happiness and excitement, and speak with intimate or enthusiastic paralanguage.

Intimacy cannot be found by emphasizing only one dialectical pole. Intimacy involves sharing warmth and togetherness as well as permitting separateness; it means being open and closed, taking risks and receiving rewards, being simultaneously predictable and novel. Intimacy is a process of celebrating change, understanding paradox, and showing closeness through rich multidimensional acts of warm, involving nonverbal communication.

DENIAL

Perhaps the least healthy way to cope with dialectical tension is through denial. Some partners refuse to recognize that their relationships go through any periods of risk, autonomy, or closedness. Baxter and Montgomery (1996) stated, "Denial represents an effort to subvert, obscure, and deny the presence of a contradiction by legitimizing only one dialectical pole to the virtual exclusion of the other poles" (p. 61). They add, "the denial response is destined to fail, the dominance of one opposing force creates an exigence for the neglected opposition" (p. 61).

Denying autonomy, for example, may propel one partner into a desperate quest for connection, thereby denying the other partner space or time apart. Like small children desperately holding their mothers and not accepting even temporary separation, friends and lovers who cling to their partners or restrict their interactions outside the relationship are viewed as immature, even pathetic. Autonomy should be viewed as a way to enhance connection, and risk as a means to making relational success even more rewarding.

DISORIENTATION

Another dysfunctional response to relational paradox is disorientation. This is a fatalistic response to contradictions, which are regarded as inevitable, negative, and unchangeable (Baxter & Montgomery, 1996). These attitudes often lead to pessimism, helplessness, and a failure to see any rewarding alternatives in one's life. Relational interactants may feel trapped in a pattern of behavior from which they can't escape. Couples who perpetuate dysfunctional cycles are typically experiencing disorientation in some form. Abusive relationships and many conflicted relationships suffer from disorientation. By nature, relationships entail paradox, and creatively dealing with these paradoxes is the only path to increased intimacy.

SUMMARY

Intimacy is located in many places. It exists in immediacy behaviors, especially prolonged nonverbal immediacy that enhances intimate connection. It exists in intimate interactions, especially when intimacy is reciprocated. It exists as an ideology, a widespread belief in our culture that life is incomplete without experiencing intimacy. It exists as a warm, comforting emotion that we experience with intimate friends. Finally, it exists in and characterizes special, close relationships.

Cognitive valence theory helps explain why intimacy develops—or fails to develop. Intimacy begins with immediacy behaviors that arouse or stimulate interaction partners. On one hand, very high arousal levels are inherently unpleasant and lead to avoidance and negative valence. Moderate arousal levels, on the other hand, activate cognitive schemata that the receiver uses to assess the appropriateness of the immediacy behaviors. Increases in immediacy behaviors that are culturally, personally, interpersonally, relationally, situationally, and state appropriate lead to attraction, reciprocity, and increased relational intimacy. Increases in immediacy behaviors that violate one or more of the cognitive schemata lead to repulsion, compensatory responses, and reduced relational intimacy.

Intimacy is dialectically balanced along four relational paradoxes: autonomy-connection, novelty-predictability, openness-closedness, and risk-reward. These relational contradictions, or paradoxes, are managed through cyclical alternation, denial, segmentation, selection, the unity of opposites, denial, and disorientation.

Part III

Implicit Influence

Nonverbal Cues of Persuasion, Deception, and Power

10

Influencing Others through Nonverbal Communication

In *The Immortals*, a novel about John F. Kennedy's romantic affair with Marilyn Monroe, Michael Korda (1992) described the initial encounter between Senator Kennedy and Monroe:

> She was wearing a tight black dress of shimmering material, which seemed several sizes too small for her, a white fox stole, costume jewelry earrings, and a cheap black patent-leather handbag. The whole outfit looked as if it might have been purchased from a thrift shop. Not that it mattered—Marilyn was beyond good taste, or bad. At this point in her life she was perhaps the biggest star in Hollywood. I took the opportunity to move closer to Jack, whose expression resembled that of a man getting his first glimpse of the Grand Canyon or Mount Everest—some natural wonder of awesome proportion and reputation. Jack closed the distance, determined to reach Marilyn before I did, took her hand, squeezed it briefly rather than shaking it, and gave her his most dashing smile. She smiled back, "I can't *believe* you're a *Senator*?" she cooed, in her tiny breathless voice. She had a charming habit of ending every sentence as if it were a question. "I thought they were all old men." She hadn't removed her hand from his. (pp. 28–29)

Influence comes in many forms. The erotic power of movie icons or political power brokers—amplified by stunningly good looks and communicated through facial expression, gait, touch, distance, and vocal inflections—makes for virtually irresistible influence. If Korda is to be believed, Jack and Marilyn both got what they wanted that night. She was nonverbally influenced by his power, charm, wealth, and good looks. He was nonverbally influenced by her stunning beauty and Hollywood stardom.

Each day of life is a game of influential moves, from small requests, such as getting one's daughter to be home on time or one's husband to take out the garbage, to major requests, such as getting your lover to accept your proposal of marriage or convincing a troubled friend to seek counseling. Much, perhaps most, of our communication is intentionally influential, persuasive, and designed to

255

change the beliefs, attitudes, or behaviors of others. Some persuasive communication is beneficial, enhancing the human spirit and condition. Some is used to cheat, seduce, deceive, or cover up. Regardless of its purpose, nonverbal behavior, in particular, determines the persuasive impact of a message, as we will see in this chapter. Unfortunately, most communication research has been preoccupied with the impact of verbal messages on persuasion. Until recently, this narrow preoccupation has caused many scholars to overlook the important persuasive effects of nonverbal communication. Moreover, the interplay of nonverbal and verbal cues makes it impossible to understand verbal persuasion without considering its nonverbal aspects.

INFLUENCING ATTITUDES AND CHANGING BEHAVIORS

At one time, the entire field of communication was focused on persuasion. In the late 1960s, when differences in ideology created conflict in our field, much like the rest of the world, communication focused on influence: How can we stop communism and communist propaganda? How can we persuade our leaders to stop the war in Vietnam? How can people of color and women gain influence in patriarchal, white America? The ideological battle was between what Rushing (1993) described as "power" and "other." All questions seemed to revolve around persuasion and social influence. As a result, the field of communication came to learn a lot about persuasion. As our field matured and branched out into research on such diversified topics as personal relationships, health, organizations, and culture, we became less preoccupied with persuasion. Of course, this does not mean that persuasion is unimportant in society today—just the contrary. Millions of messages from advertisers urge us to be conspicuous consumers; public service announcements promote safe sex, regular exercise, cancer prevention, and the benefits of education; and myriad messages at home and in the workplace influence our personal and professional behavior.

In its heyday, persuasion research rarely focused on nonverbal messages. In recent years, however, nonverbal studies, a number of active research programs, and several exciting theories have emerged that have illuminated how nonverbal behavior creates powerful persuasive outcomes. Several of these theories have generated research programs that promise to provide additional insights into the persuasion process. Although these theories have helped explain the nonverbal processes of persuasion, none has provided a great theoretical breakthrough; no theory or model has emerged as dominant. But theory building is cumulative, and nonverbal persuasion is much better understood now than it was a decade ago, as the following theories suggest.

The Direct Effects Model of Immediacy

Research has shown that increases in nonverbal immediacy substantially enhance a persuader's chance of gaining compliance and having influence on others (for more on immediacy, see chapter 8). Studies have shown that both single-channeled immediacy increases (such as increased eye contact) and multichanneled immediacy increases are associated with increased persuasion. The so-called *direct effects model* (Andersen, 1979; 1985, 1999) and a similar model of nonverbal immediacy, the *social meaning model* (Burgoon, Coker, & Coker, 1986; Burgoon, Manusov, Mineo, & Hale, 1985), predicted a linear relationship between immediacy and persuasion. For example, when an interaction partner accompanies a request with a smile, a light touch, and direct eye contact, the sender is using multichanneled immediacy behaviors to increase the likelihood that the receiver will comply.

Gaze and Persuasion

Research has provided substantial support for the social meaning and direct effects models. This is particularly true for the persuasive effects of gaze (looking at another person) and eye contact (mutual gaze into one another's eyes). In a field study, Kleinke and Singer (1979) observed the effect of gaze or no gaze on subjects' willingness to accept leaflets distributed on the street. They found that subjects were more likely to accept leaflets in a gaze condition than in the no-gaze condition. This effect was consistent for both males and females and was stronger when experimenters used no verbal communication. Similar research by Valentine (1980) indicated that bystanders were more willing to assist a disabled victim with a broken arm (by picking up change he had dropped) in an experimental gaze condition than in a no-gaze condition. This finding occurred whether the victim was alone or accompanied by a friend.

Burgoon and her colleagues (1986) provided additional empirical support for the social meaning model for gaze behavior. They tested whether a person was judged as more likely to be hired for a job when gazing versus not gazing. Specifically, they report that gaze aversion carried very negative meaning and was least persuasive, whereas sustained gaze was highly effective in interpersonal persuasion. Gaze is probably effective persuasively because it is simultaneously powerful and immediate (Andersen, 1985; Segrin, 1990). In fact, gaze can command considerable authority. In a study by Bull and Gibson-Robinson (1981), poorly dressed solicitors for charity increased their contributions dramatically when they used direct gaze. Linkey and Firestone (1990) examined a group discussion task, in which group members were asked to influence one another. These researchers found that influence was primarily a function of the visual dominance ratio (the degree to which one person looks at an interaction partner or is looked at by the interaction partner). A study by Liss, Walker, Hazelton, and Cupach (1993) showed that compliance is highly correlated with mutual gaze, indicating that eye contact is a potent predictor of persuasion. Segrin (1993) statistically compiled the results of 49 nonverbal studies, including 12 on gaze behavior. Gaze produced greater compliance than averted gaze in every one of the 12 studies. Although the effects of gaze are not overpowering, they are very consistent according to Segrin. Thus, gaze, dominant gaze, and mutual gaze all seem to have significant persuasive effects. In short, when a person is engaged in persuasive communication, looking at one's interaction partner is a major determinant of the persuader's success.

Touch and Persuasion

Like gaze, touch has positive effects on persuasion. In two compliance experiments by Willis and Hamm (1980), strangers were asked by a petitioner to comply by signing a petition or by filling out a questionnaire. In both experiments, half the strangers received touch and half received no touch; other communication cues remained constant across the two conditions. In the first experiment, strangers signed the petition 81 percent of the time in the touch condition but only 50 percent of the time in the no-touch condition. In the second experiment, strangers complied by completing the questionnaire 70 percent of the time in the touch condition but only 40 percent of the time in the no-touch condition. Likewise, other studies have found that people are more likely to fill out a questionnaire if they are touched than not touched (Guéguen, 2002). Interestingly, few subjects were aware they had been touched, even though it increased their compliance. Several studies have found that waiters and waitresses received more tips when they lightly touched customers on the shoulder, and this effect appears to be greater for cross-sex touch than same-sex touch (Ebesu-Hubbard, Tsuji, Williams, & Seatriz, 2003; Hornik, 1992). One study also found that couples consumed more alcohol in bars when the waitress touched the customer on the shoulder as compared to a non-touch, control condition (Kaufman & Mahoney, 1999). A study showed that women who touched male bus drivers compared to those who did not touch were more likely to be permitted to board the bus, despite having too little money for the fare (Guéguen & Fisher-Lokou, 2003). In yet another imaginative experiment people were more likely, when touched by a stranger, to temporarily watch over a large and dangerous-looking dog while his owner shopped, compared to those who were not touched (Guéguen & Fisher-Lokou, 2002). Results of these studies demonstrate the significant, positive effects of touch on compliance.

An investigation of touch and foot-in-the-door techniques (where a small request is followed by a larger request) showed that touch increases compliance in most experimental conditions (Goldman, Kiyohara, & Pfannensteil, 1985). In the first step of this study, an experimenter asked subjects for a small favor; the experimenter responded either positively to each subject's compliance by saying "You have been very helpful" or negatively by saying "You have not been very helpful." Next, another experimenter asked the subjects for a bigger favor. If the second experimenter used touch, the subjects were more likely to comply than if no touch accompanied the request for the bigger favor. Touch was even effective in gaining compliance following the negative-response condition. Patterson, Powell, and Lenihan (1986) conducted a touch experiment in which subjects were initially asked to score some test papers. After completing the stacks they had been given, subjects were asked to stay and score more tests. The results showed that subjects who were touched when asked to score the additional tests were more likely to comply than subjects who were not touched. The researchers attribute the increased compliance to perceptions of greater sensitivity and/or status of the experimenter in the touch condition.

In his statistical summary of thirteen studies examining the influence of touch on compliance, Segrin (1993) reported that touch showed a positive, consistent effect on compliance across the thirteen studies. Virtually all these studies compared the results of an experimenter's either touching a stranger on the arm or not touching a stranger while making a request. Little is known about the effects of persuasive touch in close relationships. Nor have researchers examined the effects of more-intimate types of touch (such as strokes, caresses, or squeezes) or touch on intimate areas of the body (such as the chest and face). Nonetheless, the available research indicates that, in general, appropriate interpersonal touch has clear, persuasive effects—a finding that is consistent with the direct effects model.

TOUCH, GAZE, AND PERSUASION

Interestingly, a number of studies have examined the persuasive impact of both touch and gaze in combination. This type of examination allows researchers to determine (1) whether one of these cues can substitute for the other, (2) their relative persuasive impact, and (3) whether they have additive or cumulative effects. Kleinke (1977) reported two such experiments that examined the effect of gaze and touch on compliance. In the first study, the experimenter left a dime in a phone booth. When a subject found the dime and the experimenter asked to have it back, the experimenter manipulated gaze and touch to produce four experimental conditions: touch and gaze, touch alone, gaze alone, and neither touch nor gaze. The touch-and-gaze condition resulted in more dimes being returned, indicating that touch and gaze have additive effects on compliance. In the second study, experimenters asked strangers in a shopping mall if they would lend them a dime. Consistent with experiment one, four combinations of touch and gaze were employed, and again the touch-and-gaze condition produced the greatest incidence of compliance. Kleinke's explanation is that touch and gaze increase attention and involvement, thereby making noncompliance more difficult. In another article, Kleinke (1980) reported two experiments that replicated the 1977 study, one in which the experimenter made a legitimate request (asking for a dime to make a phone call) and one in which the experimenter made an "illegitimate" request (asking for a dime to buy a candy bar). The results for the legitimate-request experiment reflected the finding of the 1977 study, but those for the illegitimate-request experiment did not. In the illegitimate-request experiment, the no-touch/no-gaze condition secured more compliance, possibly because the experimenter appeared more tactful or humble. A replication of Kleinke's (1977) phone booth experiment by Brockner, Pressman, Cabitt, and Moran (1982) showed that touch and gaze independently increased compliance and that touch and gaze together increased compliance even more.

Appropriate touch and gaze increase compliance with a request.

The data from these five studies suggest additive effects of both touch and eye contact consistent with the direct effects and social meaning models. Touch and eye contact are positive immediacy cues for most people that increase others' compliance. These findings have considerable practical importance. When soliciting for charity, requesting signatures for a petition, asking for a favor, or seeking assistance from a stranger, the combination of touch and gaze considerably increases one's chance of achieving compliance.

KINESIC BEHAVIOR AND PERSUASION

What effects do various bodily movements have on persuasion? A few studies provide some answers. In a study of opinion change, McGinley, LeFerve, and McGinley (1975) reported that open body positions result in more persuasion than closed body positions (keeping one's knees and feet together and one's arms folded and held close to the body). Other literature discussed in previous chapters suggests that communicators are perceived as more friendly, approachable, and warm when they use open body postures. Burgoon, Birk, and Pfau (1990) examined several kinesic behaviors for their impact on persuasion. They found that as kinesic immediacy and expressiveness increased, so did persuasiveness. Among the various kinesic behaviors they examined, facial pleasantness was the most predictive of persuasive success. In addition, more overall bodily movement and animation were correlated with persuasiveness. Liss et al. (1993) examined the effect of smiling on compliance gaining and found that more smiling resulted in greater compliance. In one set of studies, genuine smiles displayed by a fashion model influenced positive judgments of the model's attire, to a greater degree than posed smiles or neutral expressions (Peace, Miles, & Johnston, 2006).

The powerful effect of smiling goes beyond the present source of the smile; smiles enhance a receiver's disposition so that he or she is more susceptible to subsequent persuasion. In an imaginative study Guéguen and De Gail (2003) had experimenters smile at strangers on the streets, followed by another experimenter a few yards behind who dropped a set of computer diskettes. Compared to a control group, strangers who received an initial smile were significantly more likely to pick up the diskettes!

Interactional synchrony or matching, which we discussed in chapter 2 as a powerful interpersonal cue for generating connection and rapport, is also a potential source of influence and persuasion. Experimental research has shown that mirroring or imitation of another person's nonverbal behavior has positive effects on perceived persuasion and credibility, even during disagreements (Van Swol, 2003), but there was little effect on opinion change. Matching and mirroring are apparently so innately effective that they have persuasive effects even when interacting with artificial agents in immersive virtual environments (Bailenson & Yee, 2005).

VOCAL CUES AND PERSUASION

Several studies also show a positive link between vocal immediacy and persuasion. A series of studies by Buller and his associates shows that vocal immediacy cues such as a pleasant tone of voice and a fast delivery are linked to greater compliance. These effects are particularly true for individuals who are skilled decoders of nonverbal communication (Buller & Aune, 1988a, 1992; Buller & Burgoon, 1986; Buller, LePoire, Aune, & Eloy, 1992). Segrin's (1993) statistical summary of the research showed that both vocal rate and pleasantness are associated with persuasion. Burgoon et al. (1990) reported that persuasiveness increases with greater vocal fluency and pitch variety but not greater vocal pleasantness. Employing a fast, pleasant delivery style with vocal variation makes verbal communication more persuasive. This is particularly true while talking on the telephone, when other nonverbal cues are absent.

PHYSICAL APPEARANCE AND PERSUASION

Studies of compliance gaining and physical appearance show that conventional attire has positive persuasive effects. In general, "dressing up" is recommended for most persuasive situations. In a petition-signing experiment by MacNeill and Wilson (1972), experimenters obtained more signatures when dressed conventionally (in a suit and tie with short hair) than unconventionally (in a faded army jacket with long hair). In a similar study, Darley and Cooper (1972) examined the effects of countercultural or "hippie" appearance on political campaign effectiveness. They found that voters were less likely to take a leaflet from a "hippie" than from a conventionally dressed campaigner; they were also more likely to throw the leaflet away if they accepted it from the hippie rather than from the conventionally dressed campaigner. Moreover, voters attributed more radical, less acceptable views to candidates supported by hippies than to candidates supported by conventionally dressed campaigners.

Perhaps the most authoritative sort of dress is the uniform. Certainly, we are much more likely to comply with a police officer's request than a civilian's. Similarly, the uniform of medical personnel communicates authority and ensures a patient's compliance in a variety of ways: going to designated rooms, waiting a long time, taking off one's clothes, and submitting to embarrassing or painful medical procedures. The white coat or white dress is still universally worn by medical professionals to communicate authority and to ensure compliance. In Milgram's (1974) classic experiments in which he successfully persuaded participants to induce shocks (that they believed were real) to other people in laboratory learning studies, compliance was gained by an experimenter in a technician's coat worn over a white shirt and tie.

In a related study, Bushman (1988) had a female confederate randomly stop pedestrians and say, "This fellow is overparked at the meter and doesn't have any change. Give him a nickel." The woman wore different clothing in three experimental conditions. When dressed in a uniform, she gained more compliance than when dressed in business attire or casual attire. The nondescript blue uniform produced compliance 72 percent of the time, whereas only 48 percent compliance was gained in the business-attire condition and 52 percent in the casual-attire condition. In his statistical summary of nineteen studies, Segrin (1993) concluded that the more formal or high-status the clothing, the greater the compliance rate obtained. Evidently, we are more likely to permit appropriately and well-dressed individuals to approach us and to gain our trust than inappropriately or less-conventionally dressed individuals.

MULTIDIMENSIONAL IMMEDIACY AND PERSUASION

Persuaders increase immediacy and involvement through multiple channels. Several studies have examined multidimensional immediacy behaviors and persuasion. In a study of classroom compliance employing multiple indices of immediacy, J. F. Andersen (1979) found that students in a speech class were more likely to engage in communication practices (such as using an outline, maintaining eye contact, or using gestures) suggested by immediate rather than nonimmediate teachers. Burgoon et al. (1990) reported a similar finding in a study of persuasive speakers. Specifically, they found that greater persuasion was associated with vocalic behaviors (such as longer pauses, vocal pleasantness, and pitch variety), increased gaze, more smiling, greater facial expressiveness, and more overall movement.

Subsequent research has also shown that individuals use nonverbal communication to resist persuasion. In a study of rejection strategies for flirtatious advances, Trost and Engstrom (1994) reported that rejecters avoided nonverbal contact, ignored the persuader, maintained larger interpersonal spaces, acted cold and uninterested, displayed alternative relational ties (such as engagement rings), and acted nervous and uneasy.

Over the years a series of studies has shown that women are less influential than men, particularly with male audiences (Carli, 2001). Sadly, while displays of competence can be advantageous, some studies reveal that competence diminishes a woman's influence. However, research shows that if women utilize a communal style characterized by warmth, smiling, nodding, and a host of other immediacy behaviors, in combination with a competent communication style, the gender difference in persuasive effectiveness disappears. A warm, competent style seems to be particularly effective with male audiences (Carli, 2001). This is clearly a gender bias and dilemma for women: Be warm, likable, and competent and be effective, or be competent in the absence of immediacy cues and be ineffective (see chapter 5 for more on this topic).

MULTICHANNELED, MEDIATED PERSUASIVE CUES

What effect do nonverbal cues in the media have on viewers? Studies of television newscasters, for example, have shown that nonverbal behaviors influence viewers in a variety of ways. Newscasters have tremendous influence. We treat them like virtual acquaintances who are nightly guests in our homes. For many years, Walter Cronkite, the anchorman for CBS news, was considered the most credible man in America!

Studies show that the nonverbal behavior of television newscasters affects voting preferences. Friedman, Mertz, and DiMatteo (1980) reported that newscasters' facial expressions are consistently biased toward certain candidates at levels unlikely to occur by chance. In the 1976 election, Walter Cronkite, David Brinkley, and Harry Reasoner showed more favorable facial expressions when reporting on Jimmy Carter than on Gerald Ford. John Chancellor and Barbara Walters showed more positive facial affect toward Ford than Carter. Verbal content, however, showed no corresponding bias. Two studies replicated and extended these findings to the 1984 elections and show that newscasters' biased facial expressions were associated with viewers' voting behaviors (Mullen et al.,

1986). The first study found that Dan Rather of CBS and Tom Brokaw of NBC showed no facial bias when reporting on Ronald Reagan or Walter Mondale. However, Peter Jennings of ABC exhibited strong facial bias to Reagan over Mondale. The second study, which examined voters in four cities in Ohio, Missouri, Massachusetts, and Pennsylvania, showed that in each city, viewers of ABC had significantly more favorable attitudes toward Reagan than viewers of NBC or CBS. Although pro-Reagan viewers might have tuned in more to ABC, Mullen et al. (1986) believed that this study actually demonstrates a subtle, peripheral route to persuasion that occurs without deliberate, conscious consideration. In either case, this study suggests a strong association among nonverbal behavior, television viewing, and electoral decisions. More recently, on television talk shows, both the live-audience reactions and the nonverbal behavior of television talk-show hosts influenced viewer attitudes toward the issue being discussed and the credibility of the guest (Nabi & Hendrick, 2003).

Explaining the Direct Effects Model

Based on the evidence, the direct effects model (Andersen, 1985; 1999) and social meaning model (Burgoon et al., 1985) best explain nonverbal persuasive effects. Immediacy behaviors have a direct effect on compliance such that increased immediacy results in increased compliance. Moreover, the effects of various nonverbal behaviors are significant and are usually stronger than verbal message variables in their impact. As Segrin (1993) pointed out:

> The effects of nonverbal behaviors and various verbal message variables on compliance were compared. This comparison revealed that the nonverbal behaviors are as powerful, and, in some cases, more powerful than some of the message strategies that have been studied in producing compliance from others. It appears for example that whether a source gazes at and touches a target while attempting to gain compliance will be as influential in determining the outcome as whether the source gives supportive information, uses a foot-in-the-door strategy, or a one- versus two-sided message. (pp. 183–184)

But, *why* does nonverbal immediacy have such a substantial impact on compliance? Various explanations suggest that immediacy behaviors communicate power, attention, warmth, and liking. Of course, these explanations are not mutually exclusive. All of them may be valid explanations of the direct effects model to some degree, and these factors may work in concert to produce persuasive effects of immediacy.

POWER

Immediate, involving nonverbal behaviors may be more persuasive because they convey not just warmth and immediacy but also dominance and power. Low-power speech, which contains nonverbal hesitations like "ah" and "ya know," negatively affects persuasive outcomes and attitudes toward a product (Areni & Sparks, 2005). Burgoon et al. (1985) and Segrin (1990) emphasized that touch, fast speaking, official uniforms, and direct gaze may be effective behaviors of persuasion because they are powerful, not because they are immediate. Although these behaviors certainly are powerful (see chapter 12), they may be attributed to the persuasiveness of open body positions (McGinley et al., 1975), which are more submissive and vulnerable than closed body positions. The literature reviewed in this chapter on facial expressions shows that smiling is highly persuasive, even though it is usually a submissive behavior. Likewise, LaCrosse (1975) reported that head nods, a nondominant signal of affirmation, were shown to increase persuasiveness in a counseling setting. Research by Burgoon and her colleagues (1990) showed that several warm but nondominant nonverbal behaviors enhance persuasiveness, including vocal pleasantness, kinesic/proxemic immediacy, facial expressiveness, and kinesic relaxation. Dominant nonverbal behaviors, such as harsh facial expressions and the dominant "command" tone of voice, definitely give an added persuasive boost to immediacy behaviors.

As Machiavelli (1513/1947) said almost five hundred years ago, "Here the question arises; whether it is better to be loved than feared or feared than loved. The answer is it would be desirable to be both" (p. 48). Of course, this still raises questions as to why nondominant immediacy behaviors are persuasive. It may be that immediacy behaviors are persuasive for several reasons; for example, they may increase perceptions of trustworthiness and dynamism, which are both key components underlying credibility. As we will see in the following discussion, immediacy behaviors also command attention and reflect interpersonal warmth and liking.

ATTENTION

Immediacy behaviors get our attention. In virtually every theory of persuasion, attention is a necessary prerequisite to message processing and eventual compliance. For example, Petty and Cacioppo's (1986) elaboration likelihood model (discussed later in this chapter) requires message processing as a prerequisite to persuasion or attitude change. It is hard to ignore a person's persuasive request when he or she is staring you in the eyes or touching you on the arm. Mehrabian (1971a) suggested that immediacy behaviors are "approach" behaviors that increase sensory stimulation and thus turn one's focus to another person and her or his behavior. Andersen (1985) maintained that immediacy behaviors are so compelling that they create a condition in which communication must occur: "Eye contact, closer distance, and open positions almost force another person to realize that communication is commencing" (p. 2). Although more research needs to be conducted, current research and theory suggest that some of the direct effects of immediate behavior are attributable to the increased attention that immediacy behaviors produce during interaction.

WARMTH

Research on nonverbal communication shows that immediacy behaviors are perceived as warm, close, and nurturant (see Andersen, 1985; Andersen & Guerrero, 1998a). Humans, from infancy through adulthood, enjoy behaviors such as warm, protective touch, smiles, and openness, which send nonthreatening, supportive messages. Research reveals that the perception of warmth is a particularly important nonverbal behavioral outcome for many professionals, such as therapists, doctors, and trial judges, because it puts people at ease and sends positive messages (Blanck & Rosenthal, 1992; Blanck, Rosenthal, & Vannicelli, 1986). Immediacy behaviors that effectively convey warmth include touch, gaze, smiles, and postural directness. We may react positively to warm behavior because—like our parents' warm caregiving—friendly, loving behavior evokes feelings of spontaneous positivity.

Interpersonal warmth may be a basic social emotion. Immediacy behaviors produce warm feelings that are associated with intimacy, attachment, bondedness, and emotional connectedness. Andersen and Guerrero (1998a) maintained that "interpersonal warmth is the pleasant, contented, intimate feeling that occurs during positive interactions" (p. 304). Obviously, anytime a communicator can create such interpersonal warmth, he or she is setting the stage for a positive persuasive outcome.

LIKING

Immediacy behaviors may also have direct, positive effects because they signal that another person likes us. Immediacy behaviors can signal interest, inclusion, or connection even when warmth isn't present in an interaction. In his opening chapter on immediacy, Mehrabian (1971a) contends, "Such behavior patterns and many others can be understood in terms of the *immediacy principle:* People are drawn to persons they like, evaluate highly, and prefer; and they avoid or move away from things they dislike, evaluate negatively, or do not prefer" (p. 1). When people engage in affiliative behavior, we are drawn to them, we experience feelings of interest, inclusion, and attraction, and we seek to treat them positively. The automatic rule of reciprocity is the basis for much human behavior (Cialdini, 1988). A failure to respond positively to someone who is positive to us makes us seem abusive, unfair, and interpersonally isolated.

Several series of studies demonstrate clearly that immediacy behaviors inherently and directly communicate positive affect and harmonious relations (Andersen, 1979; Andersen, 1985; Andersen, Andersen, & Jensen, 1979). Nonverbal immediacy cues have clear social meanings that lead to positive persuasive effects (Burgoon, Buller, Hale, & deTurck, 1984; Burgoon et al., 1985, 1986; Strzyzewski, 1990). These findings suggest that in neutral to positive relationships (including most initial interactions), immediacy behaviors generally have direct positive effects (Andersen, 1985) for many of the reasons previously outlined.

Although the direct effects model and social meaning model are supported by the bulk of the evidence for most immediacy behaviors, other theoretical approaches also yield insights into the positive impact of nonverbal behavior on persuasion. We will discuss several of these approaches in the following sections.

Expectancy Violations Theory

Expectancy violations theory attempts to explain the persuasive impact of immediacy behavior. Early tests of this theory centered on spatial invasion. Burgoon and Jones (1976) argued that each person has cultural and personal expectations about the normal distances that should be maintained during interpersonal interaction. Research has shown that attractive, or rewarding, individuals are more persuasive if they violate interpersonal distance norms. Burgoon and Jones contend that these violations draw attention to the positive characteristics of high-reward individuals. By contrast, low-reward, or unattractive, individuals are most persuasive at normative distances because they draw less attention to their personal characteristics at normal distances.

How has this model fared? In several studies of proxemic invasion, the model received some support. Partial confirmation was provided by Stacks and Burgoon (1979), who found that rewarding communicators were more persuasive at either closer or farther distances than at normative interpersonal distances. As predicted by the model, nonrewarding individuals produced no difference in persuasiveness at close, normal, or far interpersonal distances. Two studies by Burgoon and Aho (1982) provided only partial support for the model. In both studies, distance showed no significant effect on compliance for either low-reward communicators or high-reward communicators, although reward itself produced significant effects and increased the attentiveness of receivers. This study actually supported the direct effects model and social meaning model. Albert and Dabbs (1970) reported that actual persuasion was greater at far interpersonal distances (14 to 15 feet) than at either close or moderate interpersonal distances (1 to 5 feet). Buller (1987) conducted a study in which experimenters assumed close, moderate, or far interpersonal distances while attempting to get subjects to sign petitions. Findings showed that close interpersonal distances resulted in the greatest compliance, whereas moderate and far interpersonal distances resulted in less compliance. Neither Albert and Dabbs nor Buller manipulated the reward value, but their results suggest that nonnormative distance increases compliance.

In an extension of expectancy violations theory to vocalic communication, a study by Buller and Burgoon (1986) found that pleasant voices (a positive norm violation) produced more compliance, but only for good decoders. Poor decoders complied more with hostile voices (a negative norm violation) than with neutral or pleasant voices. Although reward value was not successfully manipulated, the study provides some support for the expectancy violations model.

Two studies attempted to extend expectancy violations theory to eye behavior (Burgoon et al., 1985, 1986). Both studies employed either rewarding confederates or nonrewarding confederates and differing levels of eye gaze. The high-reward interviewees had strong qualifications, including experience, excellent grade point averages, and good references. The low-reward applicants were poorly qualified, had low grade point averages, and had little relevant work experience. Results of these studies provided little support for the expectancy violations model because the primary results showed direct persuasive effects for increased levels of gaze regardless of reward value. These results support both the social meaning model and direct effects model described earlier.

Overall, although the expectancy violations model has received some general confirmation, the support for its persuasive effects is mixed. Moreover, few of the related studies have actually tested whether expectations were violated; as such, a central tenet of the theory remains untested (Segrin, 1990). The best evidence for the persuasive effects of expectancy violations theory relates to interpersonal distance. The evidence suggests that rewarding individuals should stand closer or farther than the normative interaction distance for maximal persuasive effects. For nonrewarding communicators, standing at normative interpersonal distances may maximize persuasive effects.

Distraction Models

There is a rival approach to the expectancy violations theory in explaining the persuasive effects of nonverbal behavior. According to the so-called distraction models, if a sender's nonverbal behavior distracts a receiver, the receiver is more susceptible to persuasion. Stacks and Burgoon (1979) hypothesized that distance violations produced more persuasion because of their distracting properties. Unfortunately, they found that distance violations have no effect on a self-reported distraction measure. However, close and far distance violations were more persuasive than normative distances. Why did these distance violations produce more persuasion? One explanation is that distraction worked even though subjects were unaware of the distraction, so they could not self-report it. Another explanation is that these distance violations produced arousal effects. A subsequent study by Stacks and Burgoon (1981) reported a significant effect of both distance violations and extremes in physical attractiveness on distraction. Small persuasive effects were found for physical attractiveness and none for distance violations, providing better support for the distraction models. Similarly, in a test of the distracting effects of rapidly spoken messages on persuasion, Woodall and Burgoon (1983) showed that fast messages were more distracting than normal-rate messages, but they found no persuasive effects from the faster messages.

A meta-analysis of thirty-eight studies conducted by Buller (1986), which examined the distraction-persuasion relationship, reported that communication-irrelevant factors such as noise or visual distractions generally reduced persuasion and attitude change because they impeded the receiver's comprehension of the message. Communication-relevant distractions, however, such as highly attractive or credible sources, caused receivers to focus on these positive qualities, producing a positive effect on persuasion. If the source had low attractiveness or credibility, focusing on the speaker reduced attitude change because these negative distractions impeded believability and persuasion. In general, positively regarded sources may benefit from the receiver's focusing her or his attention on the positive characteristics of the source.

Petty and Cacioppo's (1986) work on persuasion and cognition may also help explain the process of distraction. Basically, they have shown that distraction aids the persuasion process if the message is of low quality (that is, containing weak, ambiguous arguments); for example, a distracting appearance, haptic behavior, or oculesic behavior might distract a receiver such that he or she could not concentrate on the many flaws of a so-called low-quality message. High-quality (that is, strong, clear) persuasive arguments, on the other hand, are less effective when a receiver is distracted by conspicuous nonverbal cues; the receiver cannot concentrate on the high-quality message, so its effectiveness is reduced.

Communication Accommodation Theory

Vocalic aspects of speech are crucial to persuasion. Several studies show that rapid speech enhances persuasion (Apple, Streeter, & Krauss, 1979; MacLachlan, 1979; Miller, Maruyama, Beaber, & Valone, 1976), perhaps by increasing the effort it takes to perceive the message or by improving the perceived competence of the source. However, one study (Woodall & Burgoon, 1983) found that fast speech rates did not differ from slow speech rates in their persuasive effect. The regions in which the studies were conducted offer one explanation for these conflicting results. The Apple et al. study and the MacLachlan studies were conducted in New York, and the Miller et al. study was conducted in Los Angeles—both of these cities are locations where fast speech is the norm. The Woodall and Burgoon study, in contrast, was conducted in the southeastern part of the country, where speech is considerably slower. Thus, slow speakers may be more persuasive in the South, but fast speakers may be more persuasive in the North and on the West Coast.

An even stronger explanation for these results can be found in communication accommodation theory. According to this theory (Street, 1982; Street & Brady, 1982; Street & Giles, 1982), listeners perceive speech similar to their own as more attractive, pleasant, and intelligible than others'. Moreover, a speaker typically adjusts the speech to the style or rate of the other interactant, even though most speakers are unaware of this accommodation (Street, 1982). Based on this theory, speakers who adjust to the communication rates and styles of their listeners should be more persuasive.

Several studies provide support for the persuasive effects of communication accommodation. In a study by Buller and Aune (1988a), good decoders were most likely to comply with faster messages, whereas poor decoders were not. Why did good decoders prefer faster messages? The authors showed that good decoders spoke faster; thus, as predicted by communication accommodation theory, faster speakers (that is, good decoders) preferred to listen to and were more influenced by faster speech.

A second study by Buller and Aune (1989) partially replicated the first study. Again, good decoders were found to speak faster than poor decoders. However, no effect was found for actual or perceived similarity of speech rate on compliance. Poor decoders (who generally spoke slowly) complied most with speakers with moderately slow voices, whereas good decoders (who generally spoke fast) complied most with speakers with moderately fast and very fast voices. These findings suggest that people are influenced by those who speak at the same rate as they do.

A study by Burgoon, Pfau, and their associates (1987) examined the effects of a number of communication variables on patient compliance with their physician's advice. Among the many communication variables tested, only perceived similarity was significantly related to compliance. A final study by Buller and Burgoon (1986) showed that good nonverbal decoders complied more in pleasant-voice conditions than in neutral- or hostile-voice conditions; whereas poor decoders complied most in the hostile-voice condition, moderately in the neutral-voice condition, and least in the pleasant-voice condition. Because good decoders are more affiliative, composed, and social than are poor decoders, Buller and Burgoon attribute the results to communication accommodation. People comply more with voice tones that are similar to their own.

This review shows that communication accommodation theory, as applied to nonverbal communication and persuasion, has received some support. Communicators would probably be well advised to use vocalic cues similar to their persuasive target's vocalic cues to maximize compliance. However, speech accommodation is a dynamic process in which both interactants adapt to the other's speaking style. No study of this dyadic type of social interaction has been conducted; the theory remains untested in its most complete form (Segrin, 1990). Independently, increased gaze, faster speech, and more touch are persuasive. This presents a problem for communication accommodation theory, which would have to assume that most people are higher-than-average gazers, faster-than-average speakers, and more-frequent-than-average touchers. It seems that more immediacy is probably more important than more accommodation. However, a combination of immediacy and accommodation may be highly effective given that both forms of communication reflect liking.

Emotional Arousal

Considerable evidence demonstrates that nonverbal communication behaviors, particularly immediacy behaviors, are physically and emotionally arousing (see chapters 7 and 9 for more about arousal). For example, Andersen (1985) provided a review of twenty-four studies that demonstrated that immediacy behaviors such as gaze, closer interpersonal distances, and touch produced increases in measures of physiological arousal, including galvanic skin response and heart rate. Much of the research reviewed previously in both chapters 8 and 9 suggests that immediacy behaviors result in positive, emotional mood arousal.

Evidence suggests that positive mood arousal is an explanation for the persuasive effects of nonverbal immediacy behaviors. Research has suggested that positive affective (emotional) reactions are automatic and reflect little need for analytic cognitive activity (Zajonc, 1980; 1984). As Zajonc (1984) stated:

> Only a few years ago, I published a rather speculative paper entitled "Feeling and Thinking: Preferences Need No Inferences." The argument began with the general hypothesis that affect and cognition are separate and independent systems and that although they ordinarily function conjointly, affect could be generated without a prior cognitive process. (p. 259)

Research and theory have begun to provide support for this position. Petty and Cacioppo's elaboration likelihood model makes the distinction between thoughtful analysis and "peripheral," or "primitive," affect processing. Petty and Cacioppo's biases toward thoughtful rationality are evident because they characterize "gut" feelings, intuition, and emotional feelings as *peripheral* and *primitive*. Their central argument in the elaboration likelihood model is an important one: Persuasive cues either can be thoughtful, issue-relevant, and logical, or they can be emotional, nonverbal, and contextual. Petty and Cacioppo claim that in the literature "central thought processing" appears to be more enduring. However, recent research suggests that these "peripheral" nonverbal cues, like gazing and smiling, are often more persuasive and more enduring than "central," logical, verbal message strategies such as the use of supporting evidence (Segrin, 1993).

Other researchers (Stiff, 1986; Stiff & Boster, 1987) have criticized the elaboration likelihood model and have proposed alternatives to it such as the *elasticity model*, which suggests that the parallel processing of information occurs such that we are simultaneously influenced by logical and emotional messages. Evidence seems to support the elasticity model's prediction that both logical and emotional messages are processed simultaneously.

Research on media campaigns also suggests the importance of emotional and affective information. In their research on AIDS information campaigns, Flora and Maibach (1990) reported that emotional public-service messages showing families coping with AIDS, a woman pleading with her audience to use condoms, and an intravenous drug user with AIDS explaining what she would have done differently were all more effective than rational messages featuring former Surgeon General Koop's testimony in Congress, actors discussing how to use condoms, or narrated descriptions of how AIDS is contracted. This study showed that emotional messages produced more long-term behavioral changes and information-seeking behavior about AIDS than did rational messages.

Chaudhuri and Buck (1995) reported that mood arousal strategies in advertisements are highly related to emotional, or affective, cognitions. They suggested:

> Emotional communication in advertising . . . can result in affective cognitions through the use of mood arousal strategies. Repeated pairings of a brand with a mood transfers the affect generated by the mood to the brand itself. The use of "Joe Camel" in cigarette advertising, for example, has recently drawn strong protests from anti-smoking groups. The assumption has been that certain non-verbal mood arousing cues in advertisements, such as the presence of animals, can produce affective responses that, in turn, are transferred to a favorable image for the advertised brand. (p. 425)

Chaudhuri and Buck (1995) used dozens of print and televised advertisements to demonstrate that mood-arousal processes create positive affective reactions to many commercial products.

Studies of political communication reveal the same sorts of patterns. Despite much criticism, Ronald Reagan was one of the most popular American presidents in recent memory. Although many voters disagreed with his policies and questioned both his logic and ethics, Reagan racked up huge election victories. McHugo (1985) examined emotional reactions by college students to President Reagan's expressive displays in image-only and sound-and-image conditions. Results, which were the same for both conditions, showed emotional responses consistent with Reagan's expressive displays. Attitudes toward Reagan affected listeners' self-reported emotional reactions: When Reagan was angry, viewers felt anger; when Reagan was happy, viewers reported feeling happy. McHugo (1985) concluded that expressive displays have a direct emotional impact on viewers that suggest "a possible mechanism for nonverbal behavior to influence attitudes" (p. 1526). Reagan was a "feel good" president; he created positive emotional arousal and attained electoral popularity in spite of policies or plans that had little benefit for and low popularity with the electorate in general. But "feel good" facial expression by the president is not always appreciated. More recent experimental research on President Clinton suggests that the public reacts unfavorably to positive facial expressions by presidents during crisis situations (Bucy & Bradley, 2004); evidently they expect more sober facial expressions during crises. At any rate, like face-to-face communication, facial expression and body language by newscasters and political figures have a substantial effect on viewers.

The process of nonverbal emotional arousal has been shown to work in both interpersonal relationships and mass media campaigns. Typically, nonverbal messages have an automatic validity that is virtually irrefutable. A cute baby, a gentle touch, a pretty face, and a warm smile touch our hearts and influence our behavior. Cialdini (1988) calls this our "heart of hearts," a place where our "true" feelings exist before we begin to intellectualize and rationalize a message. Instead of thinking of emotional meaning as peripheral, primitive, or illogical, we should regard it as valid intuitive information that, in addition to logic, should be taken "to heart." Of course, image manipulators both in daily interaction and in the media often employ false smiles and artificial images to exploit our heartfelt responses. My own wife, who weeps at long-distance telephone commercials, is touched by these emotionally exploitative advertisements.

Emotions are contagious. Research has shown that emotions spread quickly from person to person, largely through a nonverbal communication process (Andersen & Guerrero, 1998b; see also chapter 6). Mob panic, mass euphoria, and contagious laughter are all examples of *emotional contagion*, a term coined by Hatfield, Cacioppo, and Rapson (1994). People imitate one another's actions and get feedback from their own behavior through a process known as interpersonal facial feedback (Cappella, 1993). Direct viewing of other people's emotional behavior can change our own emotions. For example, seeing a child's face light up with joy when opening a gift usually makes us feel happy, whereas hearing a loved one angrily describe having been treated badly is likely to make us feel mad. Mirroring, or motor mimicry, is another process in which one person mimics another person's anticipated response, such as wincing when someone is about to be hit (Bavelas, Black, Chovil, Lemery, & Mullett, 1988). Although each of these mechanisms probably explains some of the reasons for emotional influence, the bottom line is this: It's easy to become sad around a sad person and to feel happy around a happy person (also see chapter 6). Contagious emotions are a powerful form of interpersonal influence. Whether it is my wife with tears in her eyes watching a long-distance commercial, my friend sending off a check after seeing a children's-fund advertisement and feeling sympathy for hungry kids, or me helping my daughter solve a problem that she is "stressed out" about, we are all influenced by the emotions around us.

Physical Attraction Theories

Upon meeting another person for the first time—before the first word is spoken and even before we have much of a chance to observe the person's nonverbal actions—we are influenced by that person's appearance (see chapter 2 for more on physical appearance). "These judgments, quick and without reflection, may be extremely important for many of the subsequent processes of social interaction (Beattie & Shovelton, 2002, p. 1). We are told, "Don't judge a book by its cover," but we still make judgments about people based on physical beauty, race, age, and biological sex. Moreover, considerable evidence indicates that physically attractive people are far more persuasive than less-attractive people. Burgoon (1983) has

Physically attractive people, such as Angelina Jolie and Brad Pitt, are inherently more persuasive than most of us because they are perceived to be more competent, honest, and intelligent than other people. (© AP Images/Michel Spingler)

written extensively about the so-called reward value of a communicator. Like it or not, physically attractive people are so "rewarding" that they can violate rules of communication and actually enhance their own reward value. Many social scientists call this a halo effect, in which one positive quality dominates other unrelated evaluations.

In a classic experiment, a woman gave an identical speech to two similar audiences. For one group, her hair, skin, and clothing were made to look unattractive; for the other group, she was attractively presented. People viewing the attractive woman were persuaded significantly more than people viewing the unattractive woman (Mills & Aronson, 1965). In three experiments, Burgoon and Aho (1982) manipulated the reward value of a shopper by controlling—among other variables—the person's physical attractiveness. In general, they found that the physically attractive shopper gained more compliance than the physically unattractive shopper.

In a study by Adams and Read (1983), physically attractive women were found to interact more frequently, be less hostile, and exhibit less compliance with another's request. They concluded, "facially attractive women may have the poise or confidence to engage in more frequent influence or persuasion attempts than lesser attractive women" (p. 157). The less attractive women were perceived to use "a highly undesirable influence style which includes demanding, interrupting, opinionated, submissive and antagonistic behavior" (p. 157). This study supports research by Chaiken (1979) that found physically attractive communicators are certainly more persuasive due to greater communication skills as well as their attractiveness. These studies suggest that physically attractive persons tend to get more practice at and more rewards from communicating and develop greater social and persuasive competence to complement their already winning looks.

A study by Puckett, Petty, Cacioppo, and Fischer (1983) indicated that physical attractiveness isn't always positively correlated with persuasion. Subjects were provided with a picture of a male author and written arguments, either strong or weak. Subjects found attractive authors to be more persuasive than unattractive authors when the essay was strong, but less persuasive than unattractive authors when the essay was weak. This suggests that men's attractiveness and competence interact to produce powerful persuasive effects.

The relationship between physical attractiveness and persuasion can be explained by several theoretical perspectives. One explanation, described earlier, is the halo effect, in which a single positive characteristic dominates other evaluations of the person. The halo effect may explain why physically attractive people are typically perceived as more credible, similar, friendly, powerful, and persuasive than less-attractive people. A second explanation is that we pay more attention to physically attractive people because they are pleasant to observe. The increased personal attention causes us to attend to their requests or arguments, resulting in increased persuasion. A third explanation is that it is reinforcing to interact with physically attractive people; these interactions provide "rewards" that condition us to comply with their requests, according to reinforcement theory. Fourth, cultural stereotypes hold that what is beautiful is good (Dion, Berscheid, & Walster, 1972). This "good" person is expected to produce good, persuasive messages. Finally, some evidence exists that affective responses to persuasion are completely separate from cognitive responses (Swann, Griffith, Piedmore, & Gaines, 1987) and even mediated by different neural modules in the human brain (Stacks & Andersen, 1989). This would explain Efran's (1974) findings (which will be discussed in the following section) that, cognitively, jurors believe physical appearance shouldn't affect their decisions, yet their actual decisions are affectly based and biased by physical appearance.

Several explanations exist for the excessive persuasive power of physical attractiveness. Probably all of the preceding explanations provide part of the picture. Right or wrong, physically attractive people are more persuasive, are used to influencing others, and have the confidence to use persuasive techniques to gain compliance from other people.

SELLING OURSELVES

The focus of persuasive messages is diverse. Parents seek to influence children. Radio talk-show hosts try to influence our political beliefs. Advertisers attempt to sell us their products. Doctors seek compliance from their patients. Often, however, persuasion involves a simpler objective: selling ourselves. We want to appear attractive to our dates, competent to our professors, conscientious to our employers, honest to the IRS, and likable to our friends. Selling ourselves is perhaps the most common objective of persuasion. Most people intuitively understand how to sell themselves. Without much thought, we know to select our best suit for an important job interview or to spend extra time on our hair before a big date. We all sell ourselves—as a date, mate, friend, employee, student, family member, and so on. Image management, once thought to be the sole province of corporate advertisers, is everybody's business. Some critics have decried the superficiality of this interpersonal sales process. In the play *My Dinner with Andre*, Andre laments the shallow roles people assume:

> One of the reasons we don't know what's going on is that when we're at one of
> these parties we're all too busy performing. We're concentrating on our own
> roles and giving a good performance, so we can't perceive what's going on

around us. That was one of the reasons Grotowski gave up the theater, you know. He just felt that people in their lives were performing so well that performance in a theater was sort of superfluous and in a way obscene. (Shawn & Gregory, 1981, p. 69)

According to Herzog (1974), the increased tendency toward fake performances and managed images is a dangerous trend, which he labels the "B.S. factor." He states, "Fakery, in other words, has come to seem a natural, quotidian part of experience. Indeed, that was the object in the first place—to make the unreal appear real, the bizarre seem ordinary, the non-thing or non-person look like a thing or person" (p. 17). If anything, fakery has become an even more refined art in the more than two decades since Herzog's identification of the B.S. factor. Political candidates are more carefully packaged than ever before. Parents manage their kindergartners' image. Interpersonal relationships turn into sales encounters. Academic resumes have become a clever form of fiction designed to "market" job applicants.

Communication researchers have identified and even condemned the superficial deceptions involved in selling oneself. Nevertheless, communication research may itself be part of the problem. Dozens of different lines of communication research have come to one overriding conclusion: Meanings lie within people; that is, the impressions we form of others are not just part of the communication game, they are the whole game. From a communication perspective, if people believe you are beautiful or credible, then you *are* beautiful or credible. The manipulation of perceptions in face-to-face communication and in the mass media is continuous. And much of this image manipulation is done through subtle, nonverbal methods. As students of communication, we should be aware of the power of image manipulation. Many people, including scholars, either are unaware of image manipulation or accept it as an inherent aspect of communication.

Traditional persuasion research has focused on how to change other people's attitudes and behaviors. But as Miller and Burgoon (1978) have noted, "most people devote the preponderance of their persuasive energies to selling *themselves*" (p. 33). Certainly, some persuasive messages deal with attitudes or issues. We all attempt to influence friends and relatives about consumer products, political candidates, and social issues. Sometimes we simply want another person to wake up, to go to the store, to go out on a date, or to take her vitamins. However, compared with these sorts of persuasive attempts, we devote much more of our energy to improving our attractiveness and credibility with others. Dressing appropriately, putting on makeup, appearing attentive to one's boss, and smiling at a friend or prospective date are all actions that seek to ingratiate and sell ourselves to other people.

Research shows that many of our nonverbal actions are crucial in determining others' reactions to us. Conversely, scholars have shown that our impressions of other people are largely a function of nonverbal communication. Results of a study by McMahon (1976) showed that in an overwhelming number of cases (84 percent), nonverbal cues were more important in forming initial impressions than verbal cues. Moreover, by creating positive impressions on others, we improve our ability to influence them. So, even when we are seeking compliance, our first task is to get others to like, respect, and believe us. For only then will our messages have much effect.

Selling Our Bodies

Although we do it subtly, most of us use our physical appearance, our bodies, and their adornment to sell ourselves. The right physique, the right "look," and the latest fashions make us more credible and attractive on the basketball court, in the corporate office, in the bedroom, and in the classroom. We spend an inordinate amount of time and money to stay in shape, buy the right clothes, and have the right hairstyle. And it works. A meta-analysis that combined the results of seventy-eight experiments revealed that physically attractive people are perceived as more sociable, dominant, sexually warm, mentally healthy, intelligent, socially skilled, and popular than less physically attractive people (Feingold, 1992). But these findings also show that there is little relationship between these perceptions and people's actual personalities.

Being physically attractive might even be a matter of life and death. Our legal system, like every other institution, is biased by our looks. Juries appear to be persuaded in favor of defendants who are physically attractive as opposed to those who are less attractive. Efran (1974) studied simulated juries who received identical fact sheets and a picture of a defendant; some juries received pictures of attractive defendants, and others were given pictures of unattractive defendants. The physically attractive defendants were evaluated as less likely to be guilty and were given less severe punishments than the unattractive defendants. This occurred despite the fact that 93 percent of the jurors said that physical appearance should not bias their verdicts. These findings suggest that we react unconsciously to physical-appearance cues. Cialdini (1988) reviewed several studies that show that "unless criminal defendants have used their attractiveness to commit a crime, good looking people are more likely to

Americans spend time working out for more than just good health. Appearance and image is a huge part of personal success and influence.

receive favorable treatment in the legal system" (p. 162). As a *20/20* report on "lookism" reported, if you are on trial for a crime, "you'd better be good looking."

Research on the role of physical appearance in politics generally shows that attractiveness is an advantage, but the research is more equivocal and mixed than research on evaluations of speakers, shoppers, or juries. Some writers have alleged that more physically attractive candidates are more electable. Folklore and research suggest that John Kennedy's physical appearance caused him to win the

Folklore and research suggest that John Kennedy's physical appearance caused him to win the televised presidential debates and possibly even the presidency against Richard Nixon. (© AP Images)

televised presidential debates and possibly even the presidency against Richard Nixon; allegedly, radio listeners preferred Nixon, whereas television viewers preferred Kennedy. An article by Vancil and Pendell (1987), however, suggested that this conclusion is a myth unsupported by the actual evidence.

Other research on physical attractiveness and electoral outcomes shows a mixed pattern of results. Andersen and Kibler (1978) found some small effects of physical attractiveness on voter preference, but these effects were wiped out by voters' perceptions of the candidates' attitude similarity and competence. Bowman (1980) studied the effect of attractiveness by showing undergraduates photographs of political candidates and asking them who they would vote for. More-attractive male candidates overwhelmingly received more votes than less-attractive male candidates. However, less-attractive female candidates received more votes than more-attractive female candidates. These findings held up regardless of whether the election was for Congress, the state legislature, the office of mayor, the school board, or a judicial seat.

Research shows a strong relationship between physical attractiveness and competence. In a study by Lewis and Bierly (1990), participants were asked to rate the competence of forty-four men and women in the U.S. House of Representatives. Whether the politician was a man or a woman, attractive members of Congress were perceived as much more competent than less-attractive members. The effect existed for both male and female respondents, although it was stronger for male respondents.

Research has shown that different styles of dress can alter people's image, either favorably or unfavorably. Showing up for a formal dinner in jeans and a T-shirt or going to basketball practice in a tuxedo would not affect one's image positively! Research on women's clothing by Harris et al. (1983) showed that a formal skirt outfit maximized others' perceptions regarding how successful, happy, feminine, interesting, attractive, and intelligent a woman was. Formal pants, however, led to positive perceptions regarding how active, happy, and successful a woman was. Dress styles do communicate and clearly enable us to sell ourselves to other people as more competent, appropriate, and attractive.

Several studies, however, have shown that attractiveness is not always an advantage. The general finding that physically attractive communicators are more persuasive does not hold true in certain circumstances. The Bowman (1980) study showed one such exception. Regarding political candidates, some voters may perceive that good looks and competence are incompatible. Indeed, women with good looks are perceived to have less need to be competent, but their less-attractive counterparts are perceived to need to develop competence to compensate for their lack of physical benefits. These findings are consistent with an organizational communication study conducted by Heilman and Saruwatari (1979), who found that physical attractiveness was a disadvantage for female job applicants for managerial positions but an advantage at lower-level nonmanagerial positions. Similar results were reported by Hocking, Walker, and Fink (1982), who asked undergraduates to evaluate the morality of two women who allegedly had premarital sexual intercourse with a man they had never met previously or with a man they had been dating for six months. Half the subjects were told the woman was very attractive; the others were told the woman was unattractive. As predicted, the attractive female was perceived as less moral, and this effect was magnified when she had just met her partner.

Unfortunately, according to these studies, attractive women are held to different standards than less-attractive women. As such, both groups are at a distinct disadvantage. An attractive woman is perceived to "have it made," presumably because males will reward her for her physical attractiveness. An attractive woman is perceived not to need to be competent to be a success in business or politics, or to resort to premarital sex to "get her man." An unattractive woman, on the other hand, cannot rely on enticing men with her beauty, so she must become competent, successful, political, and promiscuous to obtain her rewards. These findings confirm the feminist position that women are viewed as objects.

Nonetheless, in politics, employment, dating, business, and every other context, we sell ourselves with our looks. Critics may justifiably deride the superficiality of physical beauty, but it is a unique and salient form of currency in contemporary American society.

Immediacy and Interpersonal Perceptions

When selling ourselves to others, nonverbal immediacy is critical (see chapter 8). Frowns or tears can make the most beautiful person look ugly. Lack of eye contact or inappropriate interpersonal distances can make a person seem rude, deceptive, or shy. Much of the research on selling oneself reveals the powerful persuasive role of warm, positive nonverbal immediacy cues.

Perhaps the most important immediacy cue is eye contact, a behavior that simultaneously creates positive impressions of warmth, confidence, credibility, and attentiveness. Conversely, avoidance of eye contact often leads to attributions of deception, coldness, shyness, disinterest, and rudeness. In a study of interview behavior, Andersen and Coussoule (1980) reported that more continuous lookers were generally perceived as more composed, attractive, extroverted, sociable, and homophilous (similar) than those who averted eye contact.

Employment-interview research shows the importance of eye contact in getting a job. In an employment-interview simulation, Burgoon et al. (1985) found that greater eye contact positively affected the interviewer's perception of the job applicant's competence, composure, sociability, extroversion, task attraction, social attraction, physical attractiveness, intimacy, and immediacy. Most importantly, the study found that moderate to high levels of eye contact increased the likelihood of an individual's being hired, as compared to reduced eye contact.

Multichanneled immediacy cues also increase the likelihood of favorable employment interviews. McGovern (1977) experimentally examined the effects of high interviewee immediacy (increased gaze, more energy, and positive tones of voice) on the attitudes of personnel representatives. Results showed that 89 percent of the high-immediacy interviewees were invited back for a second interview, whereas none of the low-immediacy interviewees were invited back. In a similar set of experiments, Young, Beier, and Beier (1979) examined the effect of positive head movements, smiling, and eye contact on job applicants' ratings. Simultaneous use of all three of these immediacy cues by applicants produced the highest ratings. The next-highest ratings were achieved by applicants who employed a combination of eye contact and smiling, followed by eye contact alone. Minimal immediacy produced distinctly lower employment ratings. The same study also found that immediacy cues had a positive effect on employment ratings even for applicants with negative work histories. Another study by Imada and Hakel (1977) also examined the effect of immediacy (including eye contact, smiling, attentive posture, close interpersonal distances, and direct body orientation) in employment interviews. Eighty-six percent of interviewees in the high-immediacy condition were recommended for the job, whereas only 19 percent of the low-immediacy interviewees were recommended. Even in the less expressive Chinese culture research has shown that immediacy cues like smiling lead to higher job-related characteristics (Tasi, Chen, & Chui, 2005). Together these studies make it clear that increasing one's nonverbal immediacy enhances one's employment opportunities. Even in lesser-developed foraging and hunting societies, smiles seem to enhance interpersonal effectiveness. In a study by Godoy et al. (2005) among Amazonian Indians, smiling was associated with great economic and social capital and better health. Evidently, smiling is as important in the rain forest as it is in China or for American college students. A study of graduate-school selection interviews showed that positive facial nonverbal behavior, particularly eye contact, was critical to graduate-school acceptance (Anderson, 1991). High levels of eye contact fundamentally determined perceptions of competence, strength, and character and positive facial expressions were linked to both likability and perceptions of motivation.

As was the case with physical appearance, manifesting nonverbal immediacy may even be a matter of life and death! Hemsley and Doob (1978) assessed the effect of direct versus averted gaze during courtroom testimony. For all three defendants in the study, testimony accompanied by averted gaze was significantly associated with guilty verdicts. Similarly, Pryor and Buchanan (1984) created three experimental trial conditions and showed them to real jurors in a Florida courtroom. In one condition, the defendant averted eye contact, exhibited nervous self-touching behaviors, spoke nonfluently and generally appeared anxious. The defendant in another condition maintained considerable eye contact, exhibited minimal self-touching behaviors, and spoke fluently. The defendant in a third condition exhibited moderate anxiety, between the first two extremes. The immediate, relaxed defendant was less likely to be found guilty than either of the less immediate, more anxious defendants. The more immediate, less anxious defendant was perceived as more competent, trustworthy, pleasant, virtuous, reliable, and intelligent than the more anxious, less immediate defendants. Clearly, jurors judge the nonverbal behavior of trial participants and view immediate, relaxed defendants more favorably.

In the political world, nonverbal immediacy behaviors also significantly increase candidates' credibility, appropriateness, and electability. Research on nonverbal behavior in the 1988 Bush–Dukakis debates (Pfau & Kang, 1989) reveals that ratings for both George Bush (senior) and Michael Dukakis increased during those segments of the debates when each candidate exhibited immediacy behaviors. Their study revealed that greater nonverbal potency or power played little role in the debates but that greater immediacy played a significant, positive role. This was bad news for Dukakis, who employed fewer immediacy behaviors in general and whose speaking style was perceived by many as "wooden." Conversely, recent experimental research on political debates suggests that showing nonverbal signs of disagreement and nonimmediacy while listening to one's opponent are perceived as inappropriate and disrespectful (Seiter & Weger, 2005). These studies support the popular idea that warm, immediate, and upbeat candidates are preferred over their opposites.

A number of additional immediacy behaviors have a positive influence on people's interpersonal perceptions. Research has shown that more immediate behavior is viewed by recipients as more competent in providing comfort and emotional support (Jones & Guerrero 2001; Jones, 2004). Interpersonal touch has been shown to have generally positive effects on interpersonal perception (for summaries of this research see Major & Heslin, 1982; see also chapters 2 and 7). Even nonreciprocal touch can have positive effects. In one study, touchers were rated as significantly higher in status, assertiveness, and warmth than nontouchers (Major & Heslin, 1982). However, several touch-avoidance studies suggest that for highly touch-avoidant individuals, this general pattern may not hold (Andersen, Andersen, & Lustig, 1987; Andersen & Leibowitz, 1978; Sorensen, 1979), because touch avoiders dislike touchers more than nontouchers. Closer proxemic distances also tend to enhance credibility, particularly if the communicator is attractive or has high reward value (Burgoon & Jones, 1976). Experimental research shows that smiling leads to more trust and cooperative behavior (Scharlemann, Eckel, Kacelnik, & Wilson, 2001). Several studies have found that even pupil dilation produces increases in physical and social attraction, although receivers are unaware of its effects (Andersen, Todd-Mancillas, & DiClemente, 1980; Hess, 1975; Hess & Goodwin, 1974).

Vocalic Influences

A number of studies have examined vocalic, or paralinguistic, influences on interpersonal perceptions. Early research by Miller and Hewgill (1964) discovered that nonfluencies (such as stuttering, false starts, and hesitations) reduce a speaker's credibility. Pearce (1971) reported that more positive, involved, and emotional speaking styles produce perceptions of more dynamism than a scholarly, dispassionate style.

Research by Berry (1990, 1992) demonstrated that people with more attractive voices were judged to be warmer, likable, honest, dominant, and achievement oriented. Semic, Miller, and Guerrero (1996) extended Berry's research by examining how attractive and unattractive voices are perceived on answering machine messages. Like Berry, these authors found that more attractive voices were perceived as more dominant, competent, likable, and trustworthy than unattractive voices. Berry (1992) studied the combined effects of vocal attractiveness and vocal maturity. She found that people with less mature, babyish vocal qualities were perceived as less powerful and less competent but warmer and more honest than people with mature-sounding voices. Interestingly, accurate judgments about personal traits can occur very quickly. In one recent experiment raters could accurately identify top managers from lower-quality managers based on vocalic qualities judged from content-filtered speech with no verbal cues (Ambady, Krabbenhoft, & Hogan, 2006). Interestingly verbal cues did not increase the accuracy of these judgments. Research on this process called "thin slicing" has shown that people can make highly accurate judgments from just a few nonverbal cues in a very short time.

Several studies have found that faster speaking rates are correlated with more positive impressions and more persuasiveness. One study (Miller et al., 1976) discovered that faster speech increases credibility, which, in turn, increases persuasion. Presumably, people who talk relatively rapidly are confident about what they are saying; they don't hesitate or have to search for the right words because they are knowledgeable. By contrast, Apple et al. (1979) reported that slower speakers are judged as less fluent, more passive, and less truthful. MacLachlan (1979) conducted a series of studies that found that fast talkers are regarded much more favorably. Ray and Ray (1988) reported that fast-talking doctors are perceived as more competent and socially attractive than slower-talking doctors. The results generally show the benefits of faster speaking rates. However, one study by Woodall and Burgoon (1983) suggested that fast delivery only increases perceived extroversion, has little effect on perceived competence, and may actually decrease both perceived composure and character. Why did Woodall and Burgoon fail to replicate the other studies? One explanation may be found in communication accommodation theory (Street & Giles, 1982), which has shown that speakers prefer speech styles similar to their own. The initial studies (Apple et al., 1979, MacLachlan, 1979; Miller at al., 1976; Ray & Ray, 1988) were conducted in Cleveland, Los Angeles, and New York, where speech rates tend to be rapid. Woodall and Burgoon (1983) conducted their study in Florida, where the speech rate is relatively slow. Participants in each study may have reacted more favorably to speech similar to their own. In general, though, fast speech rates have more persuasive impact than slow rates. Ketrow's (1990) summary of research on voice and persuasiveness concluded that to maximize one's credibility and social attractiveness, a person should speak fluently and slightly faster than one's listeners and use a moderately loud voice, a standard dialect, and clear diction.

Of course, selling oneself is effective in the corporate, materialistic world, where power and wealth are ultimate values and the "one who dies with the most toys wins." In the final section of this chapter, we will examine the ethics of selling oneself.

ETHICS IN PERSUASION

Years ago, a colleague of mine launched an attack against all persuasion. In his explanation, he railed against persuasion as a form of dominance, enslavement, and autocratic control. He claimed persuasion leads to Nazism and exploitation of the masses. He urged us to repudiate and slay persuasion as a tool of evil dictators. The paradox, of which you may already be aware, is that a persuasive diatribe against persuasion if applied to itself would self-destruct. It is a classic example of the paradoxical struggle between the power structure and the rebel, the establishment and the revolutionary, the modernist and the postmodernist, the religious institution and the atheist, the patriarchy and the feminist, capitalism and communism.

When all is said and done, this is what Rushing (1993) eloquently described as the battle between "power" and "other." It ultimately results in great power struggles, in which adversaries become increasingly indistinguishable. So the battles between political parties, the war of the last century between capitalism and communism, al Qaeda versus the Western world, even the war between hegemonic patriarchy and overzealous feminism, all emphasize power over "power" or power over "other" in a way that diminishes the human spirit. The third character in Rushing's (1993) mythic trilogy is "spirit." According to Rushing, spirit allows interrelationship among all things. Bateson (1972) maintained that individual consciousness may pull people out of their ecological niche and disrupt the homeostatic loops of which humans are a part. Persuasion that wins a victory "over" another person, institution, or species weakens our relationships and ultimately threatens all of us.

So my friend who vehemently attempted to persuade us that all persuasion is evil missed the mark. It is egoistic, selfish persuasion, used at the expense of others, that is evil. Persuading a child to stay back from a cliff, a sick friend to see a doctor, a troubled relative to think about counseling, a rich aunt to donate to charity—these are the uses of persuasion that enhance the spirit, not diminish it. Persuasion is not the villain. It is persuasion "over" others that may be evil—my gain at your expense, your defeat for my profit. Persuasion, like fire, can warm, nourish, and illuminate. At the same time, it can also scorch, consume, and incinerate.

The tools of persuasion must be employed wisely with respect for one's receiver and with recognition of the interrelationship among all people and all things. For what goes around comes around. This is particularly true for the student of persuasion who is acquiring powerful tools from theory and research. My advice to you is this: Use persuasion wisely and ethically.

Persuasion is best used to unite the common interests of all people, of all living things. In your persuasive attempts, ask this question: Will my interaction partner and I both be better off as a result of this persuasive effort? If the answer is no, the persuasive message may have ethical problems. To understand and use persuasion is easy. To use it in a way that creates collaboration, promotes symbiosis, and enhances the human spirit is far more challenging.

SUMMARY

Nonverbal communication has often been overlooked by persuasion researchers. As this chapter demonstrates, nonverbal communication is as important as, perhaps more important than, verbal communication in persuading others to change their attitudes and behavior. The evidence best supports the direct effects model of nonverbal immediacy, which argues that direct gaze, touch, positive facial expression, attractive physical appearance, and combinations of positive, warm cues have clear and consistent persuasive effects. Nonverbal immediacy is effective because it communicates power, captures others' attention, and sends cues of warmth and liking that set the stage for influential behavior.

Other nonverbal communication/persuasion models have also received some support. Expectancy-violations theory has shown that rewarding communicators are more persuasive when they violate expectancies (for example, by using nonnormative interpersonal distances) but that unrewarding communicators are more persuasive when their behavior is consistent with expectancies (for example, by adopting normative interaction distances). Distraction models suggest that irrelevant distractions (such as traffic noise) reduce persuasion. Distractions in the form of high-status or highly attractive persuaders may enhance attraction and persuasion. This may help explain why rewarding individuals who violate expectations and create a positive distraction are influential. Communication accommodation theory suggests that we are most persuasive when we adopt our receiver's style of communication. Arousal theories have shown that nonverbal emotional appeals that stimulate receivers are often more persuasive than cool, logical appeals. Physical attraction theories have shown that attractive communicators experience a "halo effect"; that is, they are perceived by their receivers as more credible, knowledgeable, and competent—qualities that enhance their persuasive efforts. This halo effect appears to exist for both physical and vocal attractiveness.

The most common form of persuasion is selling ourselves. In our daily lives, we strive to appear competent, intelligent, attractive, and credible, primarily through impression management and nonverbal behavior. How and to what ends we use this persuasive power is a matter of ethics. Persuasion has the power to heal or hurt, protect or punish, attract or alienate. The choice is up to us.

11

Concealing and Revealing
Deception and Its Detection
through Nonverbal Cues

Yes, each new day in suburbia brings with it a new set of lies. The worst are the ones we tell ourselves right before we fall asleep. We whisper them in the dark, telling ourselves we're happy, or that he's happy. That we can change, or that he will change his mind. We persuade ourselves that we can live with our sins, or that we can live without him. Yes, each night before we fall asleep we lie to ourselves in a desperate, desperate hope that come morning—it will all be true.

—from *Desperate Housewives*

Despite the fact that lying can destroy friendships, marriages, business deals, and even presidencies, lying is widespread. In a major review of the history and legality of lying, Ford (2006) stated: "Who lies? Everyone" (p. 161). One study reported that 62 percent of all statements made in conversation are deceptive (Turner, Edgley, & Olmstead, 1975). A national survey by Patterson and Kim (1991) revealed that 91 percent of Americans lie regularly! In a diary study of lying in everyday life, people reported telling from 0 to 46 lies over one week's time (DePaulo, Kashy, Kirkendol, Wyer, & Epstein, 1996). A poll reported by Ford (1996) reported that 90 percent of Americans reported they were deceitful. Burgoon, Callister, and Hunsaker (1994) found that 85 percent of patients conceal or equivocate and about one-third outright lie when talking to their doctors; only 3 percent of patients are completely honest with their doctors. Both men and women will lie about their personal appearance, personality, past relationships, income, career skill, and intelligence to get a date, particularly if that date is high in physical attractiveness (Rowatt, Cunningham, & Druen, 1999).

Even though most of us despise liars, the ability to hide or mask one's true feelings and opinions is actually an essential part of being a competent communicator, though inept or unethical deceptions are considered incompetent. Spitzberg and Cupach (1984) suggested that when deception is both effective and appropriate, it can actually enhance perceptions of a communicator's competence, even when the deception is subsequently discovered. The key is that the deception must be situationally appropriate. It is also likely that many undetected deceptions have interpersonal benefits for the sender. Some individuals, including actors, magicians, nurses, researchers, or politicians, simply could not do their jobs without using deception. A nurse could harm a patient by revealing that his condition was worsening. A head of state cannot divulge state secrets during international negotiations. Even in our close relationships, honesty may not always be the best policy, such as when being asked to comment on your mother-in-law's hideous new dress, when tasting a close friend's disastrous new recipe, or when being asked by your romantic partner if you still feel physical attraction toward an ex-lover. These examples are illustrative of Metts' (1989) research, which demonstrated that individuals often deceive to protect their partners or their relationships.

Although we all tell lies, falling victim to a lie can be extremely infuriating, upsetting, and frustrating. Broken marital vows can result in divorce. The uncovered lies of political leaders have led to their impeachment. Lies related to business dealings are the basis of numerous lawsuits. Indeed, labeling someone a "liar" is one of the worst criticisms that can be leveled against a person.

So many paradoxes surround deception. Deception researcher Sissela Bok (1978) poses difficult questions about lying:

> Should physicians lie to dying patients so as to delay the fear and anxiety which the truth might bring them? Should professors exaggerate the excellence of their students on recommendations to give them a better chance in a tight job market? Should parents conceal from children the fact that they were adopted? Should social scientists send investigators masquerading as patients in order to learn about racial and sexual biases in diagnosis and treatment? . . . To lie, equivocate, be silent, or tell the truth in any given situation is often a hard decision. (pp. xv–xvi)

So, although we loathe being lied to and misled, such deceptions are the stuff of everyday communication. We perpetrate and are exposed to dozens of lies each day! Of course, not all people lie at the same rate. People with certain personality traits, including manipulativeness and overconcern with self-presentation, are prone to lying (Kashy & DePaulo, 1996).

Deception is not limited to human behavior. Even plants and animals employ deceptive coloration to fool enemies, trap prey, and enhance reproduction, though not consciously. Deception provides an evolutionary advantage by increasing the survival rate of a species. Verbal communication, which lends itself to the most easily produced deceptions, probably gave humans an advantage in producing collective deceptions that could disadvantage less sophisticated animals. In turn, humans learned to use this advantage on their own species. Human cooperation and altruism have often been undermined by another aspect of human nature—a desire to gain selective advantages over the group. Archaeologists Leakey and Lewin (1978) maintained:

> During the course of natural selection, individuals are certain to arise who (unconsciously) try to "cheat" in the altruism game. They may produce sham moralistic aggression, sham guilt, sham sympathy, and sham gratitude in an attempt to take more than they give, a situation that could be biologically ben-

eficial in the short term at least. Although an animal without spoken language could indulge in such "cheating" it is much more effective via the spoken word. (p. 192)

Research on chimpanzees has shown that they are capable of intentional deception (Calvin, 1991; Mitchell, 1993). According to Calvin (1991), chimpanzees, under normal circumstances, will call other chimps when they find food in abundance; when only a small amount of food is available, however, they will not call other chimps, or they may even decoy them to the wrong location. Woodruff and Premack (1979) found that chimpanzees deliberately misled "hostile" trainers who were about to steal their food but correctly informed trainers of the food's whereabouts when these trainers had previously shared food with the chimps. Premack and Premack (1983) described the results of a series of their experiments:

> Did these experiences lead the chimpanzees to lie? In these experiments, the chimpanzees showed two forms of lying: full-fledged lying and a precursor form. Only some of the animals became full-fledged liars. . . . When in the presence of the hostile trainer, all four animals did, in fact, suppress these involuntary movements . . . two of them managed to develop actual lying by misdirecting the hostile trainer to the empty container. (pp. 51–52)

These experiments have shown that chimpanzees engage in two forms of lying: the suppression of nonverbal cues that indicate food location to prevent it from being stolen and a deliberate misdirection to an empty food container. These and numerous other nonverbal actions are effective means of deception. Verbal communication, however, greatly facilitates the act of lying. Indeed, verbal communication is an inherently deceptive system (Andersen, 1999). In chapter 1, we discussed how difficult it is to fake nonverbal communication. The multichanneled, biologically based, spontaneous nonverbal system does not easily lend itself to deception. But words are "designed" to inform or to persuade others that the sender's view of reality is correct, an action that always carries with it individual biases, perceptual distortions, and self-serving rationalizations.

Of course, as receivers of potentially deceptive messages, we don't blindly accept them. We perform reality checks against what we believe to be true, and we monitor communication behaviors for signs of contradictory messages (see Ekman, 1985). Leakey and Lewin (1978) argued that like deception, detection has great survival advantages: "Just as natural selection inevitably produces would-be cheaters, it will just as inevitably give rise to individuals capable of detecting cheating. And so the game of bluff and double-bluff begins, with the new emotions of trust and suspicion being invented" (p. 192).

DEFINING DECEPTION

The most widely used definition of deception is: a conscious, intentional behavior committed with full knowledge that the information is untrue. Zuckerman, DePaulo, and Rosenthal (1981) defined deception as an intentional act that "fosters in another person a belief or understanding which the deceiver considers false" (p. 3). Knapp and Comadena (1979) noted that most studies operationalize deception as "the conscious alteration of information a person believes to be true in order to significantly change another's perceptions from what the deceiver thought they would be without the alteration" (p. 271).

Although these definitions form the basis for most deception research, they may be too narrow to characterize the many kinds of subtle deceptions common in day-to-day interaction. Burgoon, Buller, and Woodall (1996) maintained that although people do intentionally provide false information, they also conceal, omit, or exaggerate information—acts that also can be considered deceptive. Ekman (1985) suggested that there are two primary ways to deceive: to conceal and to falsify. Other scholars also include equivocation in their lists of deceptive acts (see Bavelas, Black, Chovil, & Mullett, 1990; Buller, Burgoon, Buslig, & Roiger, 1996; Burgoon, Buller, Guerrero, Afifi, & Feldman, 1996). Equivocation, for example, might involve giving a vague, ambiguous answer to a question. Certainly, concealment and equivocation can be just as misleading as falsification. Thus, both are considered forms of deception in this chapter.

To date, virtually all of the deception research has focused on deliberate, conscious, and usually verbal lies. Although considerable research has examined the nonverbal consequences of deception, such as increased anxiety, little research has examined the many subtle, nonverbal acts that constitute deception in everyday life. Some forms of nonverbal deception are processed at low levels of awareness. Research by various scholars (Andersen, Andersen, & Landgraf, 1985; Ekman, 1978; Shennum & Bugental, 1982) showed five types of behavior that could be considered deceptive commonly occur in facial expressions: (1) *simulation*, or showing feelings when you have no feelings; (2) *intensification*, giving the appearance of more feeling than you have; (3) *inhibition*, appearing to have no feelings when you really have feelings; (4) *miniaturization*, giving the appearance of having less feelings than you actually have; and (5) *masking*, covering a feeling with an expression of a feeling you are not having (see chapter 6 for a detailed discussion of the nonverbal communication of emotions).

A broad conceptualization of deception would include a lengthy list of various acts, including backstabbing, bluffing, conning, concealing, concocting, covering up, crying wolf, distorting, doctoring, entrapping, equivocating, using euphemisms, evading, exaggerating, fabricating, creating false implications, falsifying, fibbing, committing forgery and fraud, playing hoaxes, being hypocritical, impersonating, inventing, lying, masking, playing make-believe, misrepresenting, telling myths, perjuring, teasing, feigning politeness, prevaricating, putting others on, pulling ruses, simulating, spinning tall tales, spying, swindling, being two-faced, and telling untruths and white lies. Hopper and Bell (1984) reported that communicators perceive most of these acts to fall into six categories or clusters: (1) *fictions*, including exaggerating and telling tall tales and white lies; (2) *playings*, including teasing, bluffing, and playing hoaxes; (3) *lies*, including fibbing, telling untruths, and making other false verbal statements; (4) *crimes*, including entrapping, covering up, and committing forgery; (5) *masks*, including backstabbing, evading, and concealing; and (6) *unlies*, including being two-faced, backstabbing, and concealing.

SIGNS OF DECEPTION

Finding foolproof cues that accompany deceptive communication has been an age-old goal of such diverse groups as judges, juries, spouses, voters, professors, and parents. Indeed, examining the behavioral correlates of lying is one of two major streams of communication research on deception. Years ago I did deception consulting with the staff at a law-enforcement academy that trained police officers, detectives, and polygraph operators. Law-enforcement professionals have relied on the polygraph, or lie detector, as an important tool in their work. Over the past couple decades, however, courts and lawmakers have attempted to restrict the use of the polygraph, criticizing the practice as an invasion of privacy, particularly in preemployment interviews. In 1988 polygraphs were prohibited for screening employees (Ford, 2006). In light of these restrictions, law-enforcement professionals have become interested in finding a supplement to the polygraph, a way of detecting deception through nonverbal communication. In consulting with the law-enforcement academy, I focused on teaching the staff the following three important principles of detecting deception: (1) no foolproof means of detecting deception through nonverbal behavior exists now or is likely to exist in the future; (2) nonetheless, some commonalities in deceptive behavior can aid in its detection; and (3) a complex mixture of unconscious and strategic processes produce subtle changes in behavior during deceptive communication.

The Inconsistency of Deception Cues

Deception researchers have sought to discover a behavioral profile of deceptive communication. They hoped to find certain cues (for example, stuttering or shifty eyes) that always accompany deception. If they had been successful, the theoretical and practical payoffs would have been great. Unfortunately, although a few nonverbal cues have shown consistent associations with deception, these cues also are associated with many other behavioral causes.

As you will learn in this chapter, there are good theoretical reasons why no consistent set of deception cues should exist. Kraut (1980) claimed that a careful, a-priori theoretical analysis demonstrates why this is so: "People sometimes act differently when they are lying and telling the truth. But these differences are not communicants of deception per se, but instead reflect internal states like heightened cognitive processing, fear, guilt, excitement or arousal" (p. 213). At best, nonverbal cues are indirect indicants of deception. As you will see in the following discussion, research is proceeding on these indirect cues, but the process is much more complex than once believed.

Individual Differences

Individual differences in expressiveness, manipulativeness, appearance, anxiety, self-monitoring, age, and occupation that are discussed below affect how we experience and display deception. Thus, it should not be too surprising that a single checklist of deception cues that works for every individual has been hard to construct.

EXPRESSIVENESS

In a study by Riggio and Friedman (1983), dominant, extroverted, and exhibitionistic individuals displayed fewer nervous behaviors and greater skill during deception than other people. In fact, people displaying these three personality traits were so good at controlling anxiety cues that they overcontrolled them, resulting in more nervous behavior during truth telling than during deception. Similarly, another study found that expressive and socially tactful people were more successful deceivers (Riggio, Tucker, & Throckmorton, 1987). Burgoon, Buller, and Guerrero (1995) also found that social expressivity was generally associated with partner perceptions of believability. Burgoon et al. (1999) reported that socially skilled people are more expressive during both truth telling and lying, masking the difference between the two. Highly expressive people were no more likely to show deception cues when lying than when truthful (DePaulo, Blank, Swaim, & Hairfield, 1992). Conversely, unexpressive people appeared more deceptive when lying. Frank and Ekman (2004) reported that across situations the appearance of truthfulness, in both truth tellers and liars, is mainly a function of the consistency of facial behaviors. Clearly, being immediate and animated in the body, face, and voice is a major factor in disguising deception.

APPEARANCE

Research suggests that some characteristics of deceivers make them more believable to receivers. Researchers have posited that physical characteristics like age, size, and gender effect deception success. Drawing on evolutionary theory, researchers have posited that people with baby faces are perceived as weaker and warmer and evoke nurturing responses in other adults. Therefore, such persons are more believable and seem less capable of evil. Research by Masip, Garrido, and Herrero (2004) revealed that, compared to more mature-looking adults, baby-faced adults were judged as more truthful, whether or not they were lying. Baby-faced children, however, because they are perceived as immature and not capable of knowing lies from truth, were judged as less truthful. Given that women are more baby-faced than men, women are generally thought to be more trustworthy.

MANIPULATIVENESS

Research on Machiavellian individuals (manipulators) has shown an inconsistent relationship with deception. Little or no relationship between deceptive behavior and Machiavellianism has been observed (DePaulo & Rosenthal, 1979; Knapp, Hart, & Dennis, 1974; O'Hair, Cody, & McLaughlin, 1981). However, Buller and Burgoon (1994) suggested some differences in the deceptive skills of high and low Machiavellians. High Machiavellians were found to compensate manipulatively during deception through the exaggeration of such behaviors as increased eye contact.

ANXIETY

Research suggests that self-conscious and anxious individuals are poorer perpetrators of lies, just as they are poor communicators in general (see chapter 7). A study by Riggio, Tucker, and Widaman (1987) found that persons high in public self-consciousness fell apart during deception and displayed numerous deception cues, including less verbal fluency, less eye contact, fewer head movements, and more emotional reactions. Riggio, Tucker, and Throckmorton (1987) found socially anxious people to be less successful deceivers. Similarly, O'Hair, Cody, and Behnke's (1985) research showed that high communication-apprehensive individuals displayed more vocal stress during prepared lies than during prepared truths, although no difference was found for spontaneous truths and lies.

SELF-MONITORING

Research on self-monitors (individuals who are more situationally sensitive and adaptive) revealed that they were more successful deceivers than were low self-monitors (Krauss, Geller, & Olson, 1976; Miller, deTurck, & Kalbfleish, 1983). Moreover, their skills improved when they had an opportunity to practice their deceptive strategies (Miller et al., 1983). However, research by Zuckerman et al. (1981) found the opposite relationship: Self-monitoring led to less success at deceiving. Burgoon, Buller, Guerrero, and Feldman's (1994) findings may partially explain this inconsistency. They found that high and low self-monitors perceived themselves to be more successful at deception than moderate self-monitors. However, observers saw high self-monitors as the most successful deceivers. These findings indicate that high self-monitoring individuals may be their own toughest critics, in that they try to control the cues that leak deception and notice when they fail to do so. Observers, however, see high self-monitors as the most believable, presumably because they are effective in managing their behavior during deception. Similarly, a trait called public self-consciousness, the perception that you are the focus of others' attention, also has been found to be correlated with controlling behavior during deception (Vrij, Edward, & Bull, 2001).

EXPERIENCE, AGE, AND NONVERBAL ABILITY

In their review of research, Buller and Burgoon (1994) reported that people, especially women, become more skilled at lying as they get older. Deceptive skills can be learned, and advancing years provide more opportunity for practice. Recent studies show that nonverbal behavioral training that made people behave in a more credible fashion resulted in more successful deception for both adults and children (Caso, Vrij, Mann, & DeLeo, 2006; Vrij, Akehurst, Soukara, & Bull, 2004). Several studies have found that individuals who score higher in tests of nonverbal skill emit fewer deception cues. Individuals with greater nonverbal sending ability (those who can easily encode emotions nonverbally) are viewed as being more truthful (Riggio & Friedman, 1983). Similarly, studies have found that people scoring high on a measure of "social skill" emit fewer deception cues and are judged as more believable than people who are less socially skilled (Riggio, Tucker, & Widaman, 1987), especially during concealment (Burgoon, Buller, Guerrero, & Feldman, 1994).

OCCUPATION

Even when out of character, actors are probably able to pull off deception without much change in their behavior. One study showed that good actors tended to be skilled liars who could deceive observers, especially with their faces (Riggio & Friedman, 1983). Many professions require excellent acting ability to sustain lies and conceal information: Not only actors but lawyers, political candidates, diplomats, salespeople, and magicians all rely on deception in their work.

These professions probably attract already proficient deceivers who then become even more skilled as they practice their deceptive arts in their livelihoods.

Contextual Factors

In addition to individual differences, variations in context may alter the display of deception cues (see chapter 3 for more on context and nonverbal communication).

THE RELATIONSHIP

Buller and Aune (1988b) reported that deceivers behave differently with friends than with strangers. Strangers decrease eye contact during deception, but friends increase it, suggesting that nonimmediacy may be a deceptive strategy limited to strangers. Another explanation is that friends strategically manage their immediacy cues during deception to appear warm and sincere. Recent research shows that deceivers are generally more expressive and less formal when deceiving friends as opposed to strangers. Deception directed toward friends also shows more alterations in behavior than deception directed toward strangers (Buller, Burgoon, White, & Ebesu, 1994), indicating that people may be more active in managing deception when with friends. Likewise deception cues may be quite different in groups than in dyadic interaction (Frank, 2005; Marett & George, 2004).

INTERACTION

As a central part of interpersonal deception theory, Buller and Burgoon (1996) focused on the difference between noninteractive and interactive contexts in which deception occurs. They argue that in noninteractive contexts (such as a videotaped intercommunication, in which the deceiver and potential detector are not present at the same time and place), deceivers are nonimmediate, uninvolved, overaroused, negative, and impaired communicatively but that in interactive contexts, deceivers behave more strategically. Thus, in interactive contexts deceivers control their nonimmediacy, nervousness, and arousal, resulting in a somewhat stilted performance. Research has established that in interactive situations deceivers are initially less immediate and involved but become more so over time (Burgoon et al., 1999). Likewise, Vrij (2006) confirmed that in the later phases of an interaction liars appear to control their behavior more than in earlier phases. Clearly, the search for deception cues must take into account the type of relationship and communication context in which deception takes place.

PREPARATION

Prepared lies are displayed differently than spontaneous lies. O'Hair and associates (1981) found that during prepared deception, liars used shorter pauses, shorter messages, more head nods, less smiling, and more adaptors than did truth tellers. During spontaneous lies, only body adaptors increased. Prepared lies are harder to detect than unplanned lies (Bond & DePaulo, 2006). A profile of deceptive behavior must account for contextual factors.

SANCTIONING

Likewise, sanctioned deception, when an authority or the experimenter gives you permission to lie, results in a different display than unsanctioned lies (Feeley

& deTurck, 1998). In most laboratory studies of deception discussed in this chapter, deception cues associated with unsanctioned lies were employed. Unsanctioned liars are more motivated to conceal lies, and research shows that they use fewer adaptors, less eye gaze, and fewer hesitations than sanctioned liars do (Feeley & deTurck, 1998). A recent meta-analysis shows much the same thing; motivated liars showed less eye contact that unmotivated ones (DePaulo et al., 2003).

Emerging Consistencies

Among the more than 100 studies of deception and 1000 estimates of nearly 200 different cues, a few are emerging as consistent correlates of deception. Even so, none of these cues are uniquely associated with deception and vary from study to study (Andersen, 1999; Davis et al., 2005; Frank, 2005). Because of individual and contextual differences in behavior, and because emotional displays that are unrelated to deception are often present when one is deceiving, these cues are useful only in general terms, not for identifying deception in specific people under specific circumstances. Given these caveats, what does research reveal as the most likely deception cues?

GAZE

"You can't hide your lying eyes," is a sentence ingrained in our folk wisdom and is even a line from a classic song by the Eagles. Evidently, this adage rests on shaky ground, because four major statistical summaries of deception research have consistently failed to find any statistically significant, overall relationship between eye contact or eye shifts and deception (DePaulo et al., 1985, 2003; Kraut, 1980; Zuckerman et al., 1981). However, individual studies have found decreases in gaze during deception. By contrast, other studies (for example, Granhag & Strömwall, 2002; Riggio & Friedman, 1983) have found an increase in eye contact during lying, perhaps because deceivers overcompensate by consciously maintaining more direct gaze. Presumably, people know that deception is stereotypically linked with decreased eye contact, so they make sure to "look into someone's eyes" when deceiving. The lack of overall findings may indicate that across individuals and situations people engage in both more and less eye contact, washing out any overall effect. What about other eye behaviors?

PUPIL DILATION

A major summary of prior research showed a substantial increase in pupil dilation occurring during deception (DePaulo et al., 2003) which is probably due to increased arousal or cognitive activity associated with lying. Given that pupil dilation usually is correlated with positive arousal, not negative arousal (Andersen, Todd-Mancillas, & DiClemente, 1980), this finding is somewhat surprising. DePaulo et al. (2003) suggested that increased pupil dilation may be due to information processing or affective changes that occur during deception.

BLINKING

A recent study of actual criminal suspects suggested that eye blinking declines during deception due to the increased cognitive load (Vrij, 2004). However, DePaulo's (2003) prior major meta-analysis found no association of blinking with deception.

ADAPTORS

Adaptors are self-touches or object manipulations, such as twiddling one's fingers, playing with a piece of string, straightening one's clothes, or scratching an itch. Studies reveal that increased adaptors are one of the most powerful correlates of deception. Comprehensive statistical summaries of the deception literature and more recent studies have shown that increased adaptors and fidgeting are associated with deception (Caso, Macicchiolo et al., 2006; Caso, Vrij et al., 2006; DePaulo et al., 1985, 2003; Kraut, 1980; Vrij & Winkel, 1991; Zuckerman et al., 1981), although several studies failed to find such increases (Granhag & Strömwall, 2002; Koper & Miller, 1986; Vrij & Winkel, 1991). In another study, adaptors increased during factual deceptions but decreased during emotional deceptions (Comadena, 1982b). The typical finding of an increase in adaptors during deception is probably due to increased tension.

Motivation may also play a role. Deceivers who are highly motivated to escape detection may carefully control nervous gestures such as adaptors. Unfortunately for the deceiver, however, too much control may lead to a stiff, unnatural-looking manner (see Buller & Burgoon, 1996; Burgoon, Buller, & Guerrero, 1995; Burgoon & Floyd, 2000). Bond and DePaulo (2006) reported that motivation undermines deceptive skill and that highly motivated liars are easier to detect, supporting the motivation impairment hypothesis, though Burgoon and Floyd (2000) were critical of the methods in studies upon which this hypothesis is based.

BODY MOVEMENTS

Is the stereotype true that deceivers are jittery and exhibit lots of nervous body movements? Recent research suggests that truth tellers and liars do not differ in body animation, postural shifts, arm and hand movements, or foot and leg movements (DePaulo et al., 2003). However, research suggests that increased head movements are associated with deception, including up-and-down nodding behaviors, overall head mobility, chin raising, and side-to-side head shaking (Davis et al., 2005; DePaulo et al., 2003; Donaghy & Dooley, 1994). However, other research (Buller, Burgoon, White, & Ebesu, 1994) found less nodding during deception.

SMILES

Research on the relationship of smiling to deception has been confusing and contradictory; some studies have found increased smiling during deception, whereas others have reported decreased smiling. Research shows no overall statistical relationship between deception and smiling nor the mouth and eye movements that accompany true smiling (DePaulo et al., 1985, 2003; Kraut, 1980; Zuckerman et al., 1981; Vrij & Winkel, 1991). A recent meta-analysis did reveal less facial pleasantness among deceivers (DePaulo et al., 2003). Two more recent studies conducted in interactive contexts indicated that liars smile less than truth tellers, and that this trend increases across repeated interrogations (Granhag & Strömwall, 2002; Vrij, 2006).

Research suggests that true (felt) smiles are different than deceptive (unfelt) smiles, which mask other emotions, such as anxiety, contempt, or sadness (Ekman, 1988; Ekman, Friesen, & O'Sullivan, 1988). Deceptive smiles show traces of the masked emotion, and the corners of the eyes remain relatively stationary. Likewise, unfelt smiles are asymmetrical, with the smile usually portrayed more strongly on the right side of the face than the left. Felt, happy smiles, in contrast, are displayed at the corners of the eye, which fold and "smile" when someone is genuinely happy. Had previous research on deception separated these two types of smiles, a decrease in felt, happy smiles and an increase in masking smiles during deception probably would have been found.

GESTURES

Since gestures, especially illustrators, are associated with fluency of speech (see chapter 2), it is likely that gestures diminish during deception because speech is less fluent and cognitive demand is greater. Illustrators (gestures that accompany speech) decline during deception (Caso Maricchiolo et al., 2006; Caso, Vrij et al., 2006; DePaulo et al., 2003; Vrij, 2004, 2006; Vrij, Edward, Roberts, & Bull, 2000; Vrij, 2006). A series of studies by Vrij and his colleagues found that liars displayed fewer finger, hand, and arm movements than truth tellers, particularly when listening (Caso, Vrij et al., 2006; Vrij, 1994; Vrij et al., 2000; Vrij, Semin, & Bull, 1996; Vrij & Winkel, 1991), suggesting that this was not associated with speech. Perhaps the lack of gestures while listening was due to concentration on preparation for the next round of lies. Pointing gestures are less common during deception according to one recent study (Caso, Maricchiolo, et al., 2006).

One of the earliest reported and most interesting deception cues is the hand shrug (Ekman & Friesen, 1972). This gesture involves raising and lowering the hands—palm up—one or more times. Statistical reviews of previous research suggest that such gestures may not be associated with deception (DePaulo et al., 2003). However, in the Davis et al. (2005) study of criminal confessions, shoulder shrugs were associated with deception.

Hand shrugs may or may not be signs of deception. For sure, hand shrugs are signs of uncertainty.

Vocal Behaviors

Stereotypes would have us believe that liars are less enthusiastic than truth tellers. Research suggests that liars show substantially less vocal enthusiasm and immediacy than truth tellers (Burgoon et al., 1999; DePaulo et al., 2003). Studies report that deception is associated with an increase in vocal pitch (see summaries by Burgoon, Buller, & Woodall, 1996; DePaulo et al., 1985; 2003; Ekman, 1988; Sporer & Schwandt, 2006; Vrij, 2004; Zuckerman et al., 1981). This increase is probably due to heightened arousal and tension experienced while lying. Streeter, Krauss, Geller, Olson, and Apple (1979) found that highly stressful deceptive acts resulted in the greatest increase in vocal pitch. Vocal tension is another variable that has overall been found to be associated with deception (DePaulo et. al., 2003), though this finding varied from study to study.

Talkativeness

One deception cue is talkativeness. Most early studies show that liars talk less than truth tellers, particularly in response to questions (Comadena, 1982a; deTurck & Miller, 1985; Knapp et al., 1974; Vrij & Winkel, 1991). Likewise, two major recent statistical summaries of deception research report that liars use less total talk time than truth tellers relative to their partner (DePaulo et al., 2003; Sporer & Schwandt, 2006), but no difference exists between liars and truth tellers in the overall length of the interaction. Interestingly, in computer-mediated communication like e-mail and instant messaging (IM), the pattern is reversed: Liars' messages are more wordy than truth tellers' (Zhou, Burgoon, Nunamaker & Twitchell, 2004).

Speech Errors

Early research suggested that more speech errors occur during deception (Burgoon, Buller, & Woodall, 1989; DePaulo, Stone, & Lassiter, 1985; Kraut, 1980; Vrij & Winkel, 1991; Zuckerman et al., 1981). The most recent statistical research summary and subsequent studies support this early research; deception was associated with more speech errors and greater delays or response latency in answering questions (Sporer & Schwandt, 2006; Vrij, 2004; Vrij et al., 2000). However, the other recent summary of deception studies shows that liars are about as fluent as truth tellers (DePaulo et al., 2003) with two exceptions. Unprepared liars show greater response delays, and liars tend to repeat themselves more than truth tellers. Likewise, a recent study of true versus false criminal confessions found that deception was associated with word/phrase repeats and speech dysfluencies (Davis et al., 2005). DePaulo et al. (2003) reported that across dozens of studies there did not appear to be differences between liars and truth tellers in other types of dysfluencies, pauses, or disturbances. Granhag and Strömwall (2002) reported that liars use fewer pauses that truth tellers and that this difference increased over repeated interrogations. Conversely, a recent study of communication via instant messaging (IM) revealed that liars pause more briefly than truth tellers (Zhou, 2005). Likewise in IM, liars use fewer spontaneous corrections than truth tellers (Zhou, 2005). These two behaviors are likely the result of liars being aware that long pauses or corrections could be perceived as dishonest, and so they avoid such behaviors. In short, dysfluencies and repeats in particular appear to be associated with deception.

Cues Not Associated with Deception

Research demolishes some of our pet assumptions about deception. As we discussed above, behaviors like reduced eye contact, fidgeting, and ahs and ums are not very reliable signs of deception. This is why we do research: Common sense often is downright wrong! Many behaviors that one would think are associated with deception are *not* associated with it! According to the latest comprehensive statistical summary of prior research (DePaulo et al., 2003) the following are *not* associated with deception: reduced or increased eye contact, gaze aversion, eye shifts, closed eyes, smiling, head nods, hand movement, non-ah speech disturbances, filled pauses, silent pauses, head movements, object fidgeting, tense or relaxed posture, postural shifts, facial fidgeting, vocal pleasantness, facial pleasantness, and many more (for a complete list see DePaulo et al., 2003, p. 95).

Automated Deception Detection

In the past few years several research teams have developed automated systems of deception detection based on automatic, computer- and video-assisted deception detection systems (Burgoon, 2005; Meservy et al., 2005; Rothwell, Bandar, O'Shea & Mclean, 2006). These systems are capable of discerning tiny changes in a variety of nonverbal behaviors, including microbehaviors that occur at a fraction of a second. Such systems have great promise for the future as more accurate detectors of deception. While these systems may have great utility in the war on terrorism and criminal interrogations, their proponents rarely discuss issues of privacy and civil liberties associated with such effective systems. For better or worse, these systems are only about 70–80 percent accurate, though far better than either the general public or combinations of nonverbal cues can achieve (Burgoon, 2005; Meservy et al., 2005; Rothwell, et al., 2006). Recent research on deception and the brain suggest that a neurological profile of deception can achieve accurate deception detection rates in excess of 90 percent using functional magnetic resonance imagery (Kozel et al., 2005). Interestingly, several sections of the right brain hemisphere which govern nonverbal communication become more active during deception scenarios. While the jury is still out, results from these automated systems may be obtained far more quickly and more accurately than those from the prior studies discussed above, which have painstakingly recorded and analyzed hundreds of individual nonverbal behaviors.

TOWARD A THEORY OF DECEPTIVE BEHAVIOR

As mentioned earlier, a complex mix of unconscious and conscious processes are the cause of behavioral differences during deception. Perhaps the greatest benefit of research on deception is our increased theoretical understanding of the many basic processes underlying human communication. Any behavioral theory of deception must account for these numerous processes that occur during deception.

Both physical and mental changes occur during deception to cause cues to "leak." These leaks are usually involuntary, unconscious changes in nonverbal behavior. This leakage hypothesis was the basis for the original research on deception cues (see Ekman & Friesen, 1969a). Recently, scholars have recognized that deceivers also consciously and strategically alter their behavior during deception to conceal their lies, resulting in a second set of processes that produces changes in behavior during deception. As such, the difficulty in producing a profile of deception cues and in detecting deception is a function of the many types of leakage and strategic changes that occur during deception (see Buller & Burgoon, 1994; 1996).

Causes of Leakage during Deception

During deception, unconscious emotional and physical changes occur. Usually these changes are experienced as guilt, nervousness, and anxiety about getting caught. Researchers have discovered at least five primarily unconscious processes that cause leakage to occur: arousal, anxiety, negative affect, cognitive difficulty, and duping delight. Although the discussion in this chapter is limited to deception, leakage is also likely to occur in situations that evoke anger, sexual arousal, joy, fear, and anxiety. (See chapter 6 for a general discussion of emotion and chapter 7 for a discussion of anxiety.)

AROUSAL

The human mind and body prepare for activity by increasing mental and physiological arousal, including a faster heart rate, increased blood pressure, faster respiration, and changes in the electrical conductivity of the skin (see chapter 7). If arousal occurs in a negative context or if it reaches very high levels, it is experienced as anxiety. At other times, arousal can be sexual, physiological, or simply exciting. Arousal induces changes in nonverbal behaviors, including increased movement and vocalic modifications.

Polygraph testing is based on the fact that during deception key physiological indicators, such as one's heart rate, increase. According to current theory, there are at least six reasons for this increase in physiological arousal. First, because the individual often remembers past deceptions as unpleasant and traumatic, conditioned-response theory predicts that during deception the act of lying is conditioned to and associated with prior unpleasant arousal (Zuckerman et al., 1981; Sporer & Schwandt, 2006). Second, conflict theory predicts that arousal when lying is due to conflicting internal tendencies to lie and tell the truth. Third, punishment theory suggests that arousal is the result of anticipated negative consequences, should the lie be discovered (Zuckerman et al., 1981). Fourth, the guilt associated with deception can also produce arousal. Fifth, the enhanced motivation to succeed in deceiving another person may be stimulating or arousing (Zuckerman & Driver, 1985). Sixth, some individuals experience arousal because they enjoy deception and especially get pleasure from successful deception.

Many of the deception cues described earlier are due to increases in arousal (Andersen, 1999). These cues include increased speech errors, blinking, adaptors, vocal pitch, and pupil dilation. Research shows that arousal cues are most likely to be associated with deception (Buller & Aune, 1988b; Burgoon & Buller, 1994; Zuckerman & Driver, 1985). Likewise, specific tests of arousal theory have been somewhat supportive. In one experiment, deceivers in swivel chairs showed more "chair twisting"; other arousal cues, however, were actually reduced (Buller & Aune, 1988b).

Deceivers probably attempt to control arousal cues, which explains why all experiments have not found increases in arousal behaviors. Two studies of deception cues among Chinese immigrants failed to support the typical predictions of deception-induced arousal, casting doubt on whether it is a cross-cultural phenomenon (Cody et al., 1988; O'Hair, Cody, Choa, & Wang, 1989). Regardless, a large body of evidence shows that arousal-related changes do occur in people's behavior during deception.

ANXIETY

Researchers are not always able to separate arousal from anxiety. We do know, however, that some behavioral changes during deception likely result from specific increases in anxiety rather than general arousal. Guilt about lying or fear of being caught contributes to specific anxiety responses as opposed to general arousal. One of the behaviors that commonly increases during deception is the use of adaptors—self-touching or object-manipulating behaviors designed to reduce stress and anxiety. The increase in adaptors during deception is probably an attempt to reduce anxiety rather than a result of general arousal.

The most compelling evidence that suggests that nonverbal deception cues result from anxiety rather than from general arousal comes from a study comparing aroused deceivers, aroused truth tellers, and unaroused truth tellers (deTurck & Miller, 1985). Six cues, including adaptors, hand gestures, speech errors, pauses, response latency, and message duration, distinguished deceivers from *both* unaroused and aroused truth tellers. "We can conclude that behavioral configurations displayed by deceivers are not attributable to arousal per se but rather are unique to deception-induced arousal" (deTurck & Miller, 1985, p. 197). It is likely that anxiety adds to arousal results in many behavioral deception cues.

NEGATIVE AFFECT

For most people, deception is unpleasant. Many deceivers have some negative feelings for the person to whom they are lying, since it's typically an adversarial win–lose situation. Moreover, deceivers may feel guilt, anger, fear, or anxiety during the deceptive act, especially when they are lying rather than concealing or equivocating. Several scholars (Buller & Burgoon, 1994; Sporer & Schwandt, 2006; Zuckerman & Driver, 1985) have suggested that some deception cues involve leaking signs of negative feelings toward others. DePaulo et al. (1985) reported that liars make more negative statements than truth tellers. Ekman and Friesen (1969a) suggested that negative feelings during deception may be leaked via negative micromomentary expressions that occur at a fraction of a second but nonetheless influence others' perceptions. Two studies found negative vocal cues to be associated with deception. DePaulo, Rosenthal, Green, and Rosenkrantz (1982) reported that liars were judged to have more negative tones of voice than truth tellers. This study used content-filtered speech so that the judges were not aware of what was said, only the tone of voice. Buller and Aune (1988b) found that deceptive strangers were less vocally pleasant than truth-telling strangers. Although evidence is limited, it seems likely that liars communicate more negative affect than truth tellers. Research on deception in interactive contexts has also shown that deceivers show more negative affect than truth tellers (Burgoon & Buller, 1994).

COGNITIVE DIFFICULTY

Lying isn't easy. Deceivers must tell a plausible lie, monitor the receivers' reactions, control their own behavior, and seem confident. Buller and Burgoon (1994) maintained that lying is so difficult that it leads to incompetent performance, characterized by an artificial, halting, or unbelievable style. Several of the deception cues discussed previously, including dysfluencies and pupil dilation while speaking, have been found in previous studies to be more common during any difficult or cognitively demanding task (DePaulo et al., 1985; Greene, O'Hair, Cody, & Yen, 1985; Sporer & Schwandt, 2006; Vrij & Winkel, 1991; Zuckerman & Driver, 1985). It follows, then, that these deception cues may result from the cognitive difficulty experienced when lying. Cody et al. (1988) found support for the hypothesis that lying is more difficult than truth telling. Among their Chinese-immigrant sample, deceivers used briefer messages with fewer details and higher rates of speech errors than truth tellers—a finding that is consistent with the fact that lying produces signs of cognitive difficulty. Although research is still needed, these results seem to suggest that some deception cues are caused by cognitive difficulty or overload. In their theoretical overview of the deception phenomenon, Buller and Burgoon (1996) concluded that deception is a complex task that adds

> further cognitive demands beyond those associated with conducting conversation. Deceivers must strategically manipulate information to craft plausible messages "on-line" all while attending to partner reactions for information about success or failure. These tasks alone are demanding and are made more so by the special demands of creating false impressions. (p. 210)

So, conversational demands on cognitive resources are substantially increased in deceptive situations, often diverting these resources from other features of competent communication.

DUPING DELIGHT

Some liars are overconfident. Smug, excited, and pleased with their success at the deception game, these deceivers begin to emit signs of pleasure, excitement, and overconfidence, which Ekman (1985, 1988) labeled duping delight. These feelings may produce increased arousal, contributing further to the overstimulation many liars experience. Duping delight may be responsible for the occasional finding that deception produces positive affect, such as gleeful vocal tones or smiles.

Strategic Deception Cues

The five processes just described result in the involuntary leakage of deception cues. But humans are strategic creatures who influence, plan, scheme, and strategize during their deceptive attempts. Strategic deception cues are aimed at concealing deception. Buller and his colleagues (Buller & Burgoon, 1994, 1996; Buller, Burgoon, & Guerrero, 1994) argued that deception cues are a mixture of leaked (unplanned) and strategic (planned) cues. "Deceivers are concerned with appearing credible, allaying receiver suspicions, minimizing their responsibility for deceit and avoiding unpleasant consequences if deception is detected" (Buller, Burgoon, & Guerrero, 1994, p. 10). These strategic attempts to deceive produce additional changes in behavior, including reductions and (sometimes) increases in immediacy, image manipulation, arousal reduction, ambiguity increases, and leakage control.

NONIMMEDIACY

Immediacy behaviors communicate involvement, approach, and physical or psychological closeness (see chapter 8). Deception researchers have frequently witnessed reductions in immediacy by liars or attempts to disaffiliate from the target of their lies (Buller & Burgoon, 1994; Burgoon et al., 1999; DePaulo et al., 1985; White & Burgoon, 2001). Buller and Burgoon (1994) believe that nonimmediacy or withdrawal behaviors are strategic, intentional behaviors used to distance oneself from the target of a lie, to disaffiliate, and to reduce the scrutiny of probing communication. Deception research has shown that deceivers sometimes smile less, stand or sit farther away, reduce gaze, stand at less-direct body angles, and use shorter statements and answers (Buller, 1988; Buller & Burgoon, 1994; Burgoon & Buller, 1994; DePaulo et al., 1985). Similarly, research on equivocation reveals that equivocators show less pleasant, more negative cues than do nonequivocators (Buller, Burgoon, Buslig, & Roiger, 1994). Although equivocation is a mild form of deception, it is interesting that equivocators, like outright liars, manifest less immediacy.

Several deception studies have tested for immediacy effects. In their

Convicted in the WorldCom scandal, CEO Bernard Ebbers displays classic nonimmediacy behaviors in his appearance before Congress. (© AP Images/Dennis Cook)

statistical summary of prior research, Zuckerman and Driver (1985) found that "deceptive statements were more nonimmediate than truthful ones, perhaps signaling withdrawal from the content of the message" (p. 138). In a study by Buller and Aune (1988b), deceivers were significantly less immediate and involved than truth tellers, and this effect occurred throughout an entire deceptive episode. In a study of paralinguistic cues, Cody, Marston, and Foster (1984) reported that liars used fewer words, shorter messages, and longer pauses than truth tellers. Ironically, by attempting to conceal their lies through the strategy of dissociation and nonimmediacy, deceivers actually produce an additional deception cue for the attentive observer to detect.

IMMEDIACY

Paradoxically, some studies have actually found immediacy and animation to increase during deception (Davis et al., 2005; DePaulo et al., 1985; Riggio & Friedman, 1983). Evidently, deceivers use pleasant, immediate behaviors to ingratiate receivers and convince them to buy their deceptive communication. Surprisingly, some studies have even found simultaneous increases and decreases in immediacy during deception or equivocation (see Buller, Burgoon, Buslig, & Roiger, 1994). Although nonimmediacy is a more typical response in deceptive communication, some deceivers overcompensate to create a positive image. The fact that immediacy behaviors both increase and decrease during deception is paradoxical and confusing. Nonetheless, it typifies the complexity of nonverbal deception cues and illustrates why a simple profile of deceptive behaviors has remained so elusive (see chapter 8 for more about immediacy).

IMAGE MANIPULATIONS

Deceivers want to make a good impression on others; they want to be viewed as nice, honest people. To accomplish this goal, deceivers may strategically change their behavior. These image-protecting or image-management behaviors may comprise yet another set of deception cues (Buller & Burgoon, 1994, 1996; Burgoon, Buller, & Guerrero, 1995; DePaulo et al., 1985). These behaviors include pleasant, affiliative, expressive actions such as smiles, nods, vocal and kinesic expressiveness, and an avoidance of interrupting the other person (Burgoon et al., 1995; DePaulo et al., 1985). But evidence for image protection during deception is mixed. While some studies have found more image-protecting behaviors, even more studies have found reductions or no differences in these behaviors (Buller, 1988). Buller and Aune (1988b) specifically tested the hypothesis that image-protecting behaviors such as head nodding, head shaking, and general pleasantness would increase during deception; however, they found no support for that hypothesis. Burgoon, Buller, and Guerrero (1995) found that more-skilled deceivers are better able to manage their image and are more effective at deception. Thus, although not all studies indicate that image manipulation is a strategic alteration during deception, some evidence indicates that deceivers do try to maintain a more positive image in deceptive than in nondeceptive situations.

AROUSAL REDUCTION

One of the major causes of leakage, discussed previously, is arousal. People feel increased tension, stimulation, and arousal while deceiving. Buller and Aune (1988b) suggested that arousal-related leakage may be moderated by the extent to which deceivers can control this arousal. Deceivers may also actually suppress bodily activity so as not to appear nervous, aroused, or active. Charles Ingram, who was found guilty in Britain of cheating on *Who Wants to be a Millionaire,* was discovered when he and his wife showed little jubilance over winning a million pounds (well over a million dollars), which caused suspicion that their behavior was overly controlled and deceptive (Vrij, 2004). Contrary to the leakage hypothesis, Buller and Aune (1988b) found that deceivers displayed significantly fewer head and face adaptors, fewer total adaptors, less gestural animation, and softer voices than truth tellers. Moreover, they reduced those signs of arousal across the entire deceptive interaction. Buller, Strzyzewski, and Comstock (1991) reported that deceivers attempted to conceal their deceit by masking nonverbal nervousness and arousal cues. Masking was particularly evident when a receiver showed signs of suspicion. This limited evidence supports the notion that deceivers strategically reduce arousal cues. Ironically, reductions in nervous behaviors may actually constitute an additional set of deception cues.

AMBIGUITY INCREASES

One of the primary strategies employed by liars to avoid detection is to create vague, unverifiable, and uncertain messages (Buller & Burgoon, 1994). Although research suggests that this strategy involves mainly linguistic tactics, such as ambiguous or equivocal messages, some signs of uncertainty may be communicated nonverbally. One statistical summary of deception research (Zuckerman et al., 1981) reported significantly more hand shrugs (a sign of uncertainty) during deception than during truth telling. Subsequent statistical summaries report that hand shrugs fall just short of statistical significance as a deception cue. Buller and Aune (1988b) reported that hand shrugs were more prevalent among deceptive friends than with truthful friends, although this comparison did not hold up for interactions with strangers or intimates. This limited evidence suggests that future research on deception should explore other signs of vagueness or equivocation as a strategic deception cue.

LEAKAGE CONTROL

Perhaps the most common strategy employed by deceivers is to control leakage and deception cues. Zuckerman and Driver (1985) contended, "Since deceivers try not to disclose what they really think, they must exercise greater control over their behavior than do truth tellers" (p. 131). Hocking and Leathers's (1980) theory of deception cues based on leakage control argued that deceivers control three classes of behaviors: (1) those that receivers stereotype as deception cues, (2) those that the deceiver can most easily monitor, and (3) those that are most susceptible to conscious control. Hocking and Leathers suggest that Class I behaviors—including head, arm, leg, and body movements and signs of nervousness—meet all of these criteria and are most susceptible to control. Class II behaviors (such as facial expressions) are more difficult to monitor and to control. Class III behaviors (such as dysfluencies, speech rate, and vocal nervousness) cannot be consciously controlled. Considerable research supports this process of leakage control (Buller & Burgoon, 1996; Cody et al., 1984; Hocking & Leathers, 1980; Sporer & Schwandt, 2006; White & Burgoon, 2001). Research shows that across the multiple stages of an interview, deceivers try harder to be believable and control their behavior (Vrij, 2006). Thus, as mentioned earlier, eye contact is often managed during deceptive interaction. Deceivers know that people expect liars to avert their gaze. Furthermore, eye contact is a fairly easy behavior to control. Hocking and Leathers's model also explains why some studies have found deceivers to become very still, perhaps as a way to control their nervous movements.

In the absence of conscious leakage control by deceivers, one would expect lies to be accompanied by signs of arousal and nervousness, such as increases in gestures, leg and foot movements, body movements, head movements, and postural shifts. Surprisingly, statistical summaries of research do not show increases in arousal and nervousness during deception (DePaulo et al., 1985; Zuckerman & Driver, 1985). In fact, they reveal slight, though nonsignificant, decreases! Moreover, these statistical summaries of psychological studies unfortunately fail to include some communication studies that show significant decreases in these behaviors. Hocking and Leathers (1980) reported significantly fewer foot movements, one of the most controllable deception-related behaviors. Greene et al. (1985) showed that people who were asked to lie not only exhibited less foot and leg movement than truth tellers, they also continued to manifest fewer of these behaviors when they stopped lying, as compared to those who told the truth all along. Likewise, studies of computer-mediated communication reveal that compared to truth tellers, liars attempt to control behaviors like long pauses and corrections in effort to avoid online leakage (Zhou, 2005).

The best way to control strong emotions during deception, according to Ekman (1985), is to mask the emotions. Masks may include facial covering or turning away to conceal the emotional display. The best masks, of course, are false emotions, which provide camouflage to mislead the receiver. So, leakage control may also include feigned warmth or happiness or mock outrage. Evidence suggests that leakage is controlled in many ways (Ekman, 1985).

Any emerging theory of deceptive behavior needs to account for the many varieties of nonverbal leakage cues and strategic nonverbal behaviors outlined here. The complexity of these eleven interwoven processes demonstrates the theoretical basis for the inability to provide a simple taxonomy of nonverbal deception cues. Similarly, as we will learn in the next section, it is part of the reason why deception detection is so difficult.

DECEPTION DETECTION

How well can ordinary folks detect lies? Not so well! The previous discussion indicates that even researchers, employing extensive lists of nonverbal correlates of deception, are far from perfect in their detection of deception. In a number of laboratory studies, naive, untrained observers were asked to determine whether another person was lying or telling the truth, a situation with a fifty-fifty chance of a correct guess. Research shows that people do a little better than chance, even when they are highly attentive to the fact that a lie may be occurring, although there are people who are consistently better than average deception detectors (Bond & DePaulo, 2006; Frank & Ekman, 1997). Because we don't look for lies in most everyday interactions, we probably detect far fewer than half of all the lies we're told. As you will learn below, most of us are biased in favor of the truth.

Statistical summaries of research have consistently confirmed that people are poor lie detectors. Kraut (1980) reported that although people can detect lies at slightly above chance level, the mean accuracy rate across previous studies was about 57 percent, with accuracy rates rarely reaching 65 percent. Other studies corroborate this figure. Littlepage, Maddox, and Pineault (1985) report 58 percent accuracy in their deception study, with respondents judging true statements correctly 67 percent of the time and false statements correctly 51 percent of the time. McCornack and Parks' (1987) participants correctly judged deception 59 percent of the time, even though the participants were dating partners who should have been able to detect deception more easily than strangers. With dating partners, however, the truth bias is probably firmly entrenched.

People are poor deception detectors. Despite his earning the nickname "Tricky Dick" in the 1950s, American voters twice elected Nixon president in the 1960s and 1970s, regardless of his repeated lies and cover-ups. (© AP Images)

O'Sullivan, Ekman, and Friesen (1988) conducted a study in which participants viewed an honest interview and a deceptive interview. When the honest interview was shown first, the mean detection accuracy rate was 59.67, but when the deceptive interview was shown first, accuracy dropped to 48 percent and only 3 of 109 observers were 70 percent accurate in their judgments. Detection rates in a Spanish sample were about the same, 54 percent (Masip, Garrido, & Herrero, 2006), whereas Swedish observers had a detection rate of 49 percent for live interaction and 51 percent for videotaped interaction (Landstrom, Granhag, & Hartwig, 2005). A recent meta-analysis of 206 articles determined that people achieve an overall hit rate of 54 percent, a number that is highly stable across studies (Bond & DePaulo, 2006). Although this rate is just a bit above chance, it is statistically significant and represents a moderate effect size.

Intuition would suggest that ordinary, untrained observers are usually even poorer deception detectors than professionals, but such is not necessarily the case. Research shows that even people trained to detect deception, including polygraphers, judges, and customs inspectors, demonstrate no increased ability to detect deception (Kraut & Poe, 1980; Ekman & O'Sullivan, 1991, Vrij, 2004). Only secret service agents did better, achieving about a 64 percent detection rate (Ekman & O'Sullivan, 2001).

Police officers, professional interrogators, and customs inspectors sometimes have *lie biases* that make them less accurate than untrained observers. Bond and DePaulo (2006), in their summary of 19 studies that examined this topic, found that experts are no more accurate than nonexperts in deception detection. Interestingly, a study of prisoners, police detectives, patrol police, customs officers, and college students revealed that only prisoners could correctly identify deception cues, probably because they receive the best feedback about the success or failure of their deception strategies (Vrij & Semin, 1996). One recent study of criminal suspect cases judged by American graduate students in forensic pathology or criminal justice reported 62 percent accuracy rate overall and a 61 percent accuracy rate for lie detection (Davis, Markus & Walters, 2006) but no age or gender differences in detection ability. Another recent study found that for high-stakes lies from real criminals and suspects, British police officers could detect deception in the mid-70 percent range (Vrij, Mann, Robbins, & Robinson, 2006).

Interestingly, aphasics, people with destroyed left hemispheres and little verbal ability, seem to be best at detecting deception at ranges up to 70–75 percent, despite or because of their severe handicap (Etcoff, Ekman, Magee, & Frank, 2000). New techniques of interactive deception detection (Vrij, 2006) as well as the automated systems are able to detect deception at rates approaching 80 percent, and neural imaging (Kozel et al., 2005) has achieved rates in the 90 percent range.

Of course, people's poor ability at detection does not mean that most people believe themselves to be poor deception detectors. People including college students, law enforcement officers and jurors consistently report high levels of confidence in their ability to detect deception (Davis et al., 2006; Landstrom et al., 2005; Miller & Stiff, 1993; Tetterton & Warren, 2005). Worse, research reveals that confidence is typically unrelated to accuracy (DePaulo et al., 1997; Masip et al., 2003, 2006; Tetterton & Warren, 2005) and sometimes even negatively correlated (Landstrom et al., 2005). Davis et al. (2006) found a weak positive correlation (.19) between detection accuracy and confidence. Thus, most people think they are better at detecting deception than they actually are and deceive themselves about how sure they are! In the following section, we will explore some of the key reasons for people's overconfidence and poor detection ability.

Truth and Lie Biases

The biases that people hold shape the way they perceive communication. When deception is a possibility, truth and lie biases often dictate whether a receiver will actively try to detect deception in the first place. When a truth bias is operating, receivers are unlikely to look for deception unless the sender does something to "tip them off" that deception could be occurring. When a lie bias is operating, receivers are likely to be suspicious and guarded even when the sender is telling the truth. In fact, a receiver's suspicious behavior might lead a truth teller to become nervous and, thus, to appear deceptive. Alternatively, a receiver's suspicious behavior might cause a deceiver to manage her or his deceptive behavior more carefully in an attempt to avoid being detected. Either way, these biases can lead to a string of processes that ultimately result in inaccurate judgments regarding whether or not deception is occurring.

Most of us believe that others generally tell us the truth. To think that every statement is a lie would make us overly skeptical, cynical, even paranoid. Researchers have shown that a truth bias exists during everyday interactions (Levine & McCornack, 1992; McCornack & Parks, 1986; Stiff, Kim, & Ramesh, 1989). It takes an unusual event—such as receiving information that doesn't make sense or observing odd behavior on the part of an interactant—to make us suspicious. Several studies suggest that our truth biases result in low levels of suspicion in interpersonal encounters (Buller & Burgoon, 1996; Levine & McCornack,

1992). This truth bias is particularly strong for familiar and likable individuals, such as friends and lovers (Burgoon, Buller, Ebesu, & Rockwell, 1994).

As Miller and Stiff (1993) pointed out, deception detection is something of a misnomer. Virtually all of the experiments in this area of research employ both truthful and deceptive communication and ask subjects to determine whether the communicator is telling the truth. So, most of these studies are actually investigations of truth detection as well as deception detection. Indeed, studies reveal that accuracy is higher for truth detection than for deception detection, probably because of the truth bias mentioned earlier (Burgoon, Buller, Ebesu, & Rockwell, 1994; Feeley & Young, 1995; Levine, Kim, Park, & Hughes, 2006). Two recent Swedish samples attempting to detect witness deception exhibited a lie bias 56 percent of the time while observing live witness interactions and 62 percent of the time while observing videotaped interaction (Landstrom et al., 2005). This could have been due to the nature of the task or greater skepticism on the part of Swedish participants. Davis et al. (2006) found higher accuracy in detecting truth than lies among criminal justice and forensic pathology students evaluating criminal suspects' statements across found different media. A recent meta-analysis of 206 articles revealed that the truth bias results in differential success rates for the detection of truth and lies. Truth was successfully detected 61 percent of the time, whereas lies were detected only 47 percent of the time (Bond & DePaulo, 2006).

Levine et al. (1999; 2006) have demonstrated the presence of a veracity effect. The probability of a message being honest is a strong predictor of detection accuracy. If messages have a high probability of being deceptive, people's truth biases will make them relatively inaccurate. Most studies employ 50 percent lies and truths so the veracity effect is small. In everyday life where most statements are true, the truth bias would be much higher.

Certain individuals, such as used-car salespeople, politicians, and telemarketers, may violate our normal truth bias. In other words, they alert our lie biases: we *expect* a used-car salesperson to conceal certain facts about cars, and we *expect* politicians to say "no comment" when confronted by incriminating evidence. We are suspicious of their words and actions. Thus, ordinary individuals who normally have truth biases can exhibit lie biases under certain circumstances. Law enforcement officers may sometimes employ lie biases. Vrij et al. (2006) found that police officers attempting to detect high-stakes lies from real criminals and suspects have a lie accuracy rate of 73 percent and a truth accuracy rate of 70 percent. Interestingly, because people have truth and lie biases their errors are systematic. In their recent meta-analysis of more than two hundred studies, Bond and DePaulo (2006) revealed that the higher percentage of accurate truth correctly classified, the lower the percentage of accurate lies correctly classified. The correlation was −.53 between correct truth hits and correct deception hits.

Erroneous Stereotypes

Each of us has beliefs or stereotypes about how liars behave during deception. When confronted with uncertainty people use shortcuts or cognitive heuristics (Cialdini, 1988), particularly in judging deception. These shortcuts or stereotypes (such as being "shifty-eyed") are an example of an erroneous rule of

Shifty-eyed people are perceived as liars, though there is little support for this belief.

thumb about deception. A worldwide study of deception across over 70 countries showed that averted eye contact is perceived to be a sign of deception throughout the world (Global Deception Research Team, 2006). Of course, eye behavior usually is not associated with deception (DePaulo et al., 1985, 2003; Kraut, 1980; Riggio, Tucker, & Throckmorton, 1987; Zuckerman & Driver, 1985). One statistical summary of deception research reported that eight behaviors are *believed* to be associated with deception: increased speech hesitations, higher vocal pitch, more speech errors, longer response times, slower speech rates, decreased eye contact, more postural shifts, and less smiling. Unfortunately, only three of these (speech hesitations, vocal pitch, and speech errors) are actually associated with deception (DePaulo et al., 1985).

Similar surveys, not included in the former summary, have found that liars are believed to exhibit defensive gestures, shakiness, excessive movements, unnatural gestures, excessive swallowing, slow responses, and reduced eye contact; none of these behaviors, however, has been consistently associated with actual deception (Hocking, Bauchner, Kaminski, & Miller, 1979; Hocking & Leathers, 1980). Throughout the world people tend to believe that less eye contact, more postural shirts, additional self-touching, longer explanations, more stuttering, nervousness, and more gestures are associated with deception (Global Deception Research Team, 2006). The belief is widespread even among detectives and police that nervous behaviors like shifty eyes and shaking appear to be deception cues, even though research has shown they are not (Vrij, 2004). One study even reports that more-attractive communicators are perceived as less deceptive (Aune, Ching, & Levine, 1996).

In another study, researchers discovered that any weird behavior during interaction led observers to conclude that deception was occurring (Bond et al., 1992). These weird behaviors included staring excessively, closing the eyes, raising the arms, and raising the shoulders. Probably any weird or unusual behavior that violates expectancies of how people normally communicate can lead to attributions of deception.

Research has shown that receivers often falsely perceive that deception is occurring. The most common reason for disbelieving the truth is the *Othello error,* which occurs when a truth teller is falsely accused of deception based on emotional responses (such as nervousness or concern) that appear to be deceptive. The term Othello error derives from Shakespeare's famous play in which Othello misinterprets Desdemona's fear and distress over Cassio's death as evidence of her infidelity (Ekman, 1985). The Othello error illustrates that nervous movements and increases in pitch can be erroneously perceived as deception cues, even though such behavior changes are frequently the result of anger, fear, or anything that feels uncomfortable. Burgoon, Buller, Ebesu, White, and Rockwell (1996) reported that suspicion fails to improve detection accuracy. They maintain that an Othello-type error may be responsible, because when truth tellers are falsely accused they display behaviors that seem like deception. Suspicion creates a self-fulfilling prophecy: Suspicion probing leads the accused to display "deceptive-seeming" behaviors, which the accuser mistakes for deceptive behavior.

People, in general, are terrible lie detectors, yet they may be better in some contexts than most of the laboratory studies have indicated. A British researcher designed an intriguing experiment called the megalab truth test (Wiseman, 1995). Frustrated that most prior experiments had typically been conducted in research laboratories with university students, Wiseman designed a study to see if lies could be detected in the media. Wiseman filmed two interviews with Sir Robin Day, a well-known British political commentator, about his favorite films. In one interview, Day told the truth; in the other, he lied. The transcript of the interviews was printed in the *Daily Telegraph*, a large London newspaper, and the taped interviews were broadcast on both national radio and television. The public was asked to indicate by telephone which interview was truthful. Over 40,000 people responded. Radio listeners detected the lying interview 73.4 percent of the time; newspaper readers, 64.2 percent; and television viewers, only 51.8 percent. One explanation for the large discrepancy among the different forms of media is that nonverbal, visual cues actually act as distractors that enable deceivers to cover their lies with convincing nonverbal displays. These findings also suggest that in some contexts, such as radio, detection accuracy is well above the commonly reported 50 percent range. Of course, in this case, respondents knew that Sir Day was telling the truth in one situation and not the other. Without this knowledge, the truth bias may have operated so that most people would have assumed Day was telling the truth, causing the accuracy rate to go down.

Sometimes we have a feeling that someone is lying to us but we can't know for sure. When this happens, we become suspicious. Studies that measure the degree of suspicion also suggest that we may be better at deception detection than prior studies have suggested. Several studies have found that we are more suspicious of deceptive communicators than of truthful ones (Buller, Strzyzewski, & Comstock, 1991; Buller, Strzyzewski, & Hunsaker, 1991; Burgoon, Buller, Dillman, & Walther, 1995).

Although our strategies frequently throw us off track in detecting deception, liars may send signals that we do perceive accurately, at least enough to make us suspicious. Stereotypes, however, probably do not increase our accuracy. Remember that widely held stereotypes about lie detection are also shared by liars. During deception, liars are most likely to control the very cues for which we most commonly look to catch them. The communication game of hide and seek continues, with the liar frequently winning.

Collaborative Deception

The fact that many lies are actually cooperative and collusive is another factor that prevents or reduces overt deception detection. "Deception, like other communications, is mutually negotiated. Deceiver and deceived collaborate" (Knapp & Comadena, 1979, p. 272). Collaborative deception takes a number of forms. First, situations exist in which lies are expected. Bluffing in poker is a prime example of collaborative deception. Lies are expected in many sales encounters; the customer may claim limited financial resources or the existence of a better deal elsewhere, and the salesperson may quote a "rock-bottom" price. Both parties recognize the virtual certainty of deception but—as with poker—regard it as part of the sales game. Second, lies may be mutually advantageous. Consider two buddies bragging to a group about the girls they picked up or the touchdowns they once scored; they may both profit from each other's deceptions. Third, many lies, especially trivial ones, are accepted to avoid embarrassment. Morris (1977) provided the following example of such socially comfortable deception:

> If, at a dinner party, our hostess offers us a second helping of a horribly unpalatable dish, we refuse it with a polite lie. Instead of telling her the truth, we may say we are full up or on a diet. If she detects the lies and appreciates the reason for it, she is likely to let us get away with it, rather than risk introducing a note of discord into the evening. . . . Now both sides are lying and both sides know it, but the charade is allowed to run its course. (p. 107)

A fourth reason for deceptive collusion is to avoid the consequences of uncovering a lie. Parents may adopt the attitude that "ignorance is bliss" rather than probing to find out whether their daughter smokes marijuana or lives with her boyfriend. Spouses who suspect extramarital affairs may choose not to ask rather than have their lives shattered by such a revelation. Collusive lies often result in psychological denial. They are particularly common when the consequence of discovery is relational conflict or destruction.

A final type of collusive lie is the requested lie. "The most explicit form of fabrication collaboration is a formal request to be told a lie if a particularly undesirable event should occur" (Knapp & Comadena, 1979, p. 273). Thus, patients sometimes tell doctors, "Don't tell me if it's malignant." Spouses may say, "I don't want to know about your affair." This overt request to be lied to is more common than many people realize.

Collaborative lies may create a shared distorted perception of reality. Collaborative liars may actually begin to believe their fabrications (O'Hair & Cody, 1994). There is some evidence that whole groups sometimes come to believe collaborative lies. In the early twentieth century, both blacks and whites commonly believed in the "inherent inferiority of blacks." Citizens of most nations believe the lie that their country is always right. Collaborative lies are more common than most of us realize, and they deserve more investigation.

Lack of Vigilance

Most of us are unprepared to detect lies. We start with a truth bias, which for most of us is fairly persistent. Moreover, being constantly skeptical takes too

much effort; in our daily lives we are forced to sift through so many messages—
from our numerous face-to-face encounters, from computers and message
machines, from news media and advertising. So we go through life not particularly vigilant about lies, tending to accept what we're told.

One study reports that when receivers were warned about the possibility of
deception, their accuracy improved (Buller, 1989), probably due to increased vigilance. Another study shows that when receivers were told to suspect lies, they
tended to look away from the more deceptive face and tuned in to the "leakier"
body to look for deception cues (Zuckerman, Spiegel, DePaulo, & Rosenthal,
1982). These findings demonstrate that vigilance increases when lies are anticipated. As Levine (1994) argued, "deception research suggests that *receivers* may be
decidedly unmotivated to detect deception" (p. 14). Similarly, Levine et al. (2005)
found that bogus detection training produces small and variable effects, much as
does real detection training. A meta-analysis of the effects of training on deception detection reveals a small effect accounting for about a 4 percent increase in
accuracy (Frank & Feeley, 2003). All these results are probably due to a vigilance
effect, which can produce some small increases in deception detection.

(Un)familiarity

Because each person behaves somewhat differently during deception, unfamiliarity should make deception detection difficult. Research has generally
shown that behavioral familiarity is associated with improved deception detection. Miller et al. (1981) summarized several studies which show that familiarity
with a particular individual provides a baseline of observable truthful behavior
that a receiver can use to contrast with deceptive behavior. Research by Zuckerman, Koestner, and Alton (1984) shows that people can learn to detect deception
from a particular person. Subjects who were shown a person's behavior during
lying and truth telling were the most accurate in detecting subsequent lies.

A study by Feeley and Young (1995) found that increased exposure to a person's truthful behavior resulted in greater judgment accuracy for the detection of
both truthful and deceptive communicators. Comadena (1982a) reported that
familiarity produced more detection accuracy, particularly for female observers.
Female spouses were especially good deception detectors.

Interestingly, another body of research shows that we're not always better at
picking up friends' lies because we have a truth bias, as indicated in our earlier
discussion. Research has shown that relational familiarity is a two-edged sword.
In close relationships, we are less vigilant of deception and more likely to hold
truth biases. Summaries of research (Levine, 1994; Millar & Millar, 1995) suggest
that we may be less accurate in deception detection in our close, familiar relationships. Truth biases also tend to reduce suspiciousness in close relationships. One
study found that truth biases increase with familiar partners but also that these
relational truth biases were even stronger when the receiver was suspicious (Burgoon, Buller, Ebesu, & Rockwell, 1994). Levine and McCornack (1992) concluded:

> As individuals become increasingly involved in relationships, there is an
> increase in confidence in ability to judge a partner's behavior. It is likely that

when individuals are highly confident in their ability to detect deception they are less likely to scrutinize a partner's behavior actively, and more likely to rely on judgmental heuristics such as a truth bias. (p. 152)

Research suggests that different cues are useful for detecting the deception of friends and family as opposed to strangers. Voice and physical behavior aid in the detection of strangers' deception. Voice alone, however, is superior for deception detection of friends and relatives, evidently because focusing on a single channel can undermine the truth bias (Millar & Millar, 1995).

In sum, our deception-detection ability seems to improve when we develop familiarity through repeated exposure to an unfamiliar individual's behavior; in short, observable baseline data improve detection. For people we know very well, however, we have relational familiarity, and observable data are overridden by truth biases. Therefore, we might be better at detecting deception in acquaintances and casual friends, as compared to strangers (for whom we have no behavioral familiarity) and close friends, family, and lovers (for whom we have truth biases).

Individual Differences

Earlier in this chapter we examined individual differences, such as social skill, Machiavellianism, and self-consciousness, that affect people's ability to conceal their lies. But do individual differences have an effect on the ability to *detect* lies? Personality differences seem not to play an important role in deception detection. Kraut (1980) summarized the research on individual differences and concludes, "A number of findings suggest the lack of both stability and generality of individual differences in the detection of deception" (p. 213). In a summary of research on deception detection, Buller and Burgoon (1996) suggested that receivers' sensitivity skills increase their ability to detect deception. Future research, however, needs to investigate which receiving skills are most critical in the detection of deception.

Gender does appear to be related to the ability to detect deception; females are generally more accurate than males. A statistical summary of prior research showed that women were better overall detectors of deception but that detection rates were also higher in same-sex rather than opposite-sex dyads (Zuckerman et al., 1981). Other studies, not included in the former statistical summary, reveal the same pattern. Comadena (1982a) found that wives were better deception detectors than husbands. Two studies, however, found no clear gender effect in deception (Hurd & Noller, 1988; Manstead, Wagner, & MacDonald, 1984), but they did find that women were better at detecting honesty. McCornack and Parks (1987) found women to be consistently more accurate then men in detecting deception at all stages of a relationship. However, because women are generally more sensitive and polite communicators, they may decode the intended (rather than actual) message and thus be less accurate deception detectors (Burgoon, Buller, & Woodall, 1996). Although current research suggests that women are better deception detectors, more research needs to be conducted (see chapter 5 for a detailed discussion of sex and gender).

Overattribution

Overattribution occurs when prior information biases what we see. Overattribution is the basis of self-fulfilling prophecies, expectancy effects, a failure to process contradictory information, and rationalization. Often what we see is the result of what we *expect* to see rather than what we actually see! This is true in the detection of deception.

Overattribution, or anchoring as it is often called, is the tendency to make a final judgment too close to an initial one. Research shows that initial anchors, or attributions, distort respondents' own personal judgments of deception. In two studies, respondents were asked to judge if person was lying or telling the truth about that person's attitude toward a third person (Zuckerman, Koestner, Colella, & Alton, 1984; Zuckerman, Fischer, Osmun, Winkler, & Wolfson, 1987). When respondents are asked to judge another's attitudes toward a third person before judging whether the other was lying, they are less likely to conclude that the other is lying than if the judgment about lying comes first. When the possibility of deception is salient, we are prone to perceive deception. Studies have shown that in long-term or trusting relationships, detectors are less likely to make attributions of lying (Buller, 1989; Buller & Walther, 1989; McCornack & Parks, 1987). These positive relational anchors produce overattributions of honesty. Interestingly, researchers have located the areas of brain around the amygdala which are activated when someone concludes that another is being deceptive (Grezes, Frith, & Passingham, 2004).

Confusion with Other Behaviors

There is no set of behaviors that are always or even usually associated with deception. Remember, deception cues come about because of the forces we discussed above; arousal, anxiety, cognitive difficulty, duping delight and the like. Often arousal or anxiety from some other sources is confused with deceptive behavior. "There is not a single verbal, nonverbal, or physiological cue uniquely related to deception. In other words, nothing similar to Pinocchio's nose actually exists" (Vrij, 2004, p. 160).

Indirect Attributions

Earlier in this chapter we discussed how people's stereotypes about lying aren't very accurate. Research suggests that attributions about deception come indirectly from other sets of cues. Buller (1988) showed that receivers make deception attributions when a sender is highly aroused or lacking in intimacy or immediacy. Hale and Stiff (1989) reported that incongruence between verbal and nonverbal cues leads to attributions of deception. These indirect attributions that judge incongruent, aroused, or nonimmediate cues as deception may occasionally be correct. However, arousal, incongruence, and nonimmediacy are frequently the result of factors other than deception, contributing to inaccurate deception detection. Despite the fact that detecting deception may have very profound relational consequences for most individuals (Aune, Metts, & Ebesu, 1990), people are very poor at discovering acts of deception.

IMAGINING A WORLD WITHOUT DECEPTION

This chapter may seem to have concluded on a pessimistic note. Ordinary people have considerable difficulty detecting the lies of others. Undoubtedly, this means that a considerable amount of deception occurs. Certainly, over the last forty years, the public has learned that many politicians lie. Vietnam, Watergate, the Lewinsky affair, or Bush's weapons of mass deception—to name only a few examples—have demonstrated that U.S. presidents tell a number of lies to the American public. This should remind us not to trust every word emanating from high places, although it doesn't mean that all politicians are congenital liars.

Certainly, advertisers, salespeople, brokers, agents, and bankers engage in considerable deceptive behavior in an attempt to influence us. When financial gain is involved, the motivation to lie is substantial, particularly in a society where money and material objects are highly valued. Deception even occurs in personal relationships, when lying may save face, improve one's image, permit exploitation of another sexually or economically, or create artificial closeness through flattery or ingratiation.

The fact that we are all dupes of such deceptions from time to time is disturbing indeed. Our inability to separate truth from falsehood may make us wish for a world in which deception is easily detected—an appealing idea until we consider what such a world would be like. George Orwell (1949), in his novel *1984*, written half a century ago, describes a society in which thoughts can be monitored and deception detected:

> There was of course no way of knowing whether you were being watched at any given moment. How often, or on what system, the Thought Police plugged in on any individual wire was guesswork. It was even conceivable that they watched everybody all the time. But at any rate they could plug in your wire whenever they wanted to. You have to live—did live, from habit that became instinct—in the assumption that every sound you made was overheard, and except in darkness, every movement scrutinized. . . . Thoughtcrime was not a thing that could be concealed forever. You might dodge successfully for a while, even for years, but sooner or later they were bound to get you. (pp. 4, 20)

Certainly, living in paranoid fear of being caught in a lie would be far worse than living in a society in which our freedom sometimes permits exploitation. In the following passage, Orwell (1949) describes face-crime, the revelation of our deceptions through nonverbal communication.

> It was terribly dangerous to let your thoughts wander when you were in any public place or within a range of a telescreen. The smallest thing could give you away. A nervous tic, an unconscious look of anxiety, a habit of muttering to yourself—anything that carried with it the suggestion of abnormality, or having something to hide. In any case, to wear an improper expression on your face (to look incredulous when a victory was announced, for example) was itself a punishable offense. There was even a word for it in Newspeak: *face-crime*, it was called. (p. 20)

Although it seems at first that the detection and regulation of deception would be a wonderful idea, Orwell's vision of such a society should convince us otherwise.

SUMMARY

Deception, a widespread communication phenomenon, involves intentionally misleading another person. Although deception is a communication skill that has advantages for both individuals and species, it also can have extremely negative consequences. Researchers have made some strides in identifying a set of nonverbal deception cues, although considerable behavioral inconsistencies exist; these inconsistencies are due to individual differences, contextual factors, and the diverse origins of deception cues.

Deception cues comprise both leakage behaviors and strategic behavioral changes. During deception, increases may occur in arousal, anxiety, and negative affect, resulting in leakage cues. Deceivers may also leak their emotional states due to the cognitive difficulty of lying and to duping delight, the joy and excitement of successful lying. Liars also behave strategically by increasing and/or reducing immediacy, manipulating their image, attempting to reduce arousal, increasing the ambiguity of their message, and attempting to control leakage. The combination of these leakage and strategic behaviors results in a complex and often inconsistent set of deception cues.

People are poor deception detectors. Most of us (1) operate with truth biases in the majority of our interactions (only occasionally do lie biases take over), (2) possess erroneous stereotypes about deception cues, and (3) are often willing collaborators in deception. Behavioral unfamiliarity with strangers prevents good deception detection; at the same time, however, relational familiarity in close relationships creates truth biases that also prevent accurate deception detection. Overattribution is an additional cause for our inaccuracy in detecting deception.

Although we all wish we could detect deception more easily, social politeness and interpersonal effectiveness depend, to some degree, on deception. It would certainly be beneficial to be able to detect deception in salespeople and politicians, but the universal detection of deception would probably have as many disadvantages as it would advantages.

12

Positions of Power
The Nonverbal Communication of Control, Power, and Status

In *The Complete Idiot's Guide to Body Language*, Andersen (2004) recalled:

> More than a century ago, barnyard biologists observed that the "top" chicken could peck on every other chicken in the pen, but the lowliest chicken couldn't peck on any other hen. Called "dominance hierarchies," these pecking orders exist in every species and humans are no exception. (p. 127).

In his classic book, *The Power Elite*, C. Wright Mills (1956) suggested:

> As the means of information and power are centralized, some men come to occupy positions in American society from which they can look down, upon, so to speak, and their decisions mightily affect, the everyday worlds of men and women. (p. 3)

Half a century later, things have changed little. Elites exist in America with access to its powerful institutions: business, banking, communications, education, and politics. If anything, the information society of the twenty-first century has made power discrepancies even more dramatic, with the digital divide separating elite knowledge workers from information-poor manual workers.

Of course, status hierarchies have existed in every human culture throughout history. At one time, raw muscle power probably determined an individual's status and power. In modern times, however, as Morris (1977) noted, "muscle power has given way to inherited power, manipulative power, and creative power. The top musclemen have been superseded by the top inheritors, top fixers, and top talents" (p. 121).

Although the nature of power has changed, its importance has not. Holders of power still exert dominance over those with less power. One of the two most important dimensions of human relationships is the power dimension. Bertrand Russell (1938) understood the importance of this dimension when he stated, "The fundamental concept in social science is *Power*, in the same sense in which *Energy* is the fundamental concept in physics" (italics added, p. 10).

How does a person acquire power? Certainly, money, social class, education, fame, neighborhood, and family provide disproportionate access to power and status. However, an individual's own subtle behaviors can have a major effect on others' perceptions of her or his power. The charisma of some prominent people, such as John F. Kennedy, Ronald Reagan, Mother Teresa, Walter Cronkite, Bob Dylan, Michael Jordan, Tiger Woods, or Madonna, involves more than money, social class, or education.

It is appropriate to conclude a book on nonverbal communication with a chapter about power, because nonverbal power cues exist in every interaction and every nonverbal cue. Power and dominance hierarchies exist in every human culture and in other primate groups as well; so it is appropriate that we examine how power gets created nonverbally and often spontaneously. Rajecki (1983) pointed out that "dominance hierarchies seem to be a pervasive phenomenon in the primate world" (p. 86). Establishing power structures and dominance hierarchies, as you will see, is often accomplished through nonverbal codes: eye behavior, kinesic displays, material possessions, proxemic behavior, and other "positions of power."

Research on power, status, and dominance (what is sometimes the vertical dimension of social relations) reveals that nonverbal communication plays an important role in establishing one's position and determining one's interpersonal influence (Andersen & Bowman, 1990; Burgoon & Hale, 1984; Carney, Hall, & LeBeau, 2005; Duran, Jensen, Prisbell, & Rosoff, 1979; Hall, Coates, & LeBeau, 2005; Mehrabian, 1972). Power typically refers to the ability to influence others to do what one wants and to control interactions (Andersen, 2008; Berger, 1985; Burgoon & Dunbar, 2006; Ellyson & Dovidio, 1985; Patterson, 1983). Status refers to one's position in society, which generally contributes to power and dominance (Henley, 1977; Patterson, 1983; Ridgeway, 1987). Domineering behaviors are actions on the part of one person to assert control or dominance over another (Burgoon & Dunbar, 2006; Millar, Rogers-Millar, & Courtright, 1979).

If accepted by another person, then domineering behaviors become dominant ones. Often, domineering behaviors are exhibited by a domineering individual who seeks to control others. *Dominance* refers to one's position of power in relation to others (Duran et al., 1979; Patterson, 1983) and can represent either the actual state of affairs or a perceived judgment (Ellyson & Dovidio, 1985). All these terms relate to a single dimension of interpersonal behavior often labeled *control* (Burgoon & Hale, 1984; Duran et al., 1979); alternative terms for this dimension include *influence, authority, assertiveness, superiority,* and *leadership* (Duran et al., 1979; Henley, 1977).

In the following sections, the various codes of nonverbal communication are examined with respect to the hierarchical structure of human interaction. We begin where most interactions begin—upon meeting a person for the first time, when we make judgments regarding the person's physical appearance.

PHYSICAL APPEARANCE

Prior to the initiation of verbal interaction, people communicate their status and power through their physical appearance, and this information often is used as the basis for powerful first impressions (P. A. Andersen, 1984). As noted in chapter 2, the inferences we make about another person's character and status are made from how we perceive her or his appearance. Among the various impressions communicated through appearance, the nonverbal messages of dominance and status, conveyed through dress and physical size, have a major impact on interpersonal power perceptions.

Dress

One's style of dress sends a variety of messages and is often the major determinant of first impressions. Fowles (1974) contended, "Our clothes broadcast our sex, our rank and our up-to-dateness" (p. 348). Of the many statements a person makes through clothing, often the clearest messages are those regarding power and status.

Formal dress increases perceptions of dominance and control (Bickman, 1974; Brown, 1965; Mehrabian, 1976; Molloy, 1976; Morris, 1977), especially for men (Mast & Hall, 2004b). Mehrabian (1976) asserted that people who select formal dress are tapping the dominance dimension. The suit, in particular, is a symbol of dominance (Mehrabian, 1976; Molloy, 1976). Molloy, in his best-selling book, *Dress for Success,* claimed that most authority is conveyed by a dark suit but warns that black should be avoided due to its funereal overtones. He stated that the dark solid-blue suit provides particularly high credibility with the lower middle class, although he provides no specific reason for this assertion. Molloy also claimed that the pinstripe is the most authoritative pattern and that an expensive, conservative tie is a vital suit accessory, for it symbolizes respectability and responsibility (Molloy, 1976). Over three decades later, the pinstripe suit is still a symbol of authority and status. However, business attire today is often somewhat more relaxed, with business causal or a jacket with an open collar most common.

Expensive, immaculately polished shoes are also a symbol of high status (Morris, 1977). Curiously, shoes can connote dominance or submission. Mehrabian (1976) claimed that "shoes in particular can be selected to be noisy and rough (high-load in dominant ways), hushed and smooth sounding, or almost totally silent (low-load and submissive)" (p. 64). Similarly, expen-

Masculine power behaviors are expressed through the business suit, the haircut, polished shoes, decisive gestures, and long strides that still predominate in many businesses.

sive, high-fashion, or high-technology shoes such as aerobic, basketball, or running shoes, can also signal power and status. Indeed, there have been reports of children resorting to crime to get basketball shoes that cost $100 or more, prompting civil rights groups to object to the marketing of shoes to poor customers through "power ads."

A uniform is a special kind of attire that both reveals and conceals power. It identifies the wearer as part of a group structure, making the wearer's status within the group highly visible while suppressing other status cues (Joseph & Alex, 1972). The suppression of status and individuality is the reason behind the great school uniform debate in the United States. Proponents argue that school uniforms reduce socioeconomic status differences and reduce gang influence because "gang" attire would be prohibited by a uniform code. Opponents agree that uniforms reduce differences in status and individuality but argue that they suppress expression, creative individuality, and free speech.

The uniform is a nonverbal certificate of power and authority.

The uniform is also a certificate of legitimacy and can elicit conformity if it symbolizes authoritative power, as do military or police uniforms. Uniforms conceal and reveal power by suppressing individual status symbols while signaling powerful messages of authority and group status. Through the use of its uniform, a group certifies an individual as its representative and assumes responsibility for her or his behavior (Joseph & Alex, 1972). In a study by Bickman (1974), people more often complied with requests made by an experimenter dressed as a guard than one dressed as a civilian or milkman. Although a uniform affords the wearer authority at times, paradoxically, people who work in uniform generally have lower status than individuals who work in professional clothes (Koehler, Anatol, & Applbaum, 1981). For example, airline employees, including flight attendants, baggage handlers, and even pilots, usually wear uniforms, but the CEO of the airline is likely to wear a business suit. Low-status workers in establishments such as fast-food restaurants or grocery stores are also likely to wear uniforms.

High-status attire simultaneously creates perceptions of both leadership and conformity. In a classic study of pedestrian traffic, Lefkowitz, Blake, and Mouton (1955) reported that when a high-status person (communicated by that person's dress) violated a law by walking against a red light, there was a significant increase in the rate of violations by other nearby pedestrians; by contrast, when the same person dressed in low-status clothing walked against a red light, significantly fewer pedestrians followed. Another study of pedestrian behavior found that passersby resisted penetrating the boundaries of an interacting social group when the group members wore clothing of high status (Knowles, 1973). In an uncrowded college library, students fled more rapidly when their space was invaded by a well-dressed man than when invaded by a casually dressed man (Barash, 1973). In a moderately crowded library, however, the speed of flight responses was not statistically significant. Various nonverbal cues operate at a very low level of awareness. It appears that under conditions of moderate crowding, people expect to have less space, so they are less likely to react negatively. It is also unlikely that the college students (or the pedestrians in the two previous studies) were very consciously aware of the attire worn by the confederates in this experiment, but it spontaneously and nonlinguistically affected their attitudes and behavior nonetheless.

Not surprisingly, people of great wealth and high status have the prerogative to break the rules of dress. It is not uncommon to see George W. Bush, Bill Gates, or Brad Pitt in blue jeans. We all know that the super rich can afford to dress expensively, but they also have the freedom to dress shabbily and still maintain their well-established position (Henley, 1977). In addition, they can wear eccentric clothing with impunity (Morris, 1977). In short, high-status individuals have the nonverbal prerogative to dress however they please.

Gender differences in dress demonstrate an element of dominance and submission. Both men's and women's clothing is rigidly prescribed in many cultures and is governed more by fashion and social convention than by comfort or freedom of movement. Some men's dress clothing, including ties and hard-soled shoes, is not designed for comfort and women's clothing, in particular, is often quite restrictive and designed to create a submissive demeanor. In our culture, women's clothing often is tailored to emphasize bodily contours and is made of delicate materials associated with femininity (for example, silk or chiffon). The frailty of fabric and close-fitting design combine to restrict a woman's movement. A skirt, for instance, prevents certain physical activities and sitting positions, and fine fabrics compel a woman to avoid getting dirty. High heeled shoes are more attractive and sexual than they are functional. Restrictive corsets of the past made it almost impossible to breathe; today, some fashionable shoes make it almost impossible to walk. Additionally, the close-fitting design of women's clothing often precludes the incorporation of pockets, a functional aspect of most men's clothing. By being forced to carry a purse, a woman is further restricted in physical movement (Henley, 1977).

Depending on the situation women may employ different appearance strategies than men; for example, in social situations women, more than men, employ sex appeal as a power strategy. In an imaginative study of nonverbal cues at a European night club, women whose attire showed more skin, was tighter, and was shorter received less threatening nonverbal behavior from doormen than other women (Salter, Grammer, & Rikowski, 2005).

Over time, women have begun to adopt greater variety in their clothing. The fact that women can wear either traditionally feminine clothing or more-masculine, unisex clothing is indicative of the "liberation" of contemporary women. Men, however, are relegated to traditionally male clothing which increasingly covers the body. Shorts for women are often very short; for men they are usually below the knee. Most men in the United States would not wear a dress (although some men do sport earrings). This suggests that insofar as clothing is concerned, men are not as "liberated" as women because their clothing choices are more narrowly prescribed (see chapter 5 for more on gender and nonverbal communication).

Height and Size

Historically, power was about physical size and strength. Today we still talk about someone being "above" someone else rather than "down and out," "rising above" one's opponents, and being "on top." Today the importance of physical power has diminished, but it still affects our decisions. The elections of Governors Jesse Ventura in Minnesota, Arnold Schwarzenegger in California, and George W. Bush as president suggest that people often prefer tough guys over individuals with experience and competence. Height and physical size are important components of power. Tallness and largeness indicate dominance and status (Mehrabian, 1972). These attributions may derive from the physical advantage these characteristics gave our ancestors during hand-to-hand combat (Burgoon & Dunbar, 2006).

People often prefer tough guys over individuals with experience and competence. California Governor Arnold Schwarzenegger has been nicknamed "The Governator" by his supporters, in reference to his role in the *Terminator* films. (AP Images/Brian Vander Brug)

In a series of recent studies Schubert (2006) demonstrated that higher vertical positions are always viewed as more powerful whether they are objects, animals or people. Kinsbourne (2006) showed that upward movements along the vertical axis are preprogrammed into the human brain as indicants of power and triumph.

The "height is power" phenomenon places short men and most women at a disadvantage; having to look up to taller people suggests lower status and a perception of submissiveness. Actions that give the appearance of being tall or large, however, can increase a person's dominance (Scheflen, 1972). "Standing tall is in itself a good way of achieving dominance" (Henley, 1977, p. 89). In a confrontation, the act of "standing over another or the more abbreviated displays of height (i.e., raising one's head or brow while looking down) have the effect of 'cutting an opponent down to size' symbolically" (Remland, 1982a, p. 84). Beards and long hair make one's head appear larger, thereby increasing dominance (Mehrabian, 1976). Not surprisingly, a slumped posture or a curled-up position is submissive because it creates a smaller appearance (Morris, 1977).

Physical size has great significance in the business world, where height goes hand in hand with success. Tall men are more likely to be hired and to gain larger salaries and prominent positions than are shorter men (Henley, 1977). Morris (1977) indicated that being tall improves one's chances of success; here, he elaborates on the stereotypical obstacles that face a short person:

> Short men who are intensely ambitious are notorious for the savagery of their "assertiveness" when they have struggled to the top, indicating the need to compensate for their small stature. Where a tall man at the top can afford to relax, the short tyrant must remain tense, forever reestablishing his position. (p. 142)

Although the messages of power and status conveyed by physical size date back to a time when size was directly related to survival, being tall and large today still produces perceptions of power.

Physical Attraction

Men, and to a lesser degree women, benefit from greater size and height. Conversely, women, and to a lesser degree men, have higher status if they are more physically attractive. In chapter 2 we discussed the concept of the halo effect: the idea that a person with one good quality, such as physical appearance, is believed to possess other good qualities. This is both an advantage and a disadvantage for women. On one hand, attractiveness can be an additional resource for women, giving them additional power and status. Research shows that physically attractive women have higher status and power than less attractive women (Haas & Gregory 2005). On the other hand, women may feel exploited and inferior if they must use resources such as politeness and physical beauty that men do not need to deploy. Likewise, as noted in chapters 2 and 5, people have higher expectations for attractive women and to a lesser degree, attractive men, which are not really fair.

KINESICS

Kinesic behavior communicates messages of power and status via bodily positions, movements, gestures, and facial expressions (Andersen, 1984; see chapter 2). The way we move and position our bodies has a powerful, reciprocal relationship with power: Dominance is reflected in kinesic behavior, and kinesic behavior produces perceptions of dominance.

Positions

The positions in which people stand and sit reveal their relative power. Generally, powerful people occupy more space (see chapter 2). Remland (1982b) found that powerful people are more expansive while both sitting and standing. Observe people who hold their arms away from their body and their legs apart; these people exhibit power.

One particular example of an expansive body position is the arms-akimbo (hands-on-hips) position. Mehrabian (1968b) showed that people have a greater tendency to use the arms-akimbo position when addressing a low-status person than a high-status person. Likewise, Scheflen (1972) noted that individuals who hook their thumbs in their belt or use the arms-akimbo position are asserting dominance. Henley (1977) cited research studies in which receivers characterize the arms-akimbo position as a bossy and imperious behavior.

Relaxation is another power cue. Generally, higher-status individuals are more relaxed. This is probably due to the fact that those of higher power can afford to relax, whereas the weak must remain watchful (Andersen, 2008; Burgoon, Buller, & Woodall, 1996; Prisbell, 1982). Research confirms that when two strangers meet, the more relaxed individual is of higher status (Mehrabian, 1971a; Mehrabian & Friar, 1969). Likewise, high-status listeners are more relaxed than low-status listeners. Mehrabian (1969, 1972) reported that the degree of reclining and the asymmetry of limbs are important correlates of high status among seated individuals, and that rocking movements and leg and foot movements are cues emitted by high-status individuals when standing. These cues are in marked contrast to the extremely submissive cues of bodily rigidity and symmetry, such as soldiers are required to exhibit while standing at attention (Mehrabian, 1976). Similarly, people are most relaxed when interacting with a person of low status, moderately relaxed when interacting with a person of equal status, and least relaxed with a person of high status (Mehrabian, 1968a, 1968b, 1972). Recent research suggests that some studies associate relaxation with power, while other studies suggest that potency and power is the result of more active, energetic behavior. Sometimes a tense, erect posture is perceived as proud and confident rather than nervous or polite (Hall et al., 2005). Context evidently is very important in attributions about power.

As mentioned, a kinesic cue associated with higher status is limb asymmetry, which is extending the arms or legs askew (LaFrance & Mayo, 1978; Mehrabian, 1972, 1976). Superiors have the prerogative to sprawl, put their feet up, stretch, and drape their arms over the back of a chair. Leaning is another kinesic status marker. High-status individuals can lean back and appear relaxed, whereas low-status individuals must sit erect. Mehrabian (1972) maintained that status is conveyed by the expansive position, a set of high-status behaviors char-

Dominance and submission are often communicated by posture and position.

acterized by a backward leaning trunk as well as other cues. Henley (1977) asserted that dominant persons have the freedom to lean forward to express negative opinions, whereas subordinates should lean forward only to ingratiate themselves or to express positiveness. Carney et al. (2005) reported that high-power people are perceived to lean forward more than those with low power. Remland (1981) found that higher-status individuals can behave in a more relaxed and inattentive fashion than those of lower status. It is not unusual during an interaction for superiors to lean back in their chairs and to look around the room while they appear to be listening.

Several other kinesic behaviors signal power and dominance. Scheflen (1972) suggested that a sideways head tilt is a submissive posture. Carney et al. (2005) found that upward tilt is a low-power behavior whereas holding the head erect signals dominance. Similarly, Mast and Hall (2004) established that upward head tilts are judged as signs of submissiveness and downward head tilts as dominance cues, at least for women. Mehrabian and Friar (1969) found that closed, as opposed to open, arm positions are associated with higher status, at least for females. Recent studies report that open body positions are believed to be indicants of power and dominance and are actually associated with increased power (Carney, Hall, & LeBeau, 2005; Hall et al., 2005). Mehrabian (1971a) maintained that because standing is less relaxed than sitting, seated positions are high-status positions. Perhaps this explains why conventional etiquette requires people to stand in the presence of a superior.

Movements

Movement patterns also are associated with status and power. Higher-status persons have access to more people and locations and can engage in more invasive behaviors than lower-status persons (Carney et al., 2005; Mehrabian, 1971a). Indeed, it is difficult to gain access to politicians, executive officers, and celebrities, even though these individuals typically have access to their followers. Another action that conveys status is going first through a door. Traditionally, the higher-status person is permitted to enter first (Goffman, 1967). But allowing someone to enter first can also be an act of politeness and respect, as when a man opens a door for a woman and follows her through it. This commonplace act is a source of confusion in a world where power relationships are changing. Some women object to having a door opened for them because it implies their weakness or lack of equality. Most women, however, view it as polite behavior.

Actions that help others but require effort are called inconvenience displays. These behaviors communicate both respect and low status. Serving another person, walking someone to the door, and helping someone find a lost item are all behaviors typically performed by persons of lower status but are also perceived as polite and respectful acts. Morris (1977) maintained that low-ranking individuals must lower their bodies in the presence of a high-ranked person. However, it is also customary to rise in the presence of a high-status person. This kinesic contradiction may cause confusion among low-status people and is often resolved by placing the high-status person in a seated but elevated position with her or his inconvenienced and uncomfortable subordinates standing around—take, for example, a judge in a courtroom or a queen on a throne.

Pacing is a submissive behavior, which connotes waiting for a high-status person or being imprisoned, like a tiger in the zoo. Mehrabian (1976) suggested that pacing, even the relaxed sort of pacing done by college lecturers, indicates distress, avoidance, and low status. Pacing may imply an attempt to remove oneself from the environment, thus signaling submissiveness.

Gestures

Research shows that increased gestures, especially broad gestures, are believed to be powerful, dominant, and displayed by emergent leaders (Carney et al., 2005; Hall et al., 2005, Henley, 1977), though there is little objective difference between the gestures of high- and low-status people independent of talk time. Steepling, a gesture where the fingertips are raised together, is perceived as a confident, smug, and proud gesture associated with professionals and other high-status individuals (Henley, 1977). Pointing is a high-status, directive gesture that is often perceived as rude or excessively dominant. Pointing at someone is a gesture that Scheflen (1972) suggested is an act of spatial intrusion, which often occurs in escalating verbal con-

flicts that have the potential to end in acts of physical violence. Remland (1981) argued that pointing is an intrusion that communicates disrespect for another's body and can be used only by a high-status person. Pointing directions is also highly dominant—but not necessarily disrespectful. According to Henley (1977), directing another person from a distance is a prerogative reserved for authority figures.

Pointing is a high-status directive gesture that is often perceived as rude or excessively dominant.

Pointing is a primary nonverbal control behavior used to "order" another person (Scheflen, 1972; Siegel, Friedlander, & Heatherington, 1992). Dominant persons can direct others gesturally by pointing, beckoning, or halting their subordinates. Self-adaptor or self-touching gestures are perceived to be associated with low status, low power, and anxiety (see chapter 7; Carney et al., 2005; Hall et al., 2005).

Facial Expressions

The face communicates emotional and affective states better than any other part of the body (Andersen, 1984; Andersen & Guerrero, 1998b). In fact, the face actually evolved as an affective communication channel. Facial expressions are evident in all primate species, including humans (Mitchell & Maple, 1985) and often they convey messages of dominance and submission. People believe that more frequent and intense facial expressions are more likely to be displayed by powerful people and, in fact, studies show that facial expression is associated with objective power (Hall et al., 2005).

Smiling is usually an appeasement gesture among both humans and nonhuman primates. But no simple relationship exists between status and smiling. Among primates, smiling is a submissive gesture often displayed by a prostrate animal to appease a dominant aggressor. Considerable research suggests that smiling is perceived as appeasement, subordination, and submission (Hall et al., 2005; Hall, Horgan, & Carter, 2002; Henley, 1977; Keating, 1985). Smiles also communicate responsiveness, warmth, cooperativeness, and docility. Not surprisingly, women smile considerably more than men (see chapter 5). In a study by Kennedy and Camden (1983), smiling women were more likely to be interrupted than smiling men, indicating that female smiles are seen as a uniquely submissive cue. Women smiled significantly more than men when taking their speaking turn, evidently using the smile as an apology for taking their turn or as an act of submission (Kennedy & Camden, 1983). This sex difference probably reflects women's traditionally submissive status, as well as their ability to nurture and provide comfort and interpersonal warmth to others. Smiling functions as both a submissive cue and an intimacy cue (see chapter 9) and in some situations can show power.

Several studies describe contexts in which smiling can alternatively connote submissiveness or power. There are times when laughing or smiling can signify power. In adversarial situations (such as arguments, debates, or courtroom proceedings), smiling ridicules the claims of another and suggests that the argument should not be taken seriously (Remland, 1982a). Likewise, sarcastic smiles and disrespectful giggles may be used by a high-status but not a low-status person. In presidential debates, George W. Bush, Al Gore, and John Kerry could be seen sarcastically or smugly smiling at each other's claims. The effect was to politely and nonverbally dispute the opponent's claim. As Burgoon, Buller, and Woodall (1996) pointed out, sometimes nonverbal cues express sentiments that would be inappropriate or impolite to express verbally. Despite the fact that smiling is usually perceived as submissive, a subset of studies suggests it is perceived as conveying power (Hall et al., 2005). Surprisingly, despite these perceptions, the most recent meta-analysis (Hall et al., 2005) reveals no difference in smiling between powerful and less powerful people.

Other facial expressions more clearly communicate power and status. Scheflen (1972) argued that a protruded jaw is a masculine dominance expression. Henley (1977) maintained that the jutting chin, accompanied by overhanging eyebrows, a frown, drawn muscles, and the unwavering stare, constitute the stern face of authority. After observing that lowered eyebrows were a dominance and status display among nonhuman primates, Keating, Mazur, and Segall (1977) showed subjects two photographs of nearly identical faces—the only difference being that in one photograph the eyebrows were raised and in the other they were lowered. Subjects overwhelmingly selected the photographs with lowered brows as manifesting more dominance. Considerable research suggests that lowered brows are dominant, threatening signals in both human and nonhuman primates (Keating, 1985). A recent study and meta-analysis suggests that raised brows are generally perceived as submissive (Hall et al., 2005; Mast & Hall, 2004a). Conversely the "win face" or "plus face," consisting of raised eyebrows, raised chin, open eyes, and a smug expression, is a common preadolescent dominance expression (Henley, 1977; Zivin, 1982). Koehler et al. (1981) describe a facial expression that is commonly used by supervisors who are trying to refrain themselves from verbally berating a delinquent employee: A reddened face and furrowed brow, in addition to tightened shoulders, nonverbally convey control and dominance. In general angry expressions are associated with power, whereas fearful or sad faces are associated with low power (Carney et al., 2005).

A comparative study of politicians in both France and the United States reveals that facial expressions are crucial to voters' perceptions of dominance in both countries (Masters & Sullivan, 1989). It appears that a leader's dominance is a function of strong, joyful, and interested facial expressions and an absence of confused or fearful ones. Candidates who convey a sense of strength, happiness, and connectedness to voters are perceived as powerful and dominant, whereas candidates who exhibit confusion and fear are perceived as weak.

The manner in which each one of us employs facial expressions signals our power and status. Although exaggerated signs of displeasure such as boredom or disgust emphasize disagreement and disrespect for another individual, these expressions are associated with power (Carney et al., 2005; Remland, 1982a). Henley (1977) maintained that the prohibition or regulation of another person's facial expressions is a dominant move used to subordinate others. Children are frequently told, "don't stare, don't pout, and don't be angry," although they are permitted to cry (Henley, 1977). Controlling another's kinesic behavior can be a real power trip because it increases the subordinate's tension and anxiety (Buck, 1982). By contrast, facial expressiveness is associated with greater power (Carney et al., 2005).

Although subordinates are prohibited from showing certain facial expressions to higher-status persons, in general, some studies suggest low-status persons must be more facially responsive to high-status people. Hottenstein (1978) found that high-status persons emitted the same facial expressions to both high- and low-status recipients but that low-status persons showed more facial expressions to people of higher status than persons of their own rank. Head nods, according to a recent meta-analysis, are believed to be displayed by high-power people (Hall et al., 2005); but the same study showed no objective difference in the frequency of nodding between high- and low-power people. Other research suggests that head nods are perceived as submissive but warm behavior (see chapter 8) more commonly employed by lower-status people, particularly when interacting with a high-status person (Hellweg-Larsen, Cunningham, Carrico, & Pergram, 2004). This is consistent with the idea that kinesic responsiveness is required of low-status individuals, perhaps as a way to signal attentiveness and interest.

OCULESICS

The study of oculesics has shown that eye contact, or gaze, can communicate attentiveness, warmth, intimacy, control, power, and a number of other messages.

Generally, recipients of prolonged gazes perceive the looker to be more dominant than recipients of brief gazes (Thayer, 1969). This perception may have early origins, because direct gaze is a fairly universal dominance display for nonhuman primates in primitive societies—as it is in contemporary human societies (Burgoon & Saine, 1978; Carney et al., 2005; Ellsworth, Carlsmith, & Henson, 1972; LaFrance & Mayo, 1978). Research has shown that when senders increase eye contact, receivers perceive them to be more confident, effective, and of higher status (Aguinis & Henle, 2001: Cook, 1979; Hall et al. 2005; Ridgeway, Berger, & Smith, 1985; Tessler & Sushelsky, 1978).

Some studies found that people with dominant personalities employ more gaze (Fromme & Beam, 1974; Kendon & Cook, 1969; Rosa & Mazur, 1979; Strongman & Chapness, 1968), although neither Crouch and Koll (1979) nor a recent meta-analysis (Hall et al., 2005) found any relationship between objective power and gaze. People who are self-abasing and lack self-esteem tend to look downward and sideways during conversations more than their higher-esteem counterparts (Libby & Yanklevich, 1973).

Averting eye contact at key moments in a conversation may signal submissiveness, especially in women. Similarly, blinking frequently during conversations implies weakness and submissiveness (Mehrabian, 1971a). Kennedy and Camden (1983) reported that during a group discussion, women were interrupted significantly more often than men when they did not look at their conversation partner. Lamb (1981) found that women were also more likely to avert gaze during simultaneous attempts to speak first in a group. Men often gain access to the floor through the use of increased gaze, which is perceived as a powerful, dominant behavior. Averted gaze also accompanies dysfluencies, such as fragmented sentences and vocalized pauses (Cegala, Alexander, & Sokovitz, 1979), which reduce the fluency and credibility of a speaker's message.

Social status can be determined by who looks at whom. Argyle (1975) contends that individuals who receive gaze are perceived as the most powerful group members. Research shows that lower-status persons are more likely to look at persons of higher status (Burroughs, Schultz, & Autrey, 1973; Carney et al., Exline, Ellyson, & Long, 1975; Exline & Fehr, 1979; Mehrabian, 1971a; Mehrabian & Friar, 1969). This pattern is more pronounced if the high-status person shows approval (Efran, 1968; Fugita, 1974). Similarly, subjects low in assertiveness exhibit longer-duration gaze than highly assertive subjects (Alexander, 1980). In a study of a military organization, cadets who paid visual attention to low-status persons were rated lower in status (Exline et al., 1975). This finding suggests that people do not feel obligated to look at a lower-status person and may actually lose status by doing so. So, lower-status, less-dominant persons must remain visually attentive, particularly as listeners, whereas high-status individuals have the prerogative to ignore others.

The power–eye contact relationship during conversations and speeches is much clearer. Higher-status persons look more when speaking and less when listening than lower-status persons (Aguinis & Henle, 2001; Carney et al., 2005; Exline et al., 1975; Exline & Fehr, 1979; LaFrance & Mayo, 1978; Patterson, 1983). Exline et al. (1975) developed an index of visual power called the dominance ratio that is computed by dividing the length of time spent looking when listening (a

These two women are both displaying aggression and power, one actively and one passively.

polite, submissive behavior) by the length of time spent looking when speaking (a bold, dominant behavior). Lower dominance-ratio scores indicate more dominance. Research shows that people with a control orientation have lower dominance ratios, indicating that their behavior reflects their orientation (see Fehr & Exline, 1987). High-status individuals have both the ability and prerogative to maintain visual attentiveness while speaking but are not obligated to reciprocate eye contact when listening.

PROXEMICS

The interpersonal distances and spatial arrangements that occur during interactions are important indicators of power and status. "Getting in someone's face," "invading someone's space," "keeping one's distance," "and "calling someone out," are expressions that reveal the relationship between proxemics and power.

Interpersonal Distance

Most of the research on interpersonal distance and status is consistent; we provide higher-status individuals with more personal space. Mehrabian's (1969) summary of early research in this area concluded, "The distance between two communicators is positively correlated with their status discrepancy" (p. 371). Likewise, Argyle (1975) reported that "the only direct connection between dominance or status and spatial behavior is the deference shown to high-status people by keeping at a distance from them" (p. 308). Dean, Willis, and Hewitt (1975) demonstrated that interaction distance is greater when people initiate an interaction with a superior than with a peer. The initiated distance with a subordinate does not differ from peer interactions. Moreover, as the status differential becomes greater, the interaction distance increases even more (Dean, Willis, & Hewitt, 1975). One study reported that commuters at a train station accorded taller, higher-status people more space than their shorter, lower-status counter-parts (Caplan & Goldman, 1981). Compared to high-status people, lower-status people fail to defend their personal space (Bethel & Bethel, 1974). In a study by Strube and Werner (1984), type-A (control-oriented, time-pressed) individuals maintained larger personal spaces and exerted more control, regardless of their assigned role in the experiment, than type-B (more laid-back) individuals. Clearly, more space is afforded to persons of high status and high control.

Eisenberg and Smith (1971) stated that the power to defend one's own terri-tory and the right to invade another person's space are certain signs of dominance and prestige. "For a subordinate to enter the boss's office without his consent would be a clear breach of etiquette, but it is expected that the boss will saunter into the realm of any subordinate without there being the slightest complaint" (Eisenberg and Smith, 1971, p. 103). Similarly, Goldhaber's (1974) second and third rule of organizational status suggested: The higher up in the organization, the bet-ter protected your territory is. The higher up in the organization, the easier it is to invade the territory of lower-status personnel. These principles were echoed by Henley (1977) and Remland (1981). In an experiment by Leffler, Gillespie, and Conaty (1982), participants temporarily assigned to high-status roles used more space with both their bodies and possessions than did low-status participants. These findings suggest that subordinates must be careful not to violate these prox-emic rules. Limited violations may create perceptions of increased status, but obvi-ous violations may result in overt sanctions against the offending employee.

In a study of interviewee behavior, Patterson and Sechrest (1970) showed that interviewees were perceived as most dominant at a distance of four feet, least dominant at a distance of eight feet, and moderately dominant at a distance of two and six feet. Evidently, increasingly closer distances convey more dominance until excessive closeness is perceived as a violation. The result is a curvilinear relationship between dominance and distance, with close but appropriate dis-tances conveying the most dominance.

Finally, evidence suggests that the control of interpersonal distance resides with the high-status person, who can choose to be intimate or aloof. In a study of dominance and distance, Dean et al. (1975) concluded that a superior can choose a formal or an intimate distance. A subordinate must choose a formal distance. Henley (1977) summarized this research: "The proper distance to be kept in an interaction is under the control of the more powerful person" (p. 33). The preroga-tive to invade others' space clearly lies with people of high power and status (Car-ney et al., 2005). Although most studies show that power is associated with greater interpersonal distances, a meta-analysis found that closer distances are perceived as more powerful; moreover, powerful people do actually interact at closer distances (Hall et al., 2005). What is important to understand is the core principal of proxemics and power: Powerful people have the prerogative to estab-lish close or far distances from other people.

Body Orientation

Another critical proxemic power variable is the degree of body orientation between two communicators. More-direct orientations reduce the angle between two communicators; a face-to-face orientation is the most direct. Likewise, the angle of leaning (forward or backward) plays a role as well. In a study by Mehrabian (1968b), standing subjects maintained a more direct shoulder orientation to a high-status addressee than to a low-status addressee. Mehrabian (1968a) reported that body orientation is least direct toward women with low status and most direct toward disliked men of high status. In a study by Jorgenson (1975), equal-status dyads assumed a significantly more direct angle of orientation than did discrepant-status pairs; low-status pairs assumed a less direct angle of orientation than high-status pairs. Burgoon and Saine (1978) asserted that in group communication, the individual who is faced by most people probably has the most influence. Recent research suggests that powerful people are perceived to more directly orient their body toward other people (Carney et al., 2005; Hall et al., 2005), but like the research on interpersonal distance the results are somewhat inconsistent. Parallel to the research on distance, the powerful and dominant have the prerogative to orient either toward or away from other interactants.

HAPTICS

Haptics, the study of tactile communication, is both the most intimate and the most powerful form of nonverbal communication. Touch has the power to repel, disgust, insult, threaten, console, reassure, love, and arouse (Andersen, 1984; Prisbell, 1982).

Dominance and control are sometimes communicated through the initiation of touch, although touch is more likely to be perceived as an immediacy cue (see chapter 8). Touchers are perceived as more dominant and assertive than recipients of touch (Burgoon & Saine, 1978; Carney et al, 2005; Hall et al., 2005; Major, 1981; Major & Heslin, 1982). The person who initiates touch controls the interaction. The more powerful person determines whether both parties touch and what forms of touch are acceptable (Burgoon & Saine, 1978). Some specific touch behaviors indicate dominance or submission. Scheflen (1972) stated that direct poking with the index finger is a dominant, controlling act. In contrast, a person who "cuddles" to the touch of another is perceived as submissive (Henley, 1977). Likewise, powerful people are more likely to initiate handshakes than less powerful people (Carney et al., 2005).

A series of studies show that, in general, people of objectively high status touch more than those of low status (Henley, 1973; Leffler, Gillespie, & Conaty, 1982). Remland (1981) reported that in organizations superiors touch subordinates considerably more than subordinates touch superiors. Similarly, Street and Buller (1988) found that physicians socially touch patients significantly more than the reverse, signaling their superior status. However, one study (Goldstein & Jeffords, 1981), conducted in a state legislature, reports the reverse pattern: Lower-status lawmakers touched older, higher-status lawmakers more than the reverse, perhaps because they were of a less-formal generation than their seniors. The general pattern of the early results is summarized nicely by Henley (1977), who stated, "When there's a disparity of status, we observe the higher-status person to have more touch privilege than the lower-status person, who is covertly forbidden to touch at all" (p. 107). Despite these studies a recent meta-analysis of this entire body of literature shows that interpersonal touch has no association with actual power (Hall et al., 2005).

Several specific tactile behaviors are associated with dominance and power. Jones (1994) reports several studies of romantic couples that show that one partner will touch or put her or his arm around the other partner to signal possessiveness or togetherness. Interestingly, this is often done with the dominant hand (right for right-handers, left for left-handers). Siegel, Friedlander, and Heatherington (1992) reported that one touch behavior, restraining another person, is perceived as a highly controlling behavior. Obviously, any touch that constrains another person's movement is a highly dominant and controlling act. Do not be surprised if relational partners react negatively to such control.

In his book *The Right Touch,* Jones (1994) identified four progressive touch strategies that constitute power moves in interpersonal relationships (see also Jones & Yarbrough, 1985). The first is the *affection-to-compliance sequence*, in which one person softens up another with affectionate touch and then touches the person again while making a request. Jones (1994) provides this example:

> A couple was watching television together on a couch. The female first cuddled against the male. A minute later the male kissed the female. Several minutes later, the commercials came on, and the male put his arm around the female and said, "Will you get me some water, sweetie?" (p. 125)

She complied.

A second progressive touch-power sequence is the *seduction-and-rejection game* (Jones, 1994). This occurs when one person initiates flirtatious touch and then rejects the other's reciprocal approach. For example, a woman blows in her date's ear. When he attempts to engage in intimate touch, she says, "I'm not ready for that kind of relationship."

A third progressive touch-power sequence is the *power-matching move* (Jones, 1994). In this sequence, one person initiates a power touch. For instance, one male may punch another in the arm while saying, "How ya doin',?" creating a power discrepancy. The receiver of the punch then tries to equalize the relationship by punching the initiator back while saying, "Fine, how are you?"

The final touch-power sequence is the *irritate-and-mollify sequence* (Jones, 1994), in which one person initially employs a demanding or aggressive touch that is rejected because it interrupts or irritates the other; the initiator then follows up with an affectionate touch in an attempt to compensate for the first touch. A slap on a friend's butt followed by a hug or mock wrestling followed by a kiss are examples of these power sequences.

Not surprisingly, for both men and women greater power and dominance are associated with more sexual behavior (Browning, Kessler, Hatfield, & Choo, 1999). As in so many areas of life, more powerful and dominant people get what they want—including more sex.

Touch is a powerful form of nonverbal behavior. Although it can convey power, the very power of touch makes it dangerous to use outside of close relationships. Certainly, intimidating touch is not particularly effective and may provoke retaliatory touch or even legal action.

VOCALICS

Status and dominance are reflected in the way we use our voices. Studies show that social status can be detected accurately from paralinguistic cues. Harms (1961) reported that vocal cues enable listeners to distinguish among individuals who had been objectively rated for status on the Hollingshead social status index, a standard measure of status. Moe (1972) successfully replicated Harms's findings and extended them by showing that certain vocal characteristics are perceived to reflect high status and credibility. Vocal characteristics associated with higher social status and power include clearer articulation, fewer "uhs" and "ums," fewer pauses, sharper enunciation of consonants, more vocal intonation, and the ability to interrupt successfully (Argyle, 1975; Carney et al., 2005, Hall et al., 2005). Vocal variation as opposed to more monotonic vocal behavior has a strong association with both perceived and actual dominance and status (Hall et al., 2005).

Two studies have examined receivers' ability to judge dominance from vocal cues with limited success. Research by Scherer (1972) showed that listeners are able to judge dominant personalities from vocal cues in German speakers. However, Markel (1969) reported nonsignificant correlations between listeners' perceptions of vocal dominance and dominant personality types from the Minnesota Multiphasic Personality Index (MMPI). Thus, the voice is not necessarily a reliable indicant of actual dominance.

Can people alter their vocal behavior to create perceptions of more (or less) power? One experiment suggested that perceptions of leadership in women continually increase as vocal rate increases (Stang, 1973). Burgoon and Saine (1978) also noted that a fast vocal rate, high volume, and full resonance carry the sound of authority. Low pitch is also a vocal power cue (Hall et al., 2005), whereas high pitch is often associated with childish immaturity and submissiveness.

One of the most robust findings in the vocal power literature is a strong association of loudness with power and dominance, whether it is perceived power or actual power (Hall et al., 2005; Scheflen, 1972) Similarly, Mehrabian (1972) suggested that low speech volume is a metaphorical sign of weakness. Remland (1982a) argued that talking loudly is one of a cluster of behaviors that signals disrespect for another but communicates physical dominance.

Several studies have examined the relationship of laughter and power. Henley (1977) maintained that laughter is a behavior that subordinates exhibit to persons higher in status, but a recent meta-analysis shows just the opposite; laughter is perceived as dominant, but there is little concrete evidence that dominant people actually laugh more (Hall et al., 2005). Depending on the situation and relationship, laughing can reflect nervousness or submission, yet at times laughter can be an extremely dominant behavior.

Tone of voice is extraordinarily important in interpersonal interaction. One study reported that women use more competent, dominant tones of voice when communicating with their bosses as compared to communicating with their peers or subordinates, probably in an attempt to impress. Men use their most competent, dominant voice with peers, perhaps reflecting competitiveness with those of the same rank (Steckler & Rosenthal, 1985). Recent research has shown that variation in the fundamental frequency of the voice is a vocal measure of dominance that is processed unconsciously by receivers. An analysis of 19 presidential debates—including Kennedy/Nixon, Carter/Ford, Reagan/Carter, Reagan/Mondale, Bush/Dukakis, Clinton/Bush, Clinton/Dole, and Bush/Gore—found that the candidate with the more dominant fundamental frequency in his voice won the most popular votes in each election (Gregory & Gallagher, 2002). This suggests that subtle vocal cues are associated with perceptions of power and leadership.

CHRONEMICS

Our culture is extremely time-conscious. As discussed in chapter 3, we view time as a precious commodity (Andersen, 1984). The American slogan "Time is money" is indicative of how we treasure time. We try to save time, to spend it on worthwhile activities, and to avoid wasting it. As with anything valuable, the possession of time is correlated with power and status, and this association has significant communicative implications.

Waiting Time

Like money and property, the rich, the powerful, and the dominant control time. By contrast, the lives of the less privileged are filled with waiting—in crowded health-care clinics and in long lines for unemployment checks, welfare, food stamps, and temporary employment. Waiting time decreases as status increases, and the super rich are provided with luxurious facilities on the rare occasions when they must wait (Henley, 1977). Obtaining or appropriating others' time is also more easily achieved by people of high status. In many parts of the country, the person who can get a doctor's appointment on short notice is either very important or near death (Huseman, Lahiff, & Hatfield, 1976). Letting people "cool their heels" by forcing them to wait in an office is a power play that is quite effective in asserting one's authority.

Talk Time

Power and status also affect the chronemic patterns of talk time, a resource that is scarce and valuable across many interaction situations. Powerful, dominant individuals will talk more (Kendon & Cook, 1969) and hold the floor for a greater proportion of the time than will a low-dominance person (Rogers & Jones, 1975). High-status persons communicate more frequently and speak longer in group discussions (Hurwitz, Zander, & Hymovitch, 1968; Remland, 1981; Stephan, 1952; Weins, Thompson, Matarazzo, Matarazzo, & Saslow, 1965). When lower-status individuals finally do participate, their communications are more frequently directed toward those of higher status (Hurwitz et al., 1968) and often contain questions. These behaviors provide additional opportunity for high-status persons to regain the floor and spend even more time talking.

Not only do high-status individuals engage in more talk time, they interrupt more often as well (Burgoon & Saine, 1978; Hall et al., 2005; Henley, 1977; Weins et al., 1965). Even experimental subjects temporarily assigned to higher-status positions interrupt more than those assigned to low-status positions (Leffler et al., 1982). Individuals with dominant personalities interrupt more frequently (Rogers & Jones, 1975). This interruption pattern is prevalent in business organizations, where subordinates may not interrupt a boss but must immediately cede the floor when the superior interrupts them (Henley, 1977).

Higher-status people influence the actual speech patterns of lower-status individuals. Koehler et al. (1981) claimed that response latency is shorter for a subordinate, whereas a superior may take her or his time in answering. Furthermore, the length of one's speaking turn is affected by the relative status of one's interaction partner. According to Mehrabian (1968a):

> Utterance duration, for example, is a very stable quality in a person's speech, about 30 seconds long on the average. But when someone talks to a partner whose status is higher than his own, the more the high-status person nods his head the longer the speaker's utterances become. If the high-status person changes his own customary speech pattern toward longer or shorter utterances, the lower-status person will change his own speech in the same direction. (p. 54)

Mehrabian (1968a) asserts that a subordinate who does not follow the customary low-status pattern will tend to be negatively perceived by a superior.

Greetings and Meetings

Initiating or terminating a conversation is also a prerogative of the powerful, high-status person (Mehrabian, 1971a), who dictates the chronemic patterns of the interaction as well. The more powerful individual will decide when the meeting will take place, the length of the interaction, and how much time is devoted to each discussion topic (Henley, 1977). Interactions are usually terminated nonverbally, although the high-status individual can explicitly indicate through verbal communication that an interaction is over.

Work Time

Flexibility of one's work schedule is associated with status, as it symbolizes control over time. Lower-status, hourly workers are regulated by a time clock, whereas those in higher-status, managerial positions can control time by setting their own hours. The ability to control the time of others further increases one's status and power. Henley (1977) stated, "Some people have the power to annex other people's time, and the more they can annex, the more powerful they become; the more powerful they are, the more of others' time they can annex" (p. 49).

The high-status person's time in an organization is considered more valuable than that of the low-status person (Koehler et al., 1981; Remland, 1981). Higher-status individuals have the freedom to waste the time of others, yet they expect others to strictly adhere to their schedules (Goldhaber, 1974). Punctuality is demanded of subordinates, whereas superiors have the prerogative to arrive late to meetings (Koehler et al., 1981; Henley, 1977; Remland, 1981). Hurt, Scott, and McCroskey (1978) stated that waiting time in academic settings is associated with status. Increased tardiness is a perk of higher rank. A myth exists at many universities that requires one to wait longer for a full professor than an associate professor, and to wait longer for an associate professor than an assistant professor. Although no such rule really exists, most undergraduates can recite these rules verbatim.

Spending Time

How an individual spends time conveys power and status within an organization. As Koehler et al. (1981) described:

> When members of an organization are willing to devote considerable time (including spare time) in meetings, on committees, developing contacts, and the like with the aim of influencing decisions, they are likely to have an effect. They provide scarce energy reserves; they may become major information sources; they are more likely to be present when something important is under consideration. (p. 197)

Additionally, the more an individual spends time with the boss, the more her or his organizational status increases (Huseman et al., 1976).

The irreversibility of time gives it inherent value, but the particular monetary worth that business organizations place on it has made time itself a status symbol. High-status organization members are awarded more control over time, and this power enables them to attain further power and prestige within the organization.

ENVIRONMENT

We are constantly under the influence of our physical surroundings. Environmental conditions can affect an individual's thoughts, emotions, and behavior in a variety of ways. Therefore, it is not surprising that organizational communication is greatly influenced by the setting in which it occurs. Surroundings can communicate directly by projecting a particular image; they can also regulate the quality and quantity of interpersonal or group communication (Andersen, 1984). Furthermore, various characteristics of the environment can be manipulated intentionally to express dominance and status.

Territory

As indicated previously, superior height is associated with power and status; thus, it is not surprising that the height of an individual's territory symbolizes her or his relative importance (Henley, 1977). Persons of greater social or organizational value are often referred to as "high-ups," whereas persons of lesser value are referred to as "underlings" (Brown, 1965). The design of most office buildings clearly demonstrates this hierarchy: "High-rise office buildings designed to be occupied by one corporation invariably set aside the top floors for the executive eche-

Large chairs, high ceilings, great views, and lofty locations communicate power and status.

lons, frequently with the president or chairman of the board and a few key assistants occupying the topmost or penthouse floor" (Mehrabian, 1976, p. 141). Sitting in a higher position also communicates superiority—suggesting perhaps a throne—and can be achieved by offering visitors very low, soft chairs, into which they sink (Morris, 1977). Similarly, being "up front" is a position of privilege and control. First-class airplane seats are up front; lower-class seating is to the rear (Brown, 1965). In the 1950s, African Americans throughout the South were required to sit in the back of the bus, which symbolized their subservient status and lack of equality. African Americans' refusal to sit in the back of the bus was an opening shot in the battle for civil rights, increasing power for people of color in American society.

The possession of a larger space or territory is a sign of power and status. The poor must live in cramped quarters in crowded cities, whereas the rich and powerful are able to escape high density by purchasing spacious accommodations (Zlutnick & Altman, 1972). Larger territory is also a function of status within the business organization; the most important executive usually has the largest office (Eisenberg & Smith, 1971; Mehrabian, 1976; Goldhaber, 1974; Huseman et al., 1976).

Quantity of space is not the only index of high status; the elite have quality environments as well (Goldhaber, 1974). The most desirable locations, such as an office with many windows or one next to the company president, signal importance within an organization (Eisenberg & Smith, 1971; Mehrabian, 1976), as does a convenient, reserved parking space (Huseman et al., 1976). A study by Haber (1982) revealed that in the classroom, dominant individuals are most likely to occupy the center seats, whereas marginal, less-dominant individuals sit on the periphery.

Not only do high-status, high-power people possess more and better quality space, they have the prerogative to invade the territory of the lower-status, as mentioned earlier (Burgoon, Buller, & Woodall, 1996; Henley, 1977; Mehrabian, 1971a). In addition to the exclusive right to invade the territory of others, high-power people have the ability to defend their own territory (Eisenberg & Smith, 1971; Goldhaber, 1974). Low power and low status in the office are indicated by the unprotected quality of open work pits or cubicles made from temporary partitions; by contrast, the "real" walls of a closed office blocked by a receptionist's desk provide effective protection from territory invasion (Goldhaber, 1974; Huseman et al., 1976).

Executive seclusion has many advantages, but it also has drawbacks. The inaccessibility of the elite results in isolation; indeed, it is lonely at the top (Mehrabian, 1976). Some executives attempt to overcome this isolation by taking occasional walks through their subordinates' dominion, but often they find that they have become so isolated that the subordinates become anxious, clam up, feel they're being evaluated, or otherwise exhibit avoidance behavior (Mehrabian, 1976). Another detrimental consequence of upper-echelon isolation is the creation of barriers to vital upward information flow. Mehrabian (1976) stated that "management consultants are often amazed at how little many senior executives know about fairly significant interoffice matters" (p. 143).

Seating Patterns

In chapter 3 we learned that certain seating arrangements lead to increased interaction. Group seating patterns can also be employed to express dominance and status nonverbally. Research shows that high-power individuals select the most focal position in a group, particularly the end seat at a table (Heckel, 1973; Sommer, 1967). Not only is a highly visual position positively correlated with increased interaction (Hearn, 1957; Ward, 1968), it also provides more control of interaction patterns. LaFrance and Mayo (1978) asserted that "leaders must be in a position where they can see and be seen by all. This allows for more direct attempts to influence others and more efficient monitoring of the responses" (p. 100).

Not surprisingly, persons who occupy focal positions, such as the end seat of a table, are perceived as leaders (Ward, 1968) and are more likely to be selected as forepersons of juries (Strodtbeck & Hook, 1961). According to Strodtbeck and Hook, "the jurors felt that there was some intrinsic 'propriety' about the foreman being at the head of the table" (1961, p. 400).

The seating pattern of followers is quite different from that of leaders. Individuals who wish to avoid interaction choose the least-focal positions. In an early study, Hare and Bales (1963) reported that persons who sit at the corners of rectangular tables tend to contribute least to the conversation. Additionally, Sommer (1961) noted that followers will sit as close as possible to the leader. Later research on seating patterns and relative status, however, has found that many people will not attain a close position to a higher-status person but instead sit far away, closer to peers, and face the high-status person directly (Lott & Sommer, 1967). Similar behavior was noted in a study of cafeteria seating patterns, in which individuals involved in a cooperative task chose seats that were corner to corner, whereas individuals involved in a competitive task sat opposite one another (Sommer, 1965). Possibly, the more distant position with visual contact represents a challenge, a play for dominance through direct gaze.

ARTIFACTS

It should not be surprising that objects and possessions are viewed as status symbols. Half a century ago, before any research on the nonverbal communication of status and power was conducted, the suburban family of the 1950s knew that large houses, boats, and cars were symbols of success that connoted status and power.

Today, business and organizational leaders can be identified by the artifacts that accompany their status. Korda (1983) related a story about an owner of a company being wooed by a larger conglomerate. The conglomerate offered him everything: stock, a lifetime seat on the board of directors, a plane, and a limousine. But he turned it all down. It was only after offering him a couple of floors in a new building with a private elevator, a private bath and shower, and a heated towel rack that he finally accepted! Koehler et al. (1981) listed organizational status symbols, which included special parking places, luxury company cars, and office furnishings.

Considerable status revolves around the possession and use of communication devices such as blackberries, cell phones, and laptops. In an age when the telephone is often an environmental invader, a secretary, an answering service, or voice mail increases an individual's control and dominance. When one executive secretary reaches another executive secretary, a status battle of who speaks first ensues. High status requires the other person to come on the line first (Morris, 1977).

Briefcases are another organizational status symbol (Korda, 1983; Morris, 1977). Bulky briefcases are a sign of low status, because only peons have to lug around paperwork. Slimmer briefcases are much higher in status because high-status individuals need carry only vital papers. The ultimate status symbol, of course, is no briefcase at all; when you possess real power, all they want is you (Korda, 1983). As humorous as some of these examples are, status symbols have real meaning to high-power individuals. A sudden loss of these hard-won status symbols would cause feelings of hurt and reprimand.

IMMEDIACY

Up to this point, we have examined nonverbal status and power cues individually. Obviously, in real interaction, nonverbal cues are sent and received simultaneously through multiple channels and perform multiple functions. Most perceptions of status and power are the result of the receiver's gestalt perception of clusters of nonverbal cues rather than single, isolated behaviors.

The most important multichanneled construct is nonverbal immediacy. In chapter 8, immediacy behaviors were defined as clusters of cues that simultaneously communicate approach as opposed to avoidance, signal availability for communication, increase sensory stimulation and arousal, and communicate interpersonal warmth in most relationships (Andersen, Andersen, & Jensen, 1979; Andersen, 1985). Research suggests that persons of high status and power have all the options for increasing or decreasing immediacy (Andersen, 1985; Carney et al., 2005; Duran et al., 1979). Remember, high-status persons have the prerogative to increase or decrease distance, touch, and eye contact. Additionally, Mehrabian (1971) contended, "Generally, the option to increase or decrease immediacy by initiating or terminating a conversation is left to the person of high status" (p. 32). In his summary of research on power and dominance, Patterson (1983) stated:

> The pattern of findings related to encoded power and dominance suggests that high status individuals have greater flexibility in the instrumental use of nonverbal involvement than low status individuals. Thus, a high status person can typically relate to others with variable involvement and not risk the censure or disapproval a low status person would. (p. 103)

This is particularly true for initiating increased immediacy. Likewise, a movement toward intimacy is typically initiated by the person of higher status (Brown, 1965; Carney et al., 2005; Mehrabian, 1971a).

In addition to the general rule that high-status individuals have all of the immediacy options, several other findings are of interest. A study reported by Hurwitz et al. (1968) concluded that individuals with little power generally perceive they are liked more by those with more power than the situation actually justifies. Those with little power evidently reduce the threat associated with the powerful by distorting their perceptions of powerful people. Furthermore, it is possible that powerful people soften their power manipulations through increased immediacy behaviors, which lead low-status individuals to perceive they are liked.

High-status individuals use immediacy to dominate others in several ways. In a study by Geller, Goodstein, Silver, and Steinberg (1974), reducing immediacy by ignoring a person caused subjects to feel alone, withdrawn, and shy and to rate themselves less favorably than control subjects. Druckman, Rozelle, and Baxter (1982) argued that immediacy cues are interpreted quite differently in competitive as opposed to cooperative situations. In competitive settings, immediacy may be perceived as an attempt to intimidate or dominate. Burgoon and Saine (1978) reported that low-status people are likely to mirror the posture and gestures of high-status individuals, possibly in an effort to establish harmony and immediacy and to get "in sync" with the valued higher-status person. Finally, Kennedy and Camden (1983) showed that positive-affect displays help men avoid being interrupted and enable them to hold the floor. For women, however, positive affect serves as an invitation for men to interrupt them!

POWER PRINCIPLES

It is important to understand that power is always a relational construct. There can be no powerful people without powerless people. High status exists only in contrast to low status. Likewise, power is a fuzzy construct because power balances can change. Formal power can yield to informal power. Following are some power principles to keep in mind.

First, *assigned power does not equal actual power.* Organizations often produce covert power structures that have more real power than positions at the top of the organizational chart. In fact, subordinates often have far more power than they realize. Powerlessness is a state of mind that can be overcome with a change in actions and attitudes. Subordinates can organize and act collectively in their mutual interest. The power to quit, strike, or revolt resides in all subordinates. Short of acts of defiance, subordinates still have power options. Each individual has a range of power, jointly or separately. Nevertheless, although occasionally exceeding power latitudes may be advantageous, subordinates who continually challenge power and status nonverbally will irritate their superiors and usually be put in their place (Dean et al., 1975). By contrast, though, subordinates who display little or no nonverbal power relegate themselves to continuous powerlessness. Every subordinate must maintain a delicate balance between too little and too much power. A study by Remland (1982b) reported that subordinates who increase their nonverbal status displays also increase their perceived satisfaction with the superior and the organization. Low status is as much a self-inflicted phenomenon as one that is controlled by superiors. People who perceive they have more power or have more dominant personalities are most likely to express their true attitudes and emotions, perceive life as more rewarding than threatening, and experience more positive than negative emotions (Anderson & Berdahl, 2002; Berdahl & Martorana, 2006). Most people like to be in control of their lives, and these studies clearly indicate that more social power is associated with positive outcomes and emotions.

Second, *power and status are relationally based.* The rules of status and power are quite different for superiors, peers, and subordinates. As just described, the least number of options are available to the subordinate; exhibiting too much visible power is offensive and inappropriate to one's superiors. In peer relationships, however, one's latitude of options expands. Nonetheless, even among peers, too much visible power can make one seem arrogant, manipulative, greedy, or inappropriate. The latitude for peers may be greater, but sanctions still exist for consistently manifesting power inappropriate to one's position. Superiors have the widest latitudes, yet even CEOs, presidents, and dignitaries have limits on their power. Given that research shows powerful people tend to judge others more stereotypically and negatively (Brauer & Bourhis, 2006), powerful people need to remind themselves to be humble and respectful of those with less power.

Third, *power is paradoxical.* One paradox many women face in an organization is that many of their dominance or power behaviors are interpreted as something other than power (see chapter 5 for more on this issue). Loud, assertive women are still sometimes perceived as "bitchy" or "nagging," whereas men who engage in the same behavior are perceived as powerful. A study by Henley and Harmon (1985) revealed that when dominance behaviors are performed by women, they're perceived as sexual rather than dominant. These attributions deny dominance to women.

Fourth, *the less power individuals exhibit, the more power they actually have.* One study reports that when status differentials are reduced, either by decreasing the superior's nonverbal power displays or by increasing the subordinate's, the superior is rated more considerate and less aversive but no less effective (Remland, 1982b). Thus, superiors who show some nonverbal deference to subordinates may have more power in the long run by instilling satisfaction and loyalty in the subordinate. In any organization, where you stand in the power structure, who you communicate with, how much power they have, and what you can do within the appropriate behavioral parameters are essential factors in gaining and maintaining control.

Power is an interesting and elusive construct that is only beginning to be fully understood. Part of the elusiveness of power is that so much of it is conveyed nonverbally. In his classic review of power research, Berger (1985) stated:

> It can be argued that these nonverbal behaviors are more significant in determining the experience of power than are variables related to verbal content. One conclusion drawn here is that failure to take into account nonverbal behavior in the study of communication and power relationships is to doom oneself to study the tip of a very large iceberg. (p. 483)

Hopefully, this chapter has enabled you to examine a bit more of the iceberg. Future research will probe the depths of covert power that is expressed through nonverbal communication.

SUMMARY

Power and control are two of the most fundamental aspects of human behavior. Both animals and humans convey power and dominance primarily through nonverbal behavior. Prior to any verbal interaction, physical appearance communicates power and status. Our clothing broadcasts our status, wealth, fashion consciousness, and power. Formal dress, polished shoes, uniforms, and expensive basketball shoes all communicate power and leadership, as well as conformity. Very rich and high-status individuals can break the rules of dress. Some clothing, particularly women's clothing, severely restricts movement and creates subordination. Tallness and largeness also signal power and status.

Kinesic behavior sends messages of power and status through posture, position, gestures, and facial expressions. Powerful people use more space; for example, the arms-akimbo position is a particularly effective behavior for conveying power. Relaxation is usually a sign of dominance, whereas tension is a subordination display. Serving another person is a sign of subordination, as is lowering one's body or bowing in the presence of another. Larger, more frequent gestures generally communicate power, although pointing is often perceived as a powerful but rude behavior. Smiling is perceived as a submissive behavior in most circumstances, whereas a protruding jaw and lowered eyebrows, like the anger expression, communicate power. Happy, confident expressions are powerful, whereas fearful or confused expressions are subordinate.

People whose oculesic behavior includes more overall eye contact and staring are judged to be more powerful. Blinking and averting eye contact are signs of submissiveness. In groups, people are more likely to look at leaders and powerful people. High-status people look more while speaking and less when listening.

Proxemic behavior provides many cues of power and dominance. High-status people are accorded more personal space and have the prerogative to invade the space of others. Likewise, the higher people are in an organization, the more space they are afforded in terms of their office or car and at meetings. Subordinates directly face more-dominant individuals.

High-status and powerful people possess haptic freedom. They can choose to touch or not to touch other people. Low-status people have few touch prerogatives. The initiation of touch and restraining touch are signs of power, as are four touch behavioral sequences: the affection-to-compliance sequence, the seduction-and-rejection game, the power-matching move, and the irritate-and-mollify sequence. Touch is dangerous to use outside of close relationships.

Vocalic characteristics associated with power and status include clear articulation, vocal intonation, loudness, and deeper pitch. Research shows that faster-speaking individuals, particularly women, are more credible and powerful. Very high-pitched voices are associated with childish immaturity and submissiveness. Laughing is generally a subordination behavior. For example, lower-status individuals are expected to laugh at their superiors' jokes.

Power and status are related to chronemic behaviors, particularly in a time-conscious culture such as the United States, where time is money. Thus, low-status, but not high-status, individuals can be kept waiting. High-status people have greater access to talk time and interrupt more than low-status people. Powerful and high-status people can arrange meeting times and decide when a meeting will end. Flexibility of schedules is associated with high-status individuals, whereas lower-status individuals must punch clocks and be on time. For low-status people, spending time with higher-status people increases their power and status.

Environments can also convey power and status. Higher positions and larger territories are associated with greater power. Higher-status people have the right to invade the territories of others, but the reverse is not true. Power positions include the head of a table, the front of a room, and other, more visually focal locations.

Artifacts are some of the most important status symbols in today's materialistic culture. Modern communication technology, private parking spaces, and isolated offices are signs of status. The latest communication devices, expensive cars, jewelry, and slimmer briefcases are among the many objects that convey power and status.

Paradoxically, immediacy behaviors constitute their own form of power. Immediacy behaviors, which increase interpersonal closeness, are the prerogative of the powerful. Likewise, because other people value warmth and immediacy, immediacy behaviors enhance the power of an individual.

There are several principles associated with power: Assigned power does not equal actual power; power and status are relationally based; power is paradoxical; and the less power individuals exhibit, the more power they actually have.

References

Abbey, A., & Melby, C. (1986). The effects of nonverbal cues on perceptions of sexual intent. *Sex Roles, 15,* 283–298.

Acitelli, L. K., & Duck, S. W. (1987). Intimacy as the proverbial elephant. In D. Perlman & S. W. Duck (Eds.), *Intimate relationships: Development, dynamics, and deterioration* (pp. 297–308). Beverly Hills, CA: Sage.

Adams, G. R. (1977). Physical attractiveness research: Toward a developmental social psychology of beauty. *Human Development, 20,* 217–239.

Adams, G. R., & Read, D. (1983). Personality and social influence styles of attractive and unattractive college women. *Journal of Psychology, 114,* 151–157.

Adams, R. B., & Kleck, R. E. (2003). Perceived gaze direction and the processing of facial displays of emotion. *Psychological Science, 14,* 644–647.

Adams, R. B., & Kleck, R. E. (2005). Effects of direct and averted gaze on the perception of facially communicated emotion. *Emotion, 5,* 3–11.

Addington, D. W. (1968). The relationship of selected vocal characteristics to personality. *Speech Monographs, 35,* 492–505.

Afifi, W. A., & Johnson, M. L. (1993, November). *The nonverbal display of affection: Cross-sex interactions in bars.* Paper presented at the annual convention of the Speech Communication Association, Miami, FL.

Aguinis, H., & Henle, C. A. (2001). Effects of nonverbal behavior on perceptions of a female employee's power bases. *The Journal of Social Psychology, 141,* 537–549.

Aida, Y. (1993). Communication apprehension and power strategies in marital relationships. *Communication Reports, 6,* 116–121.

Aiello, J. R. (1976, April). *Effects of episodic crowding: A developmental perspective.* Paper presented at the Eastern Psychological Association Convention, New York, NY.

Aiello, J. R. (1987). Human spatial behavior. In D. Stokols & I. Altman (Eds.), *Handbook of environmental psychology* (Vol. 1, pp. 389–504). New York: Wiley.

Aiello, J. R., Epstein, Y. M., & Karlin, R. A. (1975, May). *Field experimental research on human crowding.* Paper presented at the Eastern Psychological Association Convention, New York, NY.

Aiken, L. R. (1963). The relationship of dress to selected measures of personality in undergraduate women. *Journal of Social Psychology, 59,* 119–128.

Albert, R. D., & Ah-Ha, I. (2004). Latino/Anglo-American differences in attributions to situations involving touch and silence. *International Journal of Intercultural Relations, 28,* 353–280.

Albert, S., & Dabbs, J. M. (1970). Physical distance and persuasion. *Journal of Personality and Social Psychology, 15,* 265–270.

Alexander, A. (1980, April). *An investigation of eye gaze and its relation to assertiveness.* Paper presented to the Nonverbal Division at the Eastern Communication Association Conference, Ocean City, MD.

Algoe, S. B., Buswell, B. N., & DeLamater, J. D. (2000). Gender and job status as contextual cues for the interpretation of facial expressions of emotion. *Sex Roles, 42,* 183–208.

Alibali, M. W., Heath, D. C., & Myers, H. J. (2001). Effects of visibility between speaker and listener on gesture production: Some gestures are meant to be seen. *Journal of Memory and Language, 44,* 169–188.

Allen, M. (1995, November). *Dialectical theory: Testing the relationships between tensions and relational satisfaction.* Paper presented at the Speech Communication Association Convention, Chicago, IL.

Altman, I., & Taylor, D. A. (1973). *Social penetration: The development of interpersonal relationships.* New York: Holt, Rinehart & Winston.

Altman, I., Vinsel, A., & Brown, B. B. (1981). Dialectic conceptions in social psychology: An application to social penetration and privacy regulation. In L. Berkowitz (Ed.), *Advances in experimental social psychology* (Vol. 14, pp. 107–160). New York: Academic.

Amabile, T. M., & Kabat, L. G. (1982). When self-descriptions contradict behavior: Actions to speak louder than words. *Social Cognition, 1*(4), 311–335.

Ambady, N., Bernieri, F. J., & Richeson, J. A. (2000). Toward a histology of social behavior: Judgmental accuracy from thin-slices of the behavioral stream. *Advances in Experimental Social Psychology, 32,* 201–271.

Ambady, N., & Gray, H. M. (2002). On being sad and mistaken: Mood effects on the accuracy of thin-slice judgments. *Journal of Personality and Social Psychology, 83,* 947–961.

Ambady, N., Krabbenhoft, M. A., & Hogan, D. (2006). The 30-sec sale: Using thin-slice judgments to evaluate sales effectiveness. *Journal of Consumer Psychology, 16,* 4–13.

Andersen, J. F. (1979). Teacher immediacy as a predictor of teaching effectiveness. In D. Nimmo (Ed.), *Communication yearbook 3* (pp. 543–559). New Brunswick, NJ: Transaction Books.

Andersen, J. F. (1984, April). *Nonverbal cues of immediacy and relational affect.* Paper presented at the annual convention of the Central States Speech Association, Chicago, IL.

Andersen, J. F., & Andersen, P. A. (1987). Never smile until Christmas? Casting doubt on an old myth. *Journal of Thought, 22,* 57–61.

Andersen, J. F., Andersen, P. A., & Jensen, A. D. (1979). The measurement of nonverbal immediacy. *Journal of Applied Communication Research, 7,* 153–180.

Andersen, J. F., Andersen, P. A., & Landgraf, J. (1985, May). *The development of nonverbal communication competence in childhood.* Paper presented at the annual convention of the International Communication Association, Honolulu, HI.

Andersen, J. F., Andersen, P. A., & Lustig, M. W. (1987). Opposite-sex touch avoidance: A national replication and extension. *Journal of Nonverbal Behavior, 11,* 89–109.

Andersen, J. F., Andersen, P. A., Murphy, M. A., & Wendt-Wasco, N. (1985). Teachers' reports of students' nonverbal communication in the classroom: A developmental study in grades K–12. *Communication Education, 34,* 292–307.

Andersen, J. F., Norton, R. W., & Nussbaum, J. F. (1981). Three investigations exploring relationships between perceived teacher communication behaviors and student learning. *Communication Education, 30,* 377–392.

Andersen, J. F., & Withrow, J. G. (1981). The impact of lecturer nonverbal expressiveness on improving mediated instruction. *Communication Education, 30,* 342–353.

Andersen, K., & Clevenger, T., Jr. (1963). A summary of experimental research in ethos. *Speech Monographs, 30,* 59–78.

Andersen, P. A. (1984). Nonverbal communication in the small group. In R. S. Cathcart & L. A. Samovar (Eds.), *Small group communication* (4th ed., pp. 258–275). Dubuque, IA: Brown.

Andersen, P. A. (1985). Nonverbal immediacy in interpersonal communication. In A. W. Siegman & S. Feldstein (Eds.), *Multichannel integrations of nonverbal behavior* (pp. 1–36). Hillsdale, NJ: Erlbaum.

Andersen, P. A. (1986). Consciousness, cognition, and communication. *Western Journal of Speech Communication, 50,* 87–101.

Andersen, P. A. (1987). The trait debate: A critical examination of the individual differences paradigm in intercultural communication. In B. Dervin & M. J. Voigt (Eds.), *Progress in communication sciences* (Vol. 8, pp. 47–82). Norwood, NJ: Ablex.

Andersen, P. A. (1988). Explaining intercultural differences in nonverbal communication. In L. A. Samovar & R E. Porter (Eds.), *Intercultural communication: A reader* (5th ed., pp. 272–281). Belmont, CA: Wadsworth.

Andersen, P. A. (1989, May). *A cognitive valence theory of intimate communication.* Paper presented at the International Network on Personal Relationships Conference, Iowa City, IA.

Andersen, P. A. (1991). When one cannot not communicate: A challenge to Motley's traditional communication postulates. *Communication Studies, 42,* 309–325.

Andersen, P. A. (1992a, July). *Excessive intimacy: An account analysis of behaviors, cognitive schemata, affect, and relational outcomes.* Paper presented at the 6th International Conference on Personal Relationships, Orono, ME.

Andersen, P. A. (1992b). Nonverbal communication in the small group. In R. S. Cathcart & L. A. Samovar (Eds.), *Small group communication* (6th ed., pp. 272–286). Dubuque, IA: Brown.

Andersen, P. A. (1993a). Cognitive schemata in personal relationships. In S. Duck (Ed.), *Individuals in relationships* (pp. 1–29). Newbury Park, CA: Sage.

Andersen, P. A. (1993b, July). *Steps to a communication of ecology: The interrelationships of systems in the global environmental crisis.* Paper presented at the Conference on Communication and the Environment, Big Sky, MT.

Andersen, P. A. (1997). Cues of culture: The basis of intercultural differences in nonverbal communication. In L. A. Samovar and R. E. Porter (Eds.), *Intercultural communication: A reader* (8th ed., pp. 244–256). Belmont, CA: Wadsworth.

Andersen, P. A. (1998a). Researching sex differences within sex similarities: The evolutionary consequences of reproductive differences. In D. J. Canary & K. Dindia (Eds.), *Sex differences and similarities in communication* (pp. 83–100). Mahwah, NJ: Erlbaum.

Andersen, P. A. (1998b). The cognitive valence theory of intimate communication. In T. M. Palmer & G. A. Barnett (Eds.), *Progress in communication sciences, Volume XIV: Mutual influence in interpersonal communication: Theory and research in cognition, affect, and behavior* (pp. 39–72). Stanford, CT: Ablex.

Andersen, P. A. (1999). *Nonverbal communication: Forms and functions.* (1st ed.). Mountain View CA: Mayfield.

Andersen, P. A. (2004). *The complete idiot's guide to body language.* Indianapolis: Alpha.

Andersen, P. A. (2005). The touch avoidance measure. In V. Manusov (Ed.), *The sourcebook of nonverbal measures: Going beyond words* (pp. 57–66). Mahwah, NJ: Erlbaum.

Andersen, P. A. (2006). The evolution of biological sex differences in communication. In K. Dindia & D. J. Canary (Eds.), *Sex differences and similarities in communication* (pp. 117–135). Mahwah, NJ: Erlbaum.

Andersen, P. A. (2008). Building and sustaining personal relationships: A cognitive valence explanation. In L. K. Guerrero & M. Hecht (Eds.), *The nonverbal communication reader* (3rd ed.). Long Grove, IL: Waveland

Andersen, P. A., & Andersen, J. F. (1982). Nonverbal immediacy in instruction. In L. L. Barker (Ed.), *Communication in the classroom: Original essays* (pp. 98–120). Englewood Cliffs, NJ: Prentice-Hall.

Andersen, P. A., & Andersen, J. F. (1984). The exchange of nonverbal immediacy: A critical review of dyadic models. *Journal of Nonverbal Behavior, 8,* 327–349.

Andersen, P. A., & Andersen, J. F. (2005). The measurement of nonverbal immediacy. In V. Manusov (Ed.), *The sourcebook of nonverbal measures: Going beyond words* (pp. 113–126). Mahwah, NJ: Erlbaum.

Andersen, P. A., Andersen, J. F., & Mayton, S. M. (1985). The development of nonverbal communication in the classroom: Teachers' perceptions of students in grades K–12. *Western Journal of Speech Communication, 49,* 188–203.

Andersen, P. A., & Bowman, L. (1990). Positions of power: Nonverbal influence in organizational communication. In J. A. DeVito & M. L. Hecht (Eds.), *The nonverbal communication reader* (pp. 391–411). Prospect Heights, IL: Waveland.

Andersen, P. A., & Coussoule, A. R. (1980). The perceptual world of the communication apprehensive: The effect of communication apprehension and interpersonal gaze on interpersonal perception. *Communication Quarterly, 28,* 44–54.

Andersen, P. A., Eloy, S. V., Guerrero, L. K., & Spitzberg, B. H. (1995). Romantic jealousy and relational satisfaction: A look at the impact of jealousy experience and expression. *Communication Reports, 8,* 77–85.

Andersen, P. A., Garrison, J. P., & Andersen, J. F. (1975, November). *Defining nonverbal communication: A neurophysiological explanation of nonverbal information processing.* Paper presented at the annual meeting of the Western Speech Communication Association, Seattle, WA.

Andersen, P. A., Garrison, J. P., & Andersen, J. F. (1979). Implications of a neurophysiological approach for the study of nonverbal communication. *Human Communication Research, 6,* 74–89.

Andersen, P. A., & Guerrero, L. K. (1989, February). *Avoiding communication: Verbal and nonverbal dimensions of defensiveness.* Paper presented at the annual convention of the Western Speech Communication Association, Spokane, WA.

Andersen, P. A., & Guerrero, L. K. (1998a). The bright side of relational communication: Interpersonal warmth as a social emotion. In P. A. Andersen & L. K. Guerrero (Eds.), *Handbook of communication and emotion: Research, theory, applications, and contexts* (pp. 303–324). San Diego, CA: Academic.

Andersen, P. A., & Guerrero, L. K. (1998b). Principles of communication and emotion in social interaction. In P. A. Andersen & L. K. Guerrero (Eds.), *Handbook of communication and emotion: Research, theory, applications, and contexts* (pp. 49–96). San Diego, CA: Academic.

Andersen, P. A., Guerrero, L. K., Buller, D. B., & Jorgensen, P. F. (1998). An empirical comparison of three theories of nonverbal immediacy exchange. *Human Communication Research, 24,* 501–535.

Andersen, P. A., Guerrero, L. K., & Jones, S. M. Nonverbal intimacy. (2006). In V. Manusov & M. L. Patterson (Eds.), *The Sage handbook of nonverbal communication* (pp. 259–277). Thousand Oaks, CA: Sage.

Andersen, P. A., Hecht, M. L., Hoobler, G. D., & Smallwood, M. (2002). Nonverbal communication across culture. In B. Gudykunst and B. Mody (Eds.), *Handbook of international and intercultural communication* (pp. 89–106). Thousand Oaks, CA: Sage.

Andersen, P. A., & Kibler, R. J. (1978). Candidate valence as a predictor of voter preference. *Human Communication Research, 5,* 4–14.

Andersen, P. A., & Leibowitz, K. (1978). The development and nature of the construct touch avoidance. *Environmental Psychology and Nonverbal Behavior, 3,* 89–106.

Andersen, P. A., Lustig, M. W., & Andersen, J. A. (1986). *Communication patterns across the United States: A theoretical perspective.* Paper presented at the annual convention of the International Communication Association, Chicago, IL.

Andersen, P. A., Lustig, M. W., & Andersen, J. A. (1990). Changes in latitude, changes in attitude: The relationship between climate and interpersonal communication predispositions. *Communication Quarterly, 38,* 291–311.

Andersen, P. A., & Singleton, G. W. (1978, March). *The relationship between body-type and communication avoidance.* Paper presented at the annual convention of the Eastern Communication Association, Boston, MA.

Andersen, P. A., & Sull, K. K. (1985). Out of touch, out of reach: Tactile predispositions as predictors of interpersonal distance. *Western Journal of Speech Communication, 49,* 57–72.

Andersen, P. A., & Todd-Mancillas, W. R. (1978). Scales for the measurement of homophily with public figures. *Southern Speech Communication Journal, 43,* 169–179.

Andersen, P. A., Todd-Mancillas, W. R., & DiClemente, L. (1980). The effects of pupil dilation in physical, social, and task attraction. *Australian Scan: Journal of Human Communication, 7 & 8,* 89–95.

Andersen, P. A., & Wang, H. (2006). Unraveling cultural cues: Dimensions of nonverbal communication across cultures. In L. A. Samovar, R. E. Porter, & E. R. McDaniel (Eds.), *Intercultural communication: A reader* (pp. 250–266). Belmont, CA: Wadsworth.

Anderson, C., & Berdahl, J. L. (2002). The experience of power: Examining the effects of power on approach and inhibition tendencies. *Journal of Personality and Social Psychology, 83,* 1362–1377.

Anderson, N. R. (1991). Decision making in the graduate selection interview: An experimental investigation. *Human Relations, 44,* 403–417.

Angier, N. (1995, February 22). Studying sense that picks up scents. *The San Diego Union Tribune,* p. E3.

Apple, W., Streeter, L. A., & Krauss, R. M. (1979). Effects of pitch and speech rate on personal attributions. *Journal of Personality and Social Psychology, 37,* 715–727.

Archer, D., & Akert, R. M. (1977). Words and everything else: Verbal and nonverbal cues in social interpretation. *Journal of Personality and Social Psychology, 35,* 443–449.

Areni, C. S., & Sparks, J. R. (2005). Language, power and persuasion. *Psychology and Marketing, 22,* 507–525.

Argyle, M. (1972). Non-verbal communication in human social interaction. In R. A. Hinde (Ed.), *Nonverbal communication* (pp. 248–268). Cambridge: Cambridge University Press.

Argyle, M. (1975). *Bodily communication.* New York: International Universities Press.

Aronoff, J., Woike, B. A., & Hyman, L. M. (1992). Which are the stimuli in facial displays of anger and happiness? Configurational bases of emotion recognition. *Journal of Personality and Social Psychology, 62,* 1050–1066.

Aune, K. S., & Aune, R. K. (1997, May). *Effects of relationship level and biological sex on motives for emotion management.* Paper presented at the annual meeting of the International Communication Association, Montreal, Quebec.

Aune, R. K., Ching, P. U., & Levine, T. R. (1996). Attributions of deception as a function of reward value: A test of two explanations. *Communication Quarterly, 44,* 478–486.

Aune, R. K., Metts, S., & Ebesu, A. S. (1990, November). *Managing the discovery of deception.* Paper presented at the annual meeting of the Speech Communication Association, Chicago, IL.

Babad, E. (2005). Nonverbal behavior in education. In J. A. Harrigan, R. Rosenthal, & K. R. Scherer (Eds.), *The New Handbook of Methods in Nonverbal Behavior Research* (pp. 283–311). New York: Oxford.

Badzinski, D. M. (1986, November). *Towards understanding the effects of mood on interaction processes.* Paper presented at the annual convention of the Speech Communication Association, Chicago, IL.

Bailenson, J. N., Blascovich, J., Beall, A. C., & Loomis, J. M., (2003). Interpersonal distance in immersive virtual environments. *Personality and Social Psychology Bulletin, 29,* 819–833.

Bailenson, J. N., & Yee, N. (2005). Digital chameleons: Automatic assimilation of nonverbal gestures in immersive virtual environments. *Psychological Science, 16,* 814–819.

Bakan, P. (1971). The eyes have it. *Psychology Today, 4,* 64–67.

Bakan, P., & Strayer, F. F. (1973). On reliability of conjugate lateral eye movements. *Perceptual and Motor Skills, 36,* 429–430.

Bakti, A., Baron-Cohen, S., Wheelwright, S., Connellan, J., & Ahluwalia, J. (2000). Is there an innate gaze module? Evidence from human neonates. *Infant Behavior and Development, 23,* 223–229.

Baldero, B., Rossi, N., Caterina, R., Codispoti, M., Balsomo, A., & Trombini, G. (2003). Deficit in the discrimination of nonverbal emotions in children with obesity and their mothers. *International Journal of Obesity, 27,* 191–195.

Baldwin, M. W. (1992). Relational schemas and the processing of social information. *Psychological Bulletin, 112,* 461–484.

Bandler, R., & Grinder, J. (1979). *Frogs into princes.* Moab, UT: Real People Press.

Barash, D. P. (1973). Human ethology: Personal space reiterated. *Environmental Behavior, 5,* 67–73.

Barbee, A. P., Rowatt, T. L., & Cunningham, M. R. (1998). When a friend is in need: Feelings about seeking, giving, and receiving social support. In P. A. Andersen & L. K. Guerrero (Eds.), *Handbook of communication and emotion: Research, theory, applications, and contexts* (pp. 281–301). San Diego, CA: Academic.

Bargh, J. A., & Chartrand, T. L. (1999). The unbearable automaticity of being. *American Psychologist, 54,* 462–479.

Barker, L. L., Cegala, D. J., Kibler, R. J., & Wahlers, K. J. (1979). *Groups in process: An introduction to small group communication.* Englewood Cliffs, NJ: Prentice-Hall.

Barker, L. L., & Collins, N. B. (1970). Nonverbal and kinesic research. In P. Emmert & W. D. Brooks (Eds.), *Methods of research in communication.* Boston: Houghton Mifflin.

Barnland, D. C. (1978). Communication styles in two cultures: Japan and the United States. In A. Kendon, R. M. Harris, & M. R. Key (Eds.), *Organizational behavior in face to face interaction* (pp. 427–456). The Hague: Mouton.

Barrett, K. C. (1995). A functionalist approach to shame and guilt. In J. P. Tangney & K. W. Fischer (Eds.), *Self-conscious emotions: The psychology of shame, guilt, embarrassment and pride* (pp. 25–63). New York: Guilford.

Basow, S, A., & Branam, A. C. (1998). Women and body hair: Social perceptions and attitudes. *Psychology of Women Quarterly, 22,* 637–645.

Bate, B. (1988). *Communication and the sexes.* New York: Harper & Row.

Bateson, G. B. (1972). *Steps to an ecology of mind.* New York: Balantine Books.

Baum, A., Davis, G. E., & Valins, S. (1979). Generating behavioral data for the design process. In J. R. Aiello & A. Baum (Eds.), *Residential crowding and design* (pp. 175–196). New York: Plenum.

Baumeister, R. F., Reis, H. T., & Delaspaul, P. (1995). Personal narratives about guilt: Role in action control and interpersonal relationships. *Personality and Social Psychology Bulletin, 21,* 1256–1258.

Baumeister, R. F., Stillwell, A. M., & Heatherton, T. F. (1994). Guilt: An interpersonal approach. *Psychological Bulletin, 115,* 243–267.

Baumeister, R. F., & Wotman, S. R. (1992). *Breaking hearts: The two sides of unrequited love.* New York: Guilford.

Baumgaertner, A., Buccino, G., Lange, R., McNamara, A., & Binkofski, F. (2007). Polymodal conceptual processing of human biological actions in the left inferior frontal lobe. *European Journal of Neuroscience, 25,* 881–889.

Bavelas, J. B. (1990). Behaving and communicating: A reply to Motley. *Western Journal of Speech Communication, 54,* 593–602.

Bavelas, J. B., Black, A., Chovil, N., Lemery, C. R., & Mullett, J. (1988). Form and function in motor mimicry: Topographic evidence that the primary function is communicative. *Human Communication Research, 14,* 275–299.

Bavelas, J. B., Black, A., Chovil, N., & Mullet, J. (1990). *Equivocal communication.* Newbury Park, CA: Sage.

Bavelas, J. B., Black, A., Lemery, C. R., & Mullett, J. (1986). "I'll show how you feel": Motor mimicry as a communicative act. *Journal of Personality and Social Psychology, 50,* 322–329.

Bavelas, J. B., Chovil, N., Coates, L., & Roe, L. (1995). Gestures specialized for dialogue. *Personality and Social Psychology Bulletin, 21,* 394–405.

Baxter, L. A. (1987). Cognition and communication in the relationship process. In P. McGhee, D. Clarke, & R. Burnett (Eds.), *Accounting for relationships: Social relationships of interpersonal links* (pp. 192–212). London: Methuen.

Baxter, L. A. (1988). A dialectical perspective on communication strategies in relationship development. In S. Duck (Ed.), *Handbook of personal relationships* (pp. 257–259). New York: Wiley & Sons.

Baxter, L. A. (1993). Dialectical contradictions in relationship development. In S. Petronio, J. K. Alberts, M. L. Hecht, & J. Buley (Eds.), *Contemporary perspectives on interpersonal communication.* Madison, WI: Brown & Benchmark.

Baxter, L. A. (1994). A dialogic approach to relationship maintenance. In D. Canary & L. Stafford (Eds.), *Communication and relational maintenance* (pp. 233–234). San Diego, CA: Academic.

Baxter, L. A., & Montgomery, B. M. (1996). *Relating: Dialogues and dialectics.* New York: Guilford.

Baxter, L. A., & Ward, J. (1975). Newsline. *Psychology Today, 8*(8), 28.

Baxter, L. A., & Wilmot, W. W. (1984). "Secret tests": Social strategies for acquiring information about the state of the relationship. *Human Communication Research, 11,* 171–201.

Bayes, M. A. (1970). An investigation of the behavioral cues of interpersonal warmth (Doctoral dissertation, University of Miami, 1970). *Dissertation Abstracts International, 31,* 2272B.

Beattie, G., & Shovelton, H. (2002). Blue-eyed boys? A winning smile? An experimental investigation of some core facial stimuli that may affect person perception. *Semiotica, 139,* 1–21.

Beaulieu, C. M. (2004). Intercultural study of personal space: A case study. *Journal of Applied Social Psychology, 34,* 794–805.

Beaupre, M., & Hess, U. (2005). Cross-cultural emotion recognition among Canadian ethnic groups. *Journal of Cross-Cultural Psychology, 36,* 355–370.

Beck, W. W., & Lambert, G. E. (1977). First impressions and classroom climate. *Kappa Delta Pi Record, 13*(4), 121–122.

Becker, F. D. (1973). Study of spatial markers. *Journal of Personality and Social Psychology, 26,* 439–445.

Becker-Stoll, F., Delius, A., & Scheitenberger, S. (2001). Adolescents' nonverbal emotional expressions during negotiation of a disagreement with their mothers: An attachment approach. *International Journal of Behavioral Development, 25,* 344–353.

Beebe, S. A. (1980). Effects of eye contact, posture and vocal inflection upon credibility and comprehension. *Australian Scan: Journal of Human Communication, 7–8,* 57–70.

Beier, E. G., & Sternberg, D. P. (1977). Marital communication: Subtle cues between newlyweds. *Journal of Communication, 27,* 92–97.

Bell, R. A., & Daly, J. A. (1984). The affinity-seek function in communication. *Communication Monographs, 51,* 91–115.

Bellah, R. N., Madsen, R., Sullivan, W. M., Swidler, A., & Tipton, S. (1985). *Habits of the heart: Individualism and commitment in American life.* New York: Harper & Row.

Bensafi, M., Brown, W. M., Khan, R., Levenson, B., & Sobel, N. (2004). Sniffing human sex-steroid compounds modulates mood, memory, and autonomic nervous system function in specific behavioral contexts, *Behavioral Brain Research, 152,* 11–22.

Benson, T. W., & Frandsen, K. D. (1976). An *orientation to nonverbal communication.* Chicago: Science Research Associates.

Bente, G., Donaghy, W. C., & Suwelack, D. (1998). Sex differences in body movement and visual attention: An integrated analysis of movement and gaze in mixed-sex dyads. *Journal of Nonverbal Behavior, 22,* 31–38.

Berdahl, J. L., & Martorana, P. (2006). Effects of power on emotion and expression during a controversial group discussion. *European Journal of Social Psychology, 36,* 497–509.

Berger, C. R. (1985). Social power and interpersonal communication. In M. L. Knapp & G. R. Miller (Eds.), *Handbook of interpersonal communication* (pp. 439–499). Beverly Hills, CA: Sage.

Berger, C. R. (1988). Uncertainty and information exchange in developing relationships. In S. Duck (Ed.), *Handbook of personal relationships* (pp. 239–255). New York: Wiley & Sons.

Berger, C. R., & Bradac, J. J. (1982). *Language and social knowledge: Uncertainty in interpersonal relations.* London: Edward Arnold.

Berger, C. R., & Calabrese, R. J. (1975). Some explorations in initial interaction and beyond: Toward a theory of interpersonal communication. *Human Communication Research, 1,* 99–112.

Bergland, H., Lindstrom, P., & Savik, I. (2006). Brain response to putative pheromones in lesbian women, *Proceedings of the National Academy of Sciences, 103,* 8269–8274.

Berlyne, D. E. (1960). *Conflict, arousal, and curiosity.* New York: McGraw-Hill.

Bern, S. L. (1974). The measurement of psychological androgyny. *Journal of Counseling and Clinical Psychology, 42,* 155–162.

Berry, D. S. (1990). Vocal attractiveness and vocal babyishness: Effects on stranger, self and friend impressions. *Journal of Nonverbal Behavior, 14,* 141–153.

Berry, D. S. (1992). Vocal types and stereotypes: Joint effects of vocal attractiveness and vocal maturity on person perception. *Journal of Nonverbal Behavior, 16,* 41–54.

Berscheid, E., & Walster, E. M. (1978). *Interpersonal attraction* (2nd ed.). Reading, MA: Addison-Wesley.

Bethel, E. R., & Bethel, J. A. (1974, December). *Superordinate-subordinate status relationships and defense of personal space.* Paper presented at the annual meeting of the Speech Communication Association, Chicago, IL.

Bickman, L. (1974). The social power of a uniform. *Journal of Applied Social Psychology, 4,* 47–61.

Billig, M. (1987). *Arguing and thinking: A rhetorical approach to social psychology.* New York: Cambridge University Press.

Birdwhistell, R. L. (1970). *Kinesics and context.* Philadelphia: University of Pennsylvania Press.

Biswas, A. K. (1984). *Climate and development.* Dublin, Ireland: Tycooly.

Blake, M. L., Duffy, J. R., Myers, P. S., & Tompkins, C. A. (2002). Prevalence and patterns of right hemispheric cognitive/communication deficits: Retrospective data from an inpatient rehabilitation unit. *Aphasiology, 16,* 537–547.

Blanck, P. D., & Rosenthal, R. (1982). Developing strategies for decoding "leaky" messages: On learning how and when to decode discrepant and consistent social communications. In R. S. Feldman (Ed.), *Development of nonverbal behavior in children* (pp. 203–229). New York: Springer Verlag.

Blanck, P. D., & Rosenthal, R. (1992). Nonverbal behavior in the courtroom. In R. S. Feldman (Ed.), *Applications of nonverbal behavioral theories and research* (pp. 89–115). Hillsdale, NJ: Erlbaum.

Blanck, P. D., Rosenthal, R., & Vannicelli, M. (1986). Talking to and about patients: The therapist's tone of voice. In P. D. Blanck, R. Buck, & R. Rosenthal (Eds.), *Nonverbal communication in the clinical context* (pp. 99–143). University Park, PA: Pennsylvania State University Press.

Blumstein, P., & Schwartz, P. (1983). *American couples: Money, work, sex.* New York: Morrow.

Boderman, A., Freed, D. W., & Kinnucan, M. T. (1972). Touch me, like me: Testing an encounter group assumption. *Journal of Applied Behavioral Science, 8*, 527–533.

Bogen, J. E. (1977). Some educational implications of hemispheric specialization. In W. C. Wittrock (Ed.), *The human brain* (pp. 133–152). Englewood Cliffs, NJ: Prentice-Hall.

Bok, S. (1978). *Lying: Moral choice in public and private life.* New York: Random House.

Bonanno, G., Keltner, D., Noll, J. G., Putnam, F. W., Trickett, P. K., & LeJune, J. (2002). When the face reveals what words do not: Facial expression of emotion, smiling, and the willingness to disclose childhood sexual abuse. *Journal of Personality and Social Psychology, 83*, 94–110.

Bond, C. F., & DePaulo, B. M. (2006). Accuracy of deception judgments. *Personality and Social Psychology Review, 10*, 214–234.

Bond, C. F., Omar, A., Pitre, U., Lashley, G. R., Skaggs, L. M., & Kirk, C. T. (1992). Fishy-looking liars: Judgment from expectancy violation. *Journal of Personality and Social Psychology, 63*, 969–977.

Bond, M. H. (1993). Emotions and their expression in Chinese culture. *Journal of Nonverbal Behavior, 17*, 245–262.

Boone, R. T., & Buck, R. (2003). Emotional expressivity and trustworthiness. The role of nonverbal behavior in the evolution of cooperation. *Journal of Nonverbal Behavior, 27*, 163–182.

Boroughs, M., Cafri, G., & Thompson, J. K. (2005). Male body depilation: Prevalence and associated features of body hair removal. *Sex Roles, 52*, 637–644.

Bowlby, J. (1979). *The making and breaking of affectional bonds.* London: Tavistock.

Bowman, A. (1980, April). *Physical attractiveness and electability: Looks and votes.* Paper presented at the annual meeting of the Midwest Political Science Association.

Brauer, M., & Bourhis, R. (2006). Social power. *European Journal of Social Psychology, 36*, 601–616.

Breed, G., Christiansen, E., & Larson, D. (1972). Effect of a lecturer's gaze direction upon teaching effectiveness. *Catalog of Selected Documents in Psychology, 2*, 115.

Brehm, S. S. (1985). *Intimate relationships.* New York: Random House.

Briton, N. J., & Hall, J. A. (1995). Beliefs about female and male nonverbal communication. *Sex Roles, 32*, 70–90.

Brockner, J., Pressman, B., Cabitt, J., & Moran, P. (1982). Nonverbal intimacy, sex and compliance: A field study. *Journal of Nonverbal Behavior, 6*, 253–258.

Brody, L., & Hall, J. A. (1993). Gender and emotion. In M. Lewis & J. Haviland (Eds.), *Handbook of emotions* (pp. 447–460). New York: Guilford.

Broverman, I. K., Vogel, S. R., Broverman, D. M., Clarkson, F. E., & Rosenkrantz, P. S. (1972). Sex role stereotypes: A current appraisal. *Journal of Social Issues, 28*, 59–78.

Brown, D. E. (1991). *Human universals.* Philadelphia: Temple University Press.

Brown, L. R., Kane, H., & Roodman, D. M. (1994). *Vital signs 1994: The trends that are shaping our future.* New York: Norton.

Brown, R. (1965). *Social psychology.* New York: Free Press.

Browning, J. R., Kessler, D., Hatfield, E., & Choo, P. (1999). Power, gender, and sexual behavior. *Journal of Sex Research, 36*, 342–347.

Bruneau, T. (1979). The time dimension in intercultural communication. In D. Nimmo (Ed.), *Communication yearbook 3* (pp. 423–433). New Brunswick, NJ: Transaction Books.

Buck, R. (1979). Individual differences in nonverbal sending accuracy and electrodermal responding: The externalizing-internalizing dimension. In R. Rosenthal (Ed.), *Skill in nonverbal communication: Individual differences.* Cambridge, MA: Oelgeschlager, Gunn, & Hain.

Buck, R. (1982). Spontaneous and symbolic nonverbal behavior and the ontogeny of communication. In P. S. Feldman (Ed.), *Development of nonverbal behavior in children* (pp. 29–62). New York Springer Verlag.

Buck, R. (1984). *The communication of emotion.* New York: Guilford.

Buck, R. (1988). Nonverbal communication: Spontaneous and symbolic aspects. *American Behavioral Scientist, 31*, 341–35.

Buck, R. (1995). Review of human facial expression: An evolutionary view. *Communication Theory, 5*, 393–396.

Buck, R., Miller, R. E., & Caul, W. F. (1974). Sex, personality, and physiological variables in the communication of emotion via facial expression. *Journal of Personality and Social Psychology, 30*, 587–596.

Buck, R., & VanLear, C. A. (2002). Verbal and nonverbal communication: Distinguishing symbolic, spontaneous, and pseudo-spontaneous nonverbal behavior. *Journal of Communication, 52*, 522–541.

Bucy E. P., & Bradley, S. D. (2004). Presidential expressions and viewer emotion: Counterempathic responses to televised lead displays. *Social Science Information, 43*, 59–64.

Bull, P. E. (1987). *Posture and gesture.* Oxford: Pergamon.

Bull, R., & Gibson-Robinson, E. (1981). The influence of eye-gaze, style of dress, and locality on the amounts of money donated to charity. *Human Relations, 34*, 895–905.

Buller, D. B. (1986). Distraction during persuasive communication: A meta-analytic review. *Communication Monographs, 53*, 91–114.

Buller, D. B. (1987). Communication apprehension and reactions to proxemic violations. *Journal of Nonverbal Behavior, 11*, 13–25.

Buller, D. B. (1988, November). *Nonverbal predictors of attributions during deception.* Paper presented at the annual meeting of the International Communication Association, New Orleans, LA.

Buller, D. B. (1989). *Deception by strangers, friends, and intimates: Attributional biases due to relationship development.* Unpublished manuscript, University of Arizona.

Buller, D. B., & Aune, R. K. (1988a). The effects of vocalics and nonverbal sensitivity on compliance: A speech accommodation theory explanation. *Human Communication Research, 14*, 301–332.

Buller, D. B., & Aune, R. K. (1988b, February). *Nonverbal cues to deception among friends and strangers.* Paper presented at the annual meeting of the Western Speech Communication Association, San Diego, CA.

Buller, D. B., & Aune, R. K. (1989, May). *The effects of vocalics and nonverbal sensitivity on compliance: Further tests of the speech accommodation explanation.* Paper presented at the annual meeting of the International Communication Association Convention, San Francisco, CA.

Buller, D. B., & Aune, R. K. (1992). The effects of speech rate similarity on compliance: Application of communication accommodation theory. *Western Journal of Communication, 56*, 37–53.

Buller, D. B., & Burgoon, J. K. (1986). The effects of vocalics and nonverbal sensitivity on compliance. *Human Communication Research, 13*, 126 144.

Buller, D. B., & Burgoon, J. K. (1994). Deception: Strategic and nonstrategic communication. In J. Daly & J. M. Wiemann (Eds.), *Interpersonal communication* (pp. 191–213). Hillsdale, NJ: Erlbaum.

Buller, D. B., & Burgoon, J. K. (1996). Interpersonal deception theory. *Communication Theory, 6*, 203–242.

Buller, D. B., & Burgoon, J. K. (1998). Emotional expression in the deception process. In P. A. Andersen & L. K. Guerrero (Eds.), *Handbook of communication and emotion: Research, theory, applications, and contexts* (pp. 381–402). San Diego, CA: Academic.

Buller, D. B., Burgoon, J. K., Buslig, A. L., & Roiger, J. F. (1994). Interpersonal deception: VIII. Further analysis of nonverbal and verbal correlates of equivocation from the Bavelas et al. (1990) research. *Journal of Language and Social Psychology, 13*, 396–417.

Buller, D. B., Burgoon, J. K., Buslig, A. L., & Roiger, J. F. (1996). Testing interpersonal deception theory: The language of interpersonal deception. *Communication Theory, 6*, 268–288.

Buller, D. B., Burgoon, J. K., & Guerrero, L. K. (1994, November). *Behavioral sequences in interpersonal deception.* Paper presented at the annual meeting of the Speech Communication Association Convention, New Orleans, LA.

Buller, D. B., Burgoon, J. K., White, C. H., & Ebesu, A. S. (1994). Interpersonal deception: VII. Behavioral profiles of falsification, equivocation, and concealment. *Journal of Language and Social Psychology, 13*, 366–395.

Buller, D. B., Jorgensen, P. F., Andersen, P. A., & Guerrero, L. K. (1995, June). *Correspondence among physiological, nonverbal, and perceptual measures of arousal.* Paper presented at the meeting of the International Network on Personal Relationships, Williamsburg, VA.

Buller, D. B., LePoire, B. A., Aune, R. K., & Eloy, S. V. (1992). Social perceptions as mediators of the effect of speech rate on compliance. *Human Communication Research, 19*, 286–311.

Buller, D. B., Strzyzewski, K. D., & Comstock, J. (1991). Interpersonal deception: I. Deceivers' reactions to receivers' suspicions and probing. *Communication Monographs, 58*, 1–24.

Buller, D. B., Strzyzewski, K. D., & Hunsaker, F. G. (1991). Interpersonal deception: II. The inferiority of conversational participants as deception detectors. *Communication Monographs, 58*, 25–40.

Buller, D. B., & Walther, J. B. (1989). *Deception in established relationships: Application of schema theory.* Paper presented at the annual meeting of the Western Speech Communication Association, Spokane, WA.

Bullis, C., & Horn, C. (1995). Getting a little closer: Further examination of nonverbal comforting strategies. *Communication Reports, 8,* 10.

Burgoon, J. K. (1978). Attributes of a newscaster's voice as predictors of his credibility. *Journalism Quarterly, 55,* 276–281.

Burgoon, J. K. (1980). Nonverbal communication research in the 1970s: An overview. In D. Nimmo (Ed.), *Communication yearbook 4* (pp. 179–197). New Brunswick, NJ: Transaction Books.

Burgoon, J. K. (1983). Nonverbal violations of expectations. In J. M. Wiemann & R. P. Harrison (Eds.), *Nonverbal interaction* (pp. 77–111). Beverly Hills, CA: Sage.

Burgoon, J. K. (1985a). Nonverbal signals. In M. L. Knapp & G. R. Miller (Eds.), *Handbook of interpersonal communication* (pp. 344–390). Beverly Hills, CA: Sage.

Burgoon, J. K. (1985b). The relationship of verbal and nonverbal codes. In B. Dervin & M. J. Voigt (Eds.), *Progress in communication sciences* (Vol. 6, pp. 263–298). Norwood, NJ: Ablex.

Burgoon, J. K. (1991). Relational message interpretations of touch, conversational distance, and posture. *Journal of Nonverbal Behavior, 15,* 233–259.

Burgoon, J. K. (1994). Nonverbal signals. In M. L. Knapp & G. R. Miller (Eds.), *Handbook of interpersonal communication* (2nd ed., pp. 229–285). Thousand Oaks, CA: Sage.

Burgoon, J. K. (2005, November). *Truth, deception and virtual worlds.* Keynote address at the National Communication Association Convention, Boston, MA.

Burgoon, J. K., & Aho, L. (1982). Three field experiments on the effects of violations of conversational distance. *Communication Monographs, 49,* 71–88.

Burgoon, J. K., Birk, T., & Pfau, M. (1990). Nonverbal behaviors, persuasion, and credibility. *Human Communication Research, 17,* 140–169.

Burgoon, J. K., & Buller, D. B. (1994). Interpersonal deception: III. Effects of deceit on perceived communication and nonverbal behavior dynamics. *Journal of Nonverbal Behavior, 18,* 155–184.

Burgoon, J. K., Buller, D. B., Dillman, L., & Walther, J. B. (1995). Interpersonal deception: IV. Effects of suspicion on perceived communication and nonverbal behavior dynamics. *Human Communication Research, 22,* 163–196.

Burgoon, J. K., Buller, D. B., Ebesu, A. S., & Rockwell, P. A. (1994). Interpersonal deception: V. Accuracy in deception detection. *Communication Monographs, 61,* 303–325.

Burgoon, J. K., Buller, D. B., Ebesu, A. S., White, C. H., & Rockwell, P. A. (1996). Testing interpersonal deception theory: Effects of suspicion on communication behaviors and perceptions. *Communication Theory, 6,* 243–267.

Burgoon, J. K., Buller, D. B., & Guerrero, L. K. (1995). Interpersonal deception: IX. Effects of social skill and nonverbal communication on deception success and detection accuracy. *Journal of Language and Social Psychology, 14,* 289–311.

Burgoon, J. K., Buller, D. B., Guerrero, L. K., Afifi, W. A., & Feldman, C. M. (1996). Interpersonal deception: XII. Information management dimensions underlying deceptive and truthful messages. *Communication Monographs, 63,* 50–69.

Burgoon, J. K., Buller, D. B., Guerrero, L. K., & Feldman, C. M. (1994). Interpersonal deception: VI. Effects on preinteractional and interactional factors on deceiver and observer perceptions of deception success. *Communication Studies, 45,* 263–280.

Burgoon, J. K., Buller, D. B., Hale, J. L., & deTurck, M. A. (1984). Relational messages associated with nonverbal behaviors. *Human Communication Research, 10,* 351–378.

Burgoon, J. K., Buller, D. B., White, C. H., Afifi, W., & Buslig, A. L. S. (1999). The role of conversational involvement in deceptive interpersonal interactions. *Personality and Social Psychology Bulletin, 25,* 669–686.

Burgoon, J. K., Buller, D. B., & Woodall, W. G. (1989). *Nonverbal communication: The unspoken dialogue.* New York: Harper & Row.

Burgoon, J. K., Buller, D. B., & Woodall, W. G. (1996). *Nonverbal communications: The unspoken dialogue* (2nd ed.). New York: McGraw-Hill.

Burgoon, J. K., & Coker, D. A. (1988, May). *Nonverbal expectancy violations and conversational involvement.* Paper presented at the annual convention of the International Communication Association, New Orleans, LA.

Burgoon, J. K., Coker, D. A., & Coker, R. A. (1986). Communicative effects of gaze behavior: A test of two contrasting explanations. *Human Communication Research, 12,* 495–524.

Burgoon, J. K., Dillman, L., & Stern, L. A. (1993). Adaptation in dyadic interaction: Defining and operationalizing patterns of reciprocity and compensation. *Communication Theory, 3,* 295–316.

Burgoon, J. K., & Dunbar, N. E. (2006). Nonverbal expressions of dominance and power in human relationships. In V. Manusov & M. Patterson (Eds.), *The Sage handbook of nonverbal communication* (pp. 279–297). Thousand Oaks, CA: Sage.

Burgoon, J. K., & Floyd, K, (2000). Testing for the motivation impairment effect during deceptive and truthful communication. *Western Journal of Communication, 64,* 243–267.

Burgoon, J. K., & Hale, J. L. (1984). The fundamental topoi of relational communication. *Communication Monographs, 51,* 193–214.

Burgoon, J. K., & Jones, S. B. (1976). Toward a theory of personal space expectations and their violations. *Human Communication Research, 2,* 131–146.

Burgoon, J. K., Kelley, D. L., Newton, D. A., & Keeley-Dyerson, M. P. (1989). The nature of arousal and nonverbal indices. *Human Communication Research, 16,* 217–255.

Burgoon, J. K., & Koper, R. J. (1984). Nonverbal and relational communication associated with reticence. *Human Communication Research, 10,* 601–626.

Burgoon, J. K., & LePoire, B. A. (1992). A reply from the heart: Who are Sparks and Greene and why are they saying all these horrible things? *Human Communication Research, 18,* 472–482.

Burgoon, J. K., & LePoire, B. A. (1999). Nonverbal cues and interpersonal judgments: Participant and observer perceptions of intimacy, dominance, composure and formality. *Communication Monographs, 66,* 105–124.

Burgoon, J. K., LePoire, B. A., Beutler, L. E., Bergan, J., & Engle, D. (1992). Nonverbal behaviors as indices of arousal: Extensions to the psychotherapy context. *Journal of Nonverbal Behavior, 16,* 159–178.

Burgoon, J. K., Manusov, V., Mineo, P., & Hale, J. L. (1985). Effects of gaze on hiring, credibility, attraction and relational message interpretation. *Journal of Nonverbal Behavior, 9,* 133–146.

Burgoon, J. K., & Newton, D. A. (1991). Applying a social meaning model to relational message interpretations of conversational involvement: Comparing observer and participant perspectives. *Southern Communication Journal, 66,* 96–113.

Burgoon, J. K., Pfau, M., Parrott, R., Birk, T., Coker, R., & Burgoon, M. (1987). Relational communication, satisfaction, compliance-gaining strategies, and compliance in communication between physicians and patients. *Communication Monographs, 54,* 307–324.

Burgoon, J. K., & Saine, T. (1978). *The unspoken dialogue: An introduction to nonverbal communication.* Boston: Houghton Mifflin.

Burgoon, J. K., Stern, L. A., & Dillman, L. (1995). *Interpersonal adaptation: Dyadic interaction patterns.* New York: Cambridge University Press.

Burgoon, J. K., Walther, J. B., & Baesler, E. J. (1992). Interpretations, evaluations, and consequences of interpersonal touch. *Human Communication Research, 19,* 237–263.

Burgoon, M., Callister, M., & Hunsaker, F. G. (1994). Patients who deceive: An empirical investigation of patient-physician communication. *Journal of Language and Social Psychology, 13,* 443–468.

Burleson, B. R., & Goldsmith, D. J. (1998). How the comforting process works: Alleviating emotional distress through conversationally induced reappraisals. In P. A. Andersen & L. K. Guerrero (Eds.), *Handbook of communication and emotion: Research, theory, applications, and contexts* (pp. 245–280). San Diego, CA: Academic.

Burleson, B. R., Kunkel, A. W., Samter, W., & Werking, K. J. (1996). Men's and women's evaluations of communication skills in personal relationships: When sex differences make a difference—and when they don't. *Journal of Social and Personal Relationships, 13,* 201–224.

Burroughs, W. A., Schultz, W., & Autrey, S. (1973). Quality of argument, leaders, votes, and eye contact in three-person leaderless groups. *Journal of Social Psychology, 90,* 89–93.

Burton, R. (1976). *The language of smell.* Boston: Routledge & Kegan Paul.

Bush, D. F., & Connolly, R. (1984, May). *Physician gender and nonverbal cues influence memory for health information and attitudes toward the practitioner.* Paper presented at the annual meeting of the International Communication Association, San Francisco, CA.

Bushman, B. J. (1988). The effects of apparel on compliance: A field experiment with a female authority figure. *Personality and Social Psychology Bulletin, 14,* 459–467.

Buss, D. M. (1988). From vigilance to violence: Tactics of mate retention in American undergraduates. *Ethology and Sociobiology, 9,* 291–317.

Byers, E. S., & Heinlein, L. (1989). Predicting initiations and refusals of sexual activities in married and cohabiting heterosexual couples. *Journal of Sex Research, 26,* 210–231.

Cain, W. S. (1990). Educating your nose. In J. A. Devito & M. L. Hecht (Eds.), *The nonverbal communication reader* (pp. 279–290). Prospect Heights, IL: Waveland.

Calhoun, J. B. (1962). Population density and social pathology. *Scientific American, 26*(2), 139–148.

Calvin, W. H. (1991). *The ascent of mind.* New York: Bantam.

Camras, L. A. (1982). Ethological approaches to nonverbal communication. In R. S. Feldman (Ed.), *Development of nonverbal behavior in children* (pp. 3–28). New York: Springer Verlag.

Camras, L. A., Chen, Y., Bakeman, R., Norris, K., & Cain, T. R. (2006). Culture, ethnicity, and children's facial expressions: A study of European American, mainland Chinese, Chinese American and adopted Chinese girls. *Emotion, 6,* 103–114.

Camras, L. A., Meng, Z., Ujiie, T., Dharamsi, S., Miyake, K., Oster, H., Wang, L., Cruz, J., Murdoch A., & Campos, J. (2002). Observing emotion in infants: Body behavior, and rater judgements of responses to an expectancy violating event. *Emotion, 2,* 179–193.

Camras, L. A., Oster, H., Campos, J., Campos, R., Ujiie, T., Miyake, K., Wang, L., & Meng, Z. (1998). Production of emotional facial expressions in European American, Japanese, and Chinese infants. *Developmental Psychology, 34,* 616–628.

Canary, D. J., & Cody, M. J. (1993). *Interpersonal communication: A goals-based approach.* New York: St. Martin's.

Canary, D. J., Emmers-Sommer, T. M., & Faulkner, S. (1997). *Sex and gender differences in personal relationships.* New York: Guilford.

Canary, D. J., & Hause, K. S. (1993). Is there any reason to research sex differences in communication? *Communication Quarterly, 41,* 129–144.

Canary, D. J., Spitzberg, B. H., & Semic, B. A. (1998). The experience and expression of anger in interpersonal settings. In P. A. Andersen & L. K. Guerrero (Eds.), *Handbook of communication and emotion: Research, theory, applications, and contexts* (pp. 189–213). San Diego, CA: Academic.

Caplan, M. E., & Goldman, M. (1981). Personal space violations as a function of height. *Journal of Social Psychology, 114,* 167–171.

Caporael, L. R. (1981). The paralanguage of caregiving: Baby talk to institutionalized aged. *Journal of Personality and Social Psychology, 40,* 876–884.

Cappella, J. N. (1981). Mutual influence in expressive behavior: Adult-adult and infant-adult dyadic interaction. *Psychological Bulletin, 89,* 101–132.

Cappella, J. N. (1983). Conversational involvement: Approaching and avoiding others. In J. M. Wiemann & R. P. Harrison (Eds.), *Nonverbal interaction* (pp. 113–148). Beverly Hills, CA: Sage.

Cappella, J. N. (1985). Production principles for turn-taking rules in social interaction: Socially anxious vs. socially secure persons. *Journal of Language and Social Psychology, 4,* 193–212.

Cappella, J. N. (1991a). The biological origins of automated patterns of human interaction. *Communication Theory, 1,* 4–35.

Cappella, J. N. (1991b). Mutual adaptation and relativity of measurement. In B. M. Montgomery & S. Duck (Eds.), *Studying interpersonal interaction* (pp. 103–117). New York: Guilford.

Cappella, J. N. (1993). The facial feedback hypothesis in human interaction: Review and speculation. *Journal of Language and Social Psychology, 12,* 13–29.

Cappella, J. N., & Greene, J. O. (1982). A discrepancy-arousal explanation of mutual influence in expressive behavior for adult and infant-adult interaction. *Communication Monographs, 49,* 89–114.

Cappella, J. N., & Palmer, M. T. (1990). Attitude similarity, relational history, and attraction: The mediating effect of kinesic and vocal behaviors. *Communication Monographs, 57,* 161–181.

Cardot, J., & Dodd, C. (1979, November). *Communication apprehension as a predictor of proxemic establishment.* Paper presented at the annual meeting of the Speech Communication Association, San Antonio, TX.

Carducci, B. J., & Webber, A. W. (1979). Shyness as a determinant of interpersonal distance. *Psychological Reports, 44,* 1075–1078.

Carli, L. L. (2001) Gender and social influence. *Journal of Social Issues, 57,* 725–741.

Carney, D. R., Hall, J. A., & LeBeau, L. S. (2005). Beliefs about the nonverbal expression of social power. *Journal of Nonverbal Behavior, 29,* 105–123.

Caso, L., Maricchiolo, F., Bonaiuto, M., Vrij, A., & Mann, S. (2006). The impact of deception and suspicion on different hand movements. *Journal of Nonverbal Behavior, 30,* 1–19.

Caso, L., Vrij, A., Mann, S., & De Leo, G. (2006). Deceptive responses: The impact of verbal and nonverbal countermeasures. *Legal and Criminological Psychology, 11,* 99–111.

Cegala, D. J., Alexander, A. F., & Sokovitz, S. (1979). An investigation of eye gaze and its reaction to selected verbal behavior. *Human Communication Research, 5,* 99–108.

Cegala, D. J., & Sillars, A. L. (1989). Further examination of nonverbal manifestations of interaction involvement. *Communication Reports, 2,* 39–47.

Chaiken, S. (1979). Communicator physical attractiveness and persuasion. *Journal of Personality and Social Psychology, 37,* 1387–1397.

Chartrand, T. L., & Bargh, J. A. (1999). The chameleon effect: The perceptual behavioral link of social interaction. *Journal of Personality and Social Psychology, 76,* 893–910.

Chaudhuri, A., & Buck, R. (1995). Affect, reasoning, and persuasion. *Human Communication Research, 21,* 422–441.

Chelune, G. J., Robinson, J. T., & Kommor, M. J. (1984). A cognitive interactional model of intimate relationships. In V. Derlega (Ed.), *Communication, intimacy, and close relationships* (pp. 11–40). Orlando, FL: Academic.

Cherry, C. (1966). *On human communication.* Cambridge, MA: MIT Press.

Chinoy, E. (1967). *Society.* New York: Random House.

Christiansen, C. M. (1960). Relationships between pupil achievement, pupil affect-need, teacher warmth, and teacher permissiveness. *Journal of Educational Psychology, 51,* 169–174.

Cialdini, R. B. (1984). *Influence: How and why people agree to things.* New York: Quill.

Cialdini, R. B. (1988). *Influence, science and practice.* New York: Harper Collier.

Clark, M. S., Milberg, S., & Erber, R. (1984). Effects of arousal on the judgments of others' emotions. *Journal of Personality and Social Psychology, 46,* 551–560.

Coates, E. J., & Feldman, R. S. (1996). Gender differences in nonverbal correlates of social status. *Personality and Social Psychology Bulletin, 22,* 1014–1022.

Coats, W. D., & Smidchens, U. (1966). Audience recall as a function of speaker dynamism. *Journal of Educational Psychology, 57,* 189–191.

Cody, M. J., Lee, W. S., & Chao, E. Y. (1988, September). *Telling lies: Correlates of deception among Chinese.* Paper presented at the International Congress of Psychology, Sydney, Australia.

Cody, M. J., Marston, P. J., & Foster, M. (1984, May). *Paralinguistic and verbal leakage of deception as a function of attempted control of timing of questions.* Paper presented at the annual meeting of the International Communication Association, San Francisco, CA.

Coker, D. A., & Burgoon, J. K. (1987). The nature of conversational involvement and nonverbal encoding patterns. *Human Communication Research, 13,* 463–494.

Comadena, M. E. (1982a). Accuracy in detecting deception: Intimate and friendship persons. In M. Burgoon (Ed.), *Communication yearbook 6* (pp. 446–472). Beverly Hills, CA: Sage.

Comadena, M. E. (1982b, May). *Nonverbal cues in the perception of deception.* Paper presented at the annual meeting of the Eastern Communication Association, Hartford, CT.

Comadena, M. E., & Andersen, P. A. (1978, April). *Kinesic correlates of communication apprehension: An analysis of hand movements.* Paper presented at the annual convention of the International Communication Association, Chicago, IL.

Comstock, J., Rowell, E., & Bowers, J. W. (1995). Food for thought: Teacher immediacy, student learning and curvilinearity. *Communication Education, 44,* 251–266.

Condon, J. C., & Yousef, F. (1983). *An introduction to intercultural communication.* Indianapolis: Bobbs-Merrill.

Condon, W. S., & Ogston, W. D. (1966). Sound film analysis of normal and pathological behavior patterns. *Journal of Nervous and Mental Disease, 143,* 338–347.

Condra, M. B. (1988, November). *Flirtation in developing relationships.* Paper presented at the annual convention of the Speech Communication Association, New Orleans, LA.

Conlee, C. J., Olvera, J., & Vagim, N. M. (1993). The relationship among physician nonverbal immediacy and measures of patient satisfaction with physician care. *Communication Reports, 6,* 25–33.

Cook, M. (1979). Gaze and mutual gaze in social encounters. In S. Weitz (Ed.), *Nonverbal communication: Readings with commentary* (2nd ed., pp. 77–86). New York: Oxford University Press.

Corballis, M. C. (2003). From mouth to hand: Gesture, speech, and the evolution of right-handedness. *Behavioral and Brain Sciences, 26*, 199–208.

Cortés, J. B., & Gatti, F. M. (1965). Physique and self-description of temperament. *Journal of Consulting Psychology, 29*, 432–439.

Costa, M., Dinsbach, W., Manstead, A. S. R., & Bitti, P. E. R. (2001). Social presence, embarrassment, and nonverbal behavior. *Journal of Nonverbal Behavior, 25*, 225–240.

Coulson, M. (2004). Attributing emotion to static body postures: Recognition accuracy, confusions and viewpoint dependency. *Journal of Nonverbal behavior, 24*, 117–139.

Coutts, L. M., & Schneider, F. W. (1976). Affiliative conflict theory: An investigation of the intimacy equilibrium and compensation hypothesis. *Journal of Personality and Social Psychology, 34*, 1135–1142.

Coutts, L. M., Schneider, F. W., & Montgomery, S. (1980). An investigation of the arousal model of interpersonal intimacy. *Journal of Experimental Social Psychology, 16*, 545–561.

Crawford, C. B. (1994). Effects of sex and sex-roles on avoidance of same- and opposite-sex touch. *Perceptual and Motor Skills, 70*, 107–112.

Crawford, M. (1995). *Talking difference: On gender and language.* London: Sage.

Crouch, W. W. (1980, April). *Consistency of selected eye behaviors across conversations with nine different partners.* Paper presented at the annual convention of the Eastern Communication Association, Ocean City, MD.

Crouch, W. W., & Koll, M. (1979, May). *The function of behavior in signaling dominance and submission in dyadic interactions.* Paper presented at the Eastern Communication Association, Philadelphia, PA.

Crusco, A. H., & Wetzel, C. G. (1984). The Midas touch: The effects of interpersonal touch on restaurant tipping. *Personality and Social Psychology, 10*, 512–517.

Cunningham, M. R., Roberts, A. R., Barbee, A. P., & Druen, P. B. (1995). Their ideas of beauty on the whole are the same as ours: Consistency and variability in the cross-cultural perception of female attractiveness. *Journal of Personality and Social Psychology, 68*, 261–279.

Cupach, W. R., & Metts, S. (1990). Remedial processes in embarrassing predicaments. In J. A. Anderson (Ed.), *Communication yearbook 13* (pp. 323–352). Beverly Hills, CA: Sage.

Cupach, W. R., & Metts, S. (1991). Sexuality and communication in close relationships. In K. McKinney & S. Sprecher (Eds.), *Sexuality in close relationships* (pp. 93–110). Hillsdale, NJ: Erlbaum.

Cupach, W. R., & Metts, S. (1994). *Facework.* Thousand Oaks, CA: Sage.

Cutler, W. B., Friedman, E., & McCoy, N. L. (1998). Pheromonal influences on sociosexual behavior in men. *Archives of Sexual Behavior, 27*, 1–13.

Daly, J. A., & Stafford, L. (1984). Correlates and consequences of social-communicative anxiety. In J. A. Daly & J. C. McCroskey (Eds.), *Avoiding communication: Shyness, reticence, and communication apprehension* (pp. 125–143). Beverly Hills, CA: Sage.

Daly, M., & Wilson, M. (1987). Evolutionary psychology and family violence. In C. Crawford, M. Smith, & D. Krebs (Eds.), *Sociobiology and psychology: Ideas, issues and applications* (pp. 293–309). Hillsdale, NJ: Erlbaum.

Daly, S. (1978). Behavioral correlates of social anxiety. *British Journal of Social and Clinical Psychology, 17*, 117–120.

Darley, J. M., & Cooper, J. (1972). The "clean for gene" phenomenon: The effect of students' appearance on political campaigning. *Journal of Applied Social Psychology, 2*, 24–33.

Darwin, C. (1872/1904). *The expression of emotion in man and animals.* London: John Murray.

Davis, C. (1992). Illinois: Crossroads and cross section. In J. H. Madison (Ed.), *Heartland: Comparative histories of midwestern states* (pp. 127–157). Bloomington: Indiana University Press.

Davis, F. (1973). *Inside intuition.* New York: McGraw-Hill.

Davis, M., Markus, K. A., & Walters, S. B. (2006). Judging the credibility of criminal suspect statements: Does mode of presentation matter? *Journal of Nonverbal Behavior, 30*, 181–198.

Davis, M., Markus, K., Walters, S. B., Vorus, N., & Connors, B. (2005). Behavioral cues to deception vs. topic incriminating potential in criminal confessions. *Law and Human Behavior, 29*, 483–704.

Dean, L. M., Pugh, W. M., & Gundersen, E. K. E. (1975). Spatial and perceptual components of crowding: Effects on health and satisfaction. *Environment and Behavior, 7*, 225–236.

Dean, L. M., Willis, F. N., & Hewitt, J. (1975). Initial distance among individuals equal and unequal in military rank. *Journal of Personality and Social Psychology, 32*, 294–299.

Deethardt, J. F., & Hines, D. G. (1983). Tactile communication and personality differences. *Journal of Nonverbal Behavior, 8*, 143–156.

DePaulo, B. M. (1992). Nonverbal behavior and self-presentation. *Psychological Bulletin, 111*, 203–243.

DePaulo, B. M., Blank, A., Swaim, G. W., & Hairfield, J. G. (1992). Expressiveness and expressive control. *Personality and Social Psychology Bulletin, 18*, 276–285.

DePaulo, B. M., Charlton, K., Cooper, H. Lindsay, J. J., & Muhlenbruck, L. (1997). The accuracy-confidence correlation in the detection of deception. *Personality and Social Psychology Review, 1*, 346–357.

DePaulo, B. M., Kashy, D. A., Kirkendol, S. E., Wyer, S. M., & Epstein, J. A. (1996). Lying in everyday life. *Journal of Personality and Social Psychology, 70*, 979–995.

DePaulo, B. M., Lindsay, J. L., Malone, B. E., Muhlenbruck, L., Charlton, K., & Cooper, H. (2003). Cues to deception. *Psychological Bulletin, 129*, 74–118.

DePaulo, B. M., & Rosenthal, R. (1979). Ambivalence, discrepancy, and deception in nonverbal communication. In R. Rosenthal (Ed.), *Skill in nonverbal communication* (pp. 204–248). Cambridge, MA: Oelgeschlager, Gunn, & Hain.

DePaulo, B. M., Rosenthal, R., Green, C. R., & Rosenkrantz, J. (1982). Diagnosing deceptive and mixed messages from verbal and nonverbal cues. *Journal of Experimental Social Psychology, 18*, 433–446.

DePaulo, B. M., Stone, J. I., & Lassiter, G. D. (1985). Deceiving and detecting deceit. In B. Schlenker (Ed.), *The self and social life* (pp. 323–370). New York: McGraw-Hill.

Derlega, V. J., Lewis, R. J., Harrison, S., Winstead, B. A., & Costanza, R. (1989, May). *Gender differences in the initiation and attribution of tactile intimacy.* Paper presented at the meeting of the International Network on Personal Relationships, Iowa City, IA.

Derlega, V. J., Metts, S., Petronio, S., & Margulis, S. T. (1993). *Self-disclosure.* Newbury Park, CA: Sage.

deTurck, M. A., & Miller, G. R. (1985). Deception and arousal: Isolating the behavioral correlates of deception. *Human Communication Research, 12*, 181–201.

Dillard, J. P. (1994). Rethinking the study of fear appeals: An emotional perspective. *Communication Theory, 4*, 295–323.

Dillard, J. P. (1998). The role of affect in communication, biology, and social relationships. In P. A. Andersen & L. K. Guerrero (Eds.), *The handbook of communication and emotion: Research, theory, applications, and contexts* (pp. xvii–xxxii). San Diego, CA: Academic.

Dindia, K. (1987). The effects of sex of subject and sex of partner on interruptions. *Human Communication Research, 13*, 345–371.

Dindia, K. (1997, November). *Men are from North Dakota, women are from South Dakota.* Paper presented at the annual meeting of the National Communication Association, Chicago, IL.

Dindia, K. (2006). Men are from North Dakota, women are from South Dakota. In K. Dindia & D. J. Canary (Eds.). *Sex Differences and Similarities in Communication.* (3–20). Mahwah, NJ: Erlbaum.

Dindia, K., Fitzpatrick, M. A., & Attridge, M. (1989, November). *Gaze and mutual gaze: A social relations analysis.* Paper presented at the annual convention of the Speech Communication Association, San Francisco, CA.

Dinnerstein, L., & Reimers, D. M. (1975). *Ethnic Americans: A history of immigration and assimilation.* New York: Harper & Row.

Dion, K. L. E., Berscheid, E., & Walster, E. (1972). What is beautiful is good. *Journal of Personality and Social Psychology, 24*, 285–290.

Dittman, A. T. (1972). Developmental factors in conversational behavior. *Journal of Communication, 22*, 404–423.

Dixon, J. A., & Foster, D. H. (1998). Gender, context, and backchannel responses. *Journal of Social Psychology, 138*, 134–136.

Dolin, D., & Booth-Butterfield, M. (1993). Reach out and touch someone: An analysis of nonverbal comforting responses. *Communication Quarterly, 41*, 383–393.

Donaghy, W. C., & Dooley, B. (1994). Head movement, gender, and deceptive communication. *Communication Reports, 7*, 76–87.

Doty, R. L. (Producer) (1974, November 10). Olfaction. *NOVA*. New York and Washington, DC: Public Broadcasting Service.

Doty, R. L., Snyder, P. J., Huggins, G. R., & Lowry, L. D. (1981). Endocrine, cardiovascular, and psychological correlates of olfactory sensitivity changes during the human menstrual cycle. *Journal of Comparative and Physiological Psychology, 95*, 46–60.

Dovidio, J. F., Hebl, M., Richeson, J. A., & Shelton, J. N. (2006). Nonverbal communication, race, and intergroup interaction. In V. Manusov & M. L. Patterson (Eds.), *The Sage handbook of nonverbal communication* (pp. 481–500). Thousand Oaks, CA: Sage.

Druckman, D., Rozelle, R. M., & Baxter, J. C. (1982). *Nonverbal communication: Survey, theory, and research*. Beverly Hills, CA: Sage.

Duck, S. (1988). *Relating to others*. Chicago: Dorsey.

Duck, S., & Miell, E. E. (1986). Charting the development of relationships. In R. Gilmour & S. Duck (Eds.), *The emerging field of personal relationships*. Hillsdale, NJ: Erlbaum.

Dunning, D., Li, J., & Milpass, R. S. (1998, March). *Basketball fandom and cross-race identification among European-Americans: Another look at the contact hypothesis*. Paper presented at the American Psychology-Law Society conference, Redondo Beach, CA.

Duran, R. L., Jensen, A. D., Prisbell, M., & Rosoff, J. M. (1979, February). *The control dimension of interpersonal relationships: Conceptualization, behavioral correlates and measurement*. Paper presented at the annual meeting of the Western Speech Communication Association convention, Los Angeles, CA.

Duthler, K. W. (2006). The politeness of requests made by e-mail and voicemail: Support for the hyperpersonal model. *Journal of Computer-Mediated Communication, 11*, 1–24.

Eagly, A. H., Makhijani, M. G., & Klonsky, B. G. (1992). Gender and the evaluation of leaders: A meta-analysis. *Psychological Bulletin, 111*, 3–22.

Eagly, A. H., & Wood, W. (1999). The original of sex differences in human behavior: Evolved disposition versus social roles. *American Psychologist, 54*, 408–423.

Earthworks Group. (1990). *50 simple things kids can do to save the earth*. Kansas City, MO: Andrews and McMeel.

Ebesu-Hubbard, A. S. Tsuji, A., Williams, C., & Seatriz, V. (2003). Effect of touch on gratuities in same-gender and cross-gender interaction. *Journal of Applied Social Psychology, 33*, 2427–2438.

Eckman, B. K. (1978, March). *Nonverbal correlates of anxiety*. Paper presented at the annual meeting of the Eastern Communication Association, Boston, MA.

Edmonds, E. M., & Cahoon, D. D. (1986). Attitudes concerning crimes related to clothing by female victims. *Bulletin of the Psychonomic Society, 24*, 444–446.

Efran, J. S. (1968). Looking for approval: Effects on visual behavior of approbation from persons differing in importance. *Journal of Personality and Social Psychology, 10*, 21–25.

Efran, M. G. (1974). The effect of physical appearance on the judgment of guilt, interpersonal attraction and severity of recommended punishment in a simulated jury task. *Journal of Research in Personality, 8*, 45–54.

Egland, K. L., Stelzner, M. A., Andersen, P. A., & Spitzberg, B. H. (1995). Perceived understanding, nonverbal communication, and relational satisfaction. In J. Aitken (Ed.), *Interpersonal communication processes* (pp. 1–28). Westeland, MI: Hayden-McNeill.

Egland, K. L., Stelzner, M. A., Andersen, P. A., & Spitzberg, B. H. (1997). Perceived understanding, nonverbal communication and relational satisfaction. In J. Aitken & L. Shedletsky (Eds.), *Intrapersonal communication processes* (pp. 386–395). Annandale, VA: The Speech Communication Association.

Ehrlichman, H., & Weinberger, A. (1978). Lateral eye movements and hemispheric asymmetry: A critical review. *Psychological Bulletin, 85*, 1080–1101.

Ehrlichman, H., Weiner, S. L., & Baker, A. H. (1974). Effects of verbal and spatial questions on initial gaze shifts. *Neuropsychologia, 12*, 266–277.

Eibl-Eibesfeldt, I. (1972). Similarities and differences between cultures in expressive movements. In R. A. Hinde (Ed.), *Nonverbal communication* (pp. 297–312). London: Cambridge University Press.

Eibl-Eibesfeldt, I. (1974). *Love and hate: The natural history of behavior patterns*. New York: Holt, Rinehart & Winston.

Eibl-Eibesfeldt, I. (1979). Universals in human expressive behavior. In A. Wolfgang (Ed.), *Nonverbal behavior, applications and cultural implications* (pp. 17–30). New York: Academic.

Einav, S., & Hood, B. M. (2006). Children's use of the temporal dimension of gaze for inferring preference. *Developmental Psychology, 42*, 142–152.

Eisenberg, A. M., & Smith, R. R., Jr. (1971). *Nonverbal communication*. Indianapolis: Bobbs-Merrill.

Eisenberg, N., Loyosa, S., Fabes, R. A., Guthrie, Reiser, M., Murphy, B., Shapard, S. A. Poulin, R., & Padgett, S. J. (2001). Parental socialization of children's dysregulated expression of emotion and externalizing problems. *Journal of Family Psychology, 15*, 183–205.

Ekman, P. (1965). Communication through nonverbal behavior: A source of information about an interpersonal relationship. In S. S. Tomkins & C. E. Izard (Eds.), *Affect, cognition and personality* (pp. 390–442). New York: Springer.

Ekman, P. (1972). Universal and cultural difference in the facial expression of emotion. In J. R. Cole (Ed.), *Nebraska symposium on motivation* (pp. 207–283). Lincoln: University of Nebraska Press.

Ekman, P. (1976). Movements with precise meanings. *Journal of Communication, 26*(3), 14–26.

Ekman, P. (1978). Facial expression. In A. W. Siegman & S. Feldstein (Eds.), *Nonverbal behavior and communication* (pp. 97–116). Hillsdale, NJ: Erlbaum.

Ekman, P. (1982). *Emotion in the human face*. Cambridge, England: Cambridge University Press.

Ekman, P. (1985). *Telling lies: Clues in the marketplace, politics, and marriage*. New York: Norton.

Ekman, P. (1988). Lying and nonverbal behavior: Theoretical issues and new findings. *Journal of Nonverbal Behavior, 12*, 163–175.

Ekman, P. (1993). Facial expression and emotion. *American Psychologist, 48*, 384–392.

Ekman, P., & Friesen, W. V. (1969a). Nonverbal leakage and clues to deception. *Psychiatry, 32*, 88–106.

Ekman, P., & Friesen, W. V. (1969b). The repertoire of nonverbal behavior: Categories, origins, usage and coding. *Semiotica, 1*, 49–98.

Ekman, P., & Friesen, W. V. (1972). Hand movements. *Journal of Communication, 22*, 353–374.

Ekman, P., & Friesen, W. V. (1975). *Unmasking the face: A field guide to recognizing emotions from facial clues*. Englewood Cliffs, NJ: Prentice-Hall.

Ekman, P., & Friesen, W. V. (1986). A new pan-cultural facial expression of emotion. *Motivation and Emotion, 10*, 159–168.

Ekman, P., Friesen, W. V., & Ellsworth, P. (1972). *Emotion in the human face: Guidelines for research and integration of findings*. New York: Pergamon.

Ekman, P., Friesen, W. V., & O'Sullivan, M. (1988). Smiles when lying. *Journal of Personality and Social Psychology, 54*, 414–420.

Ekman, P., & O'Sullivan, M. (1991). Who can catch a liar? *American Psychologist, 46*, 913–920.

Elazar, D. J. (1972). *American federalism: A view from the states*. New York: Thomas P. Crowell.

Elfenbein, H. A. (2006). Learning in emotion judgments: Training and the cross-cultural. *Journal of Nonverbal Behavior, 30*, 21–36.

Elfenbein, H. A., & Ambady, N. (2002). On the universality and cultural specificity of emotional recognition: A meta-analysis. *Psychological Bulletin, 128*, 205–235.

Elfenbein, H. A., & Ambady, N. (2003a). Universals and cultural differences in recognizing emotions. *Current Directions in Psychological Science, 12*, 159–164.

Elfenbein, H. A., & Ambady, N. (2003b). When familiarity breeds accuracy: Cultural exposure and facial expression recognition. *Journal of Personality and Social Psychology, 85*, 276–290.

Elfenbein, H. A., Foo, M. D., Boldry, J. G., & Tan, H. H. (2006). Dyadic effects in nonverbal communication: A variance partitioning analysis. *Cognition and Emotion, 20*, 149–159.

Elliot, S., & Jensen, A. D. (1979, May). *A summary of literature in olfactory communication: Special attention to pheromones*. Paper presented at the annual meeting of the Eastern Communication Association, Philadelphia, PA.

Elliot, S., Scott, M. D., Jensen, A. D., & McDonough, M. (1982). Perceptions of reticence: A cross-cultural investigation. In M. Burgoon (Ed.), *Communication yearbook* (pp. 591–602). New Brunswick, NJ: Transaction Books.

Ellis, L. (2006). Gender differences in smiling: An evolutionary neuroandrogenic theory. *Physiology and Behavior, 88*, 303–308.

Ellsworth, P. C., Carlsmith, J. M., & Henson, A. (1972). The stare as a stimulus of flight in human subjects. *Journal of Personality and Social Psychology, 21*, 302–311.

Ellyson, S. L., & Dovidio, J. F. (1985). Power, dominance, and nonverbal behavior: Basic concepts and issues. In S. L. Ellyson & J. F. Dovidio (Eds.), *Power, dominance, and nonverbal behavior* (pp. 1–27). New York: Springer Verlag.

Eman, V. A., Dierks-Stewart, K. J., & Tucker, R. K. (1978). Implications of sexual identity and sexually identified situations on nonverbal touch. Paper presented at the annual meeting of the Speech Communication Association, Minneapolis, MN.

Emmers, T. M., & Dindia, K. (1995). The effect of relational stage and intimacy on touch: An extension of Guerrero and Andersen. *Personal Relationships, 2,* 225–236.

Engel, R. S., & Calnon, J. M. (2004). Examining the influence of driver characteristics during traffic stops with police: Results of a National Survey. *Justice Quarterly, 19,* 41–90

Engen, T. A. (1973). The sense of smell. *Annual Review of Psychology, 24,* 187–206.

Engen, T. A. (1987). Remembering odors and their names. *American Scientist, 75,* 497–503.

Erickson, K., & Schulkin, J. (2003). Facial expressions of emotion: A cognitive neuroscience perspective. *Brain and Cognition, 52,* 52–60.

Ervin, F. R., & Martin, J. (1986). Neuropsychological bases of the primary emotions. In R. Plutchik and H. Kellerman (Eds.), *Emotion: Theory, research and experience* (Vol. 3, pp. 145–170). Orlando, FL: Academic.

Esp, B. A. (1978). The effects of teacher kinesic communication upon student learning and attitudes. *Dissertations Abstracts International, 39*(5-A), 2828.

Etcoff, N. L., Ekman, P., Magee, J. J., & Frank, M. G. (2000). Lie detection and language comprehension. *Nature, 405,* 139.

Exline, R. V., Ellyson, S. L., & Long, B. (1975). Visual behavior as an aspect of power role relationships. In P. Pliner, L. Drames, & T. Alloway (Eds.), *Nonverbal communication of aggression* (Vol. 2, pp. 21–52). New York: Plenum.

Exline, R. V., & Fehr, B. J. (1979). *Person and context in interpretation of gaze behavior.* Paper presented at the annual convention of the American Psychological Association, New York.

Exline, R. V., & Winters, L. C. (1965). Affective relations and mutual glances in dyads. In S. Tomkins & C. E. Izard (Eds.), *Affect, cognition, and personality.* New York: Springer.

Eysenck, H. J. (1963). *Experiments with drugs.* Oxford: Pergamon.

Eysenck, H. J. (1967). *The biological basis of personality.* Springfield, IL: Charles C. Thomas.

Eysenck, H. J. (1971). *Readings in extroversion-introversion: Bearings on basic psychological processes.* London: Staples.

Eysenck, H. J. (1976). Arousal, learning and memory. *Psychological Bulletin, 83,* 389–404.

Farroni, T., Csibra, G., Simion, F., & Johnson, M. H. (2002). Eye contact detection in humans from birth. *Proceedings of the National Academy of Science, 99,* 9602–9605.

Farroni, T., Menon, E., & Johnson, M. H. (2006). Factors influencing newborns' preferences for faces with eye contact. *Journal of Experimental Child Psychology, 95,* 298–308.

Feeley, T. H., & DeTurck, M. A. (1998). The behavioral correlates of sanctioned and unsanctioned deceptive communication. *Journal of Nonverbal Behavior, 22,* 189–204.

Feeley, T. H., & Young, M. J. (1995, May). *Baseline familiarity in lie detection.* Paper presented at the annual meeting of the International Communication Association Convention, Albuquerque, NM.

Fehr, B. J., & Exline, R. V. (1987). Social visual interaction: A conceptual and literature review. In A. W. Siegman & S. Feldstein (Eds.), *Nonverbal behavior and communication* (2nd ed., pp. 225–236). Hillsdale, NJ: Erlbaum.

Fehr, B., & Russell, J. A. (1984). Concept of emotion viewed from a prototype perspective. *Journal of Experimental Psychology, 113,* 464–486.

Feingold, A. (1990). Gender differences in effects of physical attraction on romantic attraction: A comparison across five research paradigms. *Journal of Personality and Social Psychology, 59,* 981–993.

Feingold, A. (1992). Good looking people are not what we think. *Psychological Bulletin, 3,* 304–341.

Feldman, R., Weller, A., Sirota, L., Eidelman. A. I. (2003). Testing a family intervention hypothesis: the contribution of mother-infant skin-to-skin contact (kangaroo care) to family interaction, proximity, and touch. *Journal of Family Psychology, 17,* 94–107.

Feldstein, S. (1972). Temporal patterns of dialogue. In A. W. Siegman & B. Pope (Eds.), *Studies in dyadic communication* (pp. 91–114). Oxford: Pergamon.

Ferguson, C. A. (1964). Baby talk in six languages. *American Anthropologist, 66,* 103–114.

Ferguson, T. J., & Stegge, H. (1995). Emotional states and traits in children: The case of shame and guilt. In J. P. Tangney & K. W. Fischer (Eds.), *Self-conscious emotions: The psychology of shame, guilt, embarrassment and pride* (pp. 174–197). New York: Guilford.

Fernandez-Dolz, J. M., & Ruiz-Belda, M. A. (1995). Are smiles a sign of happiness? Gold medal winners at the Olympic Games. *Journal of Personality and Social Psychology, 69,* 1113–1119.

Feyereisen, P. (1987). Brain pathology, lateralization, and nonverbal behavior. In R. S. Feldman & B. Rime (Eds.), *Fundamentals of nonverbal communication* (pp. 31–70). Cambridge: Cambridge University Press.

Field, T. (1999). American adolescents touch each other less and are more aggressive toward their peers than French adolescents. *Adolescence, 34,* 753–758.

Field, T. (2002). Infants' need for touch. *Human Development, 45,* 100–103.

Fielding, G. J. (1974). *Geography as a social science.* New York: Harper & Row.

Fischer, K. W., & Tangney, J. P. (1995). Self-conscious emotions and the affect revolution: Framework and overview. In J. P. Tangney & K. W. Fischer (Eds.), *Self-conscious emotions: The psychology of shame, guilt, embarrassment and pride* (pp. 3–22). New York: Guilford.

Fisher, J. D., Rytting, M., & Heslin, R. (1976). Hands touching hands: Affective and evaluative effects of an interpersonal touch. *Sociometry, 39,* 416 421.

Fitzpatrick, M. A., & Badzinski, D. (1985). All in the family: Communication in kin relationships. In M. L. Knapp & G. R Miller (Eds.), *Handbook of interpersonal communication* (pp. 687–736). Beverly Hills, CA: Sage.

Flora, J. A., & Maibach, E. W. (1990). Cognitive responses to AIDS information: The effect of issue involvement and message appeal. *Communication Research, 17,* 759–774.

Floyd, K. (2000). Affectionate same sex touch: The influence of homophobia on observers' perceptions. *The Journal of Social Psychology, 140,* 774–788.

Floyd, K., & Erbert, L. A. (2003). Relational message interpretations and nonverbal matching behavior: An application of the social meaning model. *Journal of Social Psychology, 143,* 581–597.

Floyd, K., & Morman, M. T. (1998). The measurement of affectionate communication. *Communication Quarterly, 46,* 144–163.

Floyd, K., & Ray, G. B. (2003). Human Affection Exchange IV: Vocalic predictors of perceived affection in initial interactions. *Western Journal of Communication, 67,* 56–73.

Floyd, K., Sargent, J. E., & Di Corcia, M. D. (2004). Human affective exchange VI: Further tests of reproductive probability as a predictor of men's affection with the adult sons. *Journal of Social Psychology, 144,* 191–206.

Floyd, K., & Voloudakis, M. (1999). Affectionate behavior in adult platonic relationships: Interpreting and evaluating expectancy violations. *Human Communication Research, 25,* 341–369.

Ford, C. V. (1996). *Lies! Lies! Lies! The Psychology of Deceit.* Washington, DC: American Psychology Press.

Ford, E. B. (2006). Lie detection: Historical, neuropsychiatric and legal dimensions. *International Journal of Law and Psychiatry, 29,* 159–177.

Forden, C. (1981). The influence of sex-role expectations on the perception of touch. *Sex Roles, 7,* 889–894.

Fowles, J. (1974). Why we wear clothes, ETC. A *Review of General Semantics, 31,* 343–352.

Frank, L. K. (1957). Tactile communication. *Genetic Psychology Monographs, 56,* 209–255.

Frank, M. G. (2005). Research methods in detecting deception research. In J. A. Harrigan, R. Rosenthal, & K. R. Scherer, (Eds.), *The new handbook of methods in nonverbal behavior research* (pp. 342–368). Oxford, UK: Oxford University Press.

Frank, M. G., & Ekman, P. (1997). The ability to detect deceit generalizes across different types of high stakes lies. *Journal of Personality and Social Psychology, 72,* 1429–1439.

Frank, M. G., & Ekman, P. (2004). Appearing truthful generalizes across different deception situations. *Journal of Personality and Social Psychology, 86,* 486–495.

Frank, M. G., Ekman, P., & Friesen, W. V. (1993). Behavioral markers and recognizability of the smile of enjoyment. *Journal of Personality and Social Psychology, 64,* 83–93.

Frank, M. G., & Feeley, T. H. (2003). To catch a liar: Challenges for research in lie detection training. *Journal of Applied Communication Research, 31,* 58–75.

Freud, S. (1930/1961). *Civilization and its discontents* (J. Strachey, Trans.). New York: Norton.

Frick, R. W. (1985). Communicating emotion: The role of prosodic features. *Psychological Bulletin, 97,* 412–429.

Fridlund, A. J. (1991). Evolution and facial action in reflex, social motive, and paralanguage. *Biological Psychology, 32,* 3–100.

Friedman, H. S., Mertz, T. J., & DiMatteo, M. R. (1980). Perceived bias in the facial expressions of television news broadcasters. *Journal of Communication, 30,* 103–111.

Friedman, J. N. W., Oltmanns, T. F., Gleason, M. E. J., & Turkheimer, E. (2006). Mixed impressions: Reactions of strangers to people with pathological personality traits. *Journal of Research in Personality, 40,* 395–410.

Friedman, M. (1985). Toward a reconceptualization of guilt. *Contemporary Psychoanalysis, 21,* 501–547.

Frijda, N. H., Kuipers, P., & ter Schure, E. (1989). Relations between emotion, appraisal, and emotional action readiness. *Journal of Personality and Social Psychology, 57,* 212–228.

Fromme, D. K., & Beam, D. C. (1974). Dominance and sex differences in nonverbal responses to differential eye contact. *Journal of Research in Personality, 8,* 76–87.

Fromme, D. K., Fromme, M. L., Brown, S., Daniell, J., Taylor, D. K., & Rountree, J. R. (1986). Attitudes toward touch: Cross-validation and the effects of gender and acquaintanceship. *Rassegna di Psicologia, 3,* 49–63.

Fromme, D. K., Jaynes, W. E., Taylor, D. K., Harold, E. G., Daniell, J., Rountree, J. R., & Fromme, M. L. (1989). Nonverbal behavior and attitudes toward touch. *Journal of Nonverbal Behavior, 13,* 3–14.

Frymier, A. B. (1994). A model of immediacy in the classroom. *Communication Quarterly, 42,* 133–144.

Fugita, S. S. (1974). Effects of anxiety and approval on visual interaction. *Journal of Personality and Social Psychology, 29,* 586–592.

Funder, D. C., & Ozer, D. J. (1983). Behavior as a function of the situation. *Journal of Personality and Social Psychology, 44,* 107–112.

Gaines, S. O. et al. (1998). Communication of emotions in friendships. In P. A. Andersen & L. K. Guerrero (Eds.), *Handbook of communication and emotion: Research, theory, applications, and contexts* (pp. 507–532). San Diego, CA: Academic.

Galbraith, J. K. (1951). Conditions for economic change in underdeveloped countries. *American Journal of Farm Economics, 33,* 693.

Gallaher, P. E. (1992). Individual differences in nonverbal behavior: Dimensions of style. *Journal of Personality and Social Psychology, 63,* 133–145.

Galle, O. R., & Gove, W. R. (1979). Crowding and social behavior in Chicago, 1940–1970. In J. R. Aiello & A. Baum (Eds.), *Residential crowding and design* (pp. 23–39). New York: Plenum.

Gangestad, S. W., & Thornhill, R. (1998). Menstrual cycle variations in women's preferences for the scent of symmetrical men. Proceedings of the Royal Society of London B, 265, 727–733.

Garreau, J. (1981). *The nine nations of North America.* New York: Avon Books.

Garrison, J. P., Sullivan, D. L., & Pate, L. E. (1976, December). *Interpersonal valence dimensions as discriminators of communication contexts: An empirical assessment of dyadic linkages.* Paper presented at the annual meeting of the Speech Communication Association, San Francisco, CA.

Garver-Apgar, C. E., Gangestad, S. W., Thornhill, R., Miller, R. D., & Olp, J. J. (2006). Major histocompatibility, complex alleles, sexual responsivity, and unfaithfulness in romantic couples. *Psychological Science, 17,* 830–835.

Gauger, P. W. (1952). The effect of gesture and the presence or absence of the speaker on the listening comprehension of eleventh and twelfth grade high school pupils. Cited in C. W. Dow (Ed.), Abstracts of theses in the field of speech and drama. *Speech Monographs, 19,* 116–117.

Gaulin, S. J. C. (1992). Evolution of sex differences in spatial ability. *Yearbook of Physical Anthropology, 35,* 125–151.

Geertz, C. (1973). *The interpretations of cultures.* New York: Basic Books.

Geller, D. M., Goodstein, L., Silver, M., & Steinberg, W. C. (1974). On being ignored: The effects of the violation of implicit rules of social interaction. *Sociometry, 37,* 541–556.

Gendrin, D. M., & Honeycutt, J. M. (1988, November). *The relationship between self-reported affinity-seeking competence and nonverbal immediacy behaviors among strangers and acquaintances.*

Paper presented at the annual convention of the Speech Communication Association, New Orleans, LA.

Gerbner, G., Gross, L., Morgan, M., & Signiorelli, N. (1986). Living with television: The dynamics of the cultivation process. In J. Bryant & D. Zillman (Eds.), *Perspectives on media effects* (pp. 17–41). Hillsdale, NJ: Erlbaum.

Gergen, K. J. (1991). *The saturated self: Dilemmas of identity in contemporary life.* New York: Basic Books.

Gergen, K. J., Gergen, M., & Barton, W. H. (1973). Deviance in the dark. *Psychology Today, 7,* 129–130.

Gibran, K. (1923). *The prophet.* New York: Alfred A. Knopf.

Gifford, R. (1994). A lens-mapping framework for understanding the encoding and decoding of interpersonal dispositions in nonverbal behavior. *Journal of Personality and Social Psychology, 66,* 398–412.

Giglio, K., & Lustig, M. W. (1987, February). *Teacher immediacy and student expectations as predictors of learning.* Paper presented at the annual convention of the Western Speech Communication Association, Salt Lake City, UT.

Gilbert, A. N., & Wysocki, C. J. (1987). The smell survey: Its results. *National Geographic, 174*(4), 514–525.

Giles, H., & Street, R. L. (1994). Communicator characteristics and behavior. In M. L. Knapp & G. R. Miller (Eds.), *Handbook of interpersonal communication* (2nd ed., pp. 103–161). Thousand Oaks, CA: Sage.

Glascock, J., & Ruggiero, T. E. (2006). The relationship of ethnicity and sex to professor credibility at a culturally diverse university. *Communication Education, 55,* 197–207.

Global Deception Research Team (2006). A world of lies. *Journal of Cross-Cultural Psychology, 37,* 60–74.

Godoy, R., Reyes-Garcia, V., Huanca, T., Tanner, S., Leonard, W. R., McDade, T., & Vadez, V. (2005). Do smiles have face value? Panel evidence from Amazonian Indians. *Journal of Economic Psychology, 26,* 469–490.

Goffman, E. (1959). *The presentation of self in every day life.* Garden City, NY: Doubleday-Anchor.

Goffman, E. (1967). *Interaction ritual.* Garden City, NY: Anchor Books.

Goldberg, G. N., Kiesler, C. A., & Collins, B. E. (1969). Visual behavior and face-to-face distance during interaction. *Sociometry, 32,* 43–53.

Goldhaber, G. M. (1974). *Organizational communication.* Dubuque, IA: William C. Brown.

Goldin-Meadow, S., & Wagner, S. M. (2005). How our hands help us learn. *Trends in Cognitive Science, 9,* 234–241.

Goldman, M., Kiyohara, O., & Pfannensteil, D. A. (1985). Interpersonal touch, social labeling, and the foot-in-the-door effect. *The Journal of Social Psychology, 125,* 143–147.

Goldstein, A. G., & Jeffords, J. (1981). Status and touching behavior. *Bulletin of the Psychonomic Society, 17*(2), 79–81.

Gonzaga, G. C., Turner, R. A., Keltner, D., Campos, B., & Altemus, M. (2006). Romantic love and sexual desire in close relationships. *Emotion, 6,* 163–179.

Goos, L. M., & Silverman, I. (2002). Sex-related factors in the perception of threatening facial expressions. *Journal of Nonverbal Behavior, 26,* 27–40.

Gore, A. (1992). *Earth in the balance: Ecology and the human spirit.* New York: Plume Books.

Gorham, J. (1988). The relationship between verbal teacher immediacy behaviors and student learning. *Communication Education, 37,* 40–53.

Gorham, J., & Azkahi, W. R. (1990). A comparison of teacher and student perceptions of immediacy and learning: Monitoring process and product. *Communication Education, 39,* 354–368.

Gorham, J., & Christofel, D. M. (1988, November). *The relationship of teachers' use of humor in the classroom to immediacy and student learning.* Paper presented at the annual convention of the Speech Communication Association, New Orleans, LA.

Gottman, J. M. (1979). *Marital interaction: Empirical investigations.* New York: Academic.

Grammer, K., Fink, B., & Neave, N. (2005). Human pheromones and sexual attraction. *European Journal of Obstetrics, Gynecology, and Reproductive Biology, 118,* 135–142.

Grammer, K., Kruck, K, Juette, A., & Fink, B. (2000). Non-verbal behavior as courtship signals: The role of control and choice in selecting partners. *Evolution and Human Behavior, 21,* 371–390.

Grammer, K., Renninger, L., and Fischer, B. (2004). Disco clothing, female sexual motivation, and relationship status: Is she dressed to impress? *Journal of Sex Research, 41,* 66–74.

Granhag, P. A., & Strömwell, L. A. (2002). Repeated interrogations: Verbal and nonverbal cues to deception. *Applied Cognitive Psychology, 16,* 243–257.

Grayson, B., & Stein, M. I. (1981). Attracting assault: Victim's nonverbal cues. *Journal of Communication, 31,* 68–75.

Greene, J. O., O'Hair, H. D., Cody, M. J., & Yen, C. (1985). Planning and control of behavior during deception. *Human Communication Research, 11,* 335–364.

Greene, J. O., & Sparks, G. G. (1983). Explication and test of a cognitive model of communication apprehension: A new look at an old construct. *Human Communication Research, 9,* 349–366.

Greene, J. O., & Sparks, G. G. (1992). Intellectual scrutiny as an alternative to replies from the heart: Toward clarifying the nature of arousal and its relation to nonverbal behavior. *Human Communication Research, 18,* 483–488.

Greenless, I., Buscombe, R., Thelwell, R., Holder, T., & Rimmer, M. (2005). Impact of opponents' clothing and body language on impression formation and outcome expectations. *Journal of Sports & Exercise Psychology, 27,* 39–52.

Greenwood, J. D. (1994). *Realism, identity, and emotion: Reclaiming social psychology.* Thousand Oaks, CA: Sage.

Gregory, S. W., & Gallagher, S. T. (2002). Spectral analysis of candidates' nonverbal vocal communication: Predicting U.S. presidential election outcomes. *Social Psychology Quarterly, 65,* 298–308.

Grezes, J., Frith, C., & Passingham, R. E. (2004). Brain mechanisms for inferring deceit in the actions of others. *Journal of Neuroscience, 24,* 5500–5505.

Griffin, C. H., Wilson, J. F., Langer, S., & Haist, S. A. (2003). House staff nonverbal communication skills and standardized patient satisfaction. *Journal of General Internal Medicine, 18,* 170–174.

Griffitt, W. (1970). Environmental effects on interpersonal affective behavior: Ambient effective temperature and attraction. *Journal of Personality and Social Psychology, 15,* 240–244.

Grinspan, D., Hemphill, A., & Nowicki, S. (2003). Improving the ability of elementary school-age children to identify emotion in facial expression. *Journal of Genetic Psychology, 164,* 88–100.

Gudykunst, W. B., & Kim, Y. Y. (1992). *Communicating with strangers: An approach to intercultural communication* (2nd ed.). New York: Random House.

Gudykunst, W. B., Ting-Toomey, S., & Chua, E. (1988). *Culture and interpersonal communication.* Newbury Park, CA: Sage.

Guéguen, N. (2002). Touch, awareness of touch, and compliance with a request. *Perceptual and Motor Skills, 95,* 355–360.

Guéguen, N., & De Gail, M. (2003). The effect of smiling on helping behavior: Smiling and good Samaritan behavior. *Communication Reports, 16,* 133–140.

Guéguen, N., & Fisher-Lokou, J. (2002). An evaluation of touch on a large request: A field setting. *Psychological Reports, 92,* 62–64.

Guéguen, N., & Fisher-Lokou, J. (2003). Another evaluation of touch and helping behavior. *Psychological Reports, 90,* 267–269.

Guerrero, L. K. (1994). "I'm so mad I could scream": The effects of anger expression on relational satisfaction and communication competence. *Southern Communication Journal, 59,* 125–141.

Guerrero, L. K. (1996). Attachment style differences in intimacy and involvement. *Communication Monographs, 63,* 269–292.

Guerrero, L. K. (1997). Nonverbal involvement across interactions with same-sex friends, opposite-sex friends, and romantic partners: Consistency or change? *Journal of Social and Personal Relationships, 14,* 31–59.

Guerrero, L. K., & Andersen, P. A. (1991). The waxing and waning of relational intimacy: Touch as a function of relational stage, gender and touch avoidance. *Journal of Social and Personal Relationships, 8,* 147–165.

Guerrero, L. K., & Andersen, P. A. (1994). Patterns of matching and initiation: Touch behavior and avoidance across romantic relationship stages. *Journal of Nonverbal Behavior, 18,* 137–153.

Guerrero, L. K., & Andersen, P. A. (1998a). The dark side of jealousy. In B. H. Spitzberg & W. R. Cupach (Eds.), *The dark side of close relationships.* Mahwah, NJ: Erlbaum.

Guerrero, L. K., & Andersen, P. A. (1998b). Jealousy experience and expression in romantic relationships. In P. A. Andersen & L. K. Guerrero (Eds.), *Handbook of communication and emotion: Research, theory, applications, and contexts* (pp. 155–188). San Diego, CA: Academic.

Guerrero, L. K., Andersen, P. A., Jorgensen, P. F., Spitzberg, B. H., & Eloy, S. V. (1995). Coping with the green-eyed monster: Conceptualizing and measuring communicative responses to romantic jealousy. *Western Journal of Communication, 59,* 270–304.

Guerrero, L. K., Andersen, P. A., & Trost, M. (1998). Communication and emotion: Basic concepts and approaches. In P. A. Andersen & L. K. Guerrero (Eds.), *Handbook of communication and emotion: Research, theory, applications, and contexts* (pp. 3–28). San Diego, CA: Academic.

Guerrero, L. K., & Ebesu, A. S. (1993, May). *While at play: An observational analysis of children's touch behavior.* Paper presented at the annual convention of the International Communication Association, Miami, FL.

Guerrero, L. K., & Floyd, K. (2006). *Nonverbal communication in close relationships.* Mahwah, NJ: Erlbaum.

Guerrero, L. K., Jones, S. M., & Boburka, R. R. (2006). Sex differences in emotional communication. In D. J. Canary & K. Dindia (Eds.), *Sex differences and similarities in communication* (pp. 241–261). Mahwah, NJ: Erlbaum.

Guerrero, L. K., & Miller, T. A. (1996, May). *The role of nonverbal involvement cues in videotaped distance education courses: Associations with behavioral intent and positive affective learning.* Paper presented at the annual convention of the International Communication Association, Albuquerque, NM.

Guerrero, L. K., & Reiter, R. L. (1998). Expressing emotion: Sex differences in social skills and communicative responses to anger, sadness, and jealousy. In D. J. Canary & K. Dindia (Eds.), *Sex differences and similarities in communication* (pp. 321–350). Mahwah, NJ: Erlbaum.

Gulledge, A. K., Gulledge, M. H., & Stahmann, R. F. (2003). Romantic physical affection types and relationship satisfaction. *American Journal of Family Therapy, 31,* 233–242.

Gunter, H. L. Ghaziuddin, M., & Ellis, H. D. (2002). Asperger syndrome: Tests of right hemisphere functioning and interhemispheric communication. *Journal of Autism and Developmental Disorders, 32,* 263–281.

Gur, R., & Gur, R. (1977). Correlates of conjugate lateral eye movements in man. In S. Hamad, R. W. Doty, L. Goldstein, J. Jaynes, & G. Krauthamer (Eds.), *Lateralization in the nervous system* (pp. 261–281). New York: Academic.

Gutsell, L. M., & Andersen, J. F. (1980, May). *Perceptual and behavioral responses to smiling.* Paper presented at the annual convention of the International Communication Association, Acapulco, Mexico.

Haas, A., & Gregory, S. W. (2005). The impact of physical attractiveness on women's social status and interactional power. *Sociological Forum, 20,* 449–471.

Haber, G. M. (1982). Spatial relations between dominants and marginals. *Social Psychological Quarterly, 45,* 219–228.

Halberstadt, A. G., & Eaton, K. L. (2002). A meta-analysis of family expressiveness and children's emotional expressiveness and understanding. *Marriage and Family Review, 34,* 35–62.

Halberstadt, A. G., & Saitta, M. B. (1987). Gender, nonverbal behavior, and perceived dominance: A test of the theory. *Journal of Personality and Social Psychology, 53,* 257–272.

Hale, D., & Eisen, J. (1968). *The California dream.* New York: Collier.

Hale, J. L, Lundy, J. C., & Mongeau, P. A. (1989). Perceived relational intimacy and relational message content. *Communication Research Reports, 6,* 94–99.

Hale, J. L., & Stiff, J. B. (1989). *Judgments of honesty and deceit: The impact of cue incongruence and normative influence.* Paper presented to the annual meeting of the International Communication Association, San Francisco, CA.

Hall, E. T. (1959). *The silent language.* New York: Doubleday.

Hall, E. T. (1966a). *The hidden dimension.* New York: Doubleday.

Hall, E. T. (1966b). A system of the notation of proxemic behavior. *American Anthropologist, 65,* 1003–1026.

Hall, E. T. (1968). Proxemics. *Current Anthropology, 9,* 83–109.

Hall, E. T. (1976). *Beyond culture.* Garden City, NY: Anchor Books.

Hall, E. T. (1984). *The dance of life: The other dimension of time.* Garden City, NY: Anchor.

Hall, J. A. (1978). Gender effects in decoding nonverbal cues. *Psychological Bulletin, 85,* 845–857.

Hall, J. A. (1979). Gender, gender roles, and nonverbal communication skills. In R. Rosenthal (Ed.), *Skill in nonverbal communication* (pp. 31–97). Cambridge, MA: Oelgeschlager, Gunn, & Hain.

Hall, J. A. (1984). *Nonverbal sex differences: Communication, accuracy and expressive styles.* Baltimore, MD: Johns Hopkins University Press.

Hall, J. A. (1985). Male and female nonverbal behavior. In A. W. Siegman & S. Feldstein (Eds.), *Multichannel integrations of nonverbal behavior* (pp. 195–225). Hillsdale, NJ: Erlbaum.

Hall, J. A. (1996). Touch, status, and gender at professional meetings. *Journal of Nonverbal Behavior, 20,* 23–44.

Hall, J. A. (1998). How big are nonverbal sex differences? The case of smiling and sensitivity to nonverbal cues. In D. J. Canary & K. Dindia (Eds.), *Sex differences and similarities in communication* (pp. 155–177). Mahwah, NJ: Erlbaum.

Hall, J. A. (2006). How big are nonverbal sex differences the case of smiling and nonverbal sensitivity? In K. Dindia & D. J. Canary (Eds.), *Sex differences and similarities in communication* (pp. 59–82). Mahwah, NJ: Erlbaum.

Hall, J. A., Coates, E. J., & LeBeau, L. S. (2005). Nonverbal behavior and the vertical dimension of social relations: A meta-analysis. *Psychological Bulletin, 131,* 989–924.

Hall, J. A., & Halberstadt, A. G. (1994). "Subordination" and sensitivity to nonverbal cues: A study of married working women. *Sex Roles, 31,* 149–165.

Hall, J. A., & Halberstadt, A. G. (1997). Subordination and nonverbal sensitivity: A hypothesis in search of support. In M. R. Walsh (Ed.), *Women, men, & gender: Ongoing debates* (pp. 120–133). New Haven, CT: Yale University Press.

Hall, J. A., Horgan, T. G., & Carter, J. D. (2002). Assigned and felt status in relation to observer-coded and participant reported smiling. *Journal of Nonverbal Behavior, 26,* 63–81

Hall, J. A., LeBeau, L. S., Reinoso, J. G., Thayer, F. (2001). Status, gender, and nonverbal behavior in candid and posed photographs: A study of conversations between university employees. *Sex Roles, 44,* 677–692.

Hall, J. A., Murphy, N. A., & Mast, M. S. (2006). Recall of nonverbal cues: Exploring a new definition of interpersonal sensitivity. *Journal of Nonverbal Behavior, 30,* 141–155.

Hall, J. A., & Veccia, A. M. (1990). More "touching" observations: New insights on men, women, and interpersonal touch. *Journal of Personality and Social Psychology, 59,* 1155–1162.

Hall, J. A., & Veccia, A. M. (1992). Touch asymmetry between the sexes. In C. L. Ridgeway (Ed.), *Gender, interaction, and inequality* (pp. 81–96). New York: Springer Verlag.

Halpern, D. F. (1986). *Sex differences in cognitive abilities.* Hillsdale, NJ: Erlbaum.

Hare, A., & Bales, R. (1963). Seating position and small group interaction. *Sociometry, 26,* 480–486.

Harle, M., Rockstroh, B. S., Keil, A., Wienbruch, C., & Elbert, T. R. (2004). Mapping the brain during speech comprehension: Task-specific facilitation of regional synchrony in neural networks. *BMC Neuroscience, 5,* 40–51.

Harms, L. S. (1961). Listener judgments of status cues in speech. *Quarterly Journal of Speech, 47,* 164–168.

Harner, D. P. (1973). *A review of research concerning the thermal environment and its effects on learning.* Unpublished doctoral dissertation, University of Mississippi.

Harper, R. G., Weins, A. N., & Matarazzo, J. D. (1978). *Nonverbal communication: The state of the art.* New York: John Wiley.

Harrigan, J. A. (2005). Proxemics, kinesics, and gaze. In J. A. Harrigan, R. Rosenthal, & K. Scherer (Eds.), *The new handbook of methods in nonverbal behavioral research.* Oxford, UK: Oxford University Press.

Harrigan, J. D., Oxman, T. E., & Rosenthal, R. (1985). Rapport expressed through nonverbal behavior. *Journal of Nonverbal Behavior, 9,* 95–110.

Harrington, G. M. (1955). Smiling as a measure of teacher effectiveness. *Journal of Education Research, 48,* 715–717.

Harris, M. B., James, J., Chavez, J., Fuller, M. L., Kent, S., Massanari, C., Moore, C., & Walsh, F. (1983). Clothing: Communication, compliance, and choice. *Journal of Applied Social Psychology, 13,* 88–97.

Harrison, R. P. (1974). *Beyond words: An introduction to nonverbal communication.* Englewood Cliffs, NJ: Prentice-Hall.

Haselton, M. G. (2003). The sexual overperception bias: Evidence of a systematic bias in men from a survey of naturally occurring events. *Journal of Research in Personality, 37,* 34–47.

Haselton, M. G., Mortezie, M., Pillsworth, E. G., Bleske-Recheck, A., & Frederick, D. A. (2007). Ovulatory shifts in human female ornamentation: Near ovulation, women dress to impress. *Hormones and Behavior, 51,* 40–45.

Hatfield, E. (1984). The dangers of intimacy. In V. J. Derlega (Ed.), *Communication, intimacy, and close relationships* (pp. 207–220). New York: Academic.

Hatfield, E., Cacioppo, J. T., & Rapson, R. L. (1994). *Emotional contagion.* Cambridge, England: Cambridge University Press.

Hatfield, E., & Sprecher, S. (1986). *Mirror, mirror.* Albany, NY: SUNY Press.

Havlicek, J., Dvorakova, R., Bartos, L., & Flegr, J. (2006). Non-advertised does not mean concealed: Body odor changes across the human menstrual cycle. *Ethology, 112,* 81–90.

Hayes, D., & Metzger, L. (1972). Interpersonal judgments based upon talkativeness: Fact or artifact. *Sociometry, 35,* 538–561.

Hays, R. B. (1985). A longitudinal study of friendship development. *Journal of Personality and Social Psychology, 48,* 909–924.

Hearn, G. (1957). Leadership and the spatial factor in small groups. *Journal of Abnormal and Social Psychology, 54,* 269–272.

Heaven, L., & McBrayer, D. (2000). External motivators of self-touching behaviors. *Perceptual and Motor skills, 90,* 338–342.

Hecht, M. L., Andersen, P. A., & Ribeau, S. A. (1989). The cultural dimensions of nonverbal communication. In M. K. Asante & W. B. Gudykunst (Eds.), *Handbook of international and intercultural communication* (pp. 163–185). Newbury Park, CA: Sage.

Hecht, M. L., Foster, S. H., Dunn, D. J., Willimans, J. K., Anderson, D. R., & Pulbratek, D. (1986). Nonverbal behavior of young abused and neglected children. *Communication Education, 35,* 134–142.

Heckel, R. V. (1973). Leadership and voluntary seating choice. *Psychological Reports, 32,* 141–142.

Heft, H. (1979). Background and focal environmental conditions of the home and attention in young children. *Journal of Applied Social Psychology, 9,* 47–69.

Hegstrom, T. G. (1979). Message impact: What percentage is nonverbal? *Western Journal of Speech Communication, 43,* 134–142.

Heilman, M. E., & Saruwatari, L. R. (1979). When beauty is beastly: The effects of appearance and sex on evaluations of job applicants for managerial and nonmanagerial jobs. *Organizational Behavior and Human Performance, 23,* 360–372.

Heisel, M. J., & Mongrain, M. (2004). Facial expressions and ambivalence: Looking for conflict in all the right faces. *Journal of Nonverbal Behavior, 28,* 35–52.

Helgeson, V. S., Shaver, P., & Dyer, M. (1987). Prototypes of intimacy and distance in same-sex and opposite-sex relationships. *Journal of Social and Personal Relationships, 4,* 195–233.

Helweg-Larsen, M., Cunningham, S. J., Carrico, A., & Pergram, A. (2004). To nod or not to nod: An observational study of nonverbal communication and status in male and female college students. *Psychology of Women Quarterly, 28,* 358–361.

Hemsley, G., & Doob, A. (1978). The effect of looking behavior on perceptions of a communicator's credibility. *Journal of Applied Social Psychology, 8,* 136–144.

Henchy, V. L., & Falk, E. S. (1995, February). *Public touch in lesbian and "straight" settings: An exploratory study.* Paper presented at the annual convention of the Western States Communication Association, Portland, OR.

Hendrick, S. S., & Hendrick, C. (1992). *Liking, loving, and relating* (2nd ed.). Pacific Grove, CA: Brooks/Cole.

Henley, N. M. (1973). Status and sex: Some touching observations. *Bulletin of the Psychonomic Society, 2,* 91–83.

Henley, N. M. (1977). *Body politics: Power, sex, and nonverbal communication.* Englewood Cliffs, NJ: Prentice-Hall.

Henley, N. M. (2002). Body politics and beyond. *Feminism and Psychology, 12,* 295–310.

Henley, N. M., & Harmon, S. (1985). The nonverbal semantics of power and gender. In S. L. Ellyson & J. F. Dovidio (Eds.), *Power, dominance, and nonverbal behavior* (pp. 151–164). New York: Springer Verlag.

Henningsen, D. D. (2004). Flirting with meaning: An examination of miscommunication during flirting interactions. *Sex Roles, 50*, 481–489.

Hensley, W. E. (1991). Pupillary dilation revisited: The constriction of a nonverbal cue. In J. W. Neuliep (Ed.), *Replication research in the social sciences* (pp. 97–104). Newbury Park, CA: Sage.

Hertenstein, M. J. (2002). Touch: Its communicative functions in intimacy. *Human Development, 45*, 70–94.

Hertenstein, M. J., Keltner, D., App, B., Bulleit, B. A., & Jaskolka, A. R. (2006). Touch communicates distinct emotions. *Emotion, 6*, 528–533.

Herzog, A. (1974). *The B.S. factor: The theory and technique of faking it in America.* Baltimore, MD: Penguin Books.

Heslin, R. (1974, May). *Steps toward a taxonomy of touching.* Paper presented at the annual convention of the Midwestern Psychological Association, Chicago, IL.

Heslin, R., & Alper, T. (1983). Touch: A bonding gesture. In J. M. Wiemann & R. Harrison (Eds.), *Nonverbal interaction* (pp. 47–75). Beverly Hills, CA: Sage.

Heslin, R., & Boss, D. (1980). Nonverbal intimacy in arrival and departure at an airport. *Personality and Social Psychology Bulletin, 6*, 248–252.

Hess, E. H. (1965). Attitude and pupil size. *Scientific American, 212*, 46–54.

Hess, E. H. (1975). The role of pupil size in communication. *Scientific American, 233*, 110–119.

Hess, E. H., & Goodwin, E. (1974). The present state of pupilometrics. In M. P. Janisse (Ed.), *Pupillary dynamics and behavior* (pp. 209–246). New York: Plenum.

Hess, E. H., & Petrovich, S. B. (1987). Pupillary behavior in communication. In A. W. Siegman & S. Feldstein (Eds.), *Nonverbal behavior and communication* (pp. 327–348). Hillsdale, NJ: Erlbaum.

Hess, E. H., Seltzer, A. L., & Schlien, J. M. (1965). Pupil response of hetero and homosexual males to pictures of men and women: A pilot study. *Journal of Abnormal Psychology, 70*, 165–168.

Hess, U., Adams, R. B., & Kleck, R. E. (2005). Who may frown and who should smile? Dominance, affiliation, and the display of anger and happiness. *Cognition and Emotion, 19*, 515–536.

Hess, U., Senecal, S., Kirouac, G., Herrera, P., Philippot, P., & Kleck, R. E. (2000). Emotional expressivity in men and women: Stereotypes and self-perceptions. *Cognition and Emotion, 14*, 609–642.

Heston, J. K., & Garner, P. (1972, April). *A study of personal spacing and desk arrangement in a learning environment.* Paper presented at the International Communication Association Convention, Atlanta, GA.

Hickok, G., Love-Geffen, T., & Klima, E. S. (2002). Role of the right hemisphere in sign language comprehension. *Brain and Language, 82*, 167–178.

Hickson, M., Stacks, D. W., & Moore, N-J. (2004). *Nonverbal communication: Studies and applications.* Los Angeles: Roxbury.

Hietanen, J. K., Leppanen, J. M., & Lehtonen, U. (2004). Perceptions of emotions in the hand movement quality of Finnish sign language. *Journal of Nonverbal Behavior, 28*, 53–64.

Hill, C. T., Rubin, C., & Peplau, L. A. (1976). Breakups before marriage: The end of 103 affairs. *Journal of Social Issues, 32*, 147–168.

Hill, R. D., Blackman, R. E., & Crane, D. R. (1982). The effect of the marital relationship on personal space orientation in married couples. *Journal of Social Psychology, 11*, 23–28.

Hocking, J. E., Bauchner, J., Kaminski, E. P., & Miller, G. R. (1979). Detecting deceptive communication from verbal and paralinguistic cues. *Human Communication Research, 6*, 33–46.

Hocking, J. E., & Leathers, D. G. (1980). Nonverbal indicators of deception: A new theoretical perspective. *Communication Monographs, 47*, 119–131.

Hocking, J. E., Walker, B., & Fink, E. L. (1982). The effects of physical attractiveness on the communication of attributional information. *Psychological Reports, 51*, 111–116.

Hodgins, H. S., & Belch, C. (2000). Interparental violence and nonverbal abilities. *Journal of Nonverbal Behavior, 24*, 3–24.

Hoffner, C., Cantor, J., & Thornson, E. (1988). Children's understanding of a televised narrative: Developmental differences in processing video and audio content. *Communication Research, 15*, 227–245.

Hofstede, G. (1982). *Culture's consequences* (abridged ed.). Beverly Hills, CA: Sage.

Holland, R. W., Roeder, U., van Baaren, R. B., Brandt, A. C., & Hannover, B. (2004). Don't stand so close to me: The effects of self-construal on interpersonal closeness. *Psychological Science, 15*, 237–242.

Holmes, J. G., & Rempel, J. K. (1989). Trust in close relationships. In C. Hendrick (Ed.), *Close relationships* (pp. 187–220). Newbury Park, CA: Sage.

Honeycutt, J. M., Cantrill, J. G., & Greene, R. W. (1989). Memory structures for relational escalation: A cognitive test of the sequencing of relational actions and stages. *Human Communication Research, 16*, 62–70.

Hopper, R., & Bell, R. A. (1984). Broadening the deception construct. *Quarterly Journal of Speech, 70*, 288–300.

Hornik, J. (1992). Tactile stimulation and consumer response. *Journal of Consumer Research, 19*, 449–458.

Horstman, G. (2002). Facial expressions of emotion: Does the prototype represent central tendency, frequency of instantiation, or an Ideal? *Emotion, 2*, 297–305.

Hottenstein, M. P. (1978). An exploration of the relationship between age, social status and facial gesturing (Doctoral dissertation, University of Pennsylvania, 1977). *Dissertation Abstracts International, 38*, 5648B–5649B (University Microfilms No. 78-06, 598).

Huntington, E. (1945). *Mainsprings of civilization.* New York: Wiley & Sons.

Hupka, R. B. (1981). Cultural determinants of jealousy. *Alternative Lifestyles, 4*, 310–356.

Hurd, K., & Noller, P. (1988). Decoding deception: A look at the process. *Journal of Nonverbal Behavior, 12*, 217–233.

Hurt, H. T., Scott, M. D., & McCroskey, J. C. (1978). *Communication in the classroom.* Reading, MA: Addison-Wesley.

Hurwitz, J. J., Zander, A. F., & Hymovitch, B. (1968). Some effects of power on the relations among group members. In D. Cartwright & A. Zander (Eds.), *Group dynamics* (pp. 291–297). New York: Harper & Row.

Huseman, R. C., Lahiff, J. M., & Hatfield, J. D. (1976). *Interpersonal communication in organizations.* Boston: Holbrook.

Hutson-Comeaux, S. L., & Kelly, J. R. (2002). Gender stereotypes of emotional reactions: How we judge an emotion as valid. *Sex Roles, 47*, 1–10.

Hyde, J. S. (2005). The gender similarity hypothesis. *American Psychologist, 60*, 581–592.

Hyman, R. T. (1968). The concept of an ideal teacher-student relationship: A comparison and critique. In R. T. Hyman (Ed.), *Teaching: Vantage points for study.* Philadelphia: Lippincott.

Imada, A. S., & Hakel, M. D. (1977). Influence of nonverbal communication and rater proximity on impressions and decisions in simulated employment interviews. *Journal of Applied Psychology, 62*, 295–300.

Insel, P. M., & Lindgen, A. C. (1978). *Too close for comfort: The psychology of crowding.* Englewood Cliffs, NJ: Prentice-Hall.

Iverson, J. M., & Goldin-Meadow, S. (1998). Why people gesture when they speak. *Nature, 396*, 228.

Iverson, J. M., & Goldin-Meadow, S. (2001). The resilience of gesture in talk: Gestures in blind speakers and listeners. *Developmental Science, 4*, 416–422.

Izard, C. E. (1977). *Human emotions.* New York: Plenum.

Izard, C. E. (1992). Basic emotions, relationship among emotions, and emotion-cognition relations. *Psychological Review, 99*, 561–565.

Jaffe, J. (1987). Parliamentary procedure and the brain. In A. W. Siegman and S. Feldstein (Eds.), *Nonverbal behavior and communication* (2nd ed., pp. 21–33). Hillsdale, NJ: Erlbaum.

Jaffe, J., & Anderson, S. W. (1979). Prescript to chapter 1: Communication rhythms and the evolution of language. In A. W. Siegman & S. Feldstein (Eds.), *Of speech and time: Temporal speech patterns in interpersonal contexts* (pp. 17–32). Hillsdale, NJ: Erlbaum.

Jandt, F. E. (1995). *Intercultural communication: An introduction.* Thousand Oaks, CA: Sage.

Jensen, A. D., & Andersen, P. A. (1979, May). *The relationship among communication traits, communication behaviors, and interpersonal perception variables.* Paper presented at the annual convention of the International Communication Association, Philadelphia, PA.

Jensen, J. V. (1985). Perspective on nonverbal intercultural communication. In L. A. Samovar & R. E. Porter (Eds.), *Intercultural communication: A reader* (pp. 256–272). Belmont, CA: Wadsworth.

Johnson, K. L., & Edwards, R. (1991). The effects of gender and type of romantic touch on perceptions of relational commitment. *Journal of Nonverbal Behavior, 15,* 43–54.

Johnson, K. L., & Tassinary, L. G. (2005). Perceiving sex directly and indirectly: Meaning in motion and morphology. *Psychological Science, 16,* 890–897.

Johnson, K. L., & Tassinary, L. G. (2007). Compatibility of basic social perceptions determines perceived attractiveness. *Proceedings of the National Academy of Science, 104,* 5246–5251.

Jones, S. (2004). Putting the person into person-centered and immediate emotional support. *Communication Research, 31,* 338–360.

Jones, S. E. (1994). *The right touch: Understanding and using the language of physical contact.* Cresshill, NJ: Hampton.

Jones, S. E., & Brown, B. C. (1996). Touch attitudes and touch behaviors: Recollections of early childhood touch and social self-confidence. *Journal of Nonverbal Behavior, 20,* 147–163.

Jones, S. E., & Yarbrough, E. (1985). A naturalistic study of the meanings of touch. *Communication Monographs, 52,* 19–56.

Jones, S. M., & Guerrero, L. K. (2001). The effects of nonverbal immediacy and verbal person centeredness on the emotional support process. *Human Communication Research, 27,* 567–596.

Jones, S. M., & Wirtz, J. G. (2006). How does the comforting process work? An empirical test of an appraisal-based model of comforting. *Human Communication Research, 32,* 217–243.

Jones, T. S., & Remland, M. S. (1982, May). *Cross cultural differences in self-reported touch avoidance.* Paper presented at the annual convention of the Eastern Communication Association, Hartford, CT.

Jorgenson, D. O. (1975). Field study of the relationship between status discrepancy and proxemic behavior. *Journal of Social Psychology, 97,* 173–179.

Joseph, N., & Alex, N. (1972). The uniform: A sociological perspective. *American Journal of Sociology, 77,* 719–730.

Jourard, S. M. (1966). An exploratory study of body-accessibility. *British Journal of Social and Clinical Psychology, 5,* 221–231.

Jourard, S. M., & Rubin, J. E. (1968). Self-disclosure and touching: A study of two modes of interpersonal encounter and their inter-relation. *Journal of Humanistic Psychology, 8,* 39–48.

Juslin, P. N., & Laukka, P. (2003). Communication of emotions in vocal expression and musical performance: Different channels, same code? *Psychological Bulletin, 129,* 770–814.

Kahn, A., & McGaughey, T. A. (1977). Distance and liking: When moving close produces increased liking. *Sociometry, 40,* 138–144.

Kaitz, M., Bar-Haim, Y. Lehrer, M., & Grossman, E. (2004). Adult attachment style and interpersonal distance. *Attachment and Human Development, 6,* 285–304.

Kanter, R. M. (1979). How the top is different. In R. M. Kanter & B. A. Stein (Eds.), *Life in organizations* (pp. 20–35). New York: Basic Books.

Kashy, D. A., & DePaulo, B. M. (1996). Who lies? *Journal of Personality and Social Psychology, 70,* 1037–1051.

Kaufman, D., & Mahoney, J. M. (1999). The effect of waitress touch on alcohol consumption in dyads. *Journal of Social Psychology, 139,* 261–267.

Keating, C. F. (1985). Human dominance signals: The primate in us. In S. J. Ellyson & J. F. Dovidio (Eds.), *Power, dominance and nonverbal behavior* (pp. 89–108). New York: Springer Verlag.

Keating, C. F., Mazur, A., & Segall, M. H. (1977). Facial gestures which influence the perception of status. *Sociometry, 40,* 374–378.

Keeley-Dyerson, M. P., Bailey, W., & Burgoon, J. K. (1988, May). *The effects of stress and gender on nonverbal decoding accuracy in kinesic and vocalic channels.* Paper presented at the International Communication Association Convention, New Orleans, LA.

Keeley-Dyerson, M. P., Burgoon, J. K., & Bailey, W. (1991). The effects of stress and gender on nonverbal decoding accuracy in kinesic and vocalic channels. *Human Communication Research, 17,* 584–605.

Kellerman, K. (1989). The negativity effect in initial interaction: It's all in your point of view. *Human Communication Research, 16,* 147–183.

Kelley, D. K., & Gorham, J. (1988). Effects of immediacy on recall of information. *Communication Education, 37,* 198–207.

Kelly, J. R., Murphy, J. D., Craig, T. Y., & Driscoll, D. M. (2005). The effect of nonverbal behaviors associated with sexual harassment proclivity on women's performance. *Sex Roles, 53,* 689–701.

Keltner, D. (1995). Signs of appeasement: Evidence for the distinct displays of embarrassment, amusement, and shame. *Journal of Personality and Social Psychology, 68,* 441–454.

Kendon, A. (1967). Some functions of gaze direction in social interaction. *Acta Psychologica, 26,* 22–63.

Kendon, A. (1983). Gesture and speech. In J. M. Wiemann & R. P. Harrison (Eds.), *Nonverbal interaction* (pp. 13–45). Beverly Hills, CA: Sage.

Kendon, A., & Cook, M. (1969). The consistency of gaze patterns in social interaction. *British Journal of Psychology, 60,* 481–494.

Kennedy, C. W., & Camden, C. (1983). Interruptions and nonverbal gender differences. *Journal of Nonverbal Behavior, 8,* 91–108.

Kenrick, D. T., & Keefe, R. C. (1992). Age preferences in mates reflect sex differences in human reproductive strategies. *Behavioral and Brain Sciences, 15,* 75–137.

Ketrow, S. M. (1990). Attributes of a telemarketer's voice and persuasiveness: A review and synthesis of the literature. *Journal of Direct Marketing, 4,* 7–21.

Kimura, D. (1973). The asymmetry of the human brain. *Scientific American, 231,* 70–76.

King, S. W., & Sereno, K. K. (1984). Conversational appropriateness as a conversational imperative. *The Quarterly Journal of Speech, 70,* 264–273.

Kingston, A., (1999, Nov. 3). Pubic goes public: Men are buying their wives Brazilian waxes for Valentine's Day. What's with the new obsession with grooming the female crotch? *National Post,* p. B1.

Kinsbourne, M. (2006). Gestures as embodied cognition: A neurodevelopmental interpretation. *Gesture, 6,* 205–214.

Kleck, R. (1970). Interaction distance and nonverbal agreeing responses. *British Journal of Social and Clinical Psychology, 9,* 180–182.

Kleinfeld, J. S. (1974). Effects of nonverbal warmth on the learning of Eskimo and White students. *Journal of Social Psychology, 92,* 3–9.

Kleinke, C. L. (1977). Compliance to requests made by gazing and touching experimenters in field settings. *Journal of Experimental Social Psychology, 13,* 218–223.

Kleinke, C. L. (1980). Interaction between gaze and legitimacy of request on compliance in a field setting. *Journal of Nonverbal Behavior, 5,* 3–12.

Kleinke, C. L., Meeker, F. B., & Fong, C. L. (1974). Effects of gaze, touch, and use of name on evaluation of "engaged" couples. *Journal of Research in Personality, 7,* 368–373.

Kleinke, C. L., & Singer, D. A. (1979). Influence of gaze on compliance with demanding and conciliatory requests in a field setting. *Personality and Social Psychology Bulletin, 5,* 386–390.

Klinnert, M. D., Campos, J. J., Sorce, J. F., Emde, R. N., & Svejda, M. (1983). Emotions as behavioral regulators: Social referencing in infancy. In R. Plutchik & H. Kellerman (Eds.), *Emotion: Theory, research, and experience: Vol. 2. Emotions in early development* (pp. 57–86). New York: Academic.

Kloek, J. (1961). The smell of some steroid sex hormones and their metabolites: Reflections and experiments concerning the significance of smell for the mutual relation of the sexes. *Psychiatria, Neurologia, Neurochirugia, 64,* 309–344.

Klopf, D. W., & Thompson, C. A. (1991). Nonverbal immediacy differences among Japanese, Finnish, and American university students. *Perceptual and Motor Skills, 73,* 209–210.

Knapp, M. L. (1972/1978). *Nonverbal communication in human interaction.* New York: Holt, Rinehart & Winston.

Knapp, M. L. (1978). *Social intercourse: From greeting to goodbye.* Boston, MA: Allyn & Bacon.

Knapp, M. L. (1984). *Interpersonal communication and human relationships.* Boston, MA: Allyn & Bacon.

Knapp, M. L., & Comadena, M. E. (1979). Telling it like it isn't: Deceptive communications. *Human Communication Research, 5,* 270–285.

Knapp, M. L., & Hall, J. A. (1997). *Nonverbal communication in human interaction* (3rd ed.). Fort Worth, TX: Harcourt Brace.

Knapp, M. L., & Hall, J. A. (2006). *Nonverbal communication in human interaction* (6th ed.). Belmont, CA: Wadsworth.

Knapp, M. L., Hart, R. P., & Dennis, H. S. (1974). Deception as a communication construct. *Human Communication Research, 1,* 15–29.

Knecht, S., Drager, B., Floel, A., Lohman, H., Breitenstein, C., Deppe, M., Henningsen, H., & Ringelstein, E. B. (2001). Behavioral relevance of atypical language lateralization in healthy subjects. *Brain, 124,* 1657–1665.

Kneidinger, L. M., Maple, T. L., & Tross, S. A. (2001). Touching behavior in sport: Functional components, analysis of sex differences, and ethological considerations. *Journal of Nonverbal Behavior, 25,* 43–62.

Knowles, E. S. (1973). Boundaries around group interaction: The effect of group size and member status on boundary permeability. *Journal of Personality and Social Psychology, 26,* 327–332.

Koch, S. C. (2004). Constructing gender: A lens-model inspired gender communication approach. *Sex Roles, 51,* 171–186.

Koehler, J. W., Anatol, K. W. E., & Applbaum, R. L. (1981). *Organizational communication & behavioral perspectives.* New York: Holt, Rinehart & Winston.

Koermer, C., Goldstein, M., & Forston, D. (1993). How supervisors communicatively convey immediacy to subordinates: An exploratory, qualitative investigation. *Communication Quarterly, 41,* 296–281.

Koerner, A. F., & Fitzpatrick, M. A. (2002). Nonverbal communication and marital adjustment and satisfaction: The role of decoding relationship relevant and irrelevant affect. *Communication Monographs, 69,* 33–51.

Komsi, N., Raikkonen, K., Pesonen, A., Heinonen, K., Keskivaara, P., Jarvenpaa, A., & Strandberg, T. E. (2006). Continuity of temperament from infancy to middle childhood. *Infant Behavior and Development, 29,* 494–508.

Koneya, M. (1977). Query on Ekman: Nonverbal movements or verbal surrogates? *Journal of Communication, 27,* 235–237.

Konner, M. (1987, March). The enigmatic smile. *Psychology Today, 21*(3), 42–46.

Koper, R. J., & Miller, G. R. (1986, May). *Motivation and Machiavellianism as predictors of nonverbal behavior and deception success.* Paper presented at the annual meeting of the International Communication Association, Chicago, IL.

Korda, M. (1983). Status marks—A gold-plated thermos is a man's best friend. In A. M. Katz & V. T. Katz (Eds.), *Foundations of nonverbal communication* (pp. 164–169). Carbondale: Southern Illinois University Press.

Korda, M. (1992). *The immortals.* New York: Poseidon.

Koukounas, E., & Letch, N. M. (2001). Psychological correlates of perception of sexual intent in women. *Journal of Social Psychology, 14,* 443–456.

Kowner, R. (2004). When ideals are too "far off": Physical self-ideal discrepancy and body dissatisfaction in Japan. *Genetic, Social, and General Psychology Monographs, 130,* 333–361.

Kowner, R., & Wiseman, R. (2003). Culture and status-related behavior: Japanese and American perceptions of interaction in asymmetric dyads. *Cross-Cultural Research, 37,* 178–210.

Kozel, F. A., Johnson, K. A., Mu, Q., Grensko, E. L., Laken, S. J., & George, M. S. (2005). Detecting deception using functional magnetic resonance imaging. *Biological Psychiatry, 58,* 605–623.

Krauss, R. M., Geller, V., & Olson, C. (1976, September). *Modalities and cues in the detection of deception.* Paper presented at the annual convention of the American Psychological Association, Washington, DC.

Kraut, R. E. (1980). Humans as lie detectors: Some second thoughts. *Journal of Communication, 30*(4), 209–218.

Kraut, R. E., & Johnson, R. E. (1979). Social and emotional messages of smiling: An ethological approach. *Journal of Personality and Social Psychology, 37,* 1539–1553.

Kraut, R. E., & Poe, D. (1980). On the line: The deception judgments of customs inspectors and laymen. *Journal of Personality and Social Psychology, 39,* 784–798.

LaBarre, W. (1985). Paralinguistics, kinesics, and cultural anthropology In L. A. Samovar & R. E. Porter (Eds.), *Intercultural communication: A reader* (pp. 272–279). Belmont, CA: Wadsworth.

Labre, M. P. (2002). The Brazilian wax: New hairlessness norm for women? *Journal of Communication Inquiry, 26,* 113–132.

LaCrosse, M. B. (1975). Nonverbal behavior and perceived counsellor attractiveness and persuasiveness. *Journal of Counseling Psychology, 22,* 536–566.

LaFrance, M. (2002). Smile boycotts and other body politics. *Feminism and Psychology, 12,* 319–323.

LaFrance, M., Hecht, M. L., & Paluck, E. L. (2003). The contingent smile: A meta-analysis of sex differences in smiling. *Psychological Bulletin, 129,* 305–334.

LaFrance, M., & Henley, N. M. (1997). On oppressing hypotheses: Or, differences in nonverbal sensitivity revisited. In M. R. Walsh (Ed.), *Women, men, & gender: Ongoing debates* (pp. 104–119). New Haven, CT: Yale University Press.

LaFrance, M., & Mayo, C. (1978). *Moving bodies: Nonverbal communication in social relationships.* Monterey, CA: Brooks/Cole.

Lakin, J. L., & Chartrand, T. L. (2003). Using unconscious behavioral mimicry to create affiliation and rapport. *Psychological Science, 14,* 334–339.

Lakin, J. L., & Chartrand, T. L. (2005). Exclusion and nonconscious behavioral mimicry. In K. Williams, J. Forgas, & W. van Hipple (Eds.), *The social outcast: Ostracism, social exclusion, rejection, and bullying* (pp. 279–295). New York: Taylor and Francis.

Lakin, J. L., Jefferis, V. E., Cheng, C. M., & Chartrand, T. L. (2003). The chameleon effect as social glue: Evidence for the evolutionary significant of nonconscious mimicry. *Journal of Nonverbal Behavior, 27,* 145–161.

Lamb, T. A. (1981). Nonverbal and paraverbal control in dyads and triads: Sex or power differences. *Social Psychology Quarterly, 44*(1), 49–53.

Lambert, H., & Wood, K. (2005). A comparative analysis of communication about sex, health and sexual health in India and South Africa: Implications for HIV prevention. *Culture, Health & Sexuality, 7,* 527–541.

Landstrom, S., Granhag, P. A., & Hartwig, M. (2005). Witnesses appearing live versus on video: Effects on observers' perception, veracity, assessments and memory. *Applied Cognitive Psychology, 19,* 913–933.

Langston, S. R. H., Watt, R. J., & Bruce, V. (2000). Do the eyes have it? Cues to the direction of social attention. *Trends in Cognitive Science, 4,* 50–58.

Lanutti, P. J., Laliker, M., & Hale, J. L. (2001). Violations of expectations and social-sexual communication in student/professor evaluation. *Communication Education, 50,* 69–82.

LaPlante, D., & Ambady, N. (2003). On how things are said: Voice tone, voice intensity, verbal content, and perceptions of politeness. *Journal of Language and Social Psychology, 22,* 434–441.

Larsen, K. S., & LeRoux, J. (1984). A study of same-sex touching attitudes: Scale development and personality predictors. *The Journal of Sex Research, 20,* 264–278.

Lavelli, M., & Fogel, A. (2005). Developmental changes in the relationship between infants' attention and emotion during early face-to-face communication: The two month transition. *Developmental Psychology, 41,* 265–280.

Leakey, R. E., & Lewin, R. (1978). *People of the lake: Mankind and its beginnings.* Garden City, NY: Anchor.

Leary, M. R., & Kowalski, R. M. (1995). *Social anxiety.* New York: Guilford.

Leary, M. R., & Meadows, S. (1991). Predictors, elicitors, and concomitants of social blushing. *Journal of Personality and Social Psychology, 60,* 254–262.

Leathers, D. G. (1976). *Nonverbal communication systems.* Boston: Allyn & Bacon.

Lebra, T. (1987). The cultural significance of silence in Japanese communication, *Multilingua, 6,* 343–357.

Leclerc, D., & Martin, J. N. (2004). Tour guide communication competence: French, German, and American tourists' perceptions. *International Journal of Intercultural Relations, 28,* 181–200.

Lee, J. W., & Guerrero, L. K. (2001). Types of touch in cross-sex relationships between coworkers: Perceptions of relational and emotional messages, inappropriateness, and sexual harassment. *Journal of Applied Communication Research, 29,* 197–220.

Leeds, C. H. (1950). A scale for measuring teacher-pupil attitudes and teacher-pupil rapport. *Psychological Monographs, 64,* 6.

Leffler, A., Gillespie, D. L., & Conaty, J. C. (1982). The effects of status differentiation on nonverbal behavior. *Social Psychology Quarterly, 45*(3), 161.

Lefkowitz, M., Blake, R., & Mouton, J. (1955). Status factors in pedestrian violation of traffic signals. *Journal of Abnormal and Social Psychology, 51,* 704–706.

Leibowitz, K., & Andersen, P. A. (1976, December). *The development and nature of the construct touch avoidance.* Paper presented at the annual meeting of the Speech Communication Association, San Francisco, CA.

Lemerise, E. A., & Dodge, K. A. (1993). The development of anger and hostile interactions. In M. Lewis and J. M. Haviland (Eds.), *Handbook of emotions* (pp. 537–546). New York: Guilford.

LePoire, B. A., Shepard, C., & Duggan, A. (1999). Nonverbal involvement, expressiveness, and pleasantness as predicted by parental and partner attachment style. *Communication Monographs, 66,* 293–311.

Levesque, M., Nave, C. S., & Lowe, C. A. (2006). Toward an understanding of gender differences in inferring sexual interest. *Psychology of Women Quarterly, 30,* 150–158.

Levine, T. R. (1994, May). *Conceptualizing interpersonal and relational deception.* Paper presented at the annual meeting of the Speech Communication Association, New Orleans, LA.

Levine, T. R., Feeley, T. H., McCornack, S. A., Hughes, M., & Harms, C. M. (2005). Testing the effects of nonverbal behavior training in deception detection with the inclusion of a bogus training control group. *Western Journal of Communication, 69,* 203–217.

Levine, T. R., Kim, R. K., Park, H. S., & Hughes, M. (2006). Deception detection accuracy is a predictable linear function of message veracity base-rate: A formal test of Park and Levine's probability model. *Communication Monographs, 73,* 243–260.

Levine, T. R., & McCornack, S. A. (1992). Linking love and lies: A formal test of the McCornack & Parks model of deception detection. *Journal of Social and Personal Relationships, 9,* 143–154.

Levine, T. R., Park, H. S., & McCornack, S. A. (1999). Accuracy in detecting truths and lies: Documenting the "veracity effect." *Communication Monographs, 66,* 125–144.

Levinger, G. (1980). Toward the analysis of close relationships. *Journal of Experimental Social Psychology, 16,* 510–544.

Lewis, K. E., & Bierly, M. (1990). Toward a profile of the female voter: Sex differences in perceived physical attractiveness and competence of political candidates. *Sex Roles, 22,* 1–11.

Lewis, M. (1995). Embarrassment: The emotion of self-exposure and evaluation. In J. P. Tangney & K. W. Fischer (Eds.), *Self-conscious emotions: The psychology of shame, guilt, embarrassment and pride* (pp. 198–218). New York: Guilford.

Lewis, M., & Rosenblum, L. A. (Eds.). (1974). *The effect of the infant on its caregiver.* New York: Wiley.

Lewis, P. F. (1972). Small town in Pennsylvania. *Annals of the Association of American Geographers, 62,* 323–351.

Libby, W. L., Jr., & Yanklevich, D. (1973). Personality determinants of eye contact and direction of gaze aversion. *Journal of Personality and Social Psychology, 27*(2), 197–206.

Lieberman, M. D. (2000). Intuition: A social cognitive neuroscience approach. *Psychological Bulletin, 126,* 109–137.

Light, K. C., Grewen, K. M., & Amico, J. A. (2005). More frequent partner hugs and higher ocytocin levels are linked to lower blood pressure and heart rate in premenopausal women. *Biological Psychology, 69,* 5–21.

Lindell, A. K. (2006). In your right mind: Right hemisphere contributions to language processing and production. *Neuropsychological Review, 16,* 131–148.

Linkey, H. E., & Firestone, I. J. (1990). Dyad dominance composition effects, nonverbal behaviors, and influence. *Journal of Research in Personality, 24,* 206–215.

Liss, B., Walker, M., Hazelton, V., & Cupach, W. D. (1993, February). *Mutual gaze and smiling as correlates of compliance-gaining success.* Paper presented at the annual meeting of the Western States Communication Association, Albuquerque, NM.

Littlepage, G. E., Maddox, J., & Pineault, M. A. (1985). Recognition of discrepant nonverbal messages and detection of deception. *Perceptual and Motor Skills, 60,* 119–124.

Lomax, A. (1968). *Folk song style and culture.* New Brunswick, NJ: Transaction Books.

Lott, D. F., & Sommer, R. (1967). Seating arrangements and status. *Journal of Personality and Social Psychology, 7,* 90–95.

Lower, H. M. (1980). Fear of touching as a form of communication apprehension in professional nursing students. *Australian Scan: Journal of Human Communication, 7–8,* 71–78.

Lozano, S. C., & Tversky, B. (2006). Communicative gestures facilitate problem solving for both communicators and recipients. *Journal of Memory and Language, 55,* 47–63.

Lundstrom, J. N., Goncalves, M., Esteves, F., & Olsson, M. J. (2003). Physiological effects of sub-streshold exposure to the putative human pheromone, 4, 16–androstadien-3–One. *Hormones and Behavior, 44*, 395–401.

Lundstrom, J. N., McClintock, M. K., & Olsson, M. J. (2006). Effects of reproductive state on olfactory sensitivity suggest odor specificity. *Biological Psychology, 71*, 244–247.

Lundstrom, J. N., & Olsson, M. J. (2005). Subthreshold amounts of social oderant affect mood, but not behavior, in heterosexual women when tested by a male, but not a female, experimenter. *Biological Psychology, 70*, 197–204.

Lustig, M. W., & Andersen, P. A. (1990, February). *The influence of individualism on interpersonal communication behavior and research: A synoptic view from the United States.* Paper presented at the annual meeting of the Western Speech Communication Association, Sacramento, CA.

Lustig, M. W., & Koester, J. (2003). *Intercultural competence: Interpersonal communication across culture.* New York: Harper Collins.

Luxen, M. F. (2005). Gender differences in dominance and affiliation during a demanding interaction. *Journal of Psychology, 139*, 331–347.

Macare, C. N., Hood, B. M., Milne, A. B., Rowe, A. C., & Mason, M. F. (2002). Are you looking at me? Eye gaze and person perception. *Psychological Science, 13*, 460–464.

Machiavelli, N. (1513/1947). *The prince* (T. G. Bergin, Trans.) New York: Appleton-Century-Crofts.

Mackenzie, C., & Brady, M., (2004). Communication ability in non-right handers following right hemispheric stroke. *Journal of Neurolinguistics, 17*, 301–313.

MacLachlan, J. (1979). What people really think of fast talkers. *Psychology Today, 13*(6), 112–117.

MacNeill, L., & Wilson, B. (1972). *A field study of the effects of conventional and unconventional dress on petition signing behavior.* Unpublished manuscript, Illinois State University, Normal, IL.

Magai, C., & McFadden, S. H. (1995). *The role of emotions in social and personality development: History, theory and research.* New York: Wiley.

Major, B. (1981). Gender patterns in touching behavior. In C. Mayo & N. M. Henley (Eds.), *Gender and nonverbal behavior* (pp. 15–38). New York: Springer Verlag.

Major, B., & Heslin, R. (1982). Perceptions of cross-sex and same-sex nonreciprocal touch: It is better to give than to receive. *Journal of Nonverbal Behavior, 6*, 148–162.

Major, B., Schmidlin, A. M., & Williams, L. (1990). Gender patterns in social touch: The impact of setting and age. *Journal of Personality and Social Psychology, 58*, 634–643.

Malandro, L. A., & Barker, L. (1983). *Nonverbal communication.* Reading, MA: Addison-Wesley.

Malandro, L. A., Barker, L., & Barker, D. A. (1989). *Nonverbal communication.* New York: Random House.

Mandal, M. K., & Ambady, N. (2004). Laterality of facial expressions of emotion: Universal and culture specific influences. *Behavioral Neurology, 15*, 23–34.

Mandler, G. (1975). *Mind and emotion.* New York: Wiley.

Manstead, A. S. R., Wagner, H. L., & MacDonald, C. J. (1984). Face, body, and speech as channels of communication in the detection of deception. *Basic and Applied Social Psychology, 5*, 317–332.

Manusov, V. (1991). Perceiving nonverbal messages: Effects of immediacy and encoded intent on receiver judgments. *Western Journal of Speech Communication, 55*, 235–253.

Marett, L. K., & George, J. F. (2004). Deception in the case of one sender and multiple receivers. *Group Decision and Negotiation, 13*, 29–44.

Markel, N. N. (1969). Relationship between voice-quality profiles and MMPI profiles in psychiatric patients. *Journal of Abnormal Psychology, 74*, 61–66.

Marsh, A. A., Elfenbein, H. A., & Ambady, N. (2003). Nonverbal "accents": Cultural differences in facial expressions of emotion. *Psychological Science, 14*, 373–376.

Marshall, J. E. (1984). Multiple perspectives on modularity. *Cognition, 17*, 209–242.

Marshall, L. L. (1994). Physical and psychological abuse. In W. R. Cupach & B. S. Spitzberg (Eds.), *The dark side of interpersonal communication* (pp. 281–311). Hillsdale, NJ: Erlbaum.

Marston, P. J., Hecht, M. L., Manke, M., McDaniel, S., & Reeder, J. (1998). The subjective of experience of intimacy, passion, and commitment in heterosexual loving relationships. *Personal Relationships, 5*, 15–30.

Martin, J. G., & Westie, F. R. (1959). The intolerant personality. *American Sociological Review, 24*, 521–528.

Mascolo, M. E., & Fischer, K. W. (1995). Developmental transformations in appraisals for pride, shame, and guilt. In J. P. Tangney & K. W. Fischer (Eds.), *Self-conscious emotions: The psychology of shame, guilt, embarrassment and pride* (pp. 64–113). New York: Guilford.

Masip, J., Garrido, E., & Herrero, C. (2004). Facial appearance and judgments of credibility: The effects of babyishness and age on statement credibility. *Genetic, Social and General Psychology Monographs, 129,* 269–311.

Masip, J., Garrido, E., & Herrero, C. (2006). Observers' decision moment in deception detection experiments: Its impact on judgment, accuracy, and confidence. *International Journal of Psychology, 41,* 304–319.

Maslow, A. H. (1968). *Toward a psychology of being* (2nd ed.). New York: Van Nostrand.

Mason, M. F., Tatkow, E. P., & Macrae, C. N. (2005). The look of love: Gaze shifts and person perception. *Psychological Science, 16,* 236–239.

Mast, M. S., & Hall, J. A. (2004a). When is smiling related to dominance? Assigned dominance, preference, trait dominance, and gender as moderators. *Sex Roles, 50,* 387–399.

Mast, M. S., & Hall, J. A. (2004b). Who is boss and who is not? Accuracy of judging status. *Journal of Nonverbal Behavior, 28,* 145–162.

Masters, R. D., & Sullivan, D. G. (1989). Facial displays and political leadership in France. *Behavioural Processes, 19,* 1–30.

Masters, W. H., & Johnson, V. E. (1966). *Human sexual response.* Boston: Little, Brown.

Matarazzo, J. D., Weins, A. N., & Saslow, G. (1965). Studies in interviewer speech behavior. In L. Krasner & U. P. Ullman (Eds.), *Research in behavior modification.* New York: Holt, Rinehart & Winston.

Matsumoto, D. (1991). Cultural influences on facial expressions of emotion. *Southern Communication Journal, 56,* 128–137.

Matsumoto, D. (2002). Methodological requirements to test a possible in-group advantage in judging emotions across cultures: Comment on Elfenbein and Ambady (2002) and evidence. *Psychological Bulletin, 128,* 236–242.

Matsumoto, D. (2006). Culture and nonverbal behavior. In V. Manusov & M. L. Patterson (Eds.), *The Sage handbook of nonverbal communication* (pp. 219–235). Thousand Oaks, CA: Sage.

Mayer, J. D., Solovey, P., Caruso, D. R., & Sitarenios, G. (2001). Emotional intelligence as a standard intelligence. *Emotion, 1,* 232–242.

McAdams, D. P. (1988). Personal needs and personal relationships. In S. Duck (Ed.), *Handbook of personal relationships* (pp. 7–22). New York: Wiley & Sons.

McCann, C. D., & Lalonde, R. N. (1993). Dysfunctional communication and depression: Social cognitive processes. *American Behavioral Scientist, 36,* 271–287.

McCann, K., & McKenna, H. P. (1993). An examination of touch between nurses and elderly patients in a continuing care setting in Northern Ireland. *Journal of Advanced Nursing, 18,* 838–846.

McClintock, M. K. (1971). Menstrual synchrony and suppression. *Nature, 229,* 244–245.

McClure, E. B., & Nowicki, S. (2001). Associations between social anxiety and nonverbal processing skill in preadolescent boys and girls. *Journal of Nonverbal Behavior, 25,* 3–19.

McCormick, N. B., & Jones, A. J. (1989). Gender differences in nonverbal flirtation. *Journal of Sex Education and Therapy, 15,* 271–282.

McCornack, S. A., & Parks, M. R. (1986). Deception detection and relationship development: The other side of trust. In M. L. McLaughlin (Ed.), *Communication yearbook 9* (pp. 377–389). Beverly Hills, CA: Sage.

McCornack, S. A., & Parks, M. R. (1987, May). *What women know that men don't: Sex differences in determining the truth behind deceptive messages.* Paper presented at the annual meeting of the International Communication Association, Montreal, Quebec.

McCoy, N. L., & Pitino, L. (2002). Pheromonal influences on sociosexual behavior in young women. *Physiology and Behavior, 75,* 367–375.

McCroskey, J. C. (1966). Scales for the measurement of ethos. *Speech Monographs, 33,* 65–72.

McCroskey, J. C. (1976). The effects of communication apprehension on nonverbal behavior. *Communication Quarterly, 24,* 39–44.

McCroskey, J. C. (1982). Oral communication apprehension: A reconceptualization. *Communication Yearbook, 6,* 136–170.

McCroskey, J. C., & McCain, T. A. (1974). The measurement of interpersonal attraction. *Speech Monographs, 41,* 261–266.

McCroskey, J. C., & McVetta, R. W. (1978). The relationship between communication apprehension and classroom seating preferences. *Communication Education, 27,* 99–111.

McCroskey, J. C., Richmond, V. P., & Young, T. J. (1977, March). *Interpersonal space preferences as a function of sex and communication apprehension.* Paper presented at the annual convention of the Eastern Communication Association, New York.

McCroskey, J. C., & Sheahan, M. E. (1976, April). *Seating position and participation: An alternative theoretical explanation.* Paper presented at the International Communication Association Convention, Portland, OR.

McDaniel, E. R., & Andersen, P. A. (1995, May). *Intercultural variations in tactile communication: An empirical field study.* Paper presented at the annual convention of the International Communication Association, Albuquerque, NM.

McDaniel, E. R., & Andersen, P. A. (1998). Intercultural variations in tactile communication: A field study. *Journal of Nonverbal Behavior, 22,* 59–75.

McDowell, E. E., McDowell, C. E., & Hyendahl, J. (1980, November). A *multivariate study of teacher immediacy, teaching effectiveness, and student attentiveness at the junior and senior high levels.* Paper presented at the Speech Communication Association Convention, New York.

McDowell, E. E., McDowell, C. E., Hyendahl, J., & Steil, L. K. (1980). A multivariate study of demographics, psychological sex roles, and communication apprehension. *Resources in Education, 1–18.*

McGinley, H., LaFerve, R., & McGinley, A. (1975). The influence of the communicator's body position on opinion change in others. *Journal of Personality and Social Psychology, 31,* 686–690.

McGovern, T. V. (1977). The making of a job interviewee: The effect of nonverbal behavior on an interviewer's evaluations during a selection interview (Doctoral dissertation, Southern Illinois University, 1976). *Dissertation Abstracts International* Vol. 374740B–4741B (University Microfilms No. 77-6239).

McHugo, G. J. (1985). Emotional reactions to a political leader's expressive displays. *Journal of Personality and Social Psychology, 49,* 1513–1529.

McLuhan, M. (1969). *Understanding media: The extensions of man.* New York: Penguin.

McMahon, E. M. (1976). Nonverbal communication as a function of attribution in impression formation. *Communication Monographs, 43,* 287–294.

McNeill, D. (1985). So you think gestures are nonverbal? *Psychological Review, 92,* 350–371.

Medley, D. M., & Mitzel, H. E. (1958). A technique for measuring classroom behavior. *Journal of Educational Psychology, 49,* 86–92.

Meerloo, J. A. M. (1971). A world of smells. In J. A. DeVito (Ed.), *Communication: Concepts and processes* (pp. 134–138). Englewood Cliffs, NJ: Prentice-Hall.

Mehrabian, A. (1968a). Communication without words. *Psychology Today, 2,* 52–55.

Mehrabian, A. (1968b). Inference of attitudes from the posture, orientation, and distance of a communicator. *Journal of Consulting and Clinical Psychology, 32,* 296–308.

Mehrabian, A. (1969). Significance of posture and position in the communication of attitude and status relationships. *Psychological Bulletin, 71,* 359–372.

Mehrabian, A. (1970). A semantic space for nonverbal behavior. *Journal of Consulting and Clinical Psychology, 35,* 248–257.

Mehrabian, A. (1971a). *Silent messages.* Belmont, CA: Wadsworth.

Mehrabian, A. (1971b). Verbal and nonverbal interactions of strangers in a waiting situation. *Journal of Experimental Research in Personality, 5,* 127–138.

Mehrabian, A. (1972). *Nonverbal communication.* Chicago: Aldine-Atherton.

Mehrabian, A. (1976). *Public places, private spaces.* New York: Basic Books.

Mehrabian, A., & Diamond, S. G. (1971). Seating arrangement and conversation. *Sociometry, 34,* 281–289.

Mehrabian, A., & Ferris, S. R. (1967). Inference of attitudes from nonverbal communication in two channels. *Journal of Consulting Psychology, 31,* 248–252.

Mehrabian, A., & Friar, J. T. (1969). Encoding of attitude by a seated communicator via posture and position cues. *Journal of Consulting and Clinical Psychology, 33,* 330–336.

Mehrabian, A., & Ksionsky, S. (1970). Models for affiliative and conformity behavior. *Psychological Bulletin, 74*, 110–126.

Mehrabian, A., & Weiner, M. (1967). Decoding of inconsistent communications. *Journal of Personality and Social Psychology, 6*, 109–114.

Meissner, C. A., & Brigham, J. C. (2001). Thirty years of investigating the own-race bias memory for faces: A meta-analytic review. *Psychology, Public Policy, and Law, 7*, 3–35.

Meservy, T. O., Jensen, M. L., Kruse, J., Burgoon, J. K., Nunamaker, J. F., Twitchell, D. P., Tsechpenakis, G., & Metaxes, D. N. (2005 September/October). Deception detection through automatic, unobtrusive analysis of nonverbal behavior. *IEEE Intelligent Systems*, 36–42.

Messinger, D. S., Fogel, A., & Dickson, K. L. (1999). What's in a smile? *Developmental Psychology, 35*, 701–708.

Metha, P., & Clark, M. S. (1994). Toward understanding emotions in intimate relationships. In A. I. Weber & J. H. Harvey (Eds.), *Perspectives on close relationships* (pp. 88–109). Boston, MA: Allyn & Bacon.

Metts, S. (1989). An exploratory study of deception in close relationships. *Journal of Personal and Social Relationships, 6*, 159–179.

Metts, S. (1994). Relational transgressions. In W. R. Cupach & B. H. Spitzberg (Eds.), *The dark side of interpersonal communication* (pp. 217–239). Hillsdale, NJ: Erlbaum.

Metts, S., Cupach, W. R., & Imahori, T. T. (1992). Perceptions of sexual compliance-resisting messages in three types of cross-sex relationships. *Western Journal of Communication, 56*, 1–17.

Metts, S., & Spitzberg, B. H. (1996). Sexual communication in interpersonal contexts: A scripts-based approach. In B. Burleson (Ed.), *Communication yearbook 19* (pp. 49–91). Thousand Oaks, CA: Sage.

Metts, S., Sprecher, S., & Regan, P. C. (1998). Communication and sexual desire. In P. A. Andersen & L. K. Guerrero (Eds.), *Handbook of communication and emotion: Research, theory, applications, and contexts* (pp. 353–378). San Diego, CA: Academic.

Mezzakappa, D., & Andersen, P. A. (1996, February). *Nonverbal cues of crime victims: Perceptions of convicted criminals.* Paper presented at the annual meeting of the Western States Communication Association, Pasadena, CA.

Milgram, S. (1974). *Obedience to authority.* New York: Harper & Row.

Millar, F. E., Rogers-Millar, L. E., & Courtright, J. A. (1979). Relational control and dyadic understanding: An exploratory predictive regression model. In D. Nimmo (Ed.), *Communication yearbook 3* (pp. 213–224). Beverly Hills, CA: Sage.

Millar, M., & Millar, K. (1995). Detection of deception in familiar and unfamiliar persons: The effects of information restriction. *Journal of Nonverbal Behavior, 19*, 69–84.

Miller, G. R., Bauchner, J. E., Hocking, J. E., Frontes, N. E., Kaminski, E. P., & Brandt, D. R. (1981). ". . . and nothing but the truth": How well can observers detect deceptive testimony? In B. D. Sales (Ed.), *Perspectives in law psychology: Vol. 3. The jury, judicial and trial process.* New York: Plenum.

Miller, G. R., & Burgoon, M. (1978). Persuasion research: Review and commentary. In B. D. Ruben (Ed.), *Communication yearbook 2* (pp. 29–47). New Brunswick, NJ: Transaction Books.

Miller, G. R., deTurck, M. A., & Kalbfleish, P. J. (1983). Self-monitoring, rehearsal, and self-deceptive communication. *Human Communication Research, 10*, 97–117.

Miller, G. R., & Hewgill, M. A. (1964). The effect of variations in nonfluency on audience ratings of source credibility. *Quarterly Journal of Speech, 50*, 36–44.

Miller, G. R., & Stiff, J. B. (1993). *Deceptive communication.* Newbury Park, CA: Sage.

Miller, L. (2003). Male beauty work in Japan. In J. E. Roberson & N. Suzuki (Eds.), *Men and masculinities in contemporary Japan* (pp. 37–58). Routledge Japanese Studies Series. Tokyo: Nissan Institute.

Miller, L. C., Cody, M. J., & McLaughlin, M. L. (1994). Goals and situations as fundamental constructs in interpersonal communication research. In M. L. Knapp & G. R. Miller (Eds.), *Handbook of interpersonal communication* (pp. 162–198). Thousand Oaks, CA: Sage.

Miller, L. F., Rozin, P., & Fiske, A. P. (1998). Food sharing and feeding another person suggest intimacy; two studies of American college students. *European Journal of Social Psychology, 28*, 423–236.

Miller, N., Maruyama, G., Beaber, R., & Valone, K. (1976). Speed of speech and persuasion. *Journal of Personality and Social Psychology, 34*, 615–624.

Miller, P. M., Commons, M. L., & Gutheil, T. G. (2006). Clinicians' perceptions of boundaries in Brazil and the United States. *Journal of the American Academy of Psychiatric Law, 34*, 33–41.

Miller, R. S., & Leary, M. R. (1992). Social sources and interactive functions of emotion: The case of embarrassment. In M. S. Clark (Ed.), *Review of personality and social psychology* (Vol. 14, pp. 202–221). Newbury Park, CA: Sage.

Mills, C. W. (1956). *The power elite.* London: Oxford University Press.

Mills, J., & Aronson, E. (1965). Opinion change as a function of the communicator's attractiveness and desire to influence. *Journal of Personality and Social Psychology, 1*, 173–177.

Milmoe, S., Novey, M. S., Kagan, J., & Rosenthal, R. (1974). The mother's voice: Postdicotor of aspects of her baby's behavior. In S. Weitz (Ed.), *Nonverbal communication: Readings with commentary* (pp. 250–265). New York: Oxford University Press.

Milmoe, S., Rosenthal, R., Blane, H. T., Chafetz, M. E., & Wolf, I. (1979). The doctor's voice: Postdicotor of successful referral of alcoholic patients. In S. Weitz (Ed.), *Nonverbal communication: Readings with commentary* (pp. 266–275). New York: Oxford University Press.

Mitchell, G., & Maple, T. L. (1985). Dominance in nonhuman primates. In S. L. Ellyson & J. F. Dovidio (Eds.), *Power, dominance, and nonverbal behavior* (pp. 49–66). New York: Springer Verlag.

Mitchell, R. W. (1993). Animals as liars: The human face of nonhuman duplicity. In M. Lewis & C. Saarni (Eds.), *Lying and deception in everyday life* (pp. 59–89). New York: Guilford.

Moe, J. D. (1972). Listener judgments of status cues in speech: A replication and extension. *Speech Monographs, 39*, 144–147.

Molinsky, A. L., Krabbenhoft, M. A., Ambady, N., & Choi, Y. S. (2005). Cracking the nonverbal code: Intercultural competence and gesture recognition across cultures. *Journal of Cross Cultural Psychology, 36*, 380–395.

Molloy, J. T. (1976). *Dress for success.* New York: Warner Books.

Monsour, M. (1992). Meanings of intimacy in cross-and same-sex friendships. *Journal of Social and Personal Relationships, 9*, 277–295.

Montagu, A. (1971/1978). *Touching: The human significance of the skin.* New York: Harper & Row.

Montepare, J. M., Goldstein, S. B., & Clausen, A. (1987). The identification of emotions from gait information. *Journal of Nonverbal Behavior, 11*, 33–42.

Montgomery, B. M. (1988). Quality communication in personal relationships. In S. Duck (Ed.), *Handbook of personal relationships* (pp. 343–362). New York: Wiley & Sons.

Moore, M. M., & Butler, D. L. (1989). Predictive aspects of nonverbal courtship behavior in women. *Semiotica, 76*, 205–215.

Morris, D. (1971). *Intimate behavior.* New York: Random House.

Morris, D. (1977). *Manwatching: A field guide to human behavior.* New York: Harry N. Abrams.

Morris, D. (1985). *Bodywatching.* New York: Crown.

Morton, T. L. (1977). The effects of acquaintances and distance on intimacy and reciprocity (Doctoral dissertation, University of Utah, 1976). *Dissertation Abstracts International, 37*, 3680B.

Motley, M. T. (1990). Whether one can(not) communicate: An examination through traditional communication postulates. *Western Journal of Speech Communication, 54*, 1–20.

Motley, M. T. (1991). How one may not communicate: A reply to Andersen. *Communication Studies, 42*, 326–339.

Mottet, T. P. (2000). Interactive television instructors' perceptions of students' nonverbal responsiveness and their influence on distance teaching. *Communication Education, 49*, 146–164.

Mottet, T. P., Beebe, S. A., Raffeld, P. C., & Medlock, A. L. (2004). The effects of student verbal and nonverbal responsiveness on teacher self-efficacy and job satisfaction. *Communication Education, 53*, 150–163.

Muehlenhard, C. L., Koralewski, M. A., Andrews, S. L., & Burdick, C. A. (1986). Verbal and nonverbal cues that convey interest in dating: Two studies. *Behavior Therapy, 17*, 404–419.

Muir, D. W. (2002). Adult communication with infants through touch: The forgotten sense. *Human Development, 45*, 95–99.

Mulac, A., Studley, L. B., Wiemann, J. M., & Bradac, J. J. (1987). Male/female gaze in same-sex and mixed-sex dyads: Gender-linked differences in mutual influence. *Human Communication Research, 13*, 323–343.

Mulac, A., & Wiemann, J. M. (1984). Observer-perceived communicator anxiety. In J. A. Daly & M. C. McCroskey (Eds.), *Avoiding communication: Shyness, reticence, and communication apprehension* (pp. 107–121). Beverly Hills, CA: Sage.

Mullen, B., Futrell, D., Stairs, D., Tice, D., Baumeister, R., Dawson, K., Riordan, C., Radioff, C., Goethals, G., Kennedy, J., & Rosenfeld, P. (1986). Newscasters' facial expressions and voting behavior of viewers: Can a smile elect a president? *Journal of Personality and Social Psychology, 51*, 291–295.

Murphy, E. H., & Venables, P. H. (1970). Ear asymmetry in the threshold of fusion of two clocks: A signal detection analysis. *Quarterly Journal of Experimental Psychology, 22*, 288.

Murphy, N. A. (2005). Using thin slices for behavioral coding. *Journal of Nonverbal Behavior, 29*, 235–246.

Murzynski, J., & Degelman, D. (1996). Body language of women and judgments of vulnerability of sexual assault. *Journal of Applied Social Psychology, 26*, 1617–1626.

Nabi, R., & Hendrick, A. (2003). The persuasive effect of host and audience reaction shots in television talk shows. *Journal of Communication, 53*, 527–543.

Najib, A., Lorberbaum, J. P., Kose, S., Bohning, D. E., & George, M. S. (2004). Regional brain activity in women grieving a romantic relationship breakup. *American Journal of Psychiatry, 161*, 2245–2256.

Nisbett, R. E., Peng, K., Choi, I., & Norenzayan, A. (2001). Culture and systems of thought: Holistic versus analytic cognition. *Psychological Review, 108*, 291–310.

Noller, P. (1978). Sex differences in the socialization of affectionate expression. *Developmental Psychology, 14*, 317–319.

Noller, P. (1980). Gaze in married couples. *Journal of Nonverbal Behavior, 5*, 115–129.

Noller, P. (1982). Channel consistency and inconsistency in the communications of married couples. *Journal of Personality and Social Psychology, 53*, 432–441.

Noller, P. (1984). *Nonverbal communication and marital interaction.* Oxford: Pergamon.

Noller, P. (1986). Sex differences in nonverbal communication: Advantage lost or supremacy regained? *Australian Journal of Psychology, 38*, 23–32.

Noller, P. (1987). Nonverbal communication in marriage. In D. Perlman & S. Duck (Eds.), *Intimate relationships: Development, dynamics, and deterioration* (pp. 149–175). Beverly Hills, CA: Sage.

Noller, P. (2006). Nonverbal communication in close relationships. In V. Manusov & M. Patterson (Eds.), *The Sage handbook of nonverbal communication* (pp. 304–420). Thousand Oaks, CA: Sage.

O'Brien, M. (1979). *The idea of the American South, 1920–1941.* Baltimore: Johns Hopkins University Press.

O'Hair, D., & Cody, M. J. (1994). Deception. In W. R. Cupach & B. H. Spitzberg (Eds.), *the dark side of interpersonal communication* (pp. 181–213). Hillsdale, NJ: Erlbaum.

O'Hair, D., Cody, M. J., & Behnke, R. R. (1985). Communication apprehension and vocal stress as indices of deception. *Western Journal of Speech Communication, 49*, 286–300.

O'Hair, D., Cody, M. J., Choa, E. Y., & Wang, X. (1989, February). *Vocal stress and deception detection among Chinese.* Paper presented at the annual meeting of the Western Speech Communication Association, Spokane, WA.

O'Hair, D., Cody, M. J., & McLaughlin, M. L. (1981). Prepared lies, spontaneous lies, Machiavellianism, and nonverbal communication. *Human Communication Research, 7*, 325–339.

O'Sullivan, M., Ekman, P., & Friesen, W. V. (1988). The effect of comparisons on detecting deceit. *Journal of Nonverbal Behavior, 12*, 203–215.

Oatley, K., & Johnson-Laird, P. N. (1987). Toward a cognitive theory of emotions. *Cognition and Emotion, 1*, 29–50.

Ogden, J. A. (1989). Visuospatial and other "right hemispheric" functions after long recovery periods in left-hemispherectomized subjects. *Neuropsychologia, 6*, 765–776.

Ohman, A. (1993). Fear and anxiety as emotional phenomena: Clinical phenomenology, evolutionary perspectives, and information-processing mechanisms. In M. L. Lewis & J. M. Haviland (Eds.), *Handbook of emotions* (pp. 511–536). New York: Guilford.

Olsson, S. B., Barnard, J., & Turri, L. (2006). Olfaction and identification of unrelated individuals: Examination of the masteries of human odor recognition. *Journal of Chemical Ecology, 32*, 1635–1645.

Omori, Y., & Myata, Y. (2001) Estimates of impressions based on the frequency of blinking. *Social Behavior and Personality, 29,* 159–168.

Orwell, G. (1949). *1984.* San Diego, CA: Harcourt Brace Jovanovich.

Osato, E., & Ogawa, N. (2003). The effects of seating positions on heart rates, state anxiety, and estimated interview duration in interview situations. *Psychological Reports, 93,* 755–770.

Owren, M. J., & Bachorowski, J. (2003). Reconsidering the evolution of nonlinguistic communication: The case of laughter. *Journal of Nonverbal Behavior, 27,* 183–200.

Palmer, M. T., & Simmons, K. B. (1995). Communicating intentions through nonverbal behaviors: Conscious and nonconscious encoding of liking. *Human Communication Research, 22,* 128–160.

Park, K. A., & Waters, E. (1988). Trait and relationships in developmental perspective. In S. Duck (Ed.), *Handbook of personal relationships* (pp. 161–176). New York: Wiley & Sons.

Parkinson, B. (2005). Do facial movements express emotions or communicate motives? *Personality and Social Psychology Review, 9,* 278–311.

Parks, M. (1982). Ideology in interpersonal communication: Off the couch and into the world. In M. Burgoon (Ed.), *Communication yearbook 5* (pp. 79–107). New Brunswick, NJ: Transaction Books.

Parks, M. R., & Floyd, K. (1996). Meanings for closeness and intimacy in friendship. *Journal of Social and Personal Relationships, 13,* 85–107.

Patterson, J., & Kim, P. (1991). *The day America told the truth.* New York: Prentice-Hall.

Patterson, M. L. (1973a). Compensation in nonverbal immediacy behaviors: A review. *Sociometry, 36,* 237–252.

Patterson, M. L. (1973b). Stability of nonverbal immediacy behaviors. *Journal of Experimental Social Psychology, 7,* 97–101.

Patterson, M. L. (1976). An arousal model of interpersonal intimacy. *Psychological Review, 83,* 235–245.

Patterson, M. L. (1977). Interpersonal distance, affect, and equilibrium theory. *Journal of Social Psychology, 101,* 205–214.

Patterson, M. L. (1978). The role of space in social interaction. In A. W. Siegman & S. Feldstein (Eds.), *Nonverbal behavior and communication* (pp. 265–290). Hillsdale, NJ: Erlbaum.

Patterson, M. L. (1983). *Nonverbal behavior: A functional perspective.* New York: Springer Verlag.

Patterson, M. L. (1988). Functions of nonverbal behavior in close relationships. In S. Duck (Ed.), *Handbook of personal relationships* (pp. 41–56). New York: Wiley & Sons.

Patterson, M. L. (1995). A parallel process model of nonverbal communication. *Journal of Nonverbal Communication, 19,* 330.

Patterson, M. L., & Edinger, I. A. (1987). A functional analysis of space in social interaction. In A. W. Siegman & S. Feldstein (Eds.), *Nonverbal behavior and communication* (pp. 523–562). Hillsdale, NJ: Erlbaum.

Patterson, M. L., Powell, J. L., & Lenihan, M. G. (1986). Touch, compliance, and interpersonal affect. *Journal of Nonverbal Behavior, 10,* 41–50.

Patterson, M. L., & Ritts, V. (1997). Social and communicative anxiety: A review and meta-analysis. In B. Burleson (Ed.), *Communication yearbook 20* (pp. 263–303). Thousand Oaks, CA: Sage.

Patterson, M. L., & Sechrest, L. B. (1970). Interpersonal distance and impression formation. *Journal of Personality, 38,* 161–166.

Pause, B. M. (2004). Are androgens acting pheromones in humans? *Physiology and Behavior, 83,* 21–29.

Pause, B. M., Rogalski, K. P., Sojka, B., & Ferstl, R. (1999). Sensitivity to androstenone in female subject is associated with an altered brain response to male body odor. *Physiology and Behavior, 68,* 129–137.

Peace, V., Miles, L., & Johnston, L. (2006). It doesn't matter what you wear: The impact of posed and genuine expression of happiness on product evaluation. *Social Cognition, 24,* 137–138.

Pearce, W. B. (1971). The effect of vocal cues on credibility and attitude change. *Western Speech, 35,* 176–184.

Pearson, J. C., West, R. L., & Turner, L. H. (1995). *Gender and communication* (3rd ed.). Madison, WI: Brown & Benchmark.

Pele, K., Kornreich, C., Foisy, M., & Dan, B. (2006). Recognition of emotional facial expressions in attention-deficit hyperactivity disorder. *Pediatric Neurology, 35,* 93–97.

Pell, M. C. (2005). Prosody-face interactions in emotional processing as revealed by the facial affect decision task. *Journal of Nonverbal Behavior, 29,* 193–215.

Pendell, S. D. (2002). Affection in interpersonal relationships: Not just "a fond and tender feeling." In W. B. Gudykunst (Ed.), *Communication yearbook 26* (pp. 70–115). Mahwah, NJ: Erlbaum.

Penn, D. J. (2002). The scent of genetic compatibility: Sexual selection and the major histocompatibility complex. *Ethology, 108,* 1–21.

Pennebaker, J. W., Rime, B., & Sproul, G. (1994). *Stereotype of emotional expressiveness of northerners and southerners: A cross-cultural test of Montesquieu's hypotheses.* Unpublished manuscript: Southern Methodist University.

Perlman, D., & Fehr, B. (1987). The development of intimate relationships. In D. Perlman & S. Duck (Eds.), *Intimate relationships* (pp. 13–42). Newbury Park, CA: Sage.

Peterson, A. M., Cline, R. J. W., Foster, T. S., Penner, L. A., Parrott, R. L., Keller, C. M., Naughton, M. C., Taub, J., Ruckdeschel, J. C., & Albrecht, T. L. (2007). Parents' interpersonal distance and touch behavior and child pain and distress. *Journal of Nonverbal Behavior, 31,* 79–97.

Petronio, S. (1993). Communication boundary management: A theoretical model of managing disclosure of private information between married couples. In S. Petronio, J. K. Alberts, M. L. Hecht, & J. Buley (Eds.), *Contemporary perspectives on interpersonal communication* (pp. 221–240). Madison, WI: Brown, Benchmark.

Petty, R. E., & Cacioppo, J. (1986). The elaboration likelihood model of persuasion. In L. Berkowitz (Ed.), *Advances in experimental social psychology* (Vol. 19, pp. 123–205). New York: Academic.

Pfau, M., & Kang, J. G. (1989, November). *The impact of relational and nonverbal communication in political debate influence.* Paper presented at the annual meeting of the Speech Communication Association, San Francisco, CA.

Philpot, J. S. (1983). *The relative contribution to meaning of verbal and nonverbal channels of communication: A meta-analysis.* Unpublished master's thesis, University of Nebraska.

Pilkonis, P. A. (1977). The behavioral consequences of shyness. *Journal of Personality, 45,* 596–611.

Pisano, M. D., Wall, S. M., & Foster, A. (1986). Perceptions of nonreciprocal touch in romantic relationships. *Journal of Nonverbal Behavior, 10,* 29–40.

Pittam, J., & Scherer, K. R. (1993). Vocal expression and the communication of emotion. In M. Lewis & J. M. Haviland (Eds.), *Handbook of emotions* (pp. 185–198). New York: Guilford.

Pitterman, H., & Nowicki, S. (2004). A test of the ability to identify emotion in human standing and sitting postures: The diagnostic analysis of the nonverbal accuracy-2 posture test (DANVA2–POS). *Genetic, Social and General Psychology Monographs, 130,* 146–162.

Pizzagalli, D., Koenig, T., Regard, M., & Lehmann, D. (1998). Faces and emotions: Brain electrical field sources during covert emotional processing. *Neuropsychologia, 36,* 323–332.

Planalp, S. (1985). Relational schemata: A test of alternative forms of relational knowledge as a guide to communication. *Human Communication Research, 12,* 3–29.

Planalp, S. (1998). Communicating emotion in everyday life: Cues, channels, and processes. In P. A. Andersen & L. K. Guerrero (Eds.), *Handbook of communication and emotion: Research, theory, applications, and contexts* (pp. 29–48). San Diego, CA: Academic.

Planalp, S., DeFrancisco, V. L., & Rutherford, D. (1996). Varieties of cues to emotion occurring in naturally occurring situations. *Cognition and Emotion, 10,* 137–153.

Plant, E. A., Hyde, E. A., Keltner, D., & Devine, P. (2000). The gender stereotyping of emotions. *Psychology of Women Quarterly, 24,* 81–92.

Plant, E. A., Kling, K. C., & Smith, G. L. (2004). The influence of gender and social role on the interpretation of facial expressions. *Sex Roles, 51,* 187–196.

Plax, T. G., Kearney, P., McCroskey, J. C., & Richmond, V. P. (1986). Power in the classroom IV: Verbal control strategies, nonverbal immediacy, and affective learning. *Communication Education, 35,* 43–55.

Plutchik, R. (1980). *Emotion: A psychoevolutionary synthesis.* New York: Harper & Row.

Pogue, L. L., & Ah-Yun, K. (2006). The effect of teacher nonverbal immediacy and credibility on student motivation and affective learning. *Communication Education, 55,* 331–344.

Poizner, H., Klima, E. S., & Bellugi, U. (1987). *What the hands reveal about the brain.* Cambridge, MA: MIT Press.

Porter, R. E., & Samovar, L. A. (1998). Cultural differences in emotional expression: Implications for intercultural communication. In P. A. Andersen & L. K. Guerrero (Eds.), *Handbook of communication and emotion: Research, theory, applications, and contexts* (pp. 452–472). San Diego, CA: Academic.

Portnoy, E. J. (1993). The impact of body type on perceptions of attractiveness by older individuals. *Communication Reports, 6,* 101–108.

Portnoy, E. P., & Gardner, J. M. (April, 1980). *A perceptual measure of children's development of somotypic preferences.* Paper presented at the annual meeting of the Eastern Communication Association, Ocean City, MD.

Powell, R. G., & Harville, B. (1990). The effects of teacher immediacy and clarity on instructional outcomes: An intercultural assessment. *Communication Education, 39,* 369–379.

Prager, K. J. (1995). *The psychology of intimacy.* New York: Guilford.

Prager, K. J., & Roberts, L. J. (2004). Deep intimate connection: Self and intimacy in couple relationships. In D. J. Mashek & A. P. Aron (Eds.), *Handbook of closeness and intimacy* (pp. 43–60). Mahwah, NJ: Erlbaum.

Premack, A. J., & Premack, D. (1983). *The mind of an ape.* New York: Norton.

Priest, R. F., & Sawyer, J. (1967). Proximity and peer-ship: Bases of balance in interpersonal attraction. *American Journal of Sociology, 72,* 633–649.

Prisbell, M. (1982, May). *Nonverbal communication attributes of power and status in the organizational setting.* Paper presented at the annual convention of the Eastern Communication Association, Hartford, CT.

Prosser, M. H. (1978). *The cultural dialogue: An introduction to intercultural communication.* Boston, MA: Houghton Mifflin.

Pryor, B., & Buchanan, R. W. (1984). The effects of a defendant's demeanor on juror perceptions of credibility and guilt. *Journal of Communication, 34*(3), 92–99.

Puckett, J. M., Petty, R. E., Cacioppo, J. T., & Fischer, D. L. (1983). The relative impact of age and attractiveness stereotypes on persuasion. *Journal of Gerontology, 38,* 340–343.

Ragan, P. C., & Berscheid, E. (1996). Beliefs about state, goals and objects of sexual desire. *Journal of Sex and Marital Therapy, 22,* 110–120.

Rajecki, D. W. (1983). Successful comparative psychology: Four case histories. In D. W. Rajecki (Ed.), *Comparing behavior: Studying man studying animals* (pp. 67–108). Hillsdale, NJ: Erlbaum.

Rathus, S. A., Nevid, J. S., & Fichner-Rathus, L. (1993). *Human sexuality in a world of diversity.* Boston: Allyn & Bacon.

Rawlins, W. K. (1992). *Friendship matters: Communication, dialectics, and the life course.* New York: Aldine de Gruyter.

Ray, G. B., & Floyd, K. (2006). Nonverbal expressions of liking and disliking in initial interaction: Encoding and decoding perspectives. *Southern Communication Journal, 71,* 45–65.

Ray, G. B., & Ray, E. B. (1988, November). *The relationship of paralinguistic cues to impression formation and the recall of medical messages.* Paper presented at the annual meeting of the Speech Communication Association, New Orleans, LA.

Reece, M. M., & Whitman, R. N. (1961). Warmth and expressive movements. *Psychological Reports, 8,* 76.

Reece, M. M., & Whitman, R. N. (1962). Expressive movements, warmth, and verbal reinforcement. *Journal of Abnormal and Social Psychology, 64,* 234–236.

Regan, P. C. (1996). Rhythms of desire: The association between menstrual cycle phases and female sexual desire. *The Canadian Journal of Human Sexuality, 5,* 145–156.

Register, L. M., & Henley, T. B. (1992). The phenomenology of intimacy. *Journal of Social and Personal Relationships, 9,* 467–481.

Reis, H. T., & Shaver, P. (1988). Intimacy as an interpersonal process. In S. Duck (Ed.), *Handbook of personal relationships* (pp. 367–389). New York: Wiley & Sons.

Reisenzein, R., Bordgen, S., Holtbernd, T., & Matz, D. (2006). Evidence for the strong dissociation between emotion and facial displays: The case of surprise. *Journal of Personality and Social Psychology, 91,* 295–315.

Remland, M. S. (1981). Developing leadership skills in nonverbal communication: A situational perspective. *Journal of Business Communication, 18,* 17–29.

Remland, M. S. (1982a). The implicit ad hominem fallacy: Nonverbal displays of status in the argumentative discourse. *Journal of the American Forensic Association, 19, 79–86.*

Remland, M. S. (1982b, November). *Leadership impressions and nonverbal communication in a superior-subordinate interaction.* Paper presented at the annual meeting of the Speech Communication Association, Louisville, KY.

Remland, M. S., & Jones, T. S. (1989). The effects of nonverbal involvement and communication apprehension on state anxiety, interpersonal attraction, and speech duration. *Communication Quarterly, 37, 170–183.*

Remland, M. S., Jones, T. S., & Brickman, H. (1991). Proxemic and haptic behavior in three European countries. *Journal of Nonverbal Behavior, 15, 215–232.*

Renninger, L. A., Wade, T. J., & Grammer, K. (2004). Getting the female glance: Patterns and consequences of male nonverbal behavior in courtship contexts. *Evolution and Human Behavior, 25, 416–431.*

Rich, A. L. (1974). *Interracial communication.* New York: Harper & Row.

Richards, L., Rollerson, B., & Phillips, J. (1992). Perceptions of submissiveness: Implications for victimization. *Journal of Psychology, 125, 407–411.*

Richardson, J. T. E., & Zucco, G. M. (1989). Cognition and olfaction: A review. *Psychological Bulletin, 105, 352–360.*

Richmond, V. P., Gorham, J. S., & McCroskey, J. C. (1987). The relationship between selected immediacy behaviors and cognitive learning. In M. L. McLaughlin (Ed.), *Communication yearbook 10* (pp. 574–590). Beverly Hills, CA: Sage.

Richmond, V. P., & McCroskey, J. C. (1995). *Nonverbal behavior in interpersonal relations.* Boston, MA: Allyn & Bacon.

Richmond, V. P., McCroskey, J. C., & Payne, S. K. (1987). *Nonverbal communication in interpersonal relations.* Englewood Cliffs, NJ: Prentice-Hall.

Richmond, V. P., McCroskey, J. C., Plax, T. G., & Kearney, P. (1986, November). *Teacher immediacy training and student affect.* Paper presented at the annual convention of the Speech Communication Association, Denver, CO.

Ridgeway, C. L. (1987). Nonverbal behavior, dominance, and the basis of status in task groups. *American Sociological Review, 52, 683–694.*

Ridgeway, C. L., Berger, J., & Smith, L. (1985). Nonverbal cues and status: An expectation states approach. *American Journal of Sociology, 90, 955–977.*

Riggio, R. E., & Friedman, H. S. (1983). Individual differences and cues to deception. *Journal of Personality and Social Psychology, 45, 899–915.*

Riggio, R. E., Tucker, J., & Throckmorton, B. (1987). Social skills and deception ability. *Personality and Social Psychology Bulletin, 13, 568–577.*

Riggio, R. E., Tucker, J., & Widaman, K. F. (1987). Verbal and nonverbal cues as mediators of deception ability. *Journal of Nonverbal Behavior, 11, 126–145.*

Rikowski, A., & Grammer, K. (1999). *Human body odour, symmetry and attractiveness.* Proceedings of the Royal Society of London B., 266, 869–874.

Rime, B., Mesquita, B., Philippot, P., & Boca, S. (1991). Beyond the emotional event: Six studies of the social sharing of emotion. *Cognition and Emotion, 5, 435–465.*

Ritts, V., & Patterson, M. L. (1996). Effect of social anxiety and action identification on impressions and thoughts in interaction. *Journal of Social and Clinical Psychology, 15, 191–205.*

Ritts, V., Patterson, M. L., & Tubbs, M. E. (1992). Expectations, impressions and judgments of physically attractive students. *Review of Educational Research, 62, 413–426.*

Rizzolatti, G., & Arbib, M. A. (1998) Language within our grasp. *Trends in neuroscience, 21, 188–194.*

Rizzolatti, G., & Craighero, L. (2004). The mirror neuron system. *Annual Review of Neuroscience, 27, 169–192.*

Rogers, L. E., & Millar, F. E. (1988). Relational communication. In S. Duck (Ed.), *Handbook of personal relationships* (pp. 289–306). New York: Wiley & Sons.

Rogers, L. E., & Shoemaker, F. F. (1971). *Communication of innovations: A cross-cultural approach.* New York: Free Press.

Rogers, W. T., & Jones, S. E. (1975). Effects of dominance tendencies on floor holding and interruption behavior in dyadic interaction. *Human Communication Research, 3, 291–302.*

Rosa, E., & Mazur, A. (1979). Incipient status in small groups. *Social Forces, 58,* 18–37.

Rosenfeld, H. M. (1965). Effect of an approval-seeking induction on interpersonal proximity. *Psychological Reports, 17,* 120–122.

Rosenfeld, H. M. (1966a). Approval-seeking and approval-inducing functions of verbal and nonverbal responses in the dyad. *Journal of Personality and Social Psychology, 4,* 597–605.

Rosenfeld, H. M. (1966b). Instrumental affiliative functions of face and gestural expressions. *Journal of Personality and Social Psychology, 4,* 65–72.

Rosenfeld, H. M. (1967). Nonverbal reciprocation of approval: An experimental analysis. *Journal of Experimental and Social Psychology, 3,* 102–111.

Rosenfeld, L., & Civikly, J. (1976). *With words unspoken.* New York: Holt, Rinehart & Winston.

Rosenthal, R., & DePaulo, B. M. (1979). Sex differences in accommodation in nonverbal communication. In R. Rosenthal (Ed.), *Skill in nonverbal communication: Individual differences* (pp. 68–103). Cambridge, MA: Oelgeschlager, Gunn, & Hain.

Rosenthal, R., Hall, J. A., DiMatteo, M. R., Rogers, P. L., & Archer, D. (1979). *Sensitivity to nonverbal communication: The PONS test.* Baltimore, MD: Johns Hopkins University Press.

Rosenthal, R., & Jacobson, L. (1968). *Pygmalion in the classroom: Teacher expectations and pupils' intellectual development.* New York: Holt, Rinehart & Winston.

Rosip, J. C., & Hall, J. A. (2004). Knowledge of nonverbal cues, gender and nonverbal decoding accuracy. *Journal of Nonverbal Behavior, 28,* 267–286.

Roter, D. L., Frankel, R. M., Hall, J. A., & Sluyter, D. (2006). The expression of emotion through nonverbal behavior in medical visits. *Journal of General Internal Medicine, 21,* S28–S34.

Rothman, A. D., & Nowicki, S. (2004). A measure of the ability to identify emotion in children's tone of voice. *Journal of Nonverbal Behavior, 28,* 67–92.

Rothwell, J., Bandar, Z., O'Shea, J. Mclean, D. (2006). Silent talker: A new computer-based system for the analysis of facial cues to deception. *Applied Cognitive Psychology, 20,* 757–777.

Routasalo, P., & Isola, A. (1996). The right to touch and be touched. *Nursing Ethics, 3,* 165–167.

Rowatt, W. C., Cunningham, M. R., & Druen, P. B. (1999). Lying to get a date: The effect of facial physical attractiveness on the willingness to deceive prospective dating partners. *Journal of Personal and Social Relationships, 16,* 209–223.

Ruiz-Belda, M.-A., Fernandez-Dols, J.-M., Carrera, P., & Barchard, K. (2003). Spontaneous facial expressions of happy bowlers and soccer fans. *Cognition and Emotion, 17,* 315–326.

Rushing, J. H. (1993). Power, other, and spirit in cultural texts. *Western Journal of Communication, 57,* 159–168.

Russell, B. (1938). *Power: A new social analysis.* London: Allen & Unwin.

Russell, J. A. (1989). Measures of emotion. In R. Plutchik & H. Kellerman (Eds.), *Emotion: Theory, research, and experience* (pp. 83–111). New York: Academic.

Russell, J. A. (1991). Confusions about context in the judgment of facial expressions: A reply to the contempt expression and the relativity thesis. *Motivation and Emotion, 15,* 17–184.

Russell, J. A., Bachorowski, J-A., & Fernandez-Dols, J.-M. (2003). Facial and vocal expressions of emotion. *Annual Review of Psychology, 54,* 329–349.

Russo, N. (1967). Connotation of seating arrangement. *Cornell Journal of Social Relations, 2,* 37–44.

Ryan, E. B., Bourhis, R. Y., & Knops, U. (1991). Evaluating perceptions of patronizing speech to elders. *Psychology and Aging, 6,* 442–450.

Ryans, D. G. (1960). *Characteristics of teachers.* Washington, DC: American Council on Education.

Ryans, D. G. (1964). Research on teacher behavior in the context of the teacher characteristic study. In B. J. Biddle & W. J. Ellena (Eds.), *Contemporary research on teacher effectiveness.* New York: Holt, Rinehart & Winston.

Saarni, C. (1985). Indirect processes in affect socialization. In M. Lewis & C. Saarni (Eds.), *The socialization of emotions* (pp. 187–209). New York: Plenum.

Saarni, C. (1993). Socialization of emotion. In M. Lewis & J. M. Haviland (Eds.), *Handbook of emotions* (pp. 435–446). New York: Guilford.

Sabatelli, R. M., & Rubin, M. (1986). Nonverbal expressiveness and physical attractiveness as mediators of interpersonal perceptions. *Journal of Nonverbal Behavior, 10,* 120–133.

Sadalla, E. K. (1978). Population size, structural differentiation and human behavior. *Environment and Behavior, 10,* 271–289.

Salter, F., Grammer, K., & Rikowski, A. (2005). Sex differences in negotiating with powerful males. *Human Nature, 16,* 306–321.

Samovar, L. A., & Porter, R. E. (2001). *Communication between cultures.* Belmont, CA: Wadworth.

Samovar, L. A., Porter, R. E., & Jain, N. C. (1981). *Understanding intercultural communication.* Belmont, CA: Wadsworth.

Sanders, J. A., & Wiseman, R. L. (1990). The effect of verbal and nonverbal teacher immediacy on perceived cognitive, affective, and behavioral learning in the multicultural classroom. *Communication Education, 39,* 341–353.

Sapir, E. (1928). The unconscious patterning of behavior in society. In E. S. Drummer (Ed.), *The unconscious* (pp. 114–142). New York: Knopf.

Savic, I., Berglund, H., Gulyas, B., & Roland, P. (2001). Smelling odorous sex hormone-like compounds causes sex-differentiated hypothalamic activations in humans. *Neuron, 31,* 661–668.

Savic, I., Berglund, H., & Lindstrom, P. (2005). *Brain responses to putative pheromones in homosexual men.* Proceedings of the National Academy of Science, 102, 7356–7361.

Saygin, A. P., Wilson, S. M., Dronkers, N. F., & Bates, E. (2004). *Neuropsychologia, 42,* 1788–1804.

Scafidi, F. A., Field, T. M., Schanberg, S. M., & Bauer, C. R. (1990). Massage stimulates growth in pre-term infants: A replication. *Infant Behavior & Development, 13,* 167–188.

Schachner, D. A., Shaver, P. R., & Mikulincer, M. (2005). Patterns of nonverbal behavior and sensitivity in the context of attachment relationships. *Journal of Nonverbal Behavior, 29,* 141–169.

Scharlemann, J. P. W., Eckel, C. C., Kacelnik, A., & Wilson, R. K. (2001). The value of a smile: Game theory with a human face. *Journal of Economic Psychology, 22,* 617–640.

Scheff, T. J. (1995). Conflict in family systems: The role of shame. In J. P. Tangney & K. W. Fischer (Eds.), *Self-conscious emotions: The psychology of shame, guilt, embarrassment and pride* (pp. 393–442). New York: Guilford.

Scheflen, A. E. (1965). Quasi-courtship behavior in psychotherapy. *Psychiatry, 27,* 245–257.

Scheflen, A. E. (1972). *Body language and the social order: Communication as behavior control.* Englewood Cliffs, NJ: Prentice-Hall.

Scheflen, A. E. (1974). *How behavior means.* Garden City, NY: Anchor Books.

Scherer, K. R. (1972). Judging personality from voice: A cross-cultural approach to an old issue in interpersonal perception. *Journal of Personality, 40,* 191–210.

Scherer, K. R. (1979). Acoustic noncomitants of emotional dimensions: Judging affect from synthesized tone sequences. In S. Weitz (Ed.), *Nonverbal communication: Readings with commentary* (pp. 249–253). New York: Oxford University Press.

Scherer, K. R. (2003). Vocal communication of emotion: A review of research paradigms. *Speech Communication, 40,* 227–256.

Scherer, K. R., & Ceschi, O. (2000). Criteria for emotional recognition from verbal and nonverbal expression: Studying baggage loss at the airport. *Personality and Social Psychology Bulletin, 26,* 327–329.

Scherer, K. R., & Wallbott, H. G. (1994). Evidence for universality and cultural variation of differential emotional response patterning. *Journal of Personality and Social Psychology, 66,* 310–328.

Scherwitz, L., & Helmreich, R. (1973). Interactive effects of eye contact and verbal content on interpersonal attraction in dyads. *Journal of Personality and Social Psychology, 25,* 6–14.

Schiffenbauer, A., & Schiavo, R. S. (1976). Physical distance and attraction: An intensification effect. *Journal of Experimental Social Psychology, 12,* 274–282.

Schlenker, B. R., & Leary, M. R. (1982). Social anxiety and self-presentation: A conceptualization and model. *Psychological Bulletin, 92,* 641–669.

Schlenker, B. R., & Leary, M. R. (1985). Social anxiety and communication about the self. *Journal of Language and Social Psychology, 4,* 171–192.

Schmidt, K. L., & Cohn, J. F. (2001). Human facial expression as adaptations: Evolutionary questions in facial expression research. *Yearbook of Physical Anthropology, 44,* 3–24.

Schnall, S., & Laird, J. D. (2003). Keep smiling: Enduring effects of facial expressions and postures on emotional experience and memory. *Cognition and Emotion, 17,* 787–797.

Schubert, T. W. (2006). Your highness: Vertical positions as perceptual symbols of power. *Journal of Personality and Social Psychology, 89,* 1–21.

Schwarzwald, J., Kavish, N., Shoham, M., & Waysman, M. (1977). Fear and sex-similarity as determinants of personal space. *Journal of Psychology, 96*, 55–61.

Seager, J., & Olson, A. (1986). *Women in the world atlas.* New York: Simon & Schuster.

Segrin, C. (1990, November). *Nonverbal behavior and compliance: Affiliation, arousal or dominance.* Paper presented at the annual meeting of the Speech Communication Association, Chicago, IL.

Segrin, C. (1993). The effects of nonverbal behavior on outcomes of compliance-gaining attempts. *Communication Studies, 44,* 169–187.

Segrin, C. (1998). Interpersonal communication problems associated with depression and loneliness. In P. A. Andersen & L. K. Guerrero (Eds.), *Handbook of communication and emotion: Research, theory, applications, and contexts* (pp. 216–242). San Diego, CA: Academic.

Seiter, J. S., & Weger, H. (2005). Audience perceptions of candidates' appropriateness as a function of nonverbal behaviors displayed during televised political debates. *Journal of Social Psychology, 145,* 225–235.

Selye, H. (1956). *The stress of life.* New York: McGraw-Hill.

Semic, B. A., Miller, T. A., & Guerrero, L. K. (1996, May). *The attractive voice as heard on the answering machine: Vocal determinants of first impressions.* Paper presented at the annual meeting of the International Communication Association, Chicago, IL.

Senju, A., & Hasegawa, T. (2006). Do the upright eyes have it? *Psychonomic Bulletin and Review, 13,* 223–228.

Sennett, R. (1977). *The fall of public man.* New York: Vintage Books.

Shaver, P. R., & Hazan, C. (1988, November). A biased overview of the study of love. *Journal of Social and Personal Relationships, 5,* 473–501.

Shaver, P., Schwartz, J., Kirson, D., & O'Connor, C. (1987). Emotional knowledge: Further explorations of a prototype approach. *Journal of Personality and Social Psychology, 52,* 1061–1086.

Shaver, P., Wu, S., & Schwartz, J. C. (1992). Cross-cultural similarities and differences in emotion and its representation: A prototype approach. In M. S. Clark (Ed.), *Review of personality and social psychology. Emotion* (Vol. 13, pp. 175–212). Newbury Park, CA: Sage.

Shawn, W., & Gregory, A. (1981). *My dinner with Andre.* New York: Grove.

Sheldon, W. N. (1940). *The varieties of human physique.* New York: Harper.

Shennum, W. A., & Bugental, D. B. (1982). The development of control over affective expression in nonverbal behavior. In R. S. Feldman (Ed.), *Development of nonverbal behavior in children* (pp. 101–122). New York: Springer Verlag.

Shevrin, H., & Toussieng, P. W. (1965). Vicissitudes of the need for tactile stimulation in instinctual development. *The Psychoanalytic Study of the Child, 20,* 310–339.

Siegel, S. M., Friedlander, M. L., & Heatherington, L. (1992). Nonverbal relational control in family communication. *Journal of Nonverbal Behavior, 16,* 117–139.

Siegman, A. W., & Feldstein, S. (1987). *Nonverbal behavior and communication* (2nd ed.). New York: Halsted.

Sieratzki, J. S., & Woll, B. (1996). Why do mothers cradle their babies on their left? *Lancet, 347,* 1746–1750.

Silberman, E. K., & Weingartner, H. (1986). Hemispheric lateralization of functions related to emotion. *Brain and Cognition, 5,* 322–353.

Silver, C. A., & Spitzberg, B. H. (1992, July). *Flirtation as social intercourse: Developing a measure of flirtatious behavior.* Paper presented at the Sixth International Conference on Personal Relationships, Orono, ME.

Silverman, A. F., Pressman, H. E., & Bartell, H. W. (1973). Self-esteem and tactile communication. *Journal of Humanistic Psychology, 13,* 73–77.

Sinha, S. P., & Nayyar, P. (2000). Crowding effects of density and personal space requirements among older people: The impact of self-control and social support. *The Journal of Social Psychology, 140,* 721–728.

Sitaram, K. S., & Codgell, R. T. (1976). *Foundations of intercultural communication.* Columbus, OH: Merrill.

Skuse, D. H., James, R. S., Bishop, D. V. M., & Coppin, B. (1997). Evidence from Turner's syndrome of an imprinted X-linked locus affecting cognitive function. *Nature, 387,* 705–708.

Slane, S., Dragan, W., Crandall, J., & Payne, P. (1980). Stress effects on the nonverbal behavior of sensitizers and repressors. *Journal of Psychology, 106,* 101–109.

Smith, D. E., Gier, J. A., & Willis, F. N. (1982). Interpersonal touch and compliance with a marketing request. *Basic and Applied Social Psychology, 3,* 35–38.

Smith, T. W., Ingram, R. E., & Brehm, S. S. (1983). Social anxiety, anxious self-preoccupation, and recall of self-relevant information. *Journal of Personality and Social Psychology, 44,* 1276–1283.

Sommer, R. (1961). Leadership and group geography. *Sociometry, 24,* 99–110.

Sommer, R. (1965). Leadership and small group ecology. *Sociometry, 28,* 337–348.

Sommer, R. (1967a). Small group ecology. *Psychological Bulletin, 67,* 145–151.

Sommer, R. (1967b). Sociofugal space. *American Journal of Sociology, 72,* 654–660.

Sommer, R. (1969). *Personal space.* Englewood Cliffs, NJ: Prentice-Hall.

Sorensen, G. A. (1979, May). *The effects of touch on interpersonal perceptions.* Paper presented at the annual meeting of the Eastern Communication Association, Philadelphia, PA.

Sorensen, R. C. (1973). *Adolescent sexuality in contemporary America.* New York: World Publishing.

Sparks, G. G., & Greene, J. O. (1992). On the validity of nonverbal indicators as measures of physiological arousal: A reply to Burgoon, Kelley, Newton, and Keeley-Dyerson. *Human Communication Research, 18,* 445–471.

Sperli, F., Spinelli, L. Pollo, C., & Seeck, M. (2006). Contralateral smile and laughter, but no mirth, induced by electrical stimulation of the cingulate cortex. *Epilepsia, 47,* 440–443.

Spiegel, J. P., & Machotka, P. (1974). *Messages of the body.* New York: Free Press.

Spitzberg, B. H. (1998). Sexual coercion in courtship relations. In B. H. Spitzberg & W. R. Cupach (Eds.), *The dark side of close relationships* (pp. 179–223). Mahwah NJ: Erlbaum.

Spitzberg, B. H., & Cupach, W. R. (1984). *Interpersonal communication competence.* Beverly Hills, CA: Sage.

Spitzberg, B. H., & Cupach, W. R. (1989). *Handbook of interpersonal competence research.* New York: Springer Verlag.

Spitzberg, B. H., & Cupach, W. R. (1994). Dark side denouement. In W. R. Cupach & B. H. Spitzberg (Eds.), *The dark side of interpersonal communication* (pp. 315–320). Hillsdale, NJ: Erlbaum.

Sporer, S. L. (2001a). Recognizing the faces of other ethnic groups: An integration of theories. *Psychology, Public Policy, and Law, 7,* 36–97.

Sporer, S. L. (2001b). The cross-race effect: Beyond recognition of faces in the laboratory. *Psychology, Public Policy, and Law, 7,* 170–200.

Sporer, S. L., & Schwandt, B. (2006). Paraverbal indicators of deception: A meta-analytic synthesis. *Applied Cognitive Psychology, 20,* 421–446.

Spradlin, J., & Fromme, D. K. (1989). *Parental influences on attitudes toward touch.* Unpublished manuscript, Oklahoma State University.

Stacks, D. W., & Andersen, P. A. (1989). The modular mind: Implications for intrapersonal communication. *Southern Communication Journal, 54,* 273–293.

Stacks, D. W., & Burgoon, J. K. (1979, April). *The persuasive effects of violating spatial distance expectations in small groups.* Paper presented at the annual meeting of the Southern Speech Communication Association Convention, Biloxi, MS.

Stacks, D. W., & Burgoon, J. K. (1981). The role of nonverbal behaviors as distractors in resistance to persuasion in interpersonal contexts. *Central States Speech Journal, 32,* 61–73.

Stainburn, S. (2006, May 8). Hair in the wrong places? *Crain's Chicago Business, 29,* 36.

Stang, D. J. (1973). Effect of interaction rate on ratings of leadership and liking. *Journal of Personality and Social Psychology, 27,* 405–408.

Steckler, N. A., & Rosenthal, R. (1985). Sex differences in nonverbal and verbal communication with bosses, peers, and subordinates. *Journal of Applied Psychology, 70,* 157–163.

Steinem, G. (1994). *Moving beyond words.* New York: Simon & Schuster.

Stelzner, M. A., & Egland, K. L. (1995, February). *Perceived understanding, nonverbal communication, relational satisfaction, and relational stage.* Paper presented at the annual convention of the Western States Communication Association, Portland, OR.

Stephan, F. F. (1952). The relative rate of communication between members of small groups. *American Sociological Review, 17,* 482–486.

Stern, D. (1980). *The first relationship: Mother and infant.* Cambridge, MA: Harvard University Press.

Sternberg, R. J. (1986). A triangular theory of love. *Psychological Review, 93,* 119–135.

Sternberg, R. J. (1987). *The triangle of love: Intimacy, passion, commitment.* New York: Basic Books.

Sternglanz, R. W., & DePaulo, B. M. (2004). Reading nonverbal cues to emotions: The advantages and liabilities of relationship closeness. *Journal of Nonverbal Behavior, 28,* 245–266.

Stevanoni, E., & Salmon, K. (2005). Giving memory a hand: Instructing children to gesture enhances their event recall. *Journal of Nonverbal Behavior, 29,* 217–233.

Steward, A. L., & Lupfer, M. (1987). Touching as teaching: The effect of touch on students' perceptions and performance. *Journal of Applied Psychology, 17,* 800–809.

Stier, D. S., & Hall, J. A. (1984). Gender differences in touch: An empirical and theoretical review. *Journal of Personality and Social Psychology, 47,* 440–459.

Stiff, J. B. (1986). Cognitive processing of persuasive messages: A meta-analysis review of the effects of supporting information on attitudes. *Communication Monographs, 53,* 75–89.

Stiff, J. B., & Boster, F. J. (1987). Cognitive processing: Additional thoughts and a reply to Petty, Kasner, Haugtvedt, and Cacioppo. *Communication Monographs, 54,* 233–249.

Stiff, J. B., Kim, H. J., & Ramesh, C. N. (1989, May). *Truth biases and aroused suspicion in relational deception.* Paper presented at the annual meeting of the International Communication Association, San Francisco, CA.

Stockhorst, U., & Pietrowsky, R. (2004). Olfactory perception, communication, and the nose-to-brain pathway. *Psychology and Behavior, 83,* 3–11.

Street, R. L. (1982). Evaluation of noncontent speech accommodation. *Language and Communication, 2,* 13–31.

Street, R. L., & Brady, R. M. (1982). Speech rate acceptance ranges as a function of evaluative domain, listener speech rate and communication context. *Communication Monographs, 49,* 290–308.

Street, R. L., & Buller, D. B. (1988, November). *Nonverbal response patterns in physician-patient interactions: A functional analysis.* Paper presented at the annual convention of the Speech Communication Association, New Orleans, LA.

Street, R. L., & Giles, H. (1982). Speech accommodation theory: A social cognitive approach to language and speech behavior. In M. Roloff & C. Berger (Eds.), *Social cognition and communication* (pp. 193–226). Beverly Hills, CA: Sage.

Streeter, L. A., Krauss, R. M., Geller, V., Olson, C., & Apple, W. (1979). Pitch changes during attempted deception. In S. Weitz (Ed.), *Nonverbal communication: Readings with commentary* (pp. 254–267). New York: Oxford University Press.

Strodtbeck, F. L., & Hook, L. H. (1961). The social dimensions of a twelve-man jury table. *Sociometry, 24,* 397–415.

Strongman, K. T., & Chapness, B. F. (1968). Dominance hierarchies and conflict in eye contact. *Acta Psychologica, 28,* 376–386.

Strube, M. J., & Werner, C. (1984). Personal space claims as a function of interpersonal threat: The mediating role of need for control. *Journal of Nonverbal Behavior, 8,* 195–209.

Strzyzewski, K. (1990, November). *A model of effective expression as interpersonal influence.* Paper presented at the annual meeting of the Speech Communication Association, Chicago, IL.

Swann, W. B., Griffith, J. J., Predmore, S. C., & Gaines, B. (1987). The cognitive-affective crossfire: When consistency confronts self-enhancement. *Journal of Personality and Social Psychology, 52,* 881–889.

Takala, M. (1977). Consistencies and perception of consistencies in individual psychomotion behavior. In D. Magnusson & N. S. Endler (Eds.), *Personality at the crossroads: Current issues in interactional psychology.* Hillsdale, NJ: Erlbaum.

Tangney, J. P. (1995). Shame and guilt in interpersonal relationships. In J. P. Tangney & K. W. Fischer (Eds.), *Self-conscious emotions: The psychology of shame, guilt, embarrassment and pride* (pp. 114–139). New York: Guilford.

Taraban, C. B., Hendrick, S. S., & Hendrick, C. (1998). Loving and liking. In P. A. Andersen & L. K. Guerrero (Eds.), *Handbook of communication and emotion: Research, theory, applications, and contexts* (pp. 331–351). San Diego, CA: Academic.

Tasi, W., Chen, C., & Chui, S. (2005). Exploring boundaries of the effects of applicant impression management tactics in job interviews. *Journal of Management, 31,* 108–125.

Tessler, R., & Sushelsky, L. (1978). Effects of eye contact and social status on the perception of a job applicant in an employment interviewing situation. *Journal of Vocational Behavior, 13*, 138–147.

Tetterton, V. S., & Warren, A. R. (2005). Using witness confidence can impair the ability to detect deception. *Criminal Justice and Behavior, 32*, 433–551.

Thayer, S. (1969). The effect of interpersonal looking duration on dominance judgments. *Journal of Social Psychology, 79*, 285–286.

Thayer, S. (1986). History and strategies of research on social touch. *Journal of Nonverbal Behavior, 10*, 12–28.

Thayer, S., & Schiff, W. (1974). Observer judgment of social interaction: Eye contact and relationship inferences. *Journal of Personality and Social Psychology, 30*, 110–114.

Thompson, H. S. (1971). *Fear and loathing in Las Vegas: A savage journey to the heart of the American dream.* New York: Random House.

Thompson, J. J. (1973). *Beyond words: Nonverbal communication in the classroom.* New York: Citation.

Thorne, F., Neave, N., Scholey, A., Moss, M., & Fink, B. (2002). Effect of putative male pheromones on female ratings of attractiveness: The influence of oral contraceptives and the menstrual cycle. *Neuroendocrinology Letters, 23*, 291–297.

Thornhill, R., & Gangestad, S. W. (1999). The scent of symmetry: A human sex pheromone that signals fitness? *Evolution and Human Behavior, 20*, 175–201.

Thornhill, R., & Gangestad, S. W. (2003). Evolutionary theory led to evidence for a male sex pheromone that signals symmetry. *Psychological Inquiry, 14*, 318–325.

Thornhill, R., Gangestad, S. W., Miller, G., McCollough, J. K., & Franklin, M. (2003). Major histocompatibility complex genes, symmetry, and body scent attractiveness in men and women. *Behavioral Ecology, 14*, 688–678.

Thorson, J. A., & Kasworm, C. (1984). Sunshine and suicide: Possible influences of climate on behavior. *Death Education, 8*, 125–136.

Thunberg, M., & Dimberg, U. (2000). Gender differences in facial reaction to fear-relevant stimuli. *Journal of Nonverbal Behavior, 24*, 45–51.

Tickle-Dengen, L., & Puccinelli, N. M. (1999). The nonverbal expression of negative emotions: Peer and supervisor responses to occupational therapy students' emotional attributes. *The Occupational Therapy Journal of Research, 19*, 18–39.

Tiggemann M., & Kenyon, S. J. (1998). The hairlessness norm: The removal of body hair in women. *Sex Roles, 39*, 873–885.

Tiggemann M., & Lewis, C. (2004). Attitudes toward women's body hair: Relationship with disgust sensitivity. *Psychology of Women Quarterly, 28*, 381–387.

Ting-Toomey, S. T. (1991). Intimacy expressions in three cultures: France, Japan, and the United States. *International Journal of Intercultural Relations, 15*, 29–46.

Tocqueville, A. D. (1835/1945). *Democracy in America* (Vol. 1). New York: Vintage Books.

Todd-Mancillas, W. R. (1982). Classroom environments and nonverbal behavior. In L. L. Barker (Ed.), *Communication in the classroom: Original essays* (pp. 77–97). Englewood Cliffs, NJ: Prentice-Hall.

Toerien, M., & Wilkenson, S. (2003). Gender and body hair: Constructing the feminine woman. *Women's Studies International Forum, 26*, 333–344.

Toerien, M., Wilkenson, S., & Choi, P. (2005). Bodily hair removal: The "mundane" production of normative feminity. *Sex Roles, 52*, 399–406.

Tomkins, S. S. (1962). *Affect, imagery, consciousness: Vol. 1. The positive affects.* New York: Springer Verlag.

Tomkins, S. S. (1963). *Affect, imagery, consciousness: Vol. 2. The negative affects.* New York: Springer Verlag.

Tomkins, S. S. (1984). Affect theory. In K. R. Scherer & P. Ekman (Eds.), *Approaches to emotion* (pp. 163–195). Hillsdale, NJ: Erlbaum.

Tracy, J. L., & Robins, R. W. (2004). Show your pride: Evidence for a discrete emotional expression. *Psychological Science, 15*, 194–197.

Tracy, J. L., Robins, R. W., & Lagattuta, K. H. (2005). Can children recognize pride? *Emotion, 5*, 251–257.

Trager, G. L. (1958). Paralanguage: A first approximation. *Studies in Linguistics, 13,* 1–12.

Trenholm, S., & Petrie, C. R. (1980). Reexamining body accessibility. *Australian Scan: Journal of Human Communication, 7–8,* 33–42.

Trost, M. R., & Alberts, J. K. (2006). How men and women communicate attraction: An evolutionary view. In K. Dindia & D. J. Canary (Eds.), *Sex Differences and Similarities in Communication* (pp. 317–336). Mahwah, NJ: Erlbaum

Trost, M. R., & Engstrom, C. (1994, February). *"Hit the road Jack": Strategies for rejecting flirtatious advances.* Paper presented at the annual meeting of the Western States Communication Association, San Jose, CA.

Trout, D. L., & Rosenfeld, H. M. (1980). The effect of postural lean and body congruence on the judgment of psychotherapeutic rapport. *Journal of Nonverbal Behavior, 4,* 176–190.

Tucker, D. M. (1981). Lateral brain function, emotion, and conceptualization. *Psychological Bulletin, 89,* 19–46.

Turner, R. E., Edgley, C., & Olmstead, G. (1975). Information control in conversations: Honesty is not always the best policy. *Kansas Journal of Sociology, 11,* 69–89.

Twenge, J. M. (2006). *Generation me.* New York: Free Press.

Ullman, S. E., & Knight, R. A. (1992). A multivariate model for predicting rape and physical injury outcomes during sexual assaults. *Journal of Consulting and Clinical Psychology, 60,* 28.

Uzell, D., & Horne, N. (2006). The influence of biological sex, sexuality, and gender role in interpersonal distance. *British Journal of Social Psychology, 45,* 579–597.

Vaid, J., Bellugi, U., & Poizner, H. (1989). Hand dominance for signing: Clues to brain lateralization of language. *Neuropsychologia, 27,* 949–960.

Valentine, M. E. (1980). The attenuating influence of gaze upon the bystander intervention effect. *Journal of Social Psychology, 3,* 197–203.

Van Hoofe, J. A. R. A. M. (1972). A comparative approach to the phylogeny of laughter and smiling. In R. A. Hinde (Ed.), *Non-verbal communication* (pp. 209–238). Cambridge, England: Cambridge University Press.

Van Swol, L. M. (2003). The effects of nonverbal mirroring on perceived persuasiveness, agreement with an imitator, and reciprocity in group discussion. *Communication Research, 30,* 461–480.

Vancil, D. L., & Pendell, S. D. (1987). The myth of viewer-listener disagreement in the first Kennedy-Nixon debate. *Central States Speech Journal, 38,* 16–27.

Vangelisti, A. L., & Daly, J. A. (1997). Gender differences in standards for romantic relationships. *Personal Relationships, 4,* 203–219.

Vangelisti, A. L., & Sprague, R. J. (1998). Guilt and hurt: Similarities, distinctions, and conversational strategies. In P. A. Andersen & L. K. Guerrero (Eds.), *Handbook of communication and emotion: Research, theory, applications, and contexts* (pp. 123–153). San Diego, CA: Academic.

Venezia, M., Messinger, D. S., Thorp, D., & Mundy, P. (2004). The development of anticipatory smiling. *Infancy, 6,* 397–406.

Vettin, J., & Todt, D. (2004). Laughter in conversation: Features of occurrence and acoustic structure. *Journal of Nonverbal Behavior, 28,* 93–115.

Vogel, J. J., Bowers, C. A., & Vogel, D. S. (2003). Cerebral lateralization and spatial abilities: A meta-analysis. *Brain and Cognition, 52,* 197–204.

Vollmer, J. J., & Gordon, S. A. (1975). Chemical communication. *Chemistry, 48,* 6–11.

Voyer, D., Nolan, C., & Voyer, S. (2000). The relation between experience and spatial performance in men and women. *Sex Roles, 43,* 891–915.

Vranic, A. (2003). Personal space in physically abused children. *Environment and Behavior, 35,* 550–565.

Vrij, A. (1994). The impact of information and setting on detection of deception by police detectives. *Journal of Nonverbal Behavior, 18,* 117–136.

Vrij, A. (2004). Why professionals fail to catch liars and how they can improve. *Legal and Criminal Psychology, 9,* 159–181.

Vrij, A. (2006). Challenging interviewees during interviews: The potential effects on lie detection. *Psychology, Crime & Law, 12,* 193–206.

Vrij, A., Akehurst, L., Soukara, S., & Bull, R. (2004). Let me tell you how to tell a convincing story: CBCA and reality monitoring scores as a function of age, coaching, and deception. *Canadian Journal of Behavioural Science, 36,* 113–126.

Vrij, A., Edward, K., & Bull, R. (2001). Stereotypical verbal and nonverbal responses while deceiving others. *Personality and Social Psychology Bulletin, 27*, 899–909.

Vrij, A., Edward, K., Roberts, K. P., & Bull, R. (2000). Detecting deceit via analysis of verbal and nonverbal behavior. *Journal of Nonverbal Behavior, 24*, 239–263.

Vrij, A., Mann, S., Robbins, E., & Robinson, M. (2006). Police officers ability to detect deception in high stakes situations in repeated lie detection tests. *Applied Cognitive Psychology, 20*, 741–755.

Vrij, A., & Semin, G. R. (1996). Lie experts' beliefs about nonverbal indicators of deception. *Journal of Nonverbal Behavior, 20*, 65–80.

Vrij, A., Semin, G. R., & Bull, R. (1996). Insight into behavior displayed during deception. *Human Communication Research, 22*, 544–562.

Vrij, A., & Winkel, F. W. (1991). Cultural patterns in Dutch and Surinam nonverbal behavior: An analysis of simulated police citizen encounters. *Journal of Nonverbal Behavior, 15*, 169–184.

Walster, E., Walster, G. W., & Berscheid, E. (1978). *Equity: Theory and research.* Boston, MA: Allyn & Bacon.

Ward, C. D. (1968). Seating arrangement and leadership emergence in small discussion groups. *Journal of Social Psychology, 74*, 83–90.

Ward, R. D. (1918). *Climate: Considered especially in relation to man.* New York: Putnam.

Warner, R. M., Malloy, D., Schnieder, K., Knoth, R., & Wilder, B. (1987). Rhythmic organization of social interaction and observer ratings of positive affect and involvement. *Journal of Nonverbal Behavior, 11*, 57–74.

Watson, D., & Clark, L. A. (1984). Negative affectivity: The disposition to experience aversive emotional states. *Psychological Bulletin, 96*, 465–490.

Watzlawick, P., Beavin, J. H., & Jackson, D. D. (1967). *Pragmatics of human communication.* New York: Norton.

Weiner, A. N. (1973). *Machiavellianism as a predictor of group interaction and cohesion.* Unpublished master's thesis, West Virginia University, Morgantown, WV.

Weiner, H. (1966). External chemical messengers: Emission and reception in man. *New York State Journal of Medicine, 66*, 3153–3170.

Weiner, M., Devoe, S., Rubinow, S., & Geller, J. (1972). Nonverbal behavior and nonverbal communication. *Psychological Review, 79*, 185–214.

Weiner, M., & Mehrabian, A. (1968). *Language within language: Immediacy, a channel in verbal communication.* New York: Appleton-Century-Crofts.

Weins, A. N., Thompson, S. M., Matarazzo, J. D., Matarazzo, R. G., & Saslow, G. (1965). Interview interaction behavior of supervisors, head nurses, and staff nurses. *Nursing Research, 14*, 322–329.

Weisfeld, C. C., & Stack, M. A. (2002). When I look into your eyes: An ethological analysis of gender differences in married couples' nonverbal behaviors. *Psychology, Evolution and Gender, 4*, 125–147.

Weiss, K. R. (1997, January 13). Survey finds record stress in the class of 2000. *Los Angeles Times,* p. 1.

Wells, W., & Siegel, B. (1961). Stereotyped somatypes. *Psychological Reports, 8*, 77–78.

Wertin, L., & Andersen, P. A. (1995). *Sexual harassment and cognitive schemata: A test of cognitive valence theory.* Unpublished study, School of Communication, San Diego State University.

Wertin, L., & Andersen, P. A. (1996, February). *Cognitive schemata and perceptions of sexual harassment: A test of cognitive valence theory.* Paper presented at the annual convention of the Western States Communication Association, Pasadena, CA.

Wesp, R., Hesse, J. Keutmann, D., & Wheaton, K. (2001). Gestures maintain spatial imagery. *American Journal of Psychology, 114*, 591–600.

Wheeler, D. L. (1994, November). Lessons in the signs: Researchers explore the world of the deaf to study the evolution of language. *Chronicle of Higher Education,* A6–A14.

Wheeless, L. R. (1978). A follow-up study of the relationships among trust, disclosure, and interpersonal solidarity. *Human Communication Research, 4*, 143–157.

Whicker, M. L., & Kronenfeld, J. J. (1986). *Sex role changes: Technology, politics, and policy.* New York: Praeger.

White, C. H., & Burgoon, J. K. (2001). Adaptation and communication design patterns of interaction in truthful and deceptive conversations. *Human Communication Research, 27*, 9–37.

White, G. L., & Mullen, P. E. (1989). *Jealousy: Theory, research, and clinical strategies.* New York: Guilford.

Whybrow, P. (1984). Contributions from neuroendocrinology. In K. R. Scherer & P. Ekman (Eds.), *Approaches to emotion* (pp. 59–75). Hillsdale, NJ: Erlbaum.

Wilden, A. (1972). Analog and digital communication. *Semiotica, 10,* 50–82.

Wilden, A. (1980). *System and structure.* New York: Tavistock.

Wilhelm, F. H., Kochar, A. S., Roth, W. T., & Gross, J. J., (2001). Social anxiety and response to touch: Incongruence between self-evaluative and physiological reaction. *Biological Psychology, 58,* 181–202.

Wilkins, B. M., & Andersen, P. A. (1991). Gender differences and similarities in management communication: A meta-analysis. *Management Communication Quarterly, 5,* 6–35.

Willis, F. N., & Briggs, L. F. (1992). Relationships and touch in public settings. *Journal of Nonverbal Behavior, 16,* 55–63.

Willis, F. N., & Hamm, H. (1980). The use of interpersonal touch in security compliance. *Journal of Nonverbal Behavior, 5,* 49–55.

Willis, F. N., & Rawdon, V. A. (1994). Gender and national difference in attitude toward same-gender touch. *Perceptual and Motor Skills, 78,* 1027–1034.

Wilson, B. J., & Smith, S. L. (1998). Children's responses to emotional portrayals on television. In P. A. Andersen & L. K. Guerrero (Eds.), *Handbook of communication and emotion: Research, theory, applications, and contexts* (pp. 533–569). San Diego, CA: Academic.

Wiseman, R. (1995). The megalab truth test. *Science, 373,* 391.

Witt, P. L., Wheeless, L. R., & Allen, M. (2004). A meta-analytic review of the relationship between teacher immediacy and student learning. *Communication Monographs, 71,* 184–207.

Witte, K. (1998). Fear as motivator, fear as inhibitor: Using the extended parallel process model to explain fear appeal successes and failures. In P. A. Andersen & L. K. Guerrero (Eds.), *Handbook of communication and emotion: Research, theory, applications, and contexts* (pp. 423–450). San Diego, CA: Academic.

Wood, J. T. (1996). Gender, relationships, and communication. In J. T. Wood (Ed.), *Gendered relationships* (pp. 3–19). Mountain View, CA: Mayfield.

Wood, J. T. (1997a). Clarifying the issues. *Personal Relationships, 4,* 221–228.

Wood, J. T. (1997b). *Gendered lives: Communication, gender, and culture.* Belmont, CA: Wadsworth.

Wood, J. T., & Inman, C. T. (1993). In another mode: Masculine styles of communicating closeness. *Journal of Applied Communication Research, 21,* 279–295.

Woodall, W. G., & Burgoon, J. K. (1981). The effects of nonverbal synchrony on message comprehension and persuasiveness. *Journal of Nonverbal Behavior, 5,* 207–223.

Woodall, W. G., & Burgoon, J. K. (1983). Talking fast and changing attitudes: A critique and clarification. *Journal of Nonverbal Behavior, 8,* 126–142.

Woodruff, C., & Premack, D. (1979). Intentional communication in the chimpanzee: The development of deception. *Cognition, 7,* 333–362.

Wooley, S. C., & Wooley, O. W. (1984, February). Feeling fat in a thin society. *Glamour,* 198–252.

Yabar, Y., Johnston, L., Miles, L., & Peace, V. (2006). Implicit behavioral mimicry: Investigating the impact of group membership. *Journal of Nonverbal Behavior, 30,* 97–114.

Young, D. M., Beier, E. G., & Beier, S. (1979). Beyond words: Influence of nonverbal behavior of female job applicants in the employment interview. *Personnel and Guidance Journal, 57,* 346–350.

Zajonc, R. B. (1980). Feeling and thinking: Preferences need no inferences. *American Psychologist, 35,* 151–175.

Zajonc, R. B. (1984). On primacy of affect. In K. S. Scherer & P. Ekman (Eds.), *Approaches to emotion* (pp. 259–270). Hillsdale, NJ: Erlbaum.

Zelinsky, W. (1973). *The cultural geography of the United States.* Englewood Cliffs, NJ: Prentice-Hall.

Zhang, Q., & Oetzel, J. G. (2006). Constructing and validating a teacher immediacy scale: A Chinese perspective. *Communication Education, 55,* 218–241.

Zhou, L. (2005). An empirical investigation of deception behavior in instant messaging. *IEEE Transactions on Professional Communication, 48,* 147–159.

Zhou, L. Burgoon, J. K., Nunamaker, J. F., & Twitchell, D. (2004). Automated linguistics based cues for detecting deception in text-based asynchronous computer-mediated communication: An empirical investigation. *Group Decision and Negotiation, 13,* 81–106.

Ziegler-Kratz, N., & Marshall, L. L. (1990). Impressions of therapists: The effects of gaze, smiling, and gender. *Journal of Psychology and the Behavioral Sciences, 5*, 115–129.

Zivin, G. (1982). Watching the sands shift: Conceptualizing development of nonverbal mastery. In R. S. Feldman (Ed.), *Development of nonverbal behavior in children* (pp. 63–98). New York: Springer Verlag.

Zlutnick, S., & Altman, F. (1972). Crowding and human behavior. In J. F. Wohlwill & D. H. Carson (Eds.), *Environment and the social sciences: Perspectives and applications*. Washington, DC: American Psychological Association.

Zuckerman, M., DePaulo, B. M., & Rosenthal, R. (1981). Verbal and nonverbal communication of deception. In L. Berkowitz (Ed.), *Advances in experimental social psychology* (Vol. 14, pp. 2–59). New York: Academic.

Zuckerman, M., & Driver, R. E. (1985). Telling lies: Verbal and nonverbal correlates of deception. In A. W. Siegman & S. Feldstein (Eds.), *Multichannel integrations of nonverbal behavior* (pp. 129–148). Hillsdale, NJ: Erlbaum.

Zuckerman, M., & Driver, R. E. (1989). What sounds beautiful is good: The vocal attractiveness stereotype. *Journal of Nonverbal Behavior, 13*, 67–82.

Zuckerman, M., Fischer, S. A., Osmun, R. W., Winkler, B. A., & Wolfson, L. R. (1987). Anchoring in lie detection revisited. *Journal of Nonverbal Behavior, 11*, 4–12.

Zuckerman, M., Hodgins, H., & Miyake, K. (1990). The vocal attractiveness stereotype: Replication and elaboration. *Journal of Nonverbal Behavior, 14*, 97–112.

Zuckerman, M., Koestner, R., & Alton, A. O. (1984). Learning to detect deception. *Journal of Personality and Social Psychology, 46*, 519–528.

Zuckerman, M., Koestner, R., Colella, M. J., & Alton, A. O. (1984). Anchoring in the detection of deception and leakage. *Journal of Personality and Social Psychology, 47*, 301–311.

Zuckerman, M., Spiegel, N. H., DePaulo, B. M., & Rosenthal, R. (1982). Nonverbal strategies for decoding deception. *Journal of Nonverbal Behavior, 6*, 171–187.

Zweigenhaft, R. L. (1976). Personal space in the faculty office: Desk placement and the student-faculty interaction. *Journal of Applied Psychology, 61*, 529–532.

Zweyer, K., Velker, B., & Ruch, W. (2004). Do cheerfulness, exhilaration, and humor production moderate pain tolerance? *Humor, 17*, 85–119.

Name Index

Abbey, A., 130
Acitelli, L. K., 211, 224, 228, 229, 231, 241
Adams, G. R., 34, 272
Adams, R. B., 43, 122, 145
Addington, D. W., 58
Afifi, W. A., 200, 210, 214, 286
Aguinis, H., 327, 328
Ah-Ha, I., 79, 82, 85
Aho, L., 15, 68, 197, 204, 206, 266, 272
AhYun, K., 217, 218
Aida, Y., 178
Aiello, J. R., 45, 46, 120, 121
Aiken, L. R., 33
Akehurst, L., 289
Akert, R. M., 25
Albert, R. D., 79, 82, 85
Albert, S., 266
Alberts, J. K., 117
Alex, N., 318
Alexander, A. F., 327
Algoe, S. B., 123, 124
Alibali, M. W., 38, 40
Allen, M., 217, 250
Alper, T., 88, 200, 240
Altman, F., 336
Altman, I., 207, 239, 246, 249
Alton, A. O., 309, 311
Amabile, T. M., 25
Ambady, N., 9, 11, 17, 22, 57, 81, 82, 137, 138, 139, 142, 150, 151, 280

Amico, J. A., 226
Anatol, K. W. E., 318
Andersen, J. F., 5, 19, 20, 24, 37, 38, 50, 56, 58, 60, 68, 70, 87, 88, 89, 98, 100, 126, 129, 139, 142, 143, 169, 174, 180, 185, 186, 191, 194, 197, 198, 199, 201, 202, 203, 204, 206, 209, 210, 216, 217, 218, 219, 234, 235, 243, 257, 262, 265, 268, 279, 286, 339
Andersen, K., 238
Andersen, P. A., 5, 8, 9, 10, 11, 12, 13, 14, 15, 19, 20, 22, 25, 28, 33, 34, 36, 37, 38, 43, 47, 50, 51, 56, 57, 58, 60, 68, 70, 78, 82, 83, 87, 88, 89, 90, 91, 92, 94, 96, 98, 99, 100, 103, 107, 108, 126, 129, 132, 137, 138, 139, 140, 141, 142, 143, 144, 146, 147, 149, 150, 151, 153, 155, 156, 157, 158, 159, 160, 161, 162, 163, 164, 169, 171, 173, 174, 175, 176, 177, 180, 182, 183, 184, 185, 186, 191, 192, 196, 197, 198, 199, 202, 203, 206, 207, 208, 209, 210, 213, 215, 216, 218, 223, 224,

225, 226, 227, 228, 231, 234, 235, 237, 238, 240, 243, 244, 245, 248, 257, 264, 265, 271, 273, 276, 278, 279, 286, 291, 316, 317, 322, 325, 339
Anderson, C., 340
Anderson, N. R., 278
Anderson, S. W., 40
Andrews, S. L., 214
Angier, N., 72
Applbaum, R. L., 318
Apple, W., 268, 280, 294
Arbib, M. A., 41, 166
Archer, D., 25, 127
Areni, C. S., 263
Argyle, M., 93, 197, 202, 327, 329, 332
Aronoff, J., 147
Aronson, E., 272
Attridge, A. M., 196
Aune, K. S., 122
Aune, R. K., 69, 122, 261, 268, 290, 297, 298, 299, 300, 301, 306, 312
Autrey, S., 327
Azkahi, W. R., 219

Babad, E., 217, 218
Bachorowski, J.-A., 137, 146
Badzinski, D. M., 211, 233
Baesler, E. J., 199
Bailenson, J. N., 47, 260
Bailey, W., 127, 176

Subject Index

424   Subject Index

Pulse volume, reduced, and immediacy, 171
Punctuality and immediacy, 206
Pupil dilation
    and arousal, 43–44, 53, 279
    and attraction, 43–44
    and deception, 291, 296
    and immediacy, 196–197
    and love, 159
Pupilometrics, 43, 196

Race bias, 84
Reagan, Ronald, political communication of, 270
Receiver-based definition of nonverbal communication, 16
Reciprocity, 40–41
Reduced awareness response to communication anxiety, 175–177
Redundancy, simultaneous, 23
Regulation, vocalic function of, 58
Relational communication
    and immediacy, 207–208, 213
    and intimacy, 232–234
    nonverbal vs. verbal, 27–28
    sex differences in, 131
    and touch, 51–52
Relational schemata/trajectories, 238–241
Relaxation, 202–203
    and dominance, 341
    and immediacy, 202–203, 279
    and power, 322
Religiosity, and same-sex touch, 184–185
Repetition, 57
Repetition/redundancy, vocalic function of, 57
Response latency, 69, 310

Reward value, 242–243, 266, 272. See also Interpersonal valence
Rhythmic movements, 39
Ridicule, smiling as, 301
Right Touch, The (Jones), 331
Risk/reward dialectic, 247–248

Sacred time, 70
Sadness, 149–150
Same-sex touch, 50, 96, 126, 180, 183–185, 258
Sarcasm, 26–27, 58
Saturated Self, The (Gergen), 231
Scent. See Olfactics
Schemata
    cultural, 237
    interpersonal, 238
    relational, 238–240
    self, 237–238
    situational, 240–241
    state, 241
Seasonal affective disorder, 60, 70
Seating arrangements, 62–63
Seating pattern/position, 336–337
Seduction-and-rejection game, 331
Segmentation, 249
Selection, 249
Self-adaptors, 38, 127, 157, 171, 177, 278, 292, 297, 324
Self-awareness, reduced, in communication apprehension, 179
Self-consciousness, and communication anxiety, 175–176
Self-disclosure, 225–234
Self-focus, 175–177, 189
Self-monitoring, and deception, 289
Self-presentation, 172, 273–277
Self-schemata, 237–238

Self-touching. See Self-adaptors
Selling ourselves, 273–280
Semantics vs. digital language, 28
Sender-orientation definition of nonverbal communication, 14–15
Sensitivity
    contextual, 55, 240–241
    and deception detection, 310
    and situational schemata, 240–241
Sensory stimulation, and immediacy, 192
Sex differences
    biological, 108–110
    in communication, 107–108
    in dominance, 315–341
    in haptic behavior, 50, 126–127, 184–186
    in immediacy, 210–211
    in intimacy, 229
    in kinesic behavior, 122–124
    in nonverbal perceptions and attributions, 129–131
    in nonverbal receiving ability, 127–129
    in nonverbal sending ability, 129
    in oculesic behavior, 124–125
    in physical appearance, 116–120
    in proxemic behavior, 120–121
    in relational communication, 131
    in smiling and power, 325
    social evolutionary view of, 109–110, 117–118, 121, 129
    in vocalic behavior, 125–126
    See also Gender